THE BUTTERFLIES OF AUSTRALIA

All day long I wandered about the hills, searching out wonderful paths, bowing warmly to familiar butterflies.

Vladimir Nabokov, 1924
(from a letter in Russian)

p. i: Imperial Whites (*Delias harpalyce*) mating
p. iii: Pale Green Triangles (*Graphium eurypylus*)

THE BUTTERFLIES OF AUSTRALIA

Albert Orr and Roger Kitching

Illustrated by Albert Orr

CONTENTS

Preface   vi
About the Authors   viii

PART 1: THE BIOLOGY OF BUTTERFLIES

Chapter 1: INTRODUCING THE BUTTERFLIES   2
Butterflies as Insects   2
Butterflies and Moths—the Order Lepidoptera   3
A Few Words on Names   6
The Colours of Butterflies   7
The Life Cycle of the Butterfly   8
Adult Life, Sex and Reproduction   14

Chapter 2: THE AUSTRALIAN BUTTERFLIES AND THEIR HABITATS   18
Discovery of the Australian Butterfly Fauna   18
Butterfly Families and Identification   21
Where Are Our Butterflies Found?   25
Where Did They Come From?   26
Where to Look for Butterflies in the Landscape   28
When to Look for Butterflies   32

Chapter 3: RELATIONSHIPS WITH PLANTS AND OTHER ANIMALS   34
Food Plants—the Butterfly's Prey   34
Competing for Food and Mates   41
Natural Enemies   43
Butterfly Mutualisms   47

Chapter 4: BUTTERFLIES AND HUMANS   52
Butterfly Conservation   52
Butterfly Gardening   54
Butterfly Pests   56
Becoming a Lepidopterist   57

Notes on Using This Book   60

PART 2: THE BUTTERFLIES

Chapter 5: FAMILY HESPERIIDAE—Skippers   62
    Subfamily Pyrginae—Flats   63
    Subfamily Coeliadinae—Awls   68
    Subfamily Trapezitinae—Ochres and Their Allies   72
    Subfamily Hesperiinae—Darters, Swifts and Their Allies   104

Chapter 6: FAMILY PAPILIONIDAE—Swallowtails, Birdwings,
    Triangles and Swordtails   120

Chapter 7: FAMILY PIERIDAE—Whites and Yellows   139
    Subfamily Coliadinae—Yellows   141
    Subfamily Pierinae—Whites and Jezabels   148

Chapter 8: FAMILY NYMPHALIDAE—Nymphs and Their Allies   163
    Subfamily Danainae—Tigers and Crows   165
    Subfamily Tellervinae—Hamadryad   174
    Subfamily Satyrinae—Browns   176
    Subfamily Amathusiinae—Owls   195
    Subfamilies Charaxinae and Apaturinae—Emperors   196
    Subfamily Acraeinae—Glasswings   198
    Subfamily Heliconiinae—Cruisers and Lacewings   200
    Subfamily Argynninae—Fritillaries and Their Allies   202
    Subfamily Limenitinae—Aeroplanes   204
    Subfamily Nymphalinae—Nymphs   206
    Subfamily Libytheinae—Beaks   216

Chapter 9: FAMILY LYCAENIDAE—Blues, Coppers and Hairstreaks   217
    Subfamily Riodininae—Metalmarks   220
    Subfamily Liphyrinae—Moth Butterflies   221
    Subfamily Theclinae—Hairstreaks   222
    Subfamily Polyommatinae—Blues   258

Further Reading and Societies   282
Index   285
Appendix 1: Checklist of Australian Butterflies   A1
Appendix 2: Larval Host Plants of Australian Butterflies   A9

PREFACE

There is an art to watching butterflies. A person of ordinary sensibility will generally notice a flower. It remains fixed in space. It may be approached without caution, smelled, plucked. It is easy to interact with the flower with minimal physical effort and only a basic involvement of the senses. Butterflies provide a greater challenge. Even ardent nature lovers frequently fail to notice them at all. The beauty and fascination of butterflies is at once fugitive and sublime. It is far more than a captivating pattern of wing colour. A butterfly in flight is an exquisite display of choreography with purpose. Understanding this purpose is perhaps the key to learning how to watch butterflies. We may enjoy a performance of *Swan Lake* purely for its graceful movements and gorgeous costumes, but our appreciation is greatly enhanced by knowing the story behind the dance. So it is with butterflies.

This book is intended as a guide to the greater appreciation of the butterflies we see around us. In any open space in Australia we might reasonably expect to see anywhere from half a dozen to a hundred or more different butterfly species. This book will, with a little work, allow them to be identified and, more importantly, will foster an appreciation of what butterflies are actually doing in our gardens, parks and nature reserves. More than almost any other wild animal, butterflies present ready opportunities for the observation of dramatic and fundamental life processes at close quarters. It is for this reason that they have been so inspirational and central to the development of deep understanding in many areas of biology, particularly the theory of evolution.

This work differs from almost all its predecessors in two ways. First, it has been designed to be a field guide: we expect your copy to become dog-eared and tatty with frequent use. Second, many of the butterflies we illustrate are pictured as living animals interacting with their environment, with each other and with other species of animals: in other words, appearing as you might well see them in the field. With this book in hand you should be able to identify about 98 per cent of all butterflies found in Australia. The remaining 2 per cent are very unlikely to be encountered by any but the keenest of enthusiasts: they occur as tiny isolated populations in remote places, as rare migrants to our northern shores, or are such that skilled dissection is required in order to name them.

We are fortunate to have a recent authoritative handbook to the Australian butterflies. Michael Braby's two-volume masterwork, *Butterflies of Australia*, was published in 2000 and will remain the 'bible' for serious students of butterflies for many years to come. Nevertheless, few would have the physical strength or depth of pocket to take Braby's large, heavy and very expensive volumes into the field. Our book will complement this essential reference work. We have followed Braby's conventions of higher classification, and draw on his work extensively, as we do on the books of his distinguished predecessors: Ian Common, Doug Waterhouse, Bernard D'Abrera and Charles McCubbin. The distribution maps published by Kelvin and Laurence Dunn are also an essential foundation for a work such as ours. References to these and other key works are listed at the end of the book. We have not interrupted the text with endless citations—this is a guide for a general readership, not a scientific monograph—but for those who may wish to pursue their interest further we provide a guide to further reading.

In the preparation of this book, many people have helped us immeasurably, often without knowing it. In 2001, AO's daughter, Vanessa, then nine years old, had a brief enthusiasm for butterflies which she chased in the back garden at Bramston Beach, north Queensland. There being no suitable guidebooks in print at that time, her father prepared a series of rough sketches of butterflies in life, with a short text to help her identify her catch. It was from these notes and sketches that this book was conceived. Although it has since acquired a mature scientific perspective, we hope it retains its germinal spark, first ignited in the soul of a child racing across the lawn with a net almost her own size, excitedly calling out slightly unorthodox Latin names.

From the start, while preparing this book, we have received generous and enthusiastic encouragement from our various families, friends and colleagues. It would be hard to list all of the people whose positive affirmation and moral support have sustained us and improved the final result. Many others contributed tangibly—providing information, photographs or hospitality, or by typing or editing, or suggesting themes and approaches. Therefore, for all their help, we freely acknowledge our indebtedness and offer our warmest thanks to Andrew Atkins, Sarah Boulter, Michael Braby, Keith Brown, Chris Burwell, Heather Christensen, Mabel Davis, Murdoch De Baar, Geoffrey Dyne, Heather Dyne, Rod Eastwood, Louise Egerton, Heinrich Fliedner, Jack Guyomar, David Hancock, Angela Handley, Christoph Häuser, Chris Hill, Martin Honey, Steve Johnstone, Rhondda Jones, Beverley Kitching, Kelly Lyonns, Kazuma Matsumoto, John Nielsen, Dorothy Orr, Peter Pfeitzner, Naomi Pierce, Jane Rienks, Peter Samson, Don Sands, Elly Scheermeyer, Atuhiro Shibatani, Mary Stabler, Peter Valentine, Richard Vane Wright, Peter Vukusic, Neville Yates, Patricia Yates and Myron Zalucki.

Albert Orr
Roger Kitching
Griffith University, Brisbane

ABOUT THE AUTHORS

Dr Albert Orr has had an interest in insects from childhood, and, as butterflies were the only Australian insects that could be reliably identified using a book in 1965, they became and remain his passion. Born in Maleny, Queensland, in 1953, he studied entomology and mathematics at Queensland University, graduating in 1974. He received a PhD from Griffith University in 1988 for work on butterfly mating systems, especially the evolution of the sphragis or 'chastity belt' found on the mated females of many species, including three from Australia. During his career he has carried out major studies on butterflies of all families, publishing extensively in books and journals. He spent almost ten years (1990–2000) at the Universiti Brunei Darussalam, where his research also included dragonflies, leading to the publication of three identification guides to the dragonflies of Borneo and other parts of South-East Asia, partly in collaboration with Dr Matti Hämäläinen of Helsinki University. In 2005 he shared the World Dragonfly Association award for outstanding achievement for this work. Since 2000 he has been based at Griffith University, Brisbane, as an honorary research fellow. He is editor of *The Australian Entomologist*, the principal journal publishing new information about Australian butterflies. In between short-term consultancies, conservation projects with the International Union for the Conservation of Nature and editorial work, he is devoting most of his time to popular scientific communication, and expanding his portfolio of natural history art.

Professor Roger Kitching has been the Foundation Chair of Ecology at Griffith University since 1992. He was born and educated largely in the UK, where a childhood passion for butterflies led him to a degree in zoology and entomology from Imperial College, London (1966). Subsequently he studied aquatic microcosms for which he was awarded a DPhil from the University of Oxford in 1969. He was recruited by CSIRO and moved to Australia in 1971 following a two-year research fellowship at the University of British Columbia, Canada. Five years of research on the sheep blowfly also provided a splendid opportunity to become familiar with Australian butterflies. Several papers on butterflies emerged from this period. He was appointed as one of the first staff members of the newly opened Griffith University in Brisbane in 1977. Here he supervised a group of postgraduate students, including Albert Orr, who focused on many aspects of butterfly biology. He himself continued studies on several species in three families during this period. Moving to the University of New England in Armidale, New South Wales, as Professor of Ecosystem Management in 1987, he carried out some of the first conservation assessments of Australian butterflies. He returned to Brisbane in 1992. Professor Kitching has authored, edited or co-authored eight books and over 160 scientific papers. His books include *Biology of Australian Butterflies* (CSIRO, 1999), *Food Webs and Container Habitats* (CUP, 2000) and *Arthropods of Tropical Forests* (CUP, 2003). He has served as President of the Australian Institute of Biology and the Australian Entomological Society. He was awarded the degree of Doctor of Science by Griffith University in 2003, and was appointed a member of the Order of Australia in January 2010.

PART 1

THE BIOLOGY OF BUTTERFLIES

Orchard Butterfly
(*Papilio aegeus*) courtship

1 INTRODUCING THE BUTTERFLIES

We share our lives with wildlife: in our gardens, homes and parks. We take great joy and inspiration from wildlife. Encounters with fellow mammals such as a koala or an echidna, a wallaby or a glider are always particularly exciting, but it is the bright birds and butterflies we see virtually every day that are our most direct connection with the animal world. Birds and butterflies are extremely mobile and we see them as they move. Like us, they are mostly active during the day and live their lives principally through colour vision. It is no accident that many birds and butterflies are arrayed in brilliant colours, arranged in extraordinary contrasts. And because of this beauty, which seems almost to have been specially ordered for our appreciation, we notice and relate to birds and butterflies in a way that is quite unlike our perception of lizards and spiders, mice and beetles. By contrast, butterflies pay virtually no attention to us and, should we take the trouble, we can observe their dazzling colours and fascinating lives simply by pausing a moment to look.

Many of us can name the birds we encounter daily—and there is no shortage of excellent guidebooks if we wish to confirm our decisions or extend our knowledge. This is not the case even with our most common butterflies. Perhaps the pestiferous Cabbage White and the charismatic black and orange Wanderer are part of everyday knowledge, but most people would be hard-pressed to name more than three or four kinds from their own backyards. Only in north Queensland is a native butterfly almost universally known—the brilliant Blue Mountain Butterfly, or Ulysses Butterfly (as it is called in the rest of Australia). Yet in Australia we have more or less the same number of resident species of butterflies as birds—a little over 400 in both cases. If this book succeeds as intended, then it will go some little way to rectifying this imbalance. In particular the illustrations attempt to capture the living essence of each group of butterflies, setting them in their environmental context and sometimes their human context. This, we hope, will inspire and excite others to look just a little longer at these extraordinary cohabitants of our continent.

Orchard Butterfly
(*Papilio aegeus*)

Butterflies as Insects

Butterflies are insects: they have three pairs of jointed legs and, in the adult stage, one pair of antennae ('feelers') and two pairs of wings. They have a segmented body divided clearly into three parts: a head, a thorax and an abdomen. Along with the crustaceans, millipedes, centipedes and arachnids they also have an external skeleton which they must shed to pass from life stage to life stage. Furthermore, butterflies, along with beetles, flies, bees and wasps, exhibit a complete change during their lives: metamorphosis. The adult insect is dramatically different in form and function from the immature insect—the larva or caterpillar. In between is the sedentary pupal stage, during which the cells and tissues of the insect's body are completely rearranged. This transition is one of nature's most marvellous feats. Every butterfly we see has been through it, a fact we seldom consider.

There are probably about ten million species of insect in the world: perhaps 400,000 or more in Australia alone. To cope with this vast diversity we divide the insects first into orders. There are close to 30 orders worldwide, each descended from a common ancestor, which have radiated to produce an array of species all of which share distinguishing characteristics. The four largest orders of insects are the beetles (the Coleoptera), the true two-winged flies (the Diptera), the ants, bees and wasps (collectively, the Hymenoptera), and the butterflies and moths (the Lepidoptera), distinguished by their scaled wings and coiled sucking mouthparts. The Lepidoptera also have less obvious but more or less unique features, such as high levels of potassium in their blood, chromosomes XY in females and XX in males (the reverse of most animals except birds), and the production of large quantities of sterile sperm. It would be an understatement to say that butterflies do things differently.

Even within these orders we still encounter confronting amounts of variation and diversity. So within each order there are families—groups of species that all share a common ancestor, in this case more recent than the one they share with members of other families within the same order. Finally, similar species are lumped into genera (singular: genus), implying a relatively recent common ancestry for all the species within that genus. The way this system of classification works, and the intermediate categories used in some cases (such as subfamilies and tribes), will become apparent as familiarity with the Australian butterflies grows.

Butterflies and Moths—the Order Lepidoptera

Any large, brightly coloured insect with four wings that is active during the day is usually frivolously called a 'butterfly'. Generally this will be correct, although some leafhoppers may resemble small butterflies. Therefore we must first establish whether the insect is a member of the Lepidoptera, as opposed to one of several other common insect orders. Once in the hand, this is easy. The patterns on the wings of butterflies and moths, whether they be bright or dull, are due to thousands of coloured scales, which 'tile' the wings and readily come off on our fingers. These scales give the butterflies and moths their technical name—the 'Lepidoptera'—which, from its Greek roots, simply means 'scale-wings'. Adult butterflies and moths, with a few rare exceptions, also have a feeding tube—curled like a watch spring—in place of the jaws possessed by other insects. Leafhoppers do not have these features, no matter how colourful. Other large four-winged 'fluttery' insects with coloured wings include some of the larger lacewings and sometimes dragonflies, but these have neither scales nor curled 'sucking' mouthparts. They bite (but gently).

For our specimen, the question remains: is it a butterfly or a moth? Here nature sometimes seems determined to confuse us. Many bright day-flying lepidopterans are technically not butterflies, but moths. A few rules may help. Butterflies, *in general*, have antennae with some form of knob or hook on their ends, are mostly active during the day, and generally sit with their wings folded upright over their backs. By contrast, moths, *in general*, have simply tapered or feathery antennae, are usually active at night, and perch with their wings open, often in a more or less triangular pose. But we emphasise the phrase *in general* because there are some exceptions to almost all of these rules. Although there are no butterflies with filamentous antennae, there are several groups of moths with knobbed antennae, including the rare Sun Moths. Although there are no truly nocturnal butterflies, a few species fly deep into the twilight and are attracted to the lights of houses. Some of the looper moths commonly perch with their folded wings up, and many skipper, swallowtail and nymph butterflies often perch with their wings held flat.

In general, if we apply the rules of thumb just set out we will be correct 99 per cent of the time—figuring out what went wrong with the other 1 per cent of identifications is just part of the fascination of getting to know the butterflies and moths. Opposite are shown several species of moths that are commonly confused with butterflies. All fly during the day, all have brightly coloured wings, some even sit with wings up or have knobbed antennae—and some, at first glance, confuse the experts!

Ancient origins

The Lepidoptera first appeared as a separate group of insects in the Jurassic era, sharing a world with dinosaurs and cycads. The very earliest moths probably fed on the pollen of cycads and conifers. Indeed, the living moths thought to have remained more or less unchanged from those earliest versions do just that. It was, however, in the Cretaceous period that the moths and butterflies diversified to produce the 80 or more families we see today. This huge radiation coincided with two things: the moths and butterflies evolved their greatly modified sucking mouthparts (the 'proboscis'), allowing them to feed, as adults, on nectar and other liquid food; and, second, the flowering plants diversified at the same time, creating landscapes populated with trees, shrubs and herbs not greatly different from those we experience today. It is often supposed that this simultaneous diversification of flowering plants and insects such as the Lepidoptera occurred in parallel—change in one producing a corresponding change in the other. Be that as it may, many flowering plants depend on moths and butterflies (and other insects) to achieve pollination and, in turn, the insects use the plants' leaves, stems and flowers as a food source.

As of 2010 there have been more than 20,000 species of butterflies and moths, arranged in 82 families, described as occurring in Australia. The vast majority of these are moths: only five families, comprising in total a little over 400 species, are butterflies. These five families, together with an obscure South American family, all form a single branch of the great evolutionary tree that has grown to be the modern Lepidoptera since the Jurassic era, implying that, sometime in the Cretaceous period—about 100 million years ago—they all had a single common ancestor.

INTRODUCING THE BUTTERFLIES

A Few Words on Names

The most familiar of Australian butterflies were given names by the early collectors and settlers. These were often simply descriptive—the Common Brown, the Common Grass Blue, the Orchard Swallowtail. In other instances they were more fanciful, often recalling birds or mammals—the Crow, the Blue Tiger, the Albatross and so on. In other cases they were given names that recalled familiar butterflies from Britain and Europe, sometimes with 'Australian' appended to the designation—the Australian Admiral, the Australian Fritillary and the Australian Painted Lady. Sometimes the names were fanciful and evocative—the Regent Skipper, the jezabels, the Tailed Emperor or the birdwings are examples of this type. Sometimes butterflies accumulate a whole set of alternative 'common' names. The Wanderer butterfly, which occurs in many other parts of the world, is elsewhere known as the Monarch, the Black-veined Brown and the Milkweed Butterfly—all perfectly legitimate names in English but a perfect template for confusion. For the Australian butterflies these names had more or less stabilised by the time Michael Braby's monograph on the Australian butterflies appeared in the year 2000. Even so, Braby, like preceding authors, invented many 'new' English names to suit his taste.

Common names are just that, and can never be definitive. They are based on imagination, even whimsy, and have no scientific standing. This is where scientific names come in. Ever since the celebrated Carolus Linnaeus introduced his system of classification in 1758, scientists have designated species using the so-called 'binomial system'. Essentially this means that every species is to be known by a two-word name—the first designating the genus to which the species belongs, the second the species itself. Should a species be moved from one genus to another as knowledge improves or opinions change, so the generic name may change but the species name remains absolutely fixed, with the exception that its ending may change according to the rules of Latin grammar. So, by way of example, the Common Brown Butterfly is *Heteronympha merope*. This was one of the species collected by Joseph Banks during the 1770 voyage of the *Endeavour* and described by Johann Fabricius in 1775. Fabricius called it simply *Papilio merope*, in honour of one of the several classical women called Merope known from Greek mythology. *Papilio* (Latin for 'butterfly'), was the generally accepted name for any butterfly. In 1858 a Swedish entomologist, Hans Wallengren, proposed an expansion of the then existing genera of the brown butterflies and the new generic name *Heteronympha* came into being. From then on the butterfly was known as *Heteronympha merope*. Butterfly specialists will sometimes, off-handedly, simply say *merope*, assuming their colleagues can fill in the generic name. This remains a dangerous practice, as it is perfectly possible for two species of different genera to have the same name. *Pantoporia consimilis* and *Candalides consimilis* are very different butterflies, belonging to different families; *Vanessa kershawi* and *Oreixenica kershawi* belong to different subfamilies. There are other examples. The wonder is that confusion almost never arises.

The advantage of this system of binomial scientific names is that it represents a stable system of naming with well-known rules—which are usually obeyed! The disadvantage may be that they are couched in the scientific language of Linnaeus' day—Latin. This means that the precise application of the rules of nomenclature seems, to most of us now, a black art. Yet these names have a charm and a ring to them that grow with familiarity. Just as every keen gardener has the Latin names of plants tripping easily off their tongue, so does the butterfly enthusiast.

There is also a category of name which is written as a trinomial and indicates a subspecies: for example, *Heteronympha merope salazar*. Here '*salazar*' denotes the Tasmanian form of *H. merope*. Subspecies names are applied to geographic races that do not overlap in distribution, but have the supposed potential to interbreed if they had the opportunity. Whether a geographic form represents a subspecies or a full species is often a matter of opinion, and names can be upgraded or downgraded as more information comes to hand. For example, in this book we use the combination *Jalmenus eubulus* instead of *J. evagoras eubulus*, based on recent genetic information supplied by Rod Eastwood of Harvard University. We do not use trinomials, except in a few cases where they are very distinct. Two spectacular cases of geographic variation within species are also provided by *Tisiphone abeona* and *Pseudalmenus chlorinda*, each with six named subspecies.

We will use a combination of common and scientific names in this book. Just remember—if you want definitive, authoritative names, use the scientific versions.

The Colours of Butterflies

The colours of butterflies' wings are built up like a mosaic by different-coloured overlapping scales. If you looked at a butterfly wing under a strong hand lens, you would see row upon row of flat plates, arranged on the wing membrane like the roof tiles on a house. Each scale is a single colour, due to an accumulation of various types of chemical pigments, including black or dark-brown melanin and a variety of whites, yellows and reds. Combinations of these give a lighter brown. Blue is almost always produced in a different way: that is, by the separation of light rays into their component rainbow colours by physical interference. You can see this on the playing surface of a CD, and it is called structural colour. In this case, the upper surfaces of the scales are not pigmented at all, but have a series of several very thin parallel plates, each about 0.0004 millimetres thick, separated by an airspace of about the same thickness. Behind is a dark layer containing melanin. This structure reflects light very intensely; depending on the angle of view, the hue changes. You can see this in action as you watch a Ulysses Butterfly (*Papilio ulysses*) jinking in sunlight across a dark backdrop of tropical forest. The property of changing hues with angle of view is known as iridescence, and produces a particularly vivid, sparkling effect. To illustrate this phenomenon, the fine structure of a blue scale is shown in Figure 1.1, together with an individual scale and scales as they appear on the wing.

It is possible to produce other structural colours by changing the thickness of the transparent layers in the scales and, indeed, some yellow butterflies also have scales that reflect ultraviolet light in this way; it's just not visible to our eyes. However, moving along the spectrum from blue to red means that the actual layers need to be thicker and thicker, which would take more material to develop. It is also possible that blue transmits better over long distances than green or red. Although some birds and damselflies have iridescent greens based on a very similar physical ultrastructure (that is, fine microscopic structure), the greens in the male birdwings (*Ornithoptera* spp.) actually come from a mixture of yellow chemical pigment and blue structural scales. In old specimens that have been exposed to the sun, the yellow fades and the butterfly turns blue. Recently, the physicist Peter Vukusic, of Exeter University in the UK, has demonstrated that the Ulysses Butterfly (*P. ulysses*) also has structural black in its wing margins. This is a different physical mechanism from that producing blue reflections—in fact, the structure

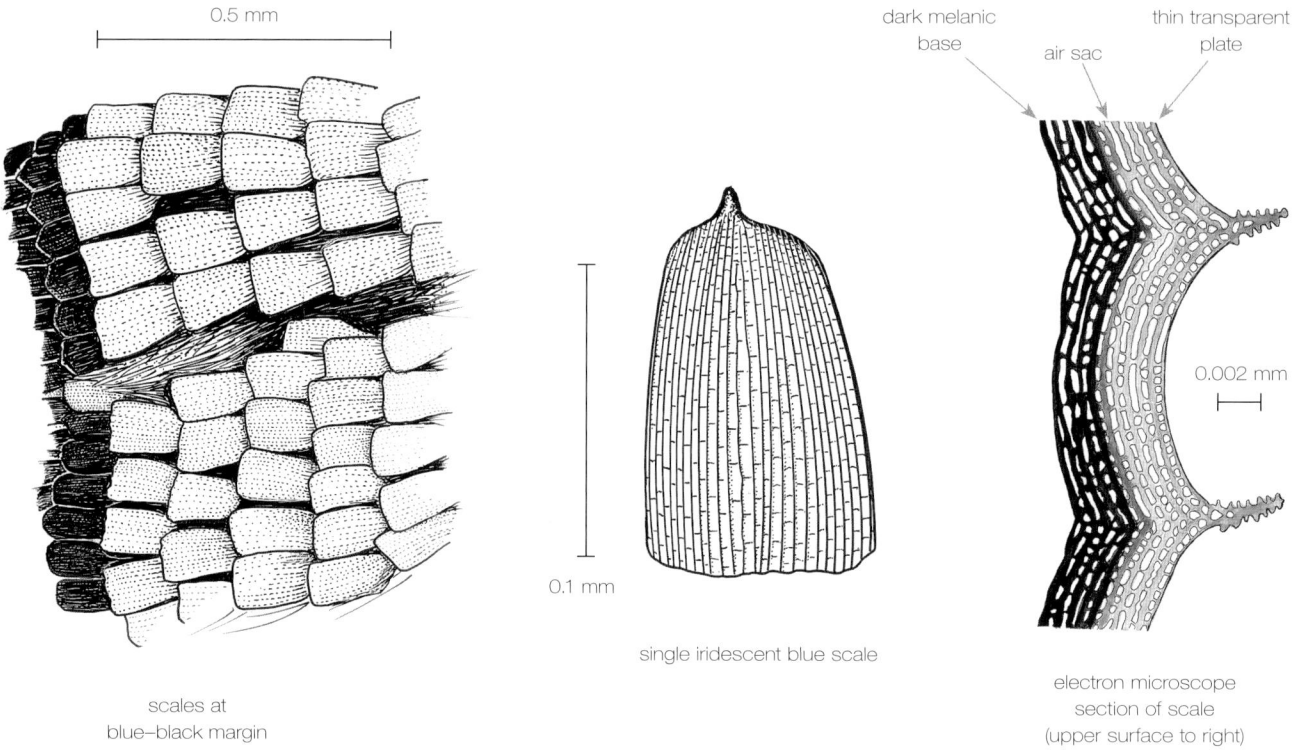

FIGURE 1.1:
Wing scales of the Ulysses Butterfly (*Papilio ulysses*) showing coarse and fine structure of blue iridescent scales, which gain their colour by physical interference of light.

absorbs light more effectively than dark pigment alone, producing a deep, velvet black. The increased contrast this very deep black provides probably enhances perception of the brilliant, iridescent blue by other butterflies and by humans.

The Life Cycle of the Butterfly

The fundamental transitions from egg to larva to pupa to adult represent the life cycle of the butterfly. We may be able to recognise each of the many species from the appearance of its larva, pupa or adult (often even the egg if we look closely), but there are features that are common to the stages and important things to be said about them. Consider, then, a single example—the Lesser Wanderer (*Danaus petilia*), found at one time or another absolutely everywhere in Australia, and hence a good choice when we wish to talk generalities.

Lifespan

First let us dispense with an old question. One of the things you will immediately be asked when people know you are interested in butterflies is 'how long do they live?' There are two problems with this question: first, the questioner usually means 'how long does the adult live?' and the second is that butterflies are basically cold-blooded. The last point is the more important one. Animals that do not control their own body temperatures internally (unlike birds and mammals) are dependent on external sources of heat to drive all their vital processes. For insects there are temperatures below which the animal can do virtually nothing—even though it doesn't die. Above that temperature, to some extent, how much of its life it gets through on a particular day depends on how warm it is. There are exceptions to this rule, such as when adults slow their activity and their metabolism during warm dry conditions, but this involves an independent physiological process and in no way changes the general principle. For insects, time is truly temperature-dependent. So whether a caterpillar lives a few days or several weeks depends on how warm it is. This is complicated somewhat by the fact that the longer a butterfly lingers in a particular life stage, the greater the chance that it will be discovered by its warm-blooded enemies, especially birds, which remain active in cool weather.

Nevertheless, depending on species and environment, normally active adults may live for as little as a week, or for two or three months. However, we should remember that the egg and the larva are just as much part of the life of the butterfly as the highly visible adult. In this case the total lifespan of a butterfly from egg to adult lasts from several weeks to about a year. This may be extended by arrested development of any stage of the life history due to unfavourable conditions such as drought.

Figure 1.2: Life cycle of the Lesser Wanderer (*Danaus petilia*).

The egg

The egg, or ovum, of the butterfly is laid by the female, usually on or near the preferred food plant (also called host plant) of the species. In the case of the Lesser Wanderer, the female seeks out one of a number of species of plants in the milkweed family (the Asclepiadaceae). These include a range of native species as well as introduced species brought into our gardens, either deliberately or by accident. Other species of butterfly may be restricted to a single species of plant (although this is less frequent); yet others will have a wide range of potential food plants. The female Lesser Wanderer will hover around the potential food plant, assessing it with the taste receptors on her front feet. If the species of plant is acceptable, she seeks out new foliage, and then, very deliberately, curves the tip of her abdomen round and lays a single shining white egg on the underside of the emerging leaf. This action is called oviposition. The Lesser Wanderer lays her eggs singly on different leaves spread over many plants; other species of butterfly lay their eggs in batches, sometimes placing as many as a hundred in a single place. Eggs vary greatly in size, shape and structure among different butterfly species; some are smooth and perfectly spherical, while others are elongate or hemispherical, with or without vertical ribbing or complex sculpturing on the surface. The shell is made of chitin, the complex carbohydrate that also forms the basis of all hard structures in insects, and is edible and nutritious.

The egg is generally the shortest of the life stages and, once laid, develops rapidly internally into a tiny larva. As the larva develops, the egg darkens and, finally, the tiny larva chews its way out of the top of the egg—a process which may last an hour or more—and immediately seeks food. Often it eats the chitinous eggshell before attacking fresh plant growth.

Butterfly eggs are susceptible to a range of natural enemies. Tiny wasps may parasitise them immediately after laying and go through *their* larval stage within the egg. True bugs may suck them dry. Ants carry off many for food. Eggs can also be very susceptible to pathogenic infections by fungi or bacteria, especially if cold weather delays their development, leaving them exposed to infection for longer than usual.

The caterpillar

The caterpillar or larva of the butterfly is often the longest lived of the life cycle stages. During this stage, food reserves must be built up for the fast and furious adult life to come. Larvae must accumulate fat and protein from their food plants, often sufficient to carry the female adult butterfly through the nutritionally expensive business of developing and laying eggs—protein is not usually part of an adult's diet at all. Males also have a great need of protein and fat, some of which they may donate to their mates during copulation. Many other nutrients, differing from species to species, must be acquired during the larval stage. In fact, the larval stage is a series of stages—five in the case of the Lesser Wanderer—each separated from the next by a shedding of the outer skin. Each of the separate stages is called an instar and their number is usually characteristic of the species: most butterflies have five, very rarely four or six.

Larvae are dedicated feeding machines. Again, in each species the larva is distinctive, but all larvae have a well-defined head capsule below which is mounted, not the sucking mouthparts of the adult, but a pair of toothed mandibles which they use to cut out portions of their food plants before eating them. Each butterfly larva has three pairs of true legs, one pair for each of the three thoracic segments behind the head. These legs are equipped with single claws at their tips and are equivalent, anatomically, to those that will be associated with each thoracic segment in the adult insect. In addition, the abdominal segments have five pairs of stubby 'prolegs' located on abdominal segments 3 to 6, with a final pair on segment 10 at the animal's posterior. These prolegs have sets of microscopic hooks, called crochets, around their blunt ends, but no true claws. All of these extra legs may be seen as safeguards; they enable the larva to keep a secure purchase on its food plant for, once dislodged, finding the right sort of plant in the right condition may be very difficult.

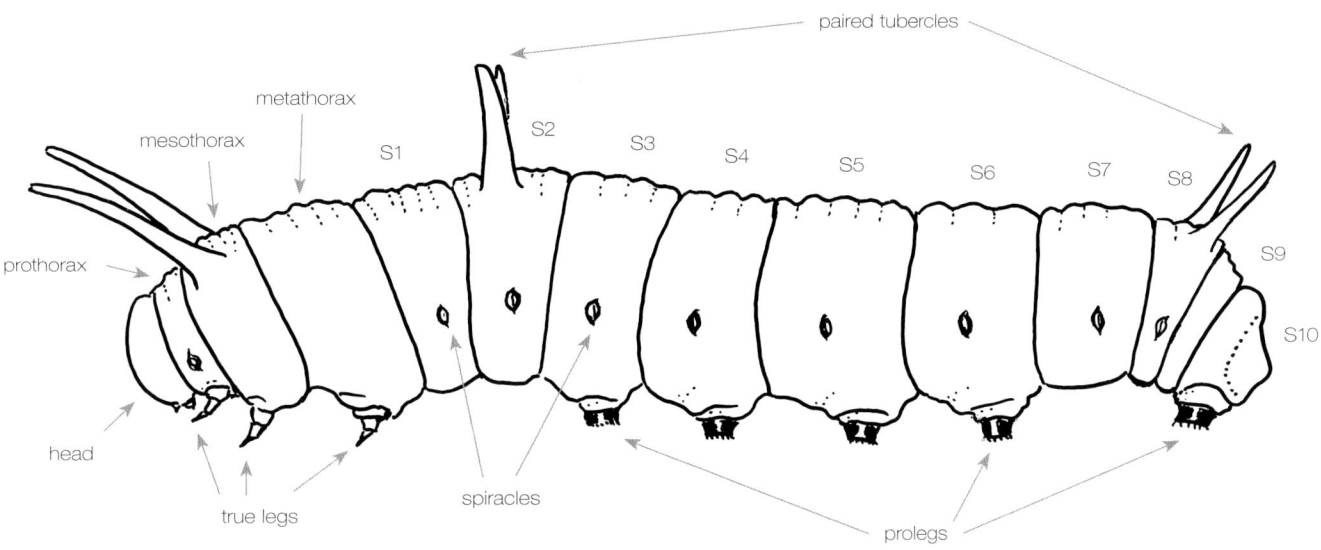

FIGURE 1.3: General larval morphology of the Lesser Wanderer (*Danaus petilia*): S1–10 refers sequentially to the segments of the abdomen, S1–8 bearing a spiracle at the side.

Along the sides of the abdomen and on the first thoracic segment are spiracles. These are the external openings of the system of air passages within the body, by which the caterpillar breathes. The larva of the Lesser Wanderer also has characteristic pairs of tubercles on its thorax and abdomen. Other species have similar processes elsewhere. Sometimes additional glandular structures are present, with defensive or other functions.

As it is often the longest stage in the butterfly's life, the larval period is also perhaps the riskiest. From the start the tiny 1st instar larvae must find foliage soft enough for them to penetrate while avoiding the defence mechanisms evolved by the plants. In the Lesser Wanderer this means that the tiny larvae must find sections of new milkweed leaf away from the major veins, which contain sticky latex evolved by the food plant as an anti-herbivore device. Later 4th and 5th instar larvae are better able to cope with tougher and more chemically protected parts of their food plants, but nevertheless must remain attached or very close to the food plant at all times.

Butterfly larvae have many natural enemies, including parasitoids such as wasps and flies, which slowly devour them alive from the inside; predators such as birds, assassin bugs or spiders; and pathogens such as fungi and bacteria. We discuss these, and the mechanisms evolved by larvae as defences, in Chapter 3.

Metamorphosis in the Black and White Tiger (*Danaus affinis*)

The final moult is achieved after the final instar larva has suspended itself by the hooks on the prolegs on its posterior end from a silken pad it has previously prepared. It stops feeding a day or two before this time and begins to contract and round out. In the case of the Lesser Wanderer and many other butterfly species, it may even move off the actual food plants and attach to nearby twigs or branches. At this stage it is called a pre-pupa. Once the final moult occurs, as it slips out of its blackened old skin, the pupa itself is revealed. For species such as the Lesser Wanderer, in which the pupa is suspended from a single support, the final contortion of ridding itself of the sloughed skin means it must hang precariously while it manoeuvres its terminal hooks around the incompletely split skin, sometimes hanging by a single thread. We might expect accidents during this stage, but they never seem to happen.

The chrysalis

The transition to the pupa or chrysalis stage of the butterfly's life cycle is one of the most extraordinary phenomena to be observed anywhere in the living world. From the moment the final larval skin is shed, the features of the adult are visible through the outer casing of the pupa. When this casing finally splits, an animal with wings, sucking mouthparts and three clearly defined body parts emerges: in short, an adult butterfly. This transition gradually becomes more and more obvious. We illustrate this in a close relative of the Lesser Wanderer, the Black and White Tiger (*Danaus affinis*).

In the pupa the final stages of development of the adult features are progressing. In all the larval stages there are small segments of true embryonic tissue that are pre-programmed to produce wings and other features characteristic of the adult. They persist and, indeed, develop very slowly throughout the larval life of the insect. These are the so-called imaginal discs ('imago' is a rather old-fashioned name for the adult stage in insects). Once in the pupal stage, hormonal control of the larval appearance is turned off and the cells of the imaginal discs divide and produce adult features. Of course, some things (legs, gut, excretory organs and so on) do not change—they are merely modified into the adult form; other features are completely new to the emerging adult.

The pupal stage can be an extremely vulnerable one for the insect. The tough outer casing is at least partially protective against natural enemies; however, pupae are attacked by specialised parasites and various predators, especially small mammals. As in the larval stage, the pupa can also be infected with bacteria or mould.

The adult

The adult or imago stage is the one we most associate with the word 'butterfly'. It is the stage that flies and the stage we most commonly notice. Anatomically there are key differences from the preceding stages. In addition to the obvious differences—two pairs of wings and a pair of antennae—there are no prolegs. The chewing mouthparts of the caterpillar have been replaced by a sucking proboscis, ideal for extracting nectar from plants, which is flanked by a pair of brush-like labial palps. The simple eyes of the larva have been replaced by large multi-lensed compound eyes—these are day-flying insects and good colour vision is essential for all their activities.

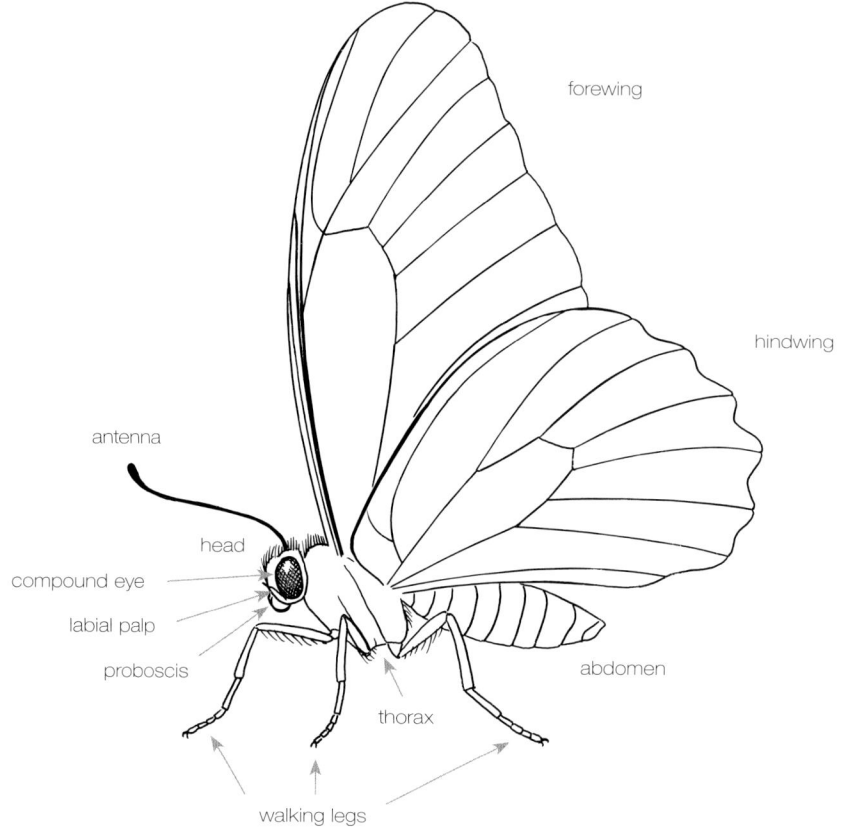

FIGURE 1.4: General external adult morphology of the Chequered Swallowtail (*Papilio demoleus*).

Upon emerging from the pupa, the fresh adult goes through a period of wing expansion as blue-greenish blood is pumped into the veins, followed by a hardening of the outer surfaces, before the insect is fully functional. During this time the animal is particularly vulnerable to predators. As a rule, the butterfly makes its maiden flight within 30 minutes to an hour after emerging, but it may take longer, especially in cool conditions.

Adult Life, Sex and Reproduction

Just as the larval stage is dedicated to feeding, the purpose of the adult stage is reproduction. In the case of females this can begin early, even before their wings are expanded. In the Common Imperial Blue (*Jalmenus evagoras*), for example, the older males sit around pupae and mate with females as soon as they emerge. When they leave the pupa, females of this species already have many mature eggs ready to be fertilised and may begin ovipositing soon after they are able to fly. Males of many other species, such as the birdwings (*Ornithoptera* spp.), actively seek out newly emerged females and mate with them before they can fly, or mate with them on their maiden flight. Indeed, most female butterflies are mated within the first day or so of emergence, although there are exceptions. Apart from the blues and their relatives, however, it is unusual for the female to emerge with mature eggs, and it takes at least several days for the first clutch to ripen, ready to lay. From then on, tiny immature eggs ripen sequentially along a female's ovaries for the remainder of her life.

Once she is able to fly, the female feeds actively, usually only on nectar, which is mainly sugar solution with sometimes very dilute amino acids—the building blocks of proteins. Females are, in most cases, subject to constant attentions from males, and the degree of control they have over mating varies greatly among different species. The male's entire purpose in life is to find and mate with females. They may do this by patrolling actively, searching for young virgins, courting older mated females ready to accept another mating, or defending territories where the females must come to obtain nectar or to oviposit. If the population is dispersed, males sometimes congregate on hilltops or other prominent landmarks, which receptive females deliberately visit in order to mate. In the Hamadryad (*Tellervo zoilus*), males display in a communal dance known as a lek, and females are drawn to the dance to seek a mate. Virgin females just three days old have been known to take the initiative in establishing genital contact. Males also need to refuel regularly with nectar, as much of their time is spent in energetic flight. In some species, males also have a great need for minerals, especially sodium and potassium, which they obtain by imbibing moisture from damp earth. Australian butterflies tend to mud-puddle, as such salt drinking is called, less than the same species in other parts of the tropics; this is especially so near the eastern coast, but the reason for this is not known.

Some butterflies mate only once: in these species, the female stores the sperm in a special sac within her body and uses the sperm to fertilise eggs throughout her life. Once mated, she will refuse further male approaches and concentrate on finding appropriate food plants on which to deposit her eggs. In other species, however, females mate many times, sometimes because they have no choice, but probably more often because, in addition to sperm, they receive a nutritious donation of proteins and fats and other substances with each mating. These nutrients can greatly enhance egg production over an individual's lifetime. When a female butterfly mates again, almost all the stored sperm from her previous male partner are neutralised, and sperm from her most recent partner fertilise her remaining eggs. In the course of evolution, males have developed mechanisms to ensure that it is *their* sperm a female uses to fertilise her eggs (so ensuring genetic continuity for the male concerned). Males often plug the sexual opening of the female with waxy materials to prevent or at least delay further mating. In extreme cases, as with the Big Greasy (*Cressida cressida*), these plugs are large and ornate, and the nutritious substances normally donated to the female are instead used to produce a hard insoluble chastity belt, called a sphragis, fixed to the outside of the female's abdomen. In the Big Greasy this lasts for the life of the female and she derives no nutrients at all from mating, since all the proteins and fats a male can spare go into the production of the sphragis. Other species hedge their bets, providing the female with a rich donation of nutrients, but leaving a small mating plug as extra—if only partial—insurance against her re-mating.

The reproductive system

In order to understand how all this works, it is necessary to understand the unusual anatomy of the female butterfly reproductive system and the process of copulation. In the female there are two reproductive openings: one (called the *ostium bursae*) lies just beneath the abdomen tip and serves for copulation; the other, at the tip of the abdomen and flanked by two small flaps, is the *oopore*, the opening of the oviduct, through which eggs are laid. It is therefore possible for a male to mate with a female and plug the ostium for life without interfering with the free passage of eggs.

During mating, the male grasps the female's abdomen tightly with his claspers (also called valves) and a dorsal hook, called the uncus (or pseuduncus). Once contact is established, the penis is inserted deep into the female's body, just reaching a large muscular sac called the *bursa copulatrix*. Into this sac, the male first secretes a large, hollow, thick-walled spermatophore, rich in fats and proteins, which will be digested later by the female. He then ejaculates sperm into the spermatophore. The sperm are quite unlike human sperm, each being simply a long thread, very thin but up to a millimetre in length. After ejaculation the penis is slowly retracted, with a hollow spermatophore stalk being produced as it is withdrawn. The end is sealed but a tiny hole is left in the side in the exact place where the opening of another female structure, the sperm duct, is located. Finally, before the female is released, a mating plug is often secreted to seal the ostium.

Soon after mating, the sperm within the female travel down the hollow stalk of the spermatophore, into the sperm duct, and up into a small blind sac called a spermatheca. This organ has a large gland that nourishes the sperm, and so they generally remain viable for the remainder of the female's life.

As each egg is laid, it passes down the oviduct past the spermatheca, and at this point a sperm is released to fertilise the egg. If another male should mate with the female, the sperm from the first male are pushed to the back of the spermatheca and cannot exit. To make this more effective, some butterflies produce many infertile but very active sperm that probably serve simply to prevent the escape of the first male's sperm.

While on the subject of reproduction, we should consider external male reproductive structures in butterflies. Many genera of butterflies contain species that are superficially very similar. Traditionally, entomologists have differentiated these on the basis of their genitalia. Indeed, there are a few genera of Australian butterflies—the whites of the genus *Elodina* for one—which can only be separated reliably by inspecting the uncus. Fortunately for the scientist, the genitalia, particularly of male butterflies, are complex and present many structures, variation in which can readily be used to separate species. Females provide less information. As an introduction to the reproductive structures (internal as well as external), we illustrate them both separately and 'in action' in Figure 1.5.

Separating males from females is generally possible by external examination. Sometimes there are dramatic differences in colour patterns on the wings, in which case the butterflies are called sexually dimorphic. The most spectacular example of this is provided by the birdwings, in which male and female differ strikingly in size, wing shape, colour and pattern. In other instances differences are subtler, with difficult cases resolved by gently squeezing the tip of the abdomen to reveal the genitalia. In general, however, female butterflies are larger, have heavier abdomens and more rounded posteriors. Males, by contrast, are generally smaller, and have slimmer abdomens with either pointed or divided (bifid) posteriors. There are also subtle differences in fore- and hindwing shape in most families. Males of many species also carry so-called sex brands on their forewings, from which pheromones (externally acting hormones) are produced to assist in mating. The placement and number of these sex brands is characteristic and in some groups, such as the small skippers, play a vital part in species identification. Other groups of butterflies, in addition, have more complex extrusible pheromone-producing organs called hair-pencils. We will deal with these in the specific accounts in Part 2.

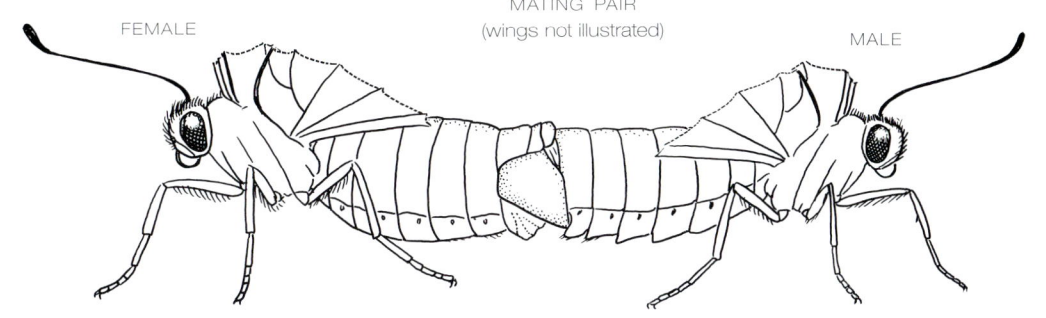
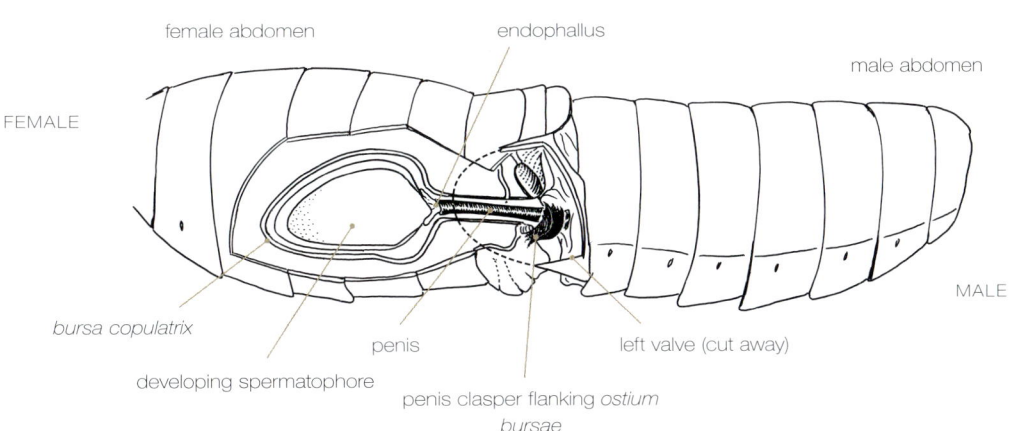

Figure 1.5: Anatomy of male and female reproductive systems and the mechanics of mating in the Orchard Butterfly (*Papilio aegeus*).

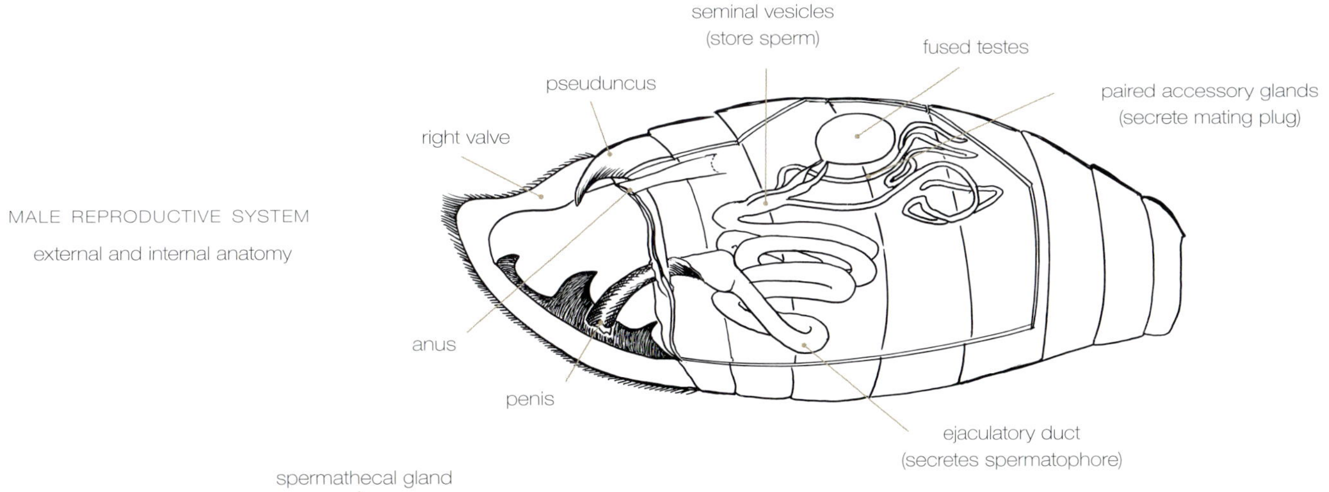

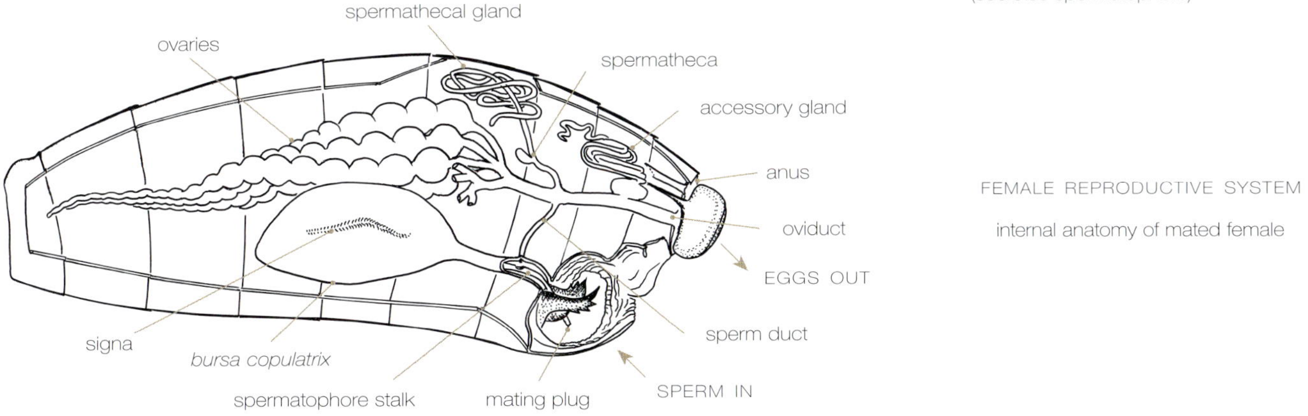

INTRODUCING THE BUTTERFLIES

2 THE AUSTRALIAN BUTTERFLIES AND THEIR HABITATS

With just 400 or so species, the Australian butterfly fauna may seem rather meagre when compared with the world total of over 17,000 species, most of which are confined to tropical rainforests. Even temperate North America, with over 700 species, significantly exceeds our total. No doubt Australia's relatively small total results from long geographic isolation and the aridity of the continent. Nevertheless, it is a highly distinctive and diverse fauna, with numerous species found nowhere else. In the right season, almost every habitat supports some butterflies, if only one of the few very widespread species. Moreover, several are specialised to highly inhospitable habitats, and these are often the most interesting species of all.

Discovery of the Australian Butterfly Fauna*

The Australian butterflies first came to the attention of Europeans when Captain Cook sailed the *Endeavour* up the east coast of Australia in 1770. He had with him naturalist Joseph Banks, later to become eminent in London, and it was Banks who wrote of his excitement at encountering mass aggregations of butterflies (probably Blue Tigers) and of hatching out a crow butterfly from its astonishing metallic-looking pupa. Banks collected 27 species of butterfly, including the first specimens of the Common Brown (*Heteronympha merope*). These 27 species were subsequently described and named in 1775 by the Danish entomologist and pupil of Linnaeus, Johann Fabricius (1745–1808). They included two so-called species of the swallowtail family, *Papilio cressida* and *Papilio harmonia*, which later proved to be, respectively, male and female of the same species we now know as the Big Greasy (*Cressida cressida*). The specimens, shown here, are still preserved in the Natural History Museum, London.

Once permanent colonies were established in Australia the butterflies attracted the interest of scientists in Europe, who clamoured for specimens. By 1805 Edward Donovan could refer to 38 species of Australian butterfly in his work *Insects*

Butterflies collected from Cooktown in 1770 by Joseph Banks

Papilio cressida

Papilio harmonia

---

* The following account is based mainly on that prepared by Max Moulds, in Kitching *et al.* (eds) (1999), listed under Further Reading and Societies, whose input we gratefully acknowledge.

18 The Butterflies of Australia

of New Holland, New Zealand, New Guinea, Otaheite and other Islands. Other naturalists of the time added descriptions of new species as they came to hand. A new phase of understanding of our butterflies began when experienced European scientists began to settle here. The most active and best known of these were the Macleays who, severally, lived in Sydney from 1826 onwards. Alexander Macleay was an outstanding and influential figure in the Royal Society and Linnaean Society in London, before being appointed to the post of Colonial Secretary of New South Wales. This meant that, almost from the beginning, Australian entomology was closely linked with the scientific establishment in Britain and Europe, then the world centre of science. The Macleays, in particular Alexander's nephew William Macleay, accumulated vast collections of insects and avidly promoted their study in Australia and New Guinea. These collections, which included the first known specimens of many species, eventually became the core of the Macleay Museum at the University of Sydney where they remain to this day. Of course, there were active naturalists in other centres, especially south-east Queensland, most notably Silvester Diggles, Thomas Lucas and William Miskin.

By the end of the nineteenth century, something like half of the Australian butterfly species we now recognise had been described and there was pressure for a general guidebook. Walker Scott had earlier set out to produce a series of volumes he called *Australian Lepidoptera and their Transformations*. Two volumes eventually appeared (1864 and 1890–98), beautifully illustrated with hand-coloured plates drawn by his daughters Harriet and Helena, but these were generally neither available nor affordable. The first genuinely popular guide was W.J. Rainbow's *A Guide to the Study of Australian Butterflies* (1907). This underrated book surely did much more to foster general interest in Australian butterflies than is generally admitted, as it was soon followed by G.A. Waterhouse and George Lyell's volume, *Butterflies of Australia*, the first really comprehensive 'modern' guide (1914). Then, in 1932, G.A. Waterhouse published a book with a much more popular title and colour illustrations, *What Butterfly is That?* This remained the standard work on Australian butterflies for over 40 years, and was in its time one of the best guides in the world. G.A. Waterhouse died in 1950 leaving a collection of more than 50,000 specimens that eventually became part of the collections of the Australian Museum in Sydney.

Many other enthusiasts of the time published accounts of life histories of our butterflies, or regional accounts, and amassed collections that eventually became core elements of our state museums (and the Australian National Insect Collection in Canberra). Just as today, most collectors were amateurs. Very few made the transition from amateur to professional, one of whom was Frederick Dodd. Dodd took up residence in Kuranda in far northern Queensland and initially made a living supplying specimens to rich overseas collectors. As that market gradually dwindled he opened a successful butterfly museum in Kuranda. The museum later became a travelling show, which toured eastern Australia to some acclaim. He also uncovered the extraordinary life cycle of the Moth Butterfly (*Liphyra brassolis*), the caterpillar of which feeds on the larvae of the green tree ants.

During the latter part of the twentieth century, science in general became more professional and a generation of full-time museum-based entomologists arose. Among these were butterfly specialists Alexander Burns in Melbourne and Norman Tindale in Adelaide. Of course, amateur interest persisted and continued to make important contributions to our knowledge of the Australian butterflies. Leonard Couchman, for example, revealed the world of Tasmanian butterflies almost single-handedly.

After the Second World War, the need for a new guide to Australian butterflies became acute. Charles Barrett and Alexander Burns published *Butterflies of Australia and New Guinea* in 1951. Although a useful and well-produced book, it was not the new guide that was needed: it described only a small selection of species, glossing over many of the smaller species, and set out to introduce the very large New Guinean fauna as well. The result was a compromise. Then, in 1964, Ian Common produced the tiny pocket guide *Australian Butterflies*. Although illustrated mostly in black and white, this invaluable booklet nevertheless enabled secure identification of virtually all the Australian species known at that time. He followed this up, in 1972, with the landmark volume *Butterflies of Australia*, co-authored with Douglas Waterhouse, nephew of G.A. Waterhouse. It is no coincidence that almost all of the colour plates used in the 1972 book were taken from the same paintings and blocks used in *What Butterfly is That?* in 1932.

In many ways, Common and Waterhouse's book marked the beginning of a new era of butterfly appreciation and study in Australia—and their book is still an essential tool for the modern student. Almost simultaneously, however, came two other notable works. In 1971, Bernard D'Abrera published *Butterflies of the Australian Region* and, in the same year, Charles McCubbin produced *Australian Butterflies*. Each was unique and, in a sense, complementary to Common and Waterhouse's book. The D'Abrera book was the first in a series that eventually illustrated almost all of the world's butterflies, apart from the skippers, which he omitted. It figures Australian butterflies comprehensively alongside their relatives from New Guinea, eastern Indonesia and the Pacific. The work relied on photographs from the unsurpassed collections of London's Natural History Museum, and D'Abrera raised the art of photographing mounted specimens to new heights. The McCubbin book was as much a work of art as a work of science and McCubbin himself painted the hundreds of illustrations, often against delightful scenic backgrounds from many parts of Australia. His subjects, though, almost always remained mounted specimens, arranged against living plants and scenic backgrounds, but indisputably dead, and spread in the museum manner or folded with tucked legs, as though removed from an envelope—another standard method of keeping specimens.

Amateur and professional students of butterflies were now well equipped and the next 25 to 30 years was a golden age for butterfly studies in Australia. State guides were produced for South Australia and Tasmania, the original locations of many of the hundreds of thousands of specimens in the nation's museums and private collections were transferred to an electronic data bank (and an extremely useful set of maps published from this database by Kelvin and Lawrence Dunn), new distribution records were accumulated, new species were described, and Australian butterfly species began to be used as focal points for all sorts of biological studies. In 1999 many of these results were summarised in a technical volume called *Biology of Australian Butterflies*, edited by Roger Kitching, Elly Scheermeyer, Rhondda Jones and Naomi Pierce.

By the new millennium, the flush of general guides from the early 1970s, although still useful, began to look a little out of date. Then Michael Braby published his monumental two-volume *Butterflies of Australia*. This summarised almost everything published about the natural history of our butterfly fauna at that time. Indeed, his book probably made the Australian butterfly fauna one of the best documented in the world. For the next several decades, all serious students of butterflies will need Braby's volumes as they provide a scientific foundation for this new century.

In spite of this history of scholarship we still know relatively little about our butterfly fauna. Even in the last few years, new species and subspecies have been described.

The full distributions and food plant ranges of many species remain to be determined. There are many life histories to be uncovered in detail. The many interactions between butterflies and other organisms are known for only a tiny number of species. The complex genetics of populations of the same or closely related species—so vital for conservation decision-making—are virtually unknown. And the ways in which our butterflies respond to human-imposed changes, such as land clearing, agriculture and, not least, climate change, remain to be documented.

Butterfly Families and Identification

The 400 or so species of Australian butterflies belong to five large families:

- the skippers—the Hesperiidae
- the swallowtails and birdwings—the Papilionidae
- the whites and yellows—the Pieridae
- the nymphs and their allies—the Nymphalidae
- the blues and hairstreaks—the Lycaenidae.

When identifying an unfamiliar butterfly, whether consciously or not, we almost always engage in a mental exercise in which the problem is resolved by a series of increasingly accurate approximations, beginning with family, then typically subfamily or tribe, before proceeding to genus and species. In this way we are able to make sense of the daunting and at first seemingly incomprehensible diversity represented by 25 subfamilies and tribes, the 98 genera, and so on. Understanding the families is a vital start to understanding butterflies.

The criteria by which families are defined are mainly structural, often quite technical. In the adult butterfly these structures may be difficult to see, especially if a specimen is observed in life. However, other characteristics, although not entirely reliable or even definable in a rigorous scientific sense, are nevertheless very helpful in placing an unfamiliar butterfly in the 'right area' for further identification. We are speaking here of a range of impressions and perceptions which collectively constitute the 'jizz' of the insect (to borrow a useful new word from the birdwatchers).

Important elements of jizz include the:

- size, ranging from tiny (wingspan less than 20 mm) to huge (wingspan more than 120 mm)
- dominant or apparent dominant colour in flight
- visible pattern on upper and/or underside
- wing shape and wing edges (whether smooth or scalloped)
- presence or absence of 'tails' on the hind wings
- build of the body (robust or slender)
- mode of flight (e.g., rapid wing beats or slow sailing)
- resting posture, and
- preferred height of activity (ground level or treetops).

What follows is a guide to the five main families and some of the very distinctive subfamilies, based on these and other impressionistic characteristics, as well as some of the more easily observed structural features.

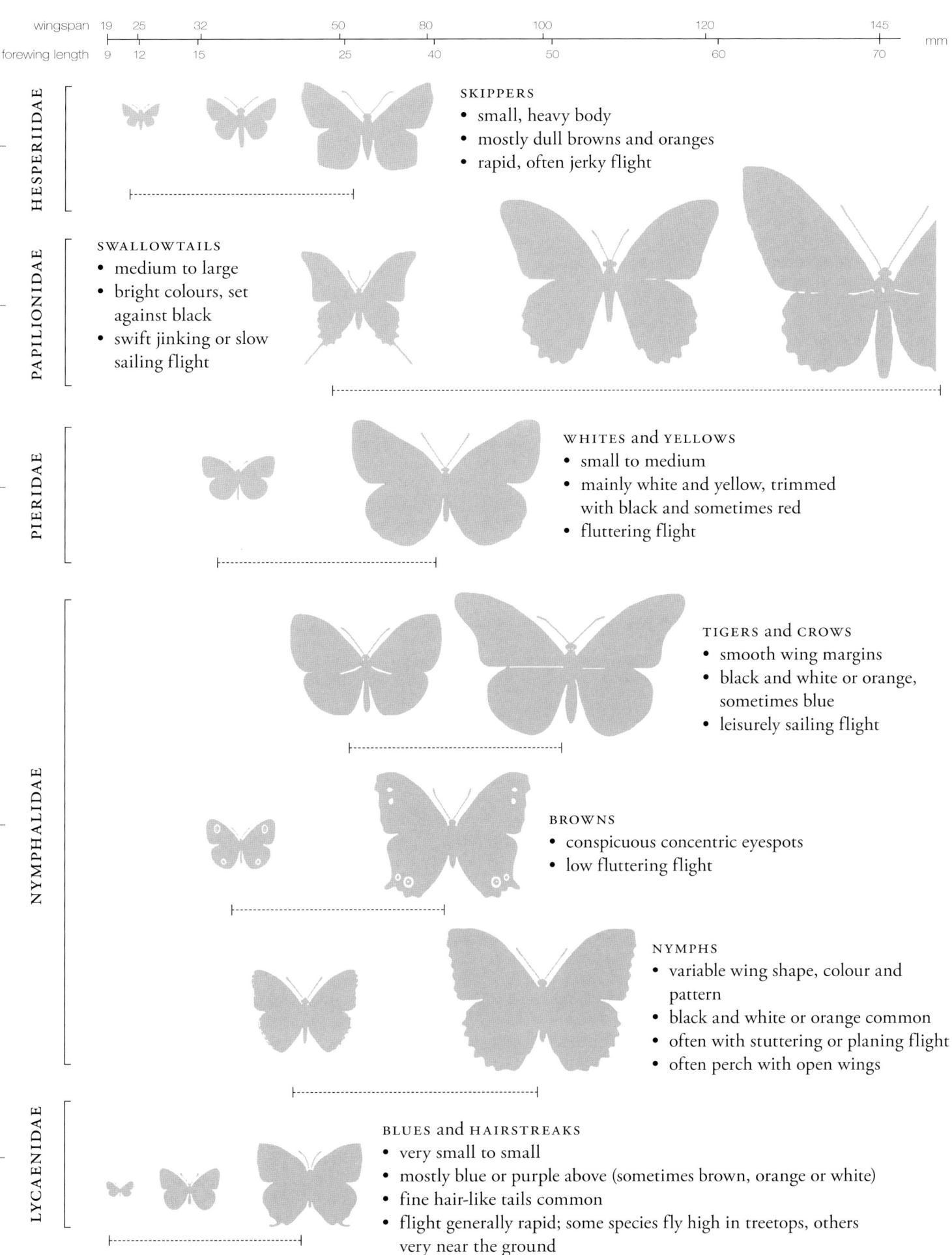

What Family?

SKIPPERS (Hesperiidae)

Mainly small with dull brown and orange colours; no eyespots or tails; robust body with antennae usually hook-tipped and always well separated at their base; often perch in the 'dart' position as shown (flat or folded in some); have rapid, jerky flight. *Main groups:* typical skippers, ochres and allies, awls and flats.

SWALLOWTAILS (Papilionidae)

Medium to very large with strong bright colours set in black; the hindwing margins are scalloped, sometimes with a strong tail; flight is swift jinking or slow sailing; very conspicuous, often seen feeding at flowers. *Main groups:* true swallowtails, triangles, swordtails and birdwings.

WHITES and YELLOWS (Pieridae)

Small to medium, mainly white, grey or yellow trimmed with black, sometimes with red spots beneath; never brown above; hindwing rounded, never with eyespots or tails; flight slow and fluttering or more rapid; perch with wings folded. *Main groups:* whites (including jezabels) and yellows.

NYMPHS and their allies (Nymphalidae)

Small to fairly large and very diverse in colour, pattern, wing shape, mode of flight and perching posture. *Main groups:* crows and tigers (sailing flight), browns (fluttering flight, always with eyespots) and true nymphs (often with planing flight, perching with open wings). Also includes distinctive and common species, such as the aeroplanes, the Tailed Emperor, the Glasswing, and the Hamadryad. Members of this family have tiny, barely visible brush-like forelegs and perch on just four legs—a feature often readily observed in nature.

BLUES and HAIRSTREAKS (Lycaenidae)

Generally small; mostly blue or purplish above but sometimes orange, brown, bronze or black and white; underside usually brownish with a fine and intricate pattern; fine hair-like tails on the hindwing associated with a 'false head' are common; flight is rapid and erratic. *Main groups:* blues and hairstreaks. There is no simple way of separating blues from hairstreaks, but hairstreaks tend to be larger and heavier in the body, whereas most blues are small and dainty. As a rule hairstreaks fly faster and higher, but there are many exceptions. The tropical Moth Butterfly also belongs in this family.

Where Are Our Butterflies Found?

We have over 400 species of butterflies in Australia. Yet in a garden in Melbourne we might be lucky to see twelve species, in Brisbane perhaps twice that number, and, in the far north, maybe 50 or 60 if we really worked at it. The shortfall between the grand total and what we see locally is because each species has a characteristic range—the geographical area within which, all else being equal, we stand a fair chance of encountering the species. We'll return to the issue of 'all else being equal' later in this section; for the moment, let's talk about geographical ranges.

If we take all of the ranges of all of the Australian butterfly species and superimpose them on a single map, we obtain the pattern shown in Figure 2.1. It shows us the contours of equal species richness—technically called isopleths—collected together in increments of 20 (west of the Great Dividing Range) or 50 species (on the east coast). When you look at Figure 2.1, it is immediately obvious that if we are interested solely in encountering the maximum possible number of species then the east coast north of Sydney is the place to be. The tropical north is especially rich, both at Cape York and in the wet tropics region around Cairns. The massive continental-scale gradients shown reflect the combination of average temperature and rainfall acting both directly on the butterflies themselves and, perhaps more importantly, on the diversity and growth rates of their many food plants. Simply to look at patterns of species richness, though, does not explain the historical question of why these patterns appear. The answer is provided by the science of biogeography.

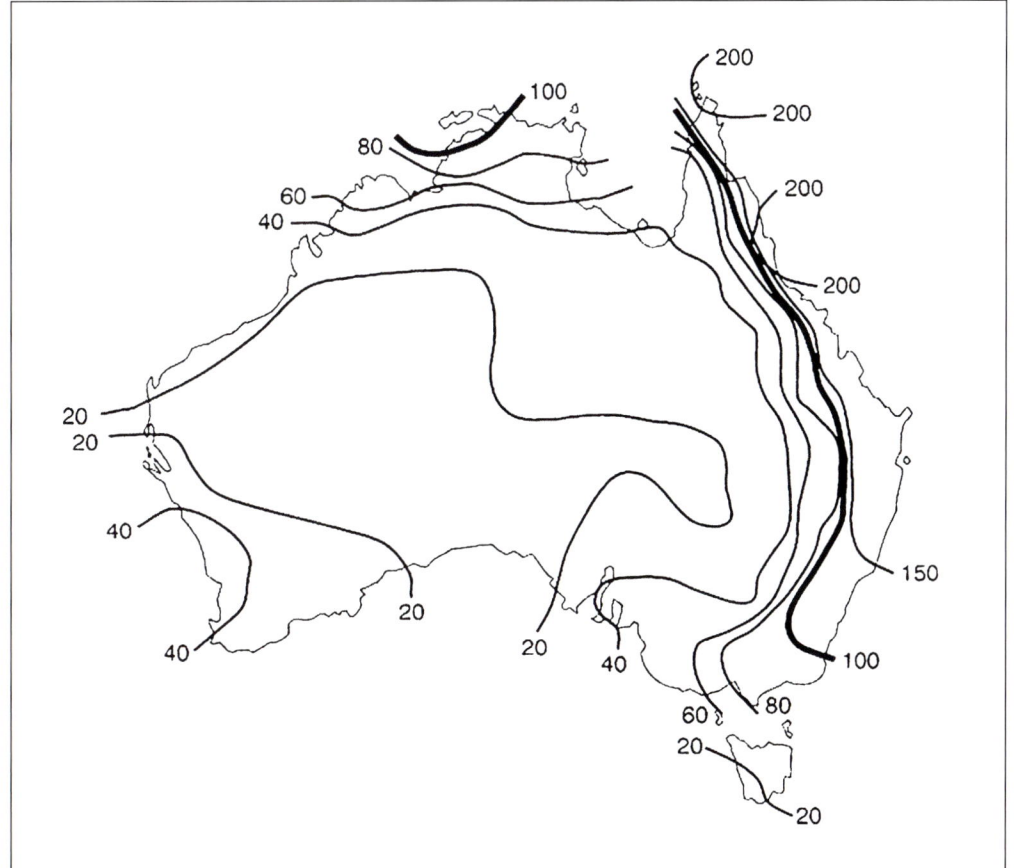

FIGURE 2.1: The distribution of Australian butterflies indicated by species richness isopleths, which show the minimum total number of species found within the areas defined.

Reproduced, with permission, from Kitching *et al.* (eds), *Biology of Australian Butterflies*, CSIRO Publishing, Melbourne, p. 63.

Where Did They Come From?

There are four issues central to understanding the origins of the Australian butterfly fauna.

Continental Drift or invasion from elsewhere?

Australia was once part of the supercontinent of Gondwana, which united the current landmasses of South America, Africa, Antarctica and Australia. Gondwana, a remnant of the unified landmass called Pangaea, existed from about 200 million years ago. In the mid-Jurassic period it began to break up into the continents (or parts of continents) that we now recognise, but the southern continents remained in close proximity for many millions of years. Of the groups of animals and plants that we recognise as typically Australian—such as the marsupials and gum trees—many have close relatives in South America and/or Africa. So what about the butterflies?

At one stage it was generally supposed that the ancestors of our butterflies invaded from Asia in geologically quite recent times (no more than twenty million years ago), reaching Australia via extensive land-bridges, which brought them within flying (or blowing) distance. Once in Australia, the process of evolutionary change and subdivision into many species then occurred. While this undoubtedly did happen, it now seems likely that the ancestors of some of our butterflies came with the continent as it broke from Gondwana, at least 60 million years ago. In recent work, Michael Braby and colleagues have shown that our jezabel butterflies (genus *Delias*) are closely related to members of several South American genera, notably *Catasticta* and its allies, and may be sister groups—that is, they all evolved from a common ancestor. All genera feed on mistletoes—a rather unusual food plant for butterflies—and have many DNA and life-history similarities. It must be stressed that the DNA results are not yet absolutely conclusive on the closeness of this relationship, but we may be sure that it will be resolved when more genes are examined. There are other groups of Australian butterflies that show similarities to South American species in other families, but the relationships now need to be confirmed genetically. Just how widespread this deep-time origin for our butterflies is remains to be seen, but there is little doubt that some of our butterflies are as fundamentally Australian as possums and bowerbirds, gum trees and lilli pillies.

Endemism and isolation

Regardless of where their ancestors came from, once isolated on parts of our continent butterflies began to evolve different appearances, behaviours and ecologies. The more isolated they were, the more differentiated they became. If species now occur only in Australia we refer to them as endemics. These tend to be smaller or more specialised species that have restricted distributions because of their environmental requirements, food plant ranges, inability to fly long distances or specialised interactions with other insect species (such as ants). Nevertheless, the wide-ranging and distinctive Dingy Swallowtail (*Papilio anactus*) is also endemic to mainland Australia. In Australia there are three regions in which local specialised endemics are particularly numerous: in the south-east and south-west of the continent, and in Tasmania. In the south-west and in Tasmania, the actual number of species present is not large but, because of their obvious geographical isolation, the species that do occur there are often different from those elsewhere in the continent. The great bulge in endemics in the south-east of the continent proper is because several evolutionary lines of cool-adapted butterflies have done particularly well there. Many of the trapezitine skippers—a whole subfamily endemic to Australia—are found here, as are the many genera of browns, such as *Heteronympha*, *Oreixenica* and *Geitoneura*. These groups do occur elsewhere, but in the south-east they predominate. This pattern of endemicity contrasts strongly with the north of the continent where isolation has not been so complete. Many of the species there, or their near relatives, occur well beyond Australia's northern limits; as long as there are occasional fresh immigrants from New Guinea or further afield, the Australian species in this region do not differentiate genetically to form separate species.

The northern connection

The richest areas of our continent in terms of sheer numbers of species are in the far north, particularly Cape York and the wet tropics region, from the Daintree to Ingham. This is partly because these areas have some of the most biodiverse and varied landscapes in Australia, with the highest rainfall and temperatures. In addition, these are the areas closest to, and in a direct path from, the biologically rich landmasses to our north. There are local endemics, but more often the species we encounter in the north have other populations across the Torres Strait in New Guinea, or even in South-East Asia. The ecological class of butterflies that have made the journey is interesting. In Australia very few rainforest butterflies are confined to the understorey, where the humidity rarely drops below 90 per cent. The Hamadryad (*Tellervo zoilus*) and the Large Green-banded Blue (*Danis danis*) in the Queensland wet tropics region are notable exceptions. In New Guinea, and even more so in tropical Asia, Africa and South America, rich groups of species of rainforest understorey butterflies have evolved, with numerous species from many families. It seems probable that, because of their habitat requirements, New Guinea and South-East Asian understorey dwellers were at no time able to cross the arid land or narrow sea barriers that have always existed between Australia and the near north.

The scattered patches of rainforest in the northern part of Cape York Peninsula—at places with evocative names like Iron Range, Bamaga and Coen, as well as on the Torres Strait Islands—are particularly rich in welcome northern invaders. The careful sampling of these remote areas has added considerable numbers of species to our known fauna over the last 30 years. Magnificent species, such as the Turquoise Emperor (*Apaturina erminea*) and the Owl (*Taenaris artemis*), occur only here in Australia, yet are widespread in New Guinea. A few species also reach our region through connections with islands like Timor and Sumba to the west; the beautiful Orange Lacewing (*Cethosia penthesilea*) is perhaps the most spectacular example. The occasional occurrence of rare vagrants—wandering individuals with no permanent population on the continent—especially in the Torres Strait, clearly show that this process of natural invasion is an ongoing one. Michael Parsons' *Butterflies of Papua New Guinea* whets our appetite for what might turn up, quite naturally, in Australia one day.

The human impact

Of course, in addition to the natural biogeographic processes that we have just discussed, humans, particularly over the last 220 years, have had massive effects on the distributions of butterflies and, in consequence, the numbers of species that we might find in a particular place. Sometimes we have added species: the Cabbage White (*Pieris rapae*) and the Wanderer (*Danaus plexippus*) were both added accidentally, either as incidental passengers with foodstuffs or as stowaways on ships. In other instances we have extended the ranges of native butterflies by our garden and commercial plantings. The citrus swallowtails (*Papilio aegeus, anactus, fuscus* and *canopus*) have all benefited from commercial and domestic plantings of citrus fruit. There are many more examples.

As Australia has developed, however, vast areas of native bushland have been destroyed, taking with them many populations of butterflies; these negative impacts have far outweighed the positive ones. Some areas have been more susceptible than others. More than half of the subtropical and tropical rainforest that existed in 1788 is gone—and this ecosystem is by far the richest in butterfly species (and virtually all other forms of land life). The brigalow belt in northern New South Wales and Queensland has been decimated, and with it specialised butterflies such as the Brigalow Blue (*Jalmenus eubulus*) and Bulloak Jewel (*Hypochrysops piceatus*).

Where to Look for Butterflies in the Landscape

As every naturalist knows, just going to a region indicated on a distribution map will not necessarily turn up the butterflies you seek. This is where an understanding of local distributions becomes vital—not only of the butterflies but of their known host plants. There is a great deal of experience involved in achieving success, but there are three factors that are especially significant in determining just where adult butterflies may be encountered. These are altitude, exact habitat type and height above the ground.

The effect of altitude

The pattern of ecosystems encountered as one ascends from sea level on the east coast is both characteristic and striking. From coastal dune systems or mangroves we progress to moist coastal plains with wet sclerophyll forest, perhaps with patches of scattered true rainforest. Then we move into tall, dry eucalypt forest. Proceeding up the massif of the Australian Alps, for example, we ascend through wet and dry sclerophyll woodland, dominated by different species of gum trees. As we enter the high country, the forests thin and shorten into woodlands and then grassy savannahs. Passing the final snowgum woodlands we climb above the tree line and find ourselves in open tundra-like short heathland covered in a rich array of alpine herbs. Extraordinarily, we can do all of this in the course of a single day's drive.

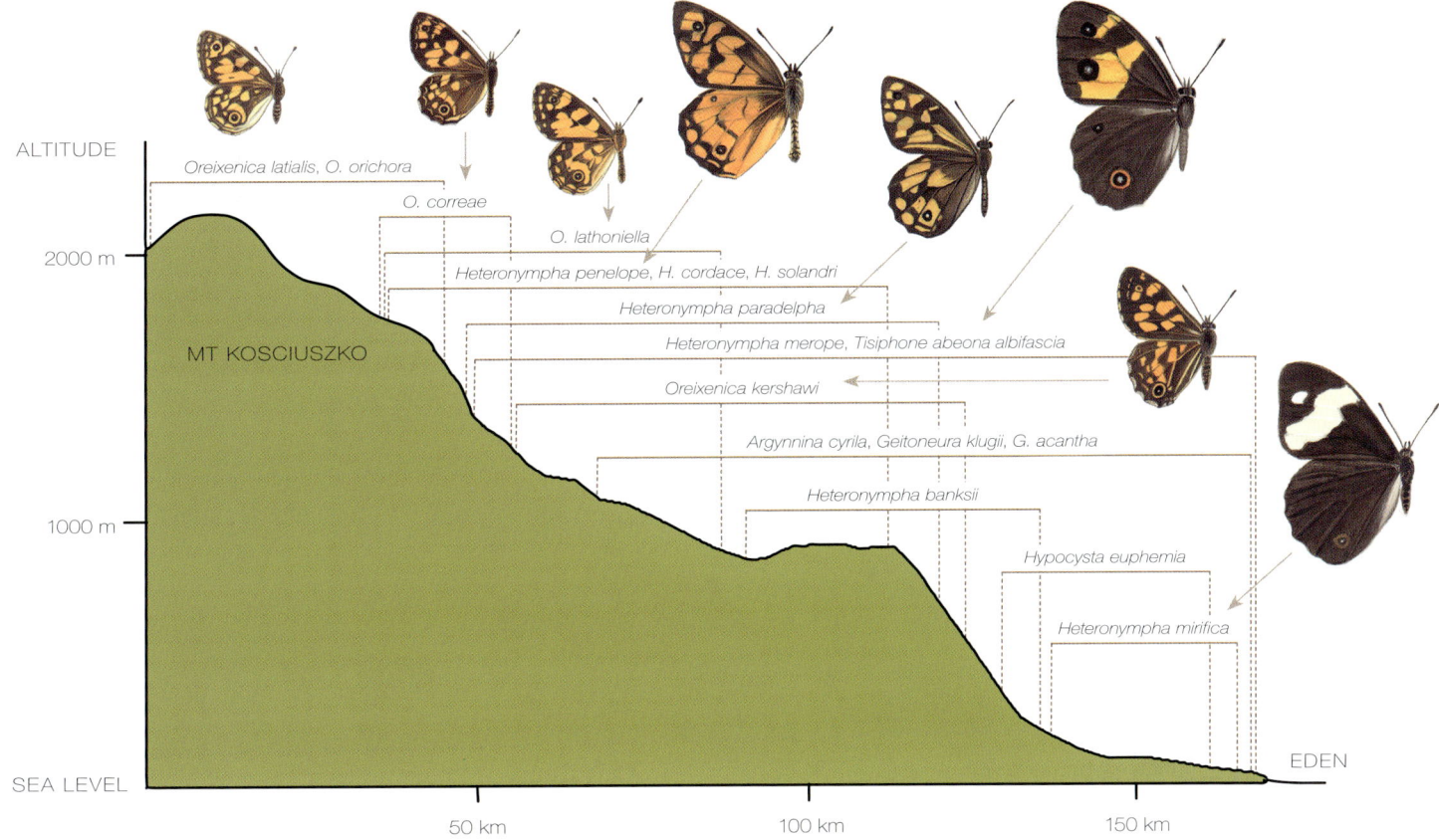

FIGURE 2.2: The altitudinal distribution of browns along a transect from the coast at Eden to the summit of Mt Kosciuszko, New South Wales.

If, however, we stop to look for butterflies we will see different species within different altitudinal zones. Figure 2.2 illustrates these changes for some of the brown butterflies (Satyrinae) that we might encounter moving from Eden to Mt Kosciuszko. This is the region where we find the greatest concentration of species of this group, all of them endemic. There are many reasons for these characteristic patterns. Particular species are more or less tolerant of extreme weather conditions; others track similarly stratified distributions of their host plants—various grasses and sedges in the case of the browns. How they came to specialise in this way is a different question.

In other parts of the continent there are different sequences of ecosystems and different sets of butterflies occur, but there is always a characteristic turnover of communities as you move away from the coast and up the ranges.

Vertical stratification and localisation within forests

Most of the places in Australia with rich butterfly assemblages occur in forests or woodlands. Many butterflies feed on the foliage of woody plants or the vines and epiphytes associated with them. Even those that specialise on low-growing herbs and grasses occur primarily in woodlands and forests. Within these ecosystems there is stratification similar to that seen along altitudinal gradients, but this time moving from the ground to the canopy high above.

Figure 2.3 shows the ground-to-canopy variation in distributions of adult butterflies seen at a particular well-known locality near Leyburn in inland south-east Queensland. This area has a mosaic of open woodland types, with scattered tall eucalypt forests interspersed with stands of old *Casuarina* or *Angophora* trees. Both eucalypts and casuarinas are heavily infested by mistletoes. Where we encounter species within the forest reflects two things: breeding sites and behaviour. So, in the high canopy, we find the four species of azures *(Ogyris* spp.) flying and often resting fairly close to clumps of their mistletoe food plants. But there is also horizontal separation. The Southern Large Azure (*Ogyris genoveva*) is found only around the pendulous mistletoe growing on eucalypts, at a site found a few hundred metres from the Bulloak stands, to which several other species are confined—namely the high-flying Bulloak Jewel (*Hypochrysops piceatus*) and three more species of azure (*Ogyris* spp.), which feed on a filamentous mistletoe that grows only on *Casuarina*. Finally, among the high fliers, the Bright Purple Jewel (*H. cyane*) is found only around the tops of the Apple Gums (*Angophora costata*), often perching well over 20 m in the canopy. Similarly, at ground level, *Lomandra*-feeding skippers seldom move more than a few metres from their patchy food plant stands. Imperial blues, such as *Jalmenus ictinus* and the almost indistinguishable *J. pseudictinus*, are confined to low *Acacia* shrubs, which host dramatically different ant species in each case, and they seldom venture far from these associates.

Other more widespread species fly mainly within a few metres of the ground, tend to perch less frequently, and are not necessarily found near their host plant or in any particular forest subtype. Many engage in long-distance movement, or feed on such generalised hosts as common grasses or weedy herbs. They are found almost everywhere, often beyond the forest margins. The Chequered Swallowtail (*Papilio demoleus*) and the Lemon Migrant (*Catopsilia pomona*) are great migrants; the Small Grass Yellow (*Eurema smilax*), Dingy Ring (*Ypthima arctoa*) and Common Grass Blue (*Zizina labradus*) are great generalists, and very low-flying. In this, and other communities, localised species present the greatest conservation challenges.

Maximum butterfly diversity is to be found in the Queensland tropics. Within this area, the greatest number of species is associated with lowland rainforest. Here, too, there is vertical stratification, with species such as the Sword-tailed Flash (*Bindahara phocides*) and the Small Oakblue (*Arhopala wildei*) almost confined to the canopy. Others, such as the triangles (*Graphium* spp.) and the Ulysses Butterfly (*Papilio ulysses*), treat the canopy and its margins like a vast amusement park, jinking wildly over the undulations of the treetops, and, without warning, diving suddenly to feed at low flowers. The Cairns Birdwing (*Ornithoptera euphorion*) also flies high, with a majestic, even floppy serenity, and seldom descends below 4 m. Few Australian butterflies are restricted to the understorey, but many, particularly nymphs and aeroplanes, are found low in sunny or semi-shaded gaps, along broad creeks or along forest margins, especially around lantana flowers.

Outside the rainforest, there is a smaller but distinct group of species associated with open grassland or woodland. Species such as the Big Greasy (*Cressida cressida*) and the Glasswing (*Acraea andromacha*) are found here, along with widespread skippers, grass blues and grass yellows, all of which avoid the rainforest. Highly localised sedge-feeding ochres and mistletoe-feeding blues also occur in highly specific localities within this general habitat. Near the coast, there is a small but very specialised community of very localised species associated with coastal swamp and mangroves. The rare Apollo Jewel (*Hypochrysops apollo*), which feeds inside ant plants (*Myrmecodia* spp.), is the most

FIGURE 2.3 (OPPOSITE): Distribution of butterflies within an open forest habitat on the Darling Downs, Queensland, showing vertical stratification, and localisation with respect to different vegetation types and host plant associations.

spectacular member of this assemblage. (Ant plants are bulbous epiphytes with pre-formed galleries occupied by ants; they depend on the ants for nourishment.) Interestingly, Australia has a relatively rich butterfly fauna occurring in mangrove forests, whereas the botanically even richer mangroves of South-East Asia, with their many ant plants, have almost no butterflies.

When to Look for Butterflies

Finally, to find butterflies, we must consider season. Australia is a huge place, with a north to south gradient in temperature and an east to west gradient in rainfall. Most of us speak of summer and winter, but in the far north these become wet and dry seasons respectively. Superimposed on these basic seasonal patterns are long periods of nearly continent-wide drought interspersed with years of extraordinary wetness.

Broadly, it is true to say that as we travel from Tasmania in the south to Cape York in the north, we progress from a temperate habitat in which adult butterflies occur only from spring to early autumn, with each species having just one generation each year, to a wet tropical habitat where most species breed all the year round with overlapping generations, so that at any time adults of most species may be on the wing. This is more or less the case even as far south as Cairns, although species such as the Cairns Birdwing (*Ornithoptera euphorion*) are uncommon in mid-winter and most species in this area occur in lower numbers during winter than just after the wet season (February to April). Exceptions are cold-loving species such as the Northern Jezabel (*Delias argenthona*) which are much more abundant in winter at these latitudes, especially in the mountains.

Moving south, even between Townsville and Mackay, winters begin to become cooler and most butterflies become scarce after May, a situation exacerbated by the reduced rainfall during the tropical dry season. South of the Tropic of Capricorn, at Rockhampton, to around Brisbane, many species of adult butterflies disappear from May until early September, with very few species at all in July and August. Exceptions are winter specialists such as the Common Jezabel (*Delias nigrina*) and some crow butterflies and relatives that overwinter as adults; they shelter for much of their time in damp warm gullies in aggregations of inactive individuals who will delay breeding until spring.

Once we reach central New South Wales, again cold-loving jezabels excepted, butterflies are seldom on the wing during the winter months (June to August), and more and more species have just a single generation per year. Even so, species such as the Common Brown (*Heteronympha merope*) may live for many months as they aestivate during the dry summer months (that is, the equivalent of hibernation but occurring in the summer rather than the winter). They neither mate nor lay eggs, but wait for the late summer rains to promote fresh grass. The larvae then develop during the winter and emerge next spring.

Phenology—the pattern of seasonal appearance of adults of different species—may be 'hard-wired' or 'soft-wired'. Soft-wired species include mainly tropical species such as the Orchard Butterfly (*Papilio aegeus*), which extends south to Sydney, and at that latitude has one or two generations each year (fewer if it reaches Melbourne); in the tropics, however, it may have six or more generations. On the other hand, species which have a southern origin, such as the Shouldered Brown (*Heteronympha penelope*), will go through only one generation regardless of conditions, spending 8–9 months as a larva, even when reared in warm conditions. In Melbourne and Adelaide, most adult butterflies are seen only during late spring, summer and early autumn. Most temperate species have distinct flight periods of between two and three months, with spring species, such as the Western Xenica (*Geitoneura minyas*), flying from September to November, and autumn species, such as the Tasmanian Ptunarra Xenica (*Oreixenica ptunarra*), flying from February to April. In the highly seasonal tropics around Darwin, few species are common in the dry season from April to August, despite the generally warm temperatures.

All butterflies outside the wet tropics region need a strategy to cope with hard times, be it winter cold or dry-season drought. As mentioned, some species remain inactive as adults through the summer (in response to dry conditions), and others overwinter as adults (in response to cool and/or dry conditions). Many enter diapause, a state of suspended development, as eggs, larvae or pupae. Among swallowtails, pupal diapause may last years during prolonged drought. The particular immature stage at which overwintering or aestivation occurs influences the time of appearance of adults. Species such as the Common Imperial Blue (*Jalmenus evagoras*), for example, in which late-summer adults lay large clusters of eggs that hatch in spring, emerge later than species that overwinter as pupae.

One response to adversity, including lack of food, is migration, and spectacular migrations are made with some predictability by many species. Along the subtropical east coast, hundreds or thousands of Caper Whites (*Belenois java*) appear over a few days in late spring, all heading more or less in the same direction, often out to sea, where most drown. Milkweed butterflies in general (*Danaus, Euploea, Tirumala* spp.) are also well known for migratory behaviour, heading south following build-ups in population, often invading locations far beyond their normal range. More modest range expansions occur in tropical species such as bushbrowns (*Mycalesis* spp.) and grass yellows (*Eurema* spp.) as they spread inland and south during the warm wet season without actual mass migration being evident.

3 RELATIONSHIPS WITH PLANTS AND OTHER ANIMALS

Common Crow (*Euploea core*) larva

Whenever we observe or contemplate a butterfly, we must bear in mind that it is part of an ecological community. It lives with other species—other butterflies, birds, reptiles, parasitic wasps, plants, and even micro-organisms. Butterflies do not interact directly with all other species with which they share a particular environment, but they do have close relationships with a surprising number. We can think of these as those species on which the butterflies 'prey'—that is, their food plants; those which prey on the butterflies—their natural enemies; and those with which the butterflies compete for food—especially herbivores or nectarivores; and, finally, those which have a mutually beneficial relationship with butterflies—the plants they pollinate or the ants that attend their larvae.

Over millennia, evolutionary responses have occurred in butterflies and in the species with which they interact. These responses may be a sort of arms race, as with predator and prey species, or a gradual adaptation to the needs of the other species, in mutually beneficial ways. This has produced such wonderful phenomena as warning coloration, mimicry and camouflage, anatomical, behavioural and ecological responses that have become genetically 'hard-wired' into particular species in consequence of long-term interactions with other species.

Food Plants—the Butterfly's Prey

All but fifteen of Australia's butterfly species have larvae that feed on living plants. The exceptions probably all feed on the larvae of ants, and spend their juvenile lives inside ant nests (although this remains to be confirmed in some of the rarer species of ant blues, *Acrodipsas* spp.). These ant-feeders are true predators, inasmuch as they are animals feeding on animals; however, the interaction between the other 390-odd species and their food plants is also predation in the broader sense that one species (the plant) suffers while the other (the larva) benefits.

In Australia there is scarcely a flowering plant that is not attacked by some Lepidoptera, although various well-known plants, such as eucalypts and *Banksia*, tend to be mainly hosts to night-flying moths rather than butterflies. The flowering plants[*]

---

[*] We are aware that serious botanists may protest, and say this view is old-fashioned or even wrong. We persist in recognising this distinction, partly because many of our readers will also understand this scheme, and partly because butterflies also appear to observe it.

can be divided into monocotyledons (those plants that send a single spear-shoot from the seed, such as grasses, sedges, gingers and palms), and the dicotyledons (those that produce two embryonic leaves upon germination and include most other flowering plants, ranging from tiny herbs and vines to rainforest trees). All but three of our herbivorous butterflies feed as larvae on flowering plants, but they do tend to be specialised to either monocotyledons or dicotyledons, with whole subfamilies of butterflies feeding on one or the other type of plant. The three exceptions that feed on non-flowering plants are the cycad-feeding blue (*Theclinesthes onycha*), which feeds on a range of naturally occurring species of cycad and relatives along our east coast, and the two species of tropical fern-feeding jewels (*Hypochrysops hippuris* and *H. theon*), which feed on several rainforest ferns. Although some of the very earliest Lepidoptera back in the Jurassic were probably originally cycad- and fern-feeders, our Cycad Blue (*Theclinesthes onycha*) and fern-feeding jewels are certainly throwbacks, so to speak, having adopted their feeding habits relatively recently; they almost certainly evolved from ancestors that fed on the foliage of flowering plants.

Feeding habits

The majority of our butterfly fauna feed as larvae on the leaves of their food plants. Sometimes they simply sit on the leaves and chew away at the edges with impressive dedication. The familiar larva of the Lesser Wanderer (*Danaus petilia*) is typical, gradually defoliating the leaves of the milkweeds on which it feeds. Watch one feeding for a few minutes and you will see the leaf disappear before your eyes. Other species scrape away at one surface of the leaf, leaving characteristic bare patches but seldom penetrating the full thickness of the leaf. The beautifully camouflaged larva of the Small Green-banded Blue (*Psychonotis caelius*) does this, feeding on the white undersides of the leaves of the red ash (*Alphitonia* spp.), common in east coast woodlands. Many species use strands of silk they produce from glands associated with their mouthparts to roll up the leaves on which they are feeding and so obtain protection from both weather and enemies. They may emerge from these shelters to feed on other foliage at night, or feed within them. They generally also use these shelters as pupation sites. Almost all of the skippers do this, pulling together the edges of the leaves of the grasses and sedges or other plants on which they feed.

However, not all herbivorous larvae feed on leaves. Some feed on buds and fully open flowers and may adopt different colour forms to match different backgrounds. This habit is common among the lycaenid butterflies, such as the tiny, *Acacia*-feeding Two-spotted Lineblue (*Nacaduba biocellata*). Other lycaenids have adapted to living in the seeds or fruits of their food plants, eating the seeds and/or flesh of berries from the inside out, emerging from the fruit only to pupate. The Bright Cornelian (*Deudorix diovis*) lives inside the seeds of rainforest trees, some of which, like the tuckeroo (*Cupaniopsis anacardioides*), are common garden trees in subtropical towns and cities. Lastly, the larva of the Apollo Jewel (*Hypochrysops apollo*), feeds inside the galleries within the swollen bulbous stem of the epiphytic ant plants (*Myrmecodia* spp.). Although they emerge from the ant nest, which is habitually part of the swollen stem, they feed on the plant tissue itself, not on ant larvae.

Many butterfly larvae feed principally at night and withdraw to shelters or other refuges during the day. We have already discussed the leaf-rolling habits of skippers. Others, like the larva of the Tailed Emperor (*Polyura sempronius*), engage in what is called 'central-place foraging'. After hatching from the egg it manufactures a silken pad close to a suitable area of foliage and spends most of the day resting on the pad, foraging out to feed on the surrounding foliage. As the larva grows, so the foraging distance increases. Just before pupation, the silken pad may be surrounded by an area of devastation, with the larva moving as much as a metre to find fresh food. Other larvae are herded by ants back and forth into ant nests or specially constructed byres. We discuss this habit at the end of the chapter.

Specialisation

A question of great importance in terms of conservation and, indeed, understanding the whole notion of why some species of butterfly are rarer than others, is that of host specialisation. Just how many species of host plants does a particular butterfly have, and what range of plant families do these represent?

Perhaps the most specialised of all Australian butterflies, in this respect, is the Mountain Iris Skipper (*Mesodina aeluropis*), which is recorded as breeding on just one colour form of the native iris (*Patersonia sericea*) in scattered locations in the subalpine woodlands of the south-east. By contrast, the Fiery Jewel (*Hypochrysops ignitus*) feeds on at least 48 species of plants from 30 genera in nineteen families, including mainly dicotyledons but also one monocotyledon. Another more familiar generalist species is the Tailed Emperor (*Polyura sempronius*), which has been found breeding on 46 species of plants belonging to 24 genera and eleven families of plants. The Common Crow (*Euploea core*) has been recorded from more food plants but of a narrower variety than *Polyura*. The Orange Palm Dart (*Cephrenes augiades*) feeds on over 130 plant species, but all of them are palms. About a fifth of our butterflies are recorded from just one species of plant, although in some cases this may reflect lack of knowledge about remote species rather than the true situation. Once we get to the level of the plant genus, however, the picture changes. Almost half of all our species are restricted, as far as we know, to just a single genus of plants. This varies from butterfly family to family—and indeed, among the skippers the figure is over 60 per cent. Of course, within each butterfly family there is a range of specialists and generalists but, overall, only about a fifth of all our butterflies feed as larvae on more than one family of plants.

There are both advantages and disadvantages of feeding on one or many food plants. Specialising on just a single species of food plant means that you might avoid having a lot of competitors for that food resource. On the other hand, you are very vulnerable should something disastrous happen to your food plant. By having alternatives, a butterfly species is able to switch to other plant species when times are tough. Inevitably, when a wide range of hosts is used, some are favoured much more than others, but it helps to have a fall-back position. Most butterfly species seem to have compromised in an evolutionary sense by becoming very efficient at exploiting one or two related groups of plants. This often produces clear patterns in which genera, tribes or even subfamilies of butterflies become closely associated with particular genera or families of plants. The birdwings (*Ornithoptera*) and their relatives, which feed only on native Dutchman's Pipes (a few species of *Aristolochia* and *Pararistolochia*), provide an excellent example; there are many other such cases.

Poisonous plants

Although we see a wide range of herbivores, from kangaroos to butterfly larvae, feeding on plants, it should not be assumed that plants are passive bystanders in this exploitation. Over time, plants have evolved an impressive array of defence mechanisms to minimise the harm caused by herbivores. These range from fearsome arrays of spines, through irritant hairs and toughening agents within leaves, to highly toxic and foul-tasting chemicals explicitly developed to give herbivores a nasty shock when they attack the plant. Undoubtedly some of these defence mechanisms evolved to deter vertebrate herbivores. Major arrays of spines and internal toxins probably belong to this category. Less dramatic arrays of hairs upon leaves and stems, and the processes of tanning in leaves, which become hardened and much less palatable with age, have probably developed to deter insect herbivores.

How do insects cope with these plant defences? Sometimes they avoid the plants with the toughest defences and switch over time to other food plants. When they persist with the more difficult food plant, the egg-laying female seeks out newly flushing leaves and buds so that the particularly sensitive young larvae will have access to softer tissue before the processes of tanning, for example, are completed. In other cases they may overcome the protective devices more directly. Sometimes the young larvae of crow butterflies (*Euploea* spp.) chew through the main veins of leaves before eating them, so restricting the flow of protective latex into the leaves.

However, day-flying butterflies and moths may have special reasons for acquiring an immunity to poisonous plants, even if it means they develop more slowly than on unprotected plant species; by exploiting the plant's anti-vertebrate poisons they can gain protection against their most formidable predators. Families of plants such as the Asclepiadaceae and Apocynaceae—for example, milkweeds and oleander—synthesise heart-poisons called cardiac glycosides, which they store in their leaves. Other plants have evolved similar mechanisms involving different poisons. Indeed because of these chemicals, toxic plants frequently also have medicinal properties which, used carefully, have therapeutic value in humans. Many common synthetic pharmaceuticals are based on compounds originally derived from such plants.

In some cases the butterflies that feed on toxic plants have developed mechanisms to extract and store these chemicals within their larvae (crow butterflies included), carrying them through to the adult stage, and then exploiting them as anti-vertebrate protective devices. A wide range of plants used by Australian butterflies contain such chemicals which, in turn, are used as protection by adult butterflies, principally against birds. In addition to the cardiac glycosides in milkweed and their relatives, probably all mistletoes contain toxins, as do the Dutchman's Pipes (*Aristolochia*), passion vines (*Passiflora*) and their relatives. *Acacia*, laurels and a range of other plants synthesise cyanides, and even citrus, figs and cabbages contain chemicals that discourage herbivores. Just how many of the butterflies that feed on these plants actually exploit and store these protective chemicals is far from fully understood. We know the habit is widespread in the tiger and crow butterflies (the subfamily Danainae). Mistletoe-feeding whites of the genus *Delias* also appear to obtain chemical protection from their food plants. The species that feed on *Aristolochia* and *Passiflora* are believed to be nearly universally toxic. On the other hand, citrus-feeders seem to be unpleasant to the taste; they are avoided by fastidious bird species and eaten without enthusiasm by hardy generalists, such as magpies and drongos. In other cases we think this mechanism may be operating but await research to confirm our suspicions.

Warning coloration

From an evolutionary point of view, being protected by poisons that have been extracted from a food plant has little advantage if the carrier of the poisons has to die before its predators—such as insectivorous birds—learn that it is so protected. As a consequence, many butterflies have developed bright warning coloration to make it easy for a predator to recognise them as soon as it has learned that they taste bad, or cause vomiting. These aposematic colours often evolve along with a tougher outer coating on the butterfly's body, so that 'tasting' is often possible without death being inevitable for the insect. In other cases, the sacrifice of one or two individuals will benefit their close relatives once particular predators have learned to associate a distinctive bright colour pattern with a bad food experience.

FIGURE 3.1: Sequence showing a naïve Spangled Drongo catching and eating a Common Jezabel (*Delias nigrina*), then vomiting shortly after.

Mimicry

One remarkable consequence of this chemical protection has been the evolution of mimicry. Mimicry in general is the process by which one species evolves to look like another to which it is not at all closely related. For this to happen there needs to be some advantage to at least one, sometimes both, of the butterfly species concerned.

Biologists recognise two distinct forms of mimicry although, when examined carefully, there appear to be many intermediate cases between these two extremes.

The most celebrated form of mimicry was that discovered by Henry Bates, an English naturalist and explorer, during his studies of butterflies on the Amazon in the mid-nineteenth century. Bates observed that some species of butterfly were advertising the fact that they are chemically protected by displaying bright warning colours, and that other species not chemically protected had evolved the same bright warning colours, apparently pretending to be the protected species. The protected species he called the 'model', the copy the 'mimic'. As long as there are not too many of the 'tasty' mimics compared with the numbers of the truly protected models, the mimic (a Batesian mimic in this case) gains protection against the predators that have learned to associate a particular warning pattern with a bad experience. In the Australian butterfly fauna the most obvious example is probably the extraordinary similarity between females of the Danaid Eggfly (*Hypolimnas misippus*) and both males and females of the Lesser Wanderer (*Danaus petilia*). The mimetic Danaid Eggfly feeds as a larva on a range of small herbs and is not chemically protected. The model, the Lesser Wanderer, like all members of its subfamily (the Danainae), feeds on a variety of milkweeds and other highly toxic plants and is chemically protected as an adult. As in this case, it often happens that only the female is a Batesian mimic. This probably occurs when females prefer males with their original sexually explicit colours. Being protected from predators is no advantage if females will not mate with you.

The second generally acknowledged form of mimicry was recognised by the German naturalist Fritz Müller, late in the nineteenth century. In Müllerian mimicry a group of species which may or may not be closely related, but all of which have some degree of chemical protection against predators, evolve to look similar. The chemical protection of each species in the 'mimicry ring' is often based on a completely different plant toxin. In this case, a predator learns to fear a whole set of species, sharing a common livery, and does not need to taste each one separately—so reducing the risk to individuals of any of the participating species of being killed by an uneducated predator. Several spectacular Müllerian mimicry rings are known, mainly in South America. There are only a few good examples of Müllerian mimicry among the Australian butterflies and day-flying moths (although the same principle of resemblance among wasps and toxic day-flying moths occurs frequently). The Orange Lacewing (*Cethosia penthesilea*) and Lesser Wanderer (*Danaus petilia*), which fly together near Darwin, are probably Müllerian mimics. Crows (*Euploea* spp.) may also show this type of resemblance, but it is difficult to say if they look similar because they are mimicking one another or simply because they are closely related.

In between are associations where neither model nor mimic is particularly good to eat, but one is much more toxic than the other. For example, the Ambrax Butterfly female (*Papilio ambrax*) mimics the Red-bodied Swallowtail (*Pachliopta polydorus*) and the Dingy Swallowtail (*Papilio anactus*) mimics the male Big Greasy (*Cressida cressida*). We would normally call this Batesian mimicry, because the model is clearly very much better protected than the mimic, but it is likely neither of the mimics is fully palatable either. Mimicry in general has never been closely studied in Australia and there are exciting opportunities for future work by enthusiasts.

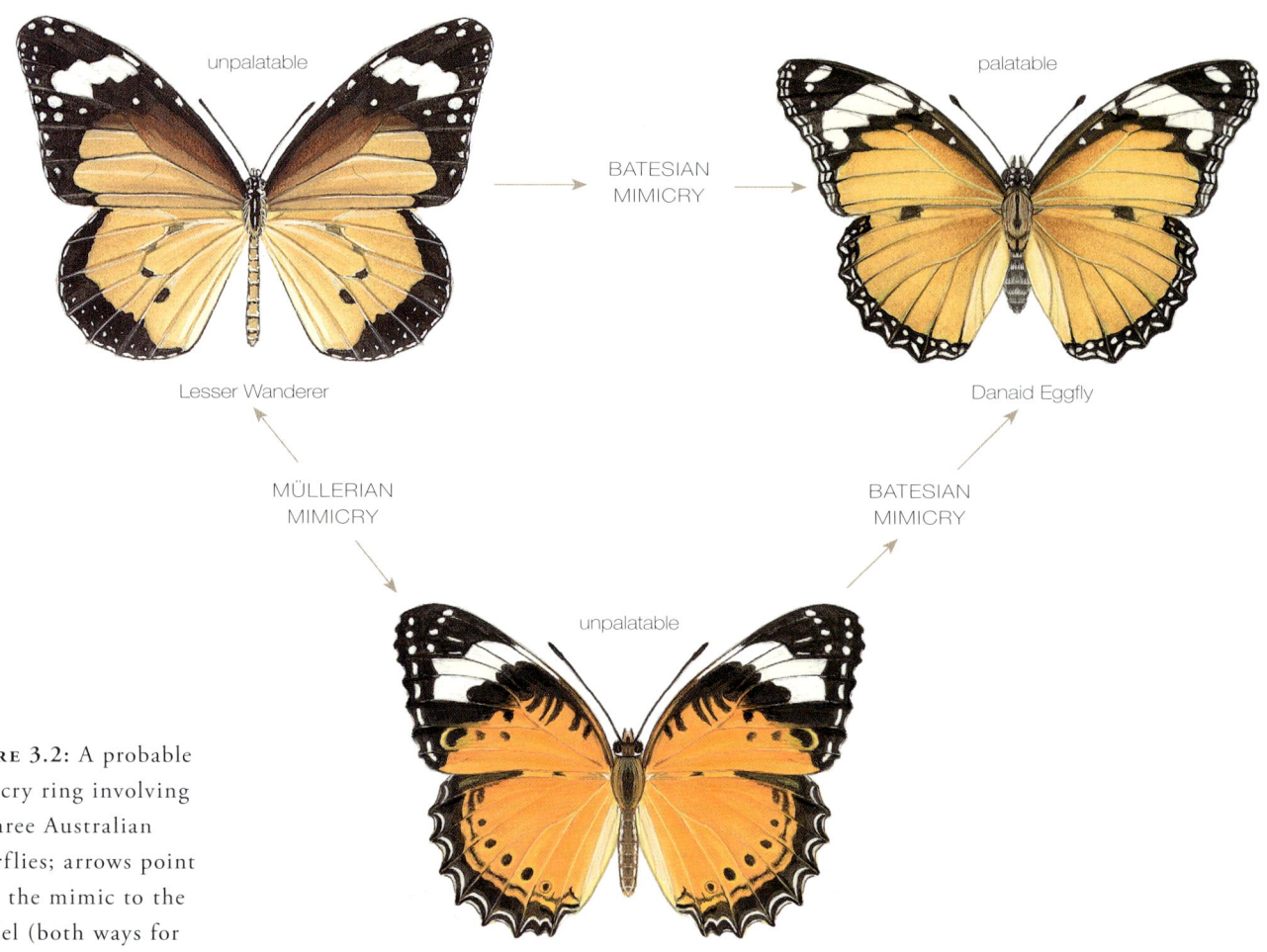

FIGURE 3.2: A probable mimicry ring involving three Australian butterflies; arrows point from the mimic to the model (both ways for Müllerian mimicry).

Danaines and pyrrolizidine alkaloids

In Australia, tiger and crow butterflies (Danainae), as well as the related Hamadryad (*Tellervo zoilus*), have exploited a second set of chemicals found in plants. This time the chemicals—with the tongue-wrenching name of pyrrolizidine alkaloids—occur in a wide range of herbaceous plants. The PAs (as they are usually known) have again evolved as defences against vertebrate herbivores. They are powerful blood poisons and may pose some public health risk as contaminants of meat. For danaine butterflies, however, they represent a readily available source of a complex organic molecule that can readily be converted by the male butterfly into sex pheromones. Species that feed as larvae on Apocynaceae obtain these chemicals from the plant, but if they have fed on Asclepiadaceae they need to obtain them as adults. Adult butterflies of both sexes can often be seen clustered around dried individuals of herbs such as *Heliotropum* and *Echium*, or vines of the family Apocynaceae such as *Parsonsia*, seeking out PAs by probing the plants with their proboscides. Often they will scratch young leaves to release a fine trickle of sap. Even individuals that obtained PAs as larvae need to top up their supplies in this way as they grow older. The poisonous chemicals also provide extra chemical protection against vertebrates and some spiders. In particular, PAs have a very bitter taste and may result in more butterflies being released unharmed than those protected by other chemicals. It is undoubtedly for this reason that females also imbibe PAs. However, it is believed that it was their role as pheromone building blocks that was the most important factor in the evolution of this unusual feeding habit.

Competing for Food and Mates

When two organisms make more or less the same demands on the environment in the same place and time then the spectre of direct competition arises. From an evolutionary point of view, direct competition is best avoided, as time and energy spent in competing is time and energy not being spent in activities which could enhance the chances of surviving to reproduce.

Ecologists recognise two forms of competition: that which occurs within a species, and that which occurs between species. Competition may also be direct or indirect: individuals may tussle physically for a scarce resource, or may take possession of a resource and defend it against all comers.

Occurrence of this process within a species—intra-specific competition—is commonplace. Obviously the most likely instance of exactly similar demands on resources in the environment is going to occur between individuals of the same species. As larvae, many species often defoliate their host plant, early developers leaving their siblings to starve; in the case of the Big Greasy (*Cressida cressida*) and also birdwings (*Ornithoptera* spp.), cannibalism of eggs and small larvae is also common. Sometimes larvae even eat freshly formed pupa.

For males, another often-contested 'resource' is females to mate with. A good example is the competition among males of the Imperial Blue butterfly (*Jalmenus evagoras*) as they wait for females to emerge from pupae clustered on top of their *Acacia* food plants. Males jostle each other as they attempt to take possession of newly emerged females with whom they mate immediately. A second example of competition is seen clearly among males of the Big Greasy. In this case males take possession of individual food plant patches—in this case the smaller species of the genus *Aristolochia*—and defend them against other patrolling males. Females approaching the plants are regarded as potential mates. In other species, male butterflies will appropriate a perch from which they can sally out to court passing females. In rainforest, the most desired perches often lie in sunny spots, and so males shift their positions throughout the day. These perches and the 'territory' that surrounds them are defended against passing males. Some species will fly out to accost any passing insect, and even fly at large dragonflies and small birds that stray into the territory.

Direct competition between species—interspecific competition—is less commonly observed. This is not surprising. If two species are in close competition there will be strong selective pressures for them to develop habits that lessen the competition. Sometimes we observe direct competition: larvae of one species encountering the egg of another on its food plant will, as likely as not, simply eat the egg along with the food plant. More commonly, though, students of competition are reduced to examining the ways in which species or individuals divide up the world to avoid competition rather than observing the interaction directly. The ecologist Joe Connell dubbed this the 'ghost of competition past'.

Competition between two species of jezabel (*Delias* spp.) for food plants

Among the Australian butterflies, we have a few excellent examples where the direct avoidance of competition is apparent. Two species of jezabels (*Delias* spp.) have been studied in detail (see the plate opposite). Both *D. argenthona* and *D. nigrina* feed as caterpillars on a range of species of mistletoe in south-east Queensland.

Although mistletoe of four species abounds in their environment, this is not the case for the fresh new shoots that are palatable to young larvae. When the two species of butterfly do occur together, each avoids the food plants on which the other species has laid eggs—even though those plants are otherwise acceptable to them. Of four species of mistletoe, two favoured ones are shared by both butterfly species, whereas two less attractive mistletoe species are eaten by one butterfly species only. When populations of both butterflies are high, each tends to utilise more its exclusive, though less attractive, host plant species. So in this case the avoidance of competition is a behavioural and immediate response to the other species. In many other species of butterflies the avoidance of competition appears to be much more 'hard-wired' and is observed as habitat segregation. We have already discussed the brown butterflies (*Oreixenica, Geitoneura, Heteronympha*) 'dividing up' altitudes and habitats in Australia's south-east. At a smaller spatial scale the set of papilionid butterflies that feeds on *Aristolochia* vines in north Queensland—*Ornithoptera euphorion, Cressida cressida* and *Pachliopta polydorus*—appear to avoid direct competition by dividing up their access to the vine by each targeting the food plant at different heights above the ground. There are many other examples where habitat partitioning (as it is called) can be interpreted as the result of the avoidance of competition. These remain just theories until butterfly enthusiasts start doing backyard experiments—as Darwin spent his life doing!

A final comment on competition may help us understand how Australian environments may differ from other parts of the world. It has been suggested that in situations where the environment itself is harsh—because of aridity, very cold winters or unpredictable weather—then competition as a mechanism for shaping ecological communities may be less important. So in tropical rainforests, which are generally thought of as very supportive of life, we may expect to see the results of tight competitive relationships as the many species that can live 'comfortably' within this climatic envelope sort themselves out by dividing available resources ever more minutely. By contrast, in a semi-desert, only a few species of butterfly are present and they must have access to a wide range of resources and alternatives just to survive in this very demanding environment. Finer subdivision of resources as a result of interspecific competition would simply result in many species disappearing. Anywhere in Australia away from the moist tropics and east coast must be regarded as a harsh environment and so, perhaps, we should expect competition to have played a less important role in sorting species/resource relationships here than elsewhere.

Natural Enemies

Just as butterflies (or at least their larvae) have a detrimental effect on the plants on which they feed, so there are many species that prey on butterflies. This in turn has led butterflies to evolve a range of mechanisms (in addition to the chemical protection and mimicry already discussed) in order to combat the assaults of these predators.

Butterflies face three general classes of threats. First, there are free-ranging predators—for example, birds, lizards, spiders and dragonflies, which attempt to eat the butterfly or its larva whole. Then there is the group of predators that eat their prey—often the larvae—from the inside out. These are generally called parasitoids—not quite 'parasites', because with many true parasites the host lives on, albeit in a less fit state than when uninfected, whereas parasitoids always kill. And finally there are the pathogens: viruses, fungi, bacteria and microsporidia which live inside the body of their host and may or may not result in the death of that host.

Predators

Adult butterflies face a variety of dangers. The birds, also free-flying and active by day, pose the biggest threat, and many of the anti-predator adaptations in butterflies seem to have evolved in response to bird predation.

While some adult butterflies adopt an active defence strategy, advertising their unpleasant taste and toxic effects with bright warning coloration, others resort to camouflage. Broadly, it is true to say that the undersides of butterflies tend to be less brightly coloured than the upperside and provide camouflage. The wings are closed above the body when at rest, with only the undersides visible. The main exceptions are the species for which there is an advantage in advertising that they taste bad, such as the jezabels (*Delias* spp.). Any butterfly enthusiast knows that once that tiny flickering blue or fluttering brown alights and closes its wings it effectively disappears. In some species, though, this camouflage is taken to almost military extremes. Examples are scattered throughout this book, but one of the most impressive is the Leafwing (*Doleschallia bisaltide*). With closed wings the underside of this species closely resembles a fallen dried leaf and even has patterning that resembles the midrib of the leaf. The Evening Brown (*Melanitis leda*) is another near-perfect mimic of a dead leaf when perched on leaf litter. This species has darker or paler seasonal forms, matching the most likely appearance of the leaf litter at particular times of the year. Along with many other species it feigns death when handled, thus reducing the risk of giving the game away to inquisitive potential predators.

Another way in which butterfly wing patterns may serve a defensive function is by developing features that direct attack away from the vital parts of the body. Large conspicuous eyespots are believed to do this, and are most often found in the Nymphalidae, especially the browns (Satyrinae). Other butterflies, especially blues and hairstreaks (Lycaenidae), have developed underside markings and tails, which when at rest combine to create the illusion of a 'super' head, at the opposite end to the true head. When perched they shuffle the hindwings restlessly, attracting attention to the area. This extraordinary phenomenon is discussed further in Chapter 9 in the account of the hairstreaks (subfamily Theclinae) in which the most spectacular examples occur. The effectiveness of these devices in averting attacks can be judged by studying the patterns of damage on butterflies' wings, generally caused by birds' beaks. Butterflies attacked while perched with shut wings generally show symmetrical damage, as the beak closes over an opposing pair of wings, whereas those intercepted in flight are more likely to have triangular tears in a single wing. Damage in which false heads have been neatly shorn off is common in hairstreaks, and many browns have triangular tears centred on their eyespots. Interestingly,

Golden Orb Weaving Spider with female Northern Jezabel caught in its web while evading a male

colourful Batesian mimics often also show severe wing damage, suggesting a bird made an indecisive attack, being unsure of the butterfly's identity, whereas species that are genuinely unpalatable are very rarely marked.

Other major predators include spiders. Web-spinning spiders, such as the Golden Orb Weaving Spider, frequently capture smaller butterflies, but find larger species difficult to subdue. It is generally believed that the deciduous scales that cover the wings of butterflies and moths help them to escape from a sticky web before the spider can reach and paralyse them. Experiments in which butterflies were deliberately flown into webs suggested that the capture rate is seldom more than 10 per cent, lending support to this idea. Other spiders are ambush predators. Crab Spiders of the family Thomisidae sit on open flowers awaiting their prey and have evolved wonderful camouflage to match the colours of the flowers. All butterflies are in danger from these 'sit and wait' predators; quite small spiders take large swallowtails and strong-bodied skippers as well as smaller prey, eating the nutritious bodies and discarding the unprofitable wings.

Several other species catch and eat adult butterflies. Certain larger dragonflies and robber flies are particularly good at this and their long spiny legs form effective 'baskets' for scooping butterflies from flower heads or catching them in flight. Other generalist predators, such as lizards or ants, will pick up adult butterflies whenever they encounter them.

The larvae and pupae of butterflies are also vulnerable to predators, especially birds. Here camouflage also plays a role in predator avoidance. Of particular interest are the larvae of the *Papilio* swallowtails, which in their early stages look like bird droppings. As the larva matures, the size of these relatively large caterpillars begins to undermine the effectiveness of the bird-dropping mimicry and the larva takes on the citrus-green colour of its host plants. In several families and subfamilies, larvae have evolved a range of spines and hairs to deter predators. These adaptations are sometimes accompanied by behaviours designed to enhance their effectiveness as defences. Larvae of the Tailed Emperor (*Polyura sempronius*), for example, use the stiff backward-pointing horns that protrude from their head capsules to deter predators, using a brisk 'head-bobbing' behaviour. Such head movements are commonly seen in other species. The larvae of the Papilionidae have an additional defence, the osmeterium—a forked, brightly coloured, erectile organ behind the head of the larvae that secretes noxious, strong-smelling chemicals. We discuss this further in the family account of the Papilionidae in Chapter 6.

Finally, in some species the larvae from a single brood of eggs cluster tightly when feeding or resting. This behaviour is seen across several families. The Glasswing (*Acraea andromacha*), the Red Lacewing (*Cethosia cydippe*) and the White Nymph (*Mynes geoffroyi*) are excellent examples from the Nymphalidae. Within the Pieridae, larvae of some of the jezabels live and feed gregariously on their mistletoe food plants. Clustering is normally associated with feeding on toxic food plants, although the Fivebar Swordtail (*Graphium aristeus*)—the only swallowtail larva to feed gregariously—may be an exception. In some species the behaviour may reduce the risk of attack by predators or parasitoids (which are not deterred by

Slender Skimmer dragonfly (*Orthetrum sabina*) with Dingy Ring

Garden Skink with Evening Brown

Juvenile Australian Magpie with Orchard Butterfly larva

plant toxins), but this subject is open to study. Among the larvae of blue butterflies, clustering is usually associated with tight relationships with ants.

Parasitoids

The often tiny insects whose larvae feed inside the eggs, larvae and pupae of butterflies come from two great orders of insects—the true flies (Diptera) and the ants, bees and wasps (Hymenoptera).

The fly family Tachinidae includes vast numbers of species and occurs nearly everywhere in the world. Virtually all tachinids are parasitoids and many of them attack the larvae of butterflies. Generally the female flies lay their eggs either on the larvae of their intended prey or on the leaves of the larval food plants. Eggs are frequently positioned near the head of the caterpillar, making it very hard for the caterpillar to remove the eggs with its jaws. When the egg is laid on the caterpillar's body, the fly larva (maggot) emerges and then burrows into the body cavity of the host. When it is placed on a leaf, the caterpillar eats the egg, which hatches internally and the maggot burrows into the body cavity of the host through the wall of the gut. The tachinid maggot then absorbs food from and feeds on the host's tissues until it matures. Eventually its oxygen demands are such that it establishes a connection with the external world by punching a hole in the body wall of the caterpillar and inserting a breathing tube through the perforation. The infested butterfly larva almost always dies, and eventually the parasitoids (and there may be several of them in a single host) either burrow out of the host and pupate in the soil or pupate within the pupal case of the butterfly, emerging as adult flies.

Tachinid fly, after emerging from Orchard Butterfly pupa

The huge insect order Hymenoptera contains about 71 very diverse families worldwide, most of which are loosely called 'wasps'. Of these, no fewer than 44 are exclusively parasitoids of other animals, principally insects. For many, their preferred or only hosts are butterflies, sometimes just the one species. Different parasitoid species may attack butterfly eggs, larvae or pupae, with the tiniest being egg parasitoids. As far as we know, all butterfly species are attacked in at least one stage of their life history. Generally the female 'wasps' insert their eggs into the bodies of their hosts. (These wasps are not to be confused with the larger hunting wasps that feed on whole prey—including butterfly larvae.) The larvae emerge within the host's body cavity and, as with the tachinids, absorb food from the body fluids of their hosts. They may also feed actively on the body tissues of the host. Unlike tachinids, they do not establish a breathing pore through the host's body wall but obtain their oxygen supply by diffusion from the blood of the host. Eventually the host dies and the parasitoids pupate just outside the resulting corpse, or within the egg or pupal shell. As with the tachinid flies, there may be many parasitoid larvae, sometimes of more than one species, within a single caterpillar. So ubiquitous are these parasitoids that a further class of 'hyperparasitoid' wasps have evolved—these prey not on the caterpillars themselves but on the parasitoid larvae within them. They even attack tiny egg parasitoids. Recent research has shown that hyperparasitoids are remarkably common in most ecosystems, but otherwise we know very little about them.

Many of the defence mechanisms evolved by caterpillars as protection against free-living predators are also effective against marauding adult female parasitoids. Nevertheless, young larvae of many families, such as swallowtails (Papilionidae) and blues (Lycaenidae) possess fine hairs, which they generally lose as they develop. These possibly play a role in defence against parasitoids while they are at their most vulnerable. The hairs of some whites (Pieridae) exude tiny droplets of noxious or irritant fluid, again a possible parasitoid deterrent. As we shall soon see, the threat posed by parasitoids has also played a major role in driving the evolution of ant-tending in lycaenid butterflies. Once a wasp or fly parasitoid has infested its host it is largely safe from physical defence mechanisms. Sometimes, though, the host will activate an immune response and encapsulate the new wasp or fly larva within itself, so preventing further damage.

Pathogens

Butterflies, like all other organisms, have their share of genuine pathogens. These are usually micro-organisms, such as bacteria, fungi or microsporidia, or viruses. In general we know little about them. A few notable exceptions, such as *Bacillus thuringiensis,* have become well known for their part in controlling pest species of Lepidoptera, including Cabbage White butterflies (*Pieris rapae*).

Some of these pathogens are lethal. These may kill their hosts and pass vast numbers of spores into the environment to infect another generation of hosts. Others are non-lethal but are suspected of having subtle negative effects on their hosts by reducing egg-laying capacity, activity or other measures of fitness. One of the more bizarre examples is that of *Wolbachia*, which affects *Hypolimnas bolina* in Asia and the Pacific, but not in Australia. This bacterium selectively kills male embryos, resulting in all-female broods from infected females, and female to male ratios up to 100:1. In these circumstances, females show increased sexual drive and promiscuity, and the males sexual fatigue; this is probably not a result of the infection itself, but rather a function of the skewed social dynamics, given the excess of females.

Butterfly Mutualisms

Ecological communities also contain species–species interactions in which both species benefit. These are 'mutualistic' interactions, and butterflies participate in many of them. Indeed, research on butterflies has helped bring this whole class of interactions into focus. Two such mutualisms are particularly noteworthy: pollination and ant–caterpillar interactions.

Butterflies as pollinators

Many species of flowers are visited and pollinated by butterflies and moths. The long extendible proboscis of the Lepidoptera is a perfect tool for probing the depths of flowers in search of nectar. Many species of flowers, in turn, have evolved structures to ensure that only butterflies and moths can reach their nectar rewards and, by so doing, collect a dusting of pollen to carry to another similar flower. Perhaps the most celebrated example of Lepidoptera pollination is that of the Madagascan orchid (*Agraecum sesquipedale*), which stores its nectar at the base of an immense floral spur that can grow to 20 cm long. Charles Darwin predicted that a moth would eventually be discovered with a proboscis length to match—and, shortly after his prediction, the hawkmoth *Xanthopan morganii* was indeed found.

Flowers that remain open during the day are those most likely to be pollinated by butterflies. They tend to be showy and scented, with reds, purples and yellows favoured. Simple nectar guides—arrangements of lines or spots—may guide the visiting butterfly to the nectar. Such signposts may exploit the butterflies' ability to see in the ultraviolet spectrum, and so may not always be obvious to the human eye. Structurally, flowers often provide a landing area on which the butterfly can perch while probing for nectar, and the flowers themselves may be individually large or arranged in compact inflorescences of smaller flowers so that a butterfly can probe from flower to flower without having to move much. Again, because of the extensible nature of the butterfly proboscis, the nectaries—the organs that secrete the nectar—are often placed at the base of floral tubes or spurs.

There is little doubt that butterflies play an important part in pollinating Australian plants, yet studies demonstrating this are few. Trevor Hawkeswood showed that over 45 per cent of the eleven species of butterflies that visited the flowers of the Corkwood Wattle (*Acacia bidwillii*) subsequently carried pollen. They were part of a large cohort of insects—including beetles, flies and wasps—involved in the pollination of this plant.

In tropical America, some butterflies are able to collect pollen in clumps on a loosely coiled proboscis and there digest it with regurgitated saliva, which they then imbibe, gaining valuable proteins. This does not mean that they do not pollinate the plant as well, because some fertile grains usually remain on the butterflies' outer mouthparts, but it does indicate that the relationship between nectar-giving plant and pollinating butterfly may not be as simple as first appears. Pollen-feeding has not yet been confirmed in any Australian butterfly, but the species most likely to exhibit this behaviour are the birdwings and their allies.

There remain many other opportunities for the study of pollination by butterflies in Australia and many interesting candidate plants for such studies: the flowers of many of the native heaths (Epacridaceae), many of the native daisies, and many red, yellow and purple flowers with tubular corollas would, at first glance, be worth investigation. Just a few words of caution are necessary: the fact that a butterfly visits a particular species of flower regularly, even gets covered in its pollen, does not demonstrate that it is necessarily a pollinator. Further, many Australian plants, particularly in forest canopies, are generalists when it comes to pollination so, even where a butterfly species is shown to be involved in pollination, it may well be part of a whole group of such mutualists. This group may even include a combination of insects and vertebrates.

Ant–caterpillar interactions

Ants are almost everywhere in Australia. For some visiting naturalists this is the 'continent of ants'. Most species of ants are generalist predators. They use their massive numbers to overwhelm everything from lizards to insect grubs and manoeuvre them back to their nests to feed their mother's vast brood of hungry larvae. Upon encountering a butterfly caterpillar, this is exactly what ants will do—except when that caterpillar is one of the hundred or so species of Australian lycaenids that are 'farmed' by ants. So why have some ants overcome their ancestral urges (so to speak) and nurtured caterpillars rather than slaughtering them?

The answer is that the butterfly larvae have something to offer the ants—three types of glands on their upper surface secrete chemicals. The most obvious of these is the so-called nectary organ (sometimes called Newcomer's Organ), which secretes a mixture

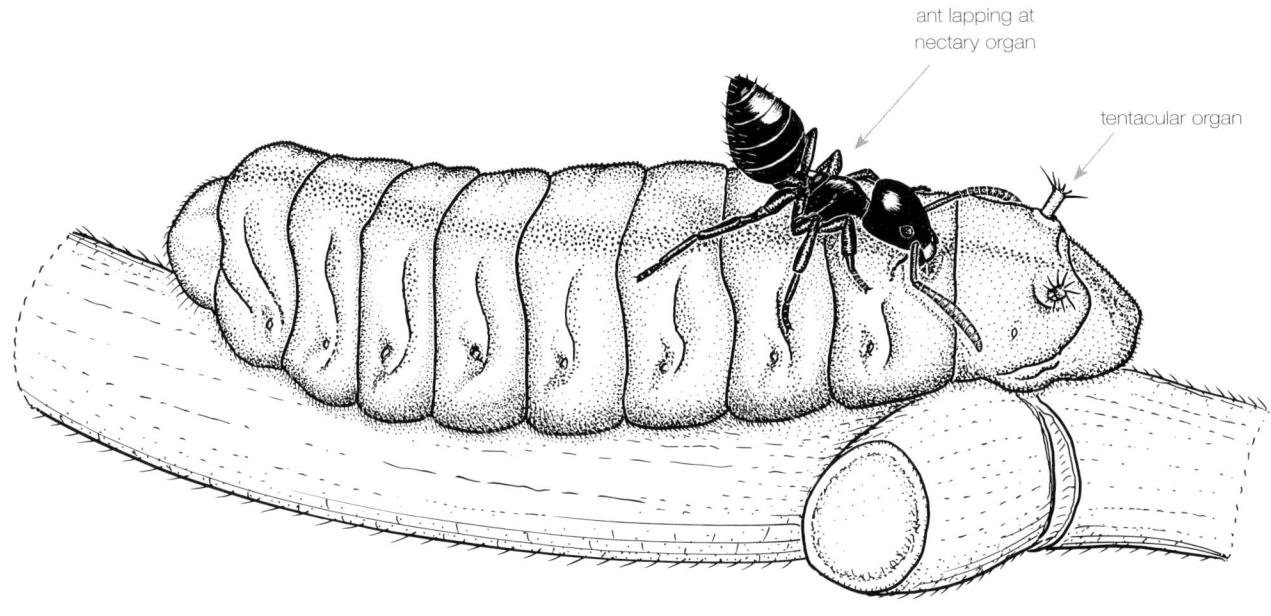

FIGURE 3.3: A *Crematogaster* ant feeding from the dorsal nectary organ of the Common Lineblue (*Nacaduba berenice*) larva.

of sugars and nitrogen-rich amino acids in solution. The ant pictured in Figure 3.3 is lapping from this gland. In addition, the larvae have sometimes hundreds of tiny glands, invisible to the naked eye, over much of the body, which secrete yet more amino acids. These are known as pore cupola organs. Finally, the paired tentacular organs pulse in and out while ants are tending the larvae, or when the larvae are trying to attract ants. These are believed to produce volatile chemicals which affect the behaviour of the ant.

Clearly there is something in this for the ants. But why would so many species of butterflies evolve to feed ants rather than doing what other species do, which is to develop mechanisms to avoid ants altogether or to protect themselves in other ways? Basically, the ants protect the larvae from both free-living predators such as large wasps and from the tiny parasitoid flies and wasps which attempt to lay their eggs in, on or close to the butterfly larvae. Indeed, in some populations of the Imperial Blue (*Jalmenus evagoras*), virtually no larvae survive to adulthood unless they are attended and protected by ants.

We divide these ant–butterfly mutualisms into a number of categories. First, a relationship may be 'obligate' or 'facultative'. In an obligate relationship the butterfly larvae are virtually never found without ants and do very poorly when the ants are absent. In facultative relationships the association is much more casual. Ants will tend the larvae from time to time but do not depend absolutely on the larvae for their well-being, and the larvae survive even when the ants are few or absent.

Among obligate relationships, again, there is considerable variety. Two examples are particularly instructive. The Imperial Blue butterfly lays its eggs in groups on a wide range of species of young wattles (*Acacia* spp.). The larvae emerge from the eggs and stay together in groups, especially during the day, and are usually covered in a dense coating of ants. Even when they spread out in the evening to feed they remain covered in ants. Ultimately they pupate, again in groups, without ever leaving the food plants, and even the pupae remain attractive to ants. When the ants are excluded artificially from either larvae or pupae, survival goes down dramatically, often to zero. The ants are so central to the well-being of the butterfly that adult females, seeking a plant on which to lay their eggs, will seek out those plants with ants above all else. Again, in artificial situations they can be induced to lay their eggs on gum tree leaves, even pieces of garden cane, as long as the ants are present. Curiously, the ants seem to ignore the adult butterflies upon emergence. In so-called coppers (*Paralucia* spp.), the butterfly larvae feed on the young shoots of blackthorn bushes (*Bursaria* spp.) and, again, are habitually attended by tiny ants. But these larvae always feed at night and spend the day not in clusters on the foliage but in shelters built by the ants at the base of the shrubs. Each evening the ants 'herd' the larvae out onto the foliage of the blackthorn and tend them while they feed. At the end of the feeding period they are accompanied back to the ant 'byres'. Eventually the butterfly larvae pupate in these shelters.

There are many variations upon this theme—in some cases the ants regurgitate food and feed the butterfly larvae, in others the ants may carry the tiny larvae from place to place. One key thing is that in most of the obligate associations there is only one species of ant involved in the relationship with a particular species of butterfly. For the same species of butterfly this may change from region to region, but in a given location a unique ant species is required. This means, of course, that for the butterfly to thrive in this location not only must its food plant be present but so must the ant. This restricts even further the patches of landscape that are suitable for the butterfly species and is yet another reason why lycaenids, more than other butterflies, often occur in small scattered populations.

These ant–butterfly interactions represent an extraordinary set of adaptations, which is particularly widespread in Australia (and, it so happens, in southern and eastern Africa). It has been suggested that the general scarcity of nitrogen in soils and plants in Australia has set the scene for this evolutionary radiation, as the ants evolve ways of obtaining this nitrogen from other sources—the butterfly larvae.

There is a fascinating complement to this story. It is tempting to think that the mutually supportive ant–butterfly interaction runs counter to the evolutionary 'nature red in tooth and claw' metaphor. In fact, these mutualisms are tightly balanced and, it seems, can slip with ease either way. That ants may revert to their predatory habits is not surprising perhaps, but for the butterfly larvae to become predatory upon the brood of the ants is much more unexpected. As we have noted already, there are fifteen species of Australian butterflies, all lycaenids but spread across three more or less unrelated genera, that do just that. In these species the female butterflies lay their eggs on plants close to the ant nest. The ants then transport the newly hatched larvae into their nest. What happens next varies a little from species to species, but ultimately results in the butterfly larvae feeding on the ant larvae through to maturity. It is generally supposed they produce chemical signals that 'turn off' the aggressive instincts of the ants during this process. Ultimately they pupate in the ant nest, making a run for it to the outside world when they emerge as adults. To aid their escape from the ants as adults they have a special class of long, loose scales that they freely shed as they leave—lubricating their way through the mass of ants to continue the next stage of their life cycle elsewhere.

How did this extraordinary switch come about? There is much speculation on this point but in at least two of the Australian genera involved (*Acrodipsas* and *Arhopala*) it seems almost certain to have arisen from ancestral species that had a mutualistic relationship with the ants. The Moth Butterfly (*Liphyra brassolis*) may be different. Its larvae are protected not by chemicals but by armour plate, and ants are hostile towards it at every stage. This species is more evolutionarily distant from the rest of the lycaenids and it is possible that its ancestors never shared a mutualism with ants.

Ant–butterfly relationships provide some of the most dramatic and unusual examples of the way butterflies are dependent on other species. Perhaps, more than any others, these associations prompt us to realise that all butterfly species are dependent on, and/or support, many other species of animals and plants in a complex network of interactions. The complexity of each species' habitat requirements, and the variety of opportunities for filling specialised niches that this provides, is probably the ultimate reason why there are so many butterfly species, even in arid Australia. That is how evolution works.

Blue Jewel (*Hypochrysops delicia*)

4 BUTTERFLIES AND HUMANS

Richmond Birdwing
(*Ornithoptera richmondia*)

Pittosporum undulatum

Only a few species of butterfly prosper in man-made habitats, such as gardens and agricultural land. Most people spend much of their lives in habitats shunned by butterflies, and so almost never see them. Scarcely any visit the concrete deserts of our inner cities, where people work to the same daily timetable as bushland butterflies. Nevertheless, butterflies have long captivated a few dedicated enthusiasts, and, increasingly, they are gaining importance in the public consciousness.

Butterfly Conservation

As Australia developed as an agricultural nation, the community at large was apathetic about the bush and all it contained. Butterflies have been collateral damage as bush was cleared.* But since the 1960s there has been new concern for biodiversity conservation. There is now an official perception that our biodiversity is an invaluable asset. However, the last 50 years has seen unprecedented levels of destruction of bushland across the nation and dramatic declines in numbers of virtually all our fauna. The dilemma that exists between ongoing development and 'improvement' from a human viewpoint, and the associated degradation of nature, raises many unsolved issues. Governments are long on rhetoric, short on conservation-positive outcomes.

Since the late 1980s, all states and the Commonwealth have enacted laws allowing species to be designated as endangered. Although in some cases they are in need of review, these laws have served us and our fauna reasonably well. We are all familiar with active programs to 'save' the Bilby, the Gouldian Finch, the Hairy-nosed Wombat and, most recently, the Tasmanian Devil. A process was established whereby the current and past distributions and population sizes of species was assessed. On this basis they could be allocated to one of several categories ranging from rare to critically endangered. These are the IUCN categories devised by the International Union for the Conservation of Nature—an international statutory body established by the United Nations and based in Geneva. Once a species is designated as being 'of conservation concern', authorities are then under pressure to produce a recovery plan in which management processes are identified that, it is hoped, will bring the species back from the brink.

When people began to notice that butterflies were less common than they had been and that some species, in particular, were very seldom seen, the idea of 'butterfly

---

* Except for one notorious case in which the habitat of a coastal population of the endangered Australian Fritillary (*Argyreus hyperbius*) was ploughed up deliberately because it attracted too much attention from butterfly collectors.

52   The Butterflies of Australia

conservation' arose. When this first came to public attention in Australia it was perhaps natural to assume that the same approach—assessing and recovering species one by one—would be applicable. After all, it was working for the Bettongs and Stick-nest Rats (more or less), so why not for butterflies? National assessments were carried out and determination of the conservation status of all species (and even subspecies) of our butterflies were made. Some states then embodied the findings in legislation. Currently seven species of butterfly are fully protected in Queensland, and several in other states. Of course, all butterflies and all other wildlife are protected in national parks, but listing a species as endangered protects it wherever it may occur. This formal protection puts restrictions on disturbing habitat, on collecting, and even on owning dried specimens of the named species. It also puts obligations on the states to draw up recovery plans for the species and to put in place management interventions to turn these plans into reality.

There are only about a dozen butterfly species that enjoy this sort of protection in Australia. Some of these species verge on being critically endangered: the Bathurst Copper (*Paralucia spinifera*) is found at only a very few highland locations close to Bathurst in New South Wales; the Bulloak Jewel (*Hypochrysops piceatus*) persists in a couple of tiny localities on Queensland's Darling Downs; and Illidge's Ant Blue (*Acrodipsas illidgei*) has a tenuous hold in its few locations in the mangroves of Moreton Bay, Queensland, beloved of developers. Some of our larger species are also under threat. There have been few, if any, sightings in Queensland of wild individuals of the Australian Fritillary (*Argyreus hyperbius*) for several years, and the Richmond Birdwing (*Ornithoptera richmondia*) has disappeared from many of its haunts along rainforest edges in south-east Queensland and northern New South Wales.

Recovery plans exist for several of these 'listed' species and recommend that, in some instances, active management is required to provide these species with the resources they need. Sometimes, as in the case of the Bathurst Copper, this means keeping some patches of its high-altitude range at the ideal post-fire stage so that young individuals of its food plant, *Bursaria* spp., as well as the ants which attend its larvae, are constantly available. In other cases, active planting of a food plant is having the desired effect of increasing numbers and infilling local ranges. Planting the vine *Pararistolochia praevenosa* as part of recovery efforts for the Richmond Birdwing in south-east Queensland, orchestrated by Don Sands, is a case in point. All recovery plans, though, stress the overarching need to stop further clearing in and around known habitats of listed species.

Such heroic interventions will sometimes be effective in leading to the recovery of populations of selected butterfly species and they should certainly be encouraged. Conservation, though, is more than preserving individual species: it is about maintaining ecological communities—the whole set of animals and plants. Indeed the legislation in some states acknowledges that whole communities of organisms may be endangered and, as a consequence, may be listed as an entity under the appropriate Act. All recovery plans for individual species, in addition to species-specific actions, recommend that the habitat of the species be preserved.

Effective butterfly conservation is as much about maintaining numbers and variety in the everyday species we encounter in our gardens, parks and reserves as it is about preserving high-profile, exceedingly rare species. In this community-level approach we are as much concerned with maintaining whole ecosystems with all their wildlife as we are in preserving butterflies exclusively. We can do this by trying to ensure that development is done thoughtfully. The advantage we have as butterfly conservationists is that even relatively small areas of natural bushland can conserve populations of many species of butterflies effectively. Under the current additional threat of climate change, maintaining natural communities of animals and plants, including butterflies, in as complete a state as possible will also give such ecosystems the best possible chance of adapting naturally to the predicted major environmental changes.

We can also take a community-level approach to butterfly conservation in our own backyards—by gardening for butterflies.

Butterfly Gardening

Taking a patch of unprepossessing builders' rubble, or recently cleared bushland, and turning it into an aesthetically pleasing and useful garden is a truly Australian thing to do. We go to great lengths to attract birds to our gardens with the planting of nectar-producing plants, the provision of feeding stations and the erection of bird-baths. Among the beauty of flowers and shrubs we may begin to notice butterflies in ways we did not previously. We may also notice that, by accident or design, some gardens attract more butterflies than others. If we want to attract and keep butterflies in our garden, just as with birds, there is much we can do. To some extent gardeners need to decide whether they wish simply to attract butterflies to their gardens from elsewhere, or if they wish to try to establish breeding populations of butterfly species on their land. From a conservation point of view, the second alternative is much to be preferred. In either case, butterflies are more likely to be attracted to partially sunny, sheltered gardens. In the warmer parts of the country, butterflies will seek out situations that provide patches of sunlight interspersed with shade. Like all flying insects they follow the fine line between being warm enough to fly freely while avoiding the drying effects of too much sun.

planting larval host plant vine
Pararistolochia praevenosa

Providing adult food

Almost all adult butterflies need a constant supply of fuel to power their activities, whether they are pursuing a mate, searching for somewhere to lay eggs, or simply foraging for further fuel. In general, the fuel source is nectar from flowers, although a few larger species will seek fallen fruit or even bird and animal droppings. From the gardener's viewpoint, providing a wide range of flowers will both keep butterflies happy and fulfil the broader aesthetic demands of the garden's human users. A very wide range of flowers will attract butterflies although those with longer corolla tubes, and those coloured red, white or purple, are said to be most attractive to butterflies.

The exact species of plant that might be planted will differ from place to place in Australia. The choice will also reflect your preference for native as opposed to exotic plantings. There are several books (such as Densey Clyne's *Attracting Butterflies to Your Garden*) and websites that will help you choose. Be aware when using these resources that, however general the authors try to be, they will almost always favour a particular region—and ensure that the resource you are using at least refers to Australia! The celebrated 'butterfly' bush (*Buddleia* spp.) routinely planted in Europe or North America to attract butterflies is widely available in Australia (and attracts more than its share of butterflies) but it thrives only in cooler climates in the south-east or, further north, at higher elevations. Plants with tubular flowers such as *Pentas* and *Penstemon* will attract larger butterflies; more open flowers or the compound flowers of daisies will pull in the smaller fry. *Buckinghamia*, *Melaleuca* and *Callistemon* blossoms may draw in masses of butterflies of all sizes. Again the choice will be location-specific. The white odorous flowers of *Cotoneaster* hedges, for example, attract browns and skippers in Canberra while the beautiful flowers of the reviled lantana attract butterflies in the subtropics and tropics.

Larval food plants

One of the first things the student of butterflies learns is where the larvae of each species are to be found. This knowledge is the key to establishing breeding populations of butterflies in the garden. Again, what can be planted and grown will depend in which part of the country the garden is situated. As a rule of thumb, if your garden lies within the mapped distribution range of a species, as indicated by the maps in this book, and is at the right altitude, then their food plants will generally grow in that area. The only exceptions are the few highly migratory species which end up far beyond their normal ranges, and food plants, from time to time.

There are well-known associations that will almost certainly bring particular species of butterfly to your garden. Planting bushes of blue-flowering *Plumbago* will attract clouds of the Zebra Blue (*Leptotes plinius*), also known as the Plumbago Blue, even though the usual garden plant is a South African relative of the butterfly's native food plant. Oleander bushes (*Nerium oleander*) will attract Common Crow butterflies (*Euploea core*), although in the subtropics these are as likely to be attracted to *Parsonsia* vines scrambling up any available tree. Citrus trees will attract the range of citrus swallowtails, and Camphor Laurel (*Cinnamomum camphorae*) and many of its relatives in the plant family Lauraceae will attract Blue Triangles (*Graphium sarpedon*) and Common Red-eyes (*Chaetocneme beata*). A Custard Apple or a Soursop (*Annona* spp.) will attract the Pale Green Triangle (*Graphium eurypylus*) and provide fruit for you. The list is very long.

Of course, planting food plants for particular butterflies can be part of an orchestrated conservation program to provide habitat for endangered or near-endangered species. As well as the Richmond Birdwing program discussed above, planting species of *Wilkeia* bushes as food for the Regent Skipper (*Euschemon rafflesia*) and *Viola betonicifolia* to encourage the Australian Fritillary (*Argyreus hyperbius*) are being trialled in some regions.

It is worth adding that many of the favoured food plants for butterflies will likely plant themselves in your garden—so don't be too keen simply to designate them as weeds and haul them out. Examples are the several species of milkweed (*Asclepias* spp., *Gomphocarpus* spp.), which are preferred food plants for both the Wanderer and Lesser Wanderer butterflies. Over much of the warm east coast the Poison Peach Bush (*Trema aspera*) will also arrive without assistance. It will almost always bring with it the Speckled Lineblue (*Catopyrops florinda*). Further, no butterfly garden should be without its patch of nettles (*Urtica* spp.), perhaps tucked away behind the shed, but vital if the Australian Admiral (*Vanessa itea*) is to join the denizens of the garden. Looking up rather than down, mistletoes in gum trees and casuarinas should always be nurtured, even if they do reduce the vigour of the tree a little. Some gardeners even go to the extent of collecting berries from wild mistletoes and rubbing them into the bark of their trees. The *Delias*, *Ogyris* and *Hypochrysops* butterflies that may then arrive will more than compensate for any minor reduction in tree growth.

It should go without saying that widespread use of insecticides and butterfly gardening simply do not mix. Most garden insecticides are broad-spectrum and do not distinguish between the pest you want to get rid of and the butterfly you wish to encourage. If you must control pests chemically, then use a very local application that will act more or less only where you place it. Sprinkling derris dust onto brassicas as a guard against the Cabbage White will be just as effective as a widespread application of a liquid spray. Even with the dust, beware of wind-blown, non-target effects.

Butterfly Pests

The Cabbage White (*Pieris rapae*) is really the only species of butterfly in Australia that can be considered a true pest. It was accidentally introduced from Europe in about 1929. Since that time it has spread over about 80 per cent of the country and few backyard cabbage plots are free from its depredations. It is also a major pest of commercially grown brassicas, including oil-crops such as rape and canola. It is generally controlled using broad-spectrum insecticides such as synthetic pyrethroids. Several attempts to introduce natural enemies to try to control the species biologically have been largely unsuccessful. Three species of parasitoid were introduced from the northern hemisphere in the 1940s and remain as viable populations in Australia. They do not, however, appear to have had any significant success in controlling populations of the butterfly. The species owes its worldwide success as a pest to its broad environmental tolerances, and the very wide range of food plants that it will utilise. That most of this wide range of food plants happens to include favoured food plants of humans produces all the requirements for an ongoing conflict.

A few species are minor pests of commercial crops—the citrus butterflies and several species of skipper that feed on rice—but none of these are of great economic importance. Other species of Australian butterfly feed on plants that are locally important as garden plants. In this respect a large range of species can be 'pests' in the sense that the gardener would rather not have his or her plants eaten by caterpillars. We have already mentioned the Cycad Blue (*Theclinesthes onycha*), which can do serious damage, especially to young or small plants. In the Queensland tropics, the Black and White Tit (*Hypolycaena danis*) is another source of annoyance. Its larvae feed on the flowers of various species of native and exotic ornamental orchids. In this case, gardeners usually consider even minimal damage intolerable, and so take strong measures to exclude it.

Since the arrival of the Cabbage White, more and more stringent quarantine procedures have been applied to keep out further unwanted pests. This has had mixed success in general (think of fire ants and European wasps) but has, to date, kept us free of another butterfly pest, the Banana Skipper (*Erionota thrax*), which is a major despoiler of commercial banana crops in Papua New Guinea and other countries to our north. An Australian-supported project to control the Banana Skipper in Papua New Guinea through introduction of a small wasp, parasitic on the skippers' eggs, was successful and has, to date, reduced the threat of accidental introduction to Australia.

Banana Skipper (*Erionota thrax*) and characteristic leaf damage

Becoming a Lepidopterist

A lepidopterist is one who studies butterflies and moths. Most lepidopterists are amateurs, and in this role have contributed hugely to our knowledge of the natural world. A few of these amateurs have added academic qualifications to their passion for butterflies and gone on to become professional scientists. Few of these people have been able to continue working with butterflies—it is a sad fact that most professional entomologists work on pest species of one sort or another, rather than on the vast majority of insects that are beneficial to humans.

Those who know and study butterflies seldom do so in a cold and considered way. They generally, often in childhood, have developed a passion for butterflies that is more than a childhood obsession. So this short section contains a few words of advice to those, like the authors, who have fallen victim to this delightful disease. It may also be useful to those who have to raise or live with them.

A deep interest in butterflies goes along with a passion to know things. There are key tools essential to feed this need.

First is the need for observation skills in the field. Butterflies live outside—not within a computer, or even the pages of a butterfly book, and there is simply no substitute for spending time, usually alone, in gardens or the bush, observing where butterflies are and what they do. Initially this learning process needs no more than a backyard with flowers. Later will come the need to record things—either as photographs, as a collection of reference specimens, and/or as notes for further use—but before all of that comes long hours spent searching and watching. This time will expose the learner to all sorts of things in addition to butterflies—the plants around or upon which they are found, the different sorts of ecosystems within which particular butterflies occur, and how flight patterns differ from day to day, hour to hour. This is what being a naturalist is all about—to see, to record and to think about the world around us—and to take joy in it along the way.

Once basic familiarity with butterflies is established, along comes the thorny question of how to develop the interest further. Traditionally this was easily answered. The young enthusiast would make a collection. This involved putting together some basic paraphernalia: a net, setting boards, killing jars, pins, chemicals and boxes in which to store the resulting dried specimens. Much of this could be made; a few items had to be bought. There are many manuals telling the beginner at great length how to catch, kill, mount, preserve and label insect collections. So why is this a difficult issue?

Over the last 50 years the amount of natural bushland around and within our cities has dwindled dramatically. It has been cleared for development of one kind or another. As a consequence, many of the species of wildlife that were once familiar have been dramatically reduced in number. One of the entirely laudable responses to this devastation has been a rise in green consciousness and a much more conservation-oriented approach to the world. Along with this change in world view has been a revision of the opinions of many on hunting as sport. The idea of going out and shooting a crocodile or a tiger or an elephant for fun or profit has become distasteful to many. A collateral casualty of this change in attitude has been the amateur butterfly collector. This is based on the mistaken impression that a modest amount of collecting will affect the population of an insect and, second, that a full appreciation of the species can be achieved passively, by watching it alive, in the field.

Each female butterfly will produce somewhere between 50 and 650 eggs during her life. In many parts of Australia there will be two or more broods a year. That butterflies are not much more common than they are is evidence of the fact that most of these eggs never make it to adulthood. Further, the life-history strategies of each species compensate for this. The removal of a small number of adults by a collector will have no perceivable impact on the local population. There are no cases in Australia where collecting has had any lasting negative effect upon a population. Only in a very small number of celebrated overseas cases where a species has already been reduced to a tiny, circumscribed population, and collecting has been on a massive, commercially motivated scale, is there a plausible suggestion that collectors made a difference to a population's viability. Of course, in Australia, listed species of conservation concern, and all species in national parks, are automatically protected from collection.

There remain hundreds of species—dozens in any one region—available to the amateur collector. No one is suggesting that such collecting should be done thoughtlessly or carelessly, but as a learning exercise it is second to none. If there is to be a next generation of butterfly enthusiasts, then at least some of them will have to be keen collectors. Some species complexes cannot readily be identified without collection, and accurate records depend upon having the specimens in the hand. Even if specimens are not to be killed and mounted, it is instructive to capture a butterfly—gently, either with a net or between the fingers—examine it closely, perhaps using a hand lens, then release it unharmed. If you have handled it properly, it will behave as though nothing has happened. Be warned, however: this takes some practice and perhaps a naturally delicate touch.

The slaughter wrought by luminescent mozzie zappers and the accidental traps represented by domestic external lights and motor vehicles eliminate vastly more insect lives than the most ardent of butterfly collectors ever could. If indignation is warranted, it should be directed at the developers, farmers and road builders who destroy, willy-nilly, huge swathes of bushland—and the invertebrates they contain—with no more than a regretful look from passers-by.

In developing any new enthusiasm for butterflies, reference material and mentors are required. A good book that covers the entire fauna and describes what is known and exciting about each species is essential. This book is just the latest in a notable series of volumes that serve this purpose. Equally important, the beginner needs stimulus from others who are knowledgeable and have sympathy for his or her newfound enthusiasm. This is where the local naturalists' clubs come in. In every state capital, and many provincial centres, there are natural history societies, sometimes even entomological societies, which provide vital stimulus and support for the novice. They present talks, run field trips and generally bring together those of like interests. These societies welcome anyone they perceive as sharing their passion for nature—and the lone butterfly lover discovers, with relief, that their obsession is not unique. As one previously solitary young American collector put it, on coming for the first time upon a valley full of waving butterfly nets, 'I thought I'd died and gone to heaven.'

NOTES ON USING THIS BOOK

The distribution maps

We provide a distribution map for every species of butterfly (and a few subspecies) described in this book. Inevitably these draw heavily on those published previously. We acknowledge the huge debt owed by all lepidopterists, including ourselves, to the compendia of locality records drawn up by the Dunns in their four-part *Review of Australian Butterflies*, and to the maps provided in Michael Braby's *Butterflies of Australia*. In addition, in our maps we have tried to accommodate new records that have been published since these works appeared.

Each map indicates the general area in which a species (or, occasionally, a subspecies) may be found. Where known records for a species occur in a number of scattered localities, we have sometimes enclosed these in a single envelope for convenience. State and territory boundaries are indicated, as are markers for the location of a selection of major cities and strategically placed towns, as shown on the map here.

In general, the filled areas enclose the known populations of each species, but it should not be supposed that the butterfly will be common or even occur throughout the enclosed area. We have drawn our 'envelopes' of occurrence generously and, where species are migratory, have included those areas where they may occur as migrants.

As a rule, we have restricted each map to a single species of butterfly. Where two species share the same map, they are indicated in different colours (orange and green). Where an overlap could not be avoided, the area of co-occurrence is shown in brown.

Sizes of adult butterflies

Throughout the text, sizes of adult butterflies are given as forewing length in millimetres, measured from the centre of the wing base to the apex. Generally, for each species a single measurement is given for the male and female. This is taken to be an approximate average of cabinet specimens and in most cases this figure can vary by at least plus or minus 5 per cent. In a few cases where unusual variation is common, a range of measurements is given. For economy of space, in some species only the male forewing length is provided. In such cases females are on average very similar in size to the males or slightly larger. Wingspan may be calculated by doubling this figure and adding a little for the breadth of the body. Note that 'wingspans' quoted in publications by Braby (2000, 2004) use another system and, hence, are not compatible with the measurements given here.

Measurements of length are not meaningful for larvae, which are constantly growing and may extend their body length depending on their posture. Among all immature stages, measurements are provided selectively for eggs only, generally in unusual or biologically interesting cases. It is usually the case that the size of the mature larva and much more compact pupa will be roughly proportional to the size of the adult's body, rather than its wing length. Body measurements of adults, however, cannot be made accurately, from either living or dead specimens.

PART 2

THE BUTTERFLIES

5 FAMILY HESPERIIDAE
Skippers

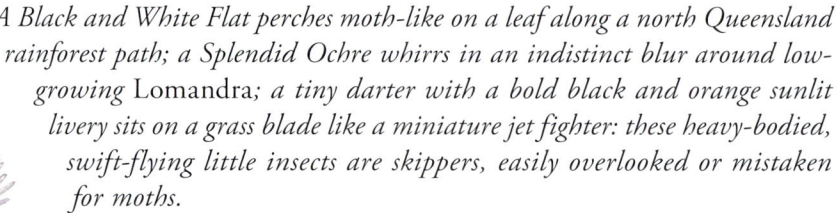

A Black and White Flat perches moth-like on a leaf along a north Queensland rainforest path; a Splendid Ochre whirrs in an indistinct blur around low-growing Lomandra; *a tiny darter with a bold black and orange sunlit livery sits on a grass blade like a miniature jet fighter: these heavy-bodied, swift-flying little insects are skippers, easily overlooked or mistaken for moths.*

The **Hesperiidae** is a very large family with about 3500 species worldwide. Many probably remain to be discovered, especially in tropical rainforests. In Australia they comprise nearly one-third of our total butterfly fauna, with 122 species. Collectively they are known as skippers, on account of the low, jerky, 'skipping' mode of flight of many species. They range from tiny to medium in size and are generally rather drab in colour, but there are exceptions. Members of the four subfamilies are known variously as flats, awls, ochres, darters and swifts.

The Hesperiidae stand apart from the rest of the butterflies, and indeed are not recognised as such by some authors. Bernard D'Abrera's lavish *Butterflies of the World* ignores them. However, they are the sister group of the remainder of the butterflies and they fly by day. Here the term 'sister group' means that they share common ancestors which were not the ancestors of any moth. It should be noted, however, that 'moth' is a very general term meaning 'member of the Lepidoptera that is not a "butterfly"', and many moths are more closely related to butterflies than they are to other groups of moths.

Walker's Grass Dart
(*Ocybadistes walkeri*)

Hesperiids differ from all other butterflies in the following ways:

- the antennae are proportionately long and are wide-set on a broad head
- the antennae often terminate in a distinct point or hook
- the cigar-shaped body is heavy in proportion to the mainly narrow wings
- the arrangement of the supporting veins in the wings has unique characteristics
- the larvae construct shelters by joining together pieces of vegetation, and
- the larvae are simple and elongate with large heads—in the Trapezitinae and Hesperiinae it is often possible to see the testes in mature larvae.

Additional easily recognised features occur in each of the four subfamilies. The Australian fauna is exceptional in being dominated by Trapezitinae (ochres and allies), which occur virtually nowhere else. Two subfamilies which contain larger species—the Pyrginae and the Coeliadinae—are much more diverse in the Asian and tropical regions to the north. Nevertheless, the Australian Pyrginae in particular contains unique and endemic members. The smaller, often lacklustre, Hesperiinae make up a substantial portion of the butterfly fauna everywhere in the world.

It is among the skippers that many opportunities exist for adding to our knowledge of the Australian butterflies. New species turn up in ones and twos year after year and much remains to be learned of their behaviour and ecology.

SUBFAMILY PYRGINAE—Flats

The worldwide subfamily **Pyrginae** includes just eight species in Australia. Most perch on leaf surfaces with their wings flat. They are generally medium-sized with a tropical or subtropical distribution. Among them is one of the strangest butterflies known to science, the Regent Skipper (*Euschemon rafflesia*), which, in the male, possesses structures normally found only in moths. The species is unique and endemic to Australia. In spite of this strange anomaly, males and females are generally very similar in appearance in all members of the subfamily, with females usually a little larger.

The larvae feed on a wide range of dicotyledons from at least seventeen families, and one broad-leafed monocotyledon (*Dioscorea*). Eggs are always laid singly, generally on a leaf of the food plant, and are fairly large and high-domed, almost spherical in some cases, with strong vertical ribbing. Larvae are rather solid, and may be brightly patterned or, more often, plain green or brownish. There is considerable variation in the form of the body and head capsule. Because the larvae feed mostly on plant species with broad, flat leaves, there is considerable scope for 'artistic expression' in the architecture of the shelters constructed. These are diverse and often beautiful, although some species are content just to join two leaves together or make a rude assemblage from leaf litter. Some will crawl into a conveniently rolled dead leaf, perhaps fixing a guy-line here and there to ensure its security. The larva normally rests inside its shelter by day and feeds at night. The pupa also forms inside the shelter, generally suspended from its roof, held by a silken girdle and an attachment at the tail. Presumably this practice reduces the risk of moisture from rainwater reaching the pupa. Pupae may also be covered in a waxy secretion, and generally have a distinctive upturned 'snout' projecting beyond the head.

Adults are commonly light brown, but several are strikingly coloured. The antennae are unusually long, much longer than half the length of the costa (the leading edge of the forewing), with an acute tip. The tip is rather mobile and may appear as strongly recurved or slightly hooked, even in the same species. In several species the hindwing has an unusual squarish outline, unique among Australian butterflies. Most species fly in the early morning or at dusk, but may also be active around the middle of the day during dull weather or in the rainforest understorey. They are sometimes attracted to lights at night.

The Western Flat (*Exometoeca nycteris*) is diurnal, and is considered to be one of the members of the subfamily that retain many ancestral features. It has no close relatives but molecular studies may show affinities with elements of the large South American pyrgine fauna.

Regent Skipper
(*Euschemon rafflesia*)

Regent Skipper and Other Flats

rafflesia

repanda

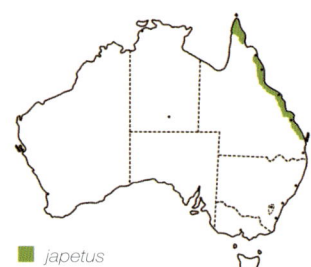
japetus

The splendid **Regent Skipper**, *Euschemon rafflesia* (fw ♂ 29 mm, ♀ 34 mm), is locally common in rainforest or neighbouring open forest where its food plants grow—*Wilkiea* species in the south and *Tetrasynandra* in the north. Tropical populations are brighter and belong to a separate subspecies, *E. rafflesia alba*. Although technically a flat, it often perches with wings half open, as well as adopting the typical flat position. Structurally *E. rafflesia* is one of the most unusual butterflies in the world. Males possess a *frenulum*—a long spine at the base of the hindwing which fits into a loop under the forewing and aids in wing coupling. This structure is found in many moth families, and its presence was once considered an important distinction between butterflies and moths. Adults are mainly active in the morning and late afternoon. They fly rapidly, usually above 2 m, perching frequently in the subcanopy. They often feed at flowers such as lantana. The large, ribbed egg is laid singly, generally on the underside of leaves of the food plant. The young larva constructs a shelter by sewing together adjacent leaves or joining a scrap of dead leaf onto the upperside of a living leaf. As the larva grows, the shelter is enlarged. It emerges to feed, mainly at night. The pupa is suspended upside down within the shelter, covered by a waxy secretion.

The **Eastern Flat**, *Netrocoryne repanda* (fw ♂ 23 mm, ♀ 25 mm), is locally common in rainforest and open eucalypt forest in eastern Australia. In the tropics a smaller, brighter subspecies, *N. repanda expansa*, occurs. The species is characterised by the very square outline to the hindwings, easily seen when it is perched flat on a leaf. Adults are active mainly in the morning and afternoon until dusk. On cloudy days they may fly at midday. Their flight is rapid, sometimes involving short bursts of flat-wing planing. They perch frequently, usually 1–3 m above the ground. The female lays relatively large, ribbed, brown eggs on leaves of the food plant. The young larva constructs its first shelter by eating a neatly circular hinged section from the leaf and folding it back onto the upper surface. Later instars and pupa may be found in rolled dead leaves, the larvae emerging to feed at night. A very wide range of host plants—all rainforest trees or shrubs—is used, including *Acmena, Alectryon, Argyrodendron, Brachychiton, Callicoma, Cryptocarya, Elaeocarpus, Endiandra, Litsea, Lophostemon, Neolitsea, Notelaea, Prunus* and *Scolopia*.

The **Pied Flat**, *Tagiades japetus* (fw ♂ 19 mm, ♀ 21 mm), is common and widespread in tropical rainforest and monsoon forest in Queensland. Adults are generally found at the edge of gaps, flying rapidly 1–3 m above the ground in sunlight in the morning and afternoon, moving into the shade in the middle of the day. They frequently perch quite low, flat on the upperside of leaves, just inside the forest understorey. They are sometimes said to resemble bird droppings. During copulation, the wings may be folded above the body. The female lays her small white eggs on the upperside of leaves of the food plant, *Dioscorea transversa*. The larvae construct elaborate shelters and feed nocturnally. The pupa is suspended from the roof of the larval shelter, possibly an adaptation to remain dry in tropical downpours.

FAMILY HESPERIIDAE—Skippers

Red-eyes and Relatives and the Western Flat

The red-eyes or dusk flats (genus *Chaetocneme*) include four large tropical and subtropical species, all of which fly at dusk, and even after dark. They are sometimes attracted to the lights of houses. In three species, the eyes are deep ruby red in life. All rest on the undersides of leaves with wings held flat. The heavily built larvae generally complete six stages (instars), instead of the usual five.

The **Common Red-eye**, *Chaetocneme beata* (fw ♂ 27 mm, ♀ 31 mm), is common in eastern rainforest and wetter open forest as well as bushy suburban gardens. Although common, it is usually only glimpsed indistinctly at dusk, as it flies rapidly within a few metres of the ground around dense vegetation. Typically it perches 2–4 m from the ground. During the day, the adult rests with wings held flat under leaves in shady places, from where it is sometimes disturbed. The egg is laid singly on the upperside of leaves of the host plant. The young larva constructs its first shelter by excising a piece of leaf and folding it back onto the upper surface. Later instars may sew two leaves together. The larva rests upside down in the shelter by day and feeds at night. The pupa is suspended within the shelter. Numerous host plant species are utilised, most commonly *Cryptocarya*, *Litsea* and *Neolitsea*, but also *Annona* (Custard Apple and Soursop), *Cinnamomum* (Camphor Laurel) and plants from nine other genera.

The **Rare Red-eye**, *Chaetocneme denitza* (fw ♂ 26 mm, ♀ 30 mm), is widespread but rare in open eucalypt forests where its host plants grow. In behaviour and life history it resembles *C. beata*. Larvae feed on eucalypts, *Lophostemon confertus*, *L. grandiflorus*, *L. suaveolens* and *Planchonia careya*.

■ beata

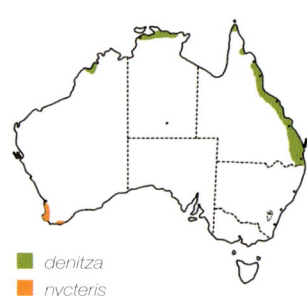
■ denitza
■ nycteris

C. beata ♂

The **Banded Red-eye**, *Chaetocneme critomedia* (fw ♂ 28 mm, ♀ 34 mm), is restricted to semi-open forest habitats on Cape York Peninsula. In behaviour and life history it resembles *C. beata* but the larva has a reddish tinge. Host plants include *Annona*, *Blephocarya*, *Cinnamomum*, *Commersonia*, *Cryptocarya*, *Endiandra*, *Litsea*, *Macaranga*, *Mallotus*, *Neolitsea* and *Syzygium*.

The **Purple Dusk Flat**, *Chaetocneme porphyropis* (fw ♂ 29 mm, ♀ 31 mm), is confined to rainforest in the Queensland wet tropics region and is nowhere common. Unlike other dusk flats, it may be active during the day from early afternoon on, when the adults keep to the forest understorey. Towards dusk they may be active in more open areas, flying swiftly 1–4 m above the ground, and perching frequently, often preferring the undersides of leaves. The life history differs from that of *C. beata* chiefly in the mature larva, which is reddish orange with distinct horns on the head. Host plants include *Cryptocarya grandis*, *Endiandra compressa*, *Litsea leefeana*, *Neolitsea dealbata* and *Cinnamomum*.

The **Western Flat**, *Exometoeca nycteris* (fw ♂ 27 mm, ♀ 31 mm), is known only from open woodland in south-west Australia. It has no near relatives and is regarded by some as a 'living fossil'. It is an uncommon and local species. Adults are active throughout the day in full sunlight, flying rapidly near the ground. Males establish territories and perch on prominent stems with wings held flat, a posture believed to display their presence to rivals. Females oviposit singly on fresh growth of their food plant, *Tetratheca hispidissima*. Larvae construct shelters on the leaf underside by drawing the edges of the leaf together. Older larvae may construct shelters on the ground from leaf litter, where pupation also occurs. The larvae emerge periodically to feed throughout the day.

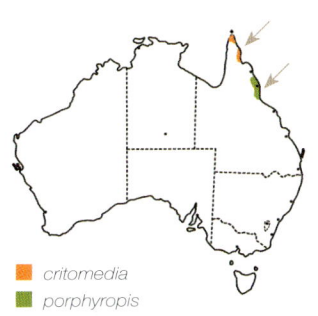

SUBFAMILY COELIADINAE—Awls

The subfamily **Coeliadinae** is confined to the Old World tropics and includes about 75 species. In Australia there are just seven species, none of which are endemic to the continent. They are called awls because the final segment of labial palp is long and slender and juts out horizontally directly in front of the eyes, resembling a bradawl.

Awls are tropical and subtropical species, with the migratory Brown Awl (*Badamia exclamationis*) just reaching the extreme east of coastal Victoria. Larval hosts are all dicotyledons, principally plants of the families Fabaceae and Malphigiaceae. The egg is relatively large, cream or dark orange, and more or less hemispherical with prominent vertical ribs. In Australian species it is always laid singly on leaves of the host plant. The larvae are cylindrical and generally boldly patterned with either transverse or longitudinal bands. As in the subfamily Pyrginae, feeding on soft broad-leafed dicotyledons gives them considerable latitude in the form of shelter construction, and the young larvae in particular have evolved several neat ways of excising one or two flaps of leaf, which are folded back to make a shelter. In the genus *Hasora* the young larvae feed from inside on the leaves of the shelter, generating a series of perforations. Shelters of older larvae may involve sewing two or more whole leaves together. The pupa is suspended within the shelter, held by a silken girdle, and is often covered in a white waxy secretion. It usually bears a strong forward-pointing, snout-like projection on its head.

The adults are small to medium in size with heavy bodies. The antennae are about half the length of the leading edge of the forewing (the costa) and terminate in a long thin tapered filament which may be strongly recurved. The forewing is very angular, with an acute apex, and the hindwing margin is sometimes elaborately curved and produced almost to make a broad short tail. All species are very swift in flight, and several fly high much of the time. All feed avidly at a wide range of flowers. An awl can generally reach nectar in the deepest corolla tubes with its long proboscis. They are basically day-flying, but tend to avoid activity during the heat of the day, and may be active feeding and ovipositing just before dusk. Species of *Hasora* perch upside down on the underside of leaves. Males of some species visit damp earth to acquire salts, and may even land on humans to imbibe their sweat.

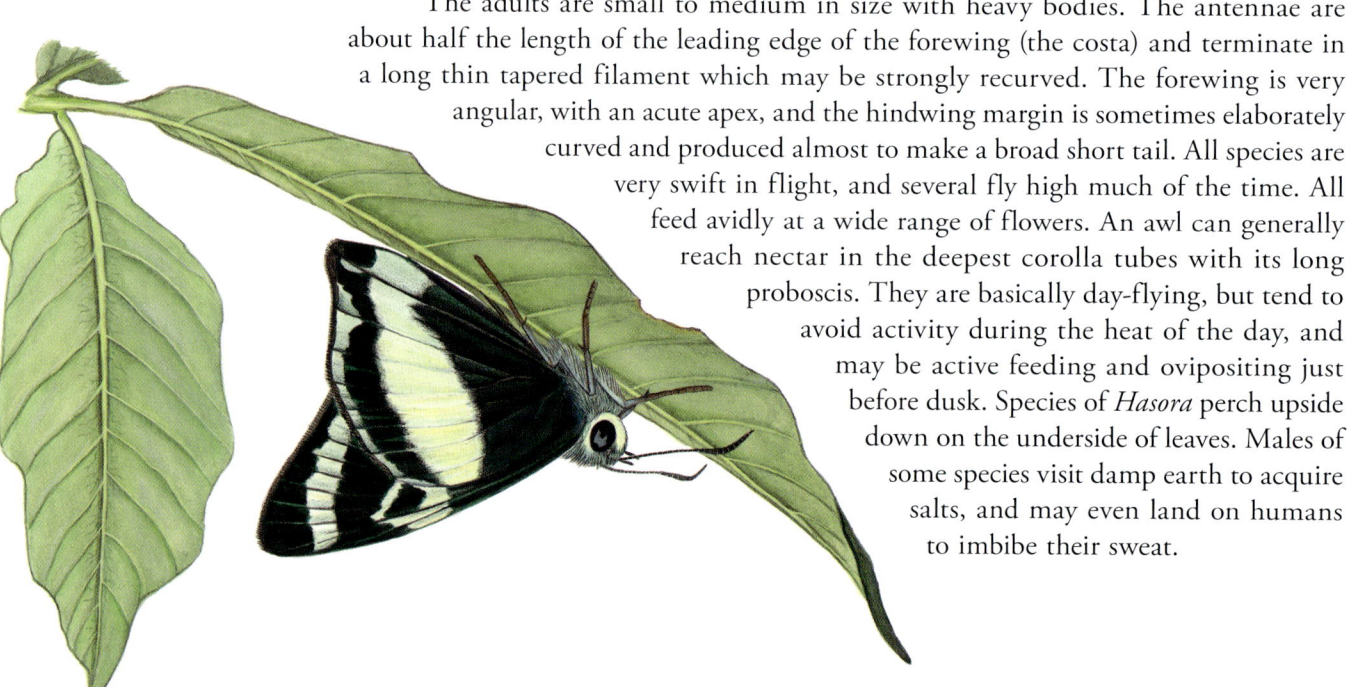

Green Awl
(*Hasora discolor*)

Awls 1

The **Peacock Awl**, *Allora doleschallii* (fw ♂ 23 mm, ♀ 26 mm), occurs locally in monsoon forest and vine scrub in North Queensland. The female shares the brilliant blue-green upperside colour of the male. Adults are normally found around the host plant, the liana *Rhyssopterys timorensis*. They fly swiftly in sunlight 1–4 m above the ground, perching frequently. Eggs are laid singly on the upperside of host plant leaves. The young larva constructs an elegant shelter made by cutting semicircular incisions in the leaf around the midrib. The flaps so created are then folded up and sewn together. The larva emerges from a small aperture on the midrib to feed at the leaf margins. As the larva grows, this structure is enlarged, becoming less regular as sometimes two or more leaves are sewn together. The pupa forms inside the shelter.

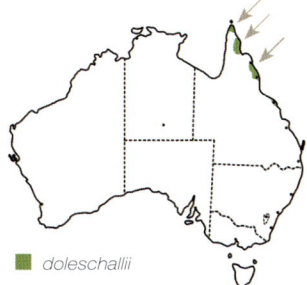
doleschallii

The **Greater Peacock Awl**, *Allora major* (fw ♂ 25 mm, ♀ 27.5 mm), is a rare species restricted to rainforest on Cape York Peninsula. Both male and female are very like *A. doleschallii* but are larger and, if anything, even more brilliantly coloured above. The white markings on the underside differ consistently, and provide a reliable means of separating the two species. Adults fly in sunlight high in the rainforest canopy. The life history is not known.

major

The **Brown Awl**, *Badamia exclamationis* (fw ♂ 24 mm, ♀ 27 mm), is a very widespread migrant found commonly in more open habitats, including gardens. It is easily recognised by its elongate forewings. Adults fly very rapidly, generally 1–3 m from the ground, and are most often seen feeding at flowers. They are fairly inactive during the hottest part of the day. Eggs are laid singly on young growth of the host plant, generally *Terminalia oblongata* or *T. catappa*. The larva constructs a rough shelter, which also serves as a pupation site, and emerges periodically to feed. Other hosts include *T. microcarpa*, *Pongamia pinnata* and *Rhyssopterys timorensis*.

exclamationis

FAMILY HESPERIIDAE—Skippers

Awls 2

discolor

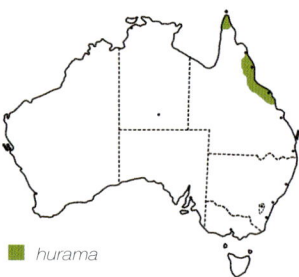
hurama

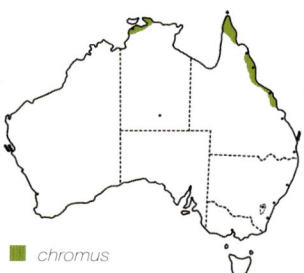
chromus

khoda

Four similar species of the genus *Hasora* occur in the eastern tropics and subtropics. Most fly by day but tend to be more active in the morning and from mid to late afternoon. They are heavy-bodied and fly swiftly, generally more than 2 m above the ground, often perching, sometimes up to 10 m above the ground. During the heat of the day and at night they perch upside down on the undersides of leaves.

The **Green Awl**, *Hasora discolor* (fw ♂ 24 mm, ♀ 25 mm), occurs locally at the margins of tropical and subtropical rainforest and along forest streams. It is usually seen feeding at flowers between 2 and 4 m, but may fly much higher. Males often descend to damp sand to drink salty fluids, and sometimes land on a human arm to imbibe sweat. The small white eggs are laid singly on new growth of the host plant, *Mucuna gigantea*. The slightly hairy, colourful larva constructs a shelter by cutting and folding a flap of leaf, or, when larger, by sewing together a whole leaflet. Feeding takes place mainly within the shelter, creating a series of distinctive holes in its surface, meaning it must periodically be reconstructed. The pupa forms inside the final shelter.

The **Broad-banded Awl**, *Hasora hurama* (fw ♂ 24 mm, ♀ 25 mm), is found locally in moist forest in tropical Queensland, especially near mangroves. During the day it often flies in shaded forest understorey, venturing to more open areas in the late afternoon. The small white eggs are laid singly on new growth of the host plant, the vine *Derris trifoliata*. The larva sews the edges of a small leaf together to make a shelter from which it emerges at night to feed. The mature larva is very like that of *H. khoda*.

The **Common Banded Awl**, *Hasora chromus* (fw ♂ 24 mm, ♀ 24 mm), is locally common in drier rainforest types and densely vegetated suburban gardens. Adults are basically diurnal and fly very rapidly 2–6 m above the ground, often feeding at flowers such as lantana. Males adopt high perches from which they defend mating territories. The small eggs are laid singly on young leaves of the tree *Pongamia pinnata*. Larval shelters are untidy and many may be found on the one tree. The mature larva is like that of *H. khoda*, but generally with broader banding.

The **Narrow-banded Awl**, *Hasora khoda* (fw ♂ 24 mm, ♀ 25 mm), is common but very local in subtropical Queensland and New South Wales. Adults are active throughout the day, generally flying and perching high (2–6 m). They feed at flowers usually in the morning, and females oviposit mainly in the late afternoon until dusk. Eggs are placed singly on fresh growth of the host plant, *Millettia megasperma* or cultivated wisteria. The larva constructs a shelter from a folded flap of excised leaf and emerges at night to feed. Later instars may sew several leaves together. Pupation takes place within the final shelter.

FAMILY HESPERIIDAE—Skippers

SUBFAMILY TRAPEZITINAE—
Ochres and Their Allies

The **Trapezitinae** is the largest subfamily of Australian skippers, with 70 species. They are endemic to Australasia and are, in fact, the only subfamily of butterflies restricted to our region. Elsewhere they occur only on the main island of New Guinea, where two small endemic genera occur, as well as three genera which also occur in Australia.

The subfamily has an unusual distribution within Australia. Whereas most butterfly groups are concentrated in the north-east of the continent, Trapezitinae attain their highest diversity in south-east Queensland. There are also several other 'hotspots' with high species numbers in the Queensland wet tropics region and south-eastern mainland Australia. They are the major skipper group in Western Australia, and a few species occur in the arid interior and in alpine areas. Unlike other groups which appear to have a southern origin, there are at present no known affinities between this subfamily and skippers in any other continent. Further clarification of this point must await comprehensive DNA studies.

Trapezitinae is considered to be separate from the subfamily Hesperiinae on the basis of several structural details, which are not readily observed. Both subfamilies have many species and both include mainly small to very small species with heavy bodies. There are, however, a few general rules that help in recognising the two groups. Trapezitinae usually perch either with wings folded above their body, half open, or sometimes fully open when perched on flowers. Only occasionally do they adopt the typical 'dart' position (that is, forewings up, hindwings down) when at rest, and if they do adopt this position they seldom hold it for long.

There are no very tiny trapezitines and the smallest species are brown with whitish or dull yellowish markings, whereas very small hesperiines are almost all black with bright-orange bands. In larger trapezitines, orange markings tend to be more broken than in similar-sized hesperiines, and their subdued colours are also a useful guide. A number of tropical trapezitines and hesperiines are mainly neutral brown with a few white markings on the forewings. In this case the forewing patterning is generally diagnostic, but also hard to see. However, in these hesperiines the tornal lobe on the hindwing (see Figure 5.2, p. 104) is generally very well developed, which is seldom the case in any trapezitine. It is a general rule that the underside markings of trapezitines are more strongly patterned than in the Hesperiinae, in which the pattern is usually diffuse beneath, but some have no pattern at all.

Separating the different species of trapezitines is yet another challenge. Only a few can reliably be identified without capture. Points to consider are size, sex (determined if necessary by squeezing the abdomen to inspect the genitalia), wing shape, upper- and underside patterns, and presence and form of a slanting—usually black—sex brand on the male forewing (see Figure 5.2, p. 104). It is also useful to consider geographical origin, associated plant species, and the fact that very few trapezitines are routinely encountered.

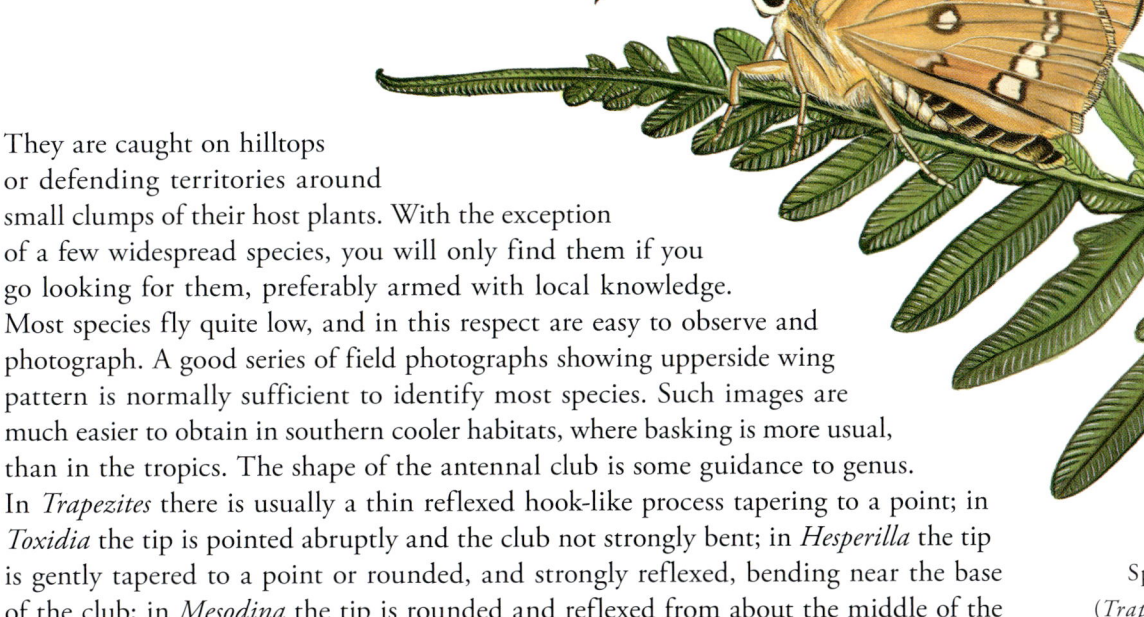

Splendid Ochre
(*Trapezites symmomus*)

They are caught on hilltops or defending territories around small clumps of their host plants. With the exception of a few widespread species, you will only find them if you go looking for them, preferably armed with local knowledge. Most species fly quite low, and in this respect are easy to observe and photograph. A good series of field photographs showing upperside wing pattern is normally sufficient to identify most species. Such images are much easier to obtain in southern cooler habitats, where basking is more usual, than in the tropics. The shape of the antennal club is some guidance to genus. In *Trapezites* there is usually a thin reflexed hook-like process tapering to a point; in *Toxidia* the tip is pointed abruptly and the club not strongly bent; in *Hesperilla* the tip is gently tapered to a point or rounded, and strongly reflexed, bending near the base of the club; in *Mesodina* the tip is rounded and reflexed from about the middle of the club. However, antennae are mobile and these features may not be apparent, especially in living specimens. Examples of antennae as they normally appear in 'set' museum specimens are shown in Figure 5.1 on page 97.

Eggs are generally hemispherical or high-domed and come in various colours. Vertical ribbing is coarse or very fine. Some are asymmetrical, oval when seen from above, and may be very large relative to the size of the adult. They are laid singly or rarely in small groups, usually on leaves of the host but sometimes on nearby leaf litter. Larvae are cylindrical or slug-like with a simple head capsule, sometimes uniquely marked. Only a very few species have any pattern on the body, which is generally dull brown or green. All build shelters near the base of their host plants and usually feed at night. The pupa forms within the shelter and has an elaborately sculptured cap on its head showing great variation in the form in different species. Some are like rabbit ears, some like bat faces, yet others like Viking helmets. Generally this structure is unique and most species can be recognised from it.

All trapezitines feed on monocotyledons. The largest genus, *Trapezites*, with eighteen species, feeds almost exclusively on *Lomandra*, except in Western Australia where plants of the family Laxmanniaceae are also utilised. Other groups feed mainly on sedges, especially *Gahnia* species, and, less frequently, grasses. The genus *Mesodina* feeds on wild irises.

Adults are active in the day, generally frequenting sunny areas. Females are almost always found near their food plants, but males of many species visit hilltops. Most species fly low but very fast, perching frequently on the ground or on the uppersides of leaves or blades of grass, adopting the positions described above. As far as we know, all are palatable to vertebrate predators.

Ochres 1

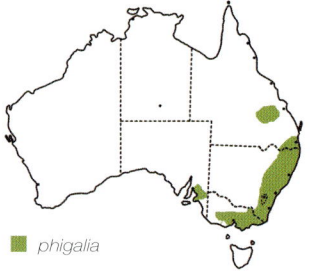
phigalia

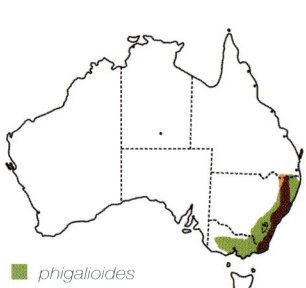
phigalioides
iacchoides

The genus *Trapezites* (the ochres) includes eighteen species—the equal-largest genus in Australia. Most species are restricted in habitat. The larvae generally feed on *Lomandra* species but in Western Australia some feed on other plants in the family Laxmanniaceae (formerly part of the Xanthorrhoeaceae).

The **Heath Ochre**, *Trapezites phigalia* (fw ♂ 16 mm, ♀ 17 mm), occurs locally in dry open forest and heath. Adults fly rapidly in sunshine, close to the ground, feeding at flowers such as *Boronia*. Males defend small territories, perching on low prominences, and often visit hilltops. The small eggs are laid singly on leaves of the host plant. The larva constructs a shelter near the leaf base and emerges at night to feed. Pupation occurs in the shelter. Host plants include several species of *Lomandra*, including *L. densiflora*, *L. fibrata*, *L. filiformis*, *L. glauca*, *L. multiflora*, *L. nana*, *L. obliqua* and *L. sororia*.

The **Montane Ochre**, *Trapezites phigalioides* (fw ♂ 15 mm, ♀ 16 mm), occurs locally in open forest from sea level to 1600 m. Its habits are similar to those of *T. phigalia*. Females lay a relatively larger egg and just one host plant, *Lomandra filiformis*, is known.

The larger **Silver-studded Ochre**, *Trapezites iacchoides* (fw ♂ 16.5 mm, ♀ 19 mm), occurs locally in damp areas in open eucalypt forest where its host plant, *Lomandra longifolia*, grows. Its life history is very similar to that of *T. phigalioides*, with the female laying a proportionally larger egg.

Ochres 2

The males of the three species featured here all have rather long and narrow wings and are particularly swift-flying. Females have much more rounded wings. The uppersides are all very similar but both sexes can be reliably identified by their underside markings, which, in the males, include large silver patches on the hindwing. Although similar in adult size, *Trapezites maheta* and *T. praxedes* lay relatively small eggs, whereas the eggs of *T. genevieveae* are large. Eggs are typically laid at the base of the host plant and the larval life histories are similar.

maheta

The **Northern Silver Ochre**, *Trapezites maheta* (fw ♂ 16 mm, ♀ 16 mm), occurs locally in open forest and heath. Adults fly and perch close to the ground, often feeding from flowers such as *Pimelea*. They are generally found near the larval host plant, *Lomandra hystrix*.

The **Southern Silver Ochre**, *Trapezites praxedes* (fw ♂ 16 mm, ♀ 16 mm), occurs in similar habitats further south. Adults, especially males, may perch quite high in the canopy of eucalypts, but are usually found nearer the ground. The main food plant is *Lomandra obliqua*, with *L. confertifolia* and *L. longifolia* also used occasionally.

praxedes
genevieveae

The **Ornate Ochre**, *Trapezites genevieveae* (fw ♂ 17 mm, ♀ 17 mm), is restricted to subtropical rainforest, where the food plant, *Lomandra spicata*, grows in small tussocks among leaf litter. Adults fly high. Males, especially, rarely descend from the canopy. Females descend lower to feed at flowers, and typically land on the forest floor to oviposit, placing their eggs on litter surrounding the base of the host plant. The larvae form shelters from leaf litter. Larvae emerge at night and leave characteristic damage on the leaves, as though the ends had been cut off using scissors.

maheta ♂

maheta ♀

maheta ♂

Lomandra spicata

genevieveae ♀ laying eggs on dead leaves

♂ praxedes ♀
underside

♂ genevieveae ♀
underside

genevieveae larva in shelter

Ochres 3

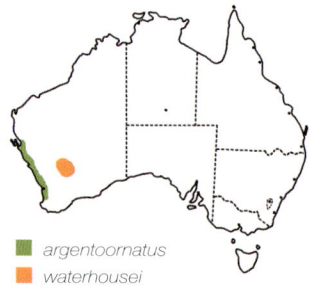

The **Yellow Ochre**, *Trapezites luteus* (fw ♂ 16 mm, ♀ 18 mm), is a rare species found very locally in the east in dry open woodland, in South Australia in semi-arid Cypress Pine woodland and mallee and, in Tasmania, in sclerophyll forest. The eastern, South Australian and Tasmanian populations are considered separate subspecies. Adults fly low and swiftly, perching on low prominences such as rocks, low shrubs or fence posts. Females lay eggs on leaves near the base of the food plant—variously, *Lomandra confertifolia*, *L. densiflora*, *L. filiformis*, *L. longifolia* and *L. multiflora*. Larvae construct shelters and feed at night.

The remaining four species all occur in the west and south of mainland Australia and are the only *Trapezites* to feed on plants other than *Lomandra*.

The **Mallee Ochre**, *Trapezites sciron* (fw ♂ 16 mm, ♀ 18 mm), is a rare and local species inhabiting arid and semi-arid habitats from western Victoria to Perth. The western and eastern forms are considered to be separate subspecies, but the differences are slight. Adults fly rapidly, near the ground, perching frequently. Males sometimes 'hilltop' along dune crests. The larva of the eastern form feeds on *Lomandra caespitosa* and *L. collina*, whereas the western form feeds on *Acanthocarpus preissii*, sometimes constructing shelters of dead leaves away from the plant. Eggs are laid on leaves of the host plants and larvae feed nocturnally.

Atkins' Ochre, *Trapezites atkinsi* (fw ♂ 15.5mm, ♀ 17 mm), is known only from a small patch of coastal heath near Point D'Entrecasteaux on the southern tip of Western Australia. No similar species occur in this location. The larvae feed on *Acanthocarpus preissii* and the habits are probably like those of the next species.

The **Silver-spotted Ochre**, *Trapezites argenteoornatus* (fw ♂ 13mm, ♀ 14 mm), occurs locally in coastal heath and dunes along the Western Australian coast. Adults fly low and rapidly, perching on low prominences such as empty snail shells. The eggs, large relative to the insect, are laid singly on stems and leaves of the host plant, *Acanthocarpus* species. The larva weaves a silken shelter incorporating the fine leaves of the plant. It emerges to feed on foliage at night.

Waterhouse's Ochre, *Trapezites waterhousei* (fw ♂ 14 mm, ♀ 16 mm), is known from only a few semi-arid woodland localities in inland Western Australia where it is found around laterite outcrops, generally near to the host plant, *Xerolirion divaricata*. Where present, it may be quite common. Adults fly close to the ground and settle frequently. Males tend to fly along the laterite ridges, perching on stones and maintaining small territories. Females flutter around the host plant. The female lays small eggs singly on the host plant, and the larval habits are probably like those of *T. argenteoornatus*. Larval shelters constructed of dead leaves and detritus have been discovered on the food plant.

FAMILY HESPERIIDAE—Skippers

Ochres 4

symmomus

The **Splendid Ochre**, *Trapezites symmomus* (fw ♂ 23 mm, ♀ 25 mm), is a common and conspicuous species in many localities in the east and south. There are three subspecies, differing slightly in the brightness of their markings. It prefers moister open forest, watercourses or rainforest margins, where its larval host plant grows, especially the common ornamental *Lomandra longifolia*. It also occurs in parkland and gardens. By far the largest of the ochres, it is also easily recognised by the nearly continuous line of silver on the hindwing underside, as opposed to the discrete spots of other species. Adults are found near their host plant, and males perch on foliage in sunny spots up to about 2 m above ground, maintaining territories. When another male encroaches, a high-speed chase usually ensues and, in low forest, the two may spiral high into the canopy. In the early to mid-morning, males also patrol patches of *Lomandra* with a quick bobbing flight, searching for freshly emerged females.

Ovipositing females flutter briskly but rather ponderously around their food plants. Typically, several leaves will be tested before a single large egg is laid on the upperside of the leaf. The young larvae form shelters by sewing leaves together, often with one looped up over another. The large older larvae are found at the base of the tussock and often incorporate fallen leaves into a large shelter, where pupation also occurs.

Lomandra longifolia

larval shelters

symmomus ♂

symmomus

symmomus

pupa in shelter

symmomus
immature stages

Variegated Blue Wren

Blue Wrens have been seen capturing and eating adults of *T. symmomus*, which must provide a large meal for such a small bird. Larvae feed at night and leave characteristic neat bite-marks on the plant, shearing off leaf ends cleanly. Other host plants sometimes used include *L. filiformis*, *L. hystrix*, *L. obliqua* and *L. spicata*.

Of all its subfamily, *T. symmomus* is probably the species most amenable to serious behavioural and ecological studies. Detailed, structured investigations of almost any aspect of its biology are likely to produce information of scientific interest.

FAMILY HESPERIIDAE—Skippers

Ochres 5

The six species shown here all range as far north as the Queensland tropics, and several are confined to this region. All occur locally. In all species eggs are laid singly, generally near the base of the *Lomandra* host. The larva makes a shelter from host plant leaves or litter at the base of the plant, and feeds at night. In some locations *Trapezites macqueeni*, *T. petalia*, *T. heteromacula* and *T. eliena* fly together.

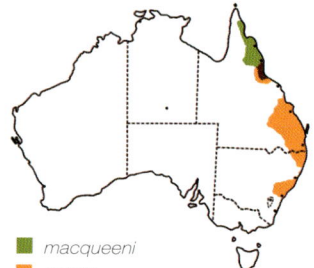

■ *macqueeni*
■ *petalia*

Macqueen's Ochre, *Trapezites macqueeni* (fw ♂ 16 mm, ♀ 18 mm), is found in dry open forests and heaths in north Queensland, generally around rocky outcrops. It is rare and local in distribution. The glossy bronzed wings of the male upperside are unique in the genus. Males frequent ridges and hilltops, perching low. Females are generally found near the food plant, *Lomandra filiformis*. Generally just one larva is found per plant.

The **Black-ringed Ochre**, *Trapezites petalia* (fw ♂ 17 mm, ♀ 17 mm), occurs in mixed eucalypt and savannah woodlands up to 1000 m in areas of moderate rainfall. Adults generally fly low in the forest understorey, perching frequently, but males also visit ridges and hilltops. Females are found near the host plant, especially *Lomandra multiflora*, but also *L. filiformis* and *L. longifolia*.

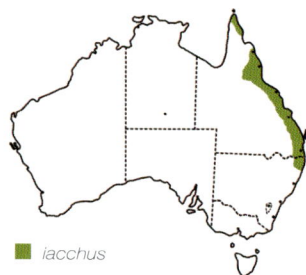

■ *iacchus*

The **Brown Ochre**, *Trapezites iacchus* (fw ♂ 19 mm, ♀ 19 mm), occurs in a range of habitats from dry eucalypt forests to wallum heath and paperbark forest. In central and north Queensland it is relatively common, displacing *T. symmomus* in moist coastal habitats. Adult males are very rapid in flight, patrolling clumps of host plant in the morning and visiting hilltops in the afternoon, patrolling or perching on low vegetation. Females tend to remain near the host plants, *Lomandra hystrix*, *L. longifolia* and *L. multiflora*.

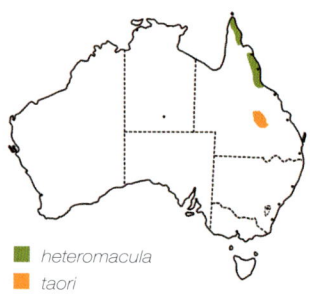

■ *heteromacula*
■ *taori*

The **Small Orange Ochre**, *Trapezites heteromacula* (fw ♂ 14.5 mm, ♀ 16 mm), is a strictly tropical species found in open eucalypt woodland, monsoon forest and rainforest borders up to 1000 m. Adults fly low, and males establish small territories in sunny clearings or on exposed slopes below hill summits. Females are sedentary and are found either feeding at flowers or seeking oviposition sites near the host plant, *Lomandra filiformis* or *L. longifolia*.

■ *eliena*

The **Orange Ochre**, *Trapezites eliena* (fw ♂ 19 mm, ♀ 21 mm), is one of the commonest and most widespread members of the genus, within its range found wherever *Lomandra* grows in open woodlands and heaths. In areas of heavy rainfall or disturbed habitats it is less common. Adults fly rapidly and are frequently seen at flowers, such as lantana, where they may perch, feeding, up to 3 m above the ground. Males commonly hilltop, especially in the afternoon, usually perching within 1.5 m of the ground. Host plants include *Lomandra confertifolia*, *L. filiformis*, *L. longifolia* and *L. multiflora*.

The **Sandstone Ochre**, *Trapezites taori* (fw ♂ 19 mm, ♀ 21 mm), is confined to a few dry sandstone areas in inland central Queensland, including Expedition Range and the Blackdown Tableland from 300–900 m. Even within these areas the insect is rare, and often flies on cliff faces where its host plant, *Lomandra confertifolia*, grows. Adults fly very rapidly, somewhat higher than most other ochres, feeding at flowers of *Banksia*, *Leptospermum* and *Xanthorrhoea*. Males establish territories in sunny clearings, on exposed hill slopes, and along cliff edges, chiefly in the afternoon.

FAMILY HESPERIIDAE—Skippers

Tropical Grass Skippers and the Blue-flash Skipper

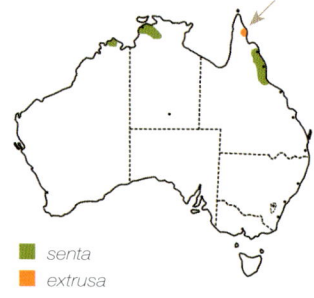
- senta
- extrusa

- xiphiphora

- crocea

- xanthomera

The five species illustrated here are tropical, with only one reaching the subtropics. All four grass skippers are small, undistinguished-looking species found locally in fairly open habitats. They are seldom recognised by casual observation. The most significant clue to field identification tends to be their location; few similar species occur so far north. As larvae they feed on grasses, building shelters and feeding at night. The known larvae have the same rather unusual form, shown for *Neohesperilla xanthomera*: swollen in the middle to posterior segments and attenuated towards the head, with a rather bulbous head capsule attached to the body. The head capsule of all species, including *N. xanthomera*, is recorded as being black and the specimen illustrated may have recently moulted. In all species the eggs are hemispherical with broad shallow fluting, and are laid singly on the underside of blades of the host grass.

The **Spotted Grass Skipper**, *Neohesperilla senta* (fw ♂ 13.5 mm, ♀ 15 mm), occurs in moist coastal eucalypt forests, where it is rare. Adults fly very rapidly just above the grass, frequently feeding from small low-growing flowers. Early in the wet season they congregate at regenerating patches burnt by fires. Larvae feed on *Themeda triandra*.

The **Sword-brand Grass Skipper**, *Neohesperilla xiphiphora* (fw ♂ 14 mm, ♀ 14 mm), occurs mainly in northern savannah, especially along creek beds. Females oviposit on grass—probably *Schizachyrium perplexum*—at the base of trees. The swift-flying males visit hilltops and perch up to 5 m high in foliage. After fires, both sexes are more common and may be found around regenerating areas with fresh grass shoots.

The **Narrow-brand Grass Skipper**, *Neohesperilla crocea* (fw ♂ 14 mm, ♀ 16 mm), is found mainly in wetter areas near rainforest or paperbark swamps. Both sexes remain around the host grass, *Chrysopogon aciculatus*. Females perch near the ground. Males maintain territories in foliage of surrounding trees, perching 3–4 m above the ground and engaging in extremely rapid territorial disputes with other males.

The **Yellow Grass Skipper**, *Neohesperilla xanthomera* (fw ♂ 16 mm, ♀ 18 mm), occurs in dry savannah woodland and open eucalypt forest, extending into northern New South Wales. It is everywhere uncommon. Males defend territories on hilltops and ridges, where they perch on the ground or on low foliage. Females occur on the lower slopes of such hills. The larvae feed on the grass genus, *Heteropogon*.

The **Blue-flash Skipper**, *Rachelia extrusa* (fw ♂ 19 mm, ♀ 21 mm), is restricted to rainforest on Cape York Peninsula. Males fly high in the canopy, dashing about rapidly as they defend their perches. Occasionally during these aerobatics you will see a flash of blue light from their brilliant iridescent upperside. The equally brilliant but slower females descend more frequently to feed at flowers such as the introduced herb *Stachytarpheta*, or to oviposit. The pink ribbed egg is placed singly on the underside of leaves of the host, *Flagellaria indica*, an understorey scrambler. Small plants are preferred. The larva has a typical, heavy trapezitine shape, and builds a shelter by rolling leaves of the host into a tube, emerging to feed at night. Older larvae may construct shelters from leaf litter. The pupa is suspended within the final shelter.

FAMILY HESPERIIDAE—Skippers

Southern Grass Skippers 1

- dominula
- sphenosema

- tillyardi

- monticolae

- cynone

The five species illustrated all have a southern or western distribution and, where reaching the eastern subtropics, are invariably montane. All are small, and most have attractive chequered markings beneath, best seen when they feed at flowers. All feed as larvae on grasses and their hemispherical fluted eggs are placed singly or in short well-spaced rows. Larvae build shelters from blades of the host grass, near its base, or from surrounding leaf litter, and feed nocturnally. Larvae of various species differ somewhat in body colour, head capsule shape and pattern.

The **Wedge Grass Skipper**, *Anisynta sphenosema* (fw ♂ 15 mm, ♀ 16 mm), occurs quite commonly along the south-west coast of Western Australia in grassy areas, especially along watercourses, and even in Perth gardens. Adults fly rapidly close to the ground, settling frequently on the ground. Females lay their eggs on debris near the host, or low on blades of the host grass, typically the native *Microlaena stipoides*, but also *Ehrharta calycina* and *E. longiflora*.

The **Two-brand Grass Skipper**, *Anisynta dominula* (fw ♂ 13–16 mm, ♀ 14–17 mm), is the most montane of all grass skippers, found mainly from 900 to 1600 m on the mainland and at sea level to 1000 m in eastern Tasmania. It exhibits considerable variation throughout its range, with the smaller western Tasmanian population considered a separate race. This form occurs from 400 to 1070 m. Adults fly low in grassy patches in open forest and subalpine woodland. They often congregate in patches of low flowers, such as daisies and dandelions, from which they sip nectar. Their social life also seems to revolve around these patches, with males driving off rivals, and matings taking place there, often after meeting on a flower. Females lay their eggs singly on blades of the host grass, *Poa* species.

The **Chequered Grass Skipper**, *Anisynta tillyardi* (fw ♂ 16 mm, ♀ 17 mm), occurs locally in moist subtropical montane areas from 900 to 1500 m. It prefers grassy areas but is sometimes found in dense thickets. Adults fly close to the ground, basking frequently in sunny patches. The female places her eggs in straight rows of up to six along the underside of a blade of the host grass, *Poa labillardieri*. The larva, with its distinctively sculptured head capsule, constructs a shelter from dead leaves at the base of the host grass tussock.

The **Mountain Grass Skipper**, *Anisynta monticolae* (fw ♂ 12 mm, ♀ 14 mm), is confined to moist open forest from 600 to 1300 m in the south-east mainland, preferring sheltered slopes and gullies. Adults fly rapidly among grass tussocks, often feeding on low flowers and basking with open wings. Females lay their eggs singly on blades of *Poa* species.

The **Mottled Grass Skipper**, *Anisynta cynone* (fw ♂ 13 mm, ♀ 14 mm), has a disjunct distribution, with a southern population occurring in grassy areas in open woodland, and coastal dunes in South Australia, and an inland population in north-central New South Wales, found in open forest grassland, especially near Gunnedah. The populations are considered to represent different races, but differences are relatively slight. Adults fly low among the grass, often perching on the ground and basking in the sun with half-opened wings. Eggs are laid singly or in rows of up to seven on blades of the host grasses, which include species of *Austrostipa*, *Brachypodium*, *Cynodon*, *Oryzopsis* and *Poa*.

FAMILY HESPERIIDAE—Skippers

Southern Grass Skippers 2

The six species featured here are mostly south-eastern in distribution, although three of the four *Toxidia* species range into the Queensland tropics and the genus is mainly tropical. Most are low-flying species, the larvae of which feed nocturnally on grass, sheltering by day in a structure made from woven grass blades and/or leaf litter. Larvae of all species are rather similar. Eggs are hemispherical with shallow fluting and are laid either on grass stems or leaves, or among debris at the base of the host plant.

compacta

The **Barred Skipper**, *Dispar compacta* (fw ♂ 13 mm, ♀ 14 mm), is common and widespread in a wide variety of open grassy forests east of the Great Dividing Range. It also occurs in subalpine areas up to 1300 m and in parks and gardens. Adults fly low over grass, with a busy skipping motion, frequently feeding from flowers. Males visit hilltops in numbers, where they may perch high in the canopy of trees growing on the summit. The eggs are laid singly on *Poa tenera* and other *Poa* species, and less commonly on the non-grasses *Gahnia* and *Lomandra*.

tasmanica

The **Two-spotted Grass Skipper**, *Pasma tasmanica* (fw ♂ 13 mm, ♀ 15 mm), occurs locally in open forest, especially in higher country up to 1280 m. In Tasmania it ranges from 0 to 900 m. Adults fly with a brisk skipping motion among grass tussocks, pausing often to feed at low flowers. Males establish small territories in sunny clearings, perching on low vegetation within 1.5 m of the ground. Eggs are laid singly on the host grass, *Microlaena stipoides* or *Poa labillardieri*, or on nearby leaf litter.

andersoni

Anderson's Grass Skipper, *Toxidia andersoni* (fw ♂ 16 mm, ♀ 18 mm), occurs in wet sclerophyll forest and rainforest margins, up to 1100 m above sea level in southern Queensland but at sea level in Victoria. It is the most southerly member of its genus. Adults fly rapidly and at moderate height (1–3 m) over grass and around low shrubs, feeding from flowers. Males hilltop, perching up to 4 m from the ground. The eggs are laid singly but sometimes in loose aggregations on leaf litter. The larva feeds on *Poa queenslandica* and *Tetrarrhena juncea*, typically starting near the base of a leaf.

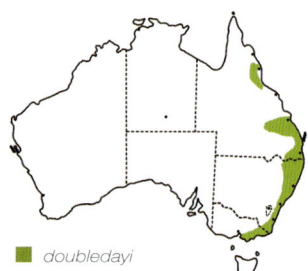
doubledayi

The **Lilac Grass Skipper**, *Toxidia doubledayi* (fw ♂ 14 mm, ♀ 15 mm), occurs in similar forest habitat, but reaches the tropics, where it is confined mainly to moist gullies in upland areas. Unlike *T. andersoni*, males do not hilltop, but establish territories in sunny patches of low foliage near the larval host grass, *Oplismenus* species. Eggs are normally laid singly in litter beneath the host.

The **White-brand Grass Skipper**, *Toxidia rietmanni* (fw ♂ 14 mm, ♀ 15 mm), has a similar distribution to *T. doubledayi* but prefers wetter habitats, being most often seen along rainforest margins, feeding on lantana. Its behaviour and life history are similar to those of *T. doubledayi*. Larval host plants include species of *Oplismenus*, *Ottochloa* and *Panicum*.

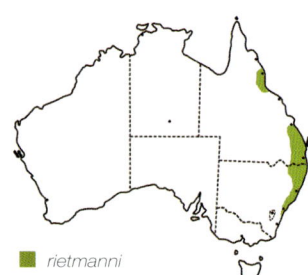
rietmanni

parvula

The **Small Grass Skipper**, *Toxidia parvula* (fw ♂ 12 mm, ♀ 14 mm), is widespread but local in open grassy forest. The adults fly very inconspicuously near the ground around a variety of grasses. Their brisk, slightly bobbing flutter is a relatively slower motion than seen in most related skippers. Their life history is poorly known.

FAMILY HESPERIIDAE—Skippers

Northern Grass Skippers 2 and Shield Skippers

peron

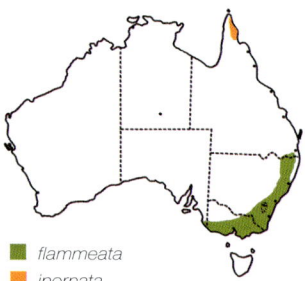
flammeata
inornata

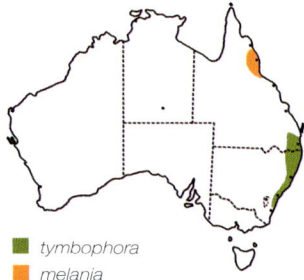
tymbophora
melania

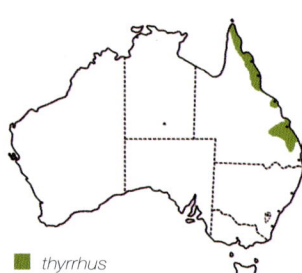
thyrrhus

These four *Toxidia* species are principally tropical and grass feeding, although *T. peron* is also found much further south and feeds on a range of monocotyledons. So far as is known, larvae construct shelters of grass blades or leaf litter and feed at night. Eggs are hemispherical and fluted.

The **Dingy Grass Skipper**, *Toxidia peron* (fw ♂ 17 mm, ♀ 17 mm), is very widespread in open forest types and rainforest edges east of the Great Dividing Range. Adults generally fly within 1–2 m of the ground in grassy places, but sometimes perch on shrubs or feed at flowers up to 3 m. Females are sometimes seen flying only centimetres above the ground, in a slowly progressive hover, as they search for places to oviposit. Males are swift in flight and often hilltop, perching in the typical dart position found most often in hesperiine skippers. Diverse food plants are used, including grasses plus *Gahnia*, *Dianella* and *Lomandra*.

The **Spotless Grass Skipper**, *Toxidia inornata* (fw ♂ 15 mm, ♀ 16 mm), is a seldom-encountered and visually undistinguished species from the rainforests of Cape York Peninsula. Adults fly low and rapidly among grass in exposed sunny edges, roadways and clearings. They perch often. The larval food plant is a grass.

The similar but larger **Dark Grass Skipper**, *Toxidia melania* (fw ♂ 18 mm, ♀ 19 mm), occurs mainly in rainforest at higher altitudes in the Queensland wet tropics region. Its habits are similar to those of *T. inornata* and, again, its food plants are grasses.

The **Dusky Grass Skipper**, *Toxidia thyrrhus* (fw ♂ 15 mm, ♀ 17 mm), is a very inconspicuous species found widely in eastern Queensland along creek beds and gullies in open eucalypt forest with grassy undergrowth. Adults fly rapidly and low in sunny places, settling frequently on grass stems or stones. Larvae feed on grasses.

The two species of shield skippers, so called because the males have a broad black patch in the middle of the forewing, have a south-eastern distribution. Their early stages are very like those of *Toxidia*, the larvae feeding nocturnally on sedges and grasses and returning before daybreak to a shelter constructed from leaf litter.

The **Bright Shield Skipper**, *Signeta flammeata* (fw ♂ 16 mm, ♀ 17.5 mm), is local but quite common in open forest and subalpine woodland along wetter parts of the Great Dividing Range. In the north it is found at higher altitudes up to 1600 m. Adults fly very rapidly within 1.5 m of the ground, usually perching within this range or a little higher. Low-growing flowers such as *Epacris*, *Leptospermum* or *Bursaria* are preferred nectar sources. At high altitudes, especially, they often perch on flowers with half-opened wings, basking as they feed. Males hilltop regularly, where they often perch high in the crowns of trees, up to 9 m above the ground. Eggs are laid singly on leaf litter near the host grasses, *Poa tenera* and *Tetrarrhena juncea*.

The **Dull Shield Skipper**, *Signeta tymbophora* (fw ♂ 15 mm, ♀ 16 mm), is rare and local, confined to patches of warm temperate rainforest, mainly at higher altitudes. Adults fly along forest margins or in sunny forest clearings, feeding from flowers such as lantana. They generally perch higher than related skippers, to exploit available patches of sunlight in their semi-shaded habitats.

FAMILY HESPERIIDAE—Skippers

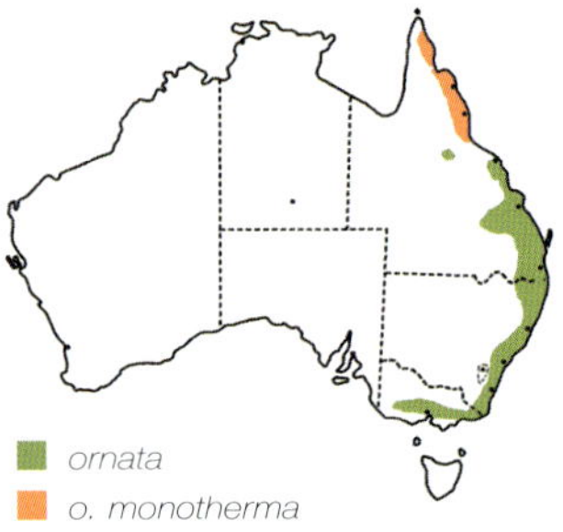

Ornate Sedge Skippers 1

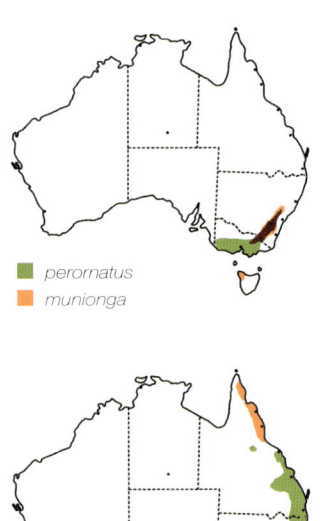

- perornatus
- munionga
- ornata
- o. monotherma

The three species featured here are distinguished by their ornate underside hindwing patterns. All feed as larvae on various species of sedges, constructing tubular silk-lined shelters near the base of the plant and emerging at night to feed.

The **Alpine Sedge Skipper**, *Oreisplanus munionga* (fw ♂ 15 mm, ♀ 18 mm), occurs in open woodland and alpine heath from 1000 to 1600 m on the mainland, and in swampy areas at sea level in Tasmania. Adults flutter low, with an almost moth-like motion, feeding from Everlasting Daisies and perching on the stems of their host. The ellipsoid egg (1.5 mm long x 1.1 mm wide) is laid singly on leaves of *Carex appressa*.

The **Mountain Sedge Skipper**, *Oreisplanus perornatus* (fw ♂ 16 mm, ♀ 20 mm), occurs in open eucalypt forest from coastal lowlands up to 1000 m, but is rare at higher altitudes. It favours boggy places, where its food plant, *Gahnia sieberiana*, grows. Adult behaviour is similar to that of *O. munionga*. The female lays relatively very large, smooth, hemispherical eggs (more than 2 mm in diameter) on the host plant leaves.

The **Spotted Sedge Skipper**, *Hesperilla ornata* (fw ♂ 17 mm, ♀ 19 mm), occurs in open eucalypt forest, heath, and along rainforest margins. Although superficially similar to *O. perornatus*, adults fly rapidly. Males visit hilltops, sometimes perching high. The female lays a large, strongly ribbed hemispherical egg on leaves of the low-growing host plants, principally *Gahnia* and, in the south, *Carex*.

The **Northern Spotted Sedge Skipper**, *H. ornata monotherma* (fw ♂ 16 mm, ♀ 18 mm), is a very distinct race and may well be a separate species.

O. munionga ♂

O. perornatus ♂

larva in shelter

O. munionga

pupa in shelter

H. ornata

H. o. ornata ♂

H. o. ornata ♀

pupa in shelter

H. o. ornata ♂

H. o. monotherma ♂

O. munionga ♂

The Butterflies of Australia

Ornate Sedge Skippers 2

Apart from *Hesperilla ornata*, three other members of the large genus *Hesperilla* have distinctive, bright underside markings. All lay strongly ribbed, hemispherical eggs on leaves of their *Gahnia* host plants. Each is specialised to one or two species of host plants, which partly explains their general rarity. Larvae construct shelters at the base of the host, feeding at night.

The **Chequered Sedge Skipper**, *Hesperilla mastersi* (fw ♂ 19 mm, ♀ 22 mm), is a rare species found locally at the margins of warm temperate rainforest. Adults fly around the host plant; males also hilltop, perching high on available vegetation. Males, especially, fly very swiftly. The larval host plant is generally *Gahnia melanocarpa*.

The **Painted Sedge Skipper**, *Hesperilla picta* (fw ♂ 17 mm, ♀ 19 mm), is found principally in sheltered gullies in moist coastal woodland and open forest. Adults fly rapidly, generally in the vicinity of patches of their host plant, *Gahnia clarkei*. They perch on nearby foliage in sunlight up to 2 or 3 m, and feed at flowers, such as lantana.

The **Silver Sedge Skipper**, *Hesperilla crypsargyra* (fw ♂ 14–15 mm, ♀ 15–17 mm), is closely related to *H. picta* and is rather like a smaller version of it. Two similar races are recognised. The larger northern one is widespread in open forest above 600 m and subalpine areas to 1500 m. Its larvae feed on *Gahnia sieberiana*. The smaller southern race occurs very locally in open, generally moist forest from 60 to 1000 m in several disjunct populations from Sydney to western Victoria. Its larvae feed on *G. microstachya*. Adults of both races fly close to the ground and visit mainly low-growing flowers.

mastersi

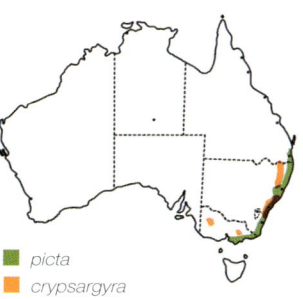
picta
crypsargyra

FAMILY HESPERIIDAE—Skippers

Southern Sedge Skippers

idothea

donnysa

flavescens

chrysotricha

The sedge skippers illustrated here all have a southern distribution, and are relatively large and brightly coloured on the upperside. Except for *Hesperilla flavescens*, they feed on a variety of *Gahnia* species and are local but generally not rare, the first two species being found in diverse habitats. The eggs in this group vary markedly in size and shape, and are laid singly on leaves of the host plant. The larvae all feed nocturnally, resting by day in shelters woven from leaves of the host near its base.

The striking **Flame Sedge Skipper**, *Hesperilla idothea* (fw ♂ 20 mm, ♀ 21 mm), occurs in open moist eucalypt forest and woodland from sea level to 1000 m. Favoured sites are sheltered slopes and gullies where, in places, it may be quite common. Adults fly swiftly. Females are mostly found near patches of host plant but males frequent hilltops, sometimes perching high in the crowns of trees. The egg is small and only slightly ovoid seen from above. *Gahnia sieberiana* and *G. radula* are the commonest host plants, but at least seven other species are recorded.

The **Varied Sedge Skipper**, *Hesperilla donnysa* (fw ♂ 17–19 mm, ♀ 20–22 mm), has several races, one in the south-east mainland, two in Western Australia and one in Tasmania. The latter is considerably larger than other forms. The species frequents a wide range of open habitats wherever its host plants grow—from coastal heath and swamp to subalpine woodland at 1500 m. Throughout its range at least fifteen species of *Gahnia* are utilised. Adults fly rapidly and near the ground. Males do not hilltop but defend territories near patches of *Gahnia*, perching on low vegetation as they keep watch. The egg is rather flattened and distinctly more ovoid in shape than that of *H. idothea*.

The **Yellow Sedge Skipper**, *Hesperilla flavescens* (fw ♂ 17 mm, ♀ 20 mm), is rare and very localised in coastal swamps between Melbourne and Adelaide. Adults fly close to the ground in the vicinity of the host plant, *Gahnia filum* (rarely *G. deusta*). Males perch on the host plant or nearby low vegetation, defending territories. The life history is very like that of *H. donnysa*.

The **Golden-haired Sedge Skipper**, *Hesperilla chrysotricha* (fw ♂ 18 mm, ♀ 20 mm), has a disjunct distribution, with eastern and western races. The differences are slight. It occurs in open swampy areas around brackish coastal estuaries and, to a lesser extent, in subcoastal open eucalypt woodland and tall *Banksia* heaths. It is very local, but common where it occurs. Adults fly low and rapidly around patches of host plant, perching up to 2 m above the ground on nearby vegetation. Males defend territories at these sites. The egg is large, flattened, and a remarkably elongate ovoid shape. The usual host plants in the east are *Gahnia trifida* and *G. filum* and, in the west, *G. decomposita* and *G. deusta*, but several other *Gahnia* species are also used.

FAMILY HESPERIIDAE—Skippers

Northern Sedge Skippers

malindeva

sarnia

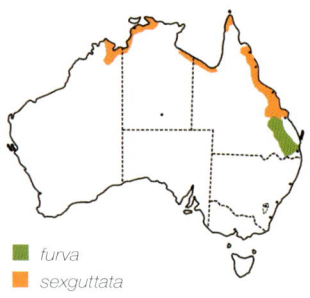
furva
sexguttata

crypsigramma

Five species of sedge skippers are virtually confined to Queensland and the Northern Territory. All are drab, with few distinguishing characteristics. All are swift in flight and occur very locally. *Hesperilla malindeva* and *H. sarnia* are distinctly larger than the other three species. The larvae feed on various types of sedges, including species of *Cyperus*, *Gahnia* and *Scleria*. As far as is known, all make tubular silk-lined shelters by sewing together adjacent leaves near the base of the plant, and feed nocturnally. Pupation occurs within the shelter. The eggs are generally hemispherical or slightly ovoid, and of medium size.

The **Two-spotted Sedge Skipper**, *Hesperilla malindeva* (fw ♂ 17 mm, ♀ 19 mm), is distinguished by two black spots, lying close together near the centre of the hindwing. No other Australian skipper is so marked. It occurs mainly in drier woodland and vine forest, especially in rocky gullies where its host plant, *Gahnia aspera*, grows. Adults are found near the host plant, flying low and feeding from flowers. Males visit hilltops.

The **Swift Sedge Skipper**, *Hesperilla sarnia* (fw ♂ 17 mm, ♀ 18 mm), is known from a few areas of open woodland on poor soils, extending well inland. It is generally a rare species. Males are usually encountered on hilltops. The larval host plants are sedges of the genus *Scleria*.

The **Riverine Sedge Skipper**, *Hesperilla sexguttata* (fw ♂ 14 mm, ♀ 16 mm), has a scattered distribution across the tropical north. It occurs in open eucalypt forest, especially along creek beds and swampy places where its host plants occur. Occasionally it occurs together with the very similar *H. furva* in Brigalow woodland. Adults fly near the food plant, perching low. Males do not hilltop. Its main host plant is *Cyperus javanicus*.

The **Grey Sedge Skipper**, *Hesperilla furva* (fw ♂ 16 mm, ♀ 16 mm), occurs in dry open eucalypt forest and brigalow, typically around sandstone or granite outcrops. It is best separated from *H. sexguttata* by the more rounded outline of the wings and greyer underside. Adults fly low around the host plant, *Scleria sphacelata*, feeding at low-growing flowers. Males visit hilltops in the afternoon.

The **Wide-brand Sedge Skipper**, *Hesperilla crypsigramma* (fw ♂ 14 mm, ♀ 14 mm), occurs over a wide range of open forest habitats and also in monsoon forest and at rainforest margins. Males are distinguished from the previous two species by their broad sex brand, females by the arrangement of their forewing spots, which lie in a distinctly curved line. Adults generally occur in rocky gullies near their host plants, *Scleria sphacelata* and *S. mackaviensis*. Males hilltop in the afternoon, perching on or near the ground.

FAMILY HESPERIIDAE—Skippers

Southern Brown Skippers

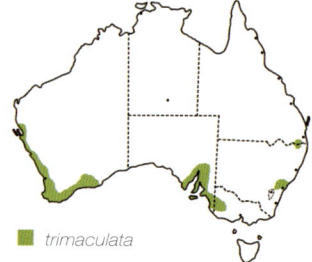
trimaculata

dirphia

There are just two species of the genus *Motasingha*, both confined to southern or western Australia. They are relatively large species, with strongly pointed wings, somewhat reminiscent of some *Hesperilla* and *Toxidia* species but, with their silver hindwing spotting, more like *Trapezites* beneath. Both species are very local and uncommon. The life history of *M. dirphia* is unknown.

The **Large Brown Skipper**, *Motasingha trimaculata* (fw ♂ 20 mm, ♀ 22 mm), has a scattered, disjunct distribution, ranging from the Queensland–New South Wales border to Western Australia. Three geographical races showing slight differences are recognised. Because it is so widespread it occurs in a wide variety of habitats, including open eucalypt forest, coastal heath and mallee. The adults are very swift-flying, and females, especially, are generally found near the host plants, feeding from flowers up to 2–3 m above the ground. Males regularly hilltop along sand ridges and other prominences. They are aggressive, attacking other males and, indeed, other insects entering their territory. The female lays her very large yellow eggs singly on leaves of the host plant—sedges of the genus *Lepidosperma* and the grassy herb *Phlebocarya ciliata*. The larvae construct tubular shelters lined with silk and feed nocturnally.

The **Western Brown Skipper**, *Motasingha dirphia* (fw ♂ 20 mm, ♀ 22 mm), is restricted to Western Australia, where it occurs in eucalypt forest, tall *Banksia* heathland and coastal heath. It overlaps with *M. trimaculata occidentalis*, from which the males may be distinguished by their broad forewing sex brand and both sexes by the pinkish cast to the underside ground colour—more a reddish earthy colour in *M. trimaculata occidentalis*. Males hilltop, but little else is known of the insect's biology.

trimaculata ♂ coastal heath, southern NSW

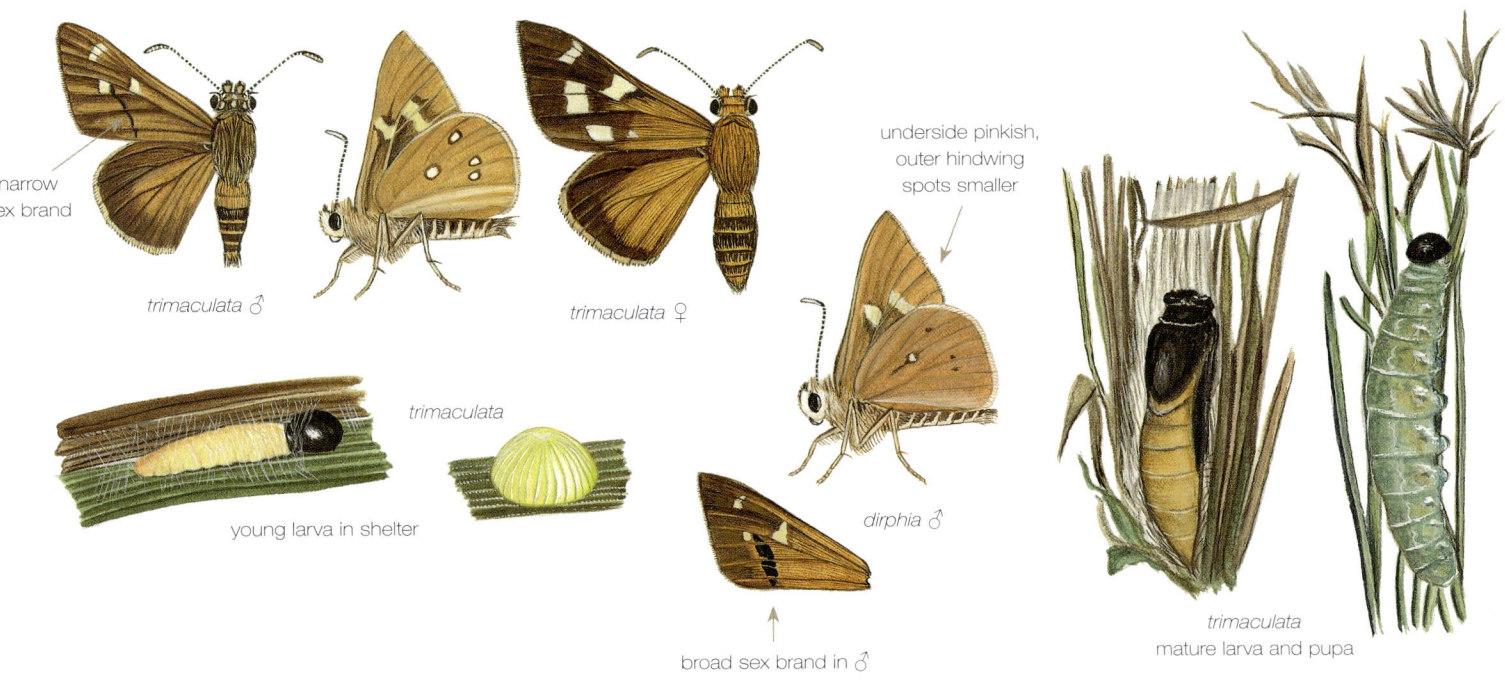

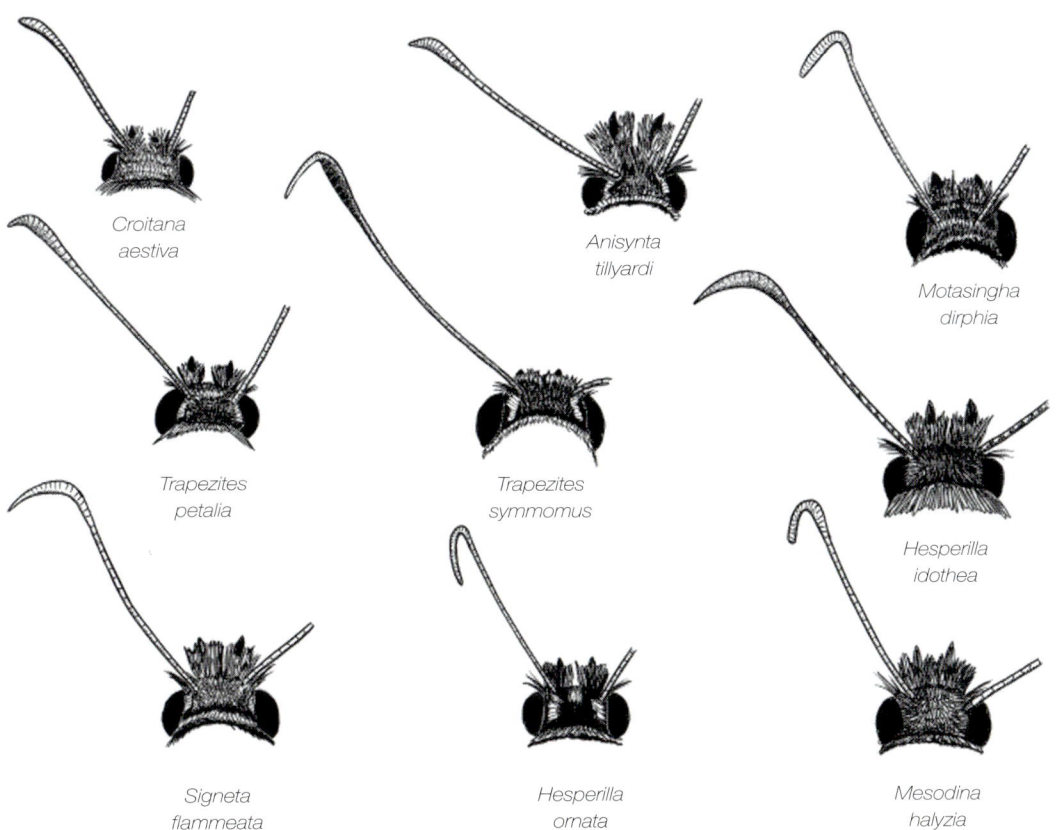

Figure 5.1: Variation in the form of the antennal club among different genera and species of ochres (Hesperiidae: Trapezitinae).

FAMILY HESPERIIDAE—Skippers

Sand Skippers 1

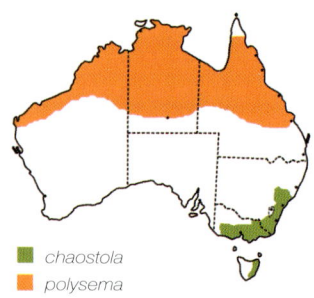

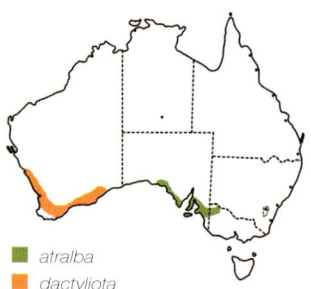

The term sand skipper is applied to a variety of species, many with inland distributions. All fly close to the ground, generally in the vicinity of the larval host plant. Larvae construct shelters near the base of the host plant and feed nocturnally.

The **Spinifex Sand Skipper**, *Proeidosa polysema* (fw ♂ 17–19 mm, ♀ 18–20 mm), has a scattered distribution across the northern part of Australia, occurring in dry open eucalypt woodland and open arid areas where its larval host plants grow. These include several species of hummock grasses of the genus *Triodia* (also incorrectly known as 'spinifex'). Adults of this round-winged species are brisk but not overly rapid in flight. Males regularly visit hilltops and dune ridges near stands of the host plant, where they perch on the ground or on low prominences. In south-central Queensland a form occurs in which the underside spots are unusually small.

Members of the genus *Antipodia* have a southern or western distribution and, as larvae, feed on sedges of the genus *Gahnia*.

The **Diamond Sand Skipper**, *Antipodia atralba* (fw ♂ 16 mm, ♀ 19 mm), occurs only in semi-arid heath and mallee in western Victoria and South Australia. It is rare and local, and most often encountered near its host, generally *Gahnia lanigera*, especially following fires. The large, ovoid egg is laid singly on leaves of the host. Males perch on the food plant to bask and maintain mating territories.

The **Western Sand Skipper**, *Antipodia dactyliota* (fw ♂ 18 mm, ♀ 18 mm), is not uncommon but is very locally distributed in Western Australia in a variety of dry habitats on sandy soils or laterite ridges, including open woodland and coastal heath. Habits are very like those of *A. atralba*, and it has at times been regarded as a race of that species. Identification is best determined from locality. The egg of *A. dactyliota* is also ovoid, but is somewhat smaller than that of *A. atralba*. The larvae feed principally on *Gahnia lanigera*, with *G. australis* and *G. ancistrophylla* occasionally utilised.

The **Heath Sand Skipper**, *Antipodia chaostola* (fw ♂ 18 mm, ♀ 19 mm), occurs in scattered populations over a range of habitats in the south-east and Tasmania. Three rather similar geographical races are recognised. It is everywhere rare, but most often encountered in open eucalypt forest and *Acacia* or *Banksia* woodland in the coastal lowlands. Less often it is found in mountain heath. In the Blue Mountains it ranges from 400 to 1000 m around sandstone escarpments. Adults are very sedentary, remaining around the host plant. The egg is large and ovoid, of similar shape and size to that of *Hesperilla chrysotricha*. It is laid singly on leaves of the host. Usual host plants are *Gahnia filifolia* and *G. radula*, with occasional hosts *G. sieberiana*, *G. microstachya* and *G. grandis*.

FAMILY HESPERIIDAE—Skippers

Sand Skippers 2

- albovenata
- aestiva
- croites
- arenaria

Four species of sand skippers inhabit arid and semi-arid areas from central to southern Australia. Their larvae feed mainly on hard spear grasses (*Austrostipa* spp.) and windmill grasses (*Enteropogon* spp.), constructing a cylindrical or tent-like structure, and feeding nocturnally. The shelters of *Herimosa* larvae open near the top, and the larva rests head upwards, with pupation also in this position. In *Croitana* the opening is at the base of the shelter and both larva and pupa rest head downwards. The egg of *Herimosa* is large and ovoid, with ribbing so fine it appears smooth. *Croitana* eggs are hemispherical and strongly fluted. Adults of most species appear in the spring, from September to November.

The **White-veined Sand Skipper**, *Herimosa albovenata* (fw ♂ 15–17 mm, ♀ 16–18 mm), occurs locally, sometimes commonly, in scattered populations across southern mainland Australia. Three geographical races are recognised, but differences are slight and nothing could be confused with this handsome skipper. It generally occurs in semi-arid open and woodland habitats with a ground cover of tussock grasses, especially around rocky outcrops and sand dunes. Adults are sedentary, remaining near their host plants, *Austrostipa scabra*, *A. eremophila* and *A. semibarbata*. They fly moderately fast, close to the ground, with a direct moth-like trajectory, perching frequently on the ground or in leaf litter.

The **Yellow Sand Skipper**, *Croitana croites* (fw ♂ 14 mm, ♀ 15 mm), occurs in Western Australia on sand dunes supporting clumps of its spear grass host plants, both on the coast and inland in open eucalypt and *Acacia* woodland. Adults fly low and rapidly, settling often on the ground or on flowers. They remain near clumps of their host plants, *Austrostipa elegantissima*, *A. platychaeta* and *A. flavescens*.

The **Inland Sand Skipper**, *Croitana arenaria* (fw ♂ 12.5 mm, ♀ 13 mm), is represented by two geographic races. *C. arenaria arenaria* occurs in open grassland in central Australia and *C. arenaria pilepudla* is found in mallee on the Eyre Peninsula in South Australia. The two races probably differ sufficiently to be regarded as separate species. In both, the wings of the female are long and narrow. Adults fly low and remain in the vicinity of their host plants—*Enteropogon acicularis* and *E. ramosus* in central Australia, *Austrostipa elegantissima* and *A. platychaeta* on the Eyre Peninsula. Males often perch on the ground or low prominences, defending small territories.

The **Desert Sand Skipper**, *Croitana aestiva* (fw ♂ 14 mm, ♀ 15 mm), is known from only a few specimens from locations in Mulga woodland west of Alice Springs. Both sexes, but particularly the females, have exceptionally long, narrow wings. Specimens have been recorded in February and April, suggesting that it may emerge mainly during good wet seasons. However, nothing more is known of its life history or behaviour.

FAMILY HESPERIIDAE—Skippers

Iris Skippers

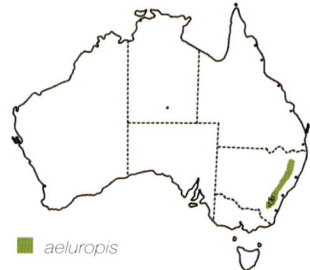

aeluropis

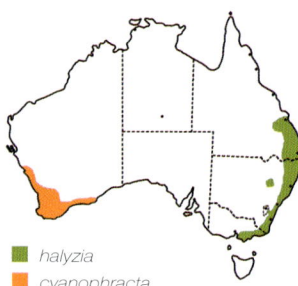

halyzia
cyanophracta

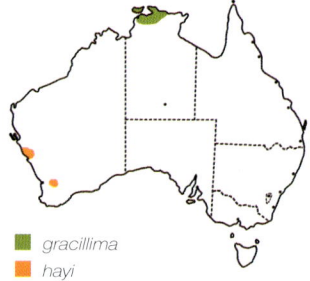

gracillima
hayi

Five species of iris skippers occur around mainland Australia, overlapping only a little in their distributions. All feed as larvae on species of wild iris (*Patersonia* spp.) and it is owing to this delightful food plant that they possess a special charm, since as adults they are all rather drab in appearance. The life histories of all species are similar, with differences noted below. Eggs are laid singly on leaves of the host plant. They are dull green, acquiring red bands as they mature. The young larvae emerge with a serpentine motion common to all skippers, then turn to eat their eggshells. The mature larvae are also generally green, with the surface of the head capsules coarsely roughened. Larvae construct shelters by sewing together 2–5 leaves of the host plant, near its base, within which they rest head downwards. Pupation occurs within the shelter, also head downwards. All species leave a distinctive series of triangular feeding excisions along the leaf edges, giving it a serrated appearance. Usually only one larva will be found per plant. In warmer habitats, nocturnal feeding is usual, but in cooler habitats larvae feed during the day. Adults fly rapidly, near the ground, almost always where *Patersonia* grows. They perch often and feed at flowers of low shrubs. Females have more rounded wings and broader forewing markings than males, and a slower, heavier flight.

The **Mountain Iris Skipper**, *Mesodina aeluropis* (fw ♂ 19 mm, ♀ 20 mm), occurs in subalpine woodland and heath from 800 to 1300 m. It is common but very local. The host plant is an alpine form of *Patersonia sericea*. Larvae feed in the afternoon and at dusk.

The **Eastern Iris Skipper**, *Mesodina halyzia* (fw ♂ 18 mm, ♀ 18 mm), is the most frequently encountered species. In the east, it is common and widespread in wetter areas of eucalypt forest and coastal heath, seldom occurring above 800 m. Larval food plants include *Patersonia fragilis*, *P. glabrata*, *P. sericea* and *P. occidentalis*. Larvae feed generally at dawn and dusk, but sometimes during the day in winter.

The **Blue Iris Skipper**, *Mesodina cyanophracta* (fw ♂ 16 mm, ♀ 17 mm), occurs commonly but very locally in jarrah forest and *Banksia* woodland in Western Australia. The larva is greyish brown rather than green, and feeds diurnally on *Patersonia occidentalis*. Adults are very active. Females often appear and lay their eggs on young plants in areas regenerating after fire.

The **Northern Iris Skipper**, *Mesodina gracillima* (fw ♂ 19 mm, ♀ 19 mm), occurs commonly but locally in eucalypt forest growing on sandy slopes near Darwin. The larval host plant is *Patersonia macrantha*. The larva feeds at night.

The **Small Iris Skipper**, *Mesodina hayi* (fw ♂ 16 mm, ♀ 17 mm), is rare and confined to two small patches of open *Allocasuarina* woodland with a heathy understorey. It overlaps with *M. cyanophracta*, but the male is easily distinguished by its smaller size and narrower wings. Females are difficult to separate. Larvae feed during the late afternoon on *Patersonia drummondii*.

FAMILY HESPERIIDAE—Skippers   103

SUBFAMILY HESPERIINAE—
Darters, Swifts and Their Allies

The subfamily **Hesperiinae** includes tiny to small, stout-bodied species, occurring mainly in the tropics and subtropics. Thirty-six species are recorded from Australia and more than 2000 worldwide. Many Australian species and most genera are widely distributed in tropical Asia. The definitive differences between the subfamilies Hesperiinae and Trapezitinae rest on details of the arrangement of the wing veins that are difficult to see, even in a mounted specimen. However, several general characteristics provide a good guide to recognising members of the subfamily. When perched, hesperiines commonly adopt the 'dart' position, with hindwings depressed and forewings erect or semi-erect, whereas trapezitines do so only rarely. In hesperiines, particularly the numerous black and orange forms, the wing pattern generally consists of continuous bands of colour, whereas in trapezitines the pattern is more broken. The underside pattern of hesperiines is generally subdued, whereas in trapezitines it may be bold and well defined. In many hesperiines the tornal lobe (see Figure 5.2) on the posterior angle of the hindwing is pronounced, especially in larger species and in males, whereas in trapezitines it is scarcely ever developed. As a rule, the more pronounced the tornal lobe, the more rapid is the flight of the butterfly. Finally, with the possible exception of the rarely seen Desert Sand Skippers, the only truly tiny skippers (forewing less than 12 mm) are all hesperiines. Many of these are very widespread and common.

The Hesperiinae can be divided into three natural groups: the *Notocrypta* group, with a single distinctive species found in north Queensland rainforests; the *Taractrocera* group, with nine genera and 29 species, including all the strongly black and orange patterned species; and the *Pelopidas* group, with three genera and six species, all greenish or yellowish brown with a pattern of small white or yellowish dots, and with the tornal lobe generally pronounced in both sexes.

The *Taractrocera* group presents major problems of identification, even at genus level. Most difficult are the 25 species in which the pattern is bold orange on dark brown or black, with an orange band along the leading margin of the forewing. Within this group a good general guide to genus is the forewing length:

- 10–14 mm = grass darts (twelve species, three genera: *Taractrocera*, *Ocybadistes*, *Suniana*)
- 13–19 mm = darters (eleven species, two genera: *Telicota* and *Arrhenes*)
- 19–24 mm = palm darts (two species of *Cephrenes*).

The tiny grass darts, *Taractrocera* and *Ocybadistes/Suniana*, may be separated from each other by the form of the antennal club, which is spoon-like and rounded in the former, and elongate and cylindrical with an acute tip in the latter. In the larger

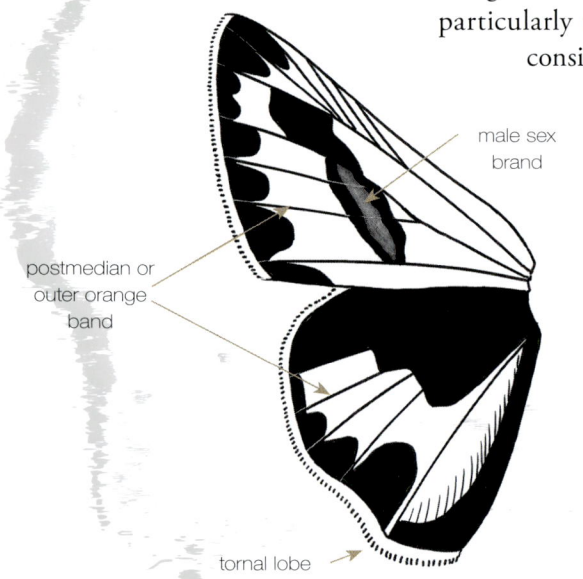

Figure 5.2: Features of the wings of a typical hesperiine.

Telicota and *Arrhenes*, the antennal club has a long, thin, apical process. As most skippers perch frequently, with experience it is possible to discern these features in the living butterfly without capture, especially with the aid of good digital macro-photography.

To identify any of these butterflies to species, however, it is generally necessary to capture a specimen, in which case various subtle but externally visible characters are useful. Males of most grass dart species can be recognised by the form of the dark sex brand on the forewing. This line or patch of slightly raised, matt black scales can be seen against the very dark-brown ground colour of the wings when viewed under strong light with a x10 hand lens or dissecting microscope. However, in worn specimens it may be quite obscure. A more visible, paler brand occurs in male darters *Telicota* and *Arrhenes* (absent from *Cephrenes*), but, although more visible, it is less variable than in grass darts, hence less useful for identification. Other clues to species identity in all genera are provided by variation in size, wing shape and wing pattern, particularly the form of the outer orange postmedian band in the forewing on both upper and undersides. In several cases, absolutely sure identification requires dissection of the genitalia, especially for females.

Early stages in the subfamily show little variation. The eggs are relatively large and hemispherical with a smooth or minutely pitted surface. They are laid singly on the leaves of the larval food plant. Newly laid eggs are white or pale yellow, often developing red markings as they mature. Larvae are elongate and smooth, generally white or pale green and sometimes marked with faint longitudinal stripes. The head capsule is also often distinctively marked. In older male larvae it is usually possible to see the embryonic testes through the transparent skin, lying as a pair of yellowish oval spots on either side of the dorsal midline, about the sixth abdominal segment. Larvae feed on monocotyledons, chiefly grasses and palms. The pupae, which are found within the larval shelters, are green or brownish, and often covered by a white waxy secretion. In some genera the pupa is elongate with a single pointed anterior process. In all hesperiine pupae the proboscis is very long, often separating from the body of the pupa towards its tip.

Hesperiines occur in a variety of habitats, from open grassland to tropical rainforest. Some species are very common and almost ubiquitous in wetter open areas of the tropics and subtropics. The adults perch in open sunlight or in sunny patches in forest. Males often engage in high-speed chases with wings audibly whirring. Ovipositing females typically fly low over grassland with a characteristic skipping motion. Hesperiine adults all possess a long proboscis (also evident in the pupae), allowing them to feed on flowers with a long corolla tube such as *Ixora* and *Pentas*. As far as we know, all species are palatable to vertebrate predators, and speed seems to be their main means of defence.

Orange Grass Dart (*Suniana sunias*)

The Banded Demon and Tropical Rainforest Swifts

waigensis

fuliginosa
atropatene

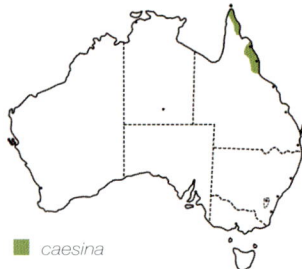

caesina

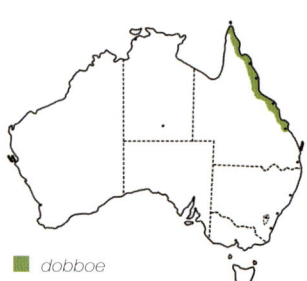

dobboe

The **Banded Demon**, *Notocrypta waigensis* (fw ♂ 19 mm, ♀ 21 mm), is a relatively large, highly conspicuous species of the tropics. Its appearance is unmistakable. It is most common in rainforests, where it occurs along the margins and also in small gaps in the understorey penetrated by sunlight. It is frequently seen perching low on the leaves of shrubs in the typical 'dart' position. The flight of territorial males is very rapid but they seldom fly far from their perch. Territorial disputes for perches between males are brief and confined. Both sexes are often seen feeding from flowers, such as *Stachytarpheta*. The proboscis is very long, enabling them to access flowers with an extended corolla tube, and they will feed in the canopy when suitable flowers are in bloom. The larvae feed on the native gingers (Zingiberaceae) *Alpinia caerulea* and *Hornstedtia scottiana*—the only Australian butterflies known to feed on this plant family. Larvae are a uniform green with a dark head, and the pupae are elongate with a short down-curved anterior horn and a very long proboscis, separated from the body of the pupa towards its tip and even extending beyond the posterior end of the body of the pupa.

The four species of rainforest swifts all belong to the *Taractrocera* group of species, which also includes all the typical black and orange hesperiines.

The **Purple Swift**, *Mimene atropatene* (fw ♂ 19 mm, ♀ 22 mm), is a little-known rainforest species from Iron Range in far north Queensland. Adults have been observed feeding on flowers of *Micromelum minutum*. The life history is unknown, but in New Guinea, where 22 species of the genus occur, larval food plants are typically climbing palms, such as *Calamus* species. Members of this genus are extremely rapid in flight.

The three species of the genus *Sabera* are all moderately small and common species occurring at tropical rainforest margins, in small clearings, and often in small sunny spots in the forest understorey.

The **Black and White Swift**, *Sabera caesina* (fw ♂ 16 mm, ♀ 16 mm), is unmistakable. The antennal club is white. Adults perch frequently either in the typical 'dart' position or with wings closed. They fly very rapidly, generally 1–3 m above the ground. Larvae feed on palms, including *Archontophoenix alexandrae*, *Calamus caryotoides* and *Normanbya normanbyi*.

The **Orange Swift**, *Sabera dobboe* (fw ♂ 17 mm, ♀ 18 mm), has similar habits to *S. caesina* but is more likely to be seen at rainforest margins than inside the forest. It is common in gardens in many towns in the north Queensland wet tropics region and often feeds at flowers. It is easily separated from other orange skippers, particularly *Telicota* species, which are about the same size, by the lack of any orange area behind the leading edge of the forewing, and by its dark underside with a distinctive yellow streak on the forewing. The larvae feed on members of the Agavaceae, including the palm lilies *Cordyline cannifolia*, *C. fruticosa*, *C. stricta* and the introduced *C. australis*.

The **White-fringed Swift**, *Sabera fuliginosa* (fw ♂ 17 mm, ♀ 18 mm), is the least common and most restricted of the three *Sabera* species. It occurs mainly in sunny patches of the rainforest understorey where it perches on leaves 1–4 m above the ground and visits flowers at rainforest margins. It is totally unmarked on its upperside except for the sex brand in the male, but is nevertheless an easily recognised species, partly because of the broad white fringe of scales along the hindwing border and partly because of its 'jizz', including its size and very rapid flight, and its preference for habitats where no remotely similar species occur. The larvae are a distinctive blue-grey in colour.

FAMILY HESPERIIDAE—Skippers

Grass Darts 1

anisomorpha

ina

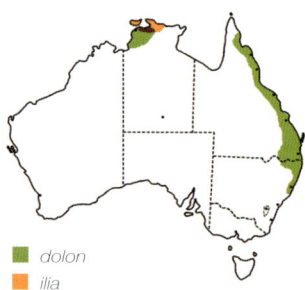
dolon
ilia

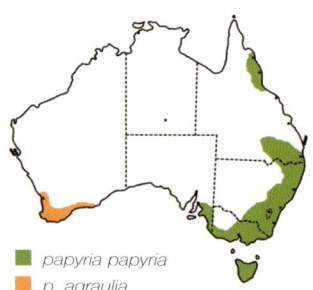
papyria papyria
p. agraulia

The five species of the genus *Taractrocera*, or spoon-clubbed grass darts, are tiny. They are distinguished by the slightly concave, spoon-like club on the antenna. At the tip is a minute hook, the apiculus, developed to varying degrees in different species. The antennae are slightly shorter relative to body size than in other grass dart genera. All species fly low in grassy areas. The males stake out tiny territories in sunny places, and perch for long periods on blades of grass or other low perches. Some species have highly specific, localised habitat preferences, whereas others are more widespread in open grassy areas in the wetter, warmer parts of Australia. However, no member of the genus is outstandingly common. Larvae feed mostly on grasses and occasionally on sedges. Known early stages are similar in all species, as illustrated for *T. anisomorpha*. The pupae is stout and rounded anteriorly.

The **Large Yellow Grass Dart**, *Taractrocera anisomorpha* (fw ♂ 12 mm, ♀ 14 mm), and the **No-brand Grass Dart**, *T. ina* (fw ♂ 12 mm, ♀ 14 mm), both occur in open woodland and grassland in northern Australia from the subtropical coast to the semi-arid interior. They differ from other *Taractrocera* by their slightly larger size and the pale yellowish underside of the hindwing. The males of these two species are most easily separated by the presence or absence of a sex brand. In both sexes the outer orange band on the forewing is more distinctly stepped in *T. ina*. The wings are more rounded in *T. ina* than in *T. anisomorpha*, especially in females. Recorded food plants for *T. anisomorpha* include *Eulalia aurea*, *Setaria paspalidioides* and introduced *Sorghum*. Native food plants of *T. ina* are not known but many introduced grasses are utilised, including *Cymbopogon*, *Oryza* (rice), *Panicum*, *Paspalum*, *Sorghum* and *Urochloa*.

The **Small Dingy Grass Dart**, *Taractrocera dolon* (fw ♂ 10 mm, ♀ 12 mm), **Northern Grass Dart**, *T. ilia* (fw ♂ 10 mm, ♀ 11 mm), **White-banded Grass Dart**, *T. papyria papyria* (fw ♂ 10 mm, ♀ 11 mm), and **Western Grass Dart**, *T. papyria agraulia* (fw ♂ 10 mm, ♀ 11 mm), are all distinctly smaller. *T. dolon* is fairly common but local in open forest near the coast. It is often found along watercourses. In both sexes the outer orange band on the hindwing generally has an extra spot anteriorly, lacking in other species except the otherwise distinctive *T. papyria*. The underside of the hindwing has broad, rather faint, markings. A distinct race, *T. d. diomedes*, occurring near Darwin, is slightly larger and brighter, but males are easily separated from *T. ina* by their sex brand, and both sexes by their hindwing markings. *T. ilia* is found only around rocky outcrops near Darwin. The upperside marking is the brightest of the genus and the underside markings are very well defined with uneven margins. The male sex brand is straight and narrow, not jagged as in *T. anisomorpha*. *T. papyria* is the most distinctive member of the genus. The eastern race, *T. papyria*, is very widespread, although rather local, in eastern Australia. It is also the only member of the genus that regularly occurs south of northern New South Wales and can be recognised by its tiny size and distinct white band on the underside of the hindwing of both sexes. This band is lacking in the southern Western Australian race *agraulia*, but as this is the only grass dart found in that region, identification is easy. The larvae of *T. dolon* have been recorded only from introduced *Sorghum*. Larval hosts of *T. ilia* are unrecorded. *T. papyria* has been recorded on a wide range of native grasses, including the genera *Austrodanthonia*, *Austrostipa*, *Cynodon*, *Echinopogon*, *Imperata*, *Microlaena*, *Phragmites* and *Poa*, introduced grasses, including *Ehrharta*, *Oryza*, *Paspalum* and *Pennisetum*, and the native sedge *Carex*.

SCHEMATIC MALE FOREWING SEX BRANDS INDICATED ON UNNATURALLY BLANCHED WINGS

Grass Darts 2

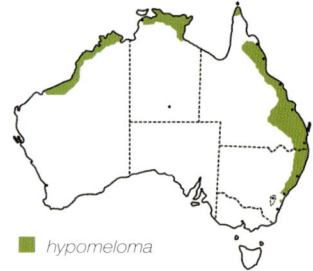
■ *hypomeloma*

■ *flavovittatus*

■ *walkeri*

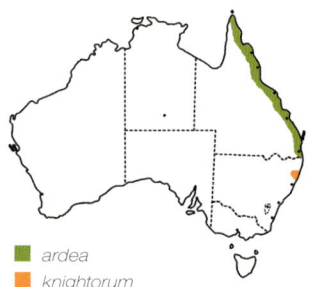
■ *ardea*
■ *knightorum*

The five species of the genus *Ocybadistes* are all tiny. They are distinguished from *Taractrocera* by the long, thickened antennal club, which has an acute tip, sometimes slightly extended to form a thin process. The antennae are relatively slightly longer than in *Taractrocera*. *Ocybadistes* species are very common and widespread in open habitats in northern and eastern Australia, with just one species, *O. knightorum*, restricted geographically. It is common to see males contesting a low perch, often just centimetres above the ground. The combative pair may fly directly above the perch in a tight whirring circle, or, in longer contests, they hover one above the other, sometimes gently ascending in tandem for a metre or two while keeping a fairly constant distance of 10–20 cm. Larvae feed mostly on grasses. Known early stages are similar. The nearly hemispherical egg is white when laid, developing a red ring and crown as it matures. The larvae are light green with black or variously patterned heads. The robust pupa is pale green or brownish with the anterior end rounded.

The **White-margined Grass Dart**, *Ocybadistes hypomeloma* (fw ♂ 12 mm, ♀ 13 mm), is slightly larger than other species. In both sexes a diagnostic feature is the thin white margin along the inner edge of the underside of the hindwing (often hard to discern in even slightly worn specimens). Other useful characters include the shape of the male sex brand, the slightly larger size, and the moderately well-developed tornal lobe in the hindwing of both sexes. *O. hypomeloma* is more active and swifter in flight than other grass darts. It is widespread in many open habitats, but local and seldom common. The larvae feed on *Themeda triandra* and *Microlaena stipoides*.

The most common, widespread and easily confused species are the **Common Grass Dart**, *Ocybadistes flavovittatus* (fw ♂ 10 mm, ♀ 11 mm), and **Walker's Grass Dart**, *O. walkeri* (fw ♂ 11 mm, ♀ 12 mm). Males are best separated by the form of the sex brand. Even if the brand itself cannot be seen in *O. flavovittatus*, at its posterior end its boundaries are clearly delimited by surrounding orange areas. In *O. walkeri* females the outer orange band on the forewing is more stepped, especially on the underside and, on the hindwing of *O. walkeri*, there is an additional anterior spot just connected to the inner margin of the outer orange band, lacking or almost lacking in *O. flavovittatus*. Both species occur in disturbed grassy habitats, including urban gardens. The life history of *O. flavovittatus* is poorly known, with its food plants simply recorded as 'grasses'. *O. walkeri* is recorded breeding on the native grasses *Cynodon dactylon*, *Imperata cylindrica*, *Thuarea involuta* and numerous genera of introduced grasses.

Knight's Grass Dart, *Ocybadistes knightorum* (fw ♂ 10 mm, ♀ 10 mm), is much darker than other species and unmistakable. It is highly restricted in its distribution, being found only in a small area near Coffs Harbour in grassy patches among *Casuarina* stands just behind the mangroves. It apparently feeds on just one species of grass, *Alexfloydia repens*, itself regarded as endangered. Within this tiny patch of habitat the butterfly is common, but it remained undiscovered until the early 1990s.

Males of the **Dark-orange Grass Dart**, *Ocybadistes ardea* (fw ♂ 10 mm, ♀ 10 mm), may be recognised by the unusual male sex brands, and distinctive forewing upperside marking. On the underside of the hindwing, the outer orange band is broad and clearly outlined by dark markings, unlike in *O. flavovittatus* and *O. walkeri*. The female might be confused with *O. flavovittatus*, but the orange markings are generally broader and more intense. *O. ardea* inhabits rainforest margins and riverine growth. It is uncommon and local. Its life history remains unknown.

Grass Darts 3

sunias

lascivia

The genus *Suniana* differs from *Ocybadistes* chiefly in the structure of the male genitalia.

The **Orange Grass Dart**, *Suniana sunias* (fw ♂ 13 mm, ♀ 13.5 mm), has upside markings and a male sex brand quite similar to the very common though slightly smaller *Ocybadistes walkeri*. It differs most clearly in the outer orange band on the forewing, which is very straight, whereas in *O. walkeri* it is at least partially stepped. Moreover, compared with *O. walkeri*, the ground colour of the underside is more orange, and the outer orange bands on the underside of both wings are more sharply defined, with transecting veins generally dark. It is quite common but local, generally frequenting swampy places and stream banks where its sedge food plant, *Leersia hexandra*, grows. It also breeds on the introduced grasses *Panicum*, *Paspalum* and *Sorghum*.

The **Dingy Grass Dart**, *Suniana lascivia* (fw ♂ 12.5 mm, ♀ 13 mm), is generally unmistakable, with the orange markings above much reduced. It occurs in several forms in the east and north in open forest and coastal vegetation. It is local and generally uncommon. Known larval food plants include *Imperata cylindrica* and introduced *Panicum* grass. Several races are recognised, with specimens from near Darwin much brighter than the illustrated specimen, with the underside marking very like *S. sunias* from the same localities. Females from this area may be difficult to separate, but in the males the sex brand is still very different. The early stages of *Suniana* are very like those of *Ocybadistes*.

♂ sunias ♀ sunias ♂ lascivia

adults of both sexes perch in low vegetation

♂ sunias

sunias

male forewing sex brands

lascivia

Darters 1

The genera *Arrhenes* and *Telicota* include species obviously larger than most grass darts. In *Arrhenes* the wings are rounded, and the hindwing tornal lobe is little developed. In *Telicota*, especially males, the forewing apex is quite acute and the hindwing tornal lobe prominent. Males of both genera have an easily visible sex brand on the forewing. The terminal process on the antennal club is often long.

The **Swamp Darter**, *Arrhenes marnas* (fw ♂ 13 mm, ♀ 14 mm), resembles, superficially, a large *Suniana sunias*, with which it shares swampy habitats and the food plant *Leersia hexandra*. Close inspection of details of the wing pattern reveals many clear differences.

The larger **Scrub Darter**, *Arrhenes dschilus* (fw ♂ 14 mm, ♀ 15 mm), flies in grassy areas in open coastal forest and along rainforest margins. Larvae feed on *Imperata cylindrica* and introduced *Panicum* and *Saccharum*. Both species are common but local.

The **Narrow-brand Darter**, *Telicota mesoptis* (fw ♂ 15 mm, ♀ 16 mm), and the **Small Darter**, *T. brachydesma* (fw ♂ 13 mm, ♀ 14 mm), are the smallest members of their genus (discussed overleaf). Both occur in wet tropical habitats, but *T. mesoptis* flies low in grassy areas in open forest or bordering rainforest. The sex brand is less oblique than in *T. augias* or *T. ancilla*. Introduced food plants include *Panicum* and *Sorghum*. In *T. brachydesma* the underside ground colour is reddish brown. It flies mainly in the rainforest canopy and is rarely encountered. Larvae feed on *Leptaspis banksii*. Like many rainforest skippers, males imbibe nutrients from bird droppings on leaves, first adding a drop of fluid from their anus to liquefy the matter.

FAMILY HESPERIIDAE—Skippers

Darters 2

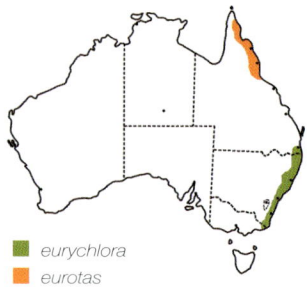
- eurychlora
- eurotas

- ancilla

- colon

- augias

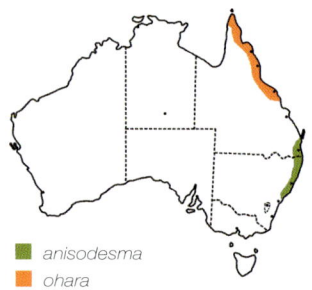
- anisodesma
- ohara

The nine species of the genus *Telicota* range in wingspan from 26 to 35 mm. The genus may generally be distinguished from grass darts and palm darts by size, the forewing having an acute apex and a pale sex brand in males, and the hindwing having a well-developed tornal lobe. Although size may be a help in identification to species, it must be realised that variation of at least 10 per cent may be expected. Details of wing shape, colour pattern and the shape and inclination of the male sex brand can help in identification, but in some cases only dissection of the genitalia will establish identity conclusively. The life history is typical for the subfamily and, as illustrated for *T. ohara*, the egg becomes pinkish with age. *Telicota* species may fly low among grass, but often perch in trees several metres above the ground. They feed at flowers such as lantana and *Pentas*, where they are sometimes ambushed by Crab Spiders (*Thomisis* sp.).

The tropical **Northern Sedge Darter**, *Telicota eurotas* (fw ♂ 15 mm, ♀ 17 mm), occurs in swampy lowland areas near forest. Larvae feed on *Scleria* species. Principal identification characters are the broad sex brand of the male, and the broad, well-defined outer orange band on the hindwing underside.

The subtropical **Southern Sedge Darter**, *Telicota eurychlora* (fw ♂ 16 mm, ♀ 17 mm), occurs along coastal streams in estuarine habitats, where larvae feed on *Cladium procerum*, and in upland swamps near rainforest. The male sex brand is narrow, and the outer orange band on the hindwing underside is narrow and obscure.

The **Greenish Darter**, *Telicota ancilla* (fw ♂ 16 mm, ♀ 17 mm), flies in open forest and along rainforest margins. Larvae feed on *Imperata cylindrica*, several other grasses and *Gahnia aspera*. The sex brand is narrow, as in *T. eurychlora*, but the hindwing tornal lobe is better developed and the underside has a greenish cast, with a better-defined outer orange band. The sex brand is set less obliquely than in *T. augias*.

The **Pale-orange Darter**, *Telicota colon* (fw ♂ 16 mm, ♀ 17 mm), is widespread and common in open wet eucalypt and coastal forests. Larvae feed on *Chrysopogon fallax*, *Ophiuros exaltatus*, *Phragmites australis* and introduced *Miscanthus* and *Sorghum*. Males are generally easily recognised by their small size, extensive palish orange marking on the upperside, with the outer band extending along the veins almost to reach the wing margin, and the broad pale sex brand. Females are generally pale, with the outer orange band on the forewing underside broad.

The **Bright-orange Darter**, *Telicota augias* (fw ♂ 16 mm, ♀ 16.5 mm), is locally common at northern rainforest margins. Larvae feed on *Flagellaria indica*. Its markings are narrower than in the similar *T. colon*, and more intensely coloured. The sex brand is narrower, darker and more obliquely set. The female forewing is rather elongate and rounded in comparison with other similar-sized darters.

The **Northern Large Darter**, *Telicota ohara* (fw ♂ 18 mm, ♀ 19 mm), occurs in tropical rainforest and riverine forest. Adults perch in the canopy but venture lower to feed at lantana and other flowers. Larvae feed on *Flagellaria indica*. *T. ohara* is darker than other darters on the underside and larger than most. Females resemble the light form of *Cephrenes augiades* but are smaller, with the underside markings better defined.

The **Southern Large Darter**, *Telicota anisodesma* (fw ♂ 18 mm, ♀ 19 mm), flies in littoral and riverine forests in the subtropics. Its habits are similar to those of *T. ohara* and the larva also feeds on *Flagellaria indica*. The male is most likely to be confused with *T. ancilla*, but the sex brand is broader and curves outward, and the underside ground colour is more orange. The female from above resembles the dark form of female *Cephrenes augiades*, but it is smaller and the underside is paler.

FAMILY HESPERIIDAE—Skippers

Palm Darts

augiades

trichopepla

The palm darts are the largest and most conspicuous of the black and orange hesperiines and also the most widespread, having been introduced to many cities around the country by the horticultural industry. They are significant pests of ornamental palms.

The more common of the two species is the **Orange Palm Dart**, *Cephrenes augiades* (fw ♂ 22 mm, ♀ 24 mm). The males are substantially larger than any species of darter (*Telicota* spp.) and lack a sex brand on the forewing upperside, which is brightly marked with orange. The underside is generally a rather bright orange-brown, but sometimes reddish brown, with the outer pale band not outlined with dark markings. The female has a light form, which has reduced orange markings above, resembling the female of the smaller and rarer *T. ohara*. However, apart from its obviously greater size, in *C. augiades* the outer orange band on the underside of the hindwing is not outlined as in *T. ohara*. There is also an uncommon dark form of the *C. augiades* female, which is almost unmarked above except for an orange suffusion at the forewing base. *C. augiades* is native to tropical and subtropical rainforest and gallery forest, wherever its palm food plants grow, but is very commonly seen in gardens and plant nurseries. Both males and females commonly feed on garden flowers. *C. augiades* larvae have been recorded feeding on more than 130 species of palms in Australia. These include species of *Archontophoenix*, *Arenga*, *Calamus*, *Carpentaria*, *Hydriastele*, *Laccospadix*, *Licuala*, *Livistona*, *Ptychosperma*, *Rhopalostylis* and *Wodyetia*.

Males maintain territories on the palm food plant or on nearby elevated vegetation, perching in bright sunlight in the 'dart' position. Territorial contests are fierce, with protagonists circling each other rapidly, with an audible whirring of wings, then breaking into high-speed chases that may extend more than 20 m into the forest canopy. Courtship also involves high-speed chases, and copulation follows if the female lands, whereupon the male alights beside her and quickly engages her genitalia with his own.

The female lays her large egg singly on the young growth of the food plant. The hemispherical egg is about 1.6 mm in diameter. When first laid it is white, but in a few days it turns yellow and develops characteristic red markings. The young larva eats the top off the eggshell from inside, then finishes the remainder after hatching. Its first task is to construct a tiny shelter, which it does by sewing together young leaves from near the tip of the frond with silk. By day it rests in the shelter, emerging at night to feed, and constructing ever larger shelters as it grows. Larvae seldom move far from their initial shelter and pupation occurs within the shelter. The pupa is pale, stout and rounded anteriorly, like that of *Telicota*. It is covered with a white waxy secretion.

The **Yellow Palm Dart**, *Cephrenes trichopepla* (fw ♂ 20 mm, ♀ 22 mm), differs from *C. augiades* in being slightly smaller and much brighter in colour. The underside is a deep chrome yellow, with the outer band of the hindwing edged with dark spots. On the underside of the hindwing is a very distinct rounded dark spot on the tornal lobe. This feature, and the general bright colour, serve to separate *C. trichopepla* immediately from *C. augiades* or any *Telicota* species, from which it also differs by the lack of a male sex brand. The female is similar in shape to female *C. augiades*, but smaller and with coloration exactly as in the male, including the distinctive dark tornal spot on the hindwing underside. The habits and habitat of *C. trichopepla* are very like those of *C. augiades*. More than 65 species of palm have been recorded as host plants, including members of the genera *Archontophoenix*, *Livistona*, *Ptychosperma* and *Wodyetia*.

FAMILY HESPERIIDAE—Skippers

Rice Skippers, *Pelopidas* and Their Allies

The *Pelopidas* group includes six species which, among other host plants, sometimes attack rice (although the Rice Swift and Yellow Swift are only recorded from this host plant overseas). All are dull in colour and swift-flying, with a well-developed tornal lobe in both sexes.

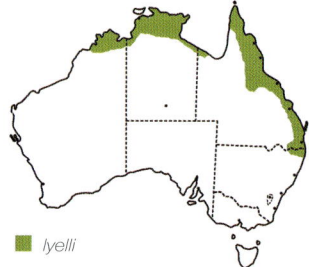

The males of **Lyell's Swift**, *Pelopidas lyelli* (fw ♂ 18 mm, ♀ 19 mm), and the **Dingy Swift**, *P. agna* (fw ♂ 18 mm, ♀ 19 mm), can both be distinguished from other rice skippers by the presence of a forewing sex brand. This is shorter, narrower and slightly less oblique in *P. agna*, and the two species differ also in the orientation of the two inner spots on the forewing, a line drawn between the two being more inwardly slanted in *P. agna* than in *P. lyelli* in both sexes. The longitudinally banded larvae are similar in both species, as are the pupae. The elongate pupae are notable for their bright green colour and long, pointed, slightly upwardly curving anterior process. Both species are widespread and common in open forest and nearby gardens, where they often visit flowers. Both feed as larvae on *Oryza* (rice) and *Sorghum*. *P. lyelli* is recorded also from introduced *Panicum* and *Pennisetum*. *P. agna* is recorded also from the native *Ischaemum australe* and introduced *Paspalum*.

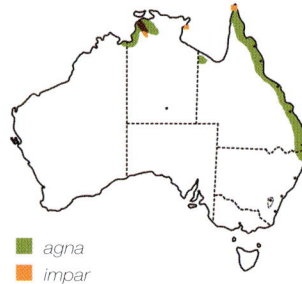

The **Yellow Swift**, *Borbo impar* (fw ♂ 18 mm, ♀ 19 mm), and **Rice Swift**, *B. cinnara* (fw ♂ 16.5 mm, ♀ 17 mm), are little-known species in Australia, occurring in rainforest edges and swampy forest only from the Cape York area in Queensland and from near Darwin. The males have no sex brand and their forewing spotting pattern differs subtly from each other and from *Pelopidas* species. Their habits are similar to those of *Pelopidas*. *B. impar* is recorded breeding on introduced *Panicum* and *Pennisetum*. *B. cinnara* is recorded from the native *Rottboellia cochinensis* in Torres Strait.

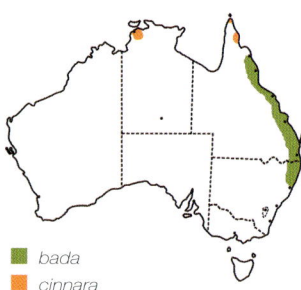

The **Grey Swift**, *Parnara bada* (fw ♂ 16 mm, ♀ 17 mm), also lacks a male sex brand and has reduced spots on the forewing of both sexes. Also unlike *Pelopidas*, it has two pale spots on the upperside of the hindwing. It is widespread in the eastern tropics and subtropics in swampy and riverine habitats. It is smaller than *Pelopidas* and *Borbo* species. It is common but local in swampy places and the banks of slow-flowing rivers where its food plant, the sedge *Leersia hexandra*, grows. It also feeds on rice. The larva is unusual among hesperiines in having a rough, almost opaque, yellowish-brown skin. The pupa is blunt anteriorly, whitish, with a relatively long proboscis. It is typically wedged in among the basal leaves of the food plant.

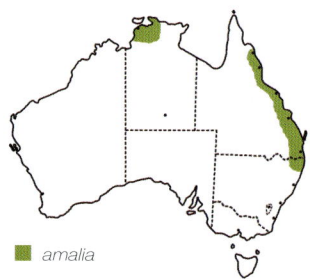

The **Hyaline Swift**, *Parnara amalia* (fw ♂ 16 mm, ♀ 17 mm), is distinctive by virtue of its markings and small size. It occurs in the same situations as *P. bada* and utilises the same food plants, but the larva is dull green rather than brown.

6 FAMILY PAPILIONIDAE
Swallowtails, Birdwings, Triangles and Swordtails

Macleay's Swallowtail (*Graphium macleayanum*)

A giant birdwing soars majestically above the city of Cairns; a Ulysses jinks across a dark wall of forest, an undulating line of electric blue flashes; massed Chequered Swallowtails fall in a dazzle of cream and black upon the garden flowers of an inland homestead; in Sydney's Royal Botanic Gardens, a quivering Blue Triangle darts from flower to flower. These are all swallowtails—the largest, most captivating and charismatic of our butterflies.

The **Papilionidae** includes about 550 species worldwide but just nineteen in Australia, making it the smallest butterfly family in terms of species numbers. Their size, bold colours and forceful presence, however, ensure they are among the best-known species. They are diverse in appearance, and generally very easy to identify, even without capture. The family name comes from the genus *Papilio*. *Papilio* is Latin for butterfly, and Carolus Linnaeus, whose 1758 classification using Latin binomial names is the basis of all modern biological nomenclature, placed every butterfly he knew in the genus *Papilio*. Later authors restricted the use of this name to certain swallowtails. Among our fauna, *P. demoleus* and *P. ulysses* still bear the names given them by Linnaeus in 1758. Of course, his specimens were collected outside Australia, and it was not until 1770 that Sir Joseph Banks collected the first truly Australian butterflies.

The term 'swallowtail' was first applied to the one English papilionid, *P. machaon*, which has short pointed tails on the hindwing. By contrast, species in Australia may have spatulate tails, long sword-tails, or none at all. Most are of northern tropical origin, and just four species are endemic. Only Macleay's Swallowtail (*Graphium macleayanum*) reaches Tasmania. Adult swallowtails differ from other families in details of their wing venation, and by the presence of a small spur on the tibia of the first pair of legs, the so-called epiphysis, also found in skippers. All six legs are fully developed. The early stages are distinctive. The egg is generally smooth, spherical and pearl-like, but may be coated with thick yellow or amber glue, which gives it a superficial ribbed pattern. It is generally laid singly on the leaves of the host plant. Larvae are swollen in the thoracic segments behind the head and have a unique, erectile, forked red or yellow structure— the osmeterium—located just behind the head. Normally it is retracted within the body but, when the larva is alarmed, it is everted suddenly and gives off a pungent odour, probably derived from food plant chemicals. This is thought to deter predators and parasitic wasps and flies. The larvae feed openly by day. Young larvae may be quite different from mature larvae and often resemble bird droppings. The pupa is anchored by its tail to a silken pad and supported with its head held upwards by a strong silk loop girdling its midriff. In many species that live in seasonal environments, pupal diapause is common during drought, when development may be arrested for many months, or even several years.

The Australian swallowtails all belong to the one subfamily, the Papilioninae, which is divided into three very distinct tribes (designated by the suffix –ini): the Graphiini, including the genera *Protographium* and *Graphium*; the Papilionini, including just the genus *Papilio*; and the Troidini, including the genera *Ornithoptera*, *Pachliopta* and *Cressida*. The primary difference separating the three tribes is their larval host plant preferences, providing us with an excellent example of butterflies as botanists. Graphiini feed mainly on Annonaceae and Lauraceae, Papilionini mainly on Rutaceae, including introduced citrus trees, and Troidini on toxic native Aristolochiaceae or Dutchman's Pipe vines.

Graphiini are believed to be generally palatable to predators, and they include the swiftest-flying and most agile members of the family. The adults' proboscis is rather short and they feed only on flowers with a relatively short corolla tube, introduced lantana being a favourite. The males and females are always similar. Males frequently probe damp soil to obtain salts.

There is little doubt that citrus-feeders among the Papilionini are only moderately palatable, but adults are sometimes taken by birds, and magpies have been seen eating mature larvae with no ill effects. *Papilio* species generally have a lively jinking flight. *P. anactus* and females of *P. ambrax*, however, mimic the unpalatable troidines *Cressida cressida* and *Pachliopta polydorus*, and their flight is generally slow and sailing, unless alarmed. In some species, such as *P. ambrax*, there is pronounced sexual dimorphism.

The Troidini are undoubtedly unpalatable to most predators. They commonly have red warning colours, and most have patches of red on the thorax and abdomen. Their flight is generally quite leisurely, with frequent intervals of gliding. Marked sexual dimorphism is common, so much so that males and females were sometimes originally described as separate species.

In both Papilionini and Troidini the proboscis is long, and they often feed at flowers with long corolla tubes, such as introduced *Pentas* or *Ixora*. However, flowers with very open nectaries, such as Umbrella Trees (*Schefflera actinophylla*), are also great favourites, especially with the Cairns Birdwing.

The Papilionidae is the one family wherein the inter-relationships among Australian genera are mostly agreed on, both from traditional analysis of visible structures, general biology and, most recently, from molecular analysis of DNA. The three major forks in the tree define the three tribes.

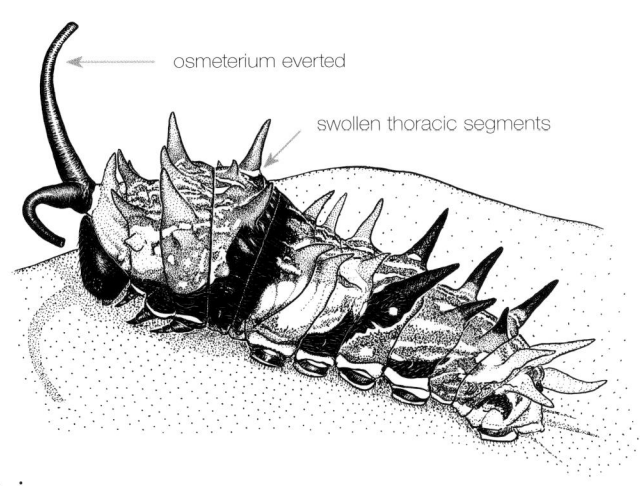

FIGURE 6.1: Orchard Butterfly (*Papilio aegeus*) larva.

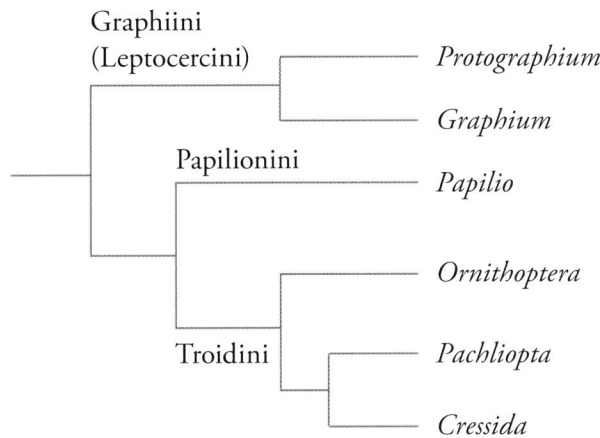

FIGURE 6.2: Evolutionary tree of swallowtail tribes and genera. There is still disagreement over the actual names to be used for the tribes, with many authors using Leptocercini rather than Graphiini.

Swordtails

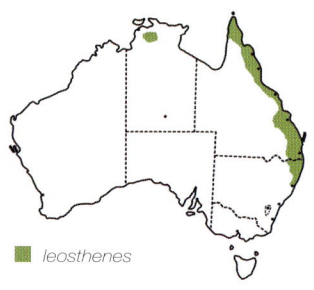
leosthenes

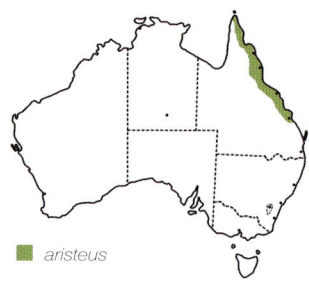
aristeus

The **Fourbar Swordtail**, *Protographium leosthenes* (fw ♂ 33 mm, ♀ 35 mm), occurs in the east and near Darwin in dry vine forest and rainforest. Its nearest relatives occur in South America. Adults fly very rapidly, usually 1–4 m above the ground, pausing often to feed at flowers. While feeding, the wings remain quivering. Males patrol stands of larval food plant and also visit hilltops. Females are sometimes seized on the wing by males and borne to the ground, and so mated. It is not certain if conventional courtship also occurs but tufts of the male scent scales on the inner margin of the hindwing are reduced compared with other species. The small pearl-like egg is laid singly on fresh growth of the host, generally the vine *Melodorum leichhardtii*. The pupa may be green or brown. Although superficially similar to *Graphium aristeus*, *P. leosthenes* is easily recognised by its narrower wings, four rather than five dark bars on the forewing and longer tails.

The **Fivebar Swordtail**, *Graphium aristeus* (fw ♂ 30 mm, ♀ 33 mm), occurs in north Queensland mainly in monsoon forest and tree savannah. It is rare in rainforest. It flies very rapidly at 2–4 m above the ground, hovering frenetically when feeding from flowers with a short corolla tube. The males often descend to the ground to feed at damp earth, extracting salts, especially sodium and potassium ions. Males also hilltop. The small pearl-like eggs are laid in clusters on young growth of the host trees, *Miliusa traceyi*, *Polyalthia nitidissima* and *Pseuduvaria froggattii*. The larvae feed gregariously. The pupa, which resembles a dead stick, forms among rocks and leaf litter. The pupal stage normally lasts up to eleven months, the adults emerging with the onset of the wet season.

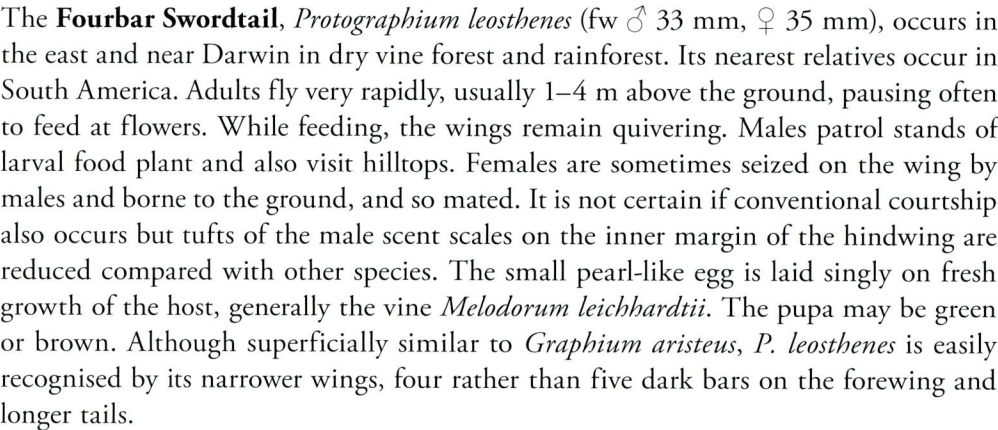

122   The Butterflies of Australia

Blue Triangle

The **Blue Triangle**, *Graphium sarpedon* (fw ♂ 41 mm, ♀ 43 mm), is one of the most familiar butterflies in the warmer parts of the east coast. Its natural habitat is mainly rainforest and monsoon forest but it is a common garden butterfly wherever introduced Camphor Laurel (*Cinnamomum camphora*) grows. It is brisk in flight, often sailing high overhead. It feeds at flowers with a short corolla tube. During courtship, the male hovers over the female, extending hemispherical brushes of long white hairs from folds in the inner margins of his hindwings. These are believed to release a sex pheromone. Most often when this behaviour is observed, the female, who may be feeding or ovipositing, simply ignores the male until he desists. Rarely a female may fold her wings, and perch with wings still, whereupon the male lands beside her and mates. Ovipositing females have an unusual behaviour in which they run the tip of their abdomen down the midrib of a leaf, often of a non-host species, presumably testing the chemical properties of the plant and assessing its suitability for oviposition. When an appropriate plant is found, the pearl-like egg is laid singly on young foliage. The larva is green and strongly humped around the thorax. The osmeterium is yellow. The pupa is green with a strong dorsal horn. Food plants include species of *Annona*, *Beilschmiedia*, *Cinnamomum*, *Clerodendrum*, *Cryptocarya*, *Doryphora*, *Endiandra*, *Geijera*, *Litsea*, *Neolitsea* and *Planchonella*.

sarpedon

FAMILY PAPILIONIDAE—Swallowtails, Birdwings, Triangles and Swordtails

Triangles and Macleay's Swallowtail

eurypylus

macfarlanei

agamemnon

macleayanum

There are three species of green triangle of similar habits. These, together with Macleay's Swallowtail, all belong to the genus *Graphium*, characterised by fork-tailed, strongly humped larvae with a yellow osmeterium and pupa with a thoracic spine. All are swift-flying, active species with a short proboscis, restricting them to flowers with a short corolla tube, such as lantana. They feed with wings quivering, darting from flower to flower, and the longer and more sickle-shaped the forewing, the more rapid is this motion. Females also lay their eggs with quivering wings. Generally courtship is as in *G. sarpedon*.

The **Pale Green Triangle**, *Graphium eurypylus* (fw ♂ 40 mm, ♀ 42 mm), is common in north-eastern coastal regions at rainforest margins, in monsoon forest and in suburban gardens. The male is pale blue above, the female pale yellowish green. There is a single row of subcostal spots on the hindwing, separating it from similar species. It flies at about 2 m and higher, and sometimes appears in great numbers, evidently migrating. Eggs are laid singly on young leaves of the host plant. Young larvae are dark brown with a white underside. Older larvae may be pale brown or olive green, generally with distinct pale rings around the spiracles along the side of the body. The pupa usually forms well away from the host tree and parasitism by tachinid flies is common. It is most commonly seen around its host plants, Custard Apples and Soursops (*Annona* spp.), but it also breeds on *Artabotrys*, *Desmos*, *Fitzalania*, *Magnolia*, *Melodorum*, *Miliusa*, *Polyalthia*, *Pseuduvaria* and *Uvaria*.

The **Green Triangle**, *Graphium macfarlanei* (fw ♂ 46 mm, ♀ 48 mm), is uncommon in north Queensland rainforest. It is particularly swift in flight, and seldom descends below about 3 m to feed briefly at nectar. The early stages are slightly different from those of *G. agamemnon*. Larval host plants include *Annona muricata*, *Desmos* species and *Rollinia deliciosa*.

The **Green-spotted Triangle**, *Graphium agamemnon* (fw ♂ 42 mm, ♀ 44 mm), is common in rainforest, monsoon forest and gardens in the eastern tropics. It is very rapid in flight, but sometimes rests within 2 m of the ground with wings held flat. Females are slightly slower-flying than males, but otherwise similar. The young larva is distinctively marked with a pale cream saddle. The mature larva is mottled green or pale pinkish brown. The pupa has a very prominent thoracic spine.

Macleay's Swallowtail, *Graphium macleayanum* (fw ♂ 34 mm, ♀ 36 mm), occurs in cooler habitats. In Queensland it is confined to mountain rainforest, but it occurs at progressively lower altitudes further south, although it has been recorded at the summit of Mt Kosciuszko. It is the only swallowtail to reach Tasmania. Adults fly high, often sailing with their tails plainly visible, but may suddenly dive quite low to feed at flowers. Males sometimes seize females in midair and carry them to the ground, but more conventional courtship also occurs. The early stages are very similar to those of *G. sarpedon*. The larvae feed on a wide range of hosts, the commonest being *Geijera salicifolia* and *Atherosperma moschatum*. Also used are species of *Cinnamomum*, *Cryptocarya*, *Endiandra*, *Daphnandra*, *Doryphora* and *Tasmannia*.

FAMILY PAPILIONIDAE—Swallowtails, Birdwings, Triangles and Swordtails

Chequered and Dingy Swallowtails

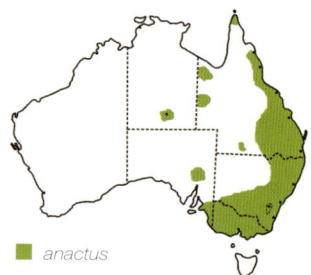

demoleus

anactus

The **Chequered Swallowtail**, *Papilio demoleus* (fw ♂ 44 mm, ♀ 46 mm), is a medium-sized swallowtail with unmistakable colouring and markings. It is a busy, active butterfly, flying with strong wing beats typically 1–2 m above the ground. Adults often feed at flowers and males at damp mud. Sometimes adults perch with wings outspread. When disturbed, they abruptly bring their forewings forward, revealing eyespots on the hindwing. This display presumably startles potential predators. It is the most widespread of our swallowtails, occurring over most of the mainland. It breeds mainly in semi-arid inland habitats, especially along watercourses and in moist gullies, but it often disperses much further afield. Occasionally, it forms mass migrations and may arrive in an area in hundreds. On 23 February 2008, vast numbers arrived at Caloundra, southern Queensland, travelling north. During the course of the day, their numbers grew from a few dozen to several hundred just before dusk. All day they remained around garden flowers, feeding and chasing one another, roosting en masse at about 5 pm on long grass tussocks in a patch of wasteland. The following morning, many fed at flowers from 7 to 9.30. Soon after, they disappeared, with none seen after 11 am. Over the next four days, no more than three individuals were seen. Previously, fewer than ten individuals had been recorded from that site in more than 40 years.

The main food plants of *P. demoleus* are legumes, native *Cullen* species, and introduced *Psoralea pinnata*, with native and cultivated citrus used occasionally. In Asia, a different subspecies of *P. demoleus* feeds mainly on citrus and is a pest. The egg is laid singly on the food plant. The larva is very distinctive. The pupa may be green or brown. Normal duration of the pupal period is 2–3 weeks, but pupae formed in March–April may remain dormant for 6–12 months.

The **Dingy Swallowtail**, *Papilio anactus* (fw ♂ 42 mm, ♀ 46 mm), is common and widespread in the east. Its native habitats include open forest and rainforest margins but it is also a common garden butterfly, especially where citrus is grown. Males and females are alike in wing pattern, and both are excellent mimics of males of *Cressida cressida*, which feeds on toxic *Aristolochia*. Males, especially, behave like *C. cressida*. They select sunny patches in lightly vegetated areas, commonly along paths, where they circle around a definite territory of 10–30 m diameter, gliding 1–2 m above the ground, sometimes perching in sunlight with wings held open. If another male appears in the territory, the occupant flies rapidly towards him, generally chasing the intruder away before resuming his leisurely patrol. These territories do not appear to contain any resource used by females such as nectar or larval food plants, and it may be that females come to these sites to meet males and mate. Males also frequently hilltop, presumably also in order to encounter receptive mates. Males do not produce a mating plug and do not harass ovipositing females. Females tend to have a more jinking flight, as do the males when alarmed, and are thus much less convincing mimics of *C. cressida*. They are most often seen around garden citrus, on which they lay their small pearl-like eggs singly. As with most swallowtails, the young and mature larvae are strikingly different. The pupa is very straight, resembling a broken twig. In addition to a wide range of native and introduced citrus, larvae also feed on *Geijera parviflora*, *Limonia acidissima* and *Poncirus trifoliata*.

FAMILY PAPILIONIDAE—Swallowtails, Birdwings, Triangles and Swordtails

Ambrax and Orchard Butterflies

aegeus

ambrax

The **Orchard Butterfly**, *Papilio aegeus* (fw ♂ 58 mm, ♀ 62 mm), is the most common large butterfly to be seen outside the north Queensland tropics. Its native habitat is principally wet open forest, and to some extent rainforest edges, but it has invaded orchards and gardens in most major centres of the east and south, and it is in these human environments that it is most often encountered. The female has, in addition to the normal form illustrated, a pale form and a dark form, both restricted to the extreme north of Queensland. The pale form is believed to mimic the Owl Butterfly (*Taenaris artemis*). Torres Strait Island populations are of a different subspecies, with minor differences from the typical race. Females are particularly striking, and have a low but erratic jinking flight. They are often observed ovipositing on fresh growth of citrus, generally supporting their weight by fluttering while the large pearl-like egg is laid. They frequently rest with wings held flat, and often feed at garden flowers, including species with long corolla tubes such as *Pentas* and *Ixora*. The males are glossy black with white markings. Flight is similar to that of the female but usually a little swifter.

Courtship is often observed. The male flies from behind the female, time and again diving under her then abruptly ascending just ahead of her, displaying his upperside colours and perhaps releasing pheromones. The male may also hover above a flying female, or one that has perched. A receptive female alights with her wings folded. Virgin females are normally intercepted and mated soon after they begin flying, and the male secretes a large internal mating plug which prevents further males from mating with her. With time, however, this plug shrinks and becomes more brittle, and can often be dislodged by another male if the female accepts a second mating. A good proportion of older females have mated twice, and some three times.

Young larvae have distinctive brown and white markings, supposed to imitate a bird dropping. Mature larvae are green with brown markings. Pupae may be green with yellowish highlights or brown, the colour matching the background. Apart from native and cultivated citrus, numerous plants are eaten by larvae, including species of *Boronia*, *Choisya*, *Clausena*, *Dinosperma*, *Eriostemon*, *Flindersia*, *Geijera*, *Halfordia*, *Leionema*, *Micromelum*, *Murraya*, *Philotheca*, *Poncirus*, *Zanthoxylum* and *Zieria*.

The **Ambrax Butterfly**, *Papilio ambrax* (fw ♂ 51 mm, ♀ 54 mm), is fairly common in rainforest in the north Queensland wet tropics region and near Mackay. The males have a rapid jinking flight, along forest paths and streams, generally 1–2 m from the ground. Females sometimes fly in this manner, especially when alarmed, but often sail quite slowly at about 2 m, and are very effective mimics of the toxic *Pachliopta polydorus*, which feeds on *Aristolochia* and occurs in similar situations. As with many palatable mimetic species, females often show evidence of bird attack on their hindwings, perhaps indicative of 'half-hearted' attacks by birds unsure of their prey. Although *P. ambrax* is superficially like a small *P. aegeus*, the two are seldom confused in nature, partly because of their size and behavioural differences, and partly because they seldom overlap, except occasionally at flowers along rainforest margins. The young larva has a bird dropping pattern similar to *P. aegeus* but lacks spines. The pupa is narrower and more elaborately sculptured than that of *P. aegeus* but exhibits similar colour variation. Host plants include native and cultivated citrus, *Clausena*, *Limonia*, *Murraya* and *Zanthoxylum*.

FAMILY PAPILIONIDAE—Swallowtails, Birdwings, Triangles and Swordtails

Ulysses Butterfly and Tailed Citrus and Northern Citrus Swallowtails

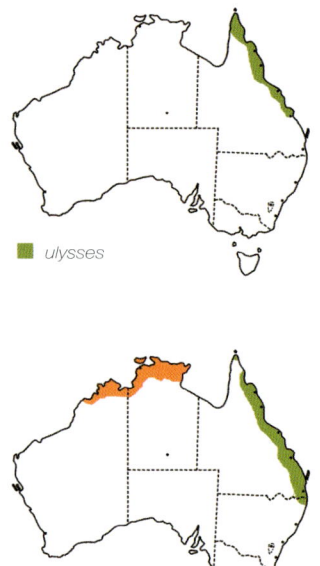

ulysses

fuscus
canopus

The magnificent **Ulysses Butterfly**, *Papilio ulysses* (fw ♂ 63 mm, ♀ 64 mm), is a very common sight in gardens and in rainforest in tropical Queensland from Mackay north. The sexes are quite similar, but the female has a smaller central blue area and often a row of small blue submarginal marks on the hindwing. The outer margin of the forewing of the male has a row of parallel sex brands, clearly visible as elongate leaf-shaped patches of dull scales. The underside of both sexes is a variegated brown, producing an effective dead-leaf effect when the butterfly perches. *P. ulysses* is a vigorous and aerobatic flier, jinking wildly around the forest canopy in a succession of blue flashes, then diving low to investigate anything shiny, such as a mirror, a car bonnet, or anything blue. During courtship, they often fly low, 1–2 m above the ground. The female flies quite slowly, but still with a bouncing erratic flight, while the more active male flies below her and regularly swoops upwards just ahead of her, possibly brushing her antennae with his androconia (pheromone-producing scales) and displaying his brilliant colour. Sometimes the male executes a full somersault in front of the female. If the female is receptive, she lands and copulation follows. The male deposits a large internal mating plug, preventing other males from mating with the female. The brilliant iridescent blue upperside colour is entirely structural, each scale having a complex multilayered interference system configured to reflect intense blue light. The black marginal scales, which include melanin pigment, also have structural properties that enable them to absorb light, creating an intense velvet black which, by heightening the contrast, probably enhances the perceived brilliance of the blue area. Larvae feed mainly on *Melicope bonwickii*, *M. elleryana*, *M. rubra* and *M. vitiflora*. Eggs are laid singly, while the female supports herself by beating her wings. The young larva has very long horns on its thorax, making hatching prolonged and strenuous. The mature larva is green, marked characteristically with white. The pupa is green and strongly bowed.

The **Tailed Citrus Swallowtail**, *Papilio fuscus* (fw ♂ 49 mm, ♀ 52 mm), is locally and seasonally common in the tropical and subtropical east, flying around rainforest margins, vine thickets, riverine forests and citrus orchards. In flight it is suggestive of a small male *P. aegeus*, but the tails are usually quite obvious. The male and female are very similar. Eggs are laid singly on young leaves of the host plant, including native and cultivated citrus, *Clausena*, *Glycosmis*, *Halfordia*, *Murraya* and *Zanthoxylum*. The larva is variable in colour. In early instars it bears the typical brown and white bird dropping pattern found in some other species of *Papilio*. Later instars may retain this pattern or be a uniform or variegated green. It has no spines. The pupa is somewhat bowed and green or pale brown. The duration of the pupal stage is variable and depends on environmental conditions. Normal development takes about two weeks, but pupae may remain dormant for as long as three years. This is believed to be a response to drought or impending drought.

The **Northern Citrus Swallowtail**, *Papilio canopus* (fw ♂ 48 mm, ♀ 51 mm), occurs in similar situations in the Northern Territory and Kimberley region of Western Australia. It has been treated by some as a subspecies of *P. fuscus*, but it has a different wing shape, is very differently marked, and our breeding experiments produced sterile offspring. Moreover, current standard world lists of swallowtail butterflies recognise the two as separate species. Its biology is very like that of *P. fuscus*.

Richmond Birdwing

richmondia

Birdwings are the largest and most popular of all butterflies. At least five lavish and expensive books, beginning in 1898, have been devoted to them. In terms of wingspan, and probably also weight, the endangered Queen Alexandra's Birdwing (*Ornithoptera alexandrae*) from northern Papua is the world's largest butterfly, with large females attaining a wingspan of 270 mm (forewing 130 mm). Three species of birdwing are known from Australia. All are very similar in appearance and behaviour and have non-overlapping ranges. There is still debate over whether any of them should be recognised as separate species rather than simply subspecies of a single widely distributed species, but experiments in which the different forms have been interbred support the three species view. The beautiful green colour of male birdwings is a combination of structural blue scales and chemical yellow pigment. Faded specimens become bluer as the yellow degrades.

The smallest member of the genus, the southern **Richmond Birdwing**, *Ornithoptera richmondia* (fw ♂ 64 mm, ♀ 73 mm), is still easily the largest Australian butterfly found outside the tropics. Formerly, it was locally and seasonally quite common in rainforest from Maryborough in Queensland south to the Richmond River in New South Wales. Occasionally, in good years, it disperses far from its breeding habitat: in 1966 a male was seen in Queen Street, Brisbane, and females were seen flying over the sea at Caloundra. In the 1990s its numbers declined alarmingly, and evidence of inbreeding depression in increasingly fragmented pockets of habitat caused concern for its long-term survival. An active program encouraging planting of its main host plant, *Pararistolochia praevenosa*, was instigated. In recent years, many more sightings have been recorded in its core habitat, where the plant has always been abundant.

Both sexes, particularly females, fly high, usually between 4 m and the height of the forest canopy. Males, especially, sail on their elongate wings, spending almost the entire day in flight. Typically, they keep to a restricted home range of a few hectares, and occasionally defend small territories around larval host plants. Sometimes they descend as low as 2–3 m to feed at flowers such as lantana, beating their wings to support their weight as they feed. Females also sail high, but often fly with a strong wing beat and direct flight path, especially when travelling between patches of forest.

Virgin females are generally discovered by males quite soon after they emerge from the pupa. The male secretes a large mating plug during copulation. Older females will sometimes re-mate, if the plug can be dislodged, and courting pairs, with the male flying below the female, are seen frequently. During this process the male periodically soars upwards, just ahead of the female, brushing her antennae with pheromones from the brushes which lie in a pocket along the inner margins of the hindwings. If the female lands, the male hovers over her, probably releasing more sex pheromones. A reluctant female will open her wings, and males seldom try to force copulation. When the female is a young virgin, sometimes with wings still soft, courtship is rather perfunctory, with the male hovering above the female for 30 seconds or less, before mating.

The egg is proportionally very large, with a diameter of about 2.3 mm. Females lay about 6–10 eggs a day, each placed carefully on the fresh growth of the host plant, *P. praevenosa* or *P. laheyana* in montane areas above 800 m. Females may produce about 180 eggs in their adult lifetime, which may last 2–3 months. Males are shorter lived, rarely surviving more than two months. The mature larva may be light grey or dark, as shown. The pupa is green, unlike other *Ornithoptera*. Development from egg to adult takes 10–14 weeks under good conditions.

FAMILY PAPILIONIDAE—Swallowtails, Birdwings, Triangles and Swordtails

Cairns and Cape York Birdwings

The **Cairns Birdwing**, *Ornithoptera euphorion* (fw ♂ 70 mm, ♀ 82 mm), differs from *O. richmondia* chiefly by its greater size and slightly more extensive green markings in the male. The two are closely related. It is common in the Queensland wet tropics region, especially near the coast, and also occurs near Mackay. Its core habitat is rainforest, including closed riverine forest, but both males and females are often seen in Cairns, and frequently visit *Hibiscus* and Umbrella Tree flowers. Males, especially, sometimes compete for these flowers with other nectarivores, such as sunbirds, and may drive them off by flying aggressively at them. It is less common for the birds to drive off the butterflies. Like all *Aristolochia*-feeders, birdwings are almost certainly unpalatable to vertebrates, although the adults may sometimes fall prey to Golden Orb Weaving Spiders (*Nephila* spp.). Generally, while feeding at flowers, both sexes support their weight by fluttering their wings. Males are known to guard feeding females with which they have mated against other males, possibly because soon after copulation the mating plug is still soft and easily dislodged, not becoming fully hardened for about a day. The eggs of *O. euphorion* are scarcely larger than those of *O. richmondia*, and a female may produce up to 300 in her lifetime. The larva of *O. euphorion* is very like that of *O. richmondia*, with light- and dark-grey forms. The pupa, however, is light brown and yellow, as in most other birdwings. Food plants include *Aristolochia acuminata*, *Pararistolochia australopithecurus*, *P. deltantha* and *P. sparusifolia*.

The **New Guinea Birdwing** from Torres Strait and New Guinea, the **Cape York Birdwing** from Cape York, and **McAlpine's Birdwing** from Iron Range on Cape York Peninsula are all distinct races of *Ornithoptera priamus*. They differ slightly from *O. richmondia* and *O. euphorion* in wing shape and the form of the markings in both sexes, but in general appearance and behaviour are very like those species. The New Guinea Birdwing (*O. priamus poseidon*, fw ♂ 80 mm, ♀ 90 mm) is on average the largest. The early stages of all races of *O. priamus* also differ from those of *O. euphorion* in that the mature larva has a white band continuing diagonally down its side from the central pale spine. The host plant is normally *Aristolochia acuminata*.

priamus poseidon ♂

5th instar larva

♀

FAMILY PAPILIONIDAE—Swallowtails, Birdwings, Triangles and Swordtails

Big Greasy

The **Big Greasy**, *Cressida cressida* (fw ♂ 37–57 mm, ♀ 31–52 mm), is common in open forest habitats in the eastern tropics and subtropics. Unusually among butterflies, males are on average considerably larger than females, and the range of size variation in both sexes is exceptional. Both sexes have tough, transparent wings with only a sparse scale covering except for the male hindwing, which has a black and white pattern with red submarginal spots on the underside—the common warning coloration found in most butterflies that feed on toxic *Aristolochia*. The tip of the abdomen is also bright red in males, and even such voracious predators as the Orb Spider (*Eriophora transmarina*) reject the red part of the male abdomen while consuming the remainder, even though they readily eat many other toxic butterfly species, suggesting that toxins are concentrated in this red patch.

The reproductive system of female *C. cressida* is unique among butterflies. Female butterflies normally receive sperm in a thick-walled package called the spermatophore. This is secreted by the male during copulation within a special receptacle termed the *bursa copulatrix* deep in the female's body. To a greater or lesser extent, females digest the spermatophore and use the proteins obtained to supplement egg production. Female *C. cressida* have no *bursa copulatrix*. The male secretions that would normally produce

a nutritious spermatophore are used instead to form a large external 'chastity belt', or sphragis, a hard and horny structure extremely resistant to chemical corrosion. This normally remains firmly clamped to the female's abdomen for the rest of her life, and prevents any other male from mating with her. Because female butterflies have separate openings for copulation and oviposition, the free passage of eggs is not impeded, although the sphragis may be a physical encumbrance to the female as she scrambles over the food plant, bending her abdomen to lay each egg. It is the completely externalised form of the female's genitalia that determines the male evolutionary response—the production of the large and wasteful external sphragis. In related butterflies, the female external genitalia generally consist of a small pocket which can hold a small plug securely, allowing the male to secrete also a very large nutritious spermatophore internally, while still preventing the female from mating with other males.

Mating behaviour in *C. cressida* is also unusual. Males patrol areas containing the larval host plant, sailing effortlessly 1–3 m above the ground, sometimes remaining on the wing almost all day. Where the host plant grows in discrete patches, these areas are fiercely defended against other males, and such is the aggression of the males that even large emperor dragonflies (*Anax* spp.) are driven off. Large males are much more successful than smaller ones in holding territory. Females are not courted but, soon after their first flight, are secured by aerial capture and forcibly mated. Large males may seize females and mate in midair. Smaller males must carry their prize to the ground. Mating lasts a minimum of fourteen hours, the bulk of the time being occupied by the period of hardening of the sphragis. Often mated females, bearing a sphragis, are also captured as they arrive to oviposit at defended host plant patches, but they are usually released after a minute or so. Females, which mainly flutter slowly above the ground, also signal their unavailability in flight by raising their abdomens and folding their hindwings down, displaying the sphragis to a male approaching from behind. Eggs, which vary greatly in size, are laid mainly on prostrate species of small-leafed *Aristolochia* growing among long grass. These include *A. chalmersii*, *A. pubera* and *A. thozetii*. The larvae, which have several colour forms, are sluggish and jerky in their movements, and evert their sweet-smelling yellow osmeteria with the greatest reluctance. Typically, larvae must travel long distances over the ground to find food, as they exhaust their small host plants, and the frequent acute shortage of larval food probably explains why so many small individuals persist in most populations. The creamy marbled pupa is attached to stones and dead grass stems, near the ground.

pupa

colour variants of mature larvae

mated ♀ abdomen

sphragis (chastity belt)

egg covered with thick secretion

FAMILY PAPILIONIDAE—Swallowtails, Birdwings, Triangles and Swordtails

Red-bodied Swallowtail

polydorus

The **Red-bodied Swallowtail**, *Pachliopta polydorus* (fw 48–51 mm), is found mainly in lowland rainforest in tropical Queensland, especially near the coast. It is local and generally rather uncommon. The adults fly slowly, usually 2–4 m above the ground, sailing or beating their wings steadily in a straight-line flightpath. They often keep to the forest understorey. Males and females are alike in colour, but the female is slightly larger with more rounded wings. As an *Aristolochia*-feeder, *P. polydorus* is undoubtedly unpalatable to vertebrate predators. Its flight and pattern is mimicked by females of *Papilio ambrax*. *Pachliopta polydorus* males probably mate with females soon after they emerge from the pupa. Courtship, if it occurs, has never been recorded. They secrete a very large spermatophore sealed by a mating plug, which probably prevents the female from re-mating, except perhaps late in life as the plug becomes brittle. The preferred food plant is *Aristolochia acuminata*, a large-leafed vine common along well-wooded lowland streams. In some situations the same plant may be utilised by *P. polydorus*, *Cressida cressida* and *Ornithoptera euphorion*, but *P. polydorus* tends to eat leaves at middle height, with *C. cressida* on lower leaves and *O. euphorion* in the canopy. *P. polydorus* also feeds on *Aristolochia chalmersii*, *A. thozetii* and several tough-leafed rainforest *Pararistolochia* species. The larvae are slow-moving and reluctant to evert their yellow osmeteria when disturbed. The ornately sculptured pupa may delay its development for more than a year in dry seasons.

FAMILY PIERIDAE
Whites and Yellows

7

On a highway somewhere, migrating Caper Whites spatter on the windscreen—their small corpses litter the verges like snow-dust; high in a eucalypt forest, gaudy jezabels flutter with a metronomic flash of black and white; in waste ground in a Brisbane park, grass yellows dance about our feet—the brilliant, buttery colours of their English cousins probably gave us the word 'butterfly'. These are the Pieridae: common, conspicuous and ubiquitous.

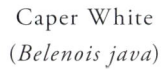

The **Pieridae** comprises about a thousand species worldwide. About 35 species are recognised from Australia, including the introduced Cabbage White. Members of the family are all small to medium-sized and coloured predominantly white, yellow or grey. Their undersides may bear red markings, but blue or green never occur, at least in Australian species. Most species have rather rounded wings with smooth, more or less unscalloped margins. The hindwings lack tails. All six legs are developed normally in both sexes. The epiphysis, a spur present on the tibia of the foreleg in Papilionidae and Hesperiidae, is lacking. All Pieridae have divided tarsal claws at the tips of their legs (Figure 7.1), readily visible under a low-power microscope.

Adults of most species are very conspicuous, flying fairly low and not too swiftly, pausing often to feed at garden flowers. Few are specialised in their habitat and half of all Australian species are migratory, several spectacularly so. The greatest number of species is found in the northern tropics, but several species occur—at least as migrants—over almost the entire mainland, and two native species reach Tasmania, where the introduced Cabbage White is also resident. Male pierids invariably court females and may have dense patches of scent scales on their wings or specialised hair brushes on the abdomen. Others have specialised scent scales known as androconia scattered over the upperside of their wings. The form of these isolated androconia is particularly elegant and tends to be characteristic to a species or genus.

When courted by unwanted males, females of all pierids display a very characteristic rejection posture. When perched, they depress their wings and lift their abdomen, exposing their genitalia. It is not known precisely why the signal has this form, but the structure of the female genitalia suggests they may have sacs that dispel an 'anti-aphrodisiac', either secreted by the female or deposited by the last male to mate with her, which deters further courting males. Female pierids seldom mate more than two or three times in their life and the males usually do not secrete physical plugs to prevent further copulation.

Caper White (*Belenois java*)

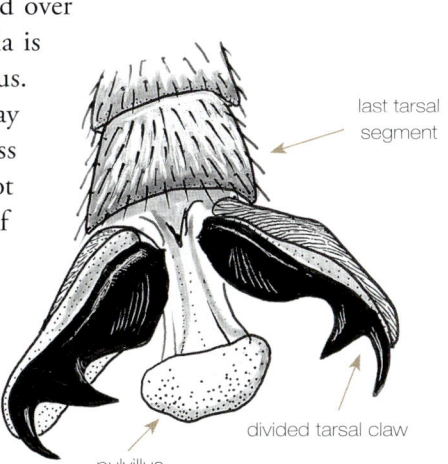

FIGURE 7.1: Tip of the mid-leg of the female Imperial White (*Delias harpalyce*), showing the bifid claws found in all members of the Pieridae.

The egg is elongate in all pierids. The larvae have a simple cylindrical shape, are plainly coloured and lack fleshy processes or branched spines. The pupa is anchored by its tail to a silken pad and supported, typically with its head upright, by a strong silk girdle.

Pierids owe their colours mainly to a class of chemicals called pterins, a name that just means 'colour from wing'. These are relatively simple chemicals with a structure based in a double pterin ring.

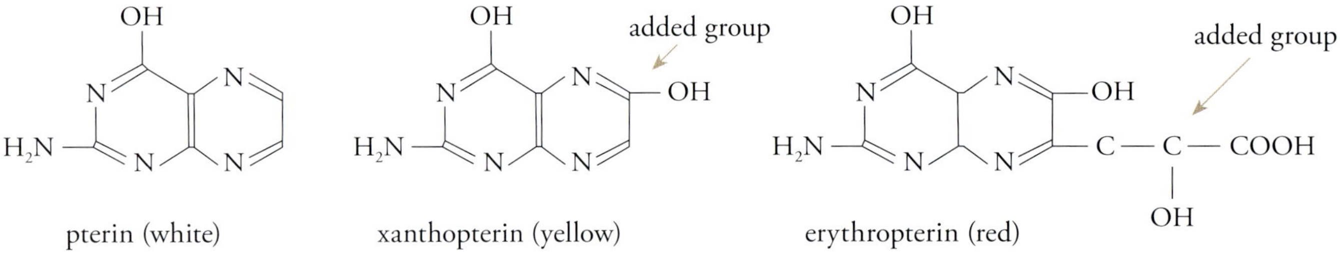

FIGURE 7.2: Pierid wing segments showing simple chemical transitions from white to yellow to red.

Many variations occur on the basic molecule, yielding whites, yellows and reds. The white colour of many pierids comes from a combination of white 'leucopterin' pigments and a physical scattering of light, caused by the fine surface texture of individual scales. This combination gives a particularly brilliant white, seldom found in other butterfly families. Xanthopterin is one of several yellow pigments, and erythropterin is red. Each is derived sequentially from the basic molecule by the addition of just one chemical group. Because of this close chemical relationship between pigments, rare developmental mistakes occur, possibly of genetic origin, in which normally red areas are substituted by yellow. Apart from melanin, which provides the black borders found in most pierids, there is often another type of coloration, invisible to us. On the uppersides of some species, iridescent ultraviolet (UV) is reflected by patches of special multilayered scales, similar to those that produce the vivid blues of the Ulysses Butterfly, but configured to reflect the shorter wavelength UV. These patches are common in species that otherwise are very similar in appearance, habits and habitat preferences. The markings are particularly distinctive in males, and no doubt aid in sex and species recognition of males by females and vice versa during courtship, given that butterflies, unlike humans, can perceive UV light.

There are two subfamilies of the Pieridae in Australia—the yellows (Coliadinae) and the whites and jezabels (Pierinae). Apart from the predominant yellow colour found in most species of the former, differences between the two groups relate to details of the wing venation and skeletal structure and are not obvious to the casual observer.

SUBFAMILY COLIADINAE—
Yellows

The subfamily **Coliadinae**, or yellows, occur worldwide and make up about a quarter of the family Pieridae. In Australia there are just eleven species in two genera. These are *Catopsilia*, the migrants, with four species, and *Eurema*, the grass yellows, with seven species. Both genera, or their near relatives, are very widely distributed throughout the tropical and subtropical regions of the world, where they are very abundant in lowland habitats ranging from rainforest to open grassland. Most Australian species are generally associated with more open habitats, but may frequent rainforest margins.

Many species exhibit strong seasonal variation, with the summer or wet-season form typically paler beneath and darker above, and the autumn/winter or dry-season form darker or more colourful beneath and with less black edging above. This variation, however, is often not clear-cut, and there may be numerous intermediate forms. In the genus *Eurema*, the more strongly marked dry-season forms are normally more easily identified, and tend to be the most frequently encountered forms in the southern parts of their ranges. In Queensland, as one drives north during summer, the lightly marked wet-season forms become progressively more prevalent—concomitantly making identification more difficult.

The eggs of all coliadines are pale, long, spindle-shaped and finely ribbed. They are laid singly on leaves of the host plant, typically legumes of the families Caesalpinaceae, Fabaceae and Mimosaceae. The larvae are cylindrical and green, often with a lateral light-coloured longitudinal line with dark edging. The pupa is smooth and pointed anteriorly and is generally pale green, rarely brownish.

Migration is common, with many species temporarily extending their ranges south or inland as climatic and local weather patterns permit. Even breeding populations are nomadic, and in most species it is rare to recapture experimentally marked individuals. Sometimes large mass migrations occur, especially among the four species of migrants (*Catopsilia* spp.).

Many coliadine species reflect distinctive species-specific patterns of ultraviolet light. This almost certainly aids both sexes to recognise potential mates of their own species, and females may use the intensity of the reflectance by males as a gauge of the youthfulness and vigour of potential mates.

Common Grass Yellow
(*Eurema hecabe*)

Migrants

pomona

pyranthe

scylla

gorgophone

Members of the genus *Catopsilia* are known as migrants because of their great powers of dispersal, and frequent though irregular mass migrations. The genus ranges throughout tropical and subtropical Asia, the Pacific and Africa. Just seven species are known, four of which reach Australia. All are similar in their habits and life histories.

The commonest and best-known species is the **Lemon Migrant**, *Catopsilia pomona* (fw ♂ 33 mm, ♀ 36 mm). It is a brisk and busy flier commonly seen dashing through gardens and open habitats, briefly pausing to feed at flowers. It is generally more common in coastal areas, but occasionally reaches inland areas and Perth. It has two seasonal forms, the dark '*crocale*' form with black antennae, and the '*pomona*' form, with pink antennae, lighter above, but more strongly patterned beneath. It was once thought that this variation was genetic but this has since been shown to be incorrect. The main factors determining the adult form (or 'morph') result from an interaction of day length and temperature acting on the development of late larval stages and early pupae. Females are more influenced by temperature, with warmer conditions producing form *crocale*, and cooler ones, *pomona*. Males, however, are more strongly influenced by day length, with longer day length during development producing form *crocale* and shorter day length producing form *pomona*. In Townsville, an abrupt switch from *crocale* to *pomona* occurred between February and March 1981, but this may take place earlier further south, and the timing from year to year may also be influenced by other factors such as rainfall. Intermediate forms also occur, especially about the time of switching of morphs.

Males and females of different morphs will interbreed freely, although different morphs of opposite sexes rarely encounter each other in nature. *C. pomona* males have a strong brand of sex scales on the upperside of the hindwing, and an overlapping brush in the forewing, used to disseminate pheromones during courtship, as a male hovers over a perched receptive female. Females lay very large numbers of relatively small eggs (1.2 x 0.5 mm). Food plants include species of *Cassia*, especially *C. fistula*, and *Senna*. Up to 150 eggs may be laid in a single day, with a lifetime output of perhaps 700–900 eggs. During the dry season, females may enter a diapause, when they do not develop or lay eggs and do not mate. This period may last for almost five months, and normally occurs in form *pomona*. By contrast, migration occurs more often in form *crocale*, with movements commonly north to south. Up to 5000 per hour, with both morphs represented, have been recorded passing an observation point in southern Queensland in late February.

The widespread **Common Migrant**, *Catopsilia pyranthe* (fw ♂ 33 mm, ♀ 36 mm), also has light and dark forms, with the former more abundant in the dry season. These differences are much less pronounced than in *C. pomona*. The species is abundant, and migratory, but tends to be found more inland and further south than *C. pomona*. Larvae feed on *Cassia brewsteri*, *C. fistula*, *Senna aciphylla*, *S. barclayana*, *S. planitiicola* and other *Senna* species.

The **Orange Migrant**, *Catopsilia scylla* (fw ♂ 33 mm, ♀ 36 mm), and **Yellow Migrant**, *C. gorgophone* (fw ♂ 32 mm, ♀ 35 mm), are both widespread, but less often encountered than the other two species. Both migrate but tend to be found around their food plants, *Senna* species, especially *S. gaudichaudii* and *S. surattensis*. All Australian *Catopsilia* species are widespread in Asia except *C. gorgophone*, which beyond Australia is found only in New Caledonia.

FAMILY PIERIDAE—Whites and Yellows 143

Grass Yellows 1

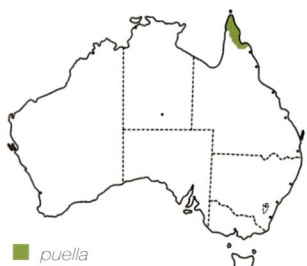
puella

hecabe

alitha

Worldwide, members of the genus *Eurema*, or grass yellows, include 66 tropical and subtropical species in all zoogeographic regions, found in habitats ranging from lowland rainforest to open savannah. They are absent from high mountain areas. There are seven species in Australia, several of which are also widespread in Asia. The species are generally very similar in appearance in both sexes, and all flutter quite slowly, generally close to the ground. Identification is usually possible by examining carefully the breadth and shape of the black margin on the upside of the wings. In dry-season forms, the pattern on the underside may also be distinctive. Size is a useful but not infallible guide, especially as developmental conditions affect size, with cooler temperatures producing larger individuals. The structure of the male genitalia is the final arbiter for difficult cases. The early stages of all species are very similar, with the tiny pupa having a distinctive 'keel'. Despite these similarities, there is a fascinating range of variation in the life-history strategies of the different species, with some utilising just one or two food plants, others feeding on many, some migrating, while others 'tough out' the dry season in a reproductive diapause. Moreover, the pattern of reflected ultraviolet (UV) light, especially in males, is generally unique and therefore diagnostic.

The most distinctive species is the **Broad-margined Grass Yellow**, *Eurema puella* (fw ♂ 20 mm, ♀ 21 mm), which flies in the sun-dappled understorey of rainforests on Cape York Peninsula. Males reflect iridescent UV from a large part of their upside yellow area. Unusually, females are white above, and the white area also reflects UV strongly. The larvae feed on *Archidendron hirsutum* and *Ventilago ecorollata*.

The remaining species all inhabit open woodland and grassland, including gardens. The largest and most often encountered in northern and eastern coastal areas is the **Common Grass Yellow**, *Eurema hecabe* (fw ♂ 20 mm, ♀ 22 mm). The male reflects UV from most of the upside yellow area. Females prefer males with bright UV reflectance. The female also reflects UV from a small basal patch on the forewing, which may assist males to distinguish them from some other species, and certainly allows males to distinguish females from other males. In advanced courtship, males flutter above females, probably wafting a downdraft of sex pheromones from a hard-to-see sex brand on the upside of the forewing. This takes place after the female has landed, presumably having already been impressed by the quality of his upside UV patch, which from below is scarcely visible to her. *E. hecabe* breeds throughout the year in the northern tropics, utilising a wide range of host plants, including species of *Acacia*, *Aeschynomene*, *Albizia*, *Breynia*, *Cassia*, *Indigofera*, *Leucaena*, *Phyllanthus*, *Senna*, *Sesbania* and *Trifolium*. The egg (1.2 x 0.4 mm) is almost as large as that of *Catopsilia pomona*. During good seasons, the species expands its range considerably to the south and may occasionally take part in large southerly migrations. Apart from its large size, *E. hecabe* is separated from all species except the smaller **Scalloped Grass Yellow**, *E. alitha* (fw ♂ 18 mm, ♀ 19 mm), by the indentation in the black margin of the forewing upside. Moreover, the winter or dry-season form has strong brown markings underneath, especially on the forewing, also found to a lesser degree in *E. alitha*, whereas the wet-season form is only slightly marked in both species. In wet- and dry-season forms of both sexes, the black margin of the wings is narrower in *E. hecabe* than in *E. alitha*, especially on the hindwing, and in *E. alitha* the indentation is normally more pronounced. *E. alitha* is a local species, only known to feed on *Glycine tabacina*. UV reflectance has not been studied in *E. alitha*.

FAMILY PIERIDAE—Whites and Yellows

Grass Yellows 2

smilax

brigitta

herla

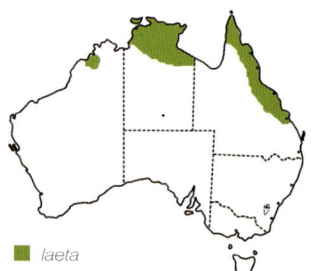

laeta

The remaining four grass yellow species are all found in open woodland and grassland. None has the scalloped indentation in the black margin of the forewing found in *Eurema hecabe* and *E. alitha*, and the margins are typically narrower. Unlike the wet-season forms of *E. hecabe* and *E. alitha*, there is little difference in the breadth of the black margins in males and females. All have a wet-season or summer form in which the underside is almost pure unmarked yellow, and a dry-season or winter form with distinctive underside markings. The precise shape and extent of the upperside black margins provide identification for wet- and dry-season forms, but dry-season forms can usually be more readily recognised by their underside. The ultraviolet (UV) reflectance patterns of males are very different in each species and probably aid in species recognition during courtship.

The most widespread species is the **Small Grass Yellow**, *Eurema smilax* (fw ♂ 16 mm, ♀ 17 mm), which extends over most of continental Australia and also reaches Lord Howe Island. It is very common, particularly in drier inland areas, and is noticeably smaller than other species, with narrower wings. The underside of the wet-season form, especially females, may be mottled with patches of dark brown, but always less strongly marked than *E. hecabe*. The male is uniquely marked with two UV patches, and also has a small elongate sex brand at the base of the underside of the forewing, visible against strong light. *E. smilax* expands its range during favourable seasons, southward in spring and autumn, and northward in autumn/winter after the tropical wet season. In the north, it breeds throughout the year, slowing during dry periods. Larvae feed on a wide range of hosts, including *Cassia fistula*, *Neptunia gracilis*, *N. monosperma*, *Senna acclinis*, *S. auriculata*, *S. coriaceae*, *S. coronilloides*, *S. nemophila*, *S. petiolaris* and *S. retusa*.

The **No-brand Grass Yellow**, *Eurema brigitta* (fw ♂ 20 mm, ♀ 22 mm), is also very common and widespread in coastal areas. It is unusual in that neither males nor females reflect UV at all, nor does the male have a visible sex brand or obvious androconial scent scales scattered over the wing. Sexual communication in this species seems strangely founded on negatives (cf. Common Grass Yellow, p. 144). Nevertheless, it breeds prolifically throughout the year in the Queensland wet tropics region and near Darwin, and expands its range considerably in the wet season or summer. Although it is an ecological opportunist, taking advantage of local conditions and ever moving to favourable areas, it is known to feed on just two plant species, *Chamaecrista nomame* and *Neptunia dimorphantha*.

Macleay's Grass Yellow, *Eurema herla* (fw ♂ 18 mm, ♀ 19 mm), is found only in Australia, where it is widespread across the north and east. The black margin on the upperside is almost restricted to the apex of the forewing. The hindwing underside of the dry-season form is a distinctive ochraceous pink with paired, curved, darker lines. The male has a small basal patch of UV-reflecting scales on the forewing. It also has overlapping basal sex brands on the underside of the forewing and the upperside of the hindwing. *E. herla* is a common and widespread species, but adults do not migrate. During the dry season, or winter, females may enter reproductive diapause when they do not mate and their ovaries cease to produce eggs. During this phase, which may last

up to six months, they may feed and even build up fat reserves. The cue to enter this state is believed to be shortening day length, as the event occurs at about the same time each year. In the spring, or wet season in the north, they mate and begin laying eggs. Larvae feed on one species of *Chamaecrista*.

The **Lined Grass Yellow**, *Eurema laeta* (fw ♂ 18 mm, ♀ 19 mm), is widespread in the north and in tropical Asia. The hindwing underside of the dry-season form is buff, with paired, straight, darker lines. The male reflects UV from most of the upperside yellow layer. It also has overlapping basal sex brands on the underside of the forewing and the upperside of the hindwing. *E. laeta* is common and widespread in the tropics. It is not migratory, but enters long periods of reproductive diapause (up to six months), when adults congregate in moist gullies. This behaviour appears to be mediated by rainfall patterns, with activity beginning soon after substantial rain. Larvae feed on one species of *Chamaecrista*.

SUBFAMILY PIERINAE—
Whites and Jezabels

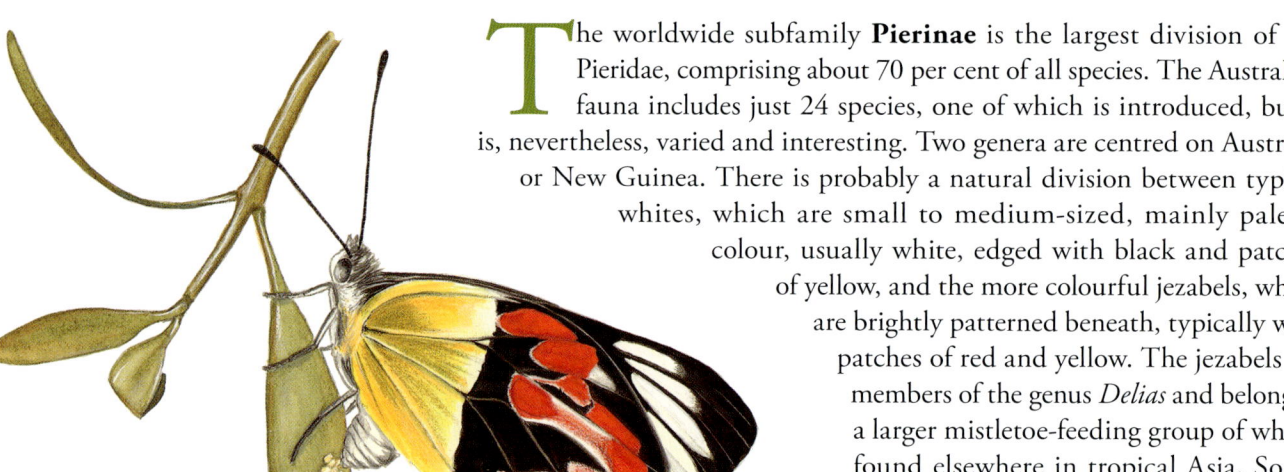

Northern Jezabel
(*Delias argenthona*)

The worldwide subfamily **Pierinae** is the largest division of the Pieridae, comprising about 70 per cent of all species. The Australian fauna includes just 24 species, one of which is introduced, but it is, nevertheless, varied and interesting. Two genera are centred on Australia or New Guinea. There is probably a natural division between typical whites, which are small to medium-sized, mainly pale in colour, usually white, edged with black and patches of yellow, and the more colourful jezabels, which are brightly patterned beneath, typically with patches of red and yellow. The jezabels are members of the genus *Delias* and belong to a larger mistletoe-feeding group of whites found elsewhere in tropical Asia, South America and Africa.

The eggs of pierines are elongate, but less so than in coliadines, and are strongly ribbed with a circlet of fine beading around the constricted top, often suggesting a tiny scent bottle. The colour ranges from white, or speckled white, to deep orange. Eggs may be laid singly or in large clusters. The larvae are generally cylindrical and uniformly coloured, either green or shades of brown, sometimes with regular yellow spotting. Jezabel larvae have variably developed long white hairs. The larvae of species which cluster their eggs are normally gregarious, especially in early instars. The pupa varies greatly in colour, ranging from bright yellow to black, brown or shades of green. It normally bears at least some spines. The larvae of typical whites feed on Capers (Capparaceae) or, in the case of the Cabbage White, Brassicaceae. Those of jezabels feed mainly on species of mistletoe (Loranthaceae and Viscaceae).

Jezabels are almost certainly unpalatable or even poisonous to vertebrate predators and are probably mimicked by a palatable nymphalid, the White Nymph (*Mynes geoffroyi*). In New Guinea, Caper-feeding *Cepora* species also appear to mimic jezabels. The introduced European Cabbage White is a serious pest, well known to gardeners and horticulturalists.

Pierines inhabit a wide variety of habitats, ranging from rainforest to semi-desert. Some species of jezabels have a temperate or montane distribution or are active in winter. Most fly with a definite flutter within a few metres of the ground and are very conspicuous. A few tropical species, especially albatrosses, are quite swift in flight. Generally, the more acute and produced the forewing tip, the faster a species flies.

Cabbage White

The **Cabbage White**, *Pieris rapae* (fw ♂ 25 mm, ♀ 26 mm), was introduced from Europe in the early twentieth century and now occupies most major centres of human population except Darwin. In the tropics it is restricted to higher country, especially the Atherton Tableland of north Queensland, where it became established in the late 1960s. It has a busy erratic flight, usually keeping near the ground. Adults are nomadic, and often appear in native habitats, but their food plants are all imported species. It is a serious horticultural pest, defoliating crops of *Brassica* (cabbages and relatives) especially, but also causing minor damage to Peppercress, Hoary Cress, *Nasturtium* and various other plants. Courtship and mating have been well studied overseas but are still not fully understood. The uppersides of the wing reflect ultraviolet (UV) broadly, and females show a preference for males reflecting an optimum intensity of UV light, neither too dull nor too bright. Androconia—specialised scent scales—are scattered over the uppersides of the wings and may release pheromones during courtship. Rather sadly, perhaps, *P. rapae* is the butterfly best known to many Australians, particularly in the south. However, it is a good insect for a young naturalist to study. It is accessible, easily observed, and females dramatically show the typical pierid rejection display when courted by unwanted males. For those wishing to learn about a butterfly's internal anatomy, we suggest without compunction this unloved insect as a good species on which to begin investigation.

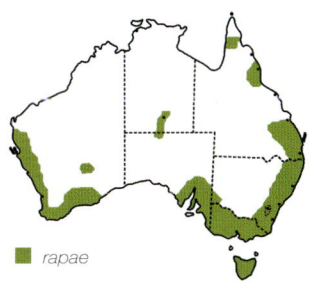

rapae

♀ displaying rejection behaviour

cabbage leaf shredded by larvae

FAMILY PIERIDAE—Whites and Yellows

Pearl Whites

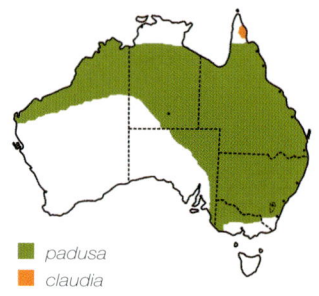
- padusa
- claudia

- parthia

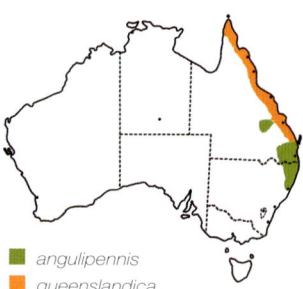
- angulipennis
- queenslandica

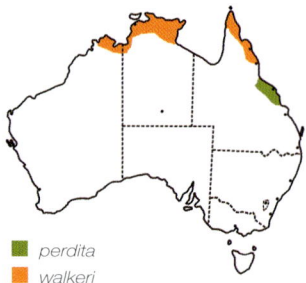
- perdita
- walkeri

The pearl whites include seven species in the genus *Elodina*. All are small and lightly built. Most inhabit moist forested areas, especially rainforest edges and gallery forest along creeks, and are restricted to the east or to the northern tropics, although two species extend more widely into the drier, open parts of the continent. All are busy fliers, generally more vigorous and swifter than the similar-sized grass yellows. Some forest species tend to fly quite high, 2–10 m above the ground, but in open country they fly lower. The life history of all species is similar. The egg is a typical 'scent bottle' form, white when first laid, developing pink mottling as it matures. It is placed singly on the underside of leaves of the food plant, one of several *Capparis* species, especially *C. canescens* and *C. sepiaria*. In *E. angulipennis*, eggs are generally laid on very old leaves, and the young larva must find its way to fresh growth before it can begin feeding. Larvae have a forked tail, virtually unique among Pieridae. All are strikingly cryptic (well-camouflaged), fitting themselves neatly into the curve of the feeding edge of their leaf. The life cycle is typically quite brief, developing from egg to adult in 30–35 days in summer. Adults often exhibit seasonal variation, dry-season forms being more strongly marked on the undersides of the hindwing.

The species can be very difficult to separate. Males and females are very alike, and species vary in wing shape, the extent and shape of the black area at the forewing apex, and the markings on the underside of the forewing, especially near the apex. Females are slightly larger than males. In some cases the best way of identifying a specimen is to consider its locality, but added confirmation may be reached in male specimens by examination of the uncus. This organ is revealed by gently pinching the tip of the abdomen, where it appears as a central, terminal prong. It is best viewed from above with a strong hand lens or dissecting microscope. Important differences are found, especially in the shape of the small projections at the base of this appendage. The species pairs *angulipennis–queenslandica* and *walkeri–claudia*, which overlap in parts of their ranges, can be reliably separated only by this method.

The most widespread species, the **Narrow-winged Pearl White**, *Elodina padusa* (fw ♂ 23 mm), occurs as a migrant over much of the continent. Its wings are slightly elongated, and it is quite swift in flight. It ranges from rainforest margins to arid areas. The pupa is slightly more elongated than in other species.

The **Chalky Pearl White**, *Elodina parthia* (fw ♂ 22 mm), is the most distinctive member of the genus. The upperside is a pale creamy white, rather than the glistening pearly white of other species, and on the underside the hindwing is relatively strongly marked with light-brown striations. It is easily recognised on the wing and prefers open forests or gardens in drier areas, especially west of the Dividing Range. It generally flies low and steadily, pausing occasionally to feed at flowers.

The **Southern Pearl White**, *Elodina angulipennis* (fw ♂ 23 mm), and the **Glistening Pearl White**, *E. queenslandica* (fw ♂ 23 mm), are externally almost identical, although the forewing underside of *E. angulipennis* is more strongly suffused with yellow at its base. Where the ranges of the two species overlap near Hervey Bay, Queensland, it may be necessary to examine the male uncus to identify a specimen with certainty. Both species differ from *E. padusa* by the different shape and pattern of the forewings, especially apparent on the underside. They frequent rainforest and vine forest and flutter rapidly, often racing high into the subcanopy.

The similar **Northern Pearl White**, *Elodina walkeri* (fw ♂ 23 mm), the **Delicate Pearl White**, *E. perdita* (fw ♂ 20 mm), and the **Cape York Pearl White**, *E. claudia* (fw ♂ 20 mm), are tropical species, with a smooth concave inner margin to the apical black patch on the forewing (toothed in other species), and little or no dark marking on the underside of the forewing. Differences in the male uncus seen from above separate them as species. *E. perdita* occurs only in coastal dune and swamp forest between Ingham and Mackay, outside the range of the other two species. *E. walkeri* occurs north of Cairns in rainforest and monsoon forest, and may overlap with *E. claudia* at Iron Range. *E. claudia* and *E. walkeri* may be separated by slight differences in the black marking on the forewing upperside, and in females of *E. claudia* the underside of the hindwing is creamy yellow. All three species are generally slightly smaller and fly more slowly and lower than *E. queenslandica*, the other rainforest species of pearl white with which they may coexist.

FAMILY PIERIDAE—Whites and Yellows

Albatrosses and Gulls

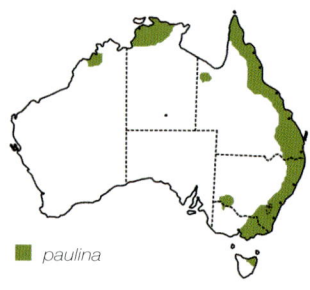
■ paulina

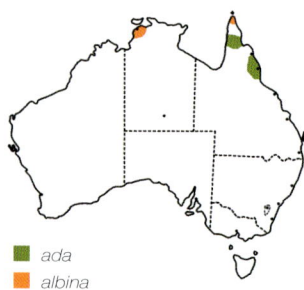
■ ada
■ albina

■ melania

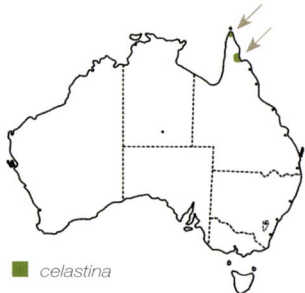
■ celastina

■ perimale

Albatrosses (*Appias* spp.) and gulls (*Cepora* spp.) are medium-sized, swift-flying whites of the Old World tropics. In Australia there are five species of *Appias* and one *Cepora*. Typically they are white above, usually with a black margin (broader in the female), and the underside of the hindwing is yellow with a variably developed black or brown marginal band. As a rule of thumb, the swiftest-flying species are those with the most acute and sharply curved forewings. Many are migratory, or at least vagrants, which means that, although very common, they are not often observed to breed. The males of *Appias* have dark hair-pencils (tufts of androconial hairs) at the tip of the abdomen, which are surely used in courtship, but little is known of this behaviour. Females of *Cepora* bear specialised scales on the abdomen which may also have a role in sexual communication. Overseas, many are evidently mimics of unpalatable, slow-flying, mistletoe-feeding genera (especially *Delias*), and they may modify their normally rapid flight to copy that of the noxious model.

The **Common Albatross**, *Appias paulina* (fw ♂ 33 mm, ♀ 34 mm), is widespread in eastern and northern Australia, and is at times very abundant. It is migratory, and sometimes reaches Tasmania. The male bears a superficial resemblance to the Cabbage White, but is larger and faster-flying. The species is most commonly found at rainforest margins but often occurs in vine forests and coastal gardens. Both sexes, but especially the females, perch frequently on leaves with the wings partly open. For such a common insect, the life history is very poorly known. The pupa illustrated is close to emergence and the colours of the female wing can be clearly seen. Earlier in its development it was grey-green or pinkish white in colour. The known larval host plants are *Capparis canescens* and *Drypetes deplanchei*.

The **White Albatross**, *Appias albina* (fw ♂ 32 mm, ♀ 33 mm), is a widespread Asian species confined in Australia to Cape York and the Northern Territory, including Darwin. Males are obvious when flying by virtue of their pure white colour and small size.

The **Orange Albatross**, *Appias ada* (fw ♂ 35 mm, ♀ 36 mm), is a tropical rainforest species generally restricted to Cape York, where it may be common. The female is very like the illustrated male, but a little darker on both upper- and undersides. Occasionally stragglers may reach the Cairns area, but it is not known to breed there. The larvae feed on *Crateva religiosa*. The early stages are very similar to those of *A. paulina*.

The **Grey Albatross**, *Appias melania* (fw ♂ 36 mm, ♀ 36 mm), is a locally common inhabitant of rainforest in the wet tropics region of north Queensland, especially in the mountains. It flies high and swiftly, and is most commonly seen feeding at lantana at the edge of rainforest, or mud-puddling. While feeding, it will often perch with wings quivering, never entirely at rest. There is a possible mimetic resemblance between this species and *Delias nysa*, a species believed to be unpalatable to birds, but the two species appear very different in flight. However, when perched, it may derive some protection from the resemblance. The larvae feed on *Drypetes* species.

A fifth albatross species (not illustrated), the **Blue Albatross**, *Appias celastina* (fw ♂ 36 mm, ♀ 36 mm), occurs rarely at Cape York.

The **Australian Gull**, *Cepora perimale* (fw ♂ 27 mm, ♀ 28 mm), is widespread and common in the east and north. It is common in coastal gardens and forest and rainforest margins, and extends well inland into drier areas. The sexes are similar, and easily distinguished from the larger female *A. paulina* by the more extensive pale spotting

in the dark marginal areas. A dry-season form, in which the underside of the hindwing is entirely brown, also occurs. The adults fly relatively rapidly, but are less aerobatic than the albatrosses. Early stages are as illustrated. The larvae feed on species of *Capparis*.

FAMILY PIERIDAE—Whites and Yellows

Caper White and Psyche

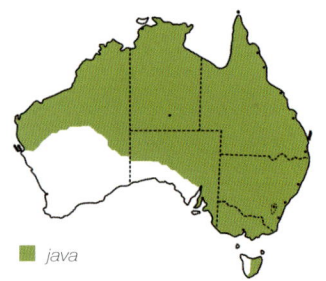
java

nina

The **Caper White**, *Belenois java* (fw ♂ 33 mm, ♀ 34 mm), belongs to a genus of open-country species common in the drier parts of tropical Asia and Africa. *B. java* is widespread within Australia, present over most of the continent and occasionally reaches Tasmania. Elsewhere it occurs in South-East Asia and the Pacific. Two subspecies are recognised; *B. java teutonia* is the normal Australian form, illustrated here. *B. java peristhene* is a Pacific form, found on New Caledonia and other islands. The latter occasionally arrives on our eastern shore as a rare transoceanic migrant. It differs from *B. java teutonia*, as the underside of the hindwing is entirely dark in the centre with a bright row of yellow spots around the margin. *B. java teutonia* varies a good deal in the extent of dark coloration, with dark and light forms recognised. This is especially evident on the upperside in females. The basis of this variation is not understood. It has been suggested they represent seasonal forms, dependent on rainfall levels during development but, as both forms may be present in the same cohort, this idea is not convincing. Another suggestion is that the differences are chemically induced, resulting from larvae feeding on different species of host plants.

B. java generally breeds west of the Great Dividing Range. Common food plants include *Capparis canescens* in the east and *C. mitchellii* in arid regions. *Apophyllum anomalum* is used in western New South Wales. Other hosts include *C. arborea*, *C. lasiantha*, *C. sepiaria*, *C. spinosa* and *C. umbonata*.

migrating *B. java*

corpses among sea wrack

They often infest trees and shrubs in enormous numbers, defoliating them completely. The eggs are laid in loose clusters, with sometimes more than a hundred eggs in a group. Larvae feed gregariously and pupation frequently takes place en masse on the skeletal remains of the host plant. Males flutter around groups of pupae and mate with females soon after they have emerged. Although courtship of older females is often observed, it rarely results in mating and it is likely that most females mate just once, soon after emergence. *B. java* is strongly migratory. During migration they fly steadily 1–3 m above the ground, sometimes descending in huge numbers on garden flowers. The patterns of migration across the entire continent are not understood, and the underlying basis of the behaviour is unclear. In most years, however, they appear in October–November flying north-east or south-east along a wide stretch of the eastern coast reaching from Townsville to Sydney. They are the harbingers of summer. Some years they appear in modest numbers, but in others they fly in many thousands for several weeks. Hundreds are killed by cars. When they reach the coast, many fly out to sea, and for days after a migration their bodies are washed up on the beach where they lie along the high-tide mark, sometimes in large numbers.

The **Psyche**, *Leptosia nina* (fw ♂ 18 mm, ♀ 20 mm), is widespread in tropical Asia. Other species of the genus occur in Africa. In Australia it is known only from isolated pockets of vine forest in the Kimberley region, especially along watercourses. It flies very weakly, low to the ground, preferring shade. The life history is not recorded from Australia but in Malaysia the egg is blue and the larvae and pupae are very like those of *Eurema hecabe*. The food plants are species of *Capparis*.

Southern Jezabels

The genus *Delias* includes more than 160 species in the Indo-Australian region, over half of which occur in the high mountains of New Guinea. It is the largest of all butterfly genera. Eight species are found in Australia. Most members of the genus prefer cooler conditions, either by remaining in temperate areas, such as the two species illustrated here, or flying at altitude and/or in winter. This habitat preference may indicate evolution in temperate habitats in what is now Antarctica, on the supercontinent of Gondwana, around 60 million years ago. All feed on mistletoes or close relatives, and are almost certainly unpalatable to vertebrate predators. *Delias* males lack discrete sex brands and probably release pheromones from specialised androconia scattered over the uppersides of the wings.

The **Imperial White**, *Delias harpalyce* (fw ♂ 39 mm, ♀ 42 mm), occurs in open eucalypt forest, mainly along the Great Dividing Range south of Warwick in southern Queensland. It is sometimes common in Canberra suburbs. The brilliant underside coloration of red and yellow on black is almost the same in both sexes. Very rarely, the red band on the female hindwing is replaced by yellow. Adults typically fly quite high, above 3 m, fluttering and sailing. In flight, the brilliant underside generally presents as black and the contrasting white upperside of the male is very obvious. The females are very dark. Males often congregate on hilltops. The eggs are laid in large clusters (up to a hundred) on the leaves of their mistletoe food plants. Common food plants include *Amyema miquelii*, *A. pendula* and *Muellerina eucalyptoides*. Other hosts include *A. congener*, *A. preissii* and *A. quandang*. The larvae feed gregariously, often in large groups of over 50 individuals. Before pupation, they spin a large silken web through the leaves and branches of the host plant and the shining black pupae are attached to this. Freshly emerged adults cling to the web. Empty pupal cases are pale yellowish brown. *D. harpalyce* has a strong preference for cool sunny conditions and during hot weather adults may aggregate in cool humid gullies. Unusually hot weather also affects development of early stages and hot seasons are typically followed by low adult population numbers.

The **Wood White**, *Delias aganippe* (fw ♂ 37 mm, ♀ 39 mm), is widespread in drier woodland habitats in southern and western Australia. The male and female undersides are very similar, and the female upperside is only slightly darker than the male. The forewings are exceptionally long and narrow, hence flight is rather rapid, with vigorous wing beats interspersed with sailing, generally 2–4 m above the ground. Males hilltop, sometimes flying tightly in large swirling aggregations of twenty or more, apparently centred around receptive females. They migrate sporadically, although seldom in huge numbers, and sometimes reach the tropical coast as far north as Townsville. Eggs are laid in clusters of up to about 70 on a variety of host plants, including several species of *Amyema*, but also the non-mistletoes, *Exocarpos* (Native Cherry) and *Santalum* species. Larvae feed gregariously and the pupae, which resemble bird droppings, may be isolated, far from the food plant, or in small groups.

FAMILY PIERIDAE—Whites and Yellows 157

Rainforest Jezabels

The three species of *Delias* illustrated here are mainly restricted to tropical and subtropical rainforest.

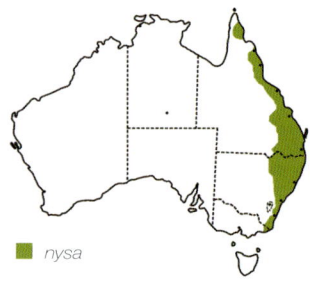
nysa

The **Nysa Jezabel**, *Delias nysa* (fw ♂ 29 mm, ♀ 29 mm), is the smallest member of the genus in Australia. In Queensland it is common in the mountains, principally at rainforest edges, but towards the south it also occurs in drier inland vine thickets. It sometimes occurs on the coast near Brisbane in late autumn, when the weather is cooler. In southern New South Wales it flies in coastal rainforest. *D. nysa* flies high, seldom below 3 m, with a strong steady flutter. It can be mistaken for a very faded *D. nigrina*, and in flight it generates a definite strobe-like flash pattern of contrasting brown and white. Eggs are laid in small clusters of 15–20 on the food plants, *Korthalsella* species. Larvae feed gregariously, at least while young. The variegated olive-green pupae are found singly, some distance from the food plant.

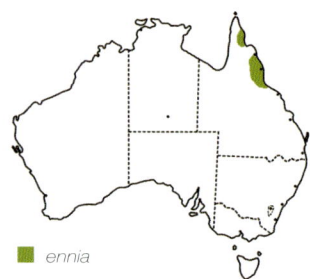
ennia

The **Yellow-banded Jezabel**, *Delias ennia nigidius* (fw ♂ 31 mm, ♀ 32 mm), is locally common in rainforest and closed gallery forest in the Queensland wet tropics region. It is commoner in the cooler months of the year. On the Atherton Tableland it is often seen at forest margins, but in the lowlands it flies in the forest understorey, normally 3–6 m above the ground, with a fairly brisk, regular flutter. Sometimes it perches on low vegetation, particularly in the heat of the day. Eggs are laid in small neat rows on leaves of the mistletoe *Notothixos leiophyllus*. Larvae feed gregariously and, when disturbed, drop from the leaf on a silken thread, climbing back up when danger is past. There are just four instars. Pupating larvae spin a loose web of silk over the host plant, and pupae may form in this web or on the vegetation or litter beneath, reached by lowering themselves on silk threads. The pupa is bright yellow. Another subspecies, *D. ennia tindalii*, occurs in rainforest at Iron Range on Cape York Peninsula. It is very different from *D. ennia nigidius* in its underside coloration, with the base of the hindwing mainly yellow and the brown band on the female much narrower. Many other races of *D. ennia* are known from New Guinea and West Papua, and a case could be made for treating many of these as separate species, thus recognising the two Australian forms as *D. nigidius* and *D. tindalii*.

aruna

The **Orange Jezabel**, *Delias aruna* (fw ♂ 40 mm, fw ♀ 41 mm), is restricted to rainforest on Cape York Peninsula. During the heat of the day the adults fly in the forest understorey with a steady flutter, appearing as a vivid series of bright orange flashes, especially in the male. Early or late in the day, they may fly higher in bright sunlight in the forest subcanopy. The larval food plant is *Dendrophthoe glabrescens*. It has long been stated in the literature that eggs are laid in clusters of up to 300, but this is not consistent with what is known about the reproductive physiology of *Delias*, and it is likely this number included the combined clutches of several females. Other reports of egg clusters of twenty seem entirely credible. The behaviour of larvae is similar to that of *D. ennia*, but in New Guinea communal pupation within a web has been reported. The pupa is bright orange with black markings.

FAMILY PIERIDAE—Whites and Yellows

Jezabels 3

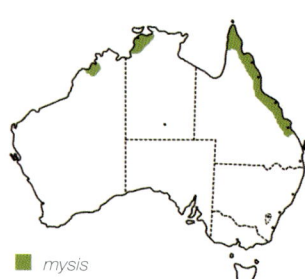

argenthona

mysis

Two mainly tropical species of *Delias* are predominantly pale with red and yellow markings on the underside.

The **Northern Jezabel**, *Delias argenthona* (fw ♂ 36 mm, ♀ 37 mm), is widespread in the east and the north. It inhabits a wide range of open forest, particularly favouring coastal paperbark woodland, mainly in the tropics and subtropics. It often occurs together with *D. nigrina* in southern Queensland. In this region it is most common in spring and autumn, and is almost confined to low-lying country. It may be very abundant. In the tropics it is found mainly in the mountains and in winter, generally in open woodland.

D. argenthona typically flies 2–6 m above the ground with a brisk flutter, sometimes engaging in rapid aerobatic movements, sometimes sailing high with wings outspread so an observer below can plainly see the gaudy underside pattern as the light shines through the wings from above. Both sexes are very fond of *Melaleuca* blossoms. Males spend much time systematically investigating vegetation as they search for young females with which to mate. Females generally mate just once in their lifetime. High-speed chases and persistent hovering courtship by males around flying or settled older females are common but seldom result in mating. Both sexes are short-lived, with a maximum lifespan of about sixteen days in warmer weather, and twenty days in winter. Females are slightly darker than males and more creamily coloured above, but they can often be recognised by their slow deliberate flutter around mistletoes as they search for sites to lay their eggs.

Where they overlap in time and space, *D. argenthona* and *D. nigrina* may come into direct competition for food. In the presence of the other species, both may switch from the most preferred shared food plant, *Dendrophthoe vitellina*, to less preferred plants not used by the other species. Eggs, touching at the bases, are laid in batches of 15–35 in disordered rows on young leaves of the food plant. Larvae feed gregariously, but may become solitary in later instars if mortality is high. Pupae mostly form alone, well removed from the host plant but, at high densities, may occur in small groups. Many mistletoes are utilised as host plants, including species of *Amyema*, *Dendrophthoe*, *Decaisnina signata*, *Diplatia furcata* and *Muellerina celastroides*, as well as the non-mistletoe *Santalum lanceolatum*. In mild winters in southern Queensland, breeding may continue through the year, with winter generations darker than earlier ones. Sometimes extremely dark females occur, which, in flight, seem almost to be another species.

The **Union Jack**, *Delias mysis* (fw ♂ 35 mm, ♀ 36 mm), is common on the coast and in the mountains of north Queensland, and is represented by a slightly different race around Darwin. Its habits are very similar to those of *D. argenthona*, but it has more rounded wings, hence a more fluttery flight. It is common in rainforest as well as gallery forest and coastal *Melaleuca* or *Casuarina* woodland, where it sometimes breeds right beside the ocean. On the coast it is more abundant in winter, but in the mountains it is seen mainly in the warmer months. As with all *Delias* species, the male hovers below the female during courtship, probably releasing sexual pheromones from the specialised androconial scales scattered over the upper sides of the wings. If she does not signal refusal, he will settle beside her and copulate. The life history is very like that of *D. argenthona*, except that egg clusters are more loosely arranged. At least one female specimen is known in which the normal red band on the hindwing underside has been replaced by yellow.

argenthona ♀
argenthona chase 
mysis ♀ 
mysis ♂  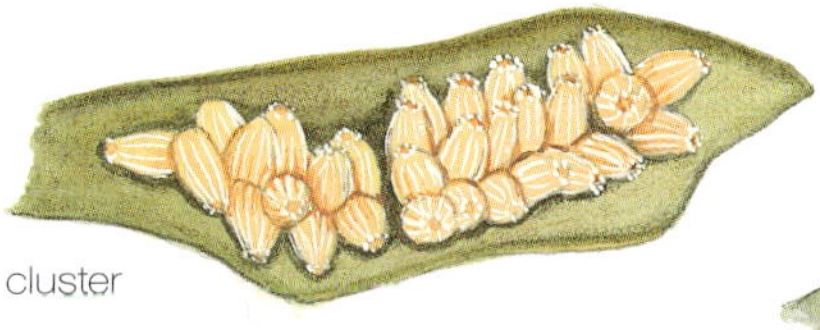
mysis ♀
egg cluster
argenthona
5th instar larva
gregarious pupae
argenthona ♀ exceptionally dark specimen collected mid-winter
mysis ♀ aberration: underside red band replaced by yellow

FAMILY PIERIDAE—Whites and Yellows

Common Jezabel

The **Common Jezabel**, *Delias nigrina* (fw ♂ 34 mm, ♀ 35 mm), is found along the east coast in upland rainforest and coastal woodland. It is a cold-loving species, and in north Queensland it is confined to the mountains, flying mainly in winter. In south Queensland it flies in the mountains in summer and on the coast in autumn and winter. During winter the lifespan extends to 4–6 weeks, almost twice that of warmer months, and females are more likely to mate twice. Further south, it is seen at progressively lower altitudes during warmer months. Males, especially, are striking to see in flight: they progress in a steady flutter of their rounded wings, with a striking stroboscopic flash pattern of intense black and white. Females, grey above, stand out less, but fly in the same manner. Flight is normally quite high, 3–7 m above the ground, depending on the habitat. Birds are known to find *D. nigrina* inedible. It is evidently mimicked by the nymphalid *Mynes geoffroyi*. Although this species does not closely replicate the *D. nigrina* underside pattern, the general flash pattern visible to a vertebrate predator is the same, especially as *M. geoffroyi* also adopts *D. nigrina*'s flight style.

D. nigrina is one of the few butterflies which remains active in light rain. In places, it may be very abundant and compete for food with *D. argenthona*, as described in the account of that species. Eggs are laid on leaves of the mistletoe host in open clusters of 10–90. Larvae are gregarious, with small yellow spots at the base of each hair. The yellow pupa has long spines and is found mostly singly, some distance from the host plant. Numerous hosts are recorded, including species of *Amyema*, *Dendrophthoe* and *Muellerina*.

gregarious larvae

nigrina

egg cluster

♂ courting; ♀ displaying refusal behaviour

FAMILY NYMPHALIDAE
Nymphs and Their Allies

8

A Common Brown fluttering around Cotoneaster flowers in a Canberra suburb, an energetic Wanderer searching for milkweeds in an overgrown Brisbane garden, or delicate Painted Ladies patrolling a Sydney herbaceous border: these are all nymphalids, which include some of the best-known and most familiar of all our butterflies.

The **Nymphalidae** is a family of small to moderately large butterflies with more than 6000 species worldwide. At present it is regarded as the largest butterfly family, but it is likely to be surpassed by the Lycaenidae, as that family becomes better known. In Australia there are 81 species of nymphalids. The family is extremely diverse, with many distinct subfamilies. They are called 'brush-footed butterflies' because the one great unifying feature of all adult nymphalids is the reduction of the forelegs to simplified stumps, which are folded close to the body when the insect is perched or walking. The reason for this reduction is not well understood but females often use their tiny forelegs to drum vigorously on the surface of a leaf before ovipositing, suggesting they have a sensory function. Nymphalids are also distinguished from all other butterflies by the fact that the pupa virtually always hangs by its rear hooks from a pad of silk without any supporting silken girdle or other structure. Beyond these features, they show great diversity in size, colour and pattern. Common names have been given to whole subfamilies—the tigers and crows (Danainae), nymphs (Nymphalinae), the browns (Satyrinae), the glasswings (Acraeinae) and so forth. Worldwide, there are seventeen subfamilies (some authorities recognise fewer) although only twelve occur in Australia.

The Nymphalidae provide an excellent example of the way in which classifications have changed in recent years. Many of the currently recognised subfamilies have at one time or another been designated as families. Originally, of course, the ways in which species were grouped together was for descriptive convenience, but as we came to understand more about evolution, so goals changed and classifications were developed which, it was supposed, reflected the way groups had evolved.

The development of molecular techniques coupled with the powerful

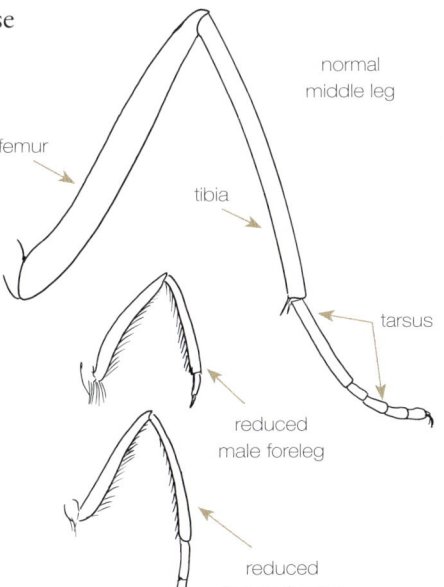

Common Eggfly
(*Hypolimnas bolina*)

FIGURE 8.1: Legs of the Common Eggfly (*Hypolimnas bolina*) showing a normal leg, with divisions, and the reduced forelegs of the male and female.

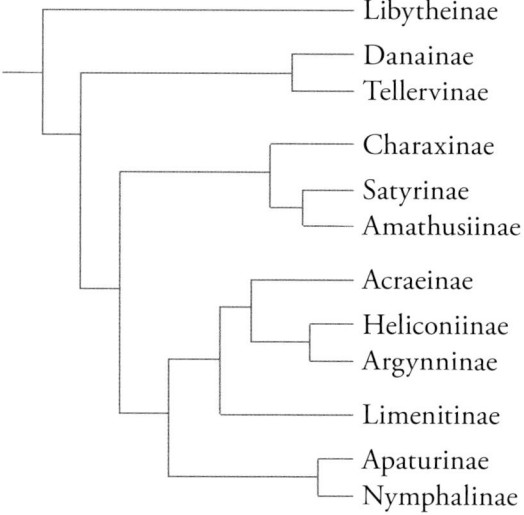

FIGURE 8.2: An evolutionary tree of Australian nymphalid subfamilies based on both morphological and molecular analysis.

statistical tools made available by modern computers has brought more certainty to the process. Building a tree of descent (a 'phylogeny') of a group of butterflies based on the successive changes that have occurred in their DNA should produce a more reliable estimate of what is related to what and how far in the past some common ancestral species might have occurred. It remains, though, a matter of opinion and judgement as to just what the scientist is going to call a 'family', a 'subfamily', a 'genus' and so on.

Only 26 of the 81 Australian brushfoot species are restricted to the continent. These endemics are all browns—the subfamily Satyrinae—and feed as larvae exclusively on monocotyledons, mainly grasses and sedges. Like many Australian endemics, these species are concentrated in the south-eastern corner of the country (with three restricted to Tasmania). The other groups of Australian nymphalids are most diverse in the tropics and have broader relationships with New Guinea and Asia. At least two species represent groups that reach their peaks of diversity in Africa. Few Australian nymphalids are currently of conservation concern, although the Australian Fritillary is a notable exception. Many of the breeding grounds of this beautiful subtropical species have been destroyed, usually accidentally for coastal development or, in at least one infamous case, deliberately. Some other local subspecies, especially certain browns, which occur as small isolated populations, are also potentially vulnerable to unintentional destruction.

With such a diverse family as the nymphalids, it is difficult to generalise about food plants. However, apart from the browns, already mentioned, and the related owls, which feed on palms, nymphalids feed on dicotyledons. In several cases, whole subfamilies have evolved in close concert with rather specialised food plants. The milkweed and hamadryad butterflies have co-evolved with the poisonous plant families Apocynaceae and Asclepiadaceae. In a similar fashion, both the Heliconiinae (the passionflower butterflies) and the Acraeinae (glasswings) have close relationships with plants in the passionflower family, Passifloraceae. On the other hand, in subfamilies such as Nymphalinae and Limenitinae, the larvae may feed on any one of a large range of flowering plant families. Because of these widely differing food preferences, some members of the family are unpalatable to birds and other predators, whereas other members are palatable. Among the palatable species are several impressive mimics, such as the female Danaid Eggfly (*Hypolimnas misippus*), which closely resembles the unpalatable Lesser Wanderer (*Danaus petilia*) in both flight and colour pattern. Such resemblances can cause confusion when it comes to identifying species, particularly when seen in flight.

SUBFAMILY DANAINAE—
Tigers and Crows

The subfamily **Danainae** contains some of the most easily observed of our butterflies. With striking wing markings and a low, leisurely flight, most species can be recognised on the wing, even from the briefest glimpse. Only in the northern tropics do some of the crow species present difficulties in identification, and it may at first be necessary to photograph or capture a specimen to be sure of its identity.

The Australian fauna includes fourteen species and three very distinctive subspecies. About half are found only in the most remote locations in the far north. There are two main groups, the crows (genus *Euploea*), and the tigers and wanderers (*Tirumala* and *Danaus*). Adults are medium to large butterflies, with bold coloration. The head and thorax are black with white spots. They are physically tough. Many have a pungent odour derived from their noxious larval food plants.

Danaine eggs are white or yellow, moderately elongate with vertical ribs, of medium to large size and always laid singly on the leaves of the host plant. Larvae are smooth and velvety. Later instars are transversely banded in black, white and yellow or orange and bear 2–4 pairs of long fleshy filaments. Pupae are smooth, shiny and compact, either green with metallic spots or entirely metallic.

The larvae feed on plants with milky sap, especially members of the Asclepiadaceae, Apocynaceae and, to a lesser extent, Moraceae (the figs). We have discussed the complex and fascinating interactions between danaines and their poisonous food plants in Chapter 3. They represent the best-understood Australian examples of chemical protection against predators, and the associated phenomena of warning coloration and some forms of mimicry.

Male danaines have a variety of scent organs, including patches of specialised scales on the forewing, known as sex brands (crows), and small pockets in the hindwing (tigers and wanderers). Males always have paired eversible organs at the tip of their abdomens called hair-pencils. These are used in courtship to dust the female with aphrodisiacs, especially in the crows. Females usually mate several times during their life, and extra matings may enhance egg production.

Some species of danaines embark on spectacular migrations. During unfavourably dry or cold weather, adults may form large aggregations in sheltered places. When migrating or aggregating, most normal reproductive activity is suspended. Adult danaines tend to be fairly long-lived, even when normally active, but individuals that overwinter may extend their lifespan by many months.

Blue Tiger
(*Tirumala hamata*)

FAMILY NYMPHALIDAE—Nymphs and Their Allies

Common Crow

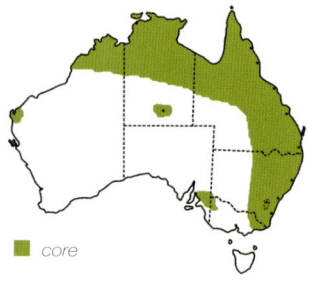

core

Outside the northern tropics, no other Australian butterfly can be confused with the **Common Crow**, *Euploea core* (fw ♂ 41 mm, ♀ 42 mm). The male differs slightly from the female in pattern, and the hind margin of the forewing is bowed downwards, whereas in the female it is straight. The male also has a dull streak on the upperside of the forewing, called a sex brand, and specialised silvery-white scales under the lower flap of the forewing.

The Common Crow occurs in a wide range of habitats, from suburban gardens to dry open inland forest. It is most abundant near the coast, especially in paperbark swamps. The large yellow eggs are laid singly on the host plant—one of a wide range of Apocynaceae (e.g. *Ichnocarpus frutescens*, *Nerium oleander*, *Parsonsia straminea*, *Parsonsia* spp.), Asclepiadaceae (e.g. *Cryptostegia* spp., *Hoya* spp., *Marsdenia* spp. and *Stephanotis* sp.) and Moraceae (e.g. *Ficus* spp.). In eastern states many gardeners know the larva as the Oleander Caterpillar. The pupa is shining silver or gold, with a metallic mirror finish—the effect is produced by complex ultrastructural means. Under optimal conditions, development takes 4–5 weeks.

The adults have a leisurely gliding flight. When normally active, feeding and breeding, adults may live 6–8 weeks. In cold or dry periods, however, adults may congregate in vast swarms in cool or warm sheltered places, mainly resting and retarding their metabolism while subsisting mainly on fat reserves. Under these circumstances, they may live at least seven months.

All host plants used confer some protection against vertebrate predators, but only the Apocynaceae provide pyrrolizidine alkaloids (PAs) for the developing larva. PAs are essential to the male butterfly's sexual success. If an individual is reared on a plant lacking PAs, it must obtain these chemicals as an adult. The flowers and withered leaves of families of plants such as the Apocynaceae, Asteraceae and Boraginaceae are rich sources of PAs and adults of both sexes often visit these natural pharmacies. The females probably do so because PAs also deter predators. Young individuals of either

core courtship: ♂ dusting perched ♀ with pheromones from hair-pencils

sex bred on Asclepiadaceae, lacking PAs, are eaten by Golden Orb Weaving Spiders (*Nephila maculata*). These same spiders release unharmed from the web any individuals rich in PAs.

Courtship in the Common Crow is complex and chemical. At least two sets of specialised scales on the male's wings may release alluring sexual odours, but the most dramatic source of aphrodisiacs are the hair-pencils. These bright yellow eversible organs are situated at the tip of the male's abdomen. During courtship, the male, having found a female, flies above and below her until she perches. Then, in a dramatic display (illustrated), he erects his hair-pencils, showering the female with aphrodisiac dust. If the female remains perched, the male lands beside her and they copulate. An unwilling female will fly away. It is believed that the hair-pencils are also everted to deter predators, and if a male butterfly is captured and held by the wings he is likely to evert them. In fact, in nature it is quite rare to see the sexual hair-pencil display, but easy to provoke the defensive display. The female genital pore (*ostium bursae*) is surrounded by a patch of yellow tissue, which she displays in the same way as the male hair-pencils when held, possibly mimicking the male.

Females mate several times, the maximum recorded being seventeen times, and almost certainly derive proteins from male secretions. These extend their life and enhance their egg production—each female lays 350–500 eggs during her life. The Common Crow may occasionally migrate, often together with the Blue Tiger (*Tirumala hamata*).

FAMILY NYMPHALIDAE—Nymphs and Their Allies

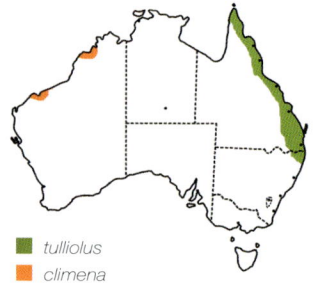
- tulliolus
- climena

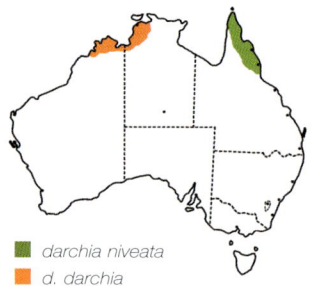
- darchia niveata
- d. darchia

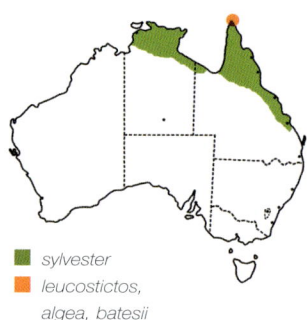
- sylvester
- leucostictos, algea, batesii

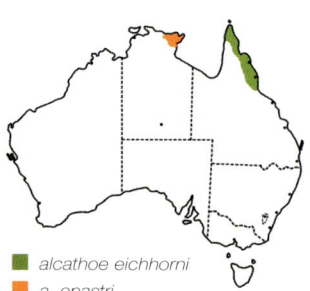
- alcathoe eichhorni
- a. enastri

Tropical Crows

Of the ten other crows found on the Australian mainland, all but one are restricted to the tropics, and only five are likely to be encountered. The remainder are rare and restricted to remote northern localities. All have similar habits to the Common Crow. In some localities several species may be found together, aggregated in dense colonies in sheltered places, especially during the northern tropical dry season. In males of all species, the hind margin of the forewing is curved to a variable extent, whereas in females it is always straight. Females are normally a little larger than males. Species with broader, more rounded wings, such as *Euploea tulliolus*, beat their wings more constantly than long-winged species, which generally have a more leisurely flight, frequently gliding. The early stages are similar to that of the Common Crow, with transversely banded larvae bearing three or four pairs of long black fleshy filaments and pupae of metallic silver or gold.

The best-known species is the **Eastern Brown Crow**, *Euploea tulliolus* (fw ♂ 37 mm). It is seldom abundant, but is often seen in habitats ranging from subtropical gardens to the margins of northern rainforests. The upperside of the male forewing is a deep velvety blue-black. Its larva feeds on *Trophis scandens*, and bears only three pairs of filaments, as in the larva of *E. darchia*, illustrated.

The **Northern Brown Crow**, *Euploea darchia darchia* (fw ♂ 34 mm), is locally common in and around Darwin. The species also has a very distinctive eastern race, the **White-margined Crow**, *E. darchia niveata* (fw ♂ 35 mm). It is rather uncommon but widespread in the coastal tropics, especially in paperbark swamps. In both subspecies the larvae feed on *Trophis scandens* and have only three pairs of filaments.

The **Two-brand Crow**, *Euploea sylvester* (fw ♂ 39 mm), and **Eichhorn's Crow**, *E. alcathoe eichhorni* (fw ♂ 41 mm), are both common at rainforest margins, along riverbeds, in coastal swamps and in gardens in the northern tropics. The two species are rather similar, but the male of *E. sylvester* has two dull parallel bars (sex brands) on its forewings whereas the male of *E. eichhorni* has none. Larvae and pupae of both species are very like those of *E. core*. Larval food plants for *E. sylvester* are *Marsdenia geminata*, *M. pleiadenia* and *Ficus racemosa*; for *E. alcathoe*, they include *Gymnanthera oblonga*, *Hoya australis*, *Marsdenia australis*, *Ficus obliqua* and *Nerium oleander*. East of Darwin is found the rare **Enastri Crow**, *E. alcathoe enastri* (fw ♂ 44 mm), which, like Eichhorn's Crow, lacks a sex brand in the male.

Of the remaining species, the **Mournful Crow**, *Euploea algea* (fw ♂ 39 mm), **Bates' Crow**, *E. batesii* (fw ♂ 44 mm), and the **Orange-flash Crow**, *E. leucostictos* (fw ♂ 38 mm), are common Papuan species occasionally found on the tip of Cape York and in the islands of Torres Strait. The **Climena Crow**, *E. climena* (fw ♂ 37 mm), has been found on the remote north-west coast, perhaps having crossed the ocean from Indonesia.

FAMILY NYMPHALIDAE—Nymphs and Their Allies

Wanderer, Lesser Wanderer and Orange Tiger

plexippus

petilia

genutia

The Wanderer and Lesser Wanderer are among our commonest and best-known butterflies. Both are open-country species, and are especially abundant in farmland or waste ground where the milkweed or wild cotton host plant (*Asclepias* spp.) grows.

The **Wanderer**, *Danaus plexippus* (fw ♂ 54 mm, ♀ 56 mm), is not a native, but reached Australia either by island hopping or as a stowaway across the Pacific from North America (where it is known as the Monarch). It became established after its host plant was artificially introduced. In North America it takes part in spectacular yearly migrations from Canada to Mexico, where hordes of butterflies overwinter in vast colonies, returning in the spring when reproductive activity recommences. Shorter migrations occur in Australia. Its great powers of flight, and high soaring abilities, are a consequence of its long, acutely tipped forewings. By contrast, the much smaller Lesser Wanderer is a low-flying, fluttering species, and this is reflected in its wing shape.

Wanderer males are sexually very aggressive. Often they patrol patches of host plant, intercepting females arriving to oviposit. Frequently, a high-speed chase ensues, with the male pursuing the female high into the air. If he manages to seize her, the pair spiral to the ground and the male may force copulation. Females normally copulate several times during their life.

Eggs are laid singly on the young leaves of the host plant, and the older larvae are very distinctively banded in black, white and yellow. The green pupa has small metallic gold spots. Development takes about four weeks. The adult butterfly may live 6–8 weeks in summer, longer in cold weather.

The **Lesser Wanderer**, *Danaus petilia* (fw ♂ 34 mm, ♀ 35 mm), is nearly ubiquitous on the Australian mainland, being absent only from dense forests, high mountains and extreme deserts. Mass movements do occur as the butterflies track suitable conditions around in different parts of the continent. Many have interpreted these as 'migrations', but they do not follow regular, repeated routes nor do they occur every year in the same fashion. Courtship is more developed in this species than in the Wanderer, and the male has a visible pocket of androconia on the upperside of the hindwings. The larva is distinctive, and feeds on a wide range of native asclepiads, including species of *Brachystelma*, *Cynanchum*, *Marsdenia*, *Rhyncharrhena* and *Sarcostemma* as well as several introduced plants, including introduced milkweeds (*Asclepias* spp.). The pupa is slightly squatter than that of *D. plexippus*. The Lesser Wanderer is mimicked by the female Danaid Eggfly (*Hypolimnas misippus*).

The **Orange Tiger**, *Danaus genutia* (fw ♂ 37 mm, ♀ 38 mm), inhabits swampy areas, including mangroves, near Darwin. Its early stages and habits are very like those of the closely related Black and White Tiger (*D. affinis*).

Males of all *Danaus* species have, on their hindwing, a small scent pouch containing sexual pheromones that can be transferred to the hair-pencils. The pouch opens on the underside of the wing, shown in detail for *D. genutia*. It is rather small in *D. plexippus*, perhaps because this species tends to mate by force as much as by chemical seduction.

FAMILY NYMPHALIDAE—Nymphs and Their Allies 171

Black and White, Brown and Blue Tigers

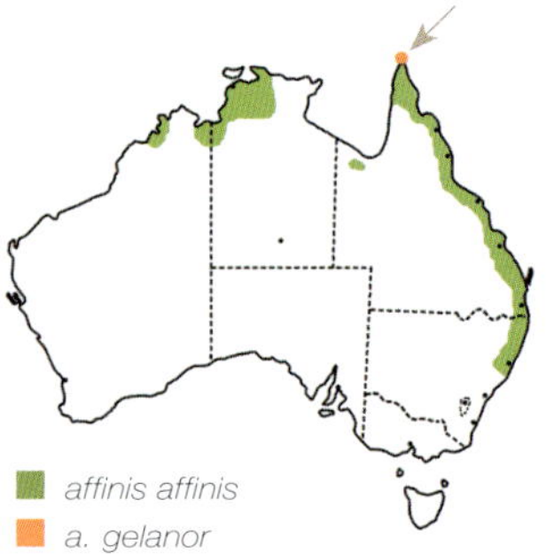

The **Black and White Tiger**, *Danaus affinis* (fw ♂ 38 mm, ♀ 38 mm), is mainly confined to coastal marshes and mangrove swamps where its larval host plant, *Cynachum carnosum*, grows among the reeds fringing the water. It is much more sedentary than either wanderer species. Females generally fly low among the reeds, whereas males fly nonchalantly 1–2 m above the ground, sometimes straying beyond the larval habitat area to visit flowers. Early stages are very like those of the Lesser Wanderer, but the larva is more strongly marked. All danaids are highly susceptible to attack by parasitoids during their development. We illustrate, opposite, the corpse of a *D. affinis* larva that died just before pupation and yielded six tachinid fly larvae. The parasitoids burrow from the corpse almost at the point of death and immediately pupate, forming small, short, cigar-like brown capsules. Adult flies hatch from these a few days later.

The Black and White Tiger exhibits sexual behaviour quite different from that of the Wanderer. In general, females lay their eggs before noon and are sexually active in the afternoon. As young butterflies, females are pursued and courted briefly by males, mating every 5–7 days. As they become older, they derive more and more of their nutrition, especially proteins, from male secondary secretions transferred during mating. Old females often mate every day, sometimes more than once if the first male was also old and depleted. In the afternoon, females perch near patches of food plant, possibly defending their patch against other females, while males patrol the general area. Passing males either discover and court perched females, or perched females chase passing males and solicit copulation by buffeting them. From captive populations we know that old females are most likely to solicit matings, and they probably are able to discriminate between old and young males, preferring the latter, where a choice is available. In captivity, female *D. affinis* may live for about twelve

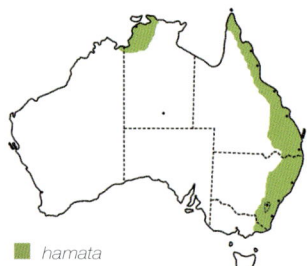

■ *affinis affinis*
■ *a. gelanor*

■ *hamata*

D. affinis ♀ ovipositing

♀ *D. affinis* giving chase to patrolling ♂

172   The Butterflies of Australia

weeks—twice as long as males—especially if they secure many matings. Egg production is also considerably enhanced by multiple mating, with a female able to produce up to 600 eggs when she mates with many males, whereas a female mated only once usually produces fewer than 300 eggs. The **Brown Tiger**, *D. affinis gelanor* (fw ♂ 39 mm), in Australia, is restricted to Torres Strait. Its general biology is very like that of the Black and White Tiger.

In summer or early autumn the **Blue Tiger**, *Tirumala hamata* (fw ♂ 46 mm, ♀ 47 mm), is sometimes one of the commonest butterflies seen in the eastern tropics and subtropics. Vast numbers congregate around the flowers of *Melaleuca* or *Buckinghamia* as they pass through on migration. They are often found roosting en masse in sheltered places, often in company with crow species. Like many other danaids, adult Blue Tigers are strongly attracted to pyrrolizidine alkaloid (PA) sources, and often scratch the young leaves of plants such as *Parsonsia* to release sap, which they imbibe. Because most specimens seen are migrants, reproductive behaviour and the early stages are seldom observed in this species. However, courtship involves extensive use of hair-pencils, as in crows. Uniquely, these are first charged with perfume from the scent pouches which open on the upperside of the wing, the opposite of *Danaus*. The egg is similar to that of the Common Crow, but white. The larva is distinctively banded in black and white and feeds on *Secamone elliptica*. The pupa has more sharply angled contours than *Danaus* species.

SUBFAMILY TELLERVINAE—
Hamadryad

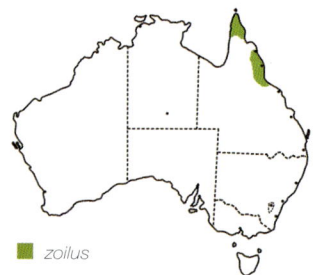

zoilus

The subfamily **Tellervinae** comprises several closely related species of the genus *Tellervo*, ranging from the Moluccas, New Guinea and north Queensland to the Solomon Islands. Unusually, the generic name comes from the Finnish national epic, the *Kalevala*, in which the character 'Tellervo' is a maid of the forest. (Most butterfly scientific names are derived from classical Greek or Latin.) Just one species occurs in northern Australia. The genus (and subfamily) is most closely related to the tigers and crows (Danainae), but in habits and appearance is very similar to a large and diverse South American group, the Ithomiinae. Hair-pencils are lacking.

The **Hamadryad**, *Tellervo zoilus* (fw ♂ 23 mm, ♀ 26 mm), flies deep in the understorey of tropical rainforest in north Queensland. It is small, very finely built, and has a weak fluttering flight. It generally flies 2–4 m above the forest floor, perching frequently on the undersides of leaves. The eyes are yellow. Males and females are very similar but males have a broad, dull central patch on the upperside of the forewing and are generally slightly smaller than females. The Hamadryad is widespread and common wherever there is suitable habitat.

Before 11 am, groups of typically 5–10 males assemble around conspicuous sunny patches in the forest and circle briskly around each other in a continuous dance. We believe this represents a lek, a behaviour where males of an animal congregate and display together to attract females. Males joining the dance are said to be lekking. Females fly to the lek, select a male, and the pair departs, settling under a nearby leaf where they copulate. In the Hamadryad, this behaviour has been definitely observed in individuals kept in large flight cages, and occasionally females, having selected a male, initiate copulation, bending the abdomen to contact and stimulate the male's genitalia.

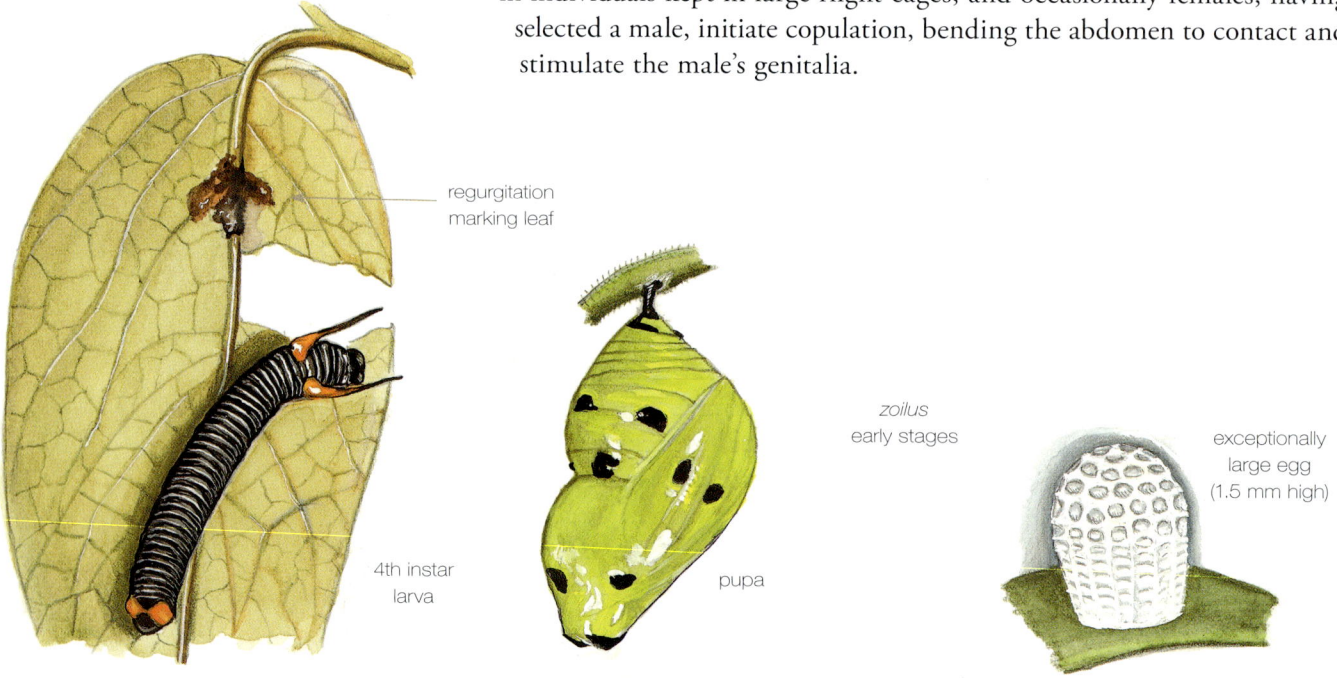

regurgitation marking leaf

4th instar larva

pupa

zoilus early stages

exceptionally large egg (1.5 mm high)

The egg of the Hamadryad is proportionally the largest of any Australian butterfly, each representing about 1 per cent of the female's body weight. Each female lays only about 40 eggs in her lifetime of about three weeks, and she mates once only, usually within a day of emerging from the pupa. The larva on hatching is very mobile. Mature larvae mark the leaves of their host plant, *Parsonsia latifolia* (Apocynaceae) with a regurgitation, perhaps as a territorial marker. There are just four instars. The yellow-green, dark-spotted pupa is squat and distorted. The entire life history, from egg to adult, may be completed in less than three weeks in warm weather.

The *Parsonsia* host plant is rich in pyrrolizidine alkaloids (PAs), and these are present in all stages of the life history. PAs protect the plant from all but a few animals which have learned to detoxify them or tolerate their poisonous effects. In the Hamadryad, PAs are incorporated into the tissues, making it unpalatable to many predators, including the Golden Orb Weaving Spider (*Nephila maculata*), which often builds its web at the edges of forest clearings favoured by male Hamadryads for their morning leks. Hamadryads caught in the webs are first tasted, then carefully cut from the web and released unharmed by the huge female spiders. PAs probably also play a role in sexual communication, but this process is not understood in this species.

SUBFAMILY SATYRINAE—
Browns

Common Brown
(*Heteronympha merope*)

The subfamily **Satyrinae**, or browns, are among our most familiar butterflies. They are principally brown or dull orange and black, and from small to medium in size. They invariably have prominent ringed eyespots, at least on the underside. They fly close to the ground, generally with a lazy fluttery motion. Most Australian species frequent open country, and are usually widespread. All are believed to be palatable to vertebrate predators and the eyespots are presumed to deflect attacks by birds and other vertebrates away from the head. Since specimens with traumatic wing damage in the region of the spots, caused by birds or lizards, are commonly encountered, the hypothesis is probably correct. Some tropical species mimic unpalatable species from other families and subfamilies. Although most species are easily observed, some of the smaller ones are difficult to identify, and sometimes it is necessary to capture a specimen and closely examine both upper- and underside patterns for reliable identification.

With about 2400 species worldwide, the subfamily is large. It is well represented even in the high Arctic and at high altitudes in the Himalayas, but the great majority of species occur in the tropics. In Australia, however, where just 34 species occur, the greatest species diversity occurs in the temperate south, especially in eastern Victoria and southern New South Wales. On ascending from sea level in this area, one encounters a continuous change in the species encountered (see Figure 2.2). Some occur only at high altitudes, even reaching the summit of Mt Kosciuszko. Three species and one genus are found only in Tasmania, the only butterflies endemic to that island state. In the tropics, there is a minor 'hotspot' near Cairns. This is due primarily to a small number of species with tropical Asian affinities. The Evening Brown (*Melanitis leda*), for example, occurs almost everywhere in the Old World tropics. However, species of ringlets (*Hypocysta*) and the Helena Brown (*Tisiphone helena*) also occur in the tropics and have no northern relatives beyond New Guinea.

The larvae feed exclusively on monocotyledons, the only major Australian butterfly group to do so apart from the large skipper subfamilies Hesperiinae and Trapezitinae. Most feed on grasses, but a few feed on sedges, mainly *Gahnia* (Swordgrass); in the far northern tropics, one species feeds on palms. The eggs are generally smooth and spherical and white or green, but in some cases they are hemispherical or cone-shaped with strong vertical ribs. They are generally laid singly or in loose groups of up to five on fresh blades of grass. Several alpine species simply drop their eggs loosely onto grass as they fly over. The larva is cylindrical or cigar-shaped, without spines, and always with a forked tail. Sometimes the head has two horns. The body is well camouflaged, either in green or brown, often with discrete longitudinal stripes. Sometimes different colour forms occur in the one species. Feeding is mostly at night. The pupa is generally suspended from vegetation but in a few southern species, especially those at high altitudes, it lies among leaf litter on the ground. Pupae that are suspended tend to be more elaborately structured, presumably having evolved an irregular outline that helps them avoid detection by predators. Southern species usually have just one generation a year, and it may take the larva the best part of a year to develop. In some cases, larvae remain inactive under a blanket of snow for several months until they are able to resume feeding.

Browns may also suspend their activity in the adult stage, with mated females delaying the production of eggs through the dry summer months, or through the tropical dry season, until fresh grass shoots are available for their young larvae. Tropical and subtropical species may have distinct wet-season (summer) and dry-season (winter) forms. The adults of tropical species are particularly partial to rotting fallen fruit or sap oozing from trees, and rarely feed from flowers. Southern species often feed on flowers of low shrubs such as *Leptospermum*, which have a short corolla tube. In any case the proboscis is never very long, so they cannot reach the nectar in many exotic garden flowers.

Most browns fly by day, and southern species are sun-loving. In the tropics, however, some species prefer forest shade, and the Evening Brown is mainly active at dusk, sometimes even coming to lights at night. In most species the male and female are similar, with the female being a little larger. Courtship and mating behaviour are generally not well understood, but it is probable that the male normally courts the female using distinctive gestures with the aid of chemical aphrodisiacs. A range of probable scent-producing organs, ranging from hair tufts to specialised scales scattered over the wing surface, are known in the subfamily. In one species, the Shouldered Brown (*Heteronympha penelope*), courtship has virtually disappeared and large-bodied males pursue and capture females, fixing a small chastity belt, or sphragis, to their abdomen to hinder subsequent matings with other males.

Dingy Rings (*Ypthima arctoa*) mating

Ringlets and Dingy Ring

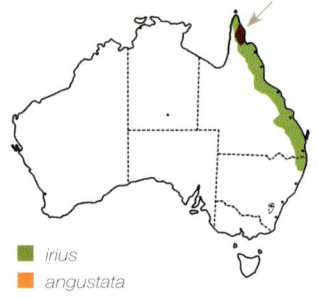

irius
angustata

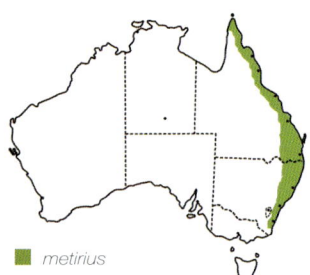

metirius

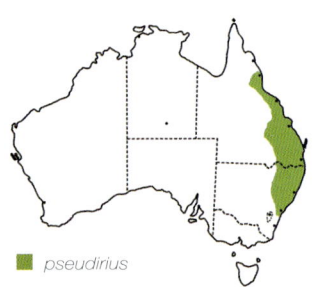

pseudirius

These are all small, low-flying, grass-feeding species. *Hypocysta* is restricted to Australia and New Guinea. The large genus *Ypthima*, with one Australian species, is widespread in the Old World tropics.

The Ringlets (genus *Hypocysta*), have a brisk, low, fluttery flight. Males, especially, perch on low vegetation in sunny spots. Species with more elongate wings tend to be more vigorous and agile in flight. They are mostly quite localised in occurrence. Larvae and pupae of all species are basically similar to those of *H. metirius* (illustrated), but can be separated by slight but clear differences in most cases. All feed on grass, but it is generally not known how specific their preferences are.

The **Black and White Ringlet**, *Hypocysta angustata* (fw ♂ 19 mm, ♀ 19 mm), is restricted to rainforest on Cape York Peninsula. It perches on low vegetation in sunny glades near its grass food plant.

The **Northern Ringlet**, *Hypocysta irius* (fw ♂ 20 mm, ♀ 23 mm), is locally common in open forest and at rainforest edges along the eastern tropical and subtropical coast. It is distinguished from the smaller *H. metirius* and *H. pseudirius* by the well-defined orange patch on the upperside of the forewing. Males perch with wings half open in sunlight on leaves and grass blades within 2–3 m of the ground, defending these sites vigorously. The female lays her smooth spherical yellow eggs on the underside of grass blades. The larvae complete just four instars, instead of the usual five.

The **Common Ringlet**, *Hypocysta metirius* (fw ♂ 19 mm, ♀ 20 mm), is widespread in open eucalypt forest and rainforest edges in the east, extending well inland in places. Its habits are very similar to those of the last species, but it is slower-flying and perches lower, within 1.5 m of the ground. Males also visit hilltops. As with all browns, specimens showing symmetrical hindwing damage near the eyespots are common, and indicative of a bird or lizard having attacked the butterfly when at rest. Larva and pupa are as illustrated, with the larva sometimes brown.

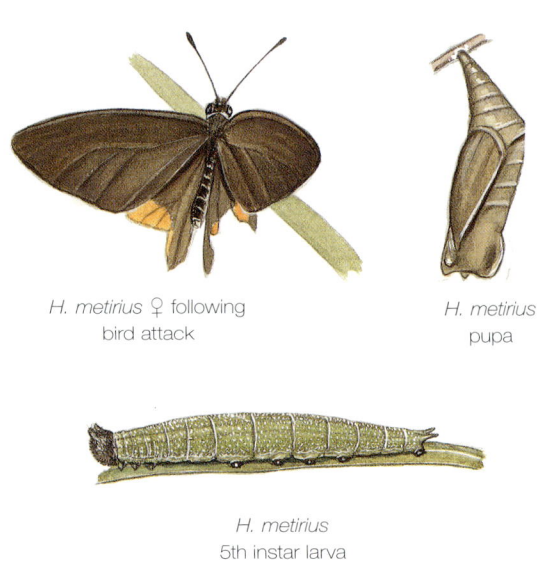

H. metirius ♀ following bird attack

H. metirius pupa

H. metirius 5th instar larva

Grey Fantail

Y. arctoa ♀ escaping

H. irius  ♂   H. angustata  ♂   H. euphemia ♂

H. metirius  ♂   H. angustata  ♂   H. adiante ♂

H. pseudirius  ♂   H. metirius  ♀   Y. arctoa ♂

The **Dingy Ringlet**, *Hypocysta pseudirius* (fw ♂ 19.5 mm, ♀ 20 mm), has a more southerly distribution than the last two species and is more common in drier inland habitats such as tropical vine thickets and brigalow scrub. It is distinguished from *H. metirius* by the smaller eyespot and the shape of the orange marking on the upperside of the hindwing, and more rounded wings. Its habits are similar to those of *H. metirius*. The larva may be green or brown and the pupa is mottled.

The **Rock Ringlet**, *Hypocysta euphemia* (fw ♂ 20 mm, ♀ 21.5 mm), occurs mainly in semi-open granite or sandstone country in New South Wales from Queensland to the Victorian border. In the northern part of its range, it is found 600–1200 m above sea level, but it occurs at lower altitudes further south. In subalpine areas, especially, it perches on rocks with wings half open in the sun.

The **Orange Ringlet**, *Hypocysta adiante* (fw ♂ 17 mm, ♀ 19 mm), is common and widespread in the east and north. It is found in a wide range of open forest habitats, but is often quite local, owing to its sedentary habits. Its flight is weak and fluttery, close to the ground. The life history is similar to other species but the larva is pinkish brown and the pupa more elongate than in other species.

The **Dingy Ring**, *Ypthima arctoa* (fw ♂ 17 mm, ♀ 19 mm), is very common and widespread in the east and north. It favours moist open woodland and grassland. It flies very low with a slower, steadier flutter than *Hypocysta* species, meandering widely over its grassland habitats, and often intruding into open pasture and gardens. Although it often perches, it does not appear to be territorial. The life history differs from *Hypocysta* mainly in the form of the pupa, which is more squat and has four transverse ridges.

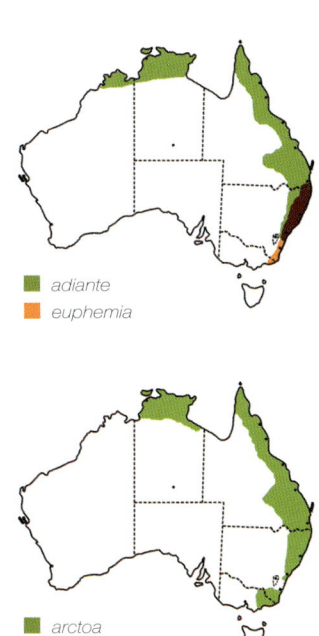

■ adiante
■ euphemia

■ arctoa

FAMILY NYMPHALIDAE—Nymphs and Their Allies

Bushbrowns

The genus *Mycalesis* is widely distributed in the rainforest regions of the Old World tropics. Just three species occur in tropical Australia. They are notable for the long tufts of hair-pencils, which doubtless release sexual pheromones during courtship, located on the upperside of the male hindwing, and opposing a shiny patch on the underside of the forewing. The eyes are hairy. Larvae and pupae of the three species are similar but recognisably different (*M. perseus* is illustrated). Mature larvae feed mainly at night. The genus *Orsotriaena* is represented by just two Indo-Australian species, one reaching Cape York. The eyes are bald and the male has an obscure patch of sex scales on the upperside of the forewing. All Australian bushbrowns are smallish butterflies with rounded wings and a slow, low, fluttery flight. They prefer semi-open habitats on the edge of rainforest, or semi-shaded swampy areas.

The **Dingy Bushbrown**, *Mycalesis perseus* (fw ♂ 20 mm, ♀ 21 mm), is widespread in wetter areas of the tropics. It is common in open woodland, at rainforest edges and in urban gardens. The adults are most active in the morning and afternoon, resting on or near the ground in shade around midday. They often feed at fallen fruits, and only rarely visit flowers. Reproductive activity is restricted mainly to the mid-afternoon. During courtship the male chases the female, approaching her from beneath, and if she lands he follows, settling directly behind her. He then depresses his hindwings while raising his forewings and vibrating them rapidly, presumably dispersing pheromones from the exposed sex scales. A receptive female remains motionless, and the male walks forward alongside her and mates. An unreceptive female turns at right angles to the male, walks away, or flies off if the male is too persistent. Females oviposit singly on young growth of various grasses, including, especially, *Themeda triandra* and also *Dichanthium sericeum*, *Heteropogon triticeus*, *Panicum maximum* and probably many other

genera. During the dry season, females may cease egg production and congregate in large numbers in moist sheltered gullies. In favourable seasons, they may expand their range considerably.

The **Cedar Bushbrown**, *Mycalesis sirius* (fw ♂ 22 mm, ♀ 24 mm), is locally common in the northern tropics. It is most abundant in coastal marshy areas around streams and paperbark swamps. Its activity pattern is like that of *M. perseus*, but unlike that species it rarely feeds from rotting fruit and is very sedentary. It has a slightly slower, more fluttery flight, as might be expected from its very rounded wings. Eggs are laid singly on fresh growth. The usual larval food plant is *Ischaemum australe*, with *Themeda triandra* and *Panicum maximum* also used.

The **Orange Bushbrown**, *Mycalesis terminus* (fw ♂ 22 mm, ♀ 24 mm), is common in the wetter parts of the Queensland tropics. It occurs alike in moist eucalypt forest and in the understorey of dense lowland forest, and in many open habitats in between. Activity patterns and mating behaviour are very like those of *M. perseus*, but males are strongly territorial, defending perches from 0.5–2 m in sunny patches along forest paths, and prominent perches along sunlit forest margins. Compared with *M. perseus* it is somewhat livelier in flight, and courtship follows a similar sequence but is very brisk and urgent. Both sexes feed at fallen fruit and sap flows. Females lay their eggs singly or in small, loose clusters on young growth of the host plant, typically *Oplismenus* species but also *Themeda triandra*, *Imperata cylindrica*, *Panicum maximum* and probably other grasses.

The **Dusky Bushbrown**, *Orsotriaena medus* (fw ♂ 23 mm, ♀ 25 mm), is confined to Cape York and the islands of Torres Strait. It is generally found in moist but rather open habitats, especially long grass such as *Imperata* and *Panicum*. Its flight is a slow bobbing flutter within 1.5 m of the ground, sometimes perching higher. Eggs are laid singly. The larva and pupa are very distinctive. Courtship and mating are normally in the afternoon. Males fly below females, exposing the sex brands on the upperside of their forewings. If a female lands, the male lands behind her, tilting his body forward, and opens and closes his wings deliberately, almost enclosing her, before manoeuvring alongside and attempting copulation.

Evening Brown and Palmfly

■ leda

■ agondas

The **Evening Brown**, *Melanitis leda* (fw ♂ 40 mm, ♀ 45 mm), is common and widespread in the north and east, ranging well into the subtropics. It occurs in a wide variety of habitats and is common in suburban parks and gardens. There are two distinct seasonal forms. The tropical wet-season or temperate summer form is smaller and paler in both sexes. The eyespots on the underside are well defined and the outline of the wings is relatively even, without strong angulations or tails. The dry-season or winter form is 1–2 mm larger and richly coloured, the underside a variegated black and pale grey, highly variable but lacking well-developed eyespots. The wing margins are strongly angulated, with small tails, especially in females. The forms are well defined, without intermediates. *M. leda* is active mainly at dawn and dusk, but may be disturbed during the day as it perches on the ground in shaded undergrowth. It then flies briefly, close to the ground, before settling again some distance from the original site. Its underside pattern in either summer or winter is well camouflaged against a backdrop of dead leaves. It flies strongly, with a bouncy, jinking motion, more like that of a swallowtail than a brown. Occasionally it is active during the day in deep rainforest or on very cloudy days, often feeding on fallen fruit. It may continue feeding well after dark and is often attracted to lights at night.

Most reproductive behaviour occurs around dusk. Males are territorial, perching with wings folded, but very alert, on vegetation at about 1 m or lower, especially along forest paths. Competing males circle around each other in aggressive encounters, beginning about a metre above the ground, but spiralling many metres into the fading sky as the contest reaches its climax. They may continue in a high-speed chase through the canopy until the winner returns to his perch. Females are intercepted as they fly past a male's perch. Pairs engage in an elaborate bobbing dance, generally with a vertical amplitude of about a metre. The male appears to present the upperside of his wings to the female, suggesting the presence of dispersed androconial scales producing sex pheromones, but this requires confirmation. These dances may continue for many minutes, but refractory females sometimes race into the canopy, or dive horizontally about a metre above the ground, thus evading the male. When a receptive female lands, the male swiftly lands quivering beside her and mates almost at once. It is likely that females mate more than once in their life. Females also oviposit at dusk, sometimes impeded by courting males.

Typically, eggs are produced in a row of three to five, on fresh growth of a suitable grass species. Larvae feed openly by day, but are highly cryptic (well-camouflaged). They are very frequently parasitised by tachinid flies, whose eggs may be found laid directly onto the larva. Larvae feed on many widespread grasses, including native *Chrysopogon*, *Heteropogon*, *Imperata*, *Leersia*, *Ophiuros*, *Themeda* and many introduced species. Because they spend much of their time on the ground, adult *M. leda* are quite often attacked by skinks and, at night, those landing on windows are eaten by geckos. Specimens with torn wings showing evidence of attacks on the eyespots are common.

The **Palmfly**, *Elymnias agondas* (fw ♂ 36 mm, ♀ 36 mm), is rare in Australia and restricted to rainforest on Cape York Peninsula. It flies in shady places with a gentle sailing or fluttering flight, the male and female mimicking, respectively, a crow or an owl butterfly, but probably the species mimicked are not found in Australia. Members of the genus elsewhere almost invariably mimic danaines or *Delias* species. Females lay their eggs singly on leaves of the food plant, the climbing palm *Calamus caryotoides* (rattan). Larvae and pupae are very distinctive.

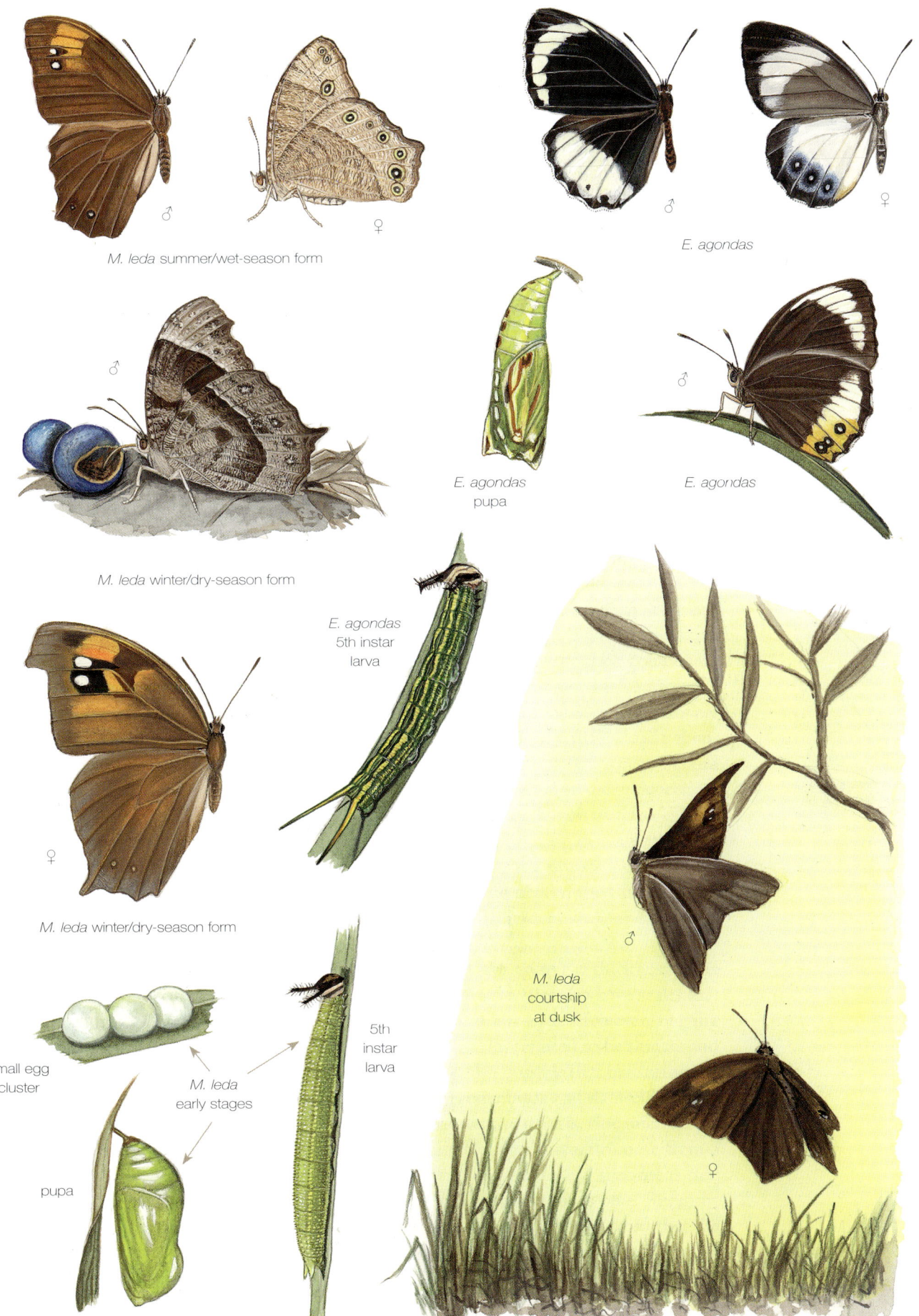

FAMILY NYMPHALIDAE—Nymphs and Their Allies 183

Larger Southern Mountain Browns

cordace

penelope

paradelpha

The **Bright-eyed Brown**, *Heteronympha cordace* (fw ♂ 24.5 mm, ♀ 26 mm), occurs from 600 to 1800 m in south-east mainland Australia, and from sea level to 1000 m in Tasmania. It is locally common in open swampy areas where its food plant, the sedge *Carex appressa*, grows. It flutters close to the ground with a weak flight, often feeding on flowers of low-growing shrubs such as *Leptospermum*. Eggs are laid singly on leaves of the food plant and the larva feeds at night, hiding in litter by day. The bright green pupa is suspended head downwards on or near the plant. Five subspecies are recognised, three in Tasmania, which differ from the typical form mainly in being smaller and, in some cases, having paler underside markings almost lacking eyespots.

The **Shouldered Brown**, *Heteronympha penelope* (fw ♂ 34 mm, ♀ 34 mm), is widespread and common in southern Australia. In the northern part of its range, it is confined to the mountains, up to 1600 m, but further south, especially in Tasmania, it also occurs at sea level. Four smaller subspecies are recognised, two in Tasmania. Preferred habitats are dry open eucalypt woodland and alpine woodland. Adults fly quite rapidly, feeding often at flowers. Unlike other members of the genus, males are larger than females by weight and are similar in wing length. They maintain territories, or patrol habitat where females are to be found. Territorial males may perch low in patches of flowers or high on leaves several metres above the ground. In some locations they visit hilltops.

Vigorous high-speed chases of passing females are common. Sometimes the female may escape by dropping from the air with folded wings, in a typical predator-avoidance manoeuvre. Mating generally occurs after the female has landed, with minimal courtship. Sometimes males seize females in midair and carry them to the ground to mate. During copulation the male secretes a sphragis, moulded in a membranous fold at the base of his genitalia and incorporating long scales which form in a dense brush flanking his claspers. During secretion of the sphragis, the male becomes almost catatonic and is supported by the female. Males and females may mate several times during their lifetime, but the male is capable of producing at most two well-formed, robust sphragides.

penelope sexual chase

cordace ♀

penelope ♀ ovipositing in flight

The males are equipped also with remarkably overdeveloped genital claspers, which are used together with the uncus as pincers to lever off any sphragis deposited by a previous male, which is particularly easy if the sphragis is frail and poorly formed. The illustration compares the relative development of these structures with those in its nearest relative, *H. paradelpha*, which does not produce a sphragis. The difference is dramatic. However, unlike females of other sphragis-producing butterflies, the female has completely normal genitalia. Females oviposit by perching and dropping their eggs, or flying over a patch of food plant, such as Snow Grass, dropping eggs as they go. The sluggish larva feeds at night, and hides in litter by day. Even at artificially high temperatures, it still requires about ten months to develop. The pupa forms among loose litter near the ground. Host plants include *Austrodanthonia*, *Poa* and *Themeda*.

The **Spotted Brown**, *Heteronympha paradelpha* (fw ♂ 26 mm, ♀ 29 mm), occurs from sea level to 1400 m in south-eastern mainland Australia, keeping to the mountains in the north. It occurs mainly in dense shaded woodland. Adults fly low, with a brisk bobbing flutter, generally close to the ground. Males may perch on sunlit eucalypt leaves 2–4 m above the ground, especially in the afternoon, when most females are ovipositing. Courtship is normal for the genus, and no sphragis is produced during copulation. The method of oviposition is the same as for *H. penelope*, with eggs dropped loosely on the grasses *Microlaena stipoides* or *Poa tenera*. The life history is similar to that of *H. penelope*. Both *H. paradelpha* and *H. penelope* fly late, from January to April.

FAMILY NYMPHALIDAE—Nymphs and Their Allies

Southern Browns

merope

solandri

banksii

mirifica

The **Common Brown**, *Heteronympha merope* (fw ♂ 34 mm, ♀ 38 mm), is one of the best-known butterflies in southern Australia. It occurs in a wide range of open and woodland habitats up to 1250 m and is common in gardens. It was first collected by Sir Joseph Banks at Botany Bay in 1770, and his specimens are now held in the Natural History Museum, London. It was also the first Australian butterfly species to be the subject of a modern ecological study, by E.D. Edwards of the CSIRO in 1973. Edwards showed that the females mate in spring when they emerge, but aestivate during the hot dry summer, delaying egg production for up to four months until conditions are more favourable. Depending on the location, the females may live up to eight months. Adults have a vigorous, somewhat jinking flight, often feeding from flowers. Males typically fly 1–4 m above the ground or even higher. Depending on the location, they may maintain territories in sunny patches, patrol large areas searching for receptive females or visit hilltops. Most females mate just once, and courtship is brief but not aggressive, unlike *H. penelope*. However, old females occasionally re-mate, which doubtless encourages persistence by males. Females signal rejection in various ways—gliding with wings outstretched, settling with wings tightly folded, or flying away at high speed—depending on the degree of male resolve. Females lay their eggs singly, or occasionally in pairs, on leaves of the host plant. Larvae, which vary greatly in colour and pattern, feed by night. The pupa forms among loose litter at the base of the host plant. Larvae feed on numerous common grasses, including *Brachypodium*, *Bromus*, *Cynodon*, *Ehrharta*, *Poa* and *Themeda*. Western and Tasmanian subspecies are smaller.

Solander's Brown, *Heteronympha solandri* (fw ♂ 28 mm, ♀ 31 mm), is common in open eucalypt forest and montane woodland from 320 to 1600 m in southern Australia. It is most common above 1000 m between December and April. It is generally low-flying, its motion a rather brisk and erratic flutter, and males may perch several metres high on sunlit foliage. The life history is similar to that of *H. banksii*; the larva is horned and the pupa suspended. Eggs are laid singly near the base of stems of the food plant, generally grasses such as *Poa* species. The larva feeds at night.

Banks' Brown, *Heteronympha banksii* (fw ♂ 27 mm, ♀ 29 mm), is common and widespread along the Great Dividing Range up to 900 m, south from the Bunya Mountains in southern Queensland. Its habitat is primarily tall, open eucalypt forest and open patches in temperate rainforest. Adults flutter erratically, with pronounced jinking, settling frequently. They typically remain close to the ground, but males may perch in sunny patches several metres high, often on tree-fern fronds, where they maintain territories. In autumn, eggs are laid singly on the leaves of the host plant—commonly *Poa tenera*, the larvae hatching soon after and feeding at night, through the winter and spring. Pupation normally occurs in December, with adults emerging from January to April.

The **Wonder Brown**, *Heteronympha mirifica* (fw ♂ 32 mm, ♀ 37 mm), is locally fairly common in south-eastern Australia. It occurs at the edges of subtropical and warm temperate rainforest and moist gullies in wet eucalypt forest from sea level to 1400 m, preferring low altitudes in the southern parts of its range. Males fly rapidly with vigorous jinking, often several metres above the ground, and often perch in high foliage. Females have a low, slow, jinking flight. They perch often, typically inconspicuously among leaf litter with wings folded so the cream forewing band is invisible. Females mate in spring and delay egg production, as in *H. merope*. The life history is somewhat like that of *H. banksii*, with a horned larva and suspended pupa. The larva feeds at night on soft grasses (*Oplismenus* sp.) or, rarely, the sedge *Gahnia clarkei*.

FAMILY NYMPHALIDAE—Nymphs and Their Allies

Southern Alpine Xenicas

■ orichora

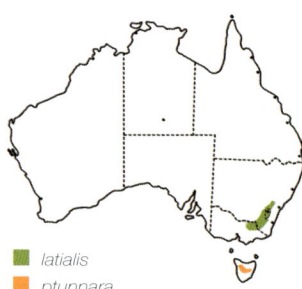
■ latialis
■ ptunnara

■ lathoniella

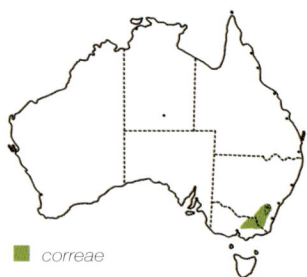
■ correae

■ kershawi

The six species of alpine xenicas are restricted to the mountains of the south-east mainland and Tasmania. Most overlap in distribution but fly at different altitudes, have short flight seasons and, to some extent, are on the wing at different times of the year. The life histories are generally similar, with some key differences. The eggs are spherical, green or pale yellow, and rather large relative to the size of the butterflies. The larvae may be brown or green, but all lack horns on the head and feed on various species of grass, especially tussock grasses and snow grasses. In high-altitude species, the pupa is smooth and lies loose on the ground. In lower-altitude species, the pupa has leaf-like flanges and is suspended from vegetation. The adults of all species fly close to the ground. Activity is restricted to sunny weather and is at its peak in the middle of the day. In late summer, several species are common on the summit of Mt Kosciuszko.

The **Spotted Alpine Xenica**, *Oreixenica orichora* (fw ♂ 17 mm, ♀ 17.5 mm), occurs from 1200 to 2100 m on the mainland, flying from December to March. The Tasmanian race, *O. orichora paludosa*, occurs from 760 to 1500 m. Adults fly in sunlight up to 1.5 m above the ground. Sexual chases are frequent and females may escape by closing their wings abruptly and dropping into the undergrowth. Females oviposit by flying over suitable grassland, dropping non-adhesive eggs as they go. The larvae feed mainly by day, but the final instar feeds at night. The pupa is similar to that of *O. latialis*.

The **Small Alpine Xenica**, *Oreixenica latialis* (fw ♂ 17 mm, ♀ 17.5 mm), occurs from 1000 to 2100 m, flying from February to April. Habits of adults are similar to those of *O. orichora* but they are slightly slower in flight, and tend to keep closer to the ground. The eggs dropped in flight by the female are adhesive and catch on the first blade of grass they touch. The larvae feed by day, and the pupa forms among loose ground litter.

The **Tasmanian Alpine Xenica**, *Oreixenica ptunarra* (fw ♂ 16.5 mm, ♀ 17 mm), occurs above 750 m in Tasmania, flying from February to April. Its biology is very like that of *O. latialis*.

The **Silver Xenica**, *Oreixenica lathoniella* (fw ♂ 18 mm, ♀ 18 mm), is the most widespread member of the genus, ranging from the Queensland border to Tasmania. Despite considerable variability, it can generally be distinguished by the well-defined large silver markings on the underside of the hindwing. The slightly smaller *O. latialis* is the most similar species, but its upperside markings are more broken, and it has narrower forewings. It is also most common at higher altitudes. Four subspecies are recognised, three in Tasmania, which may be much darker on the underside than the mainland form, *O. lathoniella herceus* (illustrated). On the mainland, it occurs mainly from 700 to 1500 m (from sea level in Victoria), flying from February to May. The Tasmanian races differ in their altitudinal preferences, but together they occur from January to March between sea level and 1000 m. Unlike high alpine species, the females lay their eggs singly on leaves of the host plant, *Microlaena stipoides*, *Poa ensiformis* or *P. labillardieri*. The pupa is suspended.

The **Orange Alpine Xenica**, *Oreixenica correae* (fw ♂ 21 mm, ♀ 22 mm), occurs between 1200 and 1800 m from December to April. Adult habits and life history are similar to those of *O. lathoniella*. Young larva feed by day, becoming more nocturnal as they mature.

The **Striped Xenica**, *Oreixenica kershawi* (fw ♂ 21 mm, ♀ 22 mm), occurs at lower altitudes than other Alpine Xenicas. It is found mainly in open eucalypt forest from 500 to 1200 m from December to April. Adults generally fly low with a weak flutter, but sometimes perch several metres above the ground. The life history is similar to that of *O. lathoniella*, the larvae feeding on *Poa* species and *Tetrarrhena juncea*.

FAMILY NYMPHALIDAE—Nymphs and Their Allies

Southern Xenicas and Forest Browns

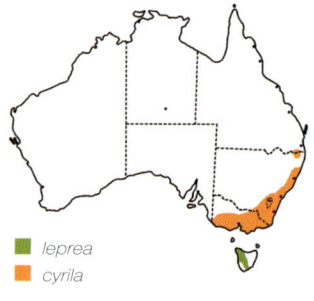
- leprea
- cyrila

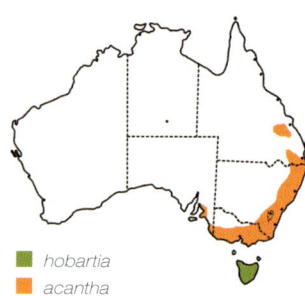
- hobartia
- acantha

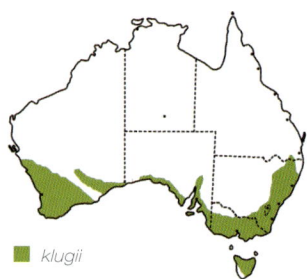
- klugii

- minyas

The **Leprea Brown**, *Nesoxenica leprea* (fw ♂ 20 mm, ♀ 21 mm), occurs in sunny glades in cool temperate *Nothofagus* forest from sea level to 1240 m in south and west Tasmania. It is the only butterfly genus restricted to Tasmania. Two subspecies are recognised; the cream-coloured *N. leprea leprea* occurs in the west, whereas the orange-coloured *N. leprea elia* occurs in three separate populations in the south, centre and north-west. Interbreeding occurs between the two subspecies, producing intermediate forms. Adults fly from September to January. They generally keep close to the ground and are most active in sunlight around noon from September to January. In the afternoon they may perch high. The life history is poorly known but larvae feed on *Uncinia tenella*.

The **Hobart Brown**, *Argynnina hobartia* (fw ♂ 18 mm, ♀ 20 mm), is also restricted to Tasmania, ranging from sea level to 1050 m in a wide range of habitats, including open eucalypt forest and grassy heath. Three subspecies are recognised, including the eastern and northern *A. hobartia hobartia*, the pale western *A. hobartia tasmanica*, and the larger alpine *A. hobartia montana*, restricted to the Cradle Mountain area. Adults are active from September to January and fly close to the ground with a gentle bobbing motion. Both sexes perch frequently in sunlight, often basking with wings open. Females flutter slowly, ovipositing on grass blades. The life history is like that of *A. cyrila*, with the pupa suspended from grass stems.

The **Forest Brown**, *Argynnina cyrila* (fw ♂ 21 mm, ♀ 22 mm), occurs in the south-east of mainland Australia from sea level in the south to over 1500 m in the New England area. Preferred habitat includes tall eucalypt forest and warm temperate rainforest. Adults are on the wing from August to January. Males, especially, fly swiftly and erratically, perching in sunlight up to 6 m high in the crowns of trees. They also visit hilltops. Females fly low, with a bobbing fluttery flight. The bright green eggs are laid singly or in small groups on the stems or leaves of the food plant, species of *Poa* and other grasses. The drab, sluggish larva remains exposed on grass blades, even when at rest.

The *Geitoneura* species, or forest xenicas, all inhabit open forest and scrubby grassland, flying low to the ground with a jerky bobbing motion. They perch frequently on or near the ground, and are most active in sunny conditions. The early stages differ markedly between species and, unlike most satyrines, their eggs are strongly ribbed and are not spherical.

The **Ringed Xenica**, *Geitoneura acantha* (fw ♂ 24 mm, ♀ 27 mm), is very distinctive. It is locally common in moister habitats on the south-east coast and tablelands of the mainland. Eggs are laid singly or in small groups on fresh blades of grass. Larvae feed at night on *Microlaena stipoides*, *Poa sieberiana*, *P. tenera* and *Themeda triandra*.

Klug's Xenica, *Geitoneura klugii* (fw ♂ 23 mm, ♀ 26 mm), is more southern and western in distribution, and generally prefers drier habitats. Towards the more northerly parts of its range it occurs up to 1400 m, whereas in Tasmania it ranges from sea level to 900 m. A small pale form (fw ♂ 18 mm, ♀ 22 mm) occurs in semi-arid areas inland from the Great Australian Bight. The egg, laid singly on fresh grass blades, is an unusual conical shape. The larva lacks horns on its head and feeds by day on *Austrostipa*, *Brachypodium*, *Ehrharta*, *Poa* and *Vulpia*.

The **Western Xenica**, *Geitoneura minyas* (fw ♂ 18.5 mm, ♀ 22 mm), is confined to south-west Australia, where it overlaps with the dark form of *G. klugii* in moist eucalypt woodland. It may be distinguished from that species by its smaller size and paler, less broken orange marking on the upperside. The hind margin of the forewing is orange, rather than dark brown. The early stages are poorly known but larvae are like those of *G. klugii* and feed on *Ehrharta* and other grasses.

FAMILY NYMPHALIDAE—Nymphs and Their Allies

Swordgrass Browns

The swordgrass browns are known only from Australia, and just two species are recognised. One of these, however, has at least five well-defined geographic races; some are so different they might be equally recognised as separate species.

The **Swordgrass Brown**, *Tisiphone abeona* (fw ♂ 31–37 mm, ♀ 33–39 mm), is locally common in a wide range of open or semi-open habitats south of Maryborough, Queensland. It generally occurs in numbers wherever large stands of its host plant grow (various species of swordgrass—actually a sedge, *Gahnia* spp.), but it is mostly very sedentary. In the last 40 years much of its former habitat has been lost due to draining of coastal swamps for agricultural and urban development. Six subspecies are recognised, none of which have ever been given separate common names. The smallest and most northerly is *T. a. rawnsleyi* (fw ♂ 31 mm, ♀ 33 mm), from coastal swamps in southern Queensland. The largest is the magnificent montane *T. a. regalis* (fw ♂ 37 mm, ♀ 39 mm), from the New England Plateau of New South Wales. Closely related to *T. a. regalis*, but brighter and smaller, is *T. a. morrisi* (fw ♂ 33 mm, ♀ 35 mm), found in isolated pockets in coastal northern New South Wales, where it is particularly threatened. Both the typical race *T. a. abeona* (fw ♂ 33 mm, ♀ 35 mm), from southern New South Wales, and *T. a. albifascia* (fw ♂ 34 mm, ♀ 36 mm), from Victoria, are more widespread and differ markedly from the other races, having a striking orange patch on the forewing; *T. a. albifascia* differs from *T. a. abeona* mainly by the more extensive white marking on the underside, especially evident in females. *T. a. aurelia* is very similar to *T. a. abeona*. Among these races there is considerable variation in preferred habitat and probably also in behaviour; the following account applies especially to the northern race, *T. a. rawnsleyi*.

All swordgrass browns are very conspicuous and fly in sunlit open areas around their food plant with a slow erratic flutter at about 1 m above the ground. They perch frequently but briefly and in colder areas they often hold their wings partly open, presumably to better absorb heat from the sun. In habitats where the host plants are more dispersed and topography allows, males may visit hilltops in order to encounter virgin females, especially in the morning. More often, however, they patrol dense patches of swordgrass, searching for freshly emerged females. Mating commonly takes place in the morning. The male lacks sex scales and it is unclear if pheromones play any role in courtship, which is perfunctory. Eggs are laid singly on leaves of the food plant, and females may test many plants before depositing one to three large eggs, singly, at different locations on the one plant. She may then inspect many more plants before again laying, perhaps 10–15 minutes later. Young larvae feed only in the early morning, and older larvae in the evening, both retreating to natural shelters among leaf litter and dead growth trapped in the heart of the plant. Numerous species of *Gahnia* are utilised in different areas.

The **Helena Brown**, *Tisiphone helena* (fw ♂ 30 mm, ♀ 32 mm), is restricted to the wet tropics region of north Queensland and is seldom common. It is most often met with in upland rainforest, but also occurs in local swampy pockets on the coast. It is sedentary, never straying far from its larval host plant. Adults fly in sunny conditions with a slow, low, leisurely flutter, in shaded or semi-shaded forest understorey. They perch often, frequently with wings half open, generally on leaves up to 2 m above the ground, or low blades of the host plant, *Gahnia sieberiana*. When alarmed, they have a surprisingly rapid jinking flight, which is unexpected given the very rounded outline of its wings. Females lay eggs singly on old dead leaves near the stem of the plant. The early stages are very similar to those of *T. abeona*.

NEW GUINEA BUTTERFLIES—
Enriching Our Fauna

A few kilometres to Australia's extreme north lies New Guinea, the second-largest island in the world. Together with its satellite islands, the Bismarck Archipelago and the Solomon Islands, New Guinea is home to nearly a thousand butterfly species. More than half the nearly 420 species recorded from Australia occur also in New Guinea, and over a hundred genera are shared. Nevertheless, in New Guinea there remain 63 genera not known from Australia, and conversely 30 Australian genera do not occur in New Guinea.

The origins of New Guinea's rich fauna are a mystery. Unlike Australia, the landmass is young in geological terms, having arisen initially from a series of islands pushed up from the ocean floor over the last 20–40 million years by the northward drift of the Australian continental mass—eventually uniting to form high mountains rising over 5000 metres. The fauna has evolved rapidly, partly from stock arriving from South-East Asia and, almost certainly, partly from stock arriving from Australia. The Asian-derived fauna may have included an earlier wave of species that arrived along a link formed by now-submerged island arcs that existed between the evolving Philippines and the emergent islands, which were to become New Guinea, and later invasions that followed a route through Sulawesi and the Moluccas, crossing narrow water barriers at some stage.

At present, however, Australia is evidently gaining species from New Guinea, and new records from the Torres Strait Islands are reported almost every year. Of the 200-odd species shared by New Guinea and Australia, more than 40 are not found south of Cape York Peninsula and half of these, in Australia, are known only from the islands of Torres Strait. The species in this category are often forest understorey species, which have a low tolerance of desiccation, and are reluctant to leave the forest to cross even quite short distances over drier grassland or savannah. They may have reached Australia as recently as 8000 years ago when the last land connection existed. They include mainly species of obvious recent tropical Asian origin, such as the Orange Archduke (*Lexias aeropa*), the Turquoise Emperor (*Apaturina erminea*) and the Orange Emperor (*Charaxes latona*), as well as several species of crows (*Euploea* spp.). Others are more enigmatic. The Harlequin (*Praetaxila segecia*) belongs to a genus almost restricted to New Guinea, where eleven species occur, but it has distant relatives in South-East Asia and none in Australia. The owls of the genus *Taenaris* are another spectacular group that just reaches the Australian mainland, with twenty species in New Guinea. The genus evidently evolved in New Guinea but, again, its distant relatives occur in South-East Asian forests.

Several interesting patterns occur among the Lycaenidae. Just two species of azure (*Ogyris* spp.) occur in southern Papua. These are evidently invaders from Australia, where fourteen species are known. Other genera, such as the jewels (*Hypochrysops* spp.), are highly diverse in Australia with eighteen species, but more so in New Guinea with 42 species. As they have few relatives in Asia, it is likely that this genus originated in Australia, but diversified in New Guinea, with several species reinvading Australia in relatively recent times. Finally, perhaps the greatest enigma of all are the jezabels (*Delias* spp.). Australia has just eight species, but in New Guinea there is an astonishing total of 116 species. The genus is also widespread in Asia, but never with more than 6–8 species in a given region, most being confined to high mountains. It is not clear at present if the ancestral stock originally reached New Guinea from Australia, or from Asia, tens of millions of years ago. However, some of our tropical species probably evolved in the New Guinea lowlands and then invaded north Queensland much more recently.

SUBFAMILY AMATHUSIINAE—
Owls

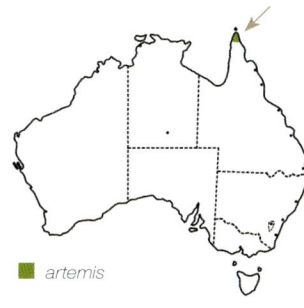
■ artemis

The subfamily **Amathusiinae** is represented on the Australian mainland by just one species, which occurs on Cape York. In Papua New Guinea there are nineteen species in the genus *Taenaris* alone, and other genera are widespread in tropical Asian rainforest. They are known as owls on account of their large prominent eyespots. The larvae feed on monocotyledons, chiefly palms in our region.

The **Artemis Owl**, *Taenaris artemis* (fw ♂ 48 mm, ♀ 51 mm), is rare on the mainland, and uncommon on the islands of Torres Strait. Its preferred habitat is swampy or littoral rainforest where the food plants, *Pandanus* or Coconut Palm, are present. Adults usually fly 2–5 m above the ground with a strong but slow flutter along a direct flightpath. They are exceptionally easy to net, providing they are not too high. The unusually coloured, round, smooth eggs are laid in very evenly spaced clusters on leaves of the food plant. Larvae feed gregariously. Their dense bristles give them a fearsome appearance, but do not cause irritations. The streamlined pupa bears a small fork anteriorly.

Within most of its Australian distribution, this large distinctive species is unmistakable in flight or at rest. However, on islands in the extreme north of Torres Strait, the paler species *Taenaris catops* was recorded nearly a hundred years ago. Many owl species will fly over open water, hence conceivably several other New Guinea species might arrive at these islands occasionally. Owls are believed to be unpalatable to vertebrate predators and *T. artemis* and similar New Guinea species are thought to be mimicked by the pale female form of *Papilio aegeus*, which also occurs in far north Queensland.

egg cluster

early stages

5th instar larva with dense bristles

artemis

FAMILY NYMPHALIDAE—Nymphs and Their Allies

SUBFAMILIES CHARAXINAE AND APATURINAE—Emperors

sempronius

latona

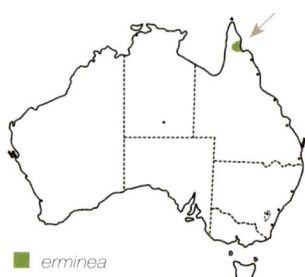
erminea

The butterflies popularly known as emperors were formerly believed to be closely related. All are medium to moderately large, swift-flying, heavy-bodied species with similar habits. Current thought is that they represent two rather distantly related subfamilies of the Nymphalidae.

The subfamily **Charaxinae** is mainly tropical and is particularly well represented in Africa. Adults very commonly have paired short, sharp, pointed tails on the hindwing. Larvae are without spines on the body, but have four recurved horns on the head capsule. The egg is spherical and nearly smooth, and the pupa is very compact and rounded.

The **Tailed Emperor**, *Polyura sempronius* (fw ♂ 47 mm, ♀ 55 mm), is common in northern and eastern Australia in a wide range of habitats, including urban areas. It flies fast and powerfully, usually 2–5 m high, sometimes sailing for long stretches with outspread wings raised slightly above the horizontal. Males very often frequent hilltops where they perch head-downwards on vegetation, waiting to intercept receptive females. Once a female has landed, courtship before mating is rather perfunctory. Disputes between rival males over a favoured perch can be violent, with an audible clashing of wings as they fly in a high, tightening spiral. Wing damage from such fights is common. Both sexes frequently imbibe fermenting sap oozing from wounds on trees, and feed also on fermenting fruit. Large yellow eggs are laid singly, usually on the upperside of host plant leaves. The larvae are highly territorial. They build a platform of leaves and spun silk from which they make sorties to feed. Larvae on their nests may show aggression towards one another; they react less to the physical proximity of a neighbour than to the distance between the two nests measured by travelling along the branches of the host tree. Larvae feed on a very large range of host plants, chiefly of the families Mimosaceae and Caesalpinaceae, but also *Brachychiton* and *Celtis*.

The **Orange Emperor**, *Charaxes latona* (fw ♂ 45 mm, ♀ 43 mm), is restricted to rainforest on Cape York Peninsula. Its flight and habits are similar to those of the Tailed Emperor, but it often flies high into the rainforest canopy where it perches. It visits hilltops, and feeds on sap and fermenting fruit on the ground. Males are attracted to animal faeces and carrion and come to baits, such as rotting prawns. The life history is very like that of the Tailed Emperor, but the larva has very distinct white chevrons on a green background. The food plant is *Cryptocarya triplinervis*.

The subfamily **Apaturinae** differs from the Charaxinae in that adults lack hindwing tails, the spineless larva usually has two forward-pointing horns, resembling a green slug, and the egg is domed with strong vertical ribs. The subfamily includes the famous European Purple Emperor (*Apatura iris*).

The **Turquoise Emperor**, *Apaturina erminea* (fw ♂ 44 mm, ♀ 44 mm), is restricted to rainforest on Cape York Peninsula. It flies in the canopy and understorey, often perching head downwards on tree trunks to imbibe sap. It is also attracted to fallen fruit. Its life history is not recorded, but *Celtis* has been suggested as a possible host plant.

FAMILY NYMPHALIDAE—Nymphs and Their Allies

SUBFAMILY ACRAEINAE—
Glasswings

andromacha

The subfamily **Acraeinae** includes about 250 species worldwide. The majority occur in tropical Africa, with numerous species also in South America. Just one species is found in Australia and the Pacific Islands. Acraeines are small to medium-sized, long-winged species. Most feed as larvae on passion vines (Passifloraceae), obtaining toxins that render the adults unpalatable to vertebrate predators. In flight, they sail lazily or flutter weakly, within a few metres of the ground. Their wings are often clear, lacking scales over much of their surface, and tough. In many species, males capture females in flight and mate by force. These species also produce an external sphragis, attached to the abdomen of mated females. The majority of species occur in open savannah habitats. Those species that occur in rainforests (almost all in Africa) do not produce a sphragis and are never clear-winged.

The **Glasswing**, *Acraea andromacha* (fw ♂ 29–30 mm, ♀ 30–32 mm), is very common and widespread in the east and north of mainland Australia, extending well inland. It prefers open forest, but is also often seen at flowers along rainforest margins and in suburban gardens. Males often congregate in large numbers on hilltops. Males and females are alike in appearance. However, the two sexes behave differently: the males sail 1–3 m above the ground almost continually as they search for females; the females flutter around likely plants as they search for oviposition sites.

Their mating behaviour is unusual, and rather similar to that of the Big Greasy (Papilionidae). Males generally discover newly emerged females as soon as they fly, capturing and carrying them to the ground where they mate forcibly. Mating lasts for 90–150 minutes and the male deposits a sphragis. As in the Big Greasy, the tough clear wings of both sexes may help avoid damage during these violent meetings. In addition to the sphragis, the male secretes a small spermatophore internally, which contains an abnormal volume of sperm, much of which remains in the *bursa copulatrix*. Mated females are also often captured and sometimes the sphragis is removed by the plier-like claspers of the male. This is made easier by the structure of the female external genitalia, which is a broad convex non-stick plate, on which the sphragis is cemented. The presence of this structure may indicate that it is in the female's interests to mate with several males. When the sphragis is removed, the female is inseminated again, with a fresh sphragis secreted by the second male. It is usual in butterflies for the sperm of the last male to be used by the female to fertilise all her remaining eggs, but in *Acraea* this may not be the case, owing to the large volume of sperm from the first male remaining in the *bursa copulatrix*. Despite their frequent success in removing the sphragis, Glasswing males are apparently less insistent than those of the Big Greasy. If a perched or ovipositing female is approached, she can deter the male by a clear rejection display, in which she flashes her hindwings. Males also briefly take down other males, but as they are not obviously territorial, and seek females by patrolling wide areas of breeding habitat or by hilltopping, this behaviour may result from mistaken sexual identity.

Females lay their small eggs in very large clusters of 20–120 on leaves of the food plant. A female can potentially produce at least 500 eggs in her lifetime. Although

they use several native food plants, such as *Adenia heterophylla*, *Passiflora aurantia*, *P. cinnabarina* and *P. herbertiana* (Passifloraceae), as well as *Hybanthus aurantiacus*, *H. enneaspermus* and *H. stellarioides* (Violaceae), they very commonly oviposit on the more abundant introduced *Passiflora* species, especially *P. suberosa* (illustrated). Eggs may be laid on cultivated passionfruit vine, but larvae do not develop. The young larvae are highly gregarious, but later instars often feed alone. The beautifully patterned, elongate pupae are found suspended on or near the host plant.

FAMILY NYMPHALIDAE—Nymphs and Their Allies

SUBFAMILY HELICONIINAE—
Cruisers and Lacewings

arsinoe

The subfamily **Heliconiinae** is best known for its long-winged, colourful, passion-vine-feeding representatives from the South American tropics. They are unpalatable to predators and significant members of the mimicry rings, recognised by the nineteenth-century naturalist and explorer Henry Walter Bates, around the same time as Charles Darwin published *On the Origin of Species* (1859). Bates' insight, that palatable species come to resemble unpalatable ones, thus gaining protection from predators, provided strong early support for Darwin's theory. The subfamily includes two Indo-Australian genera. All species feed as larvae on plants of the family Passifloraceae, and are probably unpalatable. Three species occur in tropical Australia.

The **Cruiser**, *Vindula arsinoe* (fw ♂ 47 mm, ♀ 52 mm), is common in tropical Queensland rainforest. The males fly strongly, generally 1–3 m above the ground, with frequent gliding. They often perch in sunny patches with wings half open and are aggressive towards other males. Courtship is direct, with the male landing behind a perched female, sometimes following a brisk chase, positioning himself beside her, and mating.

C. cydippe ♀ ovipositing loose cluster of eggs

Adenia heterophylla

C. cydippe pupa

C. cydippe gregarious 5th instar larvae

C. cydippe ♀ sailing flight

C. cydippe ♂

200   The Butterflies of Australia

V. arsinoe ♂

V. arsinoe ♀

C. penthesilea ♂

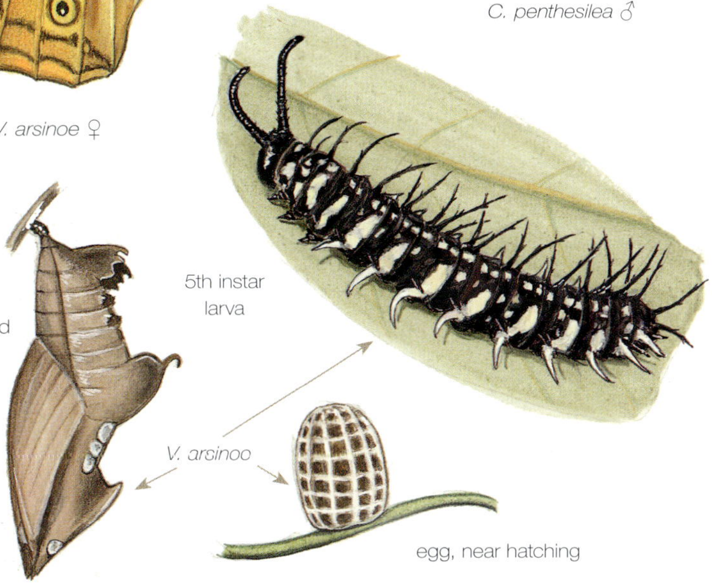

pupa, suspended

5th instar larva

V. arsinoe

egg, near hatching

Sometimes he must insinuate himself under her half-opened wings. Males often drink at damp soil, extracting salts. Females fly higher with a more pronounced flap, and also glide for short distances. The large, heavily sculptured eggs are laid singly, typically on dried tendrils of the food plant. The mature larvae resemble centipedes. The pupa is highly ornate, with broad-fringed flanges and silver spots, yet is cryptic, resembling a dead leaf. Larval food plants include *Adenia heterophylla*, *Hollrungia* species and *Passiflora aurantia*.

The **Red Lacewing**, *Cethosia cydippe* (fw ♂ 45 mm, ♀ 46 mm), is locally common in tropical Queensland rainforest. Both sexes fly with a leisurely gliding flight, typically 2–4 m from the ground. When perched with wings outspread, the brilliant red upperside presents a dramatic and unforgettable sight. The small eggs are laid in large, loose clusters on newly growing stems of the food plant, *Adenia heterophylla*. The larvae, strikingly banded in later instars, feed in groups. The pupa resembles a piece of dead leaf.

The **Orange Lacewing**, *Cethosia penthesilea* (fw ♂ 40 mm, ♀ 41 mm), is locally common in monsoon forest near Darwin. Its habits and life history are similar to those of *C. cydippe*. In flight, it is rather similar to the Lesser Wanderer (*Danaus petilia*), and the two may be Müllerian mimics of each other.

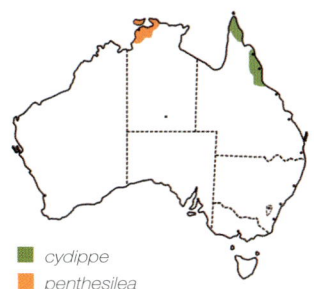

■ *cydippe*
■ *penthesilea*

FAMILY NYMPHALIDAE—Nymphs and Their Allies

SUBFAMILY ARGYNNINAE— FRITILLARIES AND THEIR ALLIES

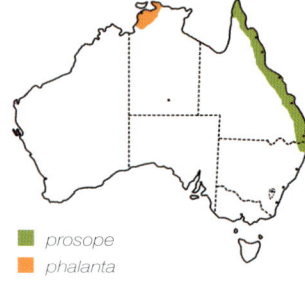

prosope
phalanta

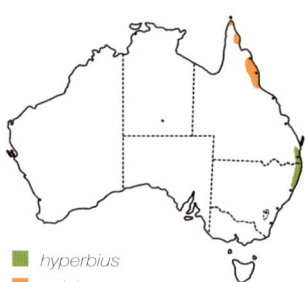

hyperbius
egista

The subfamily **Argynninae** includes numerous northern hemisphere temperate species known as fritillaries.* Fritillaries have orange-and-black spotted wings, and generally feed on violets. Australia has just one rare species. There is also a small group of tropical genera, varied in wing shape and pattern, feeding mainly on Flacourtiaceae; it is represented in Australia by three genera with one species each.

The **Rustic**, *Cupha prosope* (fw ♂ 30 mm, ♀ 32 mm), is moderately common in eastern Queensland, frequenting rainforest margins and riverine vine forests, wherever its food plant grows. Adults fly quite rapidly 1–2 m above the ground, settling frequently on leaves in sunny glades with wings half open. Males open and close their wings restlessly as they sit, and often contest desirable perches, with two antagonists disappearing into the canopy in a blur of orange. The small, rounded eggs are laid singly on young leaves of the food plant, typically *Scolopia braunii*. The larval head capsule is distinctively marked, as though wearing sunglasses. The bright green, silver-spotted pupa has several long filamentous spines, and is suspended at an angle of about 30 degrees below the leaf or twig on which it forms. Other host plants include *Flacourtia* and *Xylosma* species.

The **Vagrant**, *Vagrans egista* (fw ♂ 29 mm, ♀ 32 mm), is uncommon in lowland rainforest in Queensland's wet tropics region. Adults fly along rainforest tracks and streams, generally 2–4 m above the ground. They typically perch in sunny patches with wings closed, and sometimes males descend to extract salts from damp soil. The

---

* In Britain, especially, the term fritillary, derived from the Latin word for a gambling die, is often applied to any orange-and-black spotted butterfly (as well as a spotted tulip-like wildflower). Not all 'fritillaries' belong to the subfamily Argynninae.

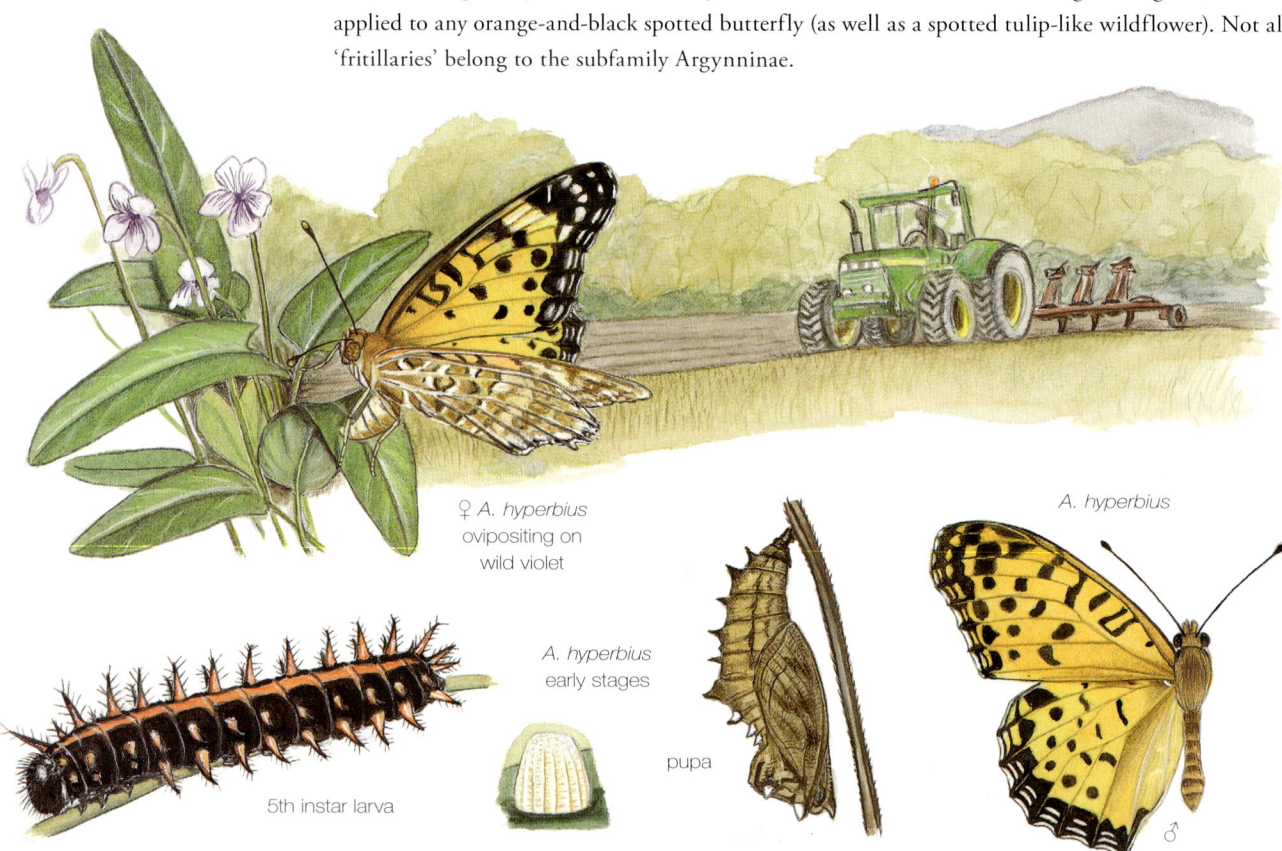

♀ *A. hyperbius* ovipositing on wild violet

A. hyperbius early stages

egg

pupa

A. hyperbius

5th instar larva

life history is very similar to that of the Rustic, the spiny green-brown larva having an almost identical black-marked orange head capsule. The host plant is *Homalium circumpinnatum*.

The **Leopard**, *Phalanta phalanta* (fw ♂ 26 mm, ♀ 27 mm), is locally common in monsoon forest near Darwin. It flies quite rapidly, usually 1–3 m above the ground, perching with half-open wings in sunny patches. The small conical egg is laid singly on new growth of the host, typically *Flacourtia territorialis*. The pupa lacks long spines. The spiny green larva has unmistakable clownish marks on its head capsule. These markings, and those on the head capsule of the Rustic and the Vagrant, suggest the head of a predatory wasp, which perhaps might deter a tiny parasitic wasp or fly.

The **Australian Fritillary**, *Argyreus hyperbius inconstans* (fw ♂ 33 mm, ♀ 35 mm), is probably Australia's most endangered butterfly and is protected in Queensland. It inhabits damp gullies in coastal areas where its host plant, *Viola betonicifolia*, grows. Its historical distribution was from Gympie to Port Macquarie, but due to urban 'development' and agricultural vandalism the only extant colony known is in northern New South Wales. The adults are quite rapid in flight, especially when disturbed, but keep low to the ground. The eggs are laid singly on leaves of the host plant and the larva, in later instars, may defoliate a plant and be forced to walk across open ground to locate more food.

SUBFAMILY LIMENITINAE—
Aeroplanes

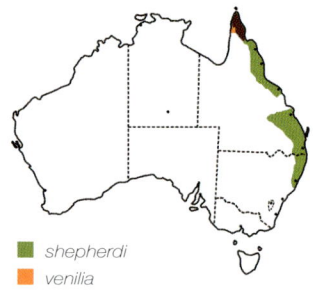

■ shepherdi
■ venilia

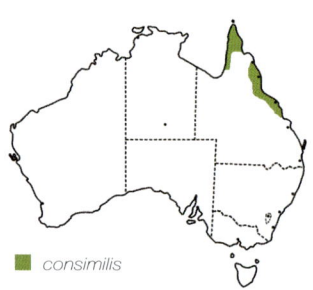

■ consimilis

■ praslini

■ aeropa

The subfamily **Limenitinae** includes five Australian species in four genera. Adults have a distinctive staccato, planing mode of flight, each wing beat followed by a short, crisp level glide of a metre or two, with wings held absolutely flat. The egg in limenitines is hairy, and the larvae and pupae are distinctive.

The **Common Aeroplane**, *Phaedyma shepherdi* (fw ♂ 33 mm, ♀ 34 mm), is common in the eastern tropics and subtropics. It frequents rainforest margins, riverine scrub and suburban gardens. Adults generally fly 2–5 m above the ground. Males perch quite high with wings half open on sunlit leaves, but typically every few minutes make brief patrols centred on their perch, flying with the typical jerky planing flight. During territorial disputes, males fly very rapidly, circling one another as they ascend to 10 m or more, but as soon as the victor returns he reverts to brisk planing. Eggs are laid singly on young growth of the host plant. The larva has wonderful disruptive coloration, accentuated by the contorted posture it adopts at rest. If a parasitoid still recognises it as a caterpillar, it may be deterred by small marks that appear to mimic the eggs of tachinid flies, suggesting that it is already infested. Larvae feed on leaves of a wide range of host plants, including *Aphananthe*, *Argyrodendron*, *Bombax*, *Brachychiton*, *Celtis*, *Cordia*, *Ehretia*, *Grewia*, *Mucuna* and *Pongamia*.

The **Cape York Aeroplane**, *Pantoporia venilia* (fw ♂ 25 mm, ♀ 27 mm), is restricted to closed forest on Cape York Peninsula. It is a nervous insect, flying 2–5 m above the ground, in short, sharp glides, perching frequently but briefly. The larva feeds on *Lepidopetalum subdichotomum*.

The **Orange Aeroplane**, *Pantoporia consimilis* (fw ♂ 20 mm, ♀ 23 mm), is common in north Queensland rainforest. Adults fly in clearings and around streams. Flight is almost always jerky planing at 1–3 m above the ground, with frequent brief perching on the upperside of sunny leaves with wings half open. The larva has disruptive black markings and adopts a hunched posture when resting. Food plants include *Austrosteenisia blackii*, *Dalbergia candenatensis* and *Derris* species.

The **Black and White Aeroplane**, *Neptis praslini* (fw ♂ 25 mm, ♀ 25 mm), is locally common in north Queensland rainforest. It is a remarkable mimic of the unpalatable Hamadryad (*Tellervo zoilus*), having not just a similar wing pattern but also yellow eyes. It flies 2–4 m above the ground with a weak flutter. When alarmed, however, it reverts to a rather absurd, weak, jerky planing, typical of its group. Males also perch frequently on the upperside of sunlit leaves, with half-open wings, whereas the Hamadryad spends much more time in flight and, when it does perch, it is invariably on the underside of leaves with closed wings. This perching behaviour by *N. praslini* is probably risky, but also integral to a male's chances of finding a mate. Larvae feed on *Briedelia penangiana*, *Erycibe coccinea* and *Phylacium bracteosum*.

The **Orange Archduke**, *Lexias aeropa* (fw ♂ 35 mm, ♀ 48 mm), is, in Australia, restricted to rainforest on Cape York Peninsula, where it is found in the understorey, perching on low vegetation and feeding on the ground at rotting fruit. It flies in a series of giant, ground-hugging glides, each broken with a strong flap of the wings. The larva, not yet known from Australia, is green with very long, lateral, finely branched spines.

FAMILY NYMPHALIDAE—Nymphs and Their Allies

SUBFAMILY NYMPHALINAE—
Nymphs

The subfamily **Nymphalinae** includes a diverse array of medium-sized to large, often very colourful butterflies. They occur worldwide and are well represented in both temperate and tropical regions. In many tropical species, colours and wing shapes are highly modified by mimicry or for camouflage, hence there is no pattern common to all members of the subfamily, although scalloped wing margins and conspicuous eyespots occur frequently.

Many earlier works on Australian butterflies treat the members of the subfamilies Heliconiinae, Argynninae and Limenitinae as falling within the Nymphalinae, largely on the basis of the morphology of their early stages. Other authors elsewhere have recognised these as separate groupings, but have accorded them the rank of tribe, which means their group name changes to end in -ini, rather than -inae (e.g. 'Limenitini'). Ultimately, the higher classification of a group will always be a matter of taste, and even if we had a complete record of the evolutionary tree of these butterflies we would still have no objective criteria for calling a group a subfamily or a tribe. However, it is important to recognise natural groupings as indicated by best available research, the most recent of which involves DNA analysis and supports the integrity of the Nymphalinae. We followed the scheme used by Braby (2000), which is in general agreement with the most recent research, itself a work in progress.

Before molecular evidence became available, the main basis for distinguishing the subfamily from others listed above was their larval host plant preferences. All feed on species of dicotyledons, commonly low-growing herbs from several largely unrelated families, including Acanthaceae, Amaranthaceae, Asteraceae, Goodeniaceae, Lamiaceae, Plantaginaceae, Portulacaceae, Scrophulariaceae, Urticaceae and others. Individual species or genera may show a preference for related plants, but as a family host plants seem to be selected mainly on the basis of growth form and palatability. So far as is known, all or most species are palatable to vertebrate and invertebrate predators, and worldwide the subfamily includes many Batesian mimics. Several species are spectacular migrants and cross oceans on a fairly regular basis.

Although the Australian fauna includes just eleven species of permanently breeding nymphalines, with an additional three recorded as occasional or rare immigrants, they are prominent members of our fauna. Almost all established species are at least locally common, tend to be very widespread within their ranges, and are low-flying and conspicuous. Males of many species are territorial and perch with wings half open, revealing striking upperside colours. Several species occur over much of the continent and three are found regularly in Tasmania. No species is endemic; the majority range throughout the Asian tropics—the Blue Argus (*Junonia orithya*) is widespread in Africa as well. Painted ladies and admirals (genus *Vanessa*) are found almost everywhere in the temperate regions of the world, and sometimes also in the tropics.

Many Nymphalinae frequently adopt a low, flat-winged, punctuated planing flight, but seldom is this as regular as in the Limenitinae, nor are the movements as crisply defined. When alarmed, they tend to fly very rapidly with a slight jinking motion. Mimetic species adopt the flight mode of their noxious models, typically slow sailing or, in the case of the White Nymph (*Mynes geoffroyi*), a steady flutter. As with the Acraeinae, some Heliconiinae, Argynninae and some Limenitinae, the larvae have branched spines, and the egg is a hemispherical dome, or a little higher, with well-defined vertical ribs. Females are often seen walking over the ground around their prostrate host plants, meticulously selecting suitable leaves on which to deposit one or two eggs. Only the White Nymph, which feeds on Stinging Trees, lays its eggs in clusters. Pupae of some species have small metallic silver or gold markings, but even so are very well camouflaged, generally mimicking dead leaves very effectively.

Blue Argus
(*Junonia orithya*)

Meadow Argus, Blue Argus and Brown Soldier

villida

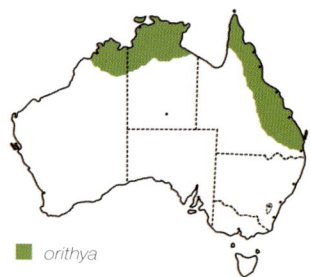
orithya

hedonia

The genus *Junonia* occurs in tropical regions throughout the world. Many are found in gardens and open wasteland, hence are among the commonest and most frequently encountered species wherever they occur. They are low-flying, typically skimming the ground in a series of fast, jerky glides with wings held flat. Many are killed on roads as a result of this habit. In Australia, they have been assigned the common names Argus, on account of their prominent eyespots, or Soldier on account of the drab brown coloration, but elsewhere they are almost universally known as pansies. They often exhibit slight seasonal variation and many species are migratory.

The **Meadow Argus**, *Junonia villida* (fw ♂ 26 mm, ♀ 28 mm), is common in suitable habitat over the entire Australian mainland and much of Tasmania. It occurs in a wide variety of open and lightly wooded habitats, including semi-arid regions, pastures and urban gardens. They are active in sunny conditions and often feed at flowers. In colder areas, they spend long periods basking with open wings. Males, especially, perch on the ground or low prominences with wings half open, guarding small territories, usually near patches of the prostrate herbs on which the larvae feed. During disputes, males spiral upwards for 10–15 m with a rapid whirring flight. Ovipositing females flutter near the ground, often walking for short distances from plant to plant. Normal flight for both sexes is a series of low (less than 0.5 m) fast glides on outspread, flattened wings, each punctuated by one or more flaps of the wings. Adults are migratory, and females may suspend egg production during the tropical dry season. Eggs are laid singly on leaves of the host plant. Larvae feed by day or night, but usually lie concealed in ground debris when not feeding. The pupa is suspended from low vegetation and is highly cryptic. *Plantago* is a common host in south-eastern Australia, but many other plants from several families are utilised. These include *Epaltes, Goodenia, Hyptis, Portulaca, Ruellia, Scabiosa, Scaevola, Stemodia, Veronica, Verbena* and others.

The **Blue Argus**, *Junonia orithya* (fw ♂ 23 mm, ♀ 26 mm), is common in open habitat in the tropical north and east. It reaches the New South Wales border in the east, but becomes increasingly rarer south of the Tropic of Capricorn. The male and female differ considerably in their upperside markings, and are easily recognised when perched with wings spread or when flying with wings held flat. Behaviour and life history is very like that of the Meadow Argus. They may suspend reproductive activity during the dry season and extend their range southward and inland during more favourable conditions. Numerous host plants are used, most of which are not shared with the Meadow Argus. These include *Angelonia, Asystasia, Brunoniella, Buchnera, Hypoestes, Justicia, Pseuderanthemum, Rostellularia, Striga, Thunbergia* and others.

The **Brown Soldier**, *Junonia hedonia* (fw ♂ 28 mm, ♀ 32 mm), is common in lowland parts of the northern and eastern tropics, and rare in subtropical coastal Queensland. It is especially abundant at the edge of riverine forest and in swampy areas. Flight is typical of the genus, but rather crisper, with the broken gliding motion better punctuated and higher, within about 2 m of the ground. Males often perch with half-open wings on leaves around this height. During hot, dry weather, both sexes perch on plant stems in shaded gullies, head downwards with wings folded so as to resemble a dead leaf. This is also the typical nocturnal roosting position. The life history is somewhat similar to that of the Meadow Argus. The usual host plant, *Hygrophilia angustifolia*, grows in moist and swampy areas.

FAMILY NYMPHALIDAE—Nymphs and Their Allies

Painted Lady and Australian Admiral

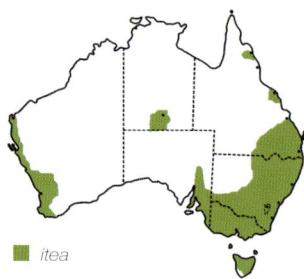

kershawi
cardui

itea

The small genus *Vanessa* is remarkable in that it has a nearly worldwide distribution, absent only from Antarctica, the high Arctic and parts of the tropics. It even includes one endemic species of admiral in New Zealand, which has one of the most impoverished butterfly faunas on earth. The adults of painted ladies, of which there are several species, are spectacular migrants, sometimes crossing oceans. In *Vanessa*, the sexes are very alike. The term 'admiral' has been used for several members of the genus *Vanessa* for at least two centuries. However, the original eighteenth-century name was 'admirable'. This linguistic curiosity fascinated the novelist and lepidopterist Vladimir Nabokov who, until his death, insisted that this archaic name was the correct one, and that admiral was a regrettable modern solecism.

The **Australian Painted Lady**, *Vanessa kershawi* (fw ♂ 29 mm, ♀ 31 mm), is widespread in open habitats over the eastern and southern parts of the Australian mainland and also Tasmania. Adults fly close to the ground in long, quick, stuttering glides on horizontal outstretched wings, punctuated mostly by a single flap of the wings. They often perch on the ground or on flowers with wings three-quarters open. In cooler latitudes, especially, they may remain in this posture for several minutes at a time, absorbing sunshine and raising their body temperature. When migrating, they tend to fly higher, up to 2 m above the ground, with more active beating of the wings. When attacked by aerial predators, such as robber flies, dragonflies or birds, they have a spectacular escape reflex whereby they fold their wings and plummet to the ground, apparently lifeless. They remain in a catatonic state for some minutes and can be picked up and laid flat on the hand, where they remain until roused. Often the presence of numerous *V. kershawi* indicates that a migration is passing through, and they do not necessarily exhibit reproductive behaviour. When they are settled in an area, males establish small territories defended from low perches. Mating is most likely to occur on or near the ground. The female lays her eggs singly on one of a wide range of hosts, including *Ammobium*, *Arctotheca*, *Bracteantha*, *Chrysocephalum*, *Gnaphalium*, *Helichrysum* and *Rhodanthe*. The drab larva makes a shelter of rolled leaves of the host, feeding mainly at night. The well-camouflaged pupa is slung from low vegetation, resembling a scrap of dead leaf.

The **European Painted Lady**, *Vanessa cardui* (fw ♂ 28 mm, ♀ 30 mm), is found from September to January in the Perth area. Migrants arrive in some years, probably from Africa, flying across the Indian Ocean, and may breed and become established

kershawi ♀ on paper daisy

210

temporarily. It can be distinguished from the very similar *V. kershawi* by the more acutely pointed forewings, straighter wing margins and the presence of more (four to five) spots towards the outer margins of the hindwing. Its biology is very like that of *V. kershawi*.

The **Australian Admiral**, *Vanessa itea* (fw ♂ 30 mm, ♀ 32 mm), is found in open areas and forest margins in the south-east and south-west of the mainland and in Tasmania. It is rapid in flight, employing the stuttering glide infrequently. It often perches high, to about 5 m, on foliage overlooking nettle patches, or on hilltops. It may also perch low in the centre of a nettle patch, if no high perches are nearby. When thus *en garde*, the wings of the male are often held half open. Both sexes feed at flowers and on sap oozing from tree trunks, perching head downwards with wings closed. The eggs are laid singly on various herbs of the nettle family, including *Parietaria*, *Pipturis*, *Soleirolia* and *Urtica*. The young larvae construct shelters of rolled leaves held together with silk, and feed at night. Older larvae may feed openly by day. The silver-spangled pupa is suspended from the host plant or nearby vegetation and is highly cryptic.

FAMILY NYMPHALIDAE—Nymphs and Their Allies

Eggflies

bolina

misippus

alimena

The genus *Hypolimnas* occurs in tropical regions throughout the Old World. Eggflies are medium-sized to large butterflies. Males of most species are highly territorial. Both sexes have a loose punctuated gliding mode of flight, or rapid jinking when alarmed. Many, especially the females, are mimics of unpalatable species, such as danaines. Mimetic species adopt the sailing flight of their noxious model. Females are sometimes polymorphic—having mimetic or non-mimetic forms concurrently.

The **Common Eggfly**, *Hypolimnas bolina* (fw ♂ 46 mm, ♀ 50 mm), is widespread and common in a wide variety of habitats, including urban gardens, in northern and eastern areas. It sometimes extends its range inland over the eastern half of the continent. Males perch on leaves with wings half to three-quarters open, displaying their bold upperside, purple-fringed white markings. The margins of these patches also reflect UV light strongly. Often the wings are slowly opened and closed with a regular rhythm. Males defend their perches aggressively, attacking not just other males but other butterflies that stray into the vicinity. When a female is located, the male courts her by flying below her with a smooth gliding action punctuated by quick, low amplitude beats, the outspread wings displaying the upperside markings. A receptive female perches on low vegetation with wings folded, and the male lands just behind her, walking alongside her, and bending his abdomen to establish genital coupling. Mating lasts 1–2 hours. The female lays her eggs singly or in small loose clusters on low-growing herbs, including *Alternanthera denticulata*, *Sida rhombifolia*, *Synedrella nodiflora* and many other genera. Larvae hide in shelters away from the food plant by day, feeding at night. Young larvae are gregarious but become solitary as they grow older.

The **Danaid Eggfly**, *Hypolimnas misippus* (fw ♂ 34 mm, ♀ 40 mm), occurs in open habitats in the tropical north and east and is rare south of Mackay. The behaviour of males is similar to that of *H. bolina*, but it is seldom as abundant. It is easily recognised by its smaller size and relatively large white patches. The female is a superb mimic of

bolina males sparring in territorial dispute

misippus ♀
(mimics *Danaus petilia*)

larger eyespots

misippus ♂

the noxious Lesser Wanderer (*Danaus petilia*), flying with the same easy sailing motion, with wings canted above the horizontal. The lacy fringe on the hindwing gives it away, at least to humans and, like many mimics, it is often damaged by birds, presumably following a hesitant attack. When alarmed, it flies with a rapid jinking motion. The life history is similar to that of *H. bolina* and the larval host plants include *Asystasia gangetica*, *Portulaca oleracea* and *Pseuderanthemum variabile*.

The **Blue Eggfly**, *Hypolimnas alimena* (fw ♂ 40 mm, ♀ 43 mm), is common at rainforest edges in the northern tropics. It is uncommon in the subtropics. Behaviour and life history is fairly similar to that of *H. bolina*, but the eggs are laid singly, the larva is solitary and darker, and the pupa is more elongate. The host plant is *Pseuderanthemum variabile*. The female has a blue-green and a rarer brown form. Near Darwin, the female form of the race *H. a. darwinensis* is almost always brown.

The **Malayan Eggfly**, *Hypolimnas anomala* (fw ♂ 42 mm, ♀ 44 mm) (not illustrated), is known from five specimens from Cape York Peninsula and near Darwin. Males and females mimic common Asian *Euploea* species not known to occur in Australia. It is the commonest eggfly species in peninsular Malaysia.

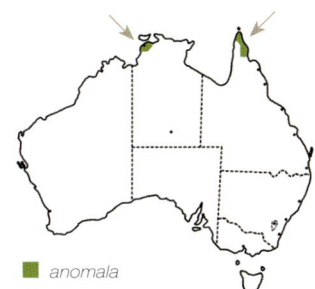

anomala

FAMILY NYMPHALIDAE—Nymphs and Their Allies

White Nymph, Leafwing and Lurcher

These three species are unrelated, specialised, tropical forest species. They exhibit a range of characteristics unusual among Australian nymphalines.

geoffroyi

The **White Nymph**, *Mynes geoffroyi* (fw ♂ 32 mm, ♀ 32 mm), is locally common in Queensland in tropical and subtropical rainforest and moist scrub. Males and females are strikingly different on the upperside but similar on the underside. The usual form, with a dark underside, is a very effective mimic of *Delias nigrina*, known to be unpalatable. It flies high (3–6 m), with a steady flutter, just like *Delias*. Although the underside pattern is not like that of *D. nigrina* in detail, it has the same general colours and, due to its mode of flight, which appears as a series of winking black and white or black and grey flashes, the illusion is very effective. Nevertheless, wing damage due to unsuccessful bird attacks is common, as is often the case with mimics. On occasions, when it occurs in open country flying between patches of forest, it may adopt an element of planing, typical of its subfamily, which is presumably a more efficient mode of flight for covering long distances. In north Queensland a form with pale undersides also occurs in both sexes, which is believed to mimic *Delias mysis*. In this form, the female is also white above. The small, ribbed eggs are laid in clusters of 15–65 on the leaves of the host plant, typically the stinging trees *Dendrocnide moroides* and *D. photinophylla*, and *Pipturus argenteus*. The extraordinary larvae are white-spangled black, with pink branching spines. They feed gregariously, grouped very closely. The elongate pupae are typically suspended from leaves of their dangerous host plant, also in groups.

bisaltide

The **Leafwing**, *Doleschallia bisaltide* (fw ♂ 38 mm, ♀ 42 mm), is common but local in rainforest and dense moist scrub in the eastern tropics and subtropics. It is sometimes found in suburban gardens. The adults are typically found in the vicinity of their low herbaceous food plant, *Pseuderanthemum variabile*. They fly rapidly for short distances within 2 m of the ground, then abruptly settle on the ground or low vegetation with wings folded. Often when watched in flight they seem to disappear, as the dead-leaf impression of the folded wings is so effective and is adopted so rapidly. The finely ribbed spherical eggs are laid singly or in small, loose groups on the leaves or buds of the host. The handsome larvae, with deep-blue iridescent spines, are sometimes found wandering over the forest floor in search of new host plants. Other host plants include *Asystasia gangetica*, *Graptophyllum*, *Ruellia* and *Strobilanthes*.

sabina

The **Lurcher**, *Yoma sabina* (fw ♂ 38 mm, ♀ 42 mm), is a rare northern rainforest species. It occurs along paths and in sunlit forest gaps, flying 1–4 m high. As its name suggests, it has a rather floppy erratic flight, but sometimes glides slowly. It frequently perches on leaves for long periods with wings held nearly flat. When it perches with wings closed on tree trunks or among leaf litter on the ground, it is almost impossible to detect, owing to its 'dead-leaf' underside pattern. The life history is similar to that of *Doleschallia bisaltide*, the eggs being laid singly on the small herbaceous food plant. Larvae must move over the forest floor to obtain food as they exhaust their small hosts, which include *Dipteracanthus bracheatus* and *Ruellia*.

FAMILY NYMPHALIDAE—Nymphs and Their Allies

SUBFAMILY LIBYTHEINAE— BEAKS

geoffroy

The worldwide subfamily **Libytheinae** comprises just twelve species in two closely related genera. They occur in most warm temperate and tropical regions, and it is usual for just one, or at most two, wide-ranging species to be present in any given region. Members of the subfamily are distinguished by their very long, projecting labial palps—processes on the front of their mouthparts flanking the proboscis, giving them their popular names of beaks or snouts. The egg is very small and elongate, resembling certain pierid eggs rather than those of other nymphalids. The larva lacks spines and the pupa is suspended at a shallow angle below a leaf or twig.

The **Beak**, *Libythea geoffroy* (fw ♂ 26 mm, ♀ 26 mm), is generally uncommon in monsoon forest or at rainforest edges in northern Australia. Western and eastern populations differ slightly and represent separate subspecies. The males perch inconspicuously on twigs and leaves in sunny glades, generally 3–6 m high, and defend their positions vigorously. Flight is rapid, especially during territorial contests, when the antagonists spiral rapidly into the sky. Females usually perch on the host plant, *Celtis paniculata*. The very small (0.65 x 0.4 mm) elongate eggs are laid singly in crevices on the food plant near new growth or inserted at the base of leaf axils. Much of the females' time is spent searching for suitable oviposition sites, and it is probable that they produce an unusually large number of eggs, given the small size of each egg. The young larvae adopt a pronounced 'S' shape when at rest, which becomes less obvious in older larva. If disturbed, they throw themselves to the ground on the end of a long silken thread, thrashing convulsively. Once danger is past, they recover their position by ascending this thread, climbing with forelegs and mouthparts. Pupae also thrash violently from side to side when disturbed.

geoffroy ♂ ♀ — perched ♂ — strongly angled pupa — 5th instar larva

FAMILY LYCAENIDAE
Blues, Coppers and Hairstreaks

A summer's walk through grass or clover will kick up a cloud of tiny blue butterflies. Purplish flickerings around Plumbago bushes, common in eastern gardens, are also blues—sometimes appearing by the hundred. The more keen-eyed will spot the tiny dark silhouettes circling the tops of our tallest trees, while the bushwalker will, from time to time, espy the gorgeous tailed butterflies we call, appropriately, imperial blues, fluttering around their masses of larvae and pupae on feathery-leaved wattle bushes. These little gems are butterflies of the family Lycaenidae—the blues, coppers and hairstreaks—representatives of the largest family of butterflies worldwide and the most diverse of our Australian families.

Common Pencilled Blue
(*Candalides absimilis*)

Worldwide, the Lycaenidae is the second-largest family of butterflies. At present, about 6000 species have been named. It is likely, however, that among this family, as with the skippers, many species are yet to be discovered and the final number may reach the 10,000-species mark. Even within Australia, each year a trickle of new species is described, or known forms are upgraded from subspecies rank, adding to our total of more than 140 species. Following Braby (2000), we recognise four subfamilies as occurring in Australia. These are the metalmarks (Riodininae), the Moth Butterfly (Liphyrinae), the hairstreaks (Theclinae) and the true blues (Polyommatinae). Riodininae and Liphyrinae are represented in Australia by just a single species each. The remaining species are roughly shared between the Theclinae and Polyommatinae.

The Lycaenidae are principally defined by features of their wing venation. In addition, in the male the front legs are almost always reduced in size yet still functional, but they are normal in the female. The antennae are set close together on the top of the head. The eyes are large and close together. Very many have orange-ringed eyespots on the underside of the hindwing associated with hair-like tails, a feature not found in other families. They range in size from tiny to (occasionally) medium-sized, but the vast majority are small. Iridescent blue or purple colouring on the upperside of the wings is very common. Their larvae are curiously flattened, or at least triangular in section, and only rarely bear spines or tubercles. The eggs are generally flattened, mandarin- or bun-shaped, with coarse or fine pitting. The pupae are short and squat, mostly rounded. They have a girdle around their midriff and may be attached to the food plant or to pads of larval silk. The larvae (and sometimes pupae) are often associated with ants.

FIGURE 9.1: Northern Large Azure (*Ogyris zosine*) larva tended by *Camponotus* ants.

tentacular organ

dorsal nectary organ

Despite their numerous species, some of which occur at high population densities, and the frequently brilliant colours on the uppersides of their wings, adult lycaenids are little noticed by the casual observer. No Australian species attains even medium size, except for the rare tropical Moth Butterfly. Those that are brilliantly coloured tend to be also very local, typically remaining very close to their larval host plant, and often flying very high. They may also be quite inactive, spending much of their day perching, so you can only rarely see the flickerings of bright blue and purple, as the sunlight flashes from their uppersides. An exception is the Common Oakblue (*Arhopala micale*) from the northern tropics, which is moderately large, flies quite low, is very active, and is also common and widespread in gardens and at forest edges. Seen in flight, its brilliant colours and stubby tails are reminiscent of a miniature Ulysses Butterfly (*Papilio ulysses*). Other species, such as the grass blues and lineblues, are very abundant and widespread, and fly conveniently at or below eye level. However, they are almost all quite drab, both on upper- and undersides, and their quick zipping motion and frequent perching make them difficult to follow. Nevertheless, for all the difficulties of observing most lycaenid species in the wild, they are very popular with collectors. Methods of obtaining the rarer specimens include using large nets with handles 7 m long; searching under bark at the base of trees for pupae, or even setting traps—consisting of pieces of corrugated cardboard bound to the trunks of host trees—where larvae pupate. Another strategy is to visit hilltops where males of many of the rarest species congregate and perch in vegetation. Of course, as with any collecting activity, the locations of the best sites are often closely guarded secrets.

Almost all our lycaenids feed on flowering plants, mostly dicotyledons, although it is difficult to generalise beyond that. Some have highly specific host plant requirements; others are restricted to one or a very small group of species. There are higher-level relationships between genera of lycaenids and related groups of food plants—examples include the mistletoe-feeding *Ogyris* species, the *Acacia*-feeding *Jalmenus* species, *Bursaria*-feeding *Paralucia* species, and so on—but even within these relationships there may be startling exceptions to the general pattern. Thus, although most species of Theclinae feed as larvae on dicotyledons, several exclusively utilise monocotyledons, or even ferns. One species of polyommatine, *Theclinesthes onycha*, feeds on cycads. It has been suggested that the development of the extraordinary relationships between ants and many lycaenid larvae may have allowed a diversification in food plant range on the part of the butterflies. As far as is known, in many cases the butterflies do not obtain chemical protection from their host plant, and therefore do not need to adapt to coping with particular plant toxins, allowing a more general diet. They are, however, protected by the ants. The ant–butterfly relationship has almost certainly allowed a small group of species to evolve predatory habits, with their larvae feeding on the larvae of the ants themselves.

We have discussed the extraordinary interactions between lycaenid larvae and ants and the specialised organs of the larvae in Chapter 3. The tentacular organs and the dorsal nectary organ, resembling a nightmarish human mouth, can be clearly seen in

Figure 9.1. This relationship, and its associated larval adaptations, remains the outstanding unique feature distinguishing the lycaenids (including the riodinines) from all other butterflies. The ant–butterfly relationship is not uniformly apparent in all lycaenids, but in one form or another it occurs in virtually all subfamilies.

Several lineages of lycaenids form large endemic or nearly endemic clusters, chief among these being the large thecline genera *Jalmenus* and *Ogyris*, and the polyommatine genus *Theclinesthes*. Others, such as *Hypochrysops*, *Philiris* and *Candalides*, are also very diverse in New Guinea but range little further. As with all the other groups of butterflies, there is a dramatic peak in species richness in the north-east owing to the many species and genera that also occur in South-East Asia. The genus *Arhopala*, for example, with four species in Australia, has nearly 40 species in Papua New Guinea and over 80 in Borneo. A great many species of lycaenid butterflies have very restricted ranges, and more than a dozen species are known only from tiny areas of the continent. Sometimes this is because they are very hard to recognise and the restrictions may be more apparent than real. In other cases, however, they are undoubtedly genuinely restricted to very small areas, and when these highly restricted ranges impinge on human needs, real conservation problems may arise. The very first cause célèbre in Australia was the case of the Eltham Copper (*Paralucia pyrodiscus lucida*), the tiny remnant populations of which were threatened by development in Victoria. The full species *Acrodipsas illidgei*, *Paralucia spinifera* and *Hypochrysops piceatus* have now overtaken the Eltham Copper as lycaenids of greatest conservation concern in Australia.

From an evolutionary point of view, there is a clear 'sister' relationship between the so-called metalmarks—the Riodininae—and the rest of the Lycaenidae. The riodinines are very diverse in the New World tropics, where they equal or outnumber other lycaenids, but much less so elsewhere. The single Australian species of this group, the Australian Harlequin (*Praetaxila segecia*), is found only on Cape York Peninsula. It also occurs in New Guinea along with some twenty related species in two genera. Recent researchers have tended to classify the two groups together as one family—the Lycaenidae—with two separate subfamilies: the Lycaeninae (the blues, coppers and hairstreaks) and the Riodininae. Equally legitimate is an approach which regards them as two separate families (Braby 2004). However, although Braby (2000) treats the Riodininae, Liphyrinae, Theclinae and Polyommatinae as equivalent subfamilies and, for convenience of reference, we follow this scheme, we note that it is certain that the Riodininae stands apart from the others.* An additional large subfamily—the Lycaeninae (the true coppers)—does not occur in Australia, although there are a few representatives in both New Zealand and New Guinea. Our four so-called 'coppers' are in fact copper-coloured Theclines! This may serve as an object lesson in the value of formal scientific names, even when authorities keep changing the endings.

---

* Strictly speaking, if we divide the whole family into two basic subfamilies—the Lycaeninae and the Riodininae (as do Common and Waterhouse, 1972)—then the subdivisions of the Lycaeninae should have a different (lower) taxonomic status (for example tribes), as are recognised in Papilionidae, and would be written as Liphyrini, Theclini and Polommatini.

SUBFAMILY RIODININAE— METALMARKS

■ *segecia*

The subfamily **Riodininae** has just one member in the far north of Australia. A number of genera occur from New Guinea and South-East Asia to tropical Africa, with one species even reaching northern Europe. However, they attain an extraordinary peak of diversity in tropical Central and South America, where they may outnumber all other lycaenids in terms of species, presenting an astonishing variety of forms, some of which apparently mimic other butterflies. As with conventional lycaenids, many of the larvae of these South American riodinines are tended by ants, but they have a quite different array of associated glandular organs, placed on different segments of the body. Many riodinines, especially in South America, have heavy metallic markings; some of them appear to have been splashed with molten silver, giving them their popular name—metalmarks.

The **Australian Harlequin**, *Praetaxila segecia* (fw ♂ 24 mm, ♀ 26 mm), occurs in tropical rainforest north from Iron Range, on Cape York Peninsula. Adults fly rapidly and erratically in the forest understorey. They perch low, typically on leaves 1–2 m high, or on the ground, either with wings folded or slightly open. They are very wary, starting at the least disturbance. The curious egg is barrel-shaped, truncate at the top, and an extraordinary shade of purple. Such eggs are unique to a section of the subfamily, although the colour is peculiar to species of the genus *Praetaxila*. They are laid in small, scattered clusters on old leaves of the larval food plant, a rainforest understorey tree, *Rapanea porosa*, usually within 2 m of the ground. The larvae feed gregariously, particularly when young. All stages of the larvae and the pupae are covered in very long hairs, possibly as a protection against parasitoids. Pupation commonly occurs in dead leaves on the ground or near the base of the tree.

♂ perching on undergrowth in forest glade

2nd instar larva

segecia ♀

♂

egg

5th instar larva

pupa

220   The Butterflies of Australia

SUBFAMILY LIPHYRINAE—
Moth Butterflies

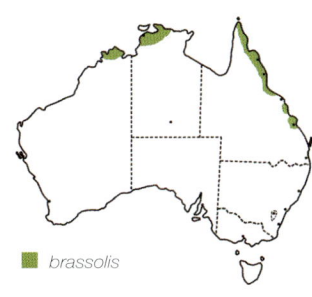

brassolis

The small subfamily **Liphyrinae** has just one member in Australia. Other genera occur in Africa. The larvae are probably all carnivorous, feeding on ant broods or plant hoppers and scale insects.

The **Moth Butterfly**, *Liphyra brassolis* (fw 41 mm, ♀ 46 mm), is confined to the wetter parts of the northern tropics, especially coastal paperbark forest. Adults mostly fly 5 m and higher, below the crowns of the trees, generally late in the afternoon and at dusk. However, the female illustrated descended to less than a metre to lay its eggs on the trunk of an orange tree at Bramston Beach, Queensland, at about 11 am in June 2001. They progress with a rapid straight-line flutter, more like a moth than a butterfly and, with their heavy and hairy bodies, are easily confused with various common larger moths.

Females lay their eggs near a nest, typically on an ant trail along a branch, and the hatchling larvae find their way into the nest to feed on the brood of the Green Tree Ant (*Oecophylla smaragdina*). They are not tolerated by the ants, and have a tough leathery shell for protection. The pupa also forms inside this shell, within the ant nest.

♀ brassolis ♂

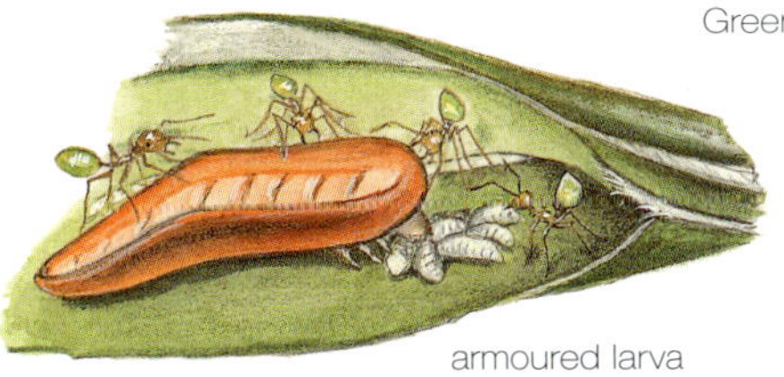

Green Tree Ant nest

armoured larva eating ant brood

pupa inside armoured larval skin

Green Tree Ant (*Oecophylla smaragdina*) worker

adult emerging covered with sticky deciduous scales that immobilise attacking ants

♀ ovipositing on ant trail near nest

The critical moment comes when the butterfly emerges from the pupa and the ants attack it. For defence, it is provided with a deep covering layer of sticky deciduous whitish scales around its abdomen. These glue up the ants' jaws and partially immobilise them so the butterfly can escape the nest. Any sticky scales the ants do not remove from the emerging butterfly dry and are shed as soon as the adult butterfly can fly. The adults have only rudimentary mouthparts and presumably feed very little after emergence—perhaps a correlate of their energy-rich larval diet. It differs fundamentally from that of other ant-eating lycaenid larvae, which dupe the ants chemically into tolerating them in their nests.

SUBFAMILY THECLINAE—
Hairstreaks

Common Imperial Blue
(*Jalmenus evagoras*)

Members of the subfamily **Theclinae** are conventionally known as the hairstreaks—a name originally bestowed on its European members, and referring to the fine tails on their hindwings and thin pale parallel streaks frequently present on the undersides. This description also works reasonably well for many Australian species, but equally applies to many polyommatines, and we can only justify the use of the term here by appealing to sentiment and tradition.* There are also many thecline species, which have quite different underside patterns. Among Australian species, only 27 per cent of theclines have tails, whereas fine hair-like tails are present in 40 per cent of polyommatines! In fact, the Theclinae are defined technically on the basis of their wing venation. As a general rule, however, they can usually be recognised by their heavier bodies and on-average larger size than most polyommatines. The larvae are generally ant-attended. A few species as larvae prey on ant broods. Unlike the Moth Butterfly, they always chemically dupe the ants into accepting them in their nests.

There are several thousands of species worldwide and just under 80 in Australia. They are divided into about eighteen tribes† (groups of related genera) of which we have representatives of six. Three of these very large tribes, though, are restricted to Australasia and contain several large genera which have diversified dramatically in Australia. These include our equal-largest genus, *Hypochrysops* (eighteen species). Other large genera include *Ogyris* (fourteen species) and *Jalmenus* (eleven species and counting), which contain many spectacular iridescent blue and black species. Others may be bright metallic orange and, in the case of *Hypochrysops*, spangled with gold or silver flecks beneath.

Many of our theclines have spectacular single or double tails on each hindwing, and about half have one or two eyespots in the angle of the hindwing. These are conventionally thought of as having evolved to deceive vertebrate predators into taking bites at the more or less dispensable hindwing of the butterfly rather than the vulnerable real head or body and, indeed, impressive symmetrical predator damage is often seen on the hindwings of otherwise active adults in the field. Generally this 'false head' effect is apparent only from the side when the wings are closed. The butterfly draws attention to the false head by constantly shuffling its hindwings, causing the antenna-like tails to wave around enticingly. In a few of our tropical and subtropical genera (*Deudorix*, *Rapala*), the presence of a roughly circular 'tornal lobe' adds to the illusion. When the butterfly

---

*   A practice which has precedence in the persistence of 'Tasmanian Tiger' for the extinct Thylacine, or 'Tiger Cat' for the extant Quoll species.

†   If the Theclini are treated as a tribe, these become subtribes, with the suffix -iti.

perches, this semi-detached flap of the hindwing is turned outwards at 90 degrees to the remainder of the wing, so as to present to a predator approaching from behind a convincing pair of false eyes—as in the individual of *Deudorix epijarbas* in Figure 9.2. This, together with the more usual underside eyespot visible from the side in the perching butterfly, produces what is effectively a double illusion. A predator approaching the butterfly from any direction, either from the side or behind, may be disoriented with respect to the position of the head, and direct its attack at the disposable tails. It seems likely that the second false head illusion, effective when viewed from behind, protects the butterflies against stalking arboreal predators, such as lizards or hunting spiders, which attack from behind. It is found in only a handful of other lycaenids worldwide. As with many other theclines, the false-head effect is enhanced by the butterfly flying inward as it lands on its perch, and then almost imperceptibly flipping around to face the other way, so that a watching predator already has the impression that the head is facing inwards before it begins its attack.

Theclines show a very large range of life-history traits. The flat, round eggs are laid singly or in clusters—sometimes even in rather haphazard piles. Often overwintering takes place in the egg, in which case the appearance of the first adults is delayed until late spring or summer. Larvae are very variable in shape and colour; those species not attended by ants tend to have extraordinary camouflage. Species attended by ants almost always have the full array of glands associated with caterpillar–ant mutualism. Some or all of these may even be present when the ant-attendance habit has been lost. Larvae may feed freely on foliage or inside fruits or seeds and may be either diurnal or nocturnal. Some, of course, spend their entire larval period within the nests of ants.

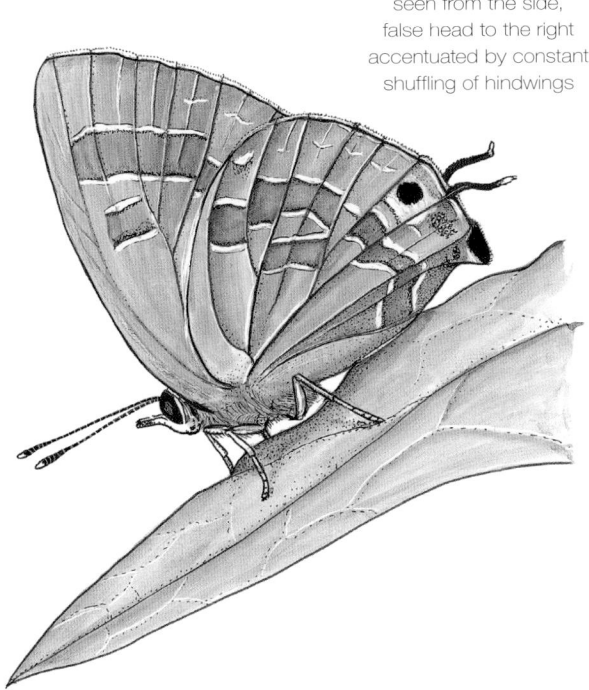
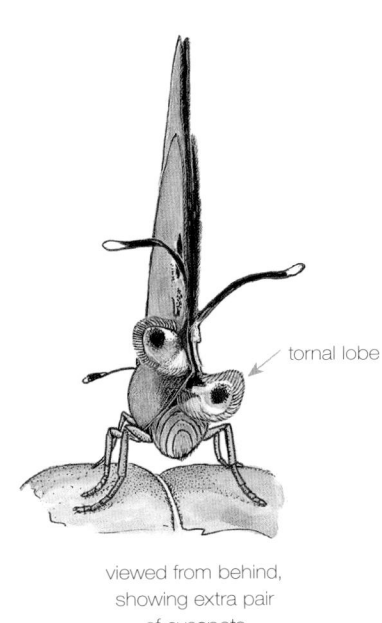

FIGURE 9.2: The Dull Cornelian (*Deudorix epijarbas*), illustrating the false-head effect.

Ant Blues

Ant blues in the genus *Acrodipsas* are all small, inconspicuous, drab and elusive. At present, ten species are known. Their chief attraction is for serious collectors; they have been so poorly known that the most recent species, *Acrodipsas decima*, was named only in 2004. They also have fascinating life histories, with larvae of probably all species living as parasites within ant colonies and feeding on the ants' brood. Females lay their eggs near an ant nest and the young larvae, which resemble ant larvae and may emit chemical signals to deceive the ants, are collected and carried unharmed into the nest by workers. As far as is known, each ant blue species is specialised to attack just one ant species. Pupation occurs inside the ant nest and the freshly emerged adults are evidently not molested—although they do have some of the same sort of deciduous scales as *Liphyra* to aid escape. The males of most species frequent prominent hilltops, presumed mating rendezvous sites where male and female can meet, and it is at these sites that most specimens are encountered. Males perch head downwards on vegetation, sometimes quite high if the situation allows, awaiting the arrival of receptive females. Their flight is very rapid. Males of most species are bronze-brown above. Females are commonly dull blue above but may be darker. The undersides of the sexes are similar.

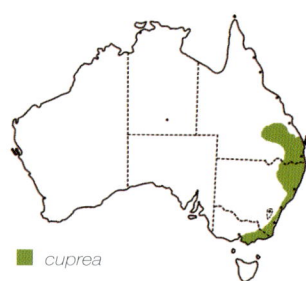
brisbanensis

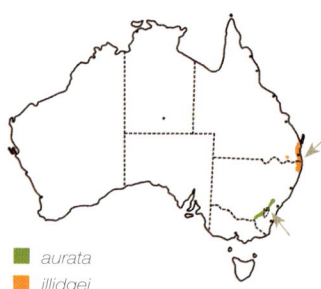
cuprea

aurata
illidgei

The ant blues fall into two groups, separable by the form of the legs. In members of the *myrmecophila* group, which includes mainly larger species, the mid-leg is normal. In the *illidgei* group, the tibia on the mid-leg is greatly reduced (Figure 9.3). This character can be seen clearly with a good hand lens. Apart from *A. illidgei* itself, the members of the *illidgei* group—*arcana*, *decima*, *hirtipes*, *melania* and *mortoni*—are all tiny (fw 10–13 mm) inhabitants of open forest and are very seldom encountered. They can be identified with confidence only by dissection and examination of the genitalia. They are not illustrated here, but they can be recognised collectively by this leg character.

Of the first group, the **Bronze Ant Blue**, *Acrodipsas brisbanensis* (fw ♂ 14 mm, ♀ 15 mm), and the **Copper Ant Blue**, *A. cuprea* (fw ♂ 14.5 mm, ♀ 16 mm), are widespread in open forest and may occur in the same locations. They differ subtly in wing shape and underside markings. These are narrower and fainter in *A. brisbanensis*. Males in some *A. cuprea* populations have a light basal dusting of metallic blue on the upperside.

The **Golden Ant Blue**, *Acrodipsas aurata* (fw ♂ 14 mm, ♀ 15 mm), easily recognised by the golden upperside of males and the dark females, is confined to the southern highlands of New South Wales. The underside is similar to that of *A. cuprea*.

The **Small Ant Blue**, *Acrodipsas myrmecophila* (fw ♂ 11 mm, ♀ 13 mm), is widespread in open forest and woodland. Apart from its small size, the wings are much narrower and more rounded than the above species.

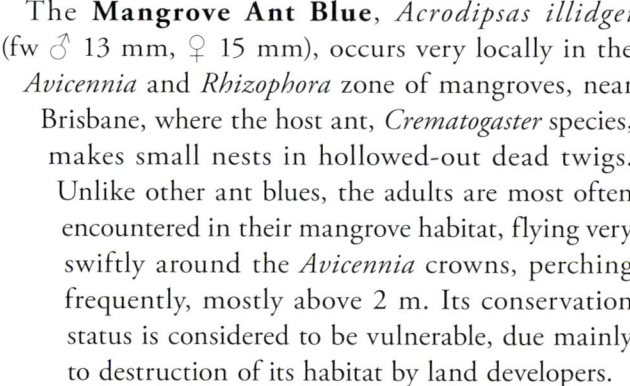

The **Mangrove Ant Blue**, *Acrodipsas illidgei* (fw ♂ 13 mm, ♀ 15 mm), occurs very locally in the *Avicennia* and *Rhizophora* zone of mangroves, near Brisbane, where the host ant, *Crematogaster* species, makes small nests in hollowed-out dead twigs. Unlike other ant blues, the adults are most often encountered in their mangrove habitat, flying very swiftly around the *Avicennia* crowns, perching frequently, mostly above 2 m. Its conservation status is considered to be vulnerable, due mainly to destruction of its habitat by land developers.

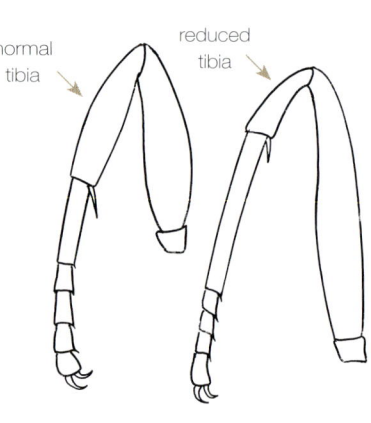

FIGURE 9.3: Mid-legs of *Acrodipsas*, showing the two types found.

FAMILY LYCAENIDAE—Blues, Coppers and Hairstreaks

Jewels 1

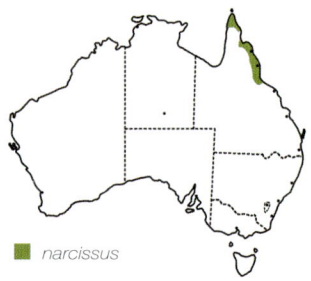
narcissus

miskini
cleon

pythias

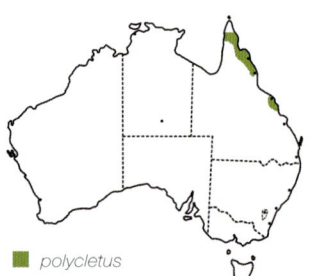
polycletus

The jewels are small to medium-sized lycaenids belonging to the genus *Hypochrysops*. With eighteen species, *Hypochrysops* equals *Trapezites* (Hesperiidae) as the largest genus in the Australian butterfly fauna. Almost all species are brilliantly coloured, with shining blues or fiery orange above, and bright red bands bordered by narrow metallic strips beneath. However, despite these ornaments, they are not conspicuous butterflies, and need to be observed closely for their sparkling gem-like beauty to be revealed. This opportunity seldom occurs. Most species fly high and rapidly, and often perch for long periods in the treetops where their presence is scarcely evident. Only rarely do they descend to feed on flowers or to oviposit. Jewels occur locally in many habitats and the larvae feed on a very wide range of host plants, usually attended by ants. The five species illustrated are tropical or subtropical.

The **Narcissus Jewel**, *Hypochrysops narcissus* (fw ♂ 16 mm, ♀ 17 mm), occurs mainly in northern mangrove and paperbark swamp. Adults fly high in the canopy, but in mangroves females, especially, may descend to feed on flowers. The flattened larvae feed on many genera of mangroves (*Aegiceras*, *Avicennia*, *Bruguiera*, *Lumnitzera* and *Rhizophora*), mistletoes (*Dendrophthoe*, *Diplatia* and *Notothixos*) and other plants (*Lophostemon* and *Terminalia*). Larvae feed by night, spending the day in shelters of rolled leaves. They are tended by the Coconut Ant (*Philidris cordatus*).

Miskin's Jewel, *Hypochrysops miskini* (fw ♂ 15 mm, ♀ 17 mm), has a disjunct distribution, occurring in two well-separated areas centred on Brisbane in the south and Cairns in the north. Males, especially, fly in the canopy of rainforest and tall wet eucalypt forest and are seldom observed. Females descend to oviposit on low-growing larval host plants. The flattened larvae feed especially on *Smilax australis*, but also on species of *Commersonia*, *Eucalyptus*, *Faradaya*, *Glochidion*, *Guioa*, *Lophostemon*, *Maesa*, *Melastoma*, *Rhodomyrtus* and *Tetrasynandra*. They are tended by the ant *Anonchomyrma gilberti*.

The **Splendid Jewel**, *Hypochrysops cleon* (fw ♂ 14 mm, ♀ 15 mm), is a high-flying rainforest canopy species known only from a few specimens from Iron Range on Cape York Peninsula. It is widespread but rare in New Guinea and the Aru Islands. Nothing is known of its early stages.

The **Peacock Jewel**, *Hypochrysops pythias* (fw ♂ 15 mm, ♀ 16 mm), is uncommon in rainforest of the North Queensland wet tropics region. Adults fly rapidly, high in the canopy and subcanopy in the vicinity of their larval host plants, descending rarely. In New Guinea, where this species is common, swarms of males may descend to obtain salt from damp earth or land on a perspiring hand or body, imbibing sweat, but such behaviour is unknown in Australia. The green and white larva resembles that of *H. polycletus*, but is more flattened. It feeds on *Commersonia bartramia* and *Trichospermum pleiostigma* and is not tended by ants.

The **Royal Jewel**, *Hypochrysops polycletus* (fw ♂ 16 mm, ♀ 18 mm), occurs at rainforest margins and especially in deciduous vine forest in the eastern tropics. It is found locally in the vicinity of its food plant, and males sometimes appear on hilltops. It is one of the more conspicuous species of jewel, flying lower, with a rapid flutter, and somewhat slower than many other species. The beautifully camouflaged larvae feed on the leaves of the woody vine *Rhyssopterys timorensis*, and are only sometimes tended by ants.

FAMILY LYCAENIDAE—Blues, Coppers and Hairstreaks

Jewels 2

ignitus

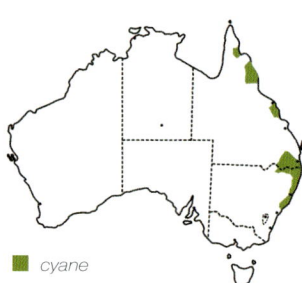

cyane

epicurus

piceatus

The four species of jewel illustrated here are found in a variety of forest habitats, often in drier areas. Although similar in general appearance, they vary greatly in their geographical ranges, habitat selection and range of host plants. In all four, the larvae are closely tended by ants.

The **Fiery Jewel**, *Hypochrysops ignitus* (fw ♂ 14–16 mm, ♀ 15–17 mm), is the most widespread species of jewel in Australia. Four geographic races are recognised which, compared with the typical specimens illustrated, differ—especially on the upperside—in the extent of the black margin. These forms, however, do not overlap with any similar species, from which the typical race is easily distinguished by the broad red bands on the underside of both sexes. The species occupies many habitats, generally of the drier open forest type, although it may also occur in heath and scrubland. Although often common, its occurrence is generally sporadic and very local. Males fly rapidly around the crowns of trees, generally at heights of 5–15 m, and they are visible only as tiny, dark, whirring dots against the sky. They are, however, commonly encountered on hilltops, where they may perch as low as 2 m, awaiting receptive females. The butterfly has a particularly intimate relationship with ants of the genus *Papyrius*. The female seeks out an ant colony around the base of a tree or sapling, and lays a large cluster of eggs on the trunk near the ground. The ants then build a 'byre' around the eggs, and as the young larvae hatch, carry them to the terminal shoots to feed by night and back to the byre or deeper in their nest for protection by day. As the larvae grow, they feed gregariously, always closely guarded by the ants. Groups of up to 30 are recorded, and if the host plant is small this can result in serious defoliation, the damage caused by their grazing creating a 'scorched-leaf' appearance. Unlike most butterflies, *H. ignitus* females apparently seek out the ant species rather than a particular host plant, as eggs and larvae have been recorded from at least 44 plant species representing seventeen families.

The **Bright Purple Jewel**, *Hypochrysops cyane* (fw ♂ 16 mm, ♀ 18 mm), is widespread in the east, but rather uncommon and local wherever it occurs. It is usually found in tall open forest, and males may visit hilltops. Otherwise the butterflies are found around the larval host plant, generally flying very high, from 10 to 20 m. Eggs are laid in clusters near fresh foliage, and larvae, when young, are gregarious. They are closely attended by ants of the genus *Anonychomyrma*. Common larval food plants are the tall trees *Angophora costata* and *Eucalyptus moluccana*, but they have also been recorded from a wide range of other plants.

The **Dull Jewel**, *Hypochrysops epicurus* (fw ♂ 15 mm, ♀ 17 mm), is confined to mangroves in the eastern subtropics. Adults usually fly rapidly around the crowns of the trees, perching for long periods so that their presence may be best revealed by beating the foliage. It is not a very common insect, but is usually not hard to find in its very restricted habitat. The larvae, which are quite similar to those of *H. piceatus*, feed on the undersides of leaves of *Avicennia marina*, leaving characteristic scarring.

The **Bulloak Jewel**, *Hypochrysops piceatus* (fw ♂ 14 mm, ♀ 16 mm), is the smallest member of the genus. It is restricted to a very few sites on the Darling Downs of southern Queensland, where stands of its host plant, the Bulloak (*Casuarina luehmannii*) grow. It is considered to be endangered due to agricultural clearing. The adults perch high in the foliage of the Bulloaks and are very sedentary. When disturbed by beating, they fly with a strong flutter, but seldom descend below about 4 m. Larvae are tended by ants of the genus *Anonychomyrma* and shelter in crevices and borer holes high on the tree.

ant byre around foot of infested plant

piceatus larva attended by ants

FAMILY LYCAENIDAE—Blues, Coppers and Hairstreaks

Jewels 3

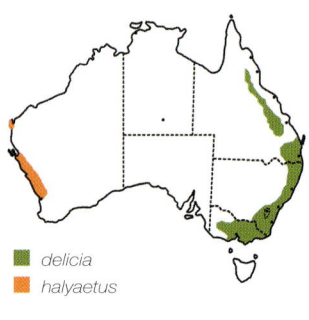

delicia
halyaetus

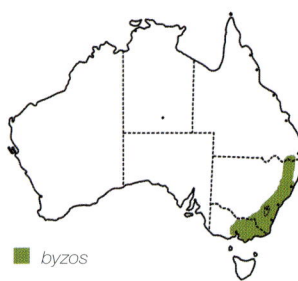

byzos

apelles

Of the many typical *Hypochrysops* species with metallic-edged red bands on the underside, the **Blue Jewel**, *Hypochrysops delicia* (fw ♂ 20 mm, ♀ 21 mm), is the largest. It is also the only eastern species in which the upperside is brilliant light blue or blue-green. The exact shade of the blue, and the extent of the black margins, are quite variable, and in the northern race, *H. delicia duaringae* (fw ♂ 17 mm, ♀ 18 mm), the black margin is greatly reduced, with the resulting effect particularly brilliant. The larvae feed at night, mainly on *Acacia* species but sometimes on *Alphitonia excelsa*, resting under bark or in borer holes by day. They are tended by *Crematogaster* ants. Eggs are normally laid in clusters in crevices in the bark of the host, with larger trees chosen when available. The preferred habitat is dry, open woodland but they occur sparsely on the coast. Males fly high in the crowns of the host trees, typically between 7 and 12 m high. They spend long periods perching, when they are all but invisible, but they can be recognised in flight by their size and quick flutter. Females sometimes descend to oviposit, and it is usually only on such rare occasions that their brilliant colours can be observed in nature.

The **Yellow-spot Jewel**, *Hypochrysops byzos* (fw ♂ 15 mm, ♀ 16 mm), is restricted to the south-east. It is widespread in open forest up to 1000 m but always confined to the vicinity of its food plant, usually *Pomaderris aspera* or *P. lanigera*. Adults perch towards the crowns of these low shrubs, often basking with half-open wings. They fly actively and rapidly, usually within 2–3 m of the ground. Females are especially conspicuous. Eggs are laid singly on the underside of leaves; by day, the superbly camouflaged larvae rest on the underside of the leaves along the midrib and at night feed on the upperside of the leaves. They are not tended by ants. The pupa also fixes itself to the underside of a leaf near the midrib. It is noteworthy that this species, like members of the related genus *Philiris*, which also lack guardian ants, adopts a strategy of open concealment by day, rather than secreting itself under bark or among dead leaves.

The **Copper Jewel**, *Hypochrysops apelles* (fw ♂ 16.5 mm, ♀ 17 mm), is one of the commonest and most easily observed of the jewels. It is found mainly in mangrove, but in Queensland north of Townsville it also occurs in open savannah woodland. In mangroves, adults may perch and fly as low as 2 m and descend even lower to feed at flowers. Eggs are laid singly or in small groups on leaves, often at the edge of a feeding scar. The very flattened larvae hide in folded leaves by day and feed at night, leaving clear grazing tracks as they take just the upper or lower layer of the leaf surface. They are closely tended by *Crematogaster* ants. The larval host plants include many species of mangroves and also, in north Queensland, numerous species of shrubs and trees, including genera such as *Acacia*, *Alphitonia*, *Commersonia* and *Eucalyptus*.

The **Western Jewel**, *Hypochrysops halyaetus* (fw ♂ 14 mm, ♀ 16 mm), is a brilliantly coloured, low-flying species locally common in coastal heath and *Banksia* woodland. Adults often feed at flowers within a metre of the ground. Eggs are laid in clusters, generally low on the food plant, and the attendant *Crematogaster* ants may construct a byre at the base of the food plant. Larvae feed on low shrubs, including *Acacia xanthina*, *Daviesia* species and *Jacksonia sternbergiana*.

FAMILY LYCAENIDAE—Blues, Coppers and Hairstreaks

Jewels 4

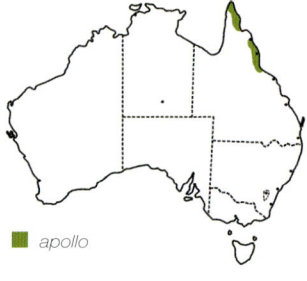
apollo

elgneri

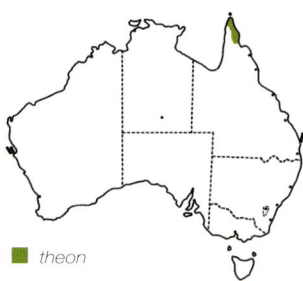
theon

hippuris

The following four species of jewel are found in the wetter parts of Cape York Peninsula in far north Queensland and are widespread in New Guinea. The southern, 'typical' race of the Apollo Jewel (*Hypochrysops apollo apollo*) is restricted to the wet tropics region, centred on Cairns. All are closely attended by the Coconut Ant (*Philidris cordatus*), but feed on different larval host plants.

The magnificent **Apollo Jewel**, *Hypochrysops apollo* (fw ♂ 20 mm, ♀ 21 mm), occurs in coastal paperbark swamp and mangrove. Its food plants are the epiphytic ant plants *Myrmecodia beccarii* and *M. tuberosa*, which grow as large stem-tubers supported by larger branches of a host tree. In both of these plant species the tuber is riddled with interconnected galleries, which provide a home for the ants. The ants, in turn, protect the plant from most herbivores, and also bring small prey items and scraps of organic matter into the galleries, providing the plant with nourishment. The butterfly larva exploits this mutualism. By offering the ants a rich nutritious secretion, while feeding on the tissue of the plant, it is not merely tolerated but is assiduously tended by the ants. It is unusual, however, for more than one larva to be present in a plant, and damage to the plant is never catastrophic, suggesting some regulation by the ants. Living inside the ants' nest, the larva has no need of concealment, hence has no cryptic pigmentation and is not flattened. At night, however, larvae may leave the galleries to feed on the sparse leaves of the plant, leaving distinctive furrows. Adults fly rapidly, mainly around the forest canopy, perching for long periods. Females descend to oviposit single eggs on the underside of the host plant tuber. A more brightly coloured subspecies occurs on the northern half of Cape York.

Elgner's Jewel, *Hypochrysops elgneri* (fw ♂ 21 mm, ♀ 22 mm), is restricted to Cape York Peninsula and Torres Strait Islands where a separate, brighter subspecies is recognised. It flies high at rainforest edges and in adjacent open forest. The flattened, dull-greenish patterned larvae feed on the mistletoes, *Dendrophthoe glabrescens* and *Notothixos* species, as well as leaves of the trees *Nauclea orientalis* and *Planchonia careya*.

The **Green-banded Jewel**, *Hypochrysops theon* (fw ♂ 19 mm, ♀ 21 mm), occurs in the rainforest understorey, where the larvae feed on the epiphytic ferns *Drynaria quercifolia* and *Platycerium hillii* (Elkhorn). Adults generally perch 1–3 m from the ground, and females, especially, are closely associated with their host plants, on which they perch for long periods, whereas males may frequent sunny patches. In pattern, it resembles the very common Large Green-banded Blue (*Danis danis*), which it may mimic.

The **Paradise Jewel**, *Hypochrysops hippuris* (fw ♂ 17.5 mm, ♀ 18 mm), is also found in rainforest gaps, especially near where its host plant, the climbing fern *Pyrrosia lanceolata*, winds over the mossy trunks of fallen trees. The curious larvae are broad and strongly flattened. The behaviour of adults is similar to that of *H. theon*, but males are swifter in flight. Both sexes evidently mimic *Danis danis*, although less convincingly than *H. theon*. Males visit hilltops. *H. cleon* and *H. hippuris* are the only Australian butterflies to feed on ferns, and perhaps the only butterflies so far known to do so worldwide. However, in the tropical rainforests of Borneo, where the topic has been studied in detail, moths belonging to several families are confirmed fern-feeders.

Myrmecodia sectioned with *apollo* larva in galleries

FAMILY LYCAENIDAE—Blues, Coppers and Hairstreaks

Diggles' Jewel and the Forest Blues

■ *digglesii*

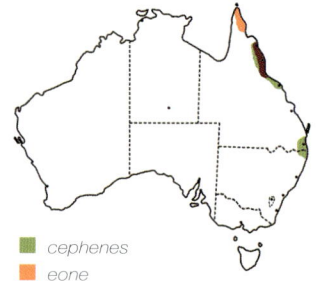
■ *cephenes*
■ *eone*

Diggles' Jewel, *Hypochrysops digglesii* (fw ♂ 17.5 mm, ♀ 18 mm), is generally an uncommon species. It occurs in open eucalypt forest and other coastal formations where its mistletoe host plants (species of *Amyema*, *Dendrophthoe* and *Muellerina*) grow. It is probably most easily observed in mangrove forests, where it flies lower, but known locations are few. Flight is very rapid, the bright upperside glinting in a sequence of quick, evanescent flashes. The strongly flattened larvae feed mainly by night, hiding in the day. They are closely tended by *Crematogaster* ants.

The **Bright Forest Blue**, *Pseudodipsas cephenes* (fw ♂ 14 mm, ♀ 15 mm), is locally common, but seldom encountered. It inhabits littoral rainforest and semi-open vegetation bordering rainforest. Males perch high, usually at 5–10 m, and dart about very rapidly. Females perch as low as 2–4 m, usually near the food plant, *Smilax australis*. Males may visit hilltops. The elongate green and brown larva feeds at night, closely attended by the ant, *Anonychomyrma gilberti*.

The **Dark Forest Blue**, *Pseudodipsas eone* (fw ♂ 12 mm, ♀ 13 mm), is similar in all aspects of its biology but has a more northerly distribution. The two species may occur together, but they seem to avoid laying their eggs on the same *Smilax* plants.

234   The Butterflies of Australia

BUTTERFLIES EVOLVING WITH ANTS

Most species of Australian blues, especially hairstreaks, are in some way associated with ants. This association can be quite loose or very close, of mutual benefit to both ant and butterfly, or, in a few cases, detrimental to the ants when the caterpillars feed on ant eggs and larvae. When the relationship is close, it is common for the larva of a butterfly species to be tended by just one ant species.

This in turn has led to interesting patterns of diversification, with groups of related butterfly species adapting to particular ant species, and remaining with them throughout evolutionary time. Now we can reconstruct the pathways of butterfly evolution using DNA analysis, it is also possible to understand how conservative (or 'hard-wired') the associations with particular ant species or species groups can be.

The imperial blues (genus *Jalmenus*) provide a good example. The relationships of the eleven species are well understood, from meticulous DNA analysis by Rod Eastwood of Harvard University, and are reproduced here with permission. Originally members of the genus were associated with small black ants of the genus *Iridomyrmex* (a complex of several very similar species). However, just as the genus was beginning to diversify, one line (*J. aridus*) evolved to associate with another type of ant, the tiny red *Froggatella kirbii*. Later, another quite different line (*J. pseudictinus*) also adopted *F. kirbii* as its host. Yet another line came to be tended by large purple *Iridomyrmex*, resulting in several related *Jalmenus* species being tended only by these ants. This has led to the remarkable situation where two butterfly species (*J. ictinus* and *J. pseudictinus*) are so similar as adults they can scarcely be told apart, but are associated with very different ants. DNA evidence also reveals that they are not very closely related. Moreover, distantly related species in several lines retain the ancestral association with small black ants.

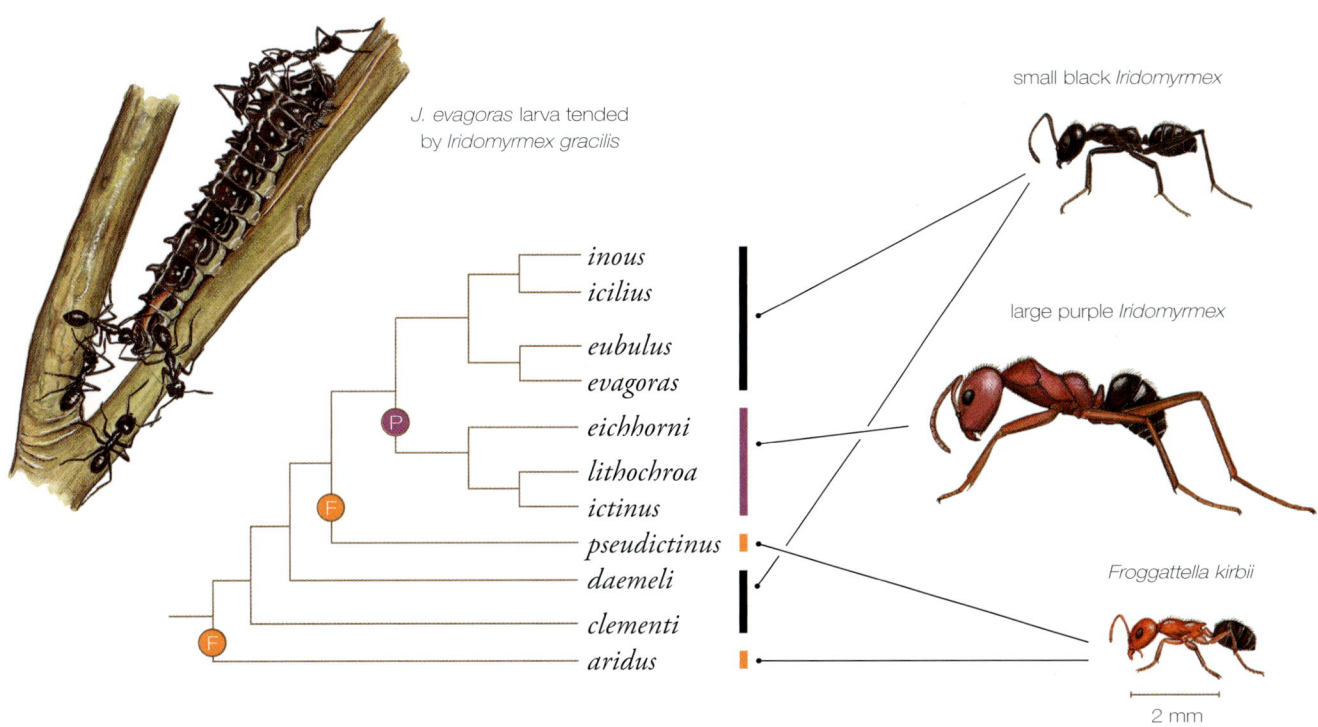

Figure 9.4: Evolutionary tree of *Jalmenus* species: P and F indicate, respectively, switches to large purple *Iridomyrmex* and *Froggatella kirbii* ants.

Moonbeams

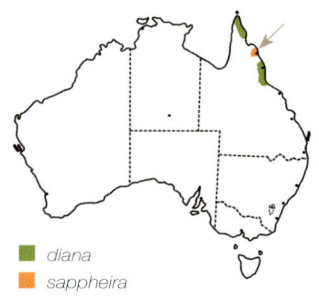
- diana
- sappheira

- fulgens

- innotata

- nitens

The moonbeams include seven species of the genus *Philiris*. In all species the underside in both sexes is pure silvery white, generally with a single black spot on the hindwing and three or four more around the margin. Females resemble the pencilled blues a little, but are usually smaller and swifter in flight, and lack the 'pencil marks' of the latter. Most species occur in tropical rainforest, and are typically seen along edges or in sunny gaps, flying and perching quite high (usually 2–7 m), although some species are probably active in the canopy where they cannot be observed from the ground. Females may fly in the understorey. Moonbeam larvae are never regularly tended by ants, and both larvae and pupae exhibit remarkable camouflage, each adapted to the leaves of its particular host plant. Larvae feed by day in full view on the underside of leaves and, unlike most ant-attended theclines, they do not shelter under bark or between leaves, but rely on their camouflage to avoid predators and parasitoids. The pupa is also attached to a leaf near the midrib, usually on the underside.

The **Diana Moonbeam**, *Philiris diana* (fw ♂ 16 mm, ♀ 17 mm), is a rare inhabitant of rainforest in the Queensland wet tropics region. Most specimens are known from Kuranda. On Cape York Peninsula a markedly different subspecies, *P. diana papuana*, occurs in open forest bordering rainforest. The larvae of both races feed on *Litsea* species.

The **Purple Moonbeam**, *Philiris fulgens* (fw ♂ 14 mm, ♀ 15 mm), is locally common in rainforest. It is almost always present at Crystal Cascades near Cairns as well as many other popular tourist spots. Although a very small butterfly, the male is quite conspicuous, with the differing colours of the fore- and hindwings upperside quite obvious as it zips around in the sunlight, often as low as 2 m above the ground. Females often fly in the understorey, 1–3 m high, when searching for plants on which to oviposit. Host plants include species of *Cryptocarya*, *Endiandra* and *Litsea*.

The **Common Moonbeam**, *Philiris innotata* (fw ♂ 14 mm, ♀ 15 mm), extends to the subtropics. It is common but inconspicuous in rainforest and semi-open riverine scrub, wherever its usual host plants, species of sandpaper fig (*Ficus opposita* and *F. coronata*), grow. Adults perch near the host plant 2–7 m above the ground and are quite inconspicuous on the wing. The larva is flattened and hairy, to better blend with the rough, textured underside of the leaf, with a definite pale line along its dorsum, suggesting a major leaf vein. The pupa normally forms under old leaves, which often bear brown scars from earlier larval feeding. It has brownish patches suggesting leaf damage.

The **Blue Moonbeam**, *Philiris nitens* (fw ♂ 13 mm, ♀ 14 mm), is locally quite common, preferring patches of disturbed areas of rainforest where its main food plant grows, the pioneer species *Macaranga involucrata*. Also utilised are *Glochidion philippicum* and *M. tanarius*. Adults fly very rapidly and are rather inconspicuous.

ziska

azula

papuana

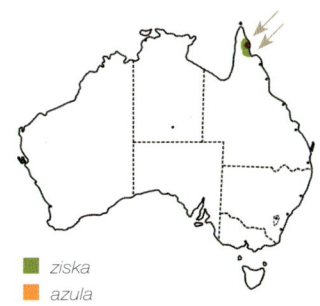

The **Sapphire Moonbeam**, *Philiris sappheira* (fw ♂ 13 mm, ♀ 13.5 mm), has similar habits, but is a rare insect, known only from a small patch of forest north of Cooktown. Its larvae feed on *Macaranga involucrata*.

Two rare rainforest species from Cape York Peninsula are the **Azure Moonbeam**, *Philiris azula* (fw ♂ 14 mm, ♀ 15 mm), and the **White-margined Moonbeam**, *P. ziska* (fw ♂ 13 mm, ♀ 13.5 mm). In both species, the males are deep blue above, with a narrower black margin than in other small species, especially *P. ziska*. In *P. ziska*, the leading edge of the hindwing has a clear white streak, easily seen when the wings are spread. Their habits are typical of the genus, and it is unlikely they could be recognised without capture.

FAMILY LYCAENIDAE—Blues, Coppers and Hairstreaks

Coppers

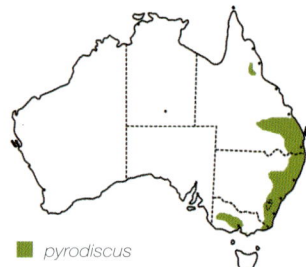
limbaria

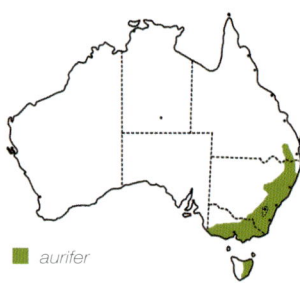
pyrodiscus

aurifer

spinifera

The coppers include four species in the two genera, *Lucia* and *Paralucia*. The genera are not closely related, nor are they allied to the true coppers (subfamily Lycaeninae) of the northern hemisphere, New Zealand and New Guinea.

The **Small Copper**, *Lucia limbaria* (fw ♂ 13 mm, ♀ 15 mm), is widespread and locally common in open grassy habitats throughout south-eastern Australia. Male and female are similar, with the latter generally larger. Adults fly rather weakly close to the ground, pausing to bask with wings half open or to feed at low flowers such as daisies or the flowers of *Oxalis* species, the larval food plants. Females lay their eggs in clusters on *Oxalis* leaves. Larvae feed by day, tended by small black *Iridomyrmex* ants. They rest underground in the nest of the attendant ants. The pupa also forms within the ant nest and lies loosely on the floor of a chamber.

The **Dull Copper**, *Paralucia pyrodiscus* (fw ♂ 16 mm, ♀ 16.5 mm), is locally common in open eucalypt forest, mainly in drier situations. Adults fly briskly but erratically within 1.5 m of the ground. Eggs are laid singly or in small groups towards the base of the host plants—*Bursaria spinosa*, but also *B. incana* and *Pittosporum spinescens*. The larvae feed by night, tended by numerous small black ants of the genus *Notoncus*. By day, they rest in the ant nest or in a small 'byre' constructed by the ants at the base of the host plant. Pupation takes place in the same situations. *P. pyrodiscus* has been divided into several geographic races, which vary greatly in the brightness of their upperside coloration. It is now considered that these forms grade into each other to a point where it is impossible to confidently delineate definite subspecies. The race *P. pyrodiscus lucida*, however, although no longer formally recognised by most authorities, deserves mention, as it is the brightest of all the forms, and is also known as the Eltham Copper, which was the subject of a famous conservation initiative in the 1990s.

The **Bright Copper**, *Paralucia aurifer* (fw ♂ 14 mm, ♀ 14.5 mm), is widespread and locally common in similar situations to those favoured by *P. pyrodiscus*, but prefers areas of higher rainfall. Its flight habits are similar. It occurs up to 1200 m and, in cooler southern and mountain habitats, it is given to basking in sunlight for long periods. Eggs are laid singly near the base of the host plant—generally *Bursaria spinosa*, but occasionally *Pittosporum multiflorum*. Larvae feed by day and remain on the plant when young, but later instars feed only by night, and are tended by small black ants of the genus *Anonychomyrma*. Pupation is within the ant nest.

The **Bathurst Copper**, *Paralucia spinifera* (fw ♂ 12 mm, ♀ 13 mm), is known from only a few very restricted localities from 900 to 1200 m in the New South Wales central highlands. Its habitat is open eucalypt woodland with a dense undergrowth of the host plant, *Bursaria spinosa*. Adults frequently bask in sunlight. The general biology and life history are very similar to that of *P. aurifer*, but the attendant ant is a different species of *Anonychomyrma*. It is not clear why it is so geographically restricted, but it is considered an endangered species and is protected by law, even on private land.

FAMILY LYCAENIDAE—Blues, Coppers and Hairstreaks

Oakblues

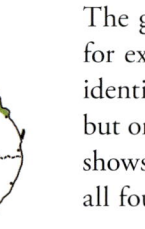
micale

centaurus

The genus *Arhopala*, or oakblues, is extremely diverse in South-East Asia. In Borneo, for example, there are more than 80 species, presenting very substantial challenges in identification. In Australia there are just four, all restricted to wet tropical habitats. All but one are associated with the Green Tree Ant (*Oecophylla smaragdina*). The landscape shows a small patch of alluvial forest in Eubanangee swamp, north Queensland, where all four species occur.

The **Common Oakblue**, *Arhopala micale* (fw ♂ 27 mm, ♀ 28 mm), is virtually ubiquitous in wetter regions of the north Queensland tropics, occurring from the beachfront to rainforest glades. It is a common garden insect in Cairns, but scarcer around Darwin. The adults are busy, highly conspicuous insects. They fly quite quickly and perch often, usually fairly low at 1–4 m above the ground. Their electric blue upperside is reminiscent of and quite as brilliant as that of the much larger swallowtail *Papilio ulysses*. The females lay their eggs singly on young shoots of the host plant, always near a nest of the ant *O. smaragdina*. The larvae feed in the open by day, usually covered by a seething mass of ants. The pupa is elongate and curiously flattened into a double 'spatula' at its posterior end. It is normally found within rolled leaves or leaf debris near the food plant. Larvae feed on a very wide range of hosts, including *Acmena*, *Buchanania*, *Calophyllum*, *Cordia*, *Cryptocarya*, *Cupaniopsis*, *Faradaya*, *Glochidion*, *Heritiera*, *Hibiscus*, *Lagerstroemia*, *Parinari*, *Ristantia*, *Syzygium*, *Terminalia* and *Xylocarpus*.

The **Dull Oakblue**, *Arhopala centaurus* (fw ♂ 26 mm, ♀ 26 mm), is slightly smaller and obviously less brilliant than *A. micale*. It is quite common in the same habitats, but far more localised. Its larvae are also tended by *O. smaragdina* on a wide range of food plants, including *Buchanania*, *Corymbia*, *Cupaniopsis*, *Dendrophthoe*, *Lagerstroemia*, *Maranthes*, *Melaleuca* and *Terminalia*.

Eubanangee Swamp, north Queensland

micale

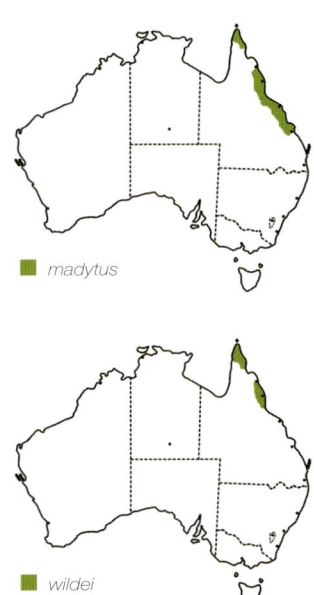

The **Bright Oakblue**, *Arhopala madytus* (fw ♂ 24.5 mm, ♀ 25 mm), is restricted to rainforest gaps and edges, and riverine forest. Its habits are similar to those of *A. micale* but, despite its common name, its upperside is less brilliant. Its larvae are tended by *O. smaragdina*. The range of hosts is limited to just two plant genera, including *Terminalia catappa*, *T. melanocarpa*, *T. sericocarpa* and *Hibiscus tiliaceus*.

The **Small Oakblue**, *Arhopala wildei* (fw ♂ 20 mm, ♀ 21 mm), is locally quite common in the canopy of lowland rainforest and riverine forest. Females, especially, may perch lower, to about 2 m, in the forest understorey. Their biology is entirely different from other species in the genus. Larvae live inside nests of the arboreal ant *Polyrhachis queenslandicus*, and feed on the ant brood, especially eggs and pupae. The female lays her eggs singly near an ant nest. On hatching, the young larva is carried into the nest by worker ants and placed with the colony's brood. The larvae exude potent secretions craved by the ants, and are at all times accepted by them. The pupa forms inside the nest, and has the characteristic elongate shape with flattened tail found in other members of the genus. However, neither larva nor pupa has strong pigmentation, suggesting that in their sheltered microhabitat they have no need of camouflage.

FAMILY LYCAENIDAE—Blues, Coppers and Hairstreaks

Bright-blue Azures

The azures comprise the large genus *Ogyris*, with fourteen species. The vernacular name is a convention rather than a description, as many species are deep blue or purple in colour rather than azure. The majority fly high and their larvae feed nocturnally on mistletoes, but a southern group known as ground azures have different habits. Most are closely associated with ants.

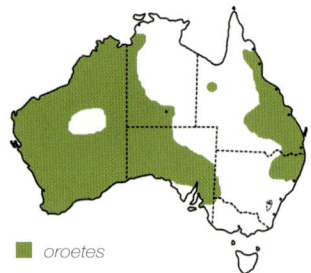
■ *amaryllis*

The **Satin Azure**, *Ogyris amaryllis* (fw ♂ 20 mm, ♀ 22 mm), occurs in a variety of habitats over most of mainland Australia. There is geographical variation in the blue colour and the extent of the black margin on the upperside, with four races recognised. The inland race, *O. amaryllis meridionalis*, ranges from the Darling Downs and Atherton Tableland in Queensland to the Western Australian coast. The typical south-eastern coastal race, *O. amaryllis amaryllis*, is illustrated. In all races, the underside forewing markings distinguish the species from other light-blue azures, especially the red marking at the base of the wing in the female. Adults fly high, generally above 4 m, perching for long periods in or near their mistletoe food plants. At about noon, courting pairs sometimes descend almost to the ground, especially if the female is evading the male, presenting a brilliant show. Mostly, however, they appear as small, dark silhouettes fluttering strongly around the treetops. Older larvae feed by night on numerous species of *Amyema*, always attended by ants from any of eight genera. They shelter by day in borer holes and in crevices where pupation also takes place. A common food near the east coast is *Amyema cambagei*, an extraordinary mistletoe which has long, thin leaves mimicking the foliage of its *Casuarina littoralis* host trees.

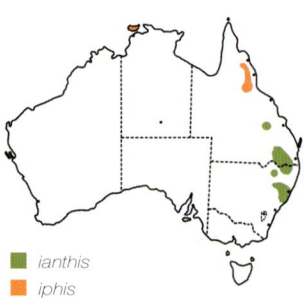
■ *oroetes*

The **Silky Azure**, *Ogyris oroetes* (fw ♂ 21.5 mm, ♀ 23 mm), is widespread but local in open eucalypt woodland and mallee. Its dark larvae feed at night on *Amyema bifurcata*, *A. miquellii* and *A. pendula*, tended by ants from any one of eleven genera. They shelter by day under bark or in ant nests, where pupation also takes place.

The **Sydney Azure**, *Ogyris ianthis* (fw ♂ 19 mm, ♀ 21 mm), is rare and very local in dry eucalypt woodland away from the coast. Male and female differ greatly. Larvae are tended by the small red ant *Froggattella kirbii*, and feed nocturnally on *Amyema linophylla*, *A. miquelii*, *A. quandang*, *Dendrophthoe glabrescens*, *D. vitellina* and *Muellerina eucalyptoides*.

■ *ianthis*
■ *iphis*

The **Orange-tipped Azure**, *Ogyris iphis* (fw ♂ 18 mm, ♀ 20 mm), is rare and local in dry inland eucalypt woodland in north Queensland. The larvae feed by night on *Amyema bifurcata*, *A. miquelii*, *A. quandang* and *Dendrophthoe glabrescens*, tended by *Froggattella kirbii*.

■ *aenone*

The **Cooktown Azure**, *Ogyris aenone* (fw ♂ 25 mm, ♀ 27 mm), has an astonishing 'disjunct' distribution, occurring in northern coastal paperbark swamp and on the Darling Downs of southern Queensland in dry scrub around stands of Bulloak. Male and female are very alike. The dark-mottled, broadly flattened larvae feed nocturnally, mainly on *Dendrophthoe vitellina*, *Diplatia furcata* and *D. tomentosa* in the north, and the *Casuarina*-mimicking *Amyema linophylla* in the south. Northern populations are associated with the Coconut Ant (*Philidris cordatus*), southern populations with *Anonychomyrma* species. The species is quite rare and very local.

FAMILY LYCAENIDAE—Blues, Coppers and Hairstreaks 243

Ground Azures

otanes

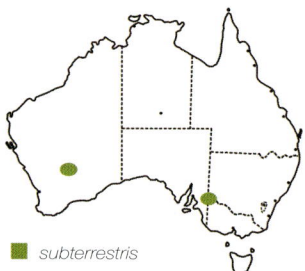
subterrestris

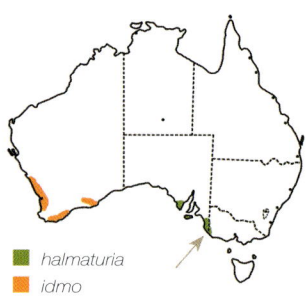
halmaturia
idmo

The ground azures include four bronzy-purple or dull-blue species found in southern mainland Australia. They form scattered populations mainly in dry, low scrubland, especially mallee. Adults fly low with a brisk flutter, within a metre of the ground, and perch on or near the ground. With one exception, larvae are probably carnivorous, feeding on the brood of their host ant.

The **Small Bronze Azure**, *Ogyris otanes* (fw ♂ 21 mm, ♀ 25 mm), occurs in mallee and coastal heath. Three subspecies are recognised, differing mainly in their underside ground colour. The typical form illustrated is from South Australia and western Victoria, where it may overlap with the very similar *O. subterrestris*. The male has a short, stubby tail on the hindwing, better developed in *O. otanes*. In the female, the outer dark band on the forewing underside is continued further than in *O. subterrestris*, and is slightly stepped. These same characteristics separate *O. otanes* from the larger *O. idmo*, where they occur together in Western Australia. Biologically, *O. otanes* differs from other ground azures. Females lay their eggs singly or in small clusters at the base of the host plant: *Choretrum glomeratum*, *C. spicatum* or *Leptomeria preissiania*. Egg parasitism is common. The virtually unpigmented larvae feed at night, closely tended by *Camponotus* ants, resting by day in the ant nest. In South Australia, the larvae often complete six instars (rather than the usual five) before pupation inside the nest. The pupa is also unusually pale. Such lack of pigmentation in the early stages is characteristic of species that spend all their time inside ant nests, such as other ground azures. The species is regarded as endangered in Victoria.

The **Arid Bronze Azure**, *Ogyris subterrestris* (fw ♂ 19–22 mm, ♀ 19–24 mm), occurs very locally in dry inland mallee. Adults fly little, and with their wings folded to show underside coloration, merge perfectly against a background of dead leaves and other vegetation. It is known from the Victoria–South Australia border region, and also from Lake Douglas, near Kalgoorlie, Western Australia. The two populations differ slightly, especially in the underside ground colour. Females lay large numbers of eggs, which are like those of *O. otanes*, on leaves and sticks around the entrance to large subterranean nests of *Camponotus* ants. The larva is pale and develops within the nest. It is believed that young larvae are fed by the ants, and later instars feed directly on the ant brood.

The **Large Bronze Azure**, *Ogyris idmo* (fw ♂ 26 mm, ♀ 28 mm), occurs in coastal heath, mallee or jarrah forest in Western Australia. Its biology is very like that of *O. subterrestris*, with larvae believed to feed on the brood of *Camponotus nigriceps* or *C. terebrans*.

Waterhouse's Azure, *Ogyris halmaturia* (fw ♂ 25 mm, ♀ 28 mm), has previously been called *O. idmo halmaturia* or *O. waterhouseri*. It is a little smaller than *O. idmo*. The male is dull purple-bronze above, with elongate rounded wings, and a fairly broad, dark margin not present in males of related species. The female is rather like that of *O. idmo*, but is blue rather than purple, and has more rounded wings. It occurs in mallee and coastal heath in South Australia and does not overlap with *O. idmo*. It flies steadily 1–2 m above the ground. The life history is similar to that of *O. subterrestris*, and it is confirmed that even young larvae feed on the ant brood. The species is considered endangered.

FAMILY LYCAENIDAE—Blues, Coppers and Hairstreaks

Large Azures

■ zosine

■ genoveva

The **Northern Large Azure**, *Ogyris zosine* (fw ♂ 27 mm, ♀ 30 mm), is widespread and found locally in a diverse range of habitats across the northern half of the continent. Although most abundant in tall open stands of eucalypt in wetter regions, it also occurs in coastal wallum in southern Queensland and *Acacia* scrubland in the arid interior. The male is always a deep bluish purple above, but the female exhibits a range of forms: in south-eastern coastal populations they are always deep purple, whereas, in the inland, they are always bright blue. The pinned (half-wing) specimens illustrated came from Slade Point, Mackay, where about one in twenty females was bright blue, with the remainder purple as shown. The habits of the butterfly vary considerably, depending on the habitat. In low heath forest they tend to frequent the highest suitable mistletoes, flying generally at about 6 m, around the crowns of the trees, occasionally descending below 3 m to perch or sip nectar from *Callistemon* flowers. In taller forest they fly higher, although they tend to remain at about the height of the most utilised clump of mistletoe, which is seldom low, but well below the crown of the host tree.

Mating follows a brief courtship. A perching male catches sight of a passing female and gives chase. Although their normal flight is a brisk flutter, chases can be very rapid. If receptive, the female perches. The male lands in front of her and, facing her, rotates his antennae around hers. This behaviour is unusual: it is common in nymphalids, but other lycaenids tend to approach directly from the side or behind. After a few seconds of this, he flips himself around to perch alongside her so rapidly the movement is scarcely perceptible, then urgently engages her genitalia by twisting his abdomen beneath hers. Once coupled, they adjust their position, facing away from each other, and remain thus, for 30–40 minutes while the sperm and accessory secretions are transferred. Most females probably mate just once, soon after emergence. They emerge from the pupa with numerous mature eggs in their ovaries, hence probably have less need of nutrients from the male than many other butterflies.

Eggs are laid singly on or near the host plant. Larvae are nocturnal and are usually tended closely by various species of sugar ants (genus *Camponotus*). When ants are absent they 'call' by rhythmically everting their tentacular organs, which probably secrete a volatile attractant (see the Lycaenidae family account). In eucalypt forest, individuals feeding on pendulous mistletoes commonly spend the day under bark or in an ant nest near the base of the host tree, and travel long distances each night to reach their food, partly guided by the ants. Even with a heavy ant guard, larvae are often attacked by braconid wasps. The resulting parasitoid larvae kill the butterfly larvae before they pupate. Pupation is under bark near the base of the tree, often en masse. The freshly formed pupa is a delicate pink, turning nearly black within two days. The empty pupal shells tend to remain long after the butterflies have emerged, thus serving to indicate the presence of the butterfly. At least thirteen mistletoe species are utilised, including species of *Amyema* and *Dendrophthoe* as well as *Decaisnina signata* and *Muellerina celastroides*.

The rather similar **Southern Large Azure**, *Ogyris genoveva* (fw ♂ 27 mm, ♀ 30 mm), is locally common in dry eucalypt forest or *Acacia* woodland in south-eastern Australia. The male is a deep royal blue, and the female is usually pale bluish green, although blue forms occur, distinguished from *O. zosine* by the larger cream spot on the forewing. It is most commonly associated with pendulous mistletoes growing on eucalypts, tended by very large *Camponotus* species, but has a wide range of hosts, including eight *Amyema* and two *Dendrophthoe* species and *Muellerina eucalyptoides*. Its behaviour and early stages are very like those of *O. zosine*.

FAMILY LYCAENIDAE—Blues, Coppers and Hairstreaks

Deep-blue and Purple Azures

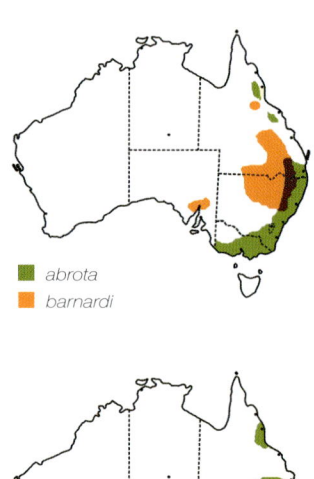

In three medium-sized species of azures, the male is deep blue to purplish, and the larvae are only weakly associated with ants. All fly rapidly and high, up to 20 m above the ground or more. All pupate under bark, occasionally high, but frequently low on the trunk of the host tree or in loose debris on the ground. Most museum specimens have been collected as pupae.

The **Dark Purple Azure**, *Ogyris abrota* (fw ♂ 23 mm, ♀ 25 mm), is locally quite common in tall eucalypt forest along the eastern Great Dividing Range. It is uncommon in lower forest on the coast. Adults fly around the crowns of trees, or perch on their mistletoe food plants. The larvae feed at night on *Amyema congener*, *Dendrophthoe vitellina*, *Muellerina celastroides* and *M. eucalyptoides*, occasionally tended by a variety of ants.

Barnard's Azure, *Ogyris barnardi* (fw ♂ 19 mm, ♀ 21 mm), is an inland species locally common in *Acacia* woodland, especially Brigalow (*Acacia harpophylla*) and Myall (a range of *Acacia* species). Its nocturnal larvae feed on *Amyema quandang*, sometimes tended by small black *Crematogaster* ants. The adults fly somewhat lower than *O. abrota* or *O. olane*, owing to the shorter stature of the vegetation in their preferred habitat.

The **Broad-margined Azure**, *Ogyris olane* (fw ♂ 20 mm, ♀ 21 mm), is widespread in dry eucalypt forest and open woodland, extending well inland, but is rare on the coast. Adults fly around their parasitic food plants and the crowns of host trees. They may also visit hilltops. Larvae feed at night, on *Amyema miquelii* and *A. pendula*, occasionally tended by a variety of small ants. Older larvae shelter near the base of the host tree, where they eventually pupate.

Australian Hairstreak

The **Australian Hairstreak**, *Pseudalmenus chlorinda* (fw ♂ 16–17 mm, ♀ 17–19 mm), is a common but very local insect in open forest and alpine woodland from the New England district of New South Wales to Tasmania. In the north of its range it is found above 1000 m, but in Tasmania it occurs at sea level. It is remarkable for its geographic variation, with four separate subspecies recognised in Tasmania alone. The most widespread race, *P. chlorinda zephyrus*, occurs in most of the south-east mainland and in the north of Tasmania. The most brilliant race is *P. chlorinda barringtonensis* from the mountains of northern New South Wales. In Tasmanian races, especially, the underside is brownish grey rather than silvery white. Adults, especially males, fly rapidly and often high around the larval host plant, typically *Acacia dealbata* or *A. melanoxylon*, but sometimes other *Acacia* species. Females tend to perch on the host plant, often basking with open wings. Females lay their eggs singly or in small groups on stems of the host plant. These are often subject to parasitism by tiny *Trichogramma* wasps. Larvae feed by day, alone or in small groups, tended by the ant *Anonychomyrma biconvexa*. Pupation usually takes place in sheltered crevices on the plant, either singly or in groups.

Cathedral Rock, Ebor, New South Wales

Imperial Blues 1

The imperial blues include eleven species in the genus *Jalmenus*. They occur in diverse open habitats over most of mainland Australia. As a result of DNA studies, the pattern of species evolution within the genus is particularly well understood. Even so, a new subspecies within the genus was named as recently as 2007, suggesting there might yet be species or subspecies within the genus awaiting discovery.

The **Common Imperial Blue**, *Jalmenus evagoras* (fw ♂ 19–21 mm, ♀ 21–23 mm), is widely distributed over south-eastern Australia. The larvae feed on numerous species of *Acacia* and are tended by several species of *Iridomyrmex* ants. The butterflies form colonies around stands of *Acacia* associated with suitable ants. Most colonies are very local and although some may persist for many years, others flourish for just a single season. The adults are very conspicuous as they flutter jerkily around their host plants, their uppersides flashing pale silvery blue or green. They usually fly quite low (1–2 m), and may perch for long periods on the leaves and stems of the plant.

When ovipositing, females respond to the presence of ants, and the ants may even encourage a female to oviposit on their tree by gently nibbling the tip of her abdomen as she probes the bark. The eggs are laid in large clusters, sometimes several deep, in crevices in the bark or in the cleft between divergent twigs. Hatching is synchronised so that eggs on the outside of a cluster emerge first, thus allowing their siblings from deeper layers to escape in their turn. Eggs are often heavily parasitised by a minute wasp (*Trichogramma* sp.). The larvae feed gregariously by day, and are generally covered by numerous ants. They exude honeydew, rich in sugars and amino acids, which the ants sip avidly. The larvae can produce sounds, variously characterised as 'grunts', 'drums' and 'hisses'. Each sound is used in a different context, but collectively they communicate either with other larvae or attendant ants, thus promoting group cohesion and attracting ants for protection when needed. Ants are probably also attracted by chemical signals. Pupae, which cluster in small groups on leaves and stems, also produce sounds made by rubbing together opposing ribbed surfaces between the fifth and sixth abdominal segments. Larvae may be heavily parasitised, both by a braconid wasp, *Apanteles* species, which emerges before the larvae can mature, and a chalcid wasp, *Brachymeria* species, which emerges from the pupa. Ants protect eggs, larvae and pupae from parasitoids. When ants are artificially excluded, parasitism increases several-fold. Moreover, the ants protect the larvae and vulnerable soft pre-pupae from a host of predators, including wasps, spiders, coccinellid beetles and other, predatory, ants.

J. evagoras has fascinating mating behaviour. Just before emergence, the pupae of both sexes emit a pheromone which is powerfully attractive to males. Typically, several males respond to this signal. Within a group of pupae they are able to determine exactly which one will soon emerge, and cluster in a tight seething scrum, jostling for position. If the emerging adult is a female, she copulates almost immediately. Often this union occurs as soon as her abdomen is free of the pupal case and, during a mating lasting 30–50 minutes, she gradually expands her wings and expels the meconium—waste from the abdomen held over from larval life. If the emerging adult is male, the waiting pack loses interest at once. Females emerge with numerous mature eggs in their ovaries; the spermatophore secreted by the male is small, and probably contributes relatively little in terms of nutrients to the female. It is likely that most females mate just once.

The **Brigalow Blue**, *Jalmenus eubulus* (fw ♂ 21 mm, ♀ 23 mm), has a similar biology to *J. evagoras*. It is confined to undisturbed patches of brigalow in inland central Queensland and was formerly considered to be a subspecies of *J. evagoras*.

FAMILY LYCAENIDAE—Blues, Coppers and Hairstreaks

Imperial Blues 2

daemeli

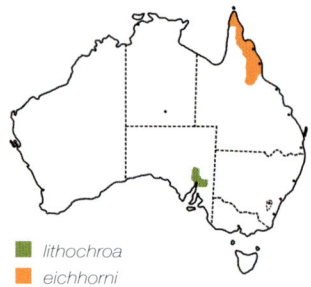

lithochroa
eichhorni

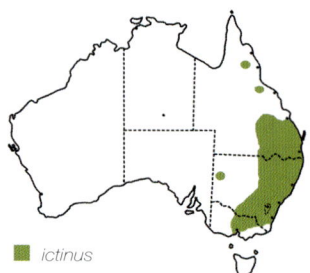

ictinus

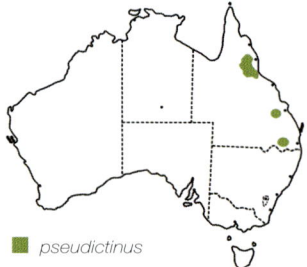

pseudictinus

Although rather similar in general appearance, other species of imperial blues are smaller and less conspicuous than *Jalmenus evagoras*. All are low-flying inhabitants of drier habitats, and are closely associated with their host plants and the ants that tend the larvae. The five species illustrated here are medium-sized, and very local in occurrence.

Daemel's Imperial Blue, *Jalmenus daemeli* (fw ♂ 17 mm, ♀ 21 mm), occurs in lightly wooded areas, preferring drier, more inland areas within its range. The underside markings are light brown, rather than black, and it cannot be confused with any other species within its range. The larvae feed on numerous species of *Acacia* and are tended by small ants of the genus *Iridomyrmex*. Adults are rarely found far from the host plant and often feed at *Acacia* blossoms. Eggs are laid in clusters, and larvae feed by day in small groups. Pupation occurs in exposed situations.

Waterhouse's Imperial Blue, *Jalmenus lithochroa* (fw ♂ 17.5 mm, ♀ 18 mm), occurs in open woodland and disturbed agricultural land in South Australia. It is slightly larger and has longer tails than *J. icilius*, the other species found in the area. Adults are normally found on or around the low-growing host plants, *Acacia pycnantha* and *A. victoriae*. Egg clusters are laid in bark crevices near the base of the host plant. Young larvae feed by night, but mature larvae feed in the daytime, attended by the large meat ants *Iridomyrmex purpureus* or *I. viridiaeneus*. The pupae are attached near the base of the host tree or in nearby debris on the ground. The species has disappeared from areas near Adelaide, owing to urban expansion.

The **Northern Imperial Blue**, *Jalmenus eichhorni* (fw ♂ 17 mm, ♀ 20 mm), occurs in dry open woodland in far north Queensland. It is easily recognised by its strong black underside markings. The broad, flattened, green and brown larvae feed by day, singly or in small groups, on various *Acacia* species, including *Acacia crassicarpa*, *A. holosericea*, *A. humifosa* and *A. leptocarpa*. They are tended by several species of *Iridomyrmex* ants. Pupation occurs in exposed situations, usually singly.

The **Stencilled Imperial Blue**, *Jalmenus ictinus* (fw ♂ 18 mm, ♀ 21 mm), is widespread in dry open woodland. It is easily distinguished from *J. evagoras* by its smaller size, the fainter and deeper blue on the upperside, and finer underside markings. Adults are found near the larval food plants, including at least nine species of *Acacia* and, rarely, *Heterodendron diversifolium*. The larvae feed openly by day, alone or in small groups, and have two rows of dorsal tubercles along their body. They are tended by the large aggressive meat ants, *Iridomyrmex purpureus* or *I. spadius*. Pupae, which may be on the host plant, or in litter at its base, also receive attention from ants.

The adults of **Macqueens's Imperial Blue**, *Jalmenus pseudictinus* (fw ♂ 18 mm, ♀ 21 mm), are indistinguishable from those of *J. ictinus* and occur in similar habitats. However, the larvae, which have similar habits, differ. Those of *J. pseudictinus* lack dorsal tubercles except at either end of the body. They are tended by the small red ants *Froggattella kirbii*. As the adults are normally found around the host plants, it is often the presence of this distinctive ant species which enables identification of the butterfly. Species such as *J. pseudictinus*, which, in the adult stage, can only be recognised indirectly, are known as cryptic species. Host plants for *J. pseudictinus* include *Acacia flavescens*, *A. harpophylla*, *A. humifusa*, *Alectryon conatus* and, rarely, *Heterodendron diversifolium*. *A. harpophylla* and *H. diversifolium* are also used by *J. ictinus*, but as the attendant ants are mutually exclusive, the two butterfly species never occur together on the same plant. *J. pseudictinus* is normally the rarer of the two.

FAMILY LYCAENIDAE—Blues, Coppers and Hairstreaks

Imperial Blues 3

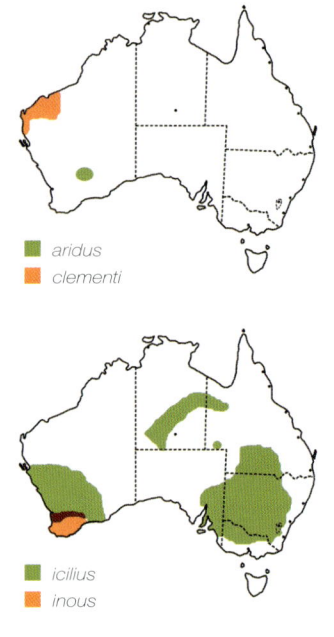

aridus
clementi

icilius
inous

Four smaller species of imperial blue occur in dry, central and western parts of Australia.

The **Inland Imperial Blue**, *Jalmenus aridus* (fw ♂ 13 mm, ♀ 14 mm), is the smallest member of the genus. It is known only from Lake Douglas, near Kalgoorlie in Western Australia. Larvae feed openly by day on *Acacia tetragonophylla* and *Senna nemophila*, attended by the small red ants, *Froggattella kirbii*. The remaining three species lack tails and are tended by small species of *Iridomyrmex* ants.

The **Turquoise Imperial Blue**, *Jalmenus clementi* (fw ♂ 14 mm, ♀ 16 mm), is restricted to the north-west, where its larvae feed by day on *Acacia alexandri*, *A. inaequilatera* and *A. tetragonophylla*.

The **Amethyst Imperial Blue**, *Jalmenus icilius* (fw ♂ 15.5 mm, ♀ 17 mm), is widely distributed over the dry central and southern inland. The larvae feed by day on numerous species of *Acacia*, as well as *Senna* and *Daviesia*.

The **Varied Imperial Blue**, *Jalmenus inous* (fw ♂ 17 mm, ♀ 18 mm), is confined to several isolated patches of habitat in the south-west. It is larger and more strongly marked on the underside, with wings more angulate than the last species, with which it overlaps. As well as the typical race *inous*, two subspecies, *notocrucifer* (meaning 'southern cross') and *bronwynae*, are recognised. Both have strong underside markings. Larvae feed mainly at night, on *Acacia rostellifera*, *A. saligna*, *Daviesia benthamii*, *D. divaricata* and *Gastrolobium microcarpum*.

aridus

clementi

icilius

icilius

icilius larva tended by *Iridomyrmex* sp.

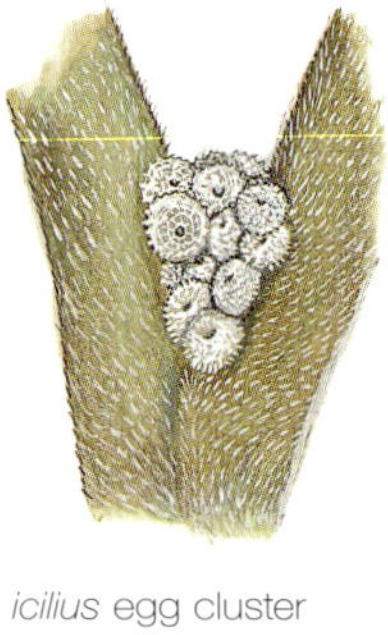

icilius egg cluster

inous

Tits and Sword-tailed Flash

The three species here are restricted to wetter regions of the tropics.

The **Black and White Tit**, *Hypolycaena danis* (fw ♂ 17.5 mm, ♀ 18 mm), is found in sunny rainforest gaps and understorey. It flies quite rapidly and perches 2–3 m above the ground. It evidently mimics females of *Psychonotis caelius*. Larvae, which are not associated with ants, feed on the Cooktown Orchid (*Dendrobium bigibbum*), as well as *D. canaliculatum* and several exotic orchids. It is a pest of concern to the ornamental flower industry in north Queensland.

The **Common Tit**, *Hypolycaena phorbas* (fw ♂ 16 mm, ♀ 19 mm), is common in a wide variety of wetter habitats, ranging from rainforest margins to gardens and mangroves. It flies 2–4 m above the ground, settling frequently. Larvae are closely tended by the ant *Oecophylla smaragdina* and feed largely at night on leaves of a very wide range of hosts from at least twelve plant families, including various species of mangrove, as well as *Cupaniopsis*, *Flagellaria*, *Lumnitzera*, *Senna* and *Terminalia*.

The **Sword-tailed Flash**, *Bindahara phocides* (fw ♂ 17 mm, ♀ 18 mm), is a spectacularly long-tailed species which occurs locally in northern tropical rainforest. Males tend to remain in the canopy and perch head downwards. Their flight is rapid and erratic. Females, which are paler beneath, may perch low in the forest understorey. The larva is quite similar to that of *Deudorix* species and feeds within the fruits of *Celastrus subspicata* and *Salacia disepala*. It is not ant-attended.

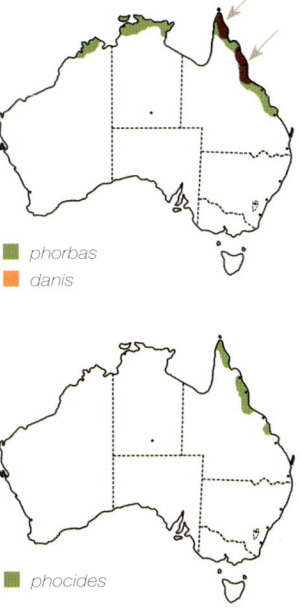

FAMILY LYCAENIDAE—Blues, Coppers and Hairstreaks

Flashes and Cornelians

■ varuna

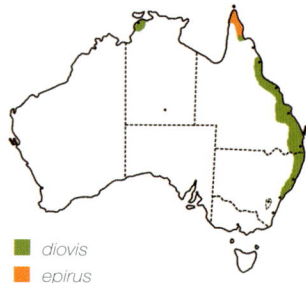
■ diovis
■ epirus

■ epijarbas

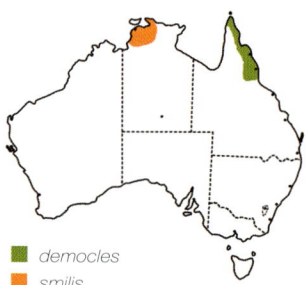
■ democles
■ smilis

The closely related genera, *Deudorix* and *Rapala*, are distinguished by the presence on the hindwing in both sexes of a semi-detached circular flap called the tornal lobe. On the upperside, this flap is marked with a definite eyespot, whereas on the underside it is dark. These features are crucial to the double false-head adaptations described in the introduction to the Theclinae.

The main difference between the two genera is in the larvae. In *Deudorix*, they feed inside fruits and seeds, hence are smooth and unpatterned with a flattened anal plate used to seal the hole as they bore into the flesh of the fruit. When older, *Rapala* larvae feed openly on buds and young foliage, and are strongly and cryptically patterned with numerous spines along the body. In neither genus are the larvae regularly tended by ants. Adults of both genera fly very rapidly and perch frequently, 2–4 m above the ground or higher. They tend to remain in the vicinity of their larval host plants, occasionally travelling several hundred metres or more to visit flowers or hilltops. The underside pattern of males and females is nearly identical in all species.

The **Indigo Flash**, *Rapala varuna* (fw ♂ 17 mm, ♀ 17 mm), is common in many habitats in the wetter regions of the north Queensland tropics, and also in low forest behind the ocean dunes in southern Queensland. The tiny bright green eggs are laid in small groups among buds of the larval host plant. The tiny young larvae burrow into buds, extruding a string of excrement, by which their presence is revealed. Older larvae emerge and feed openly among the flower heads, protected by their exquisite camouflage. A very wide range of native and introduced hosts are used, including *Acacia polystachya*, *Albizia lebbeck*, *Alphitonia excelsa*, *Cupaniopsis anacardoides*, *Dendrolobium umbellatum*, *Eriobotrya japonia*, *Jagera pseudorhus*, *Litchi chinensis*, *Pipturus argenteus* and *Pongamia pinnata*.

The **Bright Cornelian**, *Deudorix diovis* (fw ♂ 17 mm, ♀ 17.5 mm), is usually more localised than *R. varuna*. It prefers rainforest margins and monsoon forest, but also occurs commonly in gardens and littoral forest beside the sea, where it flies with *R. varuna*. The pale-green egg, much larger than that of *R. varuna*, is laid singly on fruits of the host plant. The anal plate on the larva, used to seal the entrance of the hole bored into the fruit, has two prominent pores or spiracles through which the larva breathes. Host plants are numerous and include species of *Alectryon*, *Arytera*, *Buckinghamia*, *Connarus*, *Cupaniopsis*, *Diploglottis*, *Elaeocarpus*, *Harpullia*, *Litchi*, *Macadamia*, *Pittosporum* and *Stenocarpus*.

The **Dull Cornelian**, *Deudorix epijarbas* (fw ♂ 17.5 mm, ♀ 18 mm), is much less common than the last, and confined to northern rainforest. In both sexes, the face between the eyes is white, rather than orange as it is in *D. diovis*. The female is a darker brown above. The larvae feed inside fruits of *Connarus conchocarpus*, *Litchi chinensis*, *Salacia chinensis* and *S. disepala*.

The **Orange-lobed Flash**, *Deudorix epirus* (fw ♂ 18 mm, ♀ 20 mm), is a rare rainforest species restricted to remote parts of north Queensland. Its larvae feed inside fruits and seeds of *Harpullia ramiflora*.

The **Blue Flash**, *Deudorix democles* (fw ♂ 18 mm, ♀ 21 mm), is uncommon in monsoon forest and at rainforest margins of north Queensland. The larvae feed on seeds of the vines *Strychnos lucida* or *S. minor*.

The slightly larger **Darwin Blue Flash**, *Deudorix smilis* (fw ♂ 20 mm, ♀ 23 mm), is very similar to *D. democles*, but is distinctly spotted beneath, and the blue areas on the upperside in both sexes are slightly reduced. It occurs in monsoon forest near Darwin, and the larvae feed in the fruits of *Strychnos lucida*.

FAMILY LYCAENIDAE—Blues, Coppers and Hairstreaks

SUBFAMILY POLYOMMATINAE—
Blues

Hairy Lineblue
(*Erysichton lineata*)

The remaining large subfamily of the Lycaenidae—the **Polyommatinae**—presents a dilemma. It is probably not a 'natural' group as we currently define it. That is, all members of a group should have a common ancestor and the group should include all descendents of that common ancestor. It now seems increasingly likely that although the species currently classified as polyommatines shared a common ancestor, other descendents of that ancestor are placed in other groups (most presently classified as theclines*). Nevertheless, while taxonomists wrestle with this problem, the subfamily remains a convenient grouping for the naturalist, for whom it is generally helpful in narrowing down the identity of any of our numerous blues, based on general appearance and behaviour, or 'jizz'.

The subfamily occurs worldwide and contains thousands of species, nearly 70 of which occur in Australia. In formal terms, the Polyommatinae are defined on the basis of their wing venation. As a rule of thumb, Polyommatinae are smaller, lighter species than the Theclinae, with more rounded wings and slower, lower, more fluttery flight. No polyommatine has strongly scalloped hindwings, unlike the theclines. Although in Australia more have hair-like tails than theclines, and the false-head phenomenon is common, there are no cases of double tails or extravagant 'tornal lobes'. The very common white-on-brown pattern of parallel lines on the underside, found in many lineblues and ceruleans, seldom occurs in the Theclinae, and when it does it is chiefly among the very seldom encountered ant blues.

The Polyommatinae include the many confusing, nearly uniform small blues (often browns with little or no blue dusting) that often occur profusely in pastures and gardens. A little practice, though, will show that they can be distinguished quite readily by careful examination, usually of the underside. Of course, for this purpose they often need to be captured and compared with diagnostic images, such as those presented in this book. Other larger and more dramatically patterned genera make up the remainder of the subfamily in Australia. Notable among these is the large genus *Candalides* of which we may encounter thirteen species in Australia, although even here some of the larger species are hard to separate.

Polyommatine eggs are generally very flattened, often with an apical depression. They are frequently ornamented by characteristic patterns of raised polygons. Larvae are generally squat, but otherwise are diverse in form: some are very flattened, others

---

* Such groups are called 'paraphyletic'.

deeper and slug-like. Species feeding on flowers and buds typically bear short rounded nodules on each segment, giving them a lumpy appearance. Many take on a coloration to match their background, whether on leaves or flowers. Pupae are generally small and rounded as in most other lycaenids, but in *Candalides* they are flattened and leaf-like.

In Australia, the larvae are less often attended by ants than the larvae of theclines, and even when ant-attendance does occur, the relationship is usually less well developed. This is not, however, universally the case, and the northern hemisphere species of the genus *Maculinea* and its close relatives, like some Australian theclines, are carried by worker ants into their nest and prey on the brood. Very young larvae feed on wild thyme, on which the females lay their eggs, but they are able to convince the ants—by physical and chemical mimicry—that they are lost ant larvae, needing to be rescued. Members of another Old World genus, *Niphanda*, feed as larvae on the sugary excretions of aphids, either directly or through ant regurgitations.

The subfamily is conventionally divided into four tribes, of which three are represented in Australia. The Candalidini is virtually restricted to Australia and New Guinea, with fourteen out of seventeen Australian species endemic. The genus *Nesolycaena* occurs nowhere else. The remainder of our fauna is dominated by species in the 'nominate' tribe, Polyommatini, of which only about one quarter of our species are endemic—the others are shared with New Guinea, South-East Asia and, in some cases, most of the rest of the Old World. Nevertheless, *Theclinesthes* (with five out of six species endemic) and *Neolucia* (with three out of three species endemic), give our fauna a distinctive character. Outside Australia, the various spectacular green-banded blues occur only in the Australasian region, mainly in New Guinea and the Pacific, as is the case for several other tropical rainforest groups. The third tribe represented in Australia, the Lycaenesthini, includes the mainly African genus *Anthene*; our two species are also widespread in New Guinea and eastern Indonesia.

Small Green-banded Blue
(*Psychonotis caelius*)

FAMILY LYCAENIDAE—Blues, Coppers and Hairstreaks

Pencilled Blues

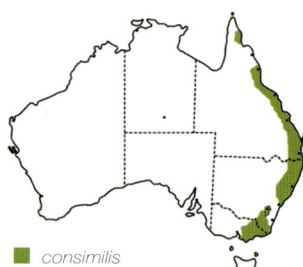

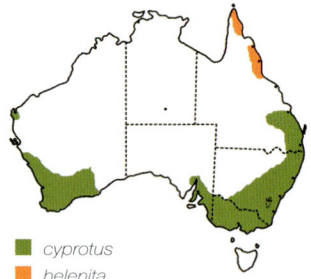

Pencilled blues include six rather similar species of the large genus *Candalides*. Typically, male and female are very different on their uppersides, but in both sexes the undersides are shining silvery white, with small, faint-grey 'pencil' marks. These vary slightly in different species but are little help for identification.

The most difficult species to separate are the **Common Pencilled Blue**, *Candalides absimilis* (fw ♂ 17.5 mm, ♀ 18 mm), the **Dark Pencilled Blue**, *C. consimilis* (fw ♂ 18 mm, ♀ 18.5 mm), and the **Trident Pencilled Blue**, *C. margarita* (fw ♂ 18 mm, ♀ 18.5 mm). All three may fly together, especially in coastal areas. The best diagnostic features for both sexes are overall wing shape and upperside coloration, especially those markings on the male forewing and the female hindwing.

The male **Northern Pencilled Blue**, *Candalides gilberti* (fw ♂ 18 mm, ♀ 18.5 mm), is very like that of *C. margarita*, but its range, centred on Darwin, is outside that of any other pencilled blue species. Its pale-blue female is distinctive.

The male **Shining Pencilled Blue**, *Candalides helenita* (fw ♂ 18 mm, ♀ 18.5 mm), is a distinctive turquoise blue above and is confined to the edges and understorey of north Queensland rainforests.

All five species tend to fly moderately high, 2–5 m above the ground, and are found in the vicinity of their host plants. Males perch in sunny spots, pursuing passing females, interweaving at high speed through the vegetation. Host plants and early stages of these five species are very variable, although the pupa is always flattened, with lateral flanges—mimicking perfectly a piece of dead leaf. *C. margarita* and *C. gilberti* feed on mistletoes (*C. margarita* on *Amyema*, *Benthamina*, *Dendrophthoe* and *Muellerina*; *C. gilberti* on *Decaisnina signata*) and have a finely pitted egg and smooth, strongly humped larva. In other species, the egg is coarsely pitted. *C. absimilis* larvae are similar to those of *margarita* but less humped, and feed on the young shoots and buds of a very wide range of hosts: species of *Alectryon*, *Brachychiton*, *Castanospermum*, *Cupaniopsis*, *Erythrina*, *Flagellaria*, *Harpullia*, *Macadamia*, *Millettia*, *Pongamia*, *Stenocarpus* and several exotics. The larvae of *C. consimilis* and *C. helenita* bear long processes. Host plants for *C. consimilis* include *Alectryon coriaceus*, *Ceratopetalum gummiferum*, *Polyscias elegans* and *P. sambucifolius*. *C. helenita* has been recorded from *Arytera pauciflora*, *Brachychiton acerifolius*, *Cryptocarya hypospodia* and *Glochidion ferdinandi*.

The **Copper Pencilled Blue**, *Candalides cyprotus* (fw ♂ 16 mm, ♀ 17 mm), which is dusky beneath, is found locally in heath or open forest in coastal, upland and inland situations. A good deal of variation occurs throughout its range. Adults fly low and perch close to the ground. Its larvae bear long processes and vary greatly in colour, but preserve a distinctive pattern of diagonal streaks. The pupae bear blunt dorsal spines. Host plants include *Conospermum taxifolium*, *Grevillea bracteosa*, *G. huegelii*, *G. juniperina*, *Hakea leucoptera* and *Jacksonia scoparia*. Larvae of pencilled blues are only rarely tended by ants.

FAMILY LYCAENIDAE—Blues, Coppers and Hairstreaks

Dusky Blues and Yellow-spot Blue

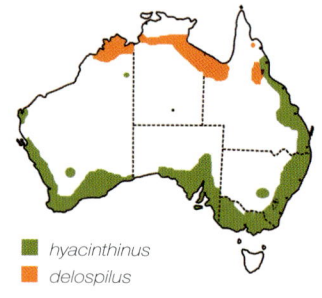

- hyacinthinus
- delospilus

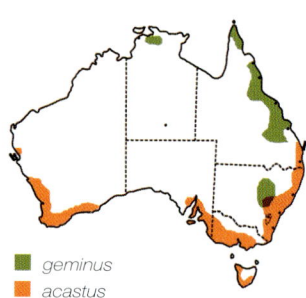

- geminus
- acastus

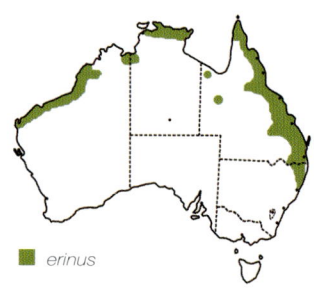

- erinus

The dusky blues include five species and one very distinct subspecies. With one exception, males are dull purple above, and females dark brown with deep blue or purple central markings. Sometimes these are reduced to a light dusting of blue or purple scales, and much variation occurs even within local populations. The underside colour and pattern, which are always very similar in both sexes, as well as overall size, provide the best means of separating the species. Wing shape may also be important. All dusky blues inhabit heath and open forest. They fly and perch close to the ground. Their larvae feed on several species of *Cassytha*, a filamentous, low-scrambling parasitic vine which grows in dense tangles over its host shrubs. Larvae and pupae are fairly similar in the various species. Eggs are coarsely pitted. The pupae are distinctively flattened, but lack the strong lateral flange found in pencilled blues. Larvae are very rarely ant-attended, and are often attacked by parasites such as tachinid flies.

The most widespread species is the **Common Dusky Blue**, *Candalides hyacinthinus* (fw ♂ 16 mm, ♀ 17.5 mm). The forewing underside bears a conspicuous pair of dark 'twin spots'. It is highly variable. In the east it is mainly coastal and subcoastal.

The southern form, the **Bright Dusky Blue**, *Candalides hyacinthinus simplex* (fw ♂ 15 mm, ♀ 16 mm), is very distinctive, with both male and female bright azure blue above. It occurs in drier habitats such as mallee. The south-western form, *C. hyacinthinus gilesi* (fw ♂ 15 mm, ♀ 16 mm), is similar to the typical eastern form but smaller and duller. It is possible these three forms may represent distinct species, but this awaits resolution.

The **Twin Dusky Blue**, *Candalides geminus* (fw ♂ 16 mm, ♀ 17 mm), also bears twin spots on the forewing and is very difficult to separate from the typical eastern *hyacinthinus*. (The genitalia, however, differ substantially.) It has a mainly eastern inland distribution, but the two species fly together in several localities. In *C. geminus*, the wing margins are more rounded and the underside markings are fainter, but this latter feature may be difficult to discern in worn specimens.

erinus ♂

Coastal heath, southern Queensland

The **Small Dusky Blue**, *Candalides erinus* (fw ♂ 13 mm, ♀ 14 mm), the third species with forewing twin spots, is mainly coastal. It is easily distinguished from *C. hyacinthinus* and *C. geminus* by its smaller size and much paler underside, which has whitish areas, especially on the hindwing.

The **Blotched Dusky Blue**, *Candalides acastus* (fw ♂ 12.5 mm, ♀ 13 mm), is similar in size to *C. erinus* but the underside is dark and blotched, and lacks a well-defined twin spot on the forewing. It is the only *Candalides* species reaching Tasmania.

The **Spotted Dusky Blue**, *Candalides delospilus* (fw ♂ 10 mm, ♀ 11 mm), is a tiny, distinctive, very local species found on sandstone or laterite outcrops in dry, northern inland habitats.

The unmistakable **Yellow-spot Blue**, *Candalides xanthospilos* (fw ♂ 15 mm, ♀ 15 mm), is locally common in heath and open forest in the east. The female is like the male, but with a brown, rather than a deep blue ground colour. Adults fly mainly 1–2 m above the ground. The larval food plants are *Pimelea linifolia*, *P. lingustrina* and *P. stricta*. The habitat illustrated shows coastal heath in southern Queensland, where *C. hyacinthinus*, *C. erinus*, *C. acastus* and *C. xanthospilos* all fly together.

■ *xanthospilos*

FAMILY LYCAENIDAE—Blues, Coppers and Hairstreaks

Rayed Blues and Opals

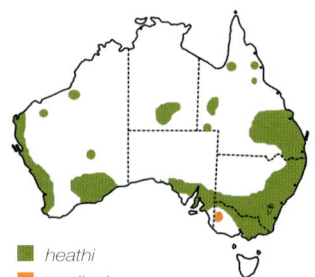

- heathi
- noelkeri

- albosericea
- urumelia

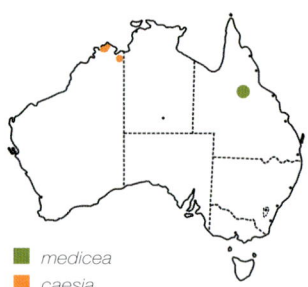

- medicea
- caesia

The rayed blues are allied to *Candalides xanthospilos*. There are two closely related species. In both, the veins on the upperside of the males are clearly delineated in golden brown against a blue or purple background. The underside in both sexes ranges from pure silvery white to grey, with small black spots along the wing margin, characteristics that enable immediate recognition of the butterflies at rest.

The **Common Rayed Blue**, *Candalides heathi* (fw ♂ 16.5 mm, ♀ 17 mm), is widespread over the continent. It occurs in a broad range of heath and open forest habitats ranging from coastal and upland areas to semi-arid woodland. Two alpine subspecies are recognised, *C. heathi alpina* from the southern New South Wales highlands and *C. heathi doddi* from the northern New South Wales highlands. Both (fw ♂ 19 mm, ♀ 20 mm) are up to 15 per cent larger than the typical form and the underside is light grey, rather than silvery white. Wherever it occurs, the species is exceedingly local, although often common. Adults fly low and perch in the vicinity of larval food plants. These include *Derwentia derwentiana*, *D. perfoliata*, *Eremophila deserti*, *E. gilesii*, *E. longifolia*, *Pimelea* species, *Plantago lanceolata*, *Prostanthera nivea* and *Stemodia florulenta*. The larvae are green to greenish yellow, rather like those of *C. margarita*, but less humped and with a slightly serrate dorsal profile. The brown to grey pupa is flattened, with weak lateral flanges.

The **Golden-rayed Blue**, *Candalides noelkeri* (fw ♂ 15 mm, ♀ 15 mm), is restricted to a small area in the Wimmera region of Victoria and is considered to be endangered. The larval host is *Myoporum parvifolium*. Larvae of rayed blues are not usually tended by ants.

The opals (genus *Nesolycaena*) are closely related to *Candalides*. They include four seldom-encountered species, all of which feed as larvae on *Boronia* species. The larvae are rather similar to those of the dusky blues and are usually not tended by ants. The pupae are slightly flattened, with weak lateral flanges. The eggs are coarsely pitted, rather like *C. erinus*. All inhabit heath or open forest with a heathy understorey and occur very locally. Adults flutter close to the ground, generally in the vicinity of the food plant, with the white uppersides flashing conspicuously.

The **Satin Opal**, *Nesolycaena albosericea* (fw ♂ 18 mm, ♀ 18 mm), occurs in coastal and inland parts of south-central Queensland. Food plants include *Boronia glabra*, *B. obovata*, *B. odorata* and *B. rosmarinifolia*.

The **Spotted Opal**, *Nesolycaena urumelia* (fw ♂ 16 mm, ♀ 17 mm), has a patchy distribution centred around Darwin, the larvae feeding on *Boronia lanceolata*.

The **Dark Opal**, *Nesolycaena medicea* (fw ♂ 16 mm, ♀ 18 mm), is known only from the White Mountains in northern central Queensland where it was discovered as recently as the 1990s. Its larvae feed on *Boronia eriantha*.

The **Kimberley Spotted Opal**, *Nesolycaena caesia* (fw ♂ 14 mm, ♀ 15 mm), is known from the eastern Kimberley region of Western Australia. Its larvae feed on *Boronia kalumburensis* and *B. wilsonii*.

FAMILY LYCAENIDAE—Blues, Coppers and Hairstreaks

Green-banded Blues and Ceruleans

The green-banded pattern on the underside has evolved several times in blues and hairstreaks. Strong resemblances between distantly related species suggest natural selection for mimetic forms. It is supposed that *Danis* and *Psychonotis* are unpalatable, and mimicked by other genera. However, insufficient is known to offer a clear explanation for this effect.

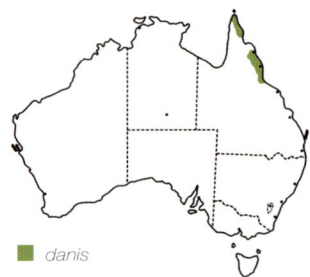

danis

The exquisite **Large Green-banded Blue**, *Danis danis* (fw ♂ 22 mm, ♀ 23 mm), is very common in rainforest in the Queensland wet tropics region. Adults occur most often in the forest understorey. Their flight is weak and fluttering and fairly low, generally 1–3 m above the ground. They perch frequently on both the upside and underside of leaves. Males, especially, may frequent small, sunny patches and perch on the upperside of the leaf. The larvae feed on new growth of *Derris* species, *Connarus conchocarpus* and *Rourea brachyandrya*. They are seldom tended by ants.

caelius

The **Small Green-banded Blue**, *Psychonotis caelius* (fw ♂ 17 mm, ♀ 17 mm), is very common in warmer and wetter habitats along the eastern coast. Adults are found near their host plant, *Alphitonia excelsa*. They fly mainly 1–3 m above the ground with a brisk fluttering flight. Ovipositing females hover around the host plant before laying their tiny, pale-green eggs singly on the underside of young leaves near the midrib. Males court the females by hovering below them when perched, then landing close behind them and rhythmically flashing their wings to display the brilliant cobalt-blue uppersides. At the peak of his excitement, the male edges so close that he may enfold her wings within his own as they close. If the female remains quiescent, the male moves alongside her and copulates. If she is unreceptive, she flies off. The pale-green, flattened larvae feed on the underside of host plant leaves and are superbly camouflaged. They are often attacked by parasitoids, especially tachinid flies. They are seldom tended by ants.

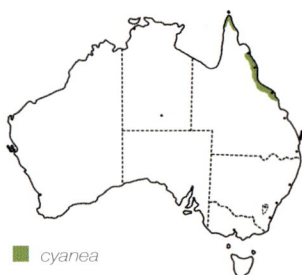

cyanea

The **Tailed Green-banded Blue**, *Nacaduba cyanea* (fw ♂ 19 mm, ♀ 19 mm), occurs in lowland tropical rainforest. It flies fairly slowly in the understorey or in sunny gaps in the forest, usually 2–4 m high, and perches frequently on the upperside of leaves. The larvae feed on *Entada phaseoloides* and are sometimes tended by small ants. Despite appearances, this species is only distantly related to *Psychonotis caelius*, which it may mimic.

aleuas

The **Bright Cerulean**, *Jamides aleuas* (fw ♂ 17 mm, ♀ 17 mm), bears a slight resemblance to the green-banded blues in its underside pattern. It flutters quite rapidly at a height of 1–5 m at rainforest margins and in sunny gaps, perching frequently on the upperside of leaves. Males are particularly brilliant in flight. The larvae feed on fresh growth of *Arytera pauciflora* and *Sarcopteryx stipata* and are occasionally tended by small ants.

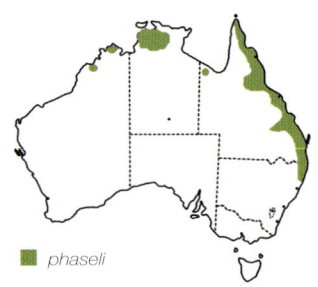

phaseli

The Dark Cerulean, *Jamides phaseli* (fw ♂ 14 mm, ♀ 15 mm), is widespread and common in open, mainly coastal forest. It is most easily confused with *Nacaduba berenice*, which may occur in the same localities, and hence is easily overlooked. It is distinguished by the broader dark margin on the upperside of the wings in the male, and on the underside by the absence of a pair of pale lines near the forewing base in both sexes. The larvae feed on *Cajanus reticulatus*, *Canavalia rosea*, *Indigofera pratensis*, *Pongamia pinnata*, *Tephrosia rufula* and introduced *Phaseolus vulgaris*. They are occasionally tended by small ants.

D. danis

D. danis ♀

P. caelius

P. caelius courtship

N. cyanea

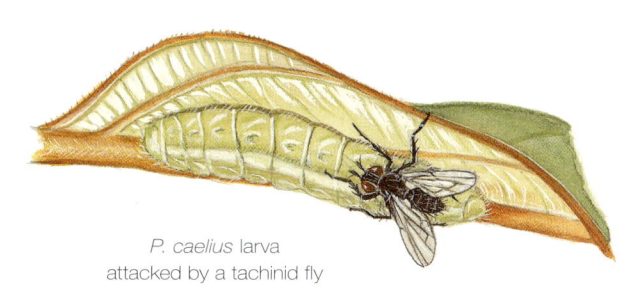

P. caelius larva attacked by a tachinid fly

J. aleuas

broad dark margin

transverse white lines absent

J. phaseli

FAMILY LYCAENIDAE—Blues, Coppers and Hairstreaks

Lineblues 1

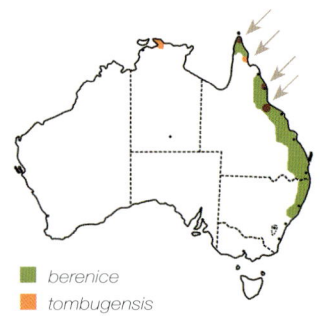

- berenice
- tombugensis

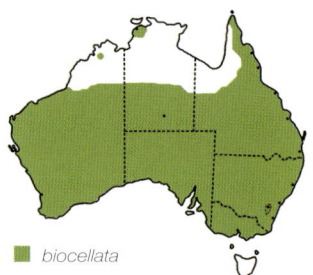

- biocellata

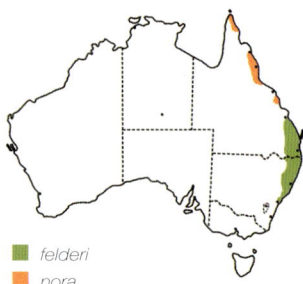

- felderi
- nora

- dubiosa

The lineblues include thirteen small to very small species in seven genera. With one exception, they are confined to the north and east, mainly near the coast. All fly moderately low in the vicinity of their larval host plants, perching frequently. Their common name derives from the series of pale parallel lines on the underside of the wings, but it should be noted that this pattern also occurs in several other polyommatine blues. Because of their small size, and the similarities among many species, they are often overlooked, although most species are quite easily observed.

The **Northern Lineblue**, *Petrelaea tombugensis* (fw ♂ 14 mm, ♀ 14 mm), is locally common in lowland rainforest in north Queensland and monsoon forest near Darwin. Its distinguishing features include the lack of a tail, and the presence of two small black spots on the hindwing underside. It is larger with a more pointed forewing than other tailless species. Adults are normally found around the larval host plant, *Terminalia catappa*. The unusual larvae feed on buds and flowers. They are not tended by ants.

The **Common Lineblue**, *Nacaduba berenice* (fw ♂ 14 mm, ♀ 14 mm), differs from the similar *Jamides phaseli* by the presence of pale lines at the base of the forewing underside. It is widespread and very abundant on the eastern coast, usually perching 1–3 m above the ground on vegetation near the larval host plants. High-speed chases with males pursuing passing females are common. The larvae are tended by numerous species of ants, large and small, and feed on young foliage and flowers of *Alectryon*, *Aphananthe*, *Arytera*, *Atalaya*, *Cupaniopsis*, *Elatostachys*, *Guioa*, *Heterodendron*, *Jagera* and *Macadamia*. Pupae are normally concealed in dead leaves, often in small groups.

The **Twin-spotted Lineblue**, *Nacaduba biocellata* (fw ♂ 12 mm, ♀ 12 mm), is found over most of mainland Australia. It is easily recognised by the two prominent dark spots on the hindwing, the lack of a tail and its small size. The female is almost entirely brown above, sometimes with a variable blue dusting basally. Adults are normally found around the buds and flowers of *Acacia* species, on which the larvae feed. They flutter briskly, usually 1–3 m above the ground. Like many flower-feeders, the larvae are coarsely nodular and very variable in colour, but often assume the yellow of wattle flowers. They are sometimes tended by small ants.

The **Short-tailed Lineblue**, *Prosotas felderi* (fw ♂ 11 mm, ♀ 11.5 mm), **Tailless Lineblue**, *P. dubiosa* (fw ♂ 11 mm, ♀ 11.5 mm), and **Long-tailed Lineblue**, *P. nora* (fw ♂ 11 mm, ♀ 11.5 mm), are all smaller species with a single large black eyespot on the underside of the hindwing. They may be separated from each other, in both sexes, by the length of the tail. The underside of females is generally paler than in males, tending to golden brown, especially in *P. felderi*. On the upperside, all *Prosotas* females resemble small versions of the female of *N. berenice*, but may be recognised by their smaller size and narrower, more strongly defined white-edged bands on the underside.

In *P. felderi* and *P. dubiosa* the short or absent tail is also diagnostic. Larvae of *P. felderi* and *P. dubiosa* feed on buds and flowers. They are smaller and slightly more humped than *N. berenice* larvae and rather variable in colour. Host plants recorded for *P. felderi* are species of *Acacia*, *Albizia*, *Alectryon coriaceus*, *Cupaniopsis anacardoides*, *Harpullia pendula* and *Litchi chinensis*. Larvae may be tended by small black ants. Host plants recorded for *P. dubiosa* are *Acacia*, *Albizia*, *Alectryon tomentosus*, *Archidendron grandiflorum*, *Harpullia pendula*, *Leucaena leucocephala*, *Litchi* and *Macadamia*. Ant-attendance has not been recorded. The host plant of *P. nora* is not known.

FAMILY LYCAENIDAE—Blues, Coppers and Hairstreaks 269

Lineblues 2

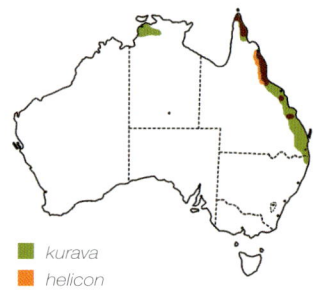
- kurava
- helicon

- lineata

- palmyra

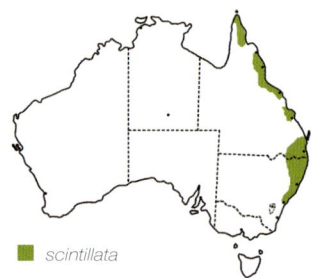
- scintillata

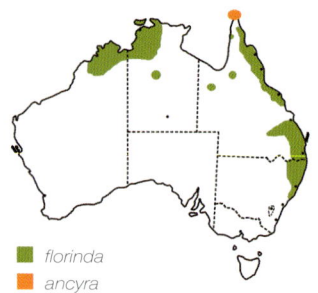
- florinda
- ancyra

Included on this page, along with three more typical lineblues, are four that are easily confused, mostly unrelated species in which the female bears white patches, especially on the forewing. Those species with elongate acute wings, such as *Ionolyce helicon*, *Erysichton* species and *Sahulana scintillata* tend to be very swift fliers, although in general habits they resemble other lineblues, perching relatively low (1–3 m) near their host plants and making frequent short flights away from these perches. Early stages tend to be quite similar in most species, with considerable colour variation within species.

The **Bronze Lineblue**, *Ionolyce helicon* (fw ♂ 11 mm, ♀ 11 mm), is locally common in rainforest and monsoon forest. The wings are very acute and angular. The larvae are green with white markings and distinctly nodular. They feed on *Allophylus cobbe* and *Entada phaseoloides*. They are evidently not attended by ants.

The **White-banded Lineblue**, *Nacaduba kurava* (fw ♂ 14 mm, ♀ 15 mm), is a pretty, rather conspicuous little species moderately common at the margins of rainforest and vine forest and, in the south of its range, it occasionally occurs in mangroves. Larvae feed on young growth of *Aegicerus corniculatum*, *Cupaniopsis anacardoides*, *Embelia curvinervia*, *Maesa haplobotrys*, *M. dependens* and *Rapanea variabilis*. They are sometimes attended by small ants.

The **Hairy Lineblue**, *Erysichton lineata* (fw ♂ 15 mm, ♀ 15 mm), is common at rainforest edges and gardens. The male and female are very different; the female is more conspicuous, with the white flash on the underside clearly visible even when it is perched. Larvae feed on buds and flowers of *Alectryon*, *Brachychiton*, *Cupaniopsis*, *Ehretia*, *Elatostachys*, *Harpullia*, *Jagera*, *Macadamia* and *Miscarytera*. They are rarely ant-attended.

The **Marbled Lineblue**, *Erysichton palmyra* (fw ♂ 15 mm, ♀ 15 mm), in flight is very similar to *E. lineata*. However, when closely examined at rest, the marbled pattern of the underside is very clear. Larvae feed on mistletoe flowers, including *Amyema cambagei*, *A. congener* and *Dendrophthoe vitellina*. They are not ant-attended. The species is rather uncommon and local, sometimes being absent even where its mistletoe food plants are abundant.

The **Glistening Lineblue**, *Sahulana scintillata* (fw ♂ 14 mm, ♀ 14.5 mm), is common in coastal eucalypt, riverine and littoral forests, and sometimes in gardens. At rest, the irregular white patch on the hindwing in both sexes can be plainly seen. The larvae are strongly marked, usually with reddish brown and white on a green ground colour, but there is much variation. They feed on buds and flowers of *Acacia disparimma*, *A. leiocalyx*, *A. maidenii*, *Albizia lebbeck*, *Alectryon coriaceus* and *Cupaniopsis anacardoides*. They are not ant-attended.

The **Speckled Lineblue**, *Catopyrops florinda* (fw ♂ 14 mm, ♀ 14.5 mm), is common and widespread at the edges of wetter forest types and gardens, wherever its host plants grow. On the underside, there are well-defined bands with intervening white patches, especially in the female. It lacks basal spots on the underside of the hindwing which are present in the similar Pale Pea Blue (*Catochrysops panormus*). Larvae feed on buds, flowers and young shoots of *Caesalpinia bonduc*, *Harpullia pendula*, *Pipturus argenteus* and *Trema tomentosa*, and are attended by ants.

The **Papuan Lineblue**, *Catopyrops ancyra* (fw ♂ 14 mm, ♀ 15 mm), is restricted to the islands of Torres Strait. The female resembles that of *C. florinda*, but the underside is like that of the *C. ancyra* male. Larvae feed on *Caesalpinia bonduc* and *Pipturus argenteus*.

FAMILY LYCAENIDAE—Blues, Coppers and Hairstreaks

Ciliate Blues and *Theclinesthes* 1

The ciliate blues include two tropical species of the genus *Anthene* and are the only members of their tribe, the Lycaenesthini, to occur in Australia. Elsewhere in the Old World tropics they are very diverse, especially in Africa. They are moderately large and heavy bodied. The wings are broad and angular and the hindwing bears three small tufts, or cilia, which give them their common name.

■ lycaenoides

The **Pale Ciliate Blue**, *Anthene lycaenoides* (fw ♂ 15.5 mm, ♀ 16 mm), is locally common in lowland rainforest and gardens in wet tropical areas, wherever its host plants grow. The larvae feed on buds, flowers and fresh shoots of *Acacia*, *Briedelia*, *Caesalpinia*, *Calliandra*, *Clerodendrum*, *Cupaniopsis*, *Faradaya*, *Flagellaria*, *Litchi*, *Pongamia*, *Rhyssopterys* and *Senna*. The larvae are somewhat nodular, like other flower-feeders, and very variable in colour. They are tended by many species of ant, chiefly the Green Tree Ant (*Oecophylla smaragdina*). The somewhat flattened pupa is green, with a yellow streak on the upperside.

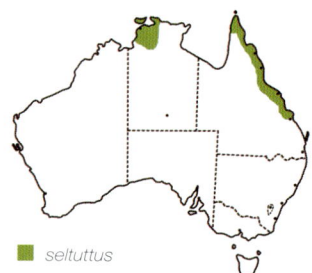
■ seltuttus

The **Dark Ciliate Blue**, *Anthene seltuttus* (fw ♂ 15 mm, ♀ 16 mm), is slightly more widespread. The female is almost entirely brown above, with a faint blue dusting towards the base of the wings. Larvae feed on young leaves of *Arytera*, *Brachychiton*, *Cassia*, *Cryptocarya*, *Cupaniopsis*, *Delonix*, *Lagerstroemia*, *Pongamia*, *Saraca*, *Schotia* and *Syzygium*. They are tended by Green Tree Ants (*O. smaragdina*). The larva and pupa bear a curious resemblance to those of the unrelated oakblues (*Arhopala* spp.), also tended by *O. smaragdina*.

The genus *Theclinesthes* includes six species, some very difficult to separate. Commonly there is a winter form, in which the underside in both sexes is darker with well-defined variegated white patches. The slug-like larvae are very variable in colour in most species, even within a single brood, and are generally ant-attended.

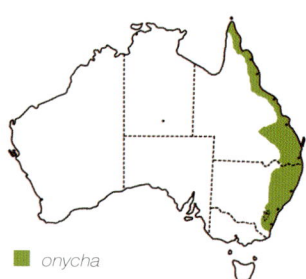
■ onycha

The **Cycad Blue**, *Theclinesthes onycha* (fw ♂ 15 mm, ♀ 16 mm), can be recognised by the strong eyespot on the hindwing underside, the brownish ground colour of the underside, and broad, indented, dark marginal band on the upperside of the male hindwing. It is a little larger than *T. miskini*. Larvae feed on the cycads *Cycas* and *Macrozamia*, the only gymnosperms consumed by any Australian butterfly. Adults occur widely in open forest and gardens but usually in the vicinity of the host plant, where they perch at 1–3 m. Flight is rapid.

■ miskini

The **Wattle Blue**, *Theclinesthes miskini* (fw ♂ 14 mm, ♀ 15 mm), which also has a strong hindwing eyespot, is slightly smaller than *T. onycha*, and the underside ground colour has a greyer tone. The dark margin to the male forewing upperside is narrow and not strongly indented. The larvae feed on young foliage of *Acacia*, especially, and also *Atalaya*, *Cajanus*, *Cathormion*, *Corymbia*, *Eucalyptus*, *Paraserianthes* and *Sesbania*. Preferred habitats are drier, more open forests, where adults perch 2–4 m above ground level.

In all remaining species, the hindwing eyespot is not prominent and the tail is short.

The **Bitter-bush Blue**, *Theclinesthes albocincta* (fw ♂ 11–14 mm, ♀ 12–15 mm), has distinct seasonal and geographic forms, with inland forms being small and mainly brown above, and coastal forms larger and pale dull blue above. Larvae range from red-brown to bright green and feed on *Adriana tomentosa* and *A. quadripartita*. Adults are low-flying and occur where the host plant grows on dunes around salt lakes or near the sea.

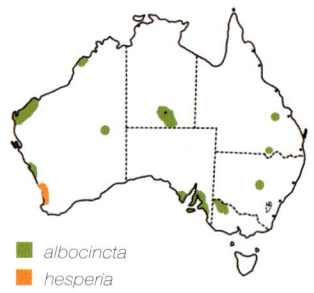
■ albocincta
■ hesperia

The **Western Bitter-bush Blue**, *Theclinesthes hesperia* (fw ♂ 14 mm, ♀ 15 mm), occurs locally in coastal sand dunes in southern Western Australia. Its range does not overlap with that of *T. albocincta*. The larval host plant is *Adriana quadripartita*.

FAMILY LYCAENIDAE—Blues, Coppers and Hairstreaks

Heath Blues and *Theclinesthes* 2

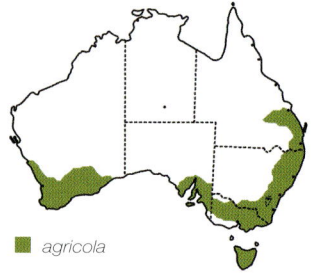
agricola

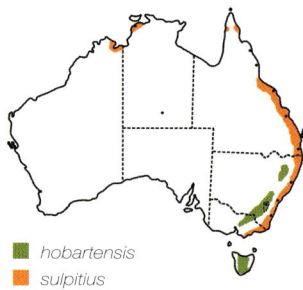
hobartensis
sulpitius

mathewi

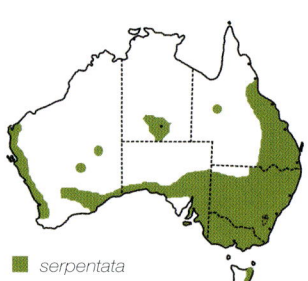
serpentata

The heath blues of the genus *Neolucia* include three small, coppery-brown species in which the wing margins are distinctly chequered. Females are coloured as the males, although they are generally somewhat lighter above and are, on average, slightly larger. The underside patterns differ clearly between the species. Adults of all species are found in heaths in various situations, and perch mostly within a metre of the ground, often with wings half open. They fly low with a brisk fluttery motion.

The **Fringed Heath Blue**, *N. agricola* (fw ♂ 12.5 mm, ♀ 13 mm), is common and widespread. It inhabits a broad range of heathland habitats, including open forest with a heath understorey, and also occurs in semi-arid, sparsely vegetated country. The larvae feed on the buds and flowers of numerous species of native peas, adapting their colour and pattern to blend with the host plant. Host plants include *Aotus ericoides*, *Bossiaea*, *Daviesia* and *Dillwynia* species, *Eutaxia microphylla*, *Jacksonia sternbergiana* and *Pultenaea* species. They are sometimes tended by small black *Iridomyrmex* ants. Like many lycaenids, the larva may be attacked by small braconid wasps, which complete their development feeding on the larva's tissues before it reaches pupation. An undescribed species of *Neolucia* close to *N. agricola* is known from Western Australia.

The **Mountain Heath Blue**, *N. hobartensis* (fw ♂ 10 mm, ♀ 10 mm), is found in heath and open forest in mountainous areas. The New England form, *N. hobartensis monticola* (fw ♂ 12 mm, ♀ 13 mm), is substantially larger. In Tasmania the species is found as low as 300 m, but in northern New South Wales is not found below 1200 m. The larvae feed on buds and flowers of *Epacris* species.

The **Dull Heath Blue**, *N. mathewi* (fw ♂ 11 mm, ♀ 11 mm), occurs locally in coastal and montane heath in the south-east. The larvae feed on buds and flowers of *Monotoca* species. Neither *N. hobartensis* nor *N. mathewi* larvae are ant-attended.

Of the two very small species of *Theclinesthes*, one, the **Saltbush Blue**, *T. serpentata* (fw ♂ 10 mm, ♀ 10.5 mm), might be confused with the heath blues on account of its size, low flight and chequered margin. However, there is no copper sheen to the upperside and the basal part of the wings is always dusted in dark blue, especially in males. The underside pattern is also distinct. It is widespread but rather local in a wide range of open or lightly forested habitats ranging from coastal mud-flats and suburban gardens to inland semi-arid saltbush scrub. It flutters briskly around its food plants, usually within a metre of the ground. Larval hosts include *Atalaya*, *Atriplex*, *Chenopodium*, *Einandia* and *Rhagodia*.

The tiny **Samphire Blue**, *Theclinesthes sulpitius* (fw ♂ 9.5 mm, ♀ 10 mm), is exceedingly common in coastal areas where its salt-loving food plants grow near the water in inlets and estuaries. Almost always, a tiny, low-flying blue found in this habitat will be this species. The male has a light-blue dusting above; the female is almost entirely brown. The wing margin is not obviously chequered. The adults often perch low on the aerial roots of mangroves. Larvae feed mainly on samphires, including *Halosarcia indica*, *Sarcocornia quinqueflora*, *Suaeda australis* and *Tecticornia australasica*, and the related *Sesuvium portulacastrum*. They are seldom ant-attended.

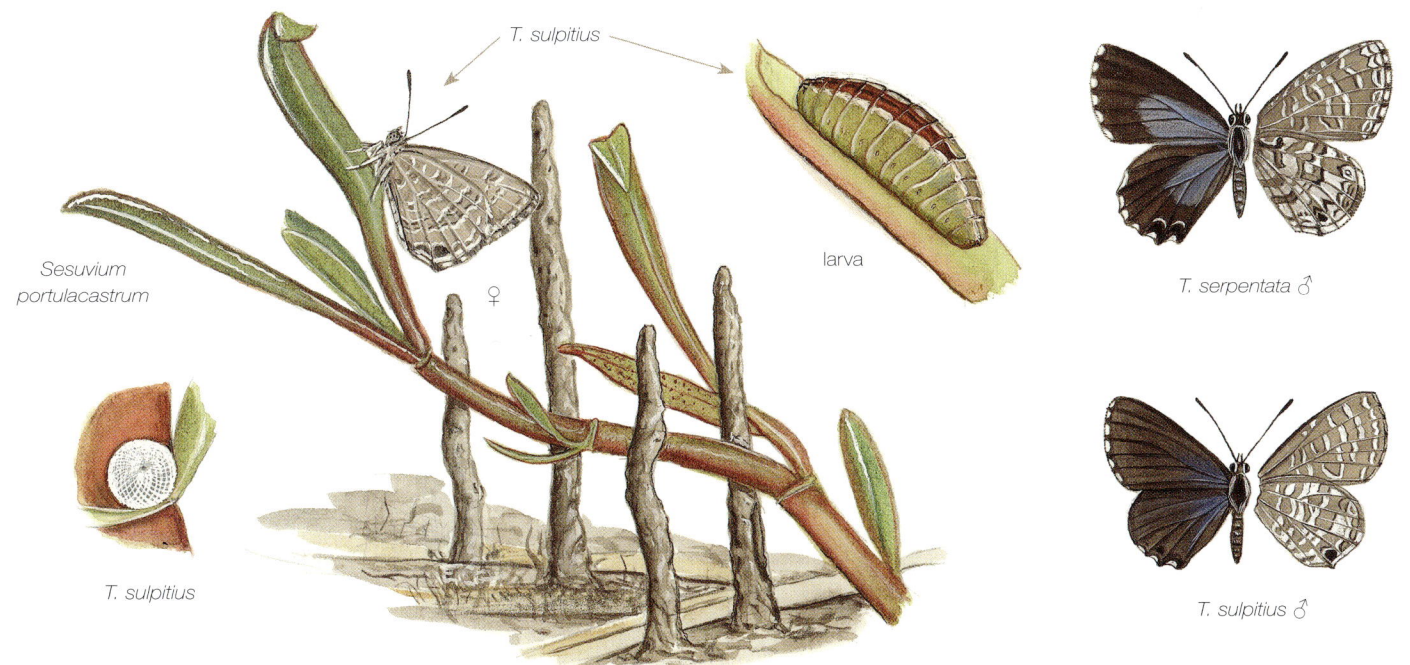

FAMILY LYCAENIDAE—Blues, Coppers and Hairstreaks

Pea Blues and the Zebra Blue

The pea blues include five small species in four diverse genera. All feed as larvae on species of native or introduced peas.

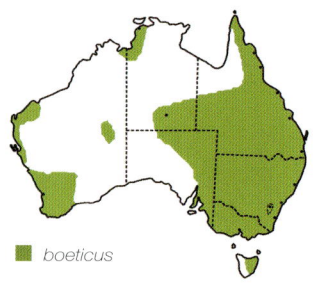
boeticus

The **Long-tailed Pea Blue**, *Lampides boeticus* (fw ♂ 17 mm, ♀ 18 mm), is a common, lively species found zipping around the larval host plants 1–3 m above the ground, perching briefly and frequently. In Australia it is found almost everywhere except in rainforests, high mountains and desert areas, and worldwide its range extends as far as Africa and western Europe. The larvae feed on buds and flowers of numerous species of pea (Fabaceae) and are sometimes ant-attended.

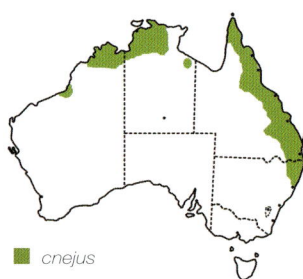
cnejus

The **Spotted Pea Blue**, *Euchrysops cnejus* (fw ♂ 15.5 mm, ♀ 16 mm), has similar habits, with a slightly more fluttery flight than *L. boeticus*. It occurs in wetter, warmer, mainly coastal areas and elsewhere is widespread in tropical Asia. Larvae feed on buds, flowers and seed-pods of the genera *Cajanus*, *Macroptilium*, *Phaseolus*, *Sesbania* and *Vigna*. They are tended by a variety of ant species.

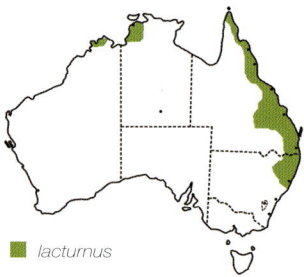
lacturnus

The **Orange-tipped Pea Blue**, *Everes lacturnus* (fw ♂ 13 mm, ♀ 13 mm), has a similar range to *E. cnejus* but tends to be more localised, owing to its greater host plant specialisation. It is also smaller and flies more slowly, perching for long periods, during which the orange patch on the underside of the hindwing is highly conspicuous. The upperside of the female is entirely brown. Like all pea blues, when perched it frequently shuffles its hindwings up and down, apparently to emphasise the 'false-head' effect created by the exaggerated eyespots and filamentous antenna-like tails. The larva feeds on flowers and seed-pods of *Desmodium heterocarpon*, and is seldom tended by ants. The pale pupa is unusually elongate and covered in very long hairs.

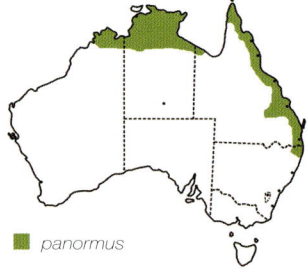
panormus

The **Pale Pea Blue**, *Catochrysops panormus* (fw ♂ 15 mm, ♀ 15 mm), is widespread and common, ranging throughout tropical Asia. It is most easily confused, both in name and appearance, with *Catopyrops florinda* (*chrysops* or 'χρυσοψ' means golden-eye, *pyrops* or 'πυροψ' means fiery eye, both evidently referring to the orange crescent around the black eyespot on the underside of the hindwing). The eyespot, however, is more prominent in *C. panormus*. Further, the male upperside is a pale chalky blue, rather than violet, and in both sexes the tail is longer; near the base of the underside of the hindwing are two or three distinct dark spots, entirely absent in *C. florinda*. Larvae feed on buds and flowers of *Cajanus*, *Crotalaria*, *Dendrolobium*, *Flemingia* and other pea genera.

The **Cobalt Pea Blue**, *Catochrysops amasea* (fw ♂ 13 mm, ♀ 14 mm), is restricted in Australia to the far north. It differs from *C. panormus* and *Catopyrops* species principally by its rounded wings and underside pattern. Larvae feed on buds and flowers of *Desmodium heterocarpon*.

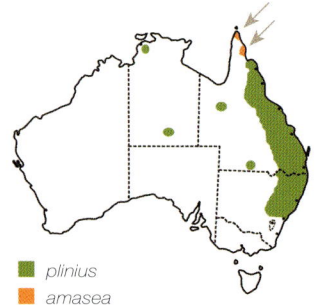
plinius
amasea

The **Zebra Blue**, *Leptotes plinius* (fw ♂ 14 mm, ♀ 14 mm), is widespread in open habitats, especially gardens. It flutters quite slowly within 1 m of the ground, perching frequently. Larvae feed on buds and flowers of *Plumbago auriculata* and *P. zeylandica* and are seldom ant-attended.

FAMILY LYCAENIDAE—Blues, Coppers and Hairstreaks

Grass Blues

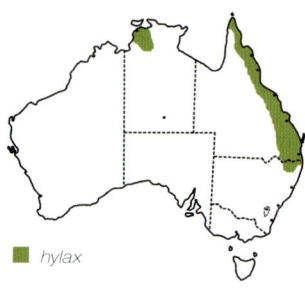
hylax

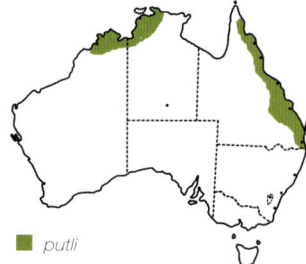
putli

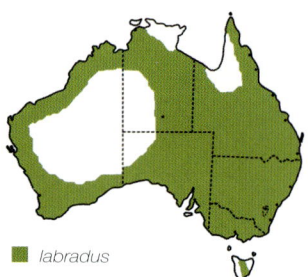
labradus

karsandra

The grass blues include five species of very small to tiny species, each in a different genus. All feed as larvae on species of prostrate dicotyledons, especially Fabaceae, which grow in grassy places. They do not feed on grass.

The **Tiny Grass Blue**, *Zizula hylax* (fw ♂ 10 mm, ♀ 11 mm), is one of the smallest butterflies in the world, easily recognised by its elongate rounded wings which are distinctly spotted beneath. The upperside of the female is almost entirely brown. It flutters daintily, low among the vegetation in grassy areas. It is widespread in wetter, warmer areas and elsewhere occurs throughout the Old World tropics. This wide distribution is believed to result largely from the ease with which it is carried by winds. Larvae feed on *Dipteracanthus australasicus*, *Hygrophilia angustifolia*, *H. costata* and *Ruellia tuberose*, and are occasionally tended by small ants.

The **Grass Jewel**, *Freyeria putli* (fw ♂ 9 mm, ♀ 9.5 mm), is probably the equal-smallest butterfly in the world, a record shared with one or two other species from the same genus from the warmer parts of the Old World. It is widespread in northern and eastern Australia and in Asia. It flies weakly among grass and around various shrubs, especially *Acacia* buds and flowers, up to about 2 m from the ground. Larvae feed on *Flemingia lineata*, *Indigofera colutea* and *I. hirsuta*. They are occasionally ant-attended.

The **Common Grass Blue**, *Zizina labradus* (fw ♂ 14 mm, ♀ 14.5 mm), is one of the most abundant and widespread butterflies in Australia and the Pacific. The brightness of the lilac upperside varies and is much reduced in females. The markings on the underside are often indistinct, particularly in worn specimens. They fly with a brisk flutter and perch often, close to the ground, frequently basking with half-open wings. Mating usually follows a brief courtship, and it is common, when walking over a field of clover, to see numerous short sexual pursuits by these diminutive insects, during which they ascend up to 2 m above the ground. Mating pairs usually perch a little above the ground, on any convenient grass stem. When disturbed, the male carries the female in a brief mating flight, seldom more than a few metres. The larvae feed on a very wide range of mostly prostrate members of the Fabaceae, or pea family, including clover and garden peas. They are sometimes tended by ants.

The **Spotted Grass Blue**, *Zizeeria karsandra* (fw ♂ 13 mm, ♀ 13 mm), is widespread but local in eastern and northern Australia, and ranges as far as north Africa. It is of similar size to *Z. labradus*, with similar habits, but the clearly defined dark spotting on the underside, easily seen when it perches, enables it to be recognised at once. Where present, it is normally abundant, but is highly sedentary. Larvae feed on *Glinus lotoides*, *G. oppositifolia*, *Tribulus cistoides* and *T. terrestris*, and are sometimes ant-attended.

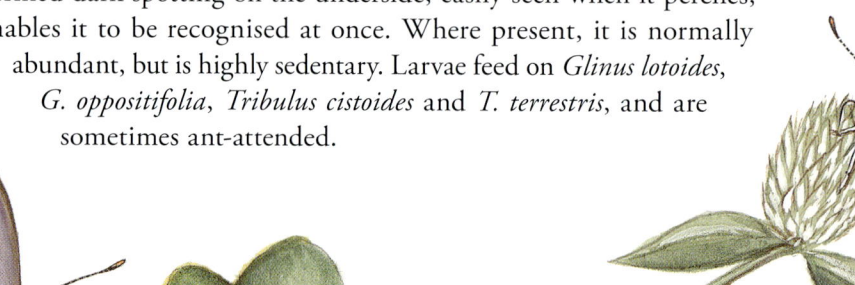

Z. labradus ♂

F. alsulus ♂

The **Black-spotted Grass Blue**, *Famegana alsulus* (fw ♂ 11 mm, ♀ 12 mm), is widespread and generally not uncommon. Its underside pattern, seen when perched, is unmistakable. It flies weakly and very low. Larval food plants include *Cajanus acutifolius*, *C. pubescens*, *Indigofera pratensis* and *Vinga lanceolata*. Larvae are sometimes ant-attended.

FAMILY LYCAENIDAE—Blues, Coppers and Hairstreaks

Some Northern Rainforest Blues

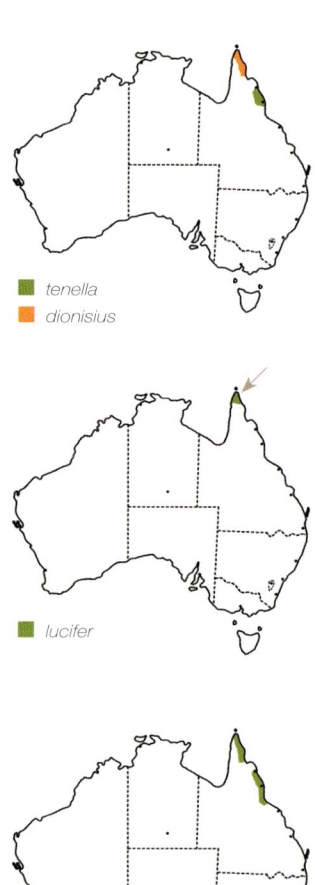

tenella
dionisius

lucifer

strongyle

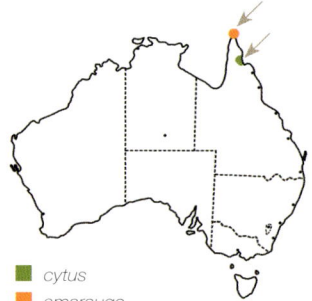

cytus
amarauge

The six species illustrated are all inhabitants of the north Queensland rainforests, most flying under the forest canopy. (Two related species of ceruleans have been discussed already, with the green-banded blues.)

The **Australian Hedge Blue**, *Udara tenella* (fw ♂ 15 mm, ♀ 15 mm), is an endemic species with many relatives very common in the mountains of New Guinea and tropical Asia. It is restricted to a small area of rainforest to the north of Cairns, with most specimens known from Kuranda. It flies mainly in the rainforest canopy, although it may descend lower around the edges. It is not especially rapid in flight and is quite conspicuous, but its rarity and arboreal habits mean it is seldom observed. The life history is unknown.

The **Pied Blue**, *Pithecops dionisius* (fw ♂ 18 mm, ♀ 18 mm), is restricted in Australia to Cape York Peninsula. It flies with a slow, deliberate flutter, generally 1–3 m above the ground beneath the rainforest canopy. When active, it typically perches on the upperside of leaves in sunny spots. The early stages are not recorded from Australia but in New Guinea the hirsute, slug-like larvae feed on flowers and seed-pods of *Desmodium ormocarpoides*, which also grows in northern Australia. The pupa is unusually shaped and covered in fine hairs, each with an expanded tip.

The **Quaker**, *Neopithecops lucifer* (fw ♂ 11.5 mm, ♀ 12 mm), has a similar distribution and occurs in the same habitats. It flies rather more briskly, but still with a pronounced flutter in the shade of the rainforest canopy, perching frequently on the upperside of leaves 1–3 m above the ground. Its small size readily distinguishes it from *P. dionisius* in flight. The larvae feed on fresh shoots of *Glycosmis trifoliata*, and are probably not tended by ants.

The **Small Pied Blue**, *Megisba strongyle* (fw ♂ 11 mm, ♀ 13 mm), is common in rainforest within the Queensland wet tropics region and further north. It flies with a brisk flutter in the understorey, perching frequently on low vegetation in sunny patches. Early in the day, males, especially, ascend to the canopy to feed on flowers, and may also be common along rainforest edges. The larva feeds on buds of *Allophylus cobbe*, *Macaranga inamoena*, *Mallotus paniculatus* and *M. philippensis*. It is not ant-attended. As with many flower- and bud-feeders, the larva is covered in fleshy, rounded nodules, the colour varying through shades of variegated reddish brown to yellowish green. The pupa is pale and lightly freckled.

The **Pale Cerulean**, *Jamides cytus* (fw ♂ 17.5 mm, ♀ 19 mm), in Australia is restricted to rainforest at Iron Range, Cape York Peninsula. It has a fairly slow fluttering flight and is found 1–3 m above the ground in the forest understorey. Females are quite different from males, with a large white patch on the underside of the forewing, which is quite evident in flight. Larvae feed on buds, flowers and fruits of *Syzygium* species and are occasionally ant-attended.

The **Shining Cerulean**, *Jamides amarauge* (fw ♂ 15.5 mm, ♀ 16 mm), is restricted in Australia to the islands of Torres Strait. Its habits are similar to those of *J. cytus* but it is distinctly livelier in flight and frequently ascends to the canopy to feed on flowers. The female is very like the male. The larvae probably feed on flowers of *Pueraria lobata*.

FAMILY LYCAENIDAE—Blues, Coppers and Hairstreaks 281

FURTHER READING AND SOCIETIES

There is an immense number of scientific papers and other articles in which the information that forms the core of material in this book first appeared. Braby's 2001 monograph contains references to most of these; others can be found with little effort through internet searches. Nevertheless, there is a relatively small number of books, each of which has been a landmark of sorts in the study of Australian butterflies. Some of these are out of print but all can be accessed through libraries. In addition, there are a few books internationally which introduce the reader to the fascination of butterflies. This is a personal and selective list and no doubt we have overlooked important works that readers can enjoy discovering for themselves.

Books on Butterflies

Ackery, P.R. and Vane-Wright, R.I. (1984), *Milkweed Butterflies: Their Cladistics and Biology, Being an Account of the Natural History of the Danainae, a Subfamily of the Nymphalidae*, British Museum (Natural History): London

Barrett, C. and Burns, A.N. (1951), *Butterflies of Australia and New Guinea*, Seward: Melbourne

Braby, M.F. (2000), *Butterflies of Australia: Their Identification, Biology and Distribution* (2 vols), CSIRO Publishing: Melbourne

—— (2004), *The Complete Field Guide to Australian Butterflies*, CSIRO Publishing: Melbourne

Burns, A.N. and Rotherham, E.R. (1969), *Australian Butterflies in Colour*, Reed: Melbourne

Common, I.F.B. (1964), *Australian Butterflies*, Jacaranda: Brisbane

Common, I.F.B. and Waterhouse, D.F. (1972), *Butterflies of Australia*, Angus & Robertson: Sydney

D'Abrera, B. (1971), *Butterflies of the Australian Region*, Lansdowne: Melbourne

Dunn, K.L. and Dunn, L.E. (1991), *Review of Australian Butterflies: Distribution, Life History and Taxonomy*, privately published: Melbourne

Emmel, T.C. (1976), *Butterflies: Their World, Their Life Cycle, Their Behaviour*, Thames & Hudson: London

Fisher, R.H. (1978), *Butterflies of South Australia*, Government Printer: Adelaide

—— (1996), *A Field Guide to Australian Butterflies*, Surrey Beatty: Chipping Norton, New South Wales

Kitching, R.L., Scheermeyer, E., Jones, R.E. and Pierce, N.E. (eds) (1999), *Biology of Australian Butterflies*, Monographs on Australian Lepidoptera 6, CSIRO Publishing: Melbourne

McCubbin, C. (1971), *Australian Butterflies*, Thomas Nelson: Melbourne

McQuillan, P. (1994), *Butterflies of Tasmania*, Tasmanian Field Naturalists Club: Hobart

Moss, J.T. (2005), *Butterfly Host Plants of South-East Queensland and Northern New South Wales*, Butterfly and other Invertebrates Club: Runcorn, Qld

Moulds, M.S. (1977), *Bibliography of the Australian Butterflies (Lepidoptera: Hesperioidea and Papilionoidea) 1773–1973*, Australian Entomological Press: Greenwich, New South Wales

New, T.R. (1991), *Butterfly Conservation*, Oxford University Press: Australia

Parsons, M. (1999), *The Butterflies of Papua New Guinea: Their Systematics and Biology*, Academic Press: London

Rainbow, W.J. (1907), *A Guide to the Study of Australian Butterflies*, Lothian: Melbourne

Russell, S.A. (2003), *An Obsession with Butterflies: Our Long Love Affair with a Singular Insect*, Perseus: Cambridge, MA

Sbordoni, V. and Forestiero, S. (1985), *The World of Butterflies*, Blandford: Poole, Dorset

Valentine, P. (1988), *Australian Tropical Butterflies*, Tropical Australia Graphics: Paluma, Qld

Waterhouse, G.A. (1932), *What Butterfly is That?*, Angus & Robertson: Sydney

Waterhouse, G.A. and Lyell, G. (1914), *The Butterflies of Australia*, Angus & Robertson: Sydney

Journals and Societies

Reports of scientific studies on Australian butterflies may be published almost anywhere in the world in a great variety of journals. Generally, at least abstracts of learned studies can be obtained by using Google Scholar, by typing the formal genus and species name of an object of interest or, more broadly, by using keywords such as the family name, butterfly, mating behaviour, and so on. However, most publications on the general natural history of Australian butterflies, including range extensions, new host plant records, descriptions of hitherto-unknown life histories and descriptions of new species group names (species and subspecies), can be found in the peer-reviewed journal, *The Australian Entomologist*, published quarterly by the Entomological Society of Queensland. It is possible to subscribe to the journal without joining the society by writing to: The Business Manager, *The Australian Entomologist*, P.O. Box 537, Indooroopilly Qld 4068, Australia. The society's website may be accessed at <www.esq.org.au>.

Other societies with a strong interest in butterflies include:

- the Butterfly and Other Invertebrates Club (Brisbane)
- the Entomological Society of New South Wales
- the Entomological Society of Victoria
- Butterfly Conservation South Australia
- the Western Australian Insect Study Society.

Websites

Sadly, websites can be ephemeral objects, rather like butterflies. Fortunately, there is Google! This search engine is also particularly valuable for obtaining information on host plants. We list overleaf a small selection of websites of relevance to the Australian butterflies.

<http://users.sa.chariot.net.au/~rbg/datasheet.htm> a site maintained by Roger Grund, focusing on South Australian butterflies

<http://museumvictoria.com.au/bioinformatics/butter>   a site maintained by Museum Victoria, focusing on Victorian species

<http://linus.socs.uts.edu.au/~don/larvae/butter.htm>   a site maintained by Don Herbison-Evans and Stella Crossley, focusing on larvae of the Australian fauna

<www.tesag.jcu.edu.au/staff/psv/butterflyTSV.html>   a site maintained by Peter Valentine illustrating and commenting on butterflies of the Townsville region of far northern Queensland

<http://geocities.com/pchew.brisbane/index.html>   a site maintained by Peter Chew and family about butterflies (and other insects) of the Brisbane region

<http://en.wikipedia.org?wiki/List_of_Butterflies_of_Tasmania>   an anonymous but quite good Wikipedia treatment of some of the butterflies found in Tasmania

<http://asgap.org.au/APOL14/jun99-1.html>   another Peter Valentine site, this time about gardening for butterflies, maintained by the Society for Growing Australian Plants (now the Australian Native Plants Society)

<www.richmondbirdwing.org.au>   one of a growing number of conservation-oriented sites; this one is maintained by the Richmond Birdwing Recovery Network

References on Plants

Anyone with more than a passing interest in butterflies needs to know quite a lot of botany as well. The main reference for plant identification in Australia is *Flora of Australia*, ABRS (1981–present), CSIRO Publishing, Melbourne. At the time of writing, 32 of the projected 59 volumes have been published, some also in revised editions. Many volumes are out of print but are available in good public libraries. There is also an online version, which covers some volumes, including most of those that are out of print. The website address is <www.environment.gov.au/biodiversity/abrs/publications/flora-of-australia/index.html>. In addition, various state and federal authorities, as well as private individuals, maintain websites with a wealth of information on the identification, classification and biology of plants. A good first point of reference is Wikipedia, which generally provides reliable information.

INDEX

Entries in **bold** indicate main entries on a subject

abeona (*Tisiphone*) 7, **192–3**, A28
abrota (*Ogyris*) 248, A20–1
absimilis (*Candalides*) 260–1, A13, A17–19, A22, A28
acantha (*Geitoneura*) 190–1, A29–30
Acanthaceae 206, A25
acastus (*Candalides*) 263, A11
Acraea andromacha 30, 45, 198–9, A14
Acraeinae 163–4, **198**
Acrodipsas
　arcana 224
　aurata 224–5
　brisbanensis 224–5
　cuprea 224–5
　decima 224
　hirtipes 224
　illidgei 53, 219, **224–5**
　melania 224
　mortoni 224
　myrmecophila 224–5
ada (*Appias*) 152–3, A14
adiante (*Hypocysta*) 179, A30
Admiral, Australian 44, 176, **210–11**
adult feeding 3, 13–15, **47–8**, 54–5, 124; *see also* bird dropping, feeding on; fruit feeding; leaf scratching; mud-puddling; nectar feeding; PA feeding; sap feeding
adult structure 13–14
aegeus (*Papilio*) 2, 17, 28, 32, 45, 46, **128–9**, A22–3
aeluropis (*Mesodina*) 36, **102–3**, A30
aenone (*Ogyris*) 242–3, A20–1
aeropa (*Lexias*) 204–5
aeroplanes 204–5
aestiva (*Croitana*) 100–1
affinis (*Danaus*) 12–13, **172–3**, A24
agamemnon (*Graphium*) 124–5, A10–11
aganippe (*Delias*) 156–7, A20–1
Agavaceae 106, A30
agna (*Pelopidas*) 118–19, A29–30
agondas (*Elymnias*) 182–3, A26
agraulia (*Taractrocera papyria*) 108–9
agricola (*Neolucia*) 274–5, A17–19
Aizoaceae A12
albatrosses 152–3
albifascia (*Tisiphone abeona*) 192–3
albina (*Appias*) 152–3
albocincta (*Theclinesthes*) 272–3, A21
albosericea (*Nesolycaena*) 264–5, A22

albovenata (*Herimosa*) 100–1, A29
alcathoe (*Euploea*) 168–9, A12, A24
aleuas (*Jamides*) 266–7, A22
algea (*Euploea*) 168–9
alimena (*Hypolimnas*) 212–13, A25
alitha (*Eurema*) 144–5, A18
alkaloids **40–1**, 166
Allora
　doleschallii 69, A21
　major 69
alpine butterflies **28**, 90, 188–9
Alpine Sedge Skipper 90
alsulus (*Famegana*) 278–9, A18
altitude, effect on distribution **28–9**, 43
amalia (*Parnara*) 118–19, A29
Amaranthaceae 206, A13
amarauge (*Jamides*) 280–1
amaryllis (*Ogyris*) 242–3, A20–1
amasea (*Catochrysops*) 276–7, A18
Amathusiinae 164, **195**
ambrax (*Papilio*) 39, 121, **128–9**, 138, A23
Ambrax Butterfly 39, **128–9**
Amethyst Imperial Blue 254
Anacardiaceae A22
anactus (*Papilio*) 26, 28, 39, 121, **126–7**, A22–3
ancilla (*Telicota*) 114–15, A28–30
ancyra (*Catopyrops*) 270–1, A12, A17
Anderson's Grass Skipper 86–7
andersoni (*Toxidia*) 86–7, A30
androconia 123, 130, 139, 149, 152, 156, 170, 182
andromacha (*Acraea*) 30, 45, **198–9**, A14
angulipennis (*Elodina*) 150–1, A14
angustata (*Hypocysta*) 178–9, A30
anisodesma (*Telicota*) 114–15, A28
anisomorpha (*Taractrocera*) 108–9, A29–30
Anisynta
　cynone 84–5, A29–30
　dominula 84–5, A30
　monticolae 84–5, A30
　sphenosema 84–5, A29
　tillyardi 84–5, A30
Annonaceae 121, A10–11
anomala (*Hypolimnas*) 213
ant attendance 36, **48–51**, 218, 222, 228–9, 230–1, 232–3, 234–5,

239, 240–1, 245, 246–7, 249, 250–1, 252–3, 254, 269, 273
ant blues 224–5
ant byres 36, 50, 228–9
ant plant 30, 32, 35, 232–3
antennae 72, 97, 104–5, 108–9, 110–11, 113, 142–3
Anthene
　lycaenoides 272–3, A16–18, A21–2, A24–5
　seltuttus 272–3, A11, A13, A17–20, A22
Antipodia
　atralba 98–9, A28
　chaostola 98–9, A28
　dactyliota 98–9, A28
antipredator defences 37–45; *see also* camouflage; chemical protection; eyespots; false head; osmeterium; PAs; unpalatability
ants and evolution 47, **235**
Apaturina erminea 27, 104, **196–7**
Apaturinae 164, **196**
apelles (*Hypochrysops*) 230–1, A14–15, A19–21, A24
Apocynaceae 37, 40, 164, 165, 166–7, 175, A23–4
apollo (*Hypochrysops*) 30, 35, **232–3**, A25
Apollo Jewel 30, 35, **232–3**
Appias
　ada 152–3, A14
　albina 152–3
　celastina 152
　melania 152–3, A21
　paulina 152–3, A14, A21
Araliaceae A23
arcana (*Acrodipsas*) 224
Archduke, Orange 204–5
arctoa (*Ypthima*) 30, 177, **178–9**, A29–30
ardea (*Ocybadistes*) 110–11
Arecaceae A26–8
arenaria (*Croitana*) 100–1, A29
argenteoornatus (*Trapezites*) 76–7, A31
argenthona (*Delias*) 32, 42–3, 44, 148, **160–1**, A20–1
Argus
　Blue 208–9
　Meadow 208–9
Argynnina
　cyrila 190–1, A30

Argynnina (continued)
    hobartia 190–1, A29
    hobartia montana 190
    hobartia tasmanica 190–1
Argyreus hyperbius 52, 53, 56, 164, **202–3**, A14
Arhopala
    centaurus 240–1, A15, A19–22
    madytus 241, A14, A19
    micale 218, **240–1**, A11, A13–14, A19–22, A24–25
    wildei 30, **241**
Arid Bronze Azure 244–5
arid zone butterflies 98–9, 100–1
aridus (*Jalmenus*) 254, A16–17
aristeus (*Graphium*) 45, **122**, A11
Aristolochia 36, 37, 41, 43, 53–4, 121, 132–8, A12
Aristolochiaceae 121, A12
Arrhenes
    dschilus 113, A29–30
    marnas 113, A29
arsinoe (*Vindula*) 200–1, A14
artemis (*Taenaris*) 27, 128, **195**, A28
Artemis Owl 27, 128, **195**
aruna (*Delias*) 158–9, A21
Asclepiadaceae 10, 37, 40, 164, 165, 166, A24
Asteraceae 166–7, 206, A25–6
Atkins' Ochre 76–7
atkinsi (*Trapezites*) 76–7, A31
atralba (*Antipodia*) 98–9, A28
atropatene (*Mimene*) 106–7
augiades (*Cephrenes*) 55, **116–17**, A26–8
augias (*Telicota*) 114–15, A28
aurata (*Acrodipsas*) 224–5
aurelia (*Tisiphone abeona*) 192–3
aurifer (*Paralucia*) 238–9, A15
Australian Admiral 56, **210–11**
Australian butterfly fauna 18, 25, Appendix 1
Australian environments 25, **28–33**
Australian Fritillary 6, 52, 53, 56, 164, **202–3**, A14
Australian Gull 152–3
Australian Hairstreak 249
Australian Harlequin 220
Australian Hedge Blue 280–1
Australian Painted Lady 6, **210–11**
awls 69–71
azula (*Philiris*) 236–7
Azure Moonbeam 236–7
azures 242–8
bada (*Parnara*) 118–19, A29

Badamia exclamationis 69, A18–19, A21
Banana Skipper 57

Banded Demon 106–7
Banded Red-eye **67**
Banks, Joseph 6, 18, 120, 186
Banks' Brown 186–7
banksii (*Heteronympha*) 186–7, A28–30
Barnard's Azure 248
barnardi (*Ogyris*) 248, A20–1
Barred Skipper 86–7
basking 73, 84–5, 88–9, 98, 180–90, 208, 210–11, 230, 238–9, 249, 275, 279
Bates, Henry Walter 39, 200
Bates' Crow 168–9
batesii (*Euploea*) 168–9
Bathurst Copper 53, 238–9
Beak 216
beata (*Chaetocneme*) 55, **66–7**, A10–12, A13, A14, A20, A21, A23
Belenois java 33, 139, **154–5**, A14
berenice (*Nacaduba*) 49, 266, **268–9**, A12, A19, A22
Big Greasy 15, 18, 30, 39, 41, **136–7**
Bindahara phocides 30, **255**, A21
binomial system **6**, 120
biocellata (*Nacaduba*) 35, **268–9**, A15–16
bird dropping, feeding on 113, 155
bird dropping, mimicry **45**, 64–5, 120, 128–31, 156
birdwings 6, 7, 14, 16, 21, 30, 32, 36, 41, 48, 52–3, 56, 121, **132–5**
bisaltide (*Doleschallia*) 44, **214–15**, A25
Bitter-bush Blue 272–3
Black and White Aeroplane 204–5
Black and White Ringlet 178–9
Black and White Swift 106–7
Black and White Tiger 12–13, **172–3**
Black and White Tit 57, **255**, A31
Black-ringed Ochre 80–1
Black-spotted Grass Blue 278–9
Blotched Dusky Blue 263
Blue Albatross 152
Blue Argus 208–9
Blue Eggfly 212–13
Blue Flash 257
Blue-flash Skipper 82–3
Blue Iris Skipper 102–3
Blue Jewel 230–1
Blue Moonbeam 236–7
Blue Mountain Butterfly **2**, 130–1
Blue Tiger 6, 18, 165, **173**
Blue Triangle 55, **123**
blues 21–4, 44, 47, **217–19**, 258–9
boeticus (*Lampides*) 276–7, A18–19
bolina (*Hypolimnas*) 47, 163, **212–13**, A13–14, A24–6
Bombacaceae A14

Boraginaceae 166, A24
Borbo
    cinnara 118–19, A30
    impar 118–19, A29–30
Braby, Michael 6, 20, 26, 60, 206, 217, 282
brachydesma (*Telicota*) 113, A29
Brassicaceae 148, A14
brassolis (*Liphyra*) 19, 50, **221**
Brigalow Blue 28, **250–1**
Bright Cerulean 266–7
Bright Copper 238–9
Bright Cornelian 35, **256–7**
Bright Dusky Blue 262–3
Bright-eyed Brown 184–5
Bright Forest Blue 234
Bright Oakblue 241
Bright-orange Darter 114–15
Bright Purple Jewel 30, **228–9**
Bright Shield Skipper 88–9
brigitta (*Eurema*) 146–7, A17
brisbanensis (*Acrodipsas*) 224–5
Broad-banded Awl 70–1
Broad-margined Azure 248
Broad-margined Grass Yellow 144–5
Bronze Ant Blue 224–5
Bronze Lineblue 270–1
Brown Awl **69**
Brown Ochre 80–1
Brown Soldier 208–9
Brown Tiger 173
browns 23, 29, 44, 95, 163–4, **176–7**
Bulloak Jewel 28, 30, 53, **228–9**
bursa copulatrix **16–17**, 136, 198
bushbrowns 180–1
butterfly gardening 54–6
byzos (*Hypochrysops*) 230–1, A13, A21

Cabbage White 2, 28, 47, 56, 148, **149**
caelius (*Psychonotis*) 35, 255, 259, **266–7**, A21
Caesalpiniaceae 141, 196, A17
caesia (*Nesolycaena*) 264–5, A22
caesina (*Sabera*) 106–7, A26–7
Cairns Birdwing 30, 32, 121, **134–5**
camouflage 34, **44–5**, 121, 122, 128–9, 130, 150–1, 176–7, 182, 201, 204–5, 206, 207–8, 211, 214–15, 226–7, 230–1, 236–7, 266–7, 274–5
Candalides
    absimilis 260–1, A13, A17–19, A22, A28
    acastus 263, A11
    consimilis 6, **260–1**, A15, A22–3
    cyprotus 260–1, A18–19
    delospilus 263, A11
    erinus 262–3, A11

geminus 262–3, A11
gilberti 260–1, A21
heathi 264–5, A19, A25
helenita 260–1, A11, A13, A21–2
hyacinthinus 262–3, A11
hyacinthinus simplex 262–3
margarita 260–1, A20–1
noelkeri 264–5, A25
xanthospilos 262–3, A19
Candalidini 259
canopus (*Papilio*) 28, **130–1**, A22–3
Cape York Aeroplane 204–5
Cape York Birdwing 134
Cape York Pearl White 151
Caper White 33, 139, **154–5**
Capparaceae 148, A14
cardiac glycosides 37
cardui (*Vanessa*) 210–11, A14
carnivorous larvae 34, **50**, 218, 221, 222, 224–5, 241
Casuarinaceae A12
Catochrysops
　amasea 276–7, A18
　panormus 276–7, A18
catops (*Taenaris*) 195, A28
Catopsilia
　gorgophone 142–3, A17
　pomona 30, **142–3**, A17
　pyranthe 142–3, A17
　scylla 142–3, A17
Catopyrops
　ancyra 270–1, A12, A17
　florinda 56, **270–1**, 276, A12, A17, A22
Cedar Bushbrown 180–1
celastina (*Appias*) 152
Celastraceae A21
centaurus (*Arhopala*) 240–1, A15, A19–22
cephenes (*Pseudodipsas*) 234, A14–15, A22–3, A31
Cephrenes
　augiades 55, **116–17**, A26–8
　trichopepla 116–17, A26–8
Cepora perimale 152–3, A14
ceruleans 266–7, 280–1
Cethosia
　cydippe 45, **200–1**, A14
　penthesilea 27, 39, **201**, A14
Chaetocneme
　beata 55, **66–7**, A10–12, A13, A14, A20, A21, A23
　critomedia 67, A10–13, A20–2
　denitza 66–7, A14, A20
　porphyropis 67, A11–12
Chalky Pearl White 150–1
chaostola (*Antipodia*) 98–9, A28
Charaxes latona 196–7, A11
Charaxinae 164, **196**

chemical protection **37–40**, 43, 121, 148, 165
Chenopodiaceae A12–13
Chequered Grass Skipper 84–5
Chequered Sedge Skipper 91
Chequered Swallowtail 14, 30, **126–7**
chlorinda (*Pseudalmenus*) 7, **249**, A15–16
chromus (*Hasora*) **70–1**, A18
Chrysobalanaceae A15
chrysotricha (*Hesperilla*) 92–3, A28
ciliate blues 272–3
cinnara (*Borbo*) 118–19, A30
citrus 28, 37, 55–6, 121, 126–30
classification 2–4, **21–4**, Part 2
claudia (*Elodina*) 151
clementi (*Jalmenus*) 254, A15–16
cleon (*Hypochrysops*) 226–7
climate, effects of **25–9**, 177, 188
climena (*Euploea*) 168–9
Climena Crow 168–9
Clusiaceae A13
cnejus (*Euchrysops*) 276–7, A18–19
Cobalt Pea Blue 276–7
Coeliadinae 62, **68**
Coliadinae 140, **141**
collecting **58–9**, 112, 210
colon (*Telicota*) 114–15, A29–30
colour aberrations 161
colour forms, larvae 35, 124–9, 132, 134, 137, 176–7, 186–7
colour forms, pupa 126, 128
colour, chemical basis 7, **140**; *see also* pigment
Combretaceae A19
Common Aeroplane 204–5
Common Albatross 152–3
Common Banded Awl 70–1
Common Brown 6, 18, 32, 176, **186–7**
Common Crow 34, 36, 55, **166–7**
Common Dusky Blue 262–3
Common Eggfly 163, **212–13**
Common Grass Blue 6, 30, **278–9**
Common Grass Dart 110–11
Common Grass Yellow 141, **144–5**
Common, Ian 20, 282
Common Imperial Blue 14, 33, 39, 41, 222, **250–1**
Common Jezabel 32, 38, **162**
Common Lineblue 49, **268–9**
Common Migrant 142–3
Common Moonbeam 236–7
Common Oakblue 218, **240–1**
Common Pencilled Blue 260–1
Common Rayed Blue 264–5
Common Red-eye 55, **66–7**
Common Ringlet 178–9
Common Tit 255

community attitudes 60–2
community, ecological 38, 42
compacta (*Dispar*) 86–7, A30
competition **41–3**, 134–5, 160, 162
Connaraceae A15
conservation 21, 30, 36, **52–4**, 58, 132, 164, 202–3, 224
consimilis (*Candalides*) 6, **260–1**, A15, A22–3
consimilis (*Pantoporia*) 6, **204–5**, A15
Convolvulaceae A24
Cooktown Azure 242–3
Copper Ant Blue 224–5
Copper Jewel 230–1
Copper Pencilled Blue 260–1
coppers 50, 217–19, **238–9**
copulation *see* mating
cordace (*Heteronympha*) 184–5, A28
core (*Euploea*) 34, 36, 55, **166–7**, A12, A23–4
Cornelian
　Bright 35, **256–7**
　Dull 223, **256–7**
correae (*Oreixenica*) 188–9, A30
courtship 5, 15, 123, 124, 128–9, 130–3, 139, 145, 160–2, 166, 167, 172–3, 174–5, 180–1, 182–3, 185, 186, 236, 247, 267
Cressida cressida 15, 18, 30, 39, 41, 43, 121, 126, **136–7**, A12
critomedia (*Chaetocneme*) **67**, A10–13, A20–2
crocea (*Neohesperilla*) 82–3, A29–30
Croitana
　aestiva 100–1
　arenaria 100–1, A29
　croites 100–1, A29–30
croites (*Croitana*) 100–1, A29–30
crows 166–9
Cruiser 200–1
crypsargyra (*Hesperilla*) 91, A28
crypsigramma (*Hesperilla*) 94–5, A28
Cunoniaceae A15
Cupha prosope 202–3, A14
cuprea (*Acrodipsas*) 224–5
cyane (*Hypochrysops*) 30, **228–9**, A16–17, A19–21
cyanea (*Nacaduba*) 266–7, A17
cyanophracta (*Mesodina*) 102–3, A30
Cycad Blue 35, 57, **272–3**
Cycadaceae A10
cycads 35, 218, A10
cydippe (*Cethosia*) 45, **200–1**, A14
cynone (*Anisynta*) 84–5, A29–30
Cyperaceae A28
cyprotus (*Candalides*) 260–1, A18–19
cyrila (*Argynnina*) 190–1, A30
cytus (*Jamides*) 280–1, A20

D'Abrera, Bernard 20, 62
dactyliota (*Antipodia*) 98–9, A28
Daemel's Imperial Blue 252–3
daemeli (*Jalmenus*) 252–3, A15–16, A20, A22
Danaid Eggfly 39, 164, 170, **212**
Danainae 37, 39, 40, 164, **165**
Danaus
    affinis 12–13, **172–3**, A24
    affinis gelanor 173
    genutia **170–1**, A24
    petilia 8–9, 11, 35, 39, **170–1**, A24
    plexippus 28, **170–1**, A24
danis (*Danis*) 27, **266–7**, A15, A22
danis (*Hypolycaena*) 57, **255**, A31
Danis danis 27, **266–7**, A15, A22
darchia (*Euploea*) 168–9, A12
Dark Cerulean 266–7
Dark Ciliate Blue 272–3
Dark Forest Blue 234
Dark Grass Skipper 88–9
Dark Opal 264–5
Dark-orange Grass Dart 110–11
Dark Pencilled Blue 260–1
Dark Purple Azure 248
dart position 34, 63, 88–9, 105, 106–7, 116–17
darters 113–15
Darwin Blue Flash 257
Darwin, Charles 43, 47, 200
day-flying moths **4–5**, 37, 39
decima (*Acrodipsas*) 224
delayed reproduction 32, 146–7, 177, 186, 208
Delias
    aganippe 156–7, A20–1
    argenthona 32, 42–3, 44, 148, **160–1**, A20–1
    aruna 158–9, A21
    ennia 158–9, A21
    ennia nigidius 158–9
    ennia tindalii 158
    harpalyce 156–7, A20–1
    mysis 160–1, A21
    nigrina 32, 38, 42–3, **162**, A20–1
    nysa 158–9, A21
Delicate Pearl White 151
delicia (*Hypochrysops*) 230–1, A15–16, A21
delospilus (*Candalides*) 263, A11
democles (*Deudorix*) 257, A23
demoleus (*Papilio*) 14, 30, **126–7**, A18, A22, A23
Demon, Banded 106–7
denitza (*Chaetocneme*) **66–7**, A14, A20
Desert Sand Skipper 100–1
Deudorix
    democles 257, A23

diovis 35, **256–7**, A13, A15, A19, A22
epijarbas 223, **256–7**, A15, A21–2, A26
epirus 257, A22
smilis 257, A23
Diamond Sand Skipper 98–9
diana (*Philiris*) 236–7, A11–12
Diana Moonbeam 236–7
diapause 33
dicotyledons 35, 63, 68, 164, 206, 218, A10
Diggles' Jewel 234
digglesii (*Hypochrysops*) 234, A20–1
Dingy Bushbrown 180–1
Dingy Grass Dart 112
Dingy Grass Skipper 88–9
Dingy Ring 30, 45, 177, **178–9**
Dingy Ringlet 179
Dingy Swallowtail 26, 39, **126–7**
Dingy Swift 118–19
dionisius (*Pithecops*) 280–1
Dioscoreaceae A31
diovis (*Deudorix*) 35, **256–7**, A13, A15, A19, A22
Dipsacaceae A25
dirphia (*Motasingha*) 96–7
discolor (*Hasora*) 68, **70–1**, A18
discovery of Australian butterflies 18–21
Dispar compacta 86–7, A30
distribution **25–31**, 52, 55, 60
DNA **26**, 121, 163, 206, 235, 250
dobboe (*Sabera*) 106–7, A30
Doleschallia bisaltide 44, **214–15**, A25
doleschallii (*Allora*) 69, A21
dolon (*Taractrocera*) 108–9, A30
dominula (*Anisynta*) 84–5, A30
donnysa (*Hesperilla*) 92–3, A28
Donovan, Edward 18
doubledayi (*Toxidia*) 86–7, A29–30
dschilus (*Arrhenes*) 113, A29–30
dubiosa (*Prosotas*) 268–9, A15–19, A22
Dull Copper 238–9
Dull Cornelian 223, **256–7**
Dull Heath Blue 274–5
Dull Jewel 228–9
Dull Oakblue 240–1
Dull Shield Skipper 88–9
Dunn, Kelvin and Lawrence 20
dusky blues 262–3
Dusky Bushbrown 181
Dusky Grass Skipper 88–9

Eastern Brown Crow 168–9
Eastern Flat 64–5
Eastern Iris Skipper 102–3
Ebenaceae A14

egg **8–10**, 15–16, 46; see also Part 2
egg clustering 33, **45–6**, 50, 84–5, 122, 148, 155, 156–8, 160–2, 183, 195, 198–9, 200–1, 207, 214, 238–9, 254, 250, 252–3, 254, 268–9
egg hatching 83, 103, 116–17, 131, 132, 261
egg parasitoids 46, 244–5, 249, 250
eggflies 212–13
egista (*Vagrans*) 202–3, A14
Eichhorn's Crow 168–9
eichhorni (*Euploea alcathoe*) 168–9
eichhorni (*Jalmenus*) 252–3, A15–16
Elaeagnaceae A19
Elaeocarpaceae A13
Elgner's Jewel 232–3
elgneri (*Hypochrysops*) 232–3, A14, A21, A25
elia (*Nesoxenica leprea*) 190–1
eliena (*Trapezites*) 80–1, A31
Elodina
    angulipennis 150–1, A14
    claudia 151
    padusa 150–1, A14
    parthia 150–1, A14
    perdita 151, A14
    queenslandica 150–1, A14
    walkeri 151, A14
Eltham Copper 219, **238–9**
Elymnias agondas 182–3, A26
Emperor
    Orange 196–7
    Tailed 6, 24, 35, 36, 45, **196–7**
    Turquoise 27, 104, **196–7**
enastri (*Euploea alcathoe*) 168–9
Enastri Crow 168–9
endangered species **52–3**, 56, 110, 132, 224, 228, 238, 244, 264
endemism **26–7**, 29, 62–3, 72, 120, 164, 176, 210, 219, 259
ennia (*Delias*) 158–9, A21
eone (*Pseudodipsas*) 234, A19, A24–5, A31
Epacridaceae 48, A14
epicurus (*Hypochrysops*) 228–9, A24
epijarbas (*Deudorix*) 223, **256–7**, A15, A21–22, A26
epirus (*Deudorix*) 257, A22
erinus (*Candalides*) 262–3, A11
Erionota thrax 57
erminea (*Apaturina*) 27, 104, **196–7**
Erysichton
    lineata 258, **270–1**, A13, A18–20, A22, A24
    palmyra 270–1, A20–1
eubulus (*Jalmenus*) 7, 28, **250–1**, A16
Euchrysops cnejus 276–7, A18–19

euphemia (*Hypocysta*) 179, A30
Euphorbiaceae A21
euphorion (*Ornithoptera*) 30, 32, 43, **134–5**, A12
Euploea
  alcathoe 168–9, A12, A24
  alcathoe eichhorni 168–9
  alcathoe enastri 168–9
  algea 168–9
  batesii 168–9
  climena 168–9
  core 34, 36, 55, **166–7**, A12, A23–4
  darchia darchia 168–9, A12
  darchia niveata 168–9
  leucostictos 168–9
  sylvester 168–9, A12, A24
  tulliolus 168–9, A12
Eupomatiaceae A10
Eurema
  alitha 144–5, A18
  brigitta 146–7, A17
  hecabe 141, **144–5**, A16–19, A21
  herla 146–7, A17
  laeta 147, A17
  puella 144–5, A17, A21
  smilax 30, **146–7**, A17
European Painted Lady 210–11
eurotas (*Telicota*) 114–15
eurychlora (*Telicota*) 114–15, A28
eurypylus (*Graphium*) 55, **124–5**, A10–11
Euschemon rafflesia 6, 56, 63, **64–5**, A11
evagoras (*Jalmenus*) 7, 14, 33, 39, 41, 222, 235, **250–1**, A15–16
Evening Brown 44, 176, **182–3**
Everes lacturnus 276–7, A18
evolutionary tree 4, 121, 163, 235
exclamationis (*Badamia*) **69**, A18–19, A21
Exometoeca nycteris 63, **67**, A22
extrusa (*Rachelia*) 82–3, A28
eyespots 24, **44**, 176, 178, 182, 195, 208–9

Fabaceae 68, 141, 276, 278, A17–19
Fabricius, Johann 6, 18
Fagaceae A12
false head 24, **44**, **223**, 256
Famegana alsulus 278–9, A18
families, recognising 21–4
felderi (*Prosotas*) 268–9, A15–17, A19, A22
female rejection 137, 139, 149, 162, 186, 198
ferns **35**, 232, A10
Fiery Jewel 36, **228–9**

Fivebar Swordtail 45, **122**
Flacourtiaceae 202, A14
Flagellariaceae A28
Flame Sedge Skipper 92–3
flammeata (*Signeta*) 88–9, A30
flats 64–5, 67
flavescens (*Hesperilla*) 92–3, A28
flavovittatus (*Ocybadistes*) 110–11, A30
florinda (*Catopyrops*) 56, **270–1**, 276, A12, A17, A22
flower-feeding larvae **35**, 57, 255, 256–7, 268–9, 270, 274–5, 276–7, 280–1
flowering plants 4, **34–5**, A10–31
food plants 10–11, 15, 25, 30–1, 34–7, 41–3, 95–6, A10–31
forced copulation 136–7, 170, 184–5, 198
forest blues 234
Forest Brown 190–1
form *crocale* 142
form *pomona* 142
Fourbar Swordtail 122
frenulum 64
Freyeria putli 278–9, A18
Fringed Heath Blue 274–5
Fritillary, Australian 6, 52, 53, 56, 164, **202–3**
fruit and seed feeding, larvae 255, 256–7
fruit feeding, adults 95, 177, 181, **182–3**, 196, 204
fulgens (*Philiris*) 236–7, A11–12
fuliginosa (*Sabera*) 106–7, A26
furva (*Hesperilla*) 94–5, A28
fuscus (*Papilio*) 28, **130–1**, A22–3

Geitoneura
  acantha 190–1, A29–30
  klugii 190–1, A29–30
  minyas 33, **190–1**, A29
gelanor (*Danaus affinis*) 173
geminus (*Candalides*) 262–3, A11
genevieveae (*Trapezites*) 75, A31
genitalia **16–17**, 150–1, 184–5, 198–9
genoveva (*Ogyris*) 30, **246–7**, A20–1
Gentianaceae A23
genutia (*Danaus*) **170–1**, A24
geoffroy (*Libythea*) 216, A12
geoffroyi (*Mynes*) 45, **214–15**, A12
geographic races **7**, 84, 91, 92, 96, 98, 100, 112, 134, 158, 188, 192, 228, 236, 238, 242, 249; *see also* subspecies
geographic variation **7**, 193, 249; *see also* geographic races; subspecies
gilberti (*Candalides*) 260–1, A21

Glasswing 24, 30, 45, **198–9**
Glistening Lineblue 270–1
Glistening Pearl White 150–1
Golden-haired Sedge Skipper 92–3
Golden-rayed Blue 264–5
Goodeniaceae 206, A25
gorgophone (*Catopsilia*) 142–3, A17
gracillima (*Mesodina*) 102–3, A30
Graphiini 121
Graphium
  agamemnon 124–5, A10–11
  aristeus 45, **122**, A11
  eurypylus 55, **124–5**, A10–11
  macfarlanei 124–5, A10–11
  macleayanum 120, **124–5**, A10–11, A23
  sarpedon 55, **123**, A10–12, A14, A23, A24
grass blues 278–9
grass darts 108–11
Grass Jewel 278–9
grass skippers 82–9
grass yellows 144–7
Greater Peacock Awl 69
Green Awl 68, **70–1**
green-banded blues 266–7
Green-banded Jewel 35, **232–3**
Green Spotted Triangle 124–5
Green Tree Ant (*Oecophylla smaragdina*) 19, 221, 240–1, 272–3
Green Triangle 124–5
Greenish Darter 114–15
gregarious larvae and pupae **45**, 122, 148, 155–7, 160–2, 200–1, 214–15, 220, 228, 250
Grey Albatross 152–3
Grey Sedge Skipper 94–5
Grey Swift 118–19
Gull, Australian 152–3

habitat destruction 52–3, 203, 224, 228
habitats 25–33; *see also* species accounts, Part 2
Haemodoraceae A30
hair-pencils **16**, 152, 165, **166–7**, 170–1, 173, 180
Hairstreak, Australian 249
hairstreaks 21–4, 44, 217–19, **222–3**
Hairy Lineblue 258, **270–1**
halmaturia (*Ogyris*) 244–5
halyaetus (*Hypochrysops*) 230–1, A16, A18
halyzia (*Mesodina*) 102–3, A30
Hamadryad 15, 24, 27, 40, **174–5**
hamata (*Tirumala*) 6, 18, 165, **173**, A24
Harlequin, Australian 220

harpalyce (*Delias*) 156–7, A20–1
Hasora
   chromus 70–1, A18
   discolor 68, **70–1**, A18
   hurama 70–1, A18
   khoda 70–1, A18–19
hayi (*Mesodina*) 102–3, A30
heath blues 274–5
Heath Ochre 74
Heath Sand Skipper 98–9
heathi (*Candalides*) 264–5, A19, A25
hecabe (*Eurema*) 141, **144–5**, A16–19, A21
Hedge Blue, Australian 280–1
hedonia (*Junonia*) 208–9, A25
helena (*Tisiphone*) 192–3, A28
Helena Brown 192–3
helenita (*Candalides*) 260–1, A11, A13, A21–2
helicon (*Ionolyce*) 270–1, A22
Heliconiinae 164, **200**, 206–7
Hemerocallidaceae A30
Herimosa albovenata 100–1, A29
herla (*Eurema*) 146–7, A17
hesperia (*Theclinesthes*) 272–3, A21
Hesperiidae 21–4, **62**
Hesperiinae 62, **104**
Hesperilla
   chrysotricha 92–3, A28
   crypsargyra 91, A28
   crypsigramma 94–5, A28
   donnysa 92–3, A28
   flavescens 92–3, A28
   furva 94–5, A28
   idothea 92–3, A28
   malindeva 94–5, A28
   mastersi 91, A28
   ornata 90, A28
   ornata monotherma 90
   picta 91, A28
   sarnia 94–5, A28
   sexguttata 94–5, A28
heteromacula (*Trapezites*) 80–1, A31
Heteronympha
   banksii 186–7, A28–30
   cordace 184–5, A28
   merope 6, 18, 32, 176, **186–7**, A29–30
   mirifica 186–7, A28–9
   paradelpha 185, A29–30
   penelope 32, **184–5**, A29–30
   solandri 186–7, A30
hilltopping 15, 73, 88–9, 156, 196, 218, 228–9
Hippocrateaceae A21
hippuris (*Hypochrysops*) 35, **232–3**, A10
hirtipes (*Acrodipsas*) 224
Hobart Brown 190–1

hobartensis (*Neolucia*) 274–5, A14
hobartia (*Argynnina*) 190–1, A29
host plant specialisation 36
human impacts 21, **28**, **52–4**, 219
hurama (*Hasora*) 70–1, A18
hyacinthinus (*Candalides*) 262–3, A11
Hyaline Swift 118–19
hylax (*Zizula*) 278–9, A25
Hymenoptera (other than ants) 3, 46, 245, 247, 249, 251, 275
hyperbius (*Argyreus*) 52, 53, 56, 164, **202–3**, A14
hyperparasitoids 46
Hypochrysops
   apelles 230–1, A14–15, A19–21, A24
   apollo 30, 35, **232–3**, A25
   byzos 230–1, A13, A21
   cleon 226–7
   cyane 30, **228–9**, A16–17, A19–21
   delicia 230–1, A15–16, A21
   digglesii 234, A20–1
   elgneri 232–3, A14, A21, A25
   epicurus 228–9, A24
   halyaetus 230–1, A16, A18
   hippuris 35, **232–3**, A10
   ignitus 36, **228–9**, A13–16, A20–4, A26, A31
   miskini 226–7, A11, A13, A15, A19–22, A25, A31
   narcissus 226–7, A15, A19–21, A24
   piceatus 28, 30, 53, 219, **228–9**, A12
   polycletus 226–7, A21
   pythias 226–7, A13
   theon 35, **232–3**, A10
Hypocysta
   adiante 179, A30
   angustata 178–9, A30
   euphemia 179, A30
   irius 178–9, A30
   metirius 178–9, A28–9
   pseudirius 179, A30
Hypolimnas
   alimena 212–13, A25
   anomala 213
   bolina 47, 163, **212–13**, A13–14, A24–6
   misippus 39, 164, 170, **212**, A13, A25
Hypolycaena
   danis 57, **255**, A31
   phorbas 255, A14–15, A17–22, A24–5, A28, A31
hypomeloma (*Ocybadistes*) 110–11, A29–30

iacchoides (*Trapezites*) 74, A31
iacchus (*Trapezites*) 80–1, A31

ianthis (*Ogyris*) 242–3, A20–1
icilius (*Jalmenus*) 254, A15–18
ictinus (*Jalmenus*) 30, **252–3**, A15–16, A22
identification **21–4**, 60
idmo (*Ogyris*) 244–5
idothea (*Hesperilla*) 92–3, A28
ignitus (*Hypochrysops*) 36, **228–9**, A13–16, A20–4, A26, A31
ilia (*Taractrocera*) 108–9
illidgei (*Acrodipsas*) 53, 219, **224–5**
imaginal discs 13
impar (*Borbo*) 118–19, A29–30
imperial blues 235, 250–4
Imperial White 156–7
ina (*Taractrocera*) 108–9, A29–30
Indigo Flash 256–7
Inland Imperial Blue 254
Inland Sand Skipper 100–1
innotata (*Philiris*) 236–7, A12
inornata (*Toxidia*) 88–9, A30
inous (*Jalmenus*) 254, A16, A18
Ionolyce helicon 270–1, A22
iphis (*Ogyris*) 242–3, A20–21
Iridaceae A30
iris skippers 102–3
irius (*Hypocysta*) 178–9, A30
itea (*Vanessa*) 56, **210–11**, A12
IUCN 52

Jalmenus
   aridus 254, A16–17
   clementi 254, A15–16
   daemeli 252–3, A15–16, A20, A22
   eichhorni 252–3, A15–16
   eubulus 7, 28, **250–1**, A16
   evagoras 7, 14, 33, 39, 41, 222, 235, **250–1**, A15–16
   icilius 254, A15–18
   ictinus 30, **252–3**, A15–16, A22
   inous 254, A16, A18
   lithochroa 252–3, A16
   pseudictinus 30, 252–3, A15–16, A22
Jamides
   aleuas 266–7, A22
   amarauge 280–1
   cytus 280–1, A20
   phaseli 266–7, A18–19
japetus (*Tagiades*) **64–5**, A31
java (*Belenois*) 33, 139, **154–5**, A14
jewels 226–33, 278–9
jezabels 158–62
jizz **21**, 106, 258
Junonia
   hedonia 208–9, A25
   orithya 208–9, A25
   villida 208–9, A13, A23–6

karsandra (*Zizeeria*) 278–9, A13, A23
kershawi (*Oreixenica*) 6, **188–9**, A30
kershawi (*Vanessa*) 6, **210–11**, A25–6
khoda (*Hasora*) 70–1, A18–19
Kimberley Spotted Opal 264–5
Klug's Xenica 190–1
klugii (*Geitoneura*) 190–1, A29–30
Knight's Grass Dart 110–11
knightorum (*Ocybadistes*) 110–11, A29
kurava (*Nacaduba*) 270–1, A15, A23

labradus (*Zizina*) 30, **278–9**, A18–19
lacewings 200–1
lacturnus (*Everes*) 276–7, A18
laeta (*Eurema*) 147, A17
Lamiaceae 206, A25
Lampides boeticus 276–7, A18–19
Large Bronze Azure 244–5
Large Brown Skipper 96–7
Large Green-banded Blue 27, **266–7**
Large Yellow Grass Dart 108–9
larva structure **9–11**, 48–9
larval feeding 10–13, **34–9**, 50; *see also* fruit and seed feeding; flower feeding; plant toxins
larval host plants 34–7; *see also* species accounts, Part 2; Appendix 2
  competition for 41–3
  gardening, provision of 54–6
lascivia (*Suniana*) 112, A29
lathoniella (*Oreixenica*) 188–9, A29–30
latialis (*Oreixenica*) 188–9
latona (*Charaxes*) 196–7, A11
Lauraceae 55, 121, A11–12
Laxmanniaceae 73, 74
leaf-marking 174–5
leaf notching (chewing veins) 37
leaf-scratching 173
Leafwing 44, **214–15**
Lecythidaceae A14
leda (*Melanitis*) 44, 176, **182–3**, A28–30
legs 11, **13–14**, 24, 120, 136, **163**, 217, **224**
lek 174–5
Lemon Migrant 30, **142–3**
Leopard 202–3
leosthenes (*Protographium*) 122, A10–11
Lepidoptera **3–4**, 19, 34–5, 37
lepidopterist, becoming 57–9
leprea (*Nesoxenica*) 190–1, A28
Leprea Brown 190–1
Leptosia nina 154–5
Leptotes plinius 55, **276–7**, A13
Lesser Wanderer 8–9, 10, 11, 13, 35, 39, 40, 56, **170–1**

leucostictos (*Euploea*) 168–9
Lexias aeropa 204–5
Libythea geoffroy 216, A12
Libytheinae 164, **216**
life cycle 8–13
lifespan **8–9**, 32, 132, 160, 162, 165, 166, 170, 172, 186
Lilac Grass Skipper 86–7
limbaria (*Lucia*) 238–9, A23
Liminitinae 164, **204**, 206–7
lineata (*Erysichton*) 258, **270–1**, A13, A18–20, A22, A24
lineblues 268–71
Lined Grass Yellow 147
Linnaeus, Carolus **6**, 18, 120
Liphyra brassolis 19, 50, **221**
Liphyrinae 217, 221
lithochroa (*Jalmenus*) 252–3, A16
localisation 28–32
Loganiaceae A23
Long-tailed Lineblue 268–9
Long-tailed Pea Blue 276–7
Loranthaceae 148, A20–1
Lucia limbaria 238–9, A23
lucida (*Paralucia pyrodiscus*) 219, **238–9**
lucifer (*Neopithecops*) 280–1, A23
Lurcher 214–15
luteus (*Trapezites*) 76–7, A31
Lycaenesthini 259, 272
Lycaenidae 21–4, 44, 47, **217–19**
lycaenoides (*Anthene*) 272–3, A16–18, A21–2, A24–5
Lyell's Swift 118–19
lyelli (*Pelopidas*) 118–19, A29–30
Lythraceae A19

macfarlanei (*Graphium*) 124–5, A10–11
Macleay, Alexander and William 19
Macleay's Grass Yellow 146–7
Macleay's Swallowtail 120, **124–5**
macleayanum (*Graphium*) 120, **124–5**, A10–11, A23
Macqueen's Imperial Blue 252–3
Macqueen's Ochre 80–1
macqueeni (*Trapezites*) 80–1, A31
madytus (*Arhopala*) 241, A14, A19
Magnoliaceae A10
maheta (*Trapezites*) 75, A31
major (*Allora*) 69
Malayan Eggfly 213
malindeva (*Hesperilla*) 94–5, A28
Mallee Ochre 76–7
Malpighiaceae 68, A21
Malvaceae A14
Mangrove Ant Blue 53, **224–5**
mangroves 28, 30, 31, 53, 170, 172, 224–5, 226–7, 228, 230–1

Marbled Lineblue 270–1
margarita (*Candalides*) 260–1, A20–1
marnas (*Arrhenes*) 113, A29
mastersi (*Hesperilla*) 91, A28
mathewi (*Neolucia*) 274–5, A14
mating **15–17**, 65, 84–5, 111, 145, 167, 175, 177, 187, 200–1, 212, 247, 251, 279
mating plug **15–17**, 126, 128, 130, 132, 134, 138
McAlpine's Birdwing 134
Meadow Argus 208–9
medicea (*Nesolycaena*) 264–5, A22
medus (*Orsotriaena*) 181, A30
Megisba strongyle 280–1, A21–2
melania (*Acrodipsas*) 224
melania (*Appias*) 152–3, A21
melania (*Toxidia*) 88–9, A30
Melanitis leda 44, 176, **182–3**, A28–30
Melastomataceae A19
Meliaceae A22
merope (*Heteronympha*) 6, 18, 32, 176, **186–7**, A29–30
Mesodina
  aeluropis 36, **102–3**, A30
  cyanophracta 102–3, A30
  gracillima 102–3, A30
  halyzia 102–3, A30
  hayi 102–3, A30
mesoptis (*Telicota*) 113, A29–30
metalmarks 220
metamorphosis 3, **12–13**
metirius (*Hypocysta*) 178–9, A28–9
micale (*Arhopala*) 218, **240–1**, A11, A13–14, A19–22, A24–5
Migrant
  Common 142–3
  Lemon 142–3
  Orange 142–3
  Yellow 142–3
migration 126, 139, 141, 142, 152, 154–5, 165, 167, 170, 173, 208, 210
Mimene atropatene 106–7
mimicry 34, **38–40**, 43, 45, 121, 126, 128, 148, 162, 164, 170, 182–3, 200–1, 204–5, 206, 212–13, 266–7
mimicry ring 39–40
Mimosaceae 141, 196, A15–17
minyas (*Geitoneura*) 33, **190–1**, A29
mirifica (*Heteronympha*) 186–7, A28–9
misippus (*Hypolimnas*) 39, 164, 170, **212**, A13, A25
Miskin's Jewel 226–7
miskini (*Hypochrysops*) 226–7, A11, A13, A15, A19–22, A25, A31

miskini (*Theclinesthes*) 272–3, A15–20, A22
mistletoe 36, 37, 42–3, 45, 148, 156–62, 234, 242–8, 261, A20–1
Molluginaceae A13
Monarch *see* Wanderer
Monimiaceae A11
monocotyledons 35, 63, 73, 105, 164, 176, 195, 218, A26
monotherma (*Hesperilla ornata*) 90
montana (*Argynnina hobartia*) 190
Montane Ochre 74
monticolae (*Anisynta*) 84–5, A30
moonbeams 236–7
Moraceae 165, A12
morrisi (*Tisiphone abeona*) 192–3
mortoni (*Acrodipsas*) 224
Motasingha
   dirphia 96–7
   trimaculata 96–7, A28, A30
Moth Butterfly 19, 24, 50, **221**
moths, day-flying **3–5**, 37, 39
Mottled Grass Skipper 84–5
Mountain Grass Skipper 84–5
Mountain Heath Blue 274–5
Mountain Iris Skipper 36, **102–3**
Mountain Sedge Skipper 90
Mournful Crow 168–9
mud-puddling **15**, 71, 122, 143, 153
munionga (*Oreisplanus*) 90, A28
mutualisms 47–51
Mycalesis
   perseus 180–1, A29–30
   sirius 180–1, A29–30
   terminus 180–1, A29–30
Mynes geoffroyi 45, **214–15**, A12
Myoporaceae A25
myrmecophila (*Acrodipsas*) 224–5
Myrsinaceae A15
Myrtaceae A19–20
mysis (*Delias*) 160–1, A21

Nacaduba
   berenice 49, 266, **268–9**, A12, A19, A22
   biocellata 35, **268–9**, A15–16
   cyanea 266–7, A17
   kurava 270–1, A15, A23
names 6–8, Appendix 1
narcissus (*Hypochrysops*) 226–7, A15, A19–21, A24
Narcissus Jewel 226–7
Narrow-banded Awl 70–1
Narrow-brand Darter 113
Narrow-brand Grass Skipper 82–3
Narrow-winged Pearl White 150–1
nectar feeding 4, 13–15, **47–8**, 69, 74, 75, 81, 83, 85, 87, 89, 90, 96, 107, 109, 115, 119, 120, 122, 127, 135, 139, 140, 145, 149, 155, 157, 159, 161, 171, 176, 184, 210, 222, 227, 231, 239, 253, 258, 275, 278
nectar plants 54–5; *see also* nectar feeding
nectary organ 49
Neohesperilla
   crocea 82–3, A29–30
   senta 82–3, A30
   xanthomera 82–3, A29
   xiphiphora 82–3, A30
Neolucia
   agricola 274–5, A17–19
   hobartensis 274–5, A14
   mathewi 274–5, A14
Neopithecops lucifer 280–1, A23
Nephila maculata 134, 167, 175; *see also* Spider, Golden Orb Weaving
Neptis praslini 204–5, A24
Nesolycaena
   albosericea 264–5, A22
   caesia 264–5, A22
   medicea 264–5, A22
   urumelia 264–5, A22
Nesoxenica
   leprea 190–1, A28
   leprea elia 190–1
Netrocoryne repanda 64–5, A11–15, A19, A20, A22, A25
New Guinea
   books on **19–20**, 282–3
   faunal connections 27, 72, 106, 134, 148, 156, 158, 164, 174, 176, 178, **194**, 195, 219, 220, 226, 232, 238, 259, 280
   pest risks 57
New Guinea Birdwing 134
nigidius (*Delias ennia*) 158–9
nigrina (*Delias*) 32, 38, 42–3, **162**, A20–1
nina (*Leptosia*) 154–5
nitens (*Philiris*) 236–7, A21
niveata (*Euploea darchia*) 168–9
No-brand Grass Dart 108–9
No-brand Grass Yellow 146–7
noelkeri (*Candalides*) 264–5, A25
nora (*Prosotas*) 268–9
Northern Brown Crow 168–9
Northern Citrus Swallowtail 28, **130–1**
Northern Grass Dart 108–9
Northern Imperial Blue 252–3
Northern Iris Skipper 102–3
Northern Jezabel 32, 44, 148, **160–1**
Northern Large Azure 218, **246–7**
Northern Large Darter 114–15
Northern Lineblue 268–9
Northern Pearl White 151

Northern Pencilled Blue 260–1
Northern Ringlet 178–9
Northern Sedge Darter 114–15
Northern Silver Ochre 75
Northern Spotted Sedge Skipper 90
Notocrypta waigensis 106–7, A30
nycteris (*Exometoeca*) 63, **67**, A22
Nymph, White 45, **214–15**
Nymphalidae 21–4, 44, 45, **163–4**
Nymphalinae 163–4, **206–7**
nymphs 21–4, 44, 45, 163–4, **206–7**
nysa (*Delias*) 158–9, A21
Nysa Jezabel 158–9

oakblues 240–1
Ochnaceae A13
ochres 74–81
Ocybadistes
   ardea 110–11
   flavovittatus 110–11, A30
   hypomeloma 110–11, A29–30
   knightorum 110–11, A29
   walkeri 62, 110–11, A29–30
Ogyris
   abrota 248, A20–1
   aenone 242–3, A20–1
   amaryllis 242–3, A20–1
   barnardi 248, A20–1
   genoveva 30, **246–7**, A20–1
   halmaturia 244–5
   ianthis 242–3, A20–1
   idmo 244–5
   iphis 242–3, A20–1
   olane 248, A20
   oroetes 242–3, A20
   otanes 244–5, A20
   subterrestris 244–5
   zosine 218, **246–7**, A20–1
ohara (*Telicota*) 114–15, A28
olane (*Ogyris*) 248, A20
Oleaceae A25
onycha (*Theclinesthes*) 35, 57, 218, **272–3**, A10
opals 264–5
Orange Aeroplane 204–5
Orange Albatross 152–3
Orange Alpine Xenica 188–9
Orange Archduke 204–5
Orange Bushbrown 180–1
Orange Emperor 196–7
Orange-flash Crow 168–9
Orange Grass Dart 105, 112
Orange Jezabel 158–9
Orange Lacewing 27, 39–40, **201**
Orange-lobed Flash 256–7
Orange Migrant 142–3
Orange Ochre 80–1
Orange Palm Dart 55, **116–17**
Orange Ringlet 179

Orange Swift 106–7
Orange Tiger 170–1
Orange-tipped Azure 242–3
Orange-tipped Pea Blue 276–7
Orchard Butterfly 2, 6, 17, 32, 45, 46, **128–9**
Orchidaceae A31
Oreisplanus
 munionga 90, A28
 perornatus 90, A28
Oreixenica
 correae 188–9, A30
 kershawi 6, **188–9**, A30
 lathoniella 188–9, A29–30
 latialis 188–9
 orichora 188–9, A30
 ptunarra 33, **188–9**
orichora (*Oreixenica*) 188–9, A30
origins of fauna **26–7**, 72, 120, 194, 219
orithya (*Junonia*) 208–9, A25
ornata (*Hesperilla*) 90, A28
Ornate Ochre 75
Ornithoptera
 euphorion 30, 32, 43, **134–5**, A12
 priamus 134, A12
 richmondia 52–3, **132–3**, A12
oroetes (*Ogyris*) 242–3, A20
Orsotriaena medus 181, A30
osmeterium 120–1, 124–5, 129, 135, 137, 138
otanes (*Ogyris*) 244–5, A20
oviposition 10, **14–15**, 75, 81, 84–5, 86–7, 103, 111, 125, 136–7, 138, 145, 148, 159, 162, 171, 172, 176, 198–9, 200–1, 202, 208–9, 212–13, 221, 231, 233, 234, 241, 243, 248, 261, 265, 269
Owl, Artemis 27, 128, **195**
owls 194–5
Oxalidaceae A23

PA feeding **40–1**, 165, 166–7, 173
Pachliopta polydorus 39, 43, 121, 128, **138**, A12
padusa (*Elodina*) 150–1, A14
Painted Lady
 Australian 6, **210–11**
 European 210–11
Painted Sedge Skipper 91
Pale Cerulean 280–1
Pale Ciliate Blue 272–3
Pale Green Triangle 55, **124–5**
Pale-orange Darter 114–15
Pale Pea Blue 276–7
palm darts 116–17
Palmfly 182–3
palmyra (*Erysichton*) 270–1, A20–1

Pandanaceae A28
panormus (*Catochrysops*) 276–7, A18
Pantoporia
 consimilis 6, **204–5**, A15
 venilia 204–5, A22
Papilio
 aegeus 2, 17, 28, 32, 45, 46, **128–9**, A22–3
 ambrax 39, 121, **128–9**, 138, A23
 anactus 26, 28, 39, 121, **126–7**, A22–3
 canopus 28, **130–1**, A22–3
 cressida 18
 demoleus 14, 30, **126–7**, A18, A22, A23
 fuscus 28, **130–1**, A22–3
 harmonia 18
 ulysses 7–8, 30, **130–1**, A23
Papilionidae 21–4, 45, 46, **120–1**
Papilionini 121
Papuan Lineblue 270–1
papuana (*Philiris diana*) 236
papyria (*Taractrocera papyria*) 108–9, A28–30
paradelpha (*Heteronympha*) 185, A29–30
Paradise Jewel 35, **232–3**
Paralucia
 aurifer 238–9, A15
 pyrodiscus 238–9, A15
 pyrodiscus lucida 219, **238–9**
 spinifera 53, 219, **238–9**, A15
parasitic wasps and flies 46, 172–3, 246–7, 267, 275
parasitoid defences 46–7
parasitoids **46–7**, 49; *see also* parasitic wasps and flies; Tachinidae
Parnara
 amalia 118–19, A29
 bada 118–19, A29
parthia (*Elodina*) 150–1, A14
parvula (*Toxidia*) 86–7, A30
PAs **40–1**, 166–7, 173, 175
Pasma tasmanica 86–7, A29–30
Passiflora 37, 199, 201, A14
Passifloraceae 164, 198–200, A14
pathogens 47
paulina (*Appias*) 152–3, A14, A21
pea blues 276–7
Peacock Awl 69
Peacock Jewel 226–7
pearl whites 150–1
Pelopidas
 agna 118–19, A29–30
 lyelli 118–19, A29–30
pencilled blues 260–1
penelope (*Heteronympha*) 32, **184–5**, A29–30

penthesilea (*Cethosia*) 27, 39, **201**, A14
perching postures **4**, **24**, **63**, 64–5, 66, **68**, 70–1, 72, 76–7, 78, 87, 91, 93, 95, 101, **104**, 106–7, 127, 153, 157, 159, 161, 163, 169, 178, 179, 180, 183, 189, 193, 195, 203, 205, 207, 211, 213, 215, 216, 217, 220, 225, 229, 231, 237, 239, 240, 245, 251, 253, 254, 255, 257, 259, 261, 262, 263, 275, 278, 279, 281; *see also* basking; dart position
perdita (*Elodina*) 151, A14
perimale (*Cepora*) 152–3, A14
peron (*Toxidia*) 88–9, A28–30
perornatus (*Oreisplanus*) 90, A28
perseus (*Mycalesis*) 180–1, A29–30
pest species 47, **56–7**, 126, 149, 255
petalia (*Trapezites*) 80–1, A31
petilia (*Danaus*) 8–9, 11, 35, 39, **170–1**, A24
Petrelaea tombugensis 268–9, A19
Phaedyma shepherdi 204–5, A12–14, A18, A24
Phalanta phalanta 202–3, A14
phaseli (*Jamides*) 266–7, A18–19
phenology 32
pheromones **16**, **40–1**, 123, 128, 130, 132, 142, 144, 149, 156, 160, 166, 170–1, 180
phigalia (*Trapezites*) 74, A31
phigalioides (*Trapezites*) 74, A31
Philiris
 azula 236–7
 diana 236–7, A11–12
 diana papuana 236
 fulgens 236–7, A11–12
 innotata 236–7, A12
 nitens 236–7, A21
 sappheira 236–7, A21
 ziska 236–7
phocides (*Bindahara*) 30, **255**, A21
phorbas (*Hypolycaena*) 255, A14–15, A17–22, A24–5, A28, A31
phylogeny 164; *see also* evolutionary tree
piceatus (*Hypochrysops*) 28, 30, 53, 219, **228–9**, A12
picta (*Hesperilla*) 91, A28
Pied Blue 280–1
Pied Flat 64–5
Pieridae 21–4, 45, 47, **139–40**
Pierinae 140, **148**
Pieris rapae 28, 47, 56, **149**, A14, A23
pigment chemistry 140; *see also* colour, chemical basis
Pithecops dionisius 280–1

Index 293

Pittosporaceae A15
plant toxins **37–41**, 121, 136, 165–75, 198–201
Plantaginaceae 206, A25
plexippus (*Danaus*) 28, **170–1**, A24
plinius (*Leptotes*) 55, **276–7**, A13
Plumbaginaceae A13
Poaceae A28–30
pollination 47–8
polycletus (*Hypochrysops*) 226–7, A21
polydorus (*Pachliopta*) 39, 43, 121, 128, **138**, A12
Polygonaceae A13
Polyommatinae 217, **258–9**
Polyommatini 259
Polypodiaceae A10
polysema (*Proeidosa*) 98–9, A30
Polyura sempronius 35, 36, 45, **196–7**, A11–17, A19, A25
pomona (*Catopsilia*) 30, **142–3**, A17
pore cupola organs 49
porphyropis (*Chaetocneme*) 67, A11–12
Portulacaceae 206, A13
Praetaxila segecia 220, A15
praslini (*Neptis*) 204–5, A24
praxedes (*Trapezites*) 75, A31
predators 11–13, 34, 37–9, **43–6**, 48–9, 79, 114–15, 134, 178, 210–11, 223, 250–1
predatory larvae *see* carnivorous larvae
priamus (*Ornithoptera*) 134, A12
proboscis 4, **13–14**, **47–8**, 68, 105, 106–7, 118, 121, 124
Proeidosa polysema 98–9, A30
prolegs 11
prosope (*Cupha*) 202–3, A14
Prosotas dubiosa 268–9, A15–19, A22
Prosotas felderi 268–9, A15–17, A19, A22
Prosotas nora 268–9
Proteaceae A19
protection, by ants *see* ant attendance
protection, legal **53**, 58, 203, 238
Protographium leosthenes 122, A10–11
Pseudalmenus chlorinda 7, **249**, A15–16
pseudictinus (*Jalmenus*) 30, **252–3**, A15–16, A22
pseudirius (*Hypocysta*) 179, A30
Pseudodipsas cephenes 234, A14–15, A22–3, A31
Pseudodipsas eone 234, A19, A24–5, A31
Psyche 154–5
Psychonotis caelius 35, 255, 259, **266–7**, A21
ptunarra (*Oreixenica*) 33, **188–9**
puella (*Eurema*) 144–5, A17, A21

pupal cap 73
Purple Dusk Flat 67
Purple Moonbeam 236–7
Purple Swift 106–7
putli (*Freyeria*) 278–9, A18
pyranthe (*Catopsilia*) 142–3, A17
Pyrginae 62, **63**
pyrodiscus (*Paralucia*) 238–9, A15
pyrrolizidine alkaloids *see* PAs; PA feeding
pythias (*Hypochrysops*) 226–7, A13

Quaker 280–1
quarantine 57
queenslandica (*Elodina*) 150–1, A14

Rachelia extrusa 82–3, A28
rafflesia (*Euschemon*) 6, 56, 63, **64–5**, A11
Rainbow 19, 283
rapae (*Pieris*) 28, 47, 56, **149**, A14, A23
Rapala varuna 256–7, A12, A15–19, A21–2
Rare Red-eye 66–7
rawnsleyi (*Tisiphone abeona*) 192–3
recovery plans 52–3
Red-bodied Swallowtail 39, **138**
red-eyes 66–7
Red Lacewing 45, **200–1**
regalis (*Tisiphone abeona*) 192–3
Regent Skipper 6, 56, 63, **64–5**
repanda (*Netrocoryne*) 64–5, A11–15, A19, A20, A22, A25
reproductive diapause *see* delayed reproduction
Resedaceae A14
Rhamnaceae A21
Rhizophoraceae A20
Rice Swift 118–19
Richmond Birdwing 52–3, 56, **132–3**
richmondia (*Ornithoptera*) 52–3, **132–3**, A12
rietmanni (*Toxidia*) 86–7, A29–30
Ringed Xenica 190–1
ringlets 178–9
Riodininae 217, 220
Riverine Sedge Skipper 94–5
Rock Ringlet 179
Rosaceae A15
Royal Jewel 226–7
Rubiaceae A25
Rustic 202–3
Rutaceae 121, A22–3

Sabera
  caesina 106–7, A26–7
  dobboe 106–7, A30
  fuliginosa 106–7, A26–7

sabina (*Yoma*) 214–15, A25
Sahulana scintillata 270–1, A15–17, A22
Saltbush Blue 274–5
Samphire Blue 274–5
sand skippers 98–101
Sandstone Ochre 80–1
Santalaceae A20
sap feeding 40, 173, **196–7**, 204–5, 211
Sapindaceae A22
Sapotaceae A14
sappheira (*Philiris*) 236–7, A21
Sapphire Moonbeam 236–7
sarnia (*Hesperilla*) 94–5, A28
sarpedon (*Graphium*) 55, **123**, A10–12, A14, A23, A24
Satin Azure 242–3
Satin Opal 264–5
Satyrinae 29, 44, 163–4, **176**
scales, on wing **3**, **7–8**, 45, 50, 105, 106, 130, 132, 139–40, 142, 146, 152, 160, 165, 166–7, 177, 180, 182, 184–5, 192, 221, 224, 262; *see also* androconia; hair-pencils; sex brand
Scalloped Grass Yellow 144–5
scent pouch 170–1, 173
scintillata (*Sahulana*) 270–1, A15–17, A22
sciron (*Trapezites*) 76–7, A31
Scrophulariaceae 206, A25
Scrub Darter 113
scylla (*Catopsilia*) 142–3, A17
season, effects of **32–3**, 120–1, 122, 130, 138, 144–7, 165, 166, 168, 170
seasonal forms **44**, 141, 142–3, 144–7, 154, 182–3, 272–3
seasonal variation 44, 141–7, 153, 160–1, 177, 182–3, 272–3
sedge skippers 88–95
segecia (*Praetaxila*) 220, A15
seltuttus (*Anthene*) 272–3, A11, A13, A17–20, A22
sempronius (*Polyura*) 35, 36, 45, **196–7**, A11–17, A19, A25
senta (*Neohesperilla*) 82–3, A30
serpentata (*Theclinesthes*) 274–5, A12–13, A22
sex brand **16**, 72, 82–3, 84–5, 86–7, 94–5, 97, **104–5**, 108–9, 110–11, 112, 113, 114–15, 118–19, 130–1, 144, 146–7, 165–9, 175, 181, 260–1
sexguttata (*Hesperilla*) 94–5, A28
shelters, larvae and pupae 35, 63, 64, 65, 66, 68, 69, 70–1, 73, 74, 75, 76–7, 78–9, 80–1, 84–5, 86–7,

90–1, 92–3, 94–5, 96–7, 98–9, 101, 105, 106–7, 109, 115, 116–17, 119
shepherdi (Phaedyma) 204–5, A12–14, A18, A24
shield skippers 88–9
Shining Cerulean 280–1
Shining Pencilled Blue 260–1
Short-tailed Lineblue 268–9
Shouldered Brown 32, **184–5**
Signeta
　flammeata 88–9, A30
　tymbophora 88–9, A28–30
Silky Azure 242–3
Silver Sedge Skipper 91
Silver-spotted Ochre 76–7
Silver-studded Ochre 74
Silver Xenica 188–9
simplex (Candalides hyacinthinus) 262–3
sirius (Mycalesis) 180–1, A29–30
skippers 4, 16, 21–4, 27, 30, 35–6, 45, 55–6, 57, **62**, 64–5, 82–3, 86–7, 96–7
Small Alpine Xenica 188–9
Small Ant Blue 224–5
Small Bronze Azure 244–5
Small Copper 238–9
Small Darter 113
Small Dingy Grass Dart 108–9
Small Dusky Blue 262–3
Small Grass Skipper 86–7
Small Grass Yellow 30, **146–7**
Small Green-banded Blue 35, 259, **266–7**
Small Iris Skipper 102–3
Small Oakblue 30, **241**
Small Orange Ochre 80–1
Small Pied Blue 280–1
Smilacaceae A31
smilax (Eurema) 30, **146–7**, A17
smilis (Deudorix) 257, A23
Solander's Brown 186–7
solandri (Heteronympha) 186–7, A30
Soldier, Brown 208–9
Southern Large Azure 30, **246–7**
Southern Large Darter 114–15
Southern Pearl White 150–1
Southern Sedge Darter 114–15
Southern Silver Ochre 75
Spangled Drongo 38
Speckled Lineblue 56, **270–1**
spermatophore **16–17**, 136–7, 138, 198, 250, 136–8
sphenosema (Anisynta) 84–5, A29
sphragis **15**, 137, 177, 184–5, 198–9
Spider, Golden Orb Weaving **44–5**, 134, 167, **175**
Spider, Orb 136

spinifera (Paralucia) 53, 219, **238–9**, A15
Spinifex Sand Skipper 98–9
Splendid Jewel 226–7
Splendid Ochre 78–9
Spotless Grass Skipper 88–9
Spotted Alpine Xenica 188–9
Spotted Brown 185
Spotted Dusky Blue 263
Spotted Grass Blue 278–9
Spotted Grass Skipper 82–3
Spotted Opal 264–5
Spotted Pea Blue 276–7
Spotted Sedge Skipper 90
Stencilled Imperial Blue 252–3
Sterculiaceae A13
Striped Xenica 188–9
strongyle (Megisba) 280–1, A21–2
structural colour **7–8**, 130–1, 132, 140
subspecies 7, 20, 53, 60, 64, 76, 78, 126, 128, 130, 132, 154, 158, 164, 165, 168, 184, 186, 188, 190, 192–3, 216, 232, 236, 238, 244, 249, 250, 254, 262, 264; *see also* geographic races
subterrestris (Ogyris) 244–5
sulpitius (Theclinesthes) 274–5, A12–13
Suniana
　lascivia 112, A29
　sunias 105, **112**, A29–30
sunias (Suniana) 105, **112**, A29–30
Surianaceae A15
swallowtails 4, 21–4, 28, 33, 45–6, 55, **120–1**, 124–7, 130–1, 138
Swamp Darter 113
Swift Sedge Skipper 94–5
swifts 106–7, 118–19
Sword-brand Grass Skipper 82–3
Sword-tailed Flash 30, **255**
Swordgrass Brown 192–3
swordtails 122
Sydney Azure 242–3
sylvester (Euploea) 168–9, A12, A24
symmomus (Trapezites) 78–9, A31

Tachinidae **46**, 172–3, 182, 204–5, 267
Taenaris
　artemis 27, 128, **195**, A28
　catops 195
Tagiades japetus 64–5, A31
Tailed Citrus Swallowtail 28, **130–1**
Tailed Emperor 6, 24, 35, 36, 45, **196–7**
Tailed Green-banded Blue 266–7
Tailless Lineblue 268–9
taori (Trapezites) 80–1, A31

Taractrocera
　anisomorpha 108–9, A29–30
　dolon 108–9, A30
　ilia 108–9
　ina 108–9, A29–30
　papyria agraulia 108–9
　papyria papyria 108–9, A28–30
tarsal drumming 171
tarsus 139, **163**
Tasmanian Alpine Xenica 33, **188–9**
tasmanica (Argynnina hobartia) 190–1
tasmanica (Pasma) 86–7, A29–30
Telicota
　ancilla 114–15, A28–30
　anisodesma 114–15, A28
　augias 114–15, A28
　brachydesma 113, A29
　colon 114–15, A29–30
　eurotas 114–15
　eurychlora 114–15, A28
　mesoptis 113, A29–30
　ohara 114–15, A28
Tellervo zoilus 15, 27, 40, **174–5**, A24
tenella (Udara) 280–1
tentacular organs 49
terminus (Mycalesis) 180–1, A29–30
territoriality 15, **51**, 96, 106, 108, 110–11, 116–17, 126, **136–7**, 181, 182, 184–5, 196, 202, 204, 208, 210–11, 212, 216
Theaceae A13
Theclinae 44, 217, **222–3**
Theclinesthes
　albocincta 272–3, A21
　hesperia 272–3, A21
　miskini 272–3, A15–20, A22
　onycha 35, 57, 218, **272–3**, A10
　serpentata 274–5, A12–13, A22
　sulpitius 274–5, A12–13
theon (Hypochrysops) 35, **232–3**, A10
Thymelaeaceae A19
thyrrhus (Toxidia) 88–9, A30
tigers 12–13, 170–3
tigers and crows 21–4, 39, 163, **165**
Tiliaceae A13
tillyardi (Anisynta) 84–5, A30
tindalii (Delias ennia) 158
Tiny Grass Blue 278–9
Tirumala hamata 6, 18, 165, **173**, A24
Tisiphone
　abeona 7, **192–3**, A28
　abeona albifascia 192–3
　abeona aurelia 192–3
　abeona morrisi 192–3
　abeona rawnsleyi 192–3
　abeona regalis 192–3
　helena 192–3, A28

Tit
  Black and White 57, **255**, A31
  Common 255
tombugensis (*Petrelaea*) 268–9, A19
Toxidia
  andersoni 86–7, A30
  doubledayi 86–7, A29–30
  inornata 88–9, A30
  melania 88–9, A30
  parvula 86–7, A30
  peron 88–9, A28–30
  rietmanni 86–7, A29–30
  thyrrhus 88–9, A30
Trapezites
  argenteoornatus 76–7, A31
  atkinsi 76–7, A31
  eliena 80–1, A31
  genevieveae 75, A31
  heteromacula 80–1, A31
  iacchoides 74, A31
  iacchus 80–1, A31
  luteus 76–7, A31
  macqueeni 80–1, A31
  maheta 75, A31
  petalia 80–1, A31
  phigalia 74, A31
  phigalioides 74, A31
  praxedes 75, A31
  sciron 76–7, A31
  symmomus 78–9, A31
  taori 80–1, A31
Trapezitinae 27, 62, **72**
Tremandraceae A22
triangles 123–5
trichopepla (*Cephrenes*) 116–17, A26–8
Trident Pencilled Blue 260–1
trimaculata (*Motasingha*) 96–7, A28, A30
Troidini 121
Tropaeolaceae A23
tulliolus (*Euploea*) 168–9, A12
Turquoise Emperor 27, 104, **196–7**
Turquoise Imperial Blue 254
Twin Dusky Blue 262–3
Twin-spotted Lineblue 35, **268–9**
Two-brand Crow 168–9
Two-brand Grass Skipper 84–5
Two-spotted Grass Skipper 86–7
Two-spotted Sedge Skipper 94–5
tymbophora (*Signeta*) 88–9, A28–30

Udara tenella 280–1
Ulmaceae A12
ulysses (*Papilio*) 7–8, 30, **130–1**, A23
Ulysses Butterfly 2, 7–8, 30, **130–1**
Union Jack 160–1
unpalatability **37–41**, 45, 121, 134, 136–7, 138, 148, 162, 164, 166–7, 170, 175
Urticaceae 206, A12
urumelia (*Nesolycaena*) 264–5, A22
UV reflectance **140–1**, 144–7, 149, 218

Vagrans egista 202–3, A14
Vagrant 202–3
Vanessa
  cardui 210–11, A14
  itea 44, 176, **210–11**, A12
  kershawi 6, **210–11**, A25–6
Varied Imperial Blue 254
Varied Sedge Skipper 92–3
varuna (*Rapala*) 256–7, A12, A15–19, A21–2
venilia (*Pantoporia*) 204–5, A22
Verbenaceae A24–5
vertical stratification 29–31
villida (*Junonia*) 208–9, A13, A23–6
Vindula arsinoe 200–1, A14
Violaceae 199, A14
Viscaceae 148, A21

waigensis (*Notocrypta*) 106–7, A30
Walker's Grass Dart 62, **110–11**
walkeri (*Elodina*) 151, A14
walkeri (*Ocybadistes*) 62, **110–11**, A29–30
Wanderer 2, 6, 28, 56, **170–1**
Wanderer, Lesser 8–9, 10, 11, 13, 35, 39, 40, 56, **170–1**
warning coloration 34, **38–40**, 44, 121, 136, 138, 165, 200–1
Waterhouse **19–20**, 282–3
Waterhouse's Azure 244–5
Waterhouse's Imperial Blue 252–3
Wattle Blue 272–3
Wedge Grass Skipper 84–5
Western Bitter-bush Blue 272–3
Western Brown Skipper 96–7
Western Flat 63, **67**
Western Grass Dart 108–9
Western Jewel 230–1
Western Sand Skipper 98–9

Western Xenica 33, **190–1**
White Albatross 152–3
White-banded Grass Dart 108–9
White-banded Lineblue 270–1
White-brand Grass Skipper 86–7
White-fringed Swift 106–7
White-margined Crow 168–9
White-margined Grass Dart 110–11
White-margined Moonbeam 236–7
White Nymph 45, **214–15**
White-veined Sand Skipper 100–1
whites 21–4, 37, 47, **139–40**, 148
Wide-brand Sedge Skipper 94–5
wildei (*Arhopala*) 30, **241**
wing shuffling 222–3, 256, 277
Winteraceae A10
Wonder Brown 186–7
Wood White 156–7

xanthomera (*Neohesperilla*) 82–3, A29
Xanthorrhoeaceae 74, A30–1
xanthospilos (*Candalides*) 262–3, A19
xenicas 188–91
xiphiphora (*Neohesperilla*) 82–3, A30

Yellow-banded Jezabel 158–9
Yellow Grass Skipper 82–3
Yellow Migrant 142–3
Yellow Ochre 76–7
Yellow Palm Dart 116–17
Yellow Sand Skipper 100–1
Yellow Sedge Skipper 92–3
Yellow-spot Blue 262–3
Yellow-spot Jewel 230–1
Yellow Swift 118–19
yellows 21–4, 139, **141**
Yoma sabina 214–15, A25
Ypthima arctoa 30, 177, **178–9**, A29–30

Zamiaceae A10
Zebra Blue 55, **276–7**
Zingiberaceae 106, A30
ziska (*Philiris*) 236–7
Zizeeria karsandra 278–9, A13, A23
Zizina labradus 30, **278–9**, A18–19
Zizula hylax 278–9, A25
zoilus (*Tellervo*) 15, 27, 40, **174–5**, A24
zosine (*Ogyris*) 218, 246–7, A20–1
Zygophyllaceae A23

Appendix 1

CHECKLIST OF AUSTRALIAN BUTTERFLIES

including species from Torres Strait and other islands of the continental shelf

The scientific name of any animal is incomplete unless it includes also the name(s) of the author(s), who first named and described it, and the date of publication. Names of authorities and their dates are placed in parentheses after the name if the species was first described as belonging to a different genus. The laws of nomenclature require that the species and subspecies names must agree with the genus in gender. Gender is determined by the endings of the names, hence if a species is transferred from a masculine to a feminine or neuter genus, and if that species name is a simple adjective, its ending will almost always need to be changed. The rules governing such cases are complex and arcane. Many Latin names have a grammatical structure which is not always obvious. Nouns in apposition, or possessive adjectives, and several other forms, do not change. However, in the following list the rules of the International Code of Zoological Nomenclature are followed to the best of our knowledge. Genera are listed in systematic order, according to their relationships, but within genera species are listed alphabetically. At the head of each genus (in bold) the author and publication date of the genus is given. For many species several subspecies have been described. The decision to accept these is often a matter of scientific judgement. We generally follow Braby (2004) in this respect, listing subspecies only when more than one is represented in Australia. Studying these names gives us much insight into their history. For example any species described by Fabricius, a Danish student of Linnaeus, in 1775, would have been collected by Joseph Banks on Cook's 1770 voyage of discovery of eastern Australia.

* remote island species, mainly Torres Straits
** rare natural immigrants
† introduced species

SUPERFAMILY HESPERIOIDEA

Family Hesperiidae

Subfamily Pyrginae

Euschemon Doubleday, 1846
Euschemon rafflesia (W.S. Macleay, 1826)
   E. r. rafflesia (W.S. Macleay, 1826)
   E. r. alba Mabille, 1903

Chaetocneme C. Felder, 1860
Chaetocneme beata (Hewitson, 1867)
Chaetocneme critomedia (Guérin-Ménville, 1831)
Chaetocneme denitza (Hewitson, 1867)
Chaetocneme porphyropis (Meyrick & Lower, 1902)

Netrocoryne C. & R. Felder, 1867
Netrocoryne repanda C. & R. Felder, 1867
   N. r. repanda C. & R. Felder, 1867
   N. r. expansa Waterhouse, 1932

Exometoeca Meyrick, 1888
Exometoeca nycteris Meyrick, 1888

Tagiades Hübner, 1819
Tagiades japetus (Stoll, 1781)
*Tagiades nestus (C. Felder, 1860)

Subfamily Coeliadinae

Allora Waterhouse & Lyell, 1914
Allora doleschallii (C. Felder, 1860)
Allora major (Rothschild, 1915)

Hasora Moore, 1881
Hasora chromus (Cramer, 1780)
Hasora discolor (C. & R. Felder, 1859)
Hasora hurama (Butler, 1870)
Hasora khoda (Mabille, 1876)

Badamia Moore, 1881
Badamia exclamationis (Fabricius, 1775)

Subfamily Trapezitinae

Rachelia Hemming, 1964
Rachelia extrusa (C. & R. Felder, 1867)

Trapezites Hübner, 1819
Trapezites argenteoornatus (Hewitson, 1868)
Trapezites atkinsi A.A.E. Williams, M.R. Williams & Hay, 1998
Trapezites eliena (Hewitson, 1868)
Trapezites genevieveae Atkins, 1997
Trapezites heteromacula, Meyrick & Lower, 1902
Trapezites iacchoides Waterhouse, 1903
Trapezites iacchus (Fabricius 1775)
Trapezites luteus (Tepper 1882)
   T. l. luteus (Tepper 1882)
   T. l. glaucus Waterhouse & Lyell, 1914
   T. l. leucon Waterhouse, 1938
Trapezites macqueeni Kerr & Sands, 1970
Trapezites maheta (Hewitson, 1877)
Trapezites petalia (Hewitson, 1868)
Trapezites phigalia (Hewitson, 1868)
Trapezites phigalioides Waterhouse, 1903
Trapezites praxedes (Plötz, 1884)
Trapezites sciron Waterhouse & Lyell, 1914
   T. s. sciron Waterhouse & Lyell, 1914
   T. s. eremicola Burns, 1948
Trapezites symmomus Hübner, 1823
   T. s. symmomus Hübner, 1823
   T. s. soma Waterhouse, 1932
   T. s. sombra Waterhouse, 1932
Trapezites taori Atkins, 1997
Trapezites waterhousei Mayo & Atkins, 1992

Anisynta Lower, 1911
Anisynta cynone (Hewitson, 1874)
   A. c. cynone (Hewitson, 1874)
   A. c. gunneda L.E. Couchman, 1954
Anisynta dominula (Plötz, 1884)
   A. d. dominula (Plötz, 1884)
   A. d. pria (Waterhouse, 1932)
Anisynta monticolae (Olliff, 1890)
Anisynta sphenosema (Meyrick & Lower, 1902)
Anisynta tillyardi Waterhouse & Lyell, 1912

Pasma Waterhouse, 1932
Pasma tasmanica (Miskin, 1889)

Dispar Waterhouse & Lyell, 1914
Dispar compacta (Butler, 1882)

Neohesperilla Waterhouse & Lyell, 1914
Neohesperilla crocea (Miskin, 1889)
Neohesperilla senta (Miskin, 1891)
Neohesperilla xanthomera (Meyrick & Lower, 1902)
Neohesperilla xiphiphora (Lower, 1911)

Toxidia Mabille, 1891
Toxidia andersoni (Kirby, 1893)
Toxidia doubledayi (C. Felder, 1862)
Toxidia inornata (Butler, 1883)
Toxidia melania (Waterhouse, 1903)
Toxidia parvula (Plötz, 1884)
Toxidia peron (Latreille, 1824)
Toxidia rietmanni (Semper, 1879)
   T. r. rietmanni (Semper, 1879)
   T. r. parasema (Lower, 1908)
Toxidia thyrrhus Mabille, 1891

Signeta Waterhouse & Lyell, 1914
Signeta flammeata (Butler, 1882)
Signeta tymbophora (Meyrick & Lower, 1902)

Oreisplanus Waterhouse & Lyell, 1914
Oreisplanus munionga (Olliff, 1890)
   O. m. munionga (Olliff, 1890)
   O. m. larana L.E. Couchman, 1962
Oreisplanus perornatus (Kirby, 1893)

Hesperilla Hewitson, 1868
Hesperilla chrysotricha (Meyrick & Lower, 1902)
   H. c. chrysotricha (Meyrick & Lower, 1902)
   H. c. cyclospila (Meyrick & Lower, 1902)
Hesperilla crypsargyra (Meyrick, 1888)
   H. c. crypsargyra (Meyrick, 1888)
   H. c. hopsoni Waterhouse, 1927
   H. c. binna Johnson & Wilson, 2005
Hesperilla crypsigramma (Meyrick & Lower, 1902)
Hesperilla donnysa Hewitson, 1868
   H. d. donnysa Hewitson, 1868
   H. d. aurantia Waterhouse, 1927
   H. d. galena Waterhouse, 1927
   H. d. albina Waterhouse, 1932
Hesperilla flavescens Waterhouse, 1927
Hesperilla furva Sands & Kerr, 1973
Hesperilla idothea (Miskin, 1889)
   H. i. idothea (Miskin, 1889)
   H. i. clara Waterhouse, 1932
Hesperilla malindeva Lower, 1911
Hesperilla mastersi Waterhouse, 1900

Hesperilla ornata (Leach, 1814)
   H. o. ornata (Leach, 1814)
   H. o. monotherma (Lower, 1907)
Hesperilla picta (Leach, 1814)
Hesperilla sarnia Atkins, 1978
Hesperilla sexguttata Herrich-Schäffer, 1869

Motasingha Watson, 1893
Motasingha dirphia (Hewitson, 1868)
Motasingha trimaculata (Tepper, 1882)
   M. t. trimaculata (Tepper, 1882)
   M. t. dilata Waterhouse, 1932
   M. t. occidentalis Moulds & Atkins, 1986

Antipodia Atkins, 1984
Antipodia atralba (Tepper, 1882)
Antipodia chaostola (Meyrick, 1888)
   A. c. chaostola (Meyrick, 1888)
   A. c. chares (Waterhouse, 1933)
   A. c. leucophaea (L.E. Couchman, 1946)
Antipodia dactyliota (Meyrick, 1888)
   A. d. dactyliota (Meyrick, 1888)
   A. d. nila (Waterhouse, 1932)

Proeidosa Atkins, 1973
Proeidosa polysema (Lower, 1908)

Herimosa Atkins, 1994
Herimosa albovenata (Waterhouse, 1940)
   H. a. albovenata (Waterhouse, 1940)
   H. a. weemala (L.E. Couchman, 1954)
   H. a. fuscata (Parsons, 1965)

Croitana Waterhouse, 1932
Croitana aestiva E.D. Edwards, 1979
Croitana arenaria E.D. Edwards, 1979
   C. a. arenaria E.D. Edwards, 1979
   C. a. pilepudla Grund, 2003
Croitana croites (Hewitson, 1874)

Mesodina Meyrick, 1901
Mesodina aeluropis Meyrick, 1901
Mesodina cyanophracta Lower, 1911
Mesodina gracillima E.D. Edwards, 1987
Mesodina halyzia (Hewitson, 1868)
Mesodina hayi E.D. Edwards & Graham, 1995

Subfamily Hesperiinae

Notocrypta de Nicéville, 1889
Notocrypta waigensis (Plötz, 1882)

Taractrocera Butler, 1870
Taractrocera anisomorpha (Lower, 1911)
Taractrocera dolon (Plötz, 1884)
   T. d. dolon (Plötz, 1884)
   T. d. diomedes Waterhouse, 1933
Taractrocera ilia Waterhouse, 1932
Taractrocera ina Waterhouse, 1932
Taractrocera papyria (Boisduval, 1832)
   T. p. papyria (Boisduval, 1832)
   T. p. agraulia (Hewitson, 1868)

Ocybadistes Heron, 1894
Ocybadistes ardea Bethune-Baker, 1906
Ocybadistes flavovittatus (Latreille, 1824)
   O. f. flavovittatus (Latreille, 1824)
   O. f. vesta (Waterhouse, 1932)
Ocybadistes hypomeloma Lower, 1911
   O. h. hypomeloma Lower, 1911
   O. h. vaga (Waterhouse, 1932)
Ocybadistes knightorum Lambkin & Donaldson, 1994
Ocybadistes walkeri Heron, 1894
   O. w. hypochlorus Lower, 1911
   O. w. olivia Waterhouse, 1933
   O. w. sothis Waterhouse, 1933

Suniana Evans, 1934
Suniana lascivia (Rosenstock, 1885)
   S. l. lascivia (Rosenstock, 1885)
   S. l. neocles (Mabille, 1891)
   S. l. lasus Waterhouse, 1937
   S. l. larrakia L.E. Couchman, 1951
Suniana sunias (C. Felder, 1860)
   S. s. rectivitta (Mabille, 1860)
   S. s. sauda Waterhouse, 1937

Arrhenes Mabille, 1904
Arrhenes dschilus (Plötz, 1885)
Arrhenes marnas (C. Felder, 1860)

Telicota Moore, 1881
Telicota ancilla (Herrich-Schäffer, 1869)
   T. a. ancilla (Herrich-Schäffer, 1869)
   T. a. baudina Evans, 1949
Telicota anisodesma Lower, 1911
Telicota augias (Linnaeus, 1763)
Telicota brachydesma Lower, 1908
Telicota colon (Fabricius, 1775)
Telicota eurotas (C. Felder, 1860)
Telicota eurychlora Lower, 1908
*Telicota kesia Evans, 1949
Telicota mesoptis Lower, 1911
Telicota ohara (Plötz, 1883)

Cephrenes Waterhouse & Lyell, 1914
Cephrenes augiades (C. Felder, 1860)
*Cephrenes moseleyi (Butler, 1884)
Cephrenes trichopepla (Lower, 1908)

Sabera Swinhoe, 1908
Sabera caesina (Hewitson, 1866)
Sabera dobboe (Plötz, 1885)
Sabera fuliginosa (Miskin, 1889)

Mimene Joicey & Talbot, 1917
Mimene atropatene (Fruhstorfer, 1911)

Pelopidas Walker, 1870
Pelopidas agna (Moore, 1866)
Pelopidas lyelli (Rothschild, 1915)

Parnara Moore, 1881
Parnara amalia (Semper, 1879)
Parnara bada (Moore, 1878)

Borbo Evans, 1949
Borbo cinnara (Wallace, 1866)
Borbo impar (Mabille, 1883)
   *B. i. tetragraphus (Mabille, 1891)
   B. i. lavinia (Waterhouse, 1932)

SUPERFAMILY PAPILIONOIDEA

Family Papilionidae

Subfamily Papilioninae

Tribe Graphiini

Protographium Munroe, 1961
Protographium leosthenes (Doubleday, 1846)
   P. l. leosthenes (Doubleday, 1846)
   P. l. geimbia (Tindale, 1927)

Graphium Scopoli, 1777
Graphium agamemnon (Linnaeus, 1758)
Graphium aristeus (Stoll, 1780)
*Graphium codrus (Cramer, 1777)
Graphium eurypylus (Linnaeus, 1758)
   G. e. lycaon (C. & R. Felder, 1865)
   *G. e. lycaonides (Rothschild, 1895)
   G. e. nyctimus (Waterhouse & Lyell, 1914)
Graphium macfarlanei (Butler, 1877)
Graphium macleayanum (Leach, 1814)
   G. m. macleayanum (Leach, 1814)

G. m. moggana L.E. Couchman, 1965
Graphium sarpedon (Linnaeus, 1758)

Tribe Papilionini

Papilio Linnaeus, 1758
Papilio aegeus Donovan, 1805
   P. a. aegeus Donovan, 1805
   **P. a. ormenus* Guérin-Ménville, 1830
Papilio ambrax Boisduval, 1832
Papilio anactus W.S. Macleay, 1826
Papilio canopus Westwood, 1842
Papilio demoleus Linnaeus, 1758
Papilio fuscus Goeze, 1779
   P. f. capaneus Westwood, 1843
   P. f. indicatus Butler, 1876
Papilio ulysses Linnaeus, 1758

Tribe Troidini

Cressida Swainson, 1832
Cressida cressida (Fabricius, 1775)
   C. c. cressida (Fabricius, 1775)
   C. c. cassandra (Waterhouse & Lyell, 1914)

Pachliopta Reakirt, 1865
Pachliopta polydorus (Linnaeus, 1763)

Ornithoptera Boisduval, 1832
Ornithoptera euphorion (Gray, 1853)
Ornithoptera priamus (Linnaeus, 1758)
   O. p. macalpinei (Moulds, 1974)
   **O. p. poseidon* (Doubleday, 1847)
   O. p. pronomus (Gray, 1853)
Ornithoptera richmondia (Gray, 1853)

Family Pieridae

Subfamily Coliadinae

Catopsilia Hübner, 1819
Catopsilia gorgophone (Boisduval, 1836)
Catopsilia pomona (Fabricius, 1775)
Catopsilia pyranthe (Linnaeus, 1758)
Catopsilia scylla (Linnaeus, 1763)

Eurema Hübner, 1819
Eurema alitha (C. & R. Felder, 1862)
Eurema brigitta (Stoll, 1780)
Eurema hecabe (Linnaeus, 1758)
Eurema herla (W.S. Macleay, 1826)
Eurema laeta (Boisduval, 1836)
Eurema puella (Boisduval, 1832)
Eurema smilax (Donovan, 1805)

Subfamily Pierinae

Elodina C. & R. Felder, 1865
Elodina angulipennis (P.H. Lucas, 1852)
Elodina claudia De Baar & Hancock, 1993
Elodina padusa (Hewitson, 1853)
Elodina parthia (Hewitson, 1853)
Elodina perdita Miskin, 1889
Elodina queenslandica De Baar & Hancock, 1993
   E. q. queenslandica De Baar & Hancock, 1993
   E. q. kuranda De Baar & Hancock, 1993
Elodina tongura Tindale 1923
Elodina walkeri Butler, 1898

Leptosia Hübner, 1818
Leptosia nina (Fabricius, 1793)

Belenois Hübner, 1819
Belenois java (Linnaeus, 1768)
   B. j. teutonia (Fabricius, 1775)
   ***B. j. peristhene* (Boisduval, 1859)

Pieris Schrank, 1801
†*Pieris rapae* (Linnaeus, 1768)

Cepora Billberg, 1820
Cepora perimale (Donovan, 1805)

Delias Hübner, 1819
Delias aganippe (Donovan, 1805)
Delias argenthona (Fabricius, 1793)
Delias aruna (Boisduval, 1832)
Delias ennia (Wallace, 1867)
   D. e. nigidius Miskin, 1884
   D. e. tindalii Joicey & Talbot, 1926
Delias harpalyce (Donovan, 1805)
Delias mysis (Fabricius, 1775)
   D. m. mysis (Fabricius, 1775)
   D. m. aestiva Butler, 1897
   **D. m. onca* Fruhstorfer, 1910
Delias nigrina (Fabricius, 1775)
Delias nysa (Fabricius, 1775)
   D. n. nysa (Fabricius, 1775)
   D. n. nivira Waterhouse & Lyell, 1914

Appias Hübner, 1819
Appias ada (Stoll, 1781)
Appias albina (Boisduval, 1836)
Appias celastina (Boisduval, 1832)
Appias melania (Fabricius, 1775)
Appias paulina (Cramer, 1777)

Family Nymphalidae

Subfamily Danainae

Euploea Fabricius, 1807
Euploea alcathoe (Godart, 1819)
   **E. a. monilifera* (Moore, 1883)
   E. a. eichhorni Staudinger, 1884
   **E. a. misenus* Miskin, 1890
   E. a. enastri Fenner, 1991
Euploea algea (Godart, 1819)
Euploea batesii C. & R. Felder, 1865
**Euploea climena (Stoll, 1782)
Euploea core (Cramer, 1780)
Euploea darchia W.S. Macleay, 1826
   E. d. darchia W.S. Macleay, 1826
   E. d. niveata (Butler, 1875)
**Euploea leucostictos* (Gmelin, 1790)
*Euploea modesta Butler, 1866
**Euploea netscheri* Snellen, 1889
Euploea sylvester (Fabricius, 1793)
   E. s. sylvester (Fabricius, 1793)
   E. s. pelor Doubleday, 1847
Euploea tulliolus (Fabricius, 1793)
   E. t. tulliolus (Fabricius, 1793)
   **E. t. dudgeonis* Grose-Smith, 1894

Danaus Kluk, 1802
Danaus affinis (Fabricius, 1775)
   D. a. affinis (Fabricius, 1775)
   **D. a. gelanor* (Waterhouse & Lyell, 1914)
**Danaus chrysippus* (Linnaeus, 1758)
   **D. c. cratippus* (C. Felder, 1860)
Danaus genutia (Cramer, 1779)
Danaus petilia (Stoll, 1790)
†*Danaus plexippus* (Linnaeus, 1758)

Tirumala Moore, 1880
Tirumala hamata (W.S. Macleay, 1826)

Subfamily Tellervinae

Tellervo Kirby, 1894
Tellervo zoilus (Fabricius, 1775)
   T. z. zoilus (Fabricius, 1775)
   T. z. gelo Waterhouse & Lyell, 1914

Subfamily Satyrinae

Melanitis Fabricius, 1807
Melanitis leda (Linnaeus, 1758)
**Melanitis amabilis* (Boisduval, 1832)
**Melanitis constantia* (Cramer, 1777)

Elymnias Hübner, 1818
Elymnias agondas (Boisduval, 1832)

Orsotriaena Wallengren, 1858
Orsotriaena medus (Fabricius, 1775)

Mycalesis Hübner, 1818
Mycalesis perseus (Fabricius, 1775)
Mycalesis sirius (Fabricius, 1775)
Mycalesis terminus (Fabricius, 1775)

Ypthima Hübner, 1818
Ypthima arctoa (Fabricius, 1775)

Hypocysta Westwood, 1851
Hypocysta adiante (Hübner, 1831)
  H. a. adiante (Hübner, 1831)
  H. a. antirius Butler, 1868
Hypocysta angustata Waterhouse & Lyell, 1914
Hypocysta euphemia Westwood, 1851
Hypocysta irius (Fabricius, 1775)
Hypocysta metirius Butler, 1875
Hypocysta pseudirius Butler, 1875

Nesoxenica Waterhouse & Lyell, 1914
Nesoxenica leprea (Hewitson, 1864)
  N. l. leprea (Hewitson, 1864)
  N. l. elia Waterhouse & Lyell, 1914

Argynnina Butler, 1867
Argynnina cyrila Waterhouse & Lyell, 1914
Argynnina hobartia (Westwood, 1851)
  A. h. hobartia (Westwood, 1851)
  A. h. tasmanica (Lyell, 1900)
  A. h. montana L.E. Couchman & R. Couchman, 1977

Oreixenica Waterhouse & Lyell, 1914
Oreixenica correae (Olliff, 1890)
Oreixenica kershawi (Miskin, 1876)
  O. k. kershawi (Miskin, 1876)
  O. k. ella (Olliff, 1888)
  O. k. kanunda Tindale, 1949
Oreixenica lathoniella (Westwood, 1851)
  O. l. lathoniella (Westwood, 1851)
  O. l. herceus Waterhouse & Lyell, 1914
  O. l. laranda Waterhouse & Lyell, 1914
  O. l. barnardi Turner, 1926
Oreixenica latialis Waterhouse & Lyell, 1914
  O. l. latialis Waterhouse & Lyell, 1914
  O. l. theddora L.E. Couchman, 1953
Oreixenica orichora (Meyrick, 1885)
  O. o. orichora (Meyrick, 1885)
  O. o. paludosa (T.P. Lucas, 1892)
Oreixenica ptunarra L.E. Couchman, 1953

Geitoneura Butler, 1867
Geitoneura acantha (Donovan, 1805)
Geitoneura klugii (Guérin-Méneville, 1830)
Geitoneura minyas (Waterhouse & Lyell, 1914)

Heteronympha Wallengren, 1858
Heteronympha banksii (Leach, 1814)
  H. b. banksii (Leach, 1814)
  H. b. mariposa Tindale, 1953
  H. b. nevina Tindale, 1953
Heteronympha cordace (Geyer, 1832)
  H. c. cordace (Geyer, 1832)
  H. c. comptena L.E. Couchman, 1954
  H. c. kurena L.E. Couchman, 1954
  H. c. legana L.E. Couchman, 1954
  H. c. wilsoni Burns, 1948
Heteronympha merope (Fabricius, 1775)
  H. m. merope (Fabricius, 1775)
  H. m. duboulayi (Butler, 1867)
  H. m. salazar Fruhstorfer, 1911
Heteronympha mirifica (Butler, 1866)
Heteronympha paradelpha Lower, 1893
Heteronympha penelope Waterhouse, 1937
  H. p. penelope Waterhouse, 1937
  H. p. alope Waterhouse, 1937
  H. p. diemeni Waterhouse, 1937
  H. p. panope Waterhouse, 1937
Heteronympha solandri Waterhouse, 1904

Tisiphone Hübner, 1819
Tisiphone abeona (Donovan, 1805)
  T. a. abeona (Donovan, 1805)
  T. a. rawnsleyi (Miskin, 1876)
  T. a. albifascia Waterhouse, 1904
  T. a. morrisi Waterhouse, 1914
  T. a. aurelia Waterhouse, 1915
  T. a. regalis Waterhouse, 1928
Tisiphone helena (Olliff, 1888)

Subfamily Amasthusiinae

Taenaris Hübner, 1819
Taenaris artemis (Snellen van Vollenhoven, 1860)
*Taenaris catops (Westwood, 1851)
*Taenaris myops (C. & R. Felder, 1860)

Subfamily Charaxinae

Polyura Billberg, 1820
Polyura sempronius (Fabricius, 1793)

Charaxes Ochsenheimer, 1816
Charaxes latona Butler, 1865

Subfamily Apaturinae

Apaturina Herrich-Schäffer, 1864
Apaturina erminea (Cramer, 1779)

Subfamily Acraeinae

Acraea Fabricius, 1807
Acraea andromacha (Fabricius, 1775)

Subfamily Heliconiinae

Cethosia Fabricius, 1807
Cethosia cydippe (Linnaeus, 1767)
Cethosia penthesilea (Cramer, 1777)

Vindula Hemming, 1934
Vindula arsinoe (Cramer, 1777)

Subfamily Argynninae

Cupha Billberg, 1820
Cupha prosope (Fabricius, 1775)

Vagrans Hemming, 1934
Vagrans egista (Cramer, 1780)

Phalanta Horsfield, 1829
Phalanta phalanta (Drury, 1773)

Argyreus Scopoli, 1777
Argyreus hyperbius (Linnaeus, 1763)

Subfamily Limenitinae

Pantoporia Hübner, 1819
Pantoporia consimilis (Boisduval, 1832)
Pantoporia venilia (Linnaeus, 1758)

Neptis Fabricius, 1807
Neptis praslini (Boisduval, 1832)

Phaedyma C. Felder, 1861
Phaedyma shepherdi (Moore, 1858)

Lexias Boisduval, 1832
Lexias aeropa (Linnaeus, 1758)

Subfamily Cyrestinae

Cyrestis Boisduval, 1832
*Cyrestis achates Butler, 1865

Subfamily Nymphalinae

Doleschallia C. & R. Felder, 1860
Doleschallia bisaltide (Cramer, 1777)

Hypolimnas Hübner, 1819
Hypolimnas alimena (Linnaeus, 1758)
   H. a. lamina Fruhstorfer, 1903
   H. a. darwinensis Waterhouse & Lyell, 1914
**Hypolimnas anomala* (Wallace, 1869)
**Hypolimnas antilope* (Cramer, 1777)
Hypolimnas bolina (Linnaeus, 1758)
Hypolimnas misippus (Linnaeus, 1764)

Yoma Doherty, 1886
Yoma sabina (Cramer, 1780)

Junonia Hübner, 1819
*Junonia erigone (Cramer, 1775)
Junonia hedonia (Linnaeus, 1764)
Junonia orithya (Linnaeus, 1758)
Junonia villida (Fabricius, 1787)

Vanessa Fabricius, 1807
**Vanessa cardui (Linnaeus, 1758)
Vanessa itea (Fabricius, 1775)
Vanessa kershawi (McCoy, 1868)

Mynes Boisduval, 1832
Mynes geoffroyi (Guérin-Ménville, 1830)

Subfamily Libytheinae

Libythea Fabricius, 1807
Libythea geoffroy Godart, 1824
   L. g. nicevillei Olliff, 1891
   L. g. genia Waterhouse, 1938

Family Lycaenidae

Subfamily Riodininae

Praetaxila Fruhstorfer, 1914
Praetaxila segecia (Hewitson, 1861)

Subfamily Liphyrinae

Liphyra Westwood, 1864
Liphyra brassolis Westwood, 1864

Subfamily Theclinae

Lucia Swainson, 1833
Lucia limbaria Swainson, 1833

Acrodipsas Sands, 1980
Acrodipsas arcana (Miller & E.D. Edwards, 1978)
Acrodipsas aurata Sands, 1997
Acrodipsas brisbanensis (Miskin, 1884)
Acrodipsas cuprea (Sands, 1965)
Acrodipsas decima (Miller & Lane, 2004)
Acrodipsas hirtipes Sands, 1980
Acrodipsas illidgei (Waterhouse & Lyell, 1914)
Acrodipsas melania Sands, 1980
Acrodipsas mortoni Sands, Miller & Kerr, 1997
Acrodipsas myrmecophila (Waterhouse & Lyell, 1913)

Paralucia Waterhouse & Turner, 1905
Paralucia aurifer (Blanchard, 1848)
Paralucia pyrodiscus (Doubleday, 1847)
   P. p. pyrodiscus (Doubleday, 1847)
   P. p. lucida (Crosby, 1951)
Paralucia spinifera E.D. Edwards & Common, 1978

Pseudodipsas C. & R. Felder, 1860
Pseudodipsas cephenes Hewitson, 1874
Pseudodipsas eone (C. & R. Felder, 1860)

Hypochrysops C. & R. Felder, 1860
Hypochrysops apelles (Fabricius, 1775)
Hypochrysops apollo Miskin, 1891
   H. a. apollo Miskin, 1891
   H. a. phoebus (Waterhouse, 1928)
Hypochrysops byzos (Boisduval, 1832)
**Hypochrysops chrysargyrus* Grose-Smith & Kirby, 1895
Hypochrysops cleon Grose-Smith, 1900
Hypochrysops cyane (Waterhouse & Lyell, 1914)
Hypochrysops delicia Hewitson, 1875
   H. d. delicia Hewitson, 1875
   H. d. duaringae (Waterhouse, 1903)
Hypochrysops digglesii (Hewitson, 1874)
Hypochrysops elgneri (Waterhouse & Lyell, 1909)
   H. e. elgneri (Waterhouse & Lyell, 1909)
   H. e. barnardi Waterhouse, 1934
Hypochrysops epicurus Miskin, 1876
Hypochrysops halyaetus Hewitson, 1874
Hypochrysops hippuris Hewitson, 1874
Hypochrysops ignitus (Leach, 1814)
   H. i. ignitus (Leach, 1814)
   H. i. olliffi Miskin, 1889
   H. i. chrysonotus Grose-Smith, 1899
   H. i. erythina (Waterhouse & Lyell, 1909)
Hypochrysops miskini (Waterhouse, 1903)
Hypochrysops narcissus (Fabricius, 1775)
   H. n. narcissus (Fabricius, 1775)
   H. n. sabirius (Fruhstorfer, 1908)
Hypochrysops piceatus Kerr, Macqueen & Sands, 1969
Hypochrysops polycletus (Linnaeus, 1758)
Hypochrysops pythias C. & R. Felder, 1865
Hypochrysops theon C. & R. Felder, 1865
   H. t. medocus (Fruhstorfer, 1908)
   H. t. cretatus Sands, 1986
   H. t. johnsoni Brown, Meyer & Weir, 2009

Philiris Röber, 1891
Philiris azula Wind & Clench, 1947
Philiris diana Waterhouse & Lyell, 1914
   P. d. diana Waterhouse & Lyell, 1914
   P. d. papuana Wind & Clench, 1947
Philiris fulgens (Grose-Smith & Kirby, 1897)
Philiris innotata (Miskin, 1874)
Philiris nitens (Grose-Smith, 1898)
   P. n. nitens (Grose-Smith, 1898)

P. n. lucina Waterhouse & Lyell, 1914
Philiris sappheira Sands, 1980
Philiris ziska (Grose-Smith, 1898)

Arhopala Boisduval, 1832
Arhopala centaurus (Fabricius, 1775)
   A. c. centaurus (Fabricius, 1775)
   A. c. asopus Waterhouse & Lyell, 1914
Arhopala madytus Fruhstorfer, 1914
Arhopala micale Blanchard, 1848
*Arhopala philander C. & R. Felder, 1865
Arhopala wildei Miskin, 1891

Ogyris Angas, 1847
Ogyris abrota (Westwood, 1851)
Ogyris aenone (Waterhouse, 1902)
Ogyris amaryllis (Hewitson, 1862)
   O. a. amaryllis (Hewitson, 1862)
   O. a. hewitsoni (Waterhouse, 1902)
   O. a. meridionalis (Bethune-Baker, 1905)
   O. a. amata (Waterhouse, 1934)
Ogyris barnardi (Miskin, 1890)
   O. b. barnardi (Miskin, 1890)
   O. b. delphis (Tindale, 1952)
Ogyris genoveva (Hewitson, 1853)
Ogyris halmaturia (Tepper, 1890)
Ogyris ianthis (Waterhouse, 1900)
Ogyris idmo (Hewitson, 1862)
   O. i. idmo (Hewitson, 1862)
Ogyris iphis (Waterhouse & Lyell, 1914)
   O. i. iphis (Waterhouse & Lyell, 1914)
   O. i. doddi (Waterhouse & Lyell, 1914)
Ogyris olane (Hewitson, 1862)
Ogyris oroetes (Hewitson, 1862)
   O. o. oroetes (Hewitson, 1862)
   O. o. apiculata (Quick, 1972)
Ogyris otanes (C. & R. Felder, 1865)
   O. o. otanes (C. & R. Felder, 1865)
   O. o. arcana Williams & Hay, 2001
   O. o. sublustris Williams & Hay, 2001
Ogyris subterrestris Field, 1999
   O. s. subterrestris Field, 1999
   O. s. petrina Field, 1999
Ogyris zosine (Hewitson, 1853)

Jalmenus Hübner, 1818
Jalmenus aridus Graham & Moulds, 1988
Jalmenus clementi H.H. Druce, 1902
Jalmenus daemeli Semper, 1879
Jalmenus eichhorni Staudinger, 1888
Jalmenus eubulus Miskin, 1876
Jalmenus evagoras (Donovan, 1805)
Jalmenus icilius Hewitson, 1865
Jalmenus ictinus Hewitson, 1865
Jalmenus inous Hewitson, 1865
   J. i. inous Hewitson, 1865
   J. i. notocrucifer Johnson, Hay & Bollam, 1992
   J. i. bronwynae Johnson & Valentine, 2007
Jalmenus lithochroa Waterhouse, 1903
Jalmenus pseudictinus Kerr & Macqueen, 1967

Pseudalmenus H.H. Druce, 1902
Pseudalmenus chlorinda (Blanchard, 1848)
   P. c. chlorinda (Blanchard, 1848)
   P. c. barringtonensis Waterhouse, 1928
   P. c. chloris Waterhouse & Lyell, 1914
   P. c. conara L.E. Couchman, 1965
   P. c. myrsilus (Westwood, 1851)
   P. c. zephyrus Waterhouse & Lyell, 1914

Hypolycaena C. & R. Felder, 1862
Hypolycaena danis (C. & R. Felder, 1865)
Hypolycaena litoralis Lambkin, Meyer, Brown & Weir, 2005
Hypolycaena phorbas (Fabricius, 1793)

Deudorix Hewitson, 1863
Deudorix democles Miskin, 1884
Deudorix diovis Hewitson, 1863
Deudorix epijarbas (Moore, 1858)
Deudorix epirus (C. Felder, 1860)
Deudorix smilis Hewitson, 1863

Rapala Moore, 1881
Rapala varuna (Horsfield, 1829)

Bindahara Moore, 1881
Bindahara phocides (Fabricius, 1793)

Subfamily Polyommatinae

Candalides Hübner, 1819
Candalides absimilis (C. Felder, 1862)
Candalides acastus (Cox, 1873)
Candalides consimilis Waterhouse, 1942
   C. c. consimilis Waterhouse, 1942
   C. c. goodingi Tindale, 1965
   C. c. toza (Kerr, 1967)
Candalides cyprotus (Olliff, 1886)
   C. c. cyprotus (Olliff, 1886)
   C. c. pallescens (Tite, 1963)
Candalides delospilus (Waterhouse, 1903)
Candalides erinus (Fabricius, 1775)
Candalides geminus E.D. Edwards & Kerr, 1978
Candalides gilberti Waterhouse, 1903
Candalides heathi (Cox, 1873)
   C. h. heathi (Cox, 1873)
   C. h. alpina Waterhouse, 1928
   C. h. doddi Burns, 1948
Candalides helenita (Semper, 1879)
Candalides hyacinthinus (Semper, 1879)
   C. h. hyacinthinus (Semper, 1879)
   C. h. simplex (Tepper, 1882)
   C. h. gilesi Williams & Bollam, 2001
Candalides margarita (Semper, 1879)
Candalides noelkeri Braby & Douglas, 2004
Candalides xanthospilos (Hübner, 1817)

Nesolycaena Waterhouse & Turner, 1905
Nesolycaena albosericea (Miskin, 1891)
Nesolycaena caesia d'Apice & Miller, 1992
Nesolycaena medicea Braby, 1996
Nesolycaena urumelia (Tindale, 1922)

Anthene Doubleday, 1847
Anthene lycaenoides (C. Felder, 1860)
Anthene seltuttus (Röber, 1886)

Petrelaea Toxopeus, 1929
Petrelaea tombugensis (Röber, 1886)

Nacaduba Moore, 1881
Nacaduba berenice (Herrich-Schäffer, 1869)
Nacaduba biocellata (C. & R. Felder, 1865)
*Nacaduba calauria (C. Felder, 1860)

Nacaduba cyanea (Cramer, 1775)
Nacaduba kurava (Moore, 1858)
   N. k. felsina Waterhouse & Lyell, 1914
   N. k. parma Waterhouse & Lyell, 1914
**Nacaduba pactolus* (C. Felder, 1860)

Erysichton Fruhstorfer, 1916
Erysichton lineata (Murray, 1874)
Erysichton palmyra (C. Felder, 1860)

Danis Fabricius, 1807
Danis danis (Cramer, 1775)
   D. d. syrius Miskin, 1890
   D. d. serapis Miskin, 1891

Nothodanis Hirowatari, 1992
**Nothodanis schaeffera* (Eschscholtz, 1821)

Psychonotis Toxopeus, 1930
Psychonotis caelius (C. & R. Felder, 1860)

Prosotas H.H. Druce, 1891
Prosotas dubiosa (Semper, 1879)
Prosotas felderi (Murray, 1874)
Prosotas nora (C. Felder, 1860)

Catopyrops Toxopeus, 1929
Catopyrops ancyra (C. Felder, 1860)
Catopyrops florinda (Butler, 1887)
   C. f. estrella (Waterhouse & Lyell, 1914)
   C. f. halys (Waterhouse, 1934)

Ionolyce Toxopeus, 1929
Ionolyce helicon (C. Felder, 1860)

Theclinesthes Röber, 1891
Theclinesthes albocincta (Waterhouse, 1903)
Theclinesthes hesperia Sibatani & Grund, 1978
   T. h. hesperia Sibatani & Grund, 1978
   T. h. littoralis Sibatani & Grund, 1978

Theclinesthes miskini (T.P. Lucas, 1889)
   T. m. miskini (T.P. Lucas, 1889)
   T. m. arnoldi (Fruhstorfer, 1916)
   T. m. eucalypti Sibatani & Grund, 1978
Theclinesthes onycha (Hewitson, 1865)
   T. o. onycha (Hewitson, 1865)
   T. o. capricornia Sibatani & Grund, 1978
Theclinesthes serpentata (Herrich-Schäffer, 1869)
   T. s. serpentata (Herrich-Schäffer, 1869)
   T. s. lavara (L. E. Couchman, 1954)
Theclinesthes sulpitius (Miskin, 1890)

Sahulana Hirowatari, 1992
Sahulana scintillata (T.P. Lucas, 1889)

Neolucia Waterhouse & Turner, 1905
Neolucia agricola (Westwood, 1851)
   N. a. agricola (Westwood, 1851)
   N. a. insulana Waterhouse & Lyell, 1914
   N. a. occidens Waterhouse & Lyell, 1914
Neolucia hobartensis (Miskin, 1890)
   N. h. hobartensis (Miskin, 1890)
   N. h. monticola Waterhouse & Lyell, 1914
Neolucia mathewi (Miskin, 1890)

Jamides Hübner, 1819
Jamides aleuas (C. & R. Felder, 1865)
*Jamides amarauge H.H. Druce, 1891
Jamides cytus (Boisduval, 1832)
**Jamides nemophilus* (Butler, 1876)
Jamides phaseli (Mathew, 1889)

Catochrysops Boisduval, 1832
Catochrysops amasea Waterhouse & Lyell, 1914

Catochrysops panormus (C. Felder, 1860)
   C. p. platissa (Herrich-Schäffer, 1869)
   C. p. papuanus Tite, 1959

Lampides Hübner, 1819
Lampides boeticus (Linnaeus, 1767)

Leptotes Scudder, 1876
Leptotes plinius (Fabricius, 1793)

Zizeeria Chapman, 1910
Zizeeria karsandra (Moore, 1865)

Zizina Chapman, 1910
Zizina labradus (Godart, 1824)
   Z. l. labradus (Godart, 1824)
   Z. l. labdalon Waterhouse & Lyell, 1914

Famegana Eliot, 1973
Famegana alsulus (Herrich-Schäffer, 1869)

Zizula Chapman, 1910
Zizula hylax (Fabricius, 1775)

Everes Hübner, 1819
Everes lacturnus Godart, 1824

Pithecops Horsfield, 1828
Pithecops dionisius (Boisduval, 1832)

Neopithecops Distant, 1884
Neopithecops lucifer (Röber, 1886)

Megisba Moore, 1881
Megisba strongyle (C. Felder, 1860)

Udara Toxopeus, 1928
Udara tenella (Miskin, 1891)

Euchrysops Butler, 1900
Euchrysops cnejus (Fabricius, 1798)

Freyeria Courvoisier, 1920
Freyeria putli (Kollar, 1844)

Appendix 2
LARVAL HOST PLANTS OF AUSTRALIAN BUTTERFLIES

Of 244 plant families recognised in the *Flora of Australia*, 105 are known to be attacked by butterfly larvae, some more than others. The table below indicates the number of host plant families attacked by major butterfly groups. When considered in relation to the number of butterfly species in each group, this gives a rough measure of degree of host plant specialisation by the group.

Butterfly Group	Number of Butterfly Species in Group	Number of Plant Families Utilised by Group
'Unorthodox' Skippers: Hesperiidae (Pyrginae + Coeliadinae)	15	19 (all dicotyledons)
'Orthodox' Skippers: Hesperiidae (Trapezitinae + Hesperiinae)	106	10 (all monocotyledons)
Swallowtails: Papilionidae	19	10 (all dicotyledons)
Whites and Yellows: Pieridae	34	12 (all dicotyledons)
Tigers, Crows and Hamadryad: Nymphalidae (Danainae + Tellervinae)	15	3 (all dicotyledons)
Browns and the Owl: Nymphalidae (Satyrinae + Amathusiinae)	35	4 (all monocotyledons)
Nymphs: Other Nymphalidae	30	31 (all dicotyledons)
Blues and Hairstreaks: Lycaenidae	148	58 (mainly dicotyledons; some non-flowering plants; Ferns and Cycads also utilised)

In this appendix, plant families are arranged in the order they appear in the *Flora of Australia*, following the well-known Cronquist system. Although this scheme is now rather dated, it is nevertheless still widely used and understood, and enables easy reference to most other botanical literature. In a few cases some recent divisions are recognised (e.g. Hemerocallidaceae [= Phormiaceae], formerly treated as part of the Liliaceae), where these do not affect the structure of the classification. On the other hand, the Euphorbiaceae, which has recently been split and rearranged, and the Sterculiaceae, which is now treated by many as defunct, are here retained.

Within each plant, family genera are arranged alphabetically. Butterfly larvae are grouped in families, indicated by the letters **H:** Hesperiidae, **Pa:** Papilionidae,

Pi: Pieridae, **N:** Nymphalidae and **L:** Lycaenidae, in that order. Within butterfly families, genera are listed as in Appendix 1: Checklist of Australian Butterflies, and species within genera are listed alphabetically. This arrangement ensures that closely related plant families appear near to each other, and it should be possible, by scanning the list, to appreciate and assess the degree of association between butterfly families and plant families. Non-native plants and butterflies are marked with an asterisk (*). For many plant species we also provide common names, generally using the name we judge most familiar, where a variety of names is available.

PTERIDOPHYTA (Ferns)

Polypodiaceae
Drynaria quercifolia (Oak-leafed Basket Fern)—
  L: *Hypochrysops theon*
Platycerium hillii (Elkhorn)—**L:** *Hypochrysops theon*
Polypodium sp.—**L:** *Hypochrysops hippuris*
Pyrrosia lanceolata—**L:** *Hypochrysops hippuris*

GYMNOSPERMAE (Non-Flowering Plants)

Cycadaceae (Cycads)
*Cycas circulus—**L:** *Theclinesthes onycha*
C. media—**L:** *Theclinesthes onycha*
C. megacarpa—**L:** *Theclinesthes onycha*
C. ophiolitica—**L:** *Theclinesthes onycha*
*C. robusta—**L:** *Theclinesthes onycha*

Zamiaceae (Cycads)
Macrozamia communis (Burrawang)—**L:** *Theclinesthes onycha*
M. pauli-guilielmi—**L:** *Theclinesthes onycha*
M. spiralis—**L:** *Theclinesthes onycha*

ANGIOSPERMAE (Flowering Plants)

DICOTYLEDONS (*non native*)

Winteraceae
Tasmannia lanceolata (Mountain Pepper Bush)—
  Pa: *Graphium macleayanum*
T. xerophila (Alpine Pepper Bush)—**Pa:** *Graphium macleayanum*

Eupomatiaceae
Eupomatia laurina (Bolwarra, Copper Laurel)—
  H: *Chaetocneme beata*

Magnoliaceae
*Magnolia sp.—**Pa:** *Graphium eurypylus*

Annonaceae (Custard Apples, Soursops and relatives)
Members of this family, and the following Monimiaceae, host mainly kite swallowtails (*Graphium* and *Protographium*), as well as a few 'atypical' skippers of the subfamily of flats (Pyrginae).
*Annona glabra (Pond Apple)—**Pa:** *Graphium agamemnon, G. eurypylus*
*A. muricata (Soursop)—**H:** *Chaetocneme critomedia,* **Pa:** *Graphium agamemnon, G. eurypylus, G. macfarlanei*
*A. reticulata (Custard Apple)—**H:** *Chaetocneme beata, C. critomedia,* **Pa:** *Graphium agamemnon, G. eurypylus, G. sarpedon*
*A. squamosa (Sweetsop)—**Pa:** *Graphium agamemnon, G. eurypylus*
Artabotrys sp.—**Pa:** *Graphium eurypylus*
Cyathostemma micranthum—**Pa:** *Graphium agamemnon*
Desmos goezeanus—**Pa:** *Graphium agamemnon, G. eurypylus*
D. wardianus—**Pa:** *Protographium leosthenes*
Desmos sp.—**Pa:** *Graphium agamemnon, G. eurypylus, G. macfarlanei*
Fitzalania heteropetala (Orange Annona)—**Pa:** *Graphium agamemnon, G. eurypylus*
Goniothalamus australis (China Pine)—**Pa:** *Graphium agamemnon*
Haplostichanthus johnsonii—**Pa:** *Graphium agamemnon*
Haplostichanthus sp.—**Pa:** *Graphium agamemnon*
Meiogyne sp.—**Pa:** *Graphium agamemnon*

Melodorum leichhardtii (Zig-zag Vine)—**H:** *Chaetocneme beata*, **Pa:** *Protographium leosthenes*, *Graphium agamemnon*, *G. eurypylus*
M. rupestrum—**Pa:** *Protographium leosthenes*, *G. eurypylus*
M. urhii—**Pa:** *Graphium agamemnon*
Melodorum sp.—**Pa:** *Graphium agamemnon*, *G. eurypylus*
Miliusa brahei (Raspberry Jelly Tree)—**Pa:** *Graphium agamemnon*, *G. eurypylus*
M. traceyi—**Pa:** *Graphium agamemnon*, *Graphium aristeus*, *G. eurypylus*
Polyalthia australis (Mast Tree)—**Pa:** *G. eurypylus*
P. michaelii (Canary Beech)—**Pa:** *Graphium agamemnon*
P. nitidissima (Canary Beech)—**Pa:** *Graphium agamemnon*, *Graphium aristeus*, *G. eurypylus*
Polyalthia sp.—**Pa:** *Graphium agamemnon*, *G. eurypylus*
Pseuduvaria froggattii (Yellowwood)—**Pa:** *Graphium agamemnon*, *Graphium aristeus*, *G. eurypylus*
P. hylandii—**Pa:** *Graphium agamemnon*
P. mulgraveana (Yellowwood)—**Pa:** *Graphium agamemnon*
P. villosa—**Pa:** *Graphium agamemnon*
Rollinia deliciosa* (Brazilian Custard Apple)—Pa:** *Graphium agamemnon*, *Graphium macfarlanei*
Uvaria concava—**Pa:** *Graphium agamemnon*, *G. eurypylus*
U. rufa—**Pa:** *Graphium agamemnon*, *G. eurypylus*
Xylopia maccreae—**Pa:** *Graphium agamemnon*
Xylopia sp.—**Pa:** *Graphium agamemnon*

Monimiaceae (Australian Sassafras and Wilkieas)

Antherosperma moschatum (Blackhearted Sassafras)—**Pa:** *Graphium macleayanum*
Daphnandra micrantha (Illawarra Socketwood)—**Pa:** *Graphium macleayanum*
D. repandula (Northern Sassafras)—**Pa:** *Graphium macleayanum*
Doryphora aromatica (Sassafras)—**Pa:** *Graphium macleayanum*, *G. sarpedon*
D. sassafras (Sassafras)—**Pa:** *Graphium macleayanum*
Tetrasynandra laxiflora (Tetra Beech)—**H:** *Euschemon rafflesia*
T. pubescens—**H:** *Euschemon rafflesia*, **L:** *Hypochrysops miskini*
Wilkiea austroqueenslandica (Smooth Wilkiea)—**H:** *Euschemon rafflesia*
W. huegeliana (Veiny Wilkiea)—**H:** *Euschemon rafflesia*
W. macrophylla (Large-leafed Wilkiea)—**H:** *Euschemon rafflesia*

Lauraceae (Laurels and Dodders)

Members of this family host mainly kite swallowtails (*Graphium*), a few 'atypical' skippers of the subfamily of flats (Hesperiidae: Pyrginae), and certain blues (Lycaenidae), especially those feeding on Dodder, a parasitic vine.

Beilschmiedia obtusifolia (Blush Walnut)—**Pa:** *Graphium sarpedon*
Cassytha aurea (Golden Dodder)—**L:** *Candalides erinus*
C. capillaris—**L:** *Candalides delospilus*, *C. erinus*
C. filiformis (Dodder)—**L:** *Candalides acastus*, *C. delospilus*, *C. erinus*
C. flindersii (Dodder)—**L:** *Candalides hyacinthinus*
C. glabella (Devil's Twine)—**L:** *Candalides acastus*
C. melantha (Large Dodder)—**L:** *Candalides hyacinthinus*
C. peninsularis (Streaked Dodder)—**L:** *Candalides acastus*, *C. hyacinthinus*
C. pubescens (Downy Dodder)—**L:** *Candalides acastus*, *C. erinus*, *C. geminus*, *C. hyacinthinus*
C. racemosa (Dodder)—**L:** *Candalides hyacinthinus*
Cinnamomum camphora* (Camphor Laurel)—H:** *Chaetocneme beata*, *C. porphyropis*, **Pa:** *Graphium macleayanum*, *G. sarpedon*, **N:** *Polyura sempronius*
C. oliveri (Oliver's Sassafras)—**H:** *Chaetocneme critomedia*, **Pa:** *Graphium macleayanum*, *G. sarpedon*
Cryptocarya corrugata (Acidwood)—**Pa:** *Graphium sarpedon*
C. densiflora (White Laurel)—**Pa:** *Graphium sarpedon*
C. erythroxylon (Pigeonberry Ash)—**H:** *Chaetocneme beata*, *Netrocoryne repanda*, **Pa:** *Graphium macleayanum*, *G. sarpedon*
C. glaucescens (Jackwood)—**H:** *Netrocoryne repanda*
C. grandis (Cinnamon Laurel)—**H:** *Chaetocneme porphyropis*
C. hypospodia (Rib-fruited Pepperberry)—**H:** *Chaetocneme critomedia*, **Pa:** *Graphium macleayanum*, *G. sarpedon*, **L:** *Arhopala micale*, *Candalides helenita*, *Anthene seltuttus*
C. mackinnoniana (Rusty Laurel)—**Pa:** *Graphium sarpedon*, **L:** *Philiris fulgens*
C. microneura (Murrogun)—**H:** *Chaetocneme beata*, *Netrocoryne repanda*, **Pa:** *Graphium macleayanum*, *G. sarpedon*
C. murrayi (Murray's Laurel)—**Pa:** *Graphium sarpedon*, **L:** *Philiris fulgens*
C. triplinervis (Three-veined Laurel)—**H:** *Chaetocneme critomedia*, *Netrocoryne repanda*, **Pa:** *Graphium macleayanum*, *G. sarpedon*, **N:** *Charaxes latona*
Cryptocarya sp.—**H:** *Chaetocneme critomedia*
Cryptocarya sp. aff. *rigida*—**H:** *Chaetocneme beata*, *C. porphyropis*, *Netrocoryne repanda*
Endiandra compressa (White Bark)—**H:** *Chaetocneme porphyropis*
E. discolor (Rose Walnut)—**Pa:** *Graphium macleayanum*
E. glauca (Brown Walnut)—**H:** *Chaetocneme critomedia*
E. hypotephra (Northern Rose Walnut)—**L:** *Philiris fulgens*
E. impressicosta (Steelbutt)—**Pa:** *Graphium sarpedon*
E. pubens (Hairy Walnut)—**Pa:** *Graphium macleayanum*
E. sieberi (Hard Corkwood)—**H:** *Netrocoryne repanda*
Litsea bindoniana (Bollywood)—**H:** *Netrocoryne repanda*, **Pa:** *Graphium sarpedon*
L. breviumbellata (Bollywood)—**H:** *Chaetocneme critomedia*, *Netrocoryne repanda*, **Pa:** *Graphium sarpedon*, **L:** *Philiris diana*, *P. fulgens*
L. glutinosa (Bollywood)—**H:** *Chaetocneme critomedia*, **Pa:** *Graphium sarpedon*

L. leefeana (Brown Bolly Gum)—**H:** *Chaetocneme beata, C. porphyropis, Netrocoryne repanda,* **Pa:** *Graphium sarpedon,* **L:** *Philiris fulgens*
L. macrophylla—**H:** *Chaetocneme critomedia*
L. reticulata (Bollywood)—**Pa:** *Graphium sarpedon*
Litsea sp.—**L:** *Philiris diana*
Neolitsea australiensis (Green Bolly Gum)—
   H: *Chaetocneme critomedia,* **Pa:** *Graphium sarpedon*
N. dealbata (Hairy-leaved Bolly Gum)—**H:** *Chaetocneme beata, C. critomedia, C. porphyropis, Netrocoryne repanda,* **Pa:** *Graphium sarpedon*
Neolitsea sp.—**H:** *Netrocoryne repanda*

Aristolochiaceae (Dutchman's Pipes)

Aristolochias, or Dutchman's pipes, host the larvae of all troidine swallowtails, birdwings, the Big Greasy and the Red-bodied Swallowtail. Few other Lepidoptera attack them. The species in the genus *Aristolochia* generally have soft leaves, those of *Pararistolochia* being very hard-leaved.

Aristolochia acuminata—**Pa:** *Cressida cressida, Pachliopta polydorus, Ornithoptera euphorion, O. priamus*
A. chalmersii—**Pa:** *Cressida cressida, Pachliopta polydorus, Ornithoptera priamus*
*A. elegans (Cultivated Dutchman's Pipe)—**Pa:** *Cressida cressida, Ornithoptera euphorion* (larvae of both said to sometimes feed on flowers)
A. holzei—**Pa:** *Cressida cressida*
A. indica (Birthwort)—**Pa:** *Ornithoptera euphorion*
A. meridionalis—**Pa:** *Cressida cressida*
A. pubera—**Pa:** *Cressida cressida, Ornithoptera euphorion*
A. thozetii—**Pa:** *Cressida cressida, Pachliopta polydorus, Ornithoptera euphorion*
Pararistolochia australopithecurus—**Pa:** *Pachliopta polydorus, Ornithoptera euphorion*
P. deltantha—**Pa:** *Pachliopta polydorus, Ornithoptera euphorion*
P. laheyana—**Pa:** *Ornithoptera richmondia*
P. linearifolia—**Pa:** *Pachliopta polydorus*
P. peninsulensis—**Pa:** *Pachliopta polydorus*
P. praevenosa (Richmond Birdwing Vine)—
   Pa: *Ornithoptera richmondia*
P. sparusifolia—**Pa:** *Ornithoptera euphorion*

Ulmaceae (Elms and Hackberries)

Aphananthe philippinensis (Native Elm)—**N:** *Phaedyma shepherdi,* **L:** *Nacaduba berenice*
*Celtis occidentalis (Hackberry)—**N:** *Polyura sempronius*
C. paniculata—**N:** *Polyura sempronius, Phaedyma shepherdi, Libythea geoffroy*
C. philippensis—**N:** *Polyura sempronius, Phaedyma shepherdi*
*C. sinensis—**N:** *Polyura sempronius, Phaedyma shepherdi*
Celtis sp. aff. *timorensis*—**N:** *Phaedyma shepherdi*
Trema tomentosa (Poison Peach)—**L:** *Catopyrops florinda*

Moraceae (Figs)

Only certain crows (Nymphalidae, *Euploea* sp.) and the Common Moonbeam (Lycaenidae, *Philiris innotata*) are known to feed on figs.

*Ficus benghalensis—**L:** *Philiris innotata*
F. benjamina (Weeping Fig)—**N:** *Euploea core*
*F. carica (Common Fig)—**L:** *Philiris innotata*
F. congesta (Cluster Fig)—**L:** *Philiris innotata*
F. coronata (Sandpaper Fig)—**N:** *Euploea core,* **L:** *Philiris innotata*
*F. lyrata—**N:** *Euploea core*
F. microcarpa (Small-fruited Fig)—**N:** *Euploea core*
*F. natalensis—**N:** *Euploea core*
F. obliqua (Small Leafed Fig)—**N:** *Euploea alcathoe, E. core*
F. opposita (Sandpaper Fig)—**L:** *Philiris innotata,* **N:** *Euploea core*
F. platypoda (Australian Rock Fig)—**N:** *Euploea core*
F. racemosa (Cluster Fig)—**N:** *Euploea sylvester*
F. rubiginosa (Port Jackson Fig)—**N:** *Euploea core*
F. virens (Curtain Fig)—**N:** *Euploea core*
Ficus sp. **N:** *Euploea core,* **L:** *Philiris innotata*
Trophis scandens (Burney Vine)—**N:** *Euploea darchia, E. tulliolus*

Urticaceae (Nettles and Stinging Trees)

Dendrocnide moroides (Gympie Tree)—**N:** *Mynes geoffroyi*
D. photinophylla (Shining Leaf stinging Tree)—**N:** *Mynes geoffroyi*
Parietaria debilis (Native Pellitory)—**N:** *Vanessa itea*
*P. judaica—**N:** *Vanessa itea*
Pipturus argenteus (Native Mulberry)—**N:** *Vanessa itea, Mynes geoffroyi,* **L:** *Rapala varuna, Catopyrops ancyra, C. florinda*
*Soleirolia soleirolii—**N:** *Vanessa itea*
Urtica incisa (Stinging Nettle)—**N:** *Vanessa itea*
*U. urens—**N:** *Vanessa itea*

Fagaceae (Oaks)

*Quercus palustris (Pin Oak)—**N:** *Polyura sempronius*

Casuarinaceae

Allocasuarina luehmannii (Bulloak)—**L:** *Hypochrysops piceatus*

Aizoaceae

Sesuvium portulacastrum (Sea Purslane)—**L:** *Theclinesthes sulpitius*

Chenopodiaceae (Saltbushes and Samphires)

Species of this family are host to just two species of blues (Lycaenidae, *Theclinesthes* sp.).

Atriplex australasica (Green Saltbush)—**L:** *Theclinesthes serpentata*
A. eichleri (Eichler's Saltbush)—**L:** *Theclinesthes serpentata*
A. elachophylla (Annual Saltbush)—**L:** *Theclinesthes serpentata*
A. holocarpa (Pop Saltbush)—**L:** *Theclinesthes serpentata*
A. leptocarpa (Slender-fruit Saltbush)—**L:** *Theclinesthes serpentata*
A. limbata (Spreading Saltbush)—**L:** *Theclinesthes serpentata*

A. lindleyi (Eastern Flat-top Saltbush)—**L:** *Theclinesthes serpentata*
A. muelleri (Annual Saltbush)—**L:** *Theclinesthes serpentata*
A. nummularia (Old Man Saltbush)—**L:** *Theclinesthes serpentata*
A. obconica (Saltbush)—**L:** *Theclinesthes serpentata*
A. paludosa (Marsh Saltbush)—**L:** *Theclinesthes serpentata*
A. pseudocampanulata (Mealy Saltbush)—**L:** *Theclinesthes serpentata*
A. pumilio (Mat Saltbush)—**L:** *Theclinesthes serpentata*
A. quinii (Kidney-fruit Saltbush)—**L:** *Theclinesthes serpentata*
A. rhagodioides (Silver Saltbush)—**L:** *Theclinesthes serpentata*
A. semibaccata (Spreading Saltbush, Berry Saltbush)— **L:** *Theclinesthes serpentata*
A. spongiosa (Little Pop Saltbush)—**L:** *Theclinesthes serpentata*
A. suberecta (Sprawling Saltbush)—**L:** *Theclinesthes serpentata*
A. velutinella (Sandhill Saltbush)—**L:** *Theclinesthes serpentata*
A. vesicaria (Bladder Saltbush)—**L:** *Theclinesthes serpentata*
*Chenopodium album (Fat Hen)—**L:** *Theclinesthes serpentata*
C. nitrariaceum (Nitre Goosefoot)—**L:** *Theclinesthes serpentata*
Einadia hastata (Berry Saltbush)—**L:** *Theclinesthes serpentata*
E. nutans (Climbing Saltbush)—**L:** *Theclinesthes serpentata*
Halosarcia indica (Samphire)—**L:** *Theclinesthes sulpitius*
Rhagodia candolleana (Sea Berry Saltbush)— **L:** *Theclinesthes serpentata*
R. crassifolia (Spiny Saltbush)—**L:** *Theclinesthes serpentata*
R. eremaea (Tall Saltbush)—**L:** *Theclinesthes serpentata*
R. parabolica (Fragrant Saltbush)—**L:** *Theclinesthes serpentata*
R. preissii (Mallee Saltbush)—**L:** *Theclinesthes serpentata*
R. spinescens (Thorny Saltbush)—**L:** *Theclinesthes serpentata*
Sarcocornia quinqueflora (Beaded Glasswort)— **L:** *Theclinesthes sulpitius*
Suaeda australis (Seablite)—**L:** *Theclinesthes sulpitius*
Tecticornia australasica (Samphire)—**L:** *Theclinesthes sulpitius*

Amaranthaceae (Amaranths)
Alternanthera angustifolia (Narrowleaf Joyweed)— **N:** *Hypolimnas bolina*
A. denticulata (Calico Plant)—**N:** *Hypolimnas bolina*
*A. sessilis—**N:** *Hypolimnas bolina*

Portulacaceae (Purslane or Pigweed)
Portulaca oleracea (Pigweed)—**N:** *Hypolimnas misippus, Junonia villida*

Molluginaceae (Carpet Weeds) (= Aizoaceae)
Glinus lotoides (Hairy Carpet Weed)—**L:** *Zizeeria karsandra*
G. oppositifolia (Slender Carpet Weed)—**L:** *Zizeeria karsandra*

Polygonaceae (Docks and Knotweeds)
Persicaria prostrata (Creeping Knotweed)— **N:** *Hypolimnas bolina*

Plumbaginaceae (Plumbagos)
*Plumbago auriculata (Plumbago)—**L:** *Leptotes plinius*
P. zeylanica (Native Plumbago)—**L:** *Leptotes plinius*

Ochnaceae (Mickey Mouse Plant)
*Ochna serrulata (Mickey Mouse Plant)—**N:** *Polyura sempronius*

Theaceae (Tea family)
*Camelia sp.—**L:** *Hypochrysops ignitus*

Clusiaceae
Calophyllum inophyllum (Mastwood, Ball Nut)— **L:** *Arhopala micale*

Elaeocarpaceae (Quandongs)
Elaeocarpus angustifolius (Quandong)—**L:** *Deudorix diovis*
E. obovatus (Hard Quandong)—**L:** *Hypochrysops ignitus*
E. reticulatus (Blueberry Ash)—**H:** *Netrocoryne repanda*

Tiliaceae
Grewia papuana—**N:** *Phaedyma shepherdi*
Trichospermum pleiostigma (Whitfield Ash)— **L:** *Hypochrysops pythias*

Sterculiaceae (Kurrajongs and allies)
Brachychiton acerifolius (Illawarra Flame Tree)— **N:** *Polyura sempronius, Phaedyma shepherdi,* **L:** *Candalides absimilis, C. helenita, Anthene seltuttus, Erysichton lineata*
B. australis (Broad-leafed Bottle Tree)—**N:** *Polyura sempronius, Phaedyma shepherdi*
B. discolor (Lace Tree)—**N:** *Polyura sempronius, Phaedyma shepherdi*
B. paradoxus (Red-flowered Kurrajong)—**L:** *Hypochrysops ignitus*
B. populneus (Kurrajong)—**H:** *Netrocoryne repanda,* **N:** *Polyura sempronius, Phaedyma shepherdi,* **L:** *Candalides absimilis*
Commersonia bartramia (Brown Kurrajong)— **H:** *Chaetocneme critomedia,* **L:** *Hypochrysops miskini, H. pythias*
C. fraseri (Brush Kurrajong)—**L:** *Hypochrysops byzos*
Commersonia sp.—**H:** *Chaetocneme beata*
Heritiera littoralis (Looking-glass Mangrove)— **L:** *Arhopala micale*
Rulingia salviifolia—**L:** *Hypochrysops byzos*
Sterculia sp. (Tropical Chestnuts)—**N:** *Polyura sempronius*

Bombacaceae
Bombax ceiba (Red Silk Cotton Tree)—**N:** *Phaedyma shepherdi*

Malvaceae (Mallow family)
Argyrodendron actinophyllum (Black Booyong)—**N:** *Polyura sempronius, Phaedyma shepherdi*
Hibiscus tiliaceus (Cotton tree)—**L:** *Arhopala madytus, A. micale*
*Hibiscus sp.—**H:** *Chaetocneme beata*
*Lavatera arborea (Tree Mallow)—**N:** *Vanessa cardui*
*Sida acuta (Spinyhead)—**N:** *Hypolimnas bolina*
S. rhombifolia (Paddy's Lucerne)—**N:** *Hypolimnas bolina*

Lecythidaceae (Brazil Nut family)
Barringtonia sp.—**L:** *Hypochrysops apelles*
Planchonia careya (Cocky Apple)—**H:** *Chaetocneme denitza*, **L:** *Hypochrysops apelles, H. elgneri, H. ignitus, Hypolycaena phorbas*

Flacourtiaceae
This family is mainly host to a group of fritillary allies (Nymphalidae: Argynninae), including three closely related genera, *Cupha, Phalanta* and *Vagrans*.
*Flacourtia indica (Governor's Plum)—**N:** *Cupha prosope*
*F. inermis (Lori Lori)—**N:** *Phalanta phalanta*
F. jangomas (Indian Plum)—**N:** *Cupha prosope*
*F. rukam—**N:** *Phalanta phalanta*
F. territorialis—**N:** *Phalanta phalanta*
Flacourtia sp.—**N:** *Cupha prosope*
Homalium circumpinnatum (Brown Boxwood)—**N:** *Vagrans egista*
Scolopia braunii (Flint Wood)—**H:** *Netrocoryne repanda*, **N:** *Cupha prosope*
Xylosma ovatum—**N:** *Cupha prosope*
X. terrae-reginae—**N:** *Cupha prosope*
Xylosma sp.—**N:** *Cupha prosope*

Violaceae (Violets and Spadeflowers)
This family hosts only the Glasswing (Nymphalidae: Acraeinae) and the Australian Fritillary (Nymphalidae: Argynninae).
Hybanthus aurantiacus (Scrub Violet)—**N:** *Acraea andromacha*
H. enneaspermus (Spade Flower)—**N:** *Acraea andromacha*
H. stellaroides (Spade Flower)—**N:** *Acraea andromacha*
Viola betonicifolia (Native Violet)—**N:** *Argyreus hyperbius*

Passifloraceae (Passion Vines)
This family hosts only the Glasswing (Nymphalidae: Acraeinae, *Acraea andromacha*) and the Cruiser (*Vindula arsinoe*) and two lacewings (*Cethosia* sp.) (all Nymphalidae: Heliconiinae).
Adenia heterophylla—**N:** *Acraea andromacha, Cethosia cydippe, C. penthesilea, Vindula arsinoe*
Hollrungia sp.—**N:** *Cethosia cydippe, Vindula arsinoe*
Passiflora aurantia—**N:** *Acraea andromacha, Vindula arsinoe*
P. cinnabarina—**N:** *Acraea andromacha*
P. foetida—**N:** *Acraea andromacha*
P. herbertiana—**N:** *Acraea andromacha*
*P. mollissima—**N:** *Acraea andromacha*
*P. suberosa—**N:** *Acraea andromacha*
*P. subpeltata—**N:** *Acraea andromacha*

Capparaceae (Caper family)
Members of the Caper family host only whites (Pieridae: Pierinae).
Apophyllum anomalum (Currant Bush)—**Pi:** *Belenois java*
Capparis arborea (Native Pomegranate)—**Pi:** *Elodina angulipennis, E. parthia, Belenois java, Cepora perimale*
C. canescens (Dog Caper)—**Pi:** *Elodina angulipennis, E. padusa, E. parthia, Belenois java, Cepora perimale*
C. lasiantha (Nepine)—**Pi:** *Elodina padusa, Belenois java*
C. mitchellii (Wild Orange)—**Pi:** *Elodina padusa, Belenois java*
C. sarmentosa—**Pi:** *Elodina angulipennis, E. parthia, E. queenslandica, Belenois java, Cepora perimale*
C. sepiaria (Wild Orange)—**Pi:** *Elodina perdita, E. queenslandica, E. walkeri, Appias paulina, Belenois java, Cepora perimale*
C. spinosa (Wild Passionfruit)—**Pi:** *Elodina parthia, Belenois java*
C. umbonata (Bush Orange)—**Pi:** *Belenois java*
*Cleome sp.—**Pi:** **Pieris rapae*
Crateva religiosa (Temple Tree)—**Pi:** *Appias ada*

Brassicaceae (Cabbage and Mustard family)
*Brassica sp.—**Pi:** **Pieris rapae*
*Hirschfeldia incana (Greek Mustard)—**Pi:** **Pieris rapae*
*Lepidium africanum—**Pi:** **Pieris rapae*
*Sisymbrium officinale (Hedge Mustard)—**Pi:** **Pieris rapae*

Resedaceae (Mignonettes)
*Reseda sp.—Pi: **Pieris rapae*

Epacridaceae (Heath family)
Brachyloma daphnoides (Daphne Heath)—**L:** *Hypochrysops ignitus*
Epacris breviflora (Drumstick Heath)—**L:** *Neolucia hobartensis*
E. paludosa (Swamp Heath)—**L:** *Neolucia hobartensis*
E. petrophila (Snow Heath)—**L:** *Neolucia hobartensis*
Epacris sp.—**L:** *Neolucia hobartensis*
Monotoca elliptica (Tree Broom-heath)—**L:** *Neolucia mathewi*
M. oreophila (Mountain Broom-heath)—**L:** *Neolucia mathewi*

Sapotaceae
Planchonella queenslandica (Blush Coondoo)—**Pa:** *Graphium sarpedon*

Ebenaceae (Ebony and Persimmon family)
Diospyros fasciculosa (Grey Ebony)—**L:** *Pseudodipsas cephenes*

Myrsinaceae (Muttonwoods and allies)

Aegiceras corniculatum (River Mangrove)—
  L: *Hypochrysops narcissus, Hypolycaena phorbas, Nacaduba kurava*
Embelia curvinervia—**L:** *Nacaduba kurava*
Maesa dependens—**L:** *Hypochrysops miskini, Nacaduba kurava*
M. haplobotrys—**L:** *Nacaduba kurava*
Rapanea porosa (Salmon Muttonwood)—**L:** *Praetaxila segecia*
R. variabilis (Muttonwood)—**L:** *Nacaduba kurava*

Connaraceae

Connarus conchocarpus (Conch Vine)—**L:** *Deudorix diovis, D. epijarbas, Danis danis*
Rourea coccinea—**L:** *Danis danis*

Cunoniaceae

Callicoma serratifolia (Black Wattle)—**H:** *Netrocoryne repanda*
Ceratopetalum gummiferum (NSW Christmas Bush)—
  L: *Candalides consimilis*

Pittosporaceae

Bursaria incana—**L:** *Paralucia pyrodiscus*
B. spinosa (Blackthorn)—**L:** *Paralucia aurifer, P. pyrodiscus, P. spinifera*
Pittosporum multiflorum (Orange Thorn)—**L:** *Paralucia aurifer*
P. spinescens (Wallaby Apple)—**L:** *Paralucia pyrodiscus*
P. undulatum (Mock Orange)—**L:** *Deudorix diovis*

Rosaceae (Rose family)

*Eriobotrya japonica (Loquat)—**L:** *Rapala varuna*
*Prunus sp.—**H:** *Netrocoryne repanda,* **L:** *Hypochrysops ignitus*
*Rosa sp.—**L:** *Hypochrysops ignitus*
*Rubus fruticosus (Blackberry)—**L:** *Hypochrysops ignitus*

Chrysobalanaceae

Maranthes corymbosa—**L:** *Arhopala centaurus*
Parinari nonda (Nonda Plum)—**L:** *Arhopala micale*

Surianaceae

Guilfoylia monostylis—**N:** *Polyura sempronius*

Mimosaceae (Wattles and allies)

This large family is primarily host to endemic blues and hairstreaks, but many species are attacked by the Tailed Emperor (*Polyura sempronius*), and some are host plants for various grass yellows (*Eurema* spp.). Because of the difficulties of identifying *Acacia* species, it is sometimes impossible to say with certainty which of several similar species actually provided the host plant record.

Acacia acradenia—**L:** *Nacaduba biocellata, Theclinesthes miskini*
A. acuminata (Raspberry Jam Wattle)—**L:** *Jalmenus icilius*
A. alexandri—**L:** *Jalmenus clementi, Theclinesthes miskini*
A. anceps (Port Lincoln Wattle)—**L:** *Jalmenus icilius, Nacaduba biocellata, Theclinesthes miskini*
A. aneura (Mulga)—**L:** *Jalmenus icilius, Nacaduba biocellata*
A. aulacocarpa—see *A. disparrima*
A. auriculiformis (Northern Black Wattle)—**L:** *Prosotas dubiosa, Theclinesthes miskini*
A. baileyana (Cootamundra Wattle)—**Pi:** *Eurema hecabe,* **N:** *Polyura sempronius,* **L:** *Hypochrysops delicia*
A. bancroftii (Bancroft's Wattle)—**L:** *Jalmenus daemeli*
A. betchei—**L:** *Nacaduba biocellata*
A. bidwillii (Dogwood)—**L:** *Jalmenus daemeli, J. icilius, Nacaduba biocellata*
A. binervata (Two-veined Hickory)—**L:** *Jalmenus evagoras*
A. binervia (Coast Myall)—**L:** *Hypochrysops delicia*
A. brachybotrya (Grey Mulga)—**L:** *Nacaduba biocellata*
A. calamifolia (Wallowa)—**L:** *Jalmenus icilius, Nacaduba biocellata*
A. concurrens (Black Wattle)—**L:** *Prosotas felderi*; also see *A. leiocalyx*
A. conferta—**L:** *Nacaduba biocellata*
A. coriacea (Dogwood)—**L:** *Nacaduba biocellata*
A. crassicarpa (Thick-podded Salwood)—**L:** *Jalmenus eichhorni, Theclinesthes miskini*
A. cyclops (Red-eyed Wattle)—**L:** *Nacaduba biocellata*
A. dealbata (Silver Wattle)—**N:** *Polyura sempronius,* **L:** *Hypochrysops delicia, Jalmenus evagoras, J. icilius, J. ictinus, Pseudalmenus chlorinda*
A. deanei (Green-barked Wattle)—**Pi:** *Eurema hecabe,* **N:** *Polyura sempronius,* **L:** *Jalmenus icilius, Nacaduba biocellata*
A. decurrens (Green-barked Wattle)—**N:** *Polyura sempronius,* **L:** *Hypochrysops delicia, H. ignitus, Jalmenus daemeli, J. evagoras, J. ictinus, Pseudalmenus chlorinda, Nacaduba biocellata*
A. difficilis—**L:** *Theclinesthes miskini*
A. disparrima (Hickory Wattle)—**L:** *Hypochrysops delicia, H. ignitus, Jalmenus evagoras, Nacaduba biocellata, Prosotas dubiosa, P. felderi, Theclinesthes miskini, Sahulana scintillata*
A. elata (Cedar Wattle)—**L:** *Pseudalmenus chlorinda*
A. erinacea (Prickly Wattle)—**L:** *Nacaduba biocellata*
A. falcata (Sickle-leaf Wattle)—**L:** *Jalmenus evagoras, Prosotas felderi*
A. filicifolia (Fern-leafed Wattle)—**L:** *Jalmenus evagoras*
A. fimbriata (Brisbane Wattle)—**L:** *Jalmenus evagoras*
A. flavescens (Red Wattle)—**L:** *Pseudodipsas cephenes, Hypochrysops apelles, H. delicia, H. ignitus, Jalmenus pseudictinus, Theclinesthes miskini*
A. floribunda (Catkin Wattle)—**L:** *Jalmenus evagoras, Prosotas felderi*
A. gentistifolia—**L:** *Jalmenus evagoras*
A. glaucocarpa (Feathery Wattle)—**N:** *Polyura sempronius* **L:** *Jalmenus daemeli*
A. granitica (Granite Wattle)—**L:** *Prosotas felderi*
A. halliana—**L:** *Nacaduba biocellata*

A. harpophylla (Brigalow)—**L:** *Jalmenus daemeli, J. eubulus, J. icilius, J. ictinus, J. pseudictinus, Theclinesthes miskini*
A. hemignosta—**L:** *Prosotas dubiosa*
A. holosericea (Silver-leafed Wattle)—**L:** *Hypochrysops ignitus, Jalmenus eichhorni, Theclinesthes miskini*
A. humifusa—**L:** *Hypochrysops cyane, Jalmenus eichhorni, J. pseudictinus*
A. implexa (Hickory Wattle)—**L:** *Hypochrysops delicia, Jalmenus evagoras, J. ictinus, Nacaduba biocellata*
A. inaequilatera—**L:** *Jalmenus clementi*
A. ingramii—**L:** *Jalmenus evagoras*
A. irrorata (Green-barked Wattle)—**L:** *Hypochrysops delicia, Jalmenus daemeli, J. evagoras, Nacaduba biocellata*
A. juncifolia (Rush Wattle)—**L:** *Hypochrysops ignitus*
A. karroo*—L:** *Nacaduba biocellata*
A. leiocalyx (Black Wattle)—**L:** *Hypochrysops delicia, Jalmenus daemeli, J. evagoras, J. ictinus, Prosotas dubiosa, P. felderi, Sahulana scintillata*
A. leiophylla (Coast Golden Wattle)—**L:** *Hypochrysops ignitus*
A. leptocarpa (North Coast Wattle)—**L:** *Jalmenus eichhorni*
A. leucoclada (Northern Silver Wattle)—**L:** *Jalmenus daemeli, J. evagoras*
A. ligulata (Sandhill Wattle)—**L:** *Jalmenus inous, Nacaduba biocellata*
A. longifolia (Sallow Wattle)—**N:** *Polyura sempronius,* **L:** *Hypochrysops ignitus, Jalmenus evagoras*
A. loroloba—see *A. deanei*
A. macradenia (Zig-zag Wattle)—**L:** *Jalmenus daemeli, J. evagoras*
A. maidenii (Maiden's Wattle)—**Pi:** *Eurema hecabe,* **N:** *Polyura sempronius,* **L:** *Jalmenus evagoras, Nacaduba biocellata, Prosotas dubiosa, Sahulana scintillata*
A. mangium (Hickory Wattle)—**L:** *Hypochrysops ignitus, Nacaduba biocellata, Prosotas dubiosa, Theclinesthes miskini*
A. mearnsii (Black Wattle)—**N:** *Polyura sempronius,* **L:** *Hypochrysops delicia, H. ignitus, Jalmenus evagoras, J. icilius, J. ictinus, Pseudalmenus chlorinda, Nacaduba biocellata*
A. melanoxylon (Blackwood)—**Pi:** *Eurema hecabe,* **N:** *Polyura sempronius,* **L:** *Hypochrysops delicia, Jalmenus evagoras, J. ictinus, Pseudalmenus chlorinda*
A. nematophylla—**L:** *Nacaduba biocellata*
A. neriifolia (Silver Wattle)—**N:** *Polyura sempronius,* **L:** *Hypochrysops ignitus, Jalmenus daemeli, J. evagoras, Theclinesthes miskini*
A. nilotica*—Pi:** *Eurema hecabe*
A. obtusifolia (Stiff-leaf Wattle)—**L:** *Pseudalmenus chlorinda*
A. oshanesii—see *A. decurrens*
A. oswaldii (Umbrella Wattle)—**L:** *Nacaduba biocellata*
A. papyrocarpa (Western Myall)—**L:** *Nacaduba biocellata*
A. parramattensis (Parramatta Wattle)—**L:** *Hypochrysops delicia, Jalmenus evagoras, J. icilius*

A. pendula (Weeping Myall)—**L:** *Jalmenus daemeli, J. icilius, J. ictinus*
A. penninervis (Mountain Hickory)—**L:** *Jalmenus evagoras, Nacaduba biocellata, Prosotas felderi*
A. podalyriifolia (Silver Wattle)—**N:** *Polyura sempronius,* **L:** *Prosotas felderi*
A. polybotrya (Western Silver Wattle)—**L:** *Jalmenus evagoras*
A. polystachya—**L:** *Rapala varuna, Anthene lycaenoides, Nacaduba biocellata, Prosotas dubiosa*
A. pravissima (Oven's Wattle)—**L:** *Pseudalmenus chlorinda*
A. pycnantha (Golden Wattle)—**L:** *Hypochrysops delicia, H. ignitus, Jalmenus evagoras, J. lithochroa, J. icilius, Nacaduba biocellata, Theclinesthes miskini*
A. quornensis (Quorn Wattle)—**L:** *Nacaduba biocellata*
A. retinodes (Wirilda)—**L:** *Jalmenus icilius, Nacaduba biocellata*
A. rigens (Needle Wattle)—**L:** *Nacaduba biocellata*
A. rostellifera (Summer-scented Wattle)—**L:** *Jalmenus inous*
A. rubida (Red-stemmed Wattle)—**Pi:** *Eurema hecabe,* **L:** *Jalmenus evagoras, J. icilius, J. ictinus*
A. rupicola (Rock Wattle)—**L:** *Nacaduba biocellata*
A. salicina (Coobah)—**L:** *Nacaduba biocellata, Theclinesthes miskini*
A. saligna (Golden Wreath Wattle)—**N:** *Polyura sempronius,* **L:** *Hypochrysops ignitus, Jalmenus icilius, J. inous, Nacaduba biocellata, Theclinesthes miskini*
A. sclerophylla (Hard-leafed Wattle)—**L:** *Nacaduba biocellata*
A. sophorae (Coastal Wattle)—**L:** *Prosotas felderi*
A. spectabilis (Mudgee Wattle)—**Pi:** *Eurema hecabe,* **N:** *Polyura sempronius,* **L:** *Hypochrysops delicia, Jalmenus evagoras*
A. stenophylla (River Cooba)—**L:** *Nacaduba biocellata*
A. terminalis (Sunshine Wattle)—**L:** *Jalmenus evagoras, Pseudalmenus chlorinda*
A. tetragonophylla (Dead Finish)—**L:** *Jalmenus aridus, J. clementi, Nacaduba biocellata, Theclinesthes miskini*
A. trachyphloia (Golden Feather Wattle)— **L:** *Pseudalmenus chlorinda*
A. tumida—**L:** *Hypochrysops ignitus*
A. victoriae (Prickly Wattle)—**L:** *Jalmenus lithochroa, J. icilius, Nacaduba biocellata, Prosotas dubiosa, Theclinesthes miskini*
A. xanthina (White-stemmed Wattle)—**L:** *Hypochrysops halyaetus*
Acacia sp.—**L:** *Hypochrysops delicia, Sahulana scintillata*
Adenanthera abrosperma (Giddy Giddy)—**N:** *Polyura sempronius*
Albizia canescens (Sleeping Tree)—**N:** *Polyura sempronius*
A. julibrissin*—Pi:** *Eurema hecabe*
A. lebbeck* (Siris Tree)—Pi:** *Eurema hecabe,* **N:** *Polyura sempronius,* **L:** *Rapala varuna, Prosotas dubiosa, P. felderi, Sahulana scintillata*
A. procera—**N:** *Polyura sempronius*
A. retusa—**N:** *Polyura sempronius*

Archidendron grandiflorum (Pink Lace Flower)—
  L: *Prosotas dubiosa*
A. hirsutum—**Pi:** *Eurema puella*
Calliandra houstoniana*—L:** *Anthene lycaenoides*
C. surinamensis* (Powder Puff Flower)—N:** *Polyura sempronius*, **L:** *Anthene lycaenoides*
Cathormion umbellatum—**L:** *Theclinesthes miskini*
Entada phaseoloides (Match Box Bean)—**L:** *Nacaduba cyanea*
Leucaena leucocephala*—Pi:** *Eurema hecabe*, **L:** *Prosotas dubiosa*
*Mimosa pigra (Giant Sensitive Tree)—**N:** *Polyura sempronius*
Neptunia dimorphantha (Sensitive Plant)—**Pi:** *Eurema brigitta*
N. gracilis (Sensitive Plant)—**Pi:** *Eurema smilax*
N. monosperma—**Pi:** *Eurema smilax*
Pararchidendron pruinosum (Snow Wood)—**N:** *Polyura sempronius*
Paraserianthes lophantha (Crested Wattle)—**N:** *Polyura sempronius*, **L:** *Rapala varuna*, ?*Prosotas dubiosa*, ?*P. felderi*, ?*Sahulana scintillata*
P. toona (Red Cedar)—**N:** *Polyura sempronius*

Caesalpiniaceae (Bauhinia family)

This family hosts most yellows (Pieridae: Coliadinae), as well as the Tailed Emperor (*Polyura sempronius*; Nymphalidae: Charaxinae), and several blues and hairstreaks (Lycaenidae).

Caesalpinia bonduc (Tartary Maw)—**L:** *Anthene lycaenoides*, *Catopyrops ancyra*, *C. florinda*
C. crista—**L:** *Anthene lycaenoides*
C. ferrea* (Leopard Tree)—N:** *Polyura sempronius*
C. gilliesii (Bird-of-Paradise Shrub)—**N:** *Polyura sempronius*
C. mexicana*—N:** *Polyura sempronius*
Cassia auriculata—**L:** *Anthene lycaenoides*
C. brewsteri (Native Laburnum, Cigar Bush)—
  Pi: *Catopsilia pomona*, *C. pyranthe*, **N:** *Polyura sempronius*, **L:** *Candalides absimilis*
C. fistula* (Cascara, Golden Shower)—Pi:** *Catopsilia pomona*, *C. pyranthe*, *Eurema smilax*, **N:** *Polyura sempronius*, **L:** *Hypolycaena phorbas*, *Candalides absimilis*, *Anthene lycaenoides*, *A. seltuttus*
C. javanica (Pink Shower)—**Pi:** *Catopsilia pomona*, **N:** *Polyura sempronius*
C. marksiana (Brush Cassia)—**Pi:** *Catopsilia pomona*, **N:** *Polyura sempronius*
C. queenslandica (Cassia)—**Pi:** *Catopsilia pomona*, **N:** *Polyura sempronius*
C. siamea* (Kassod Tree)—Pi:** *Catopsilia pomona*
C. tomentella (Little Cigar Cassia)—**Pi:** *Catopsilia pomona*, **N:** ?*Polyura sempronius*
Cassia sp.—**Pi:** *Catopsilia pyranthe*, *Eurema hecabe*
Chamaecrista nomame (Five-leaf Cassia)—**Pi:** *Eurema brigitta*
Chamaecrista sp.—**Pi:** *E. herla*, *E. laeta*

*Delonix regia (Poinciana)—**N:** *Polyura sempronius*, **L:** *Anthene seltuttus*
Peltophorum pterocarpum (Golden Flame Tree)—
  N: *Polyura sempronius*
Saraca thaipingensis*—L:** *Anthene seltuttus*
**Schizolobium parahybum* (Yellow Jacaranda)—
  N: *Polyura sempronius*
**Schotia brachypetala* (Drunken Parrot Tree)—
  L: *Anthene seltuttus*
Senna acclinis (Rainforest Cassia)—**Pi:** *Catopsilia gorgophone*, *Eurema hecabe*, *E. smilax*
S. aciphylla (Sprawling Cassia)—**Pi:** *Catopsilia pyranthe*
S. alata* (Candle Bush)—Pi:** *Catopsilia pomona*, *C. pyranthe*, *Eurema smilax*, **N:** *Polyura sempronius*, **L:** *Hypolycaena phorbas*, *Anthene lycaenoides*
S. artemisioides (Silver Cassia, Senna)—**L:** *Jalmenus icilius*
S. auriculata*—Pi:** *Catopsilia gorgophone*, *C. scylla*, *Eurema hecabe*, *E. smilax*, **L:** *Candalides absimilis*
S. barclayana (Pepper-leaf Senna)—**Pi:** *Catopsilia pyranthe*
S. coriaceae—**Pi:** *Eurema smilax*
S. coronilloides (Brigalow Senna)—**Pi:** *Catopsilia pomona*, *Eurema hecabe*, *E. smilax*
S. didymobotrya*—Pi:** *Catopsilia pomona*, *C. pyranthe*, **N:** *Polyura sempronius*
S. gaudichaudii (= *retusa*) (Climbing Cassia)—
  Pi: *Catopsilia gorgophone*, *C. scylla*, *Eurema hecabe*, *E. smilax*, **L:** *Anthene lycaenoides*
S. leptoclada—**Pi:** *Catopsilia scylla*
S. magnifolia (Weedy Cassia)—**Pi:** *Catopsilia pomona*
S. marksiana (Brush Senna)—**Pi:** *Catopsilia pomona*, **N:** *Polyura sempronius*
S. nemophila (Punty Bush, Desert Cassia)—**Pi:** *Eurema smilax*, **L:** *Jalmenus aridus*, *J. icilius*
S. odorata (Scented Senna)—**Pi:** *Catopsilia pomona*
S. petiolaris (Grey Cassia)—**Pi:** *Eurema smilax*
S. planitiicola (Arsenic Bush)—**Pi:** *Catopsilia pyranthe*
S. pleurocarpa (Chocolate Bush)—**Pi:** *Catopsilia pomona*
S. queenslandica (Queensland Cassia)—**Pi:** *Catopsilia pomona*
S. surattensis* (Scrambled Egg Plant)—Pi:** *Catopsilia gorgophone*, *C. scylla*, *Eurema hecabe*, **N:** *Polyura sempronius*, **L:** *Anthene lycaenoides*
S. venusta (Candlestick Cassia)—**Pi:** *Catopsilia pomona*, *C. pyranthe*
Senna sp.—**Pi:** *Eurema smilax*

Fabaceae (Peas and Legumes)

Peas are hosts to butterflies of every family, but the main group feeding on them are blues (Lycaenidae: Polyommatinae).

Aeschynomene hirsuta*—Pi:** *Eurema hecabe*
A. indica (Buddha Pea)—**Pi:** *Eurema hecabe*
Aotus ericoides (Golden Pea)—**L:** *Neolucia agricola*
Austrosteenisia blackii (Blood Vine)—**N:** *Pantoporia consimilis*
Bossiaea carinalis—**L:** *Neolucia agricola*

B. rhombifolia—**L:** *Neolucia agricola*
Cajanus acutifolius—**L:** *Famegana alsulus*
C. cajan (Pigeon Pea)—**L:** *Euchrysops cnejus*
C. pubescens—**L:** *Famegana alsulus*
C. reticulatus—**L:** *Prosotas dubiosa, Theclinesthes miskini, Jamides phaseli, Catochrysops panormus, Lampides boeticus, Euchrysops cnejus*
Callerya megasperma (Native Wisteria)—**H:** *Hasora khoda*, **L:** *Candalides absimilis*
Canavalia rosea (Coastal Jack-bean)—**L:** *Jamides phaseli*
Castanospermum australe (Blackbean Tree)— **L:** *Hypolycaena phorbas, Candalides absimilis*
Chamaecytisus proliferus (Tagasaste)—**L:** *Lampides boeticus*
Crotalaria alata (Rattlebox)—**L:** *Catochrysops panormus, Lampides boeticus, Zizina labradus*
C. cunninghamii (Green Bird Flower)—**L:** *Lampides boeticus*
C. eremaea (Desert Rattlepod)—**L:** *Lampides boeticus*
*C. goreensis (Gambia Pea)—**L:** *Lampides boeticus*
C. mitchellii (Yellow Rattlepod)—**L:** *Lampides boeticus*
*C. mucronata—**L:** *Lampides boeticus*
C. novaehollandiae—**L:** *Lampides boeticus*
*C. pallida (Streaked Rattlepod)—**L:** *Catochrysops panormus, Lampides boeticus, Zizina labradus*
Cullen australasicum (Native Scurf-pea)—**Pa:** *Papilio demoleus*
C. badoconum—**Pa:** *Papilio demoleus*
C. balsamicum—**Pa:** *Papilio demoleus*
C. cinereum—**Pa:** *Papilio demoleus*
C. microcephalum (Dusky Scurf-pea)—**L:** *Zizina labradus*
C. patens (Spreading Scurf-pea)—**Pa:** *Papilio demoleus*, **L:** *Lampides boeticus, Zizina labradus*
C. pustulatum—**Pa:** *Papilio demoleus*
C. tenax (Emu-foot)—**Pa:** *Papilio demoleus*, **L:** *Zizina labradus*
Dalbergia candenatensis—**N:** *Pantoporia consimilis*
*D. sissoo (Himalayan Raintree)—**L:** *Prosotas dubiosa*
Daviesia angulata (Bitter Pea)—**L:** *Neolucia agricola*
D. benthamii (Spiny Bitter Pea)—**L:** *Jalmenus icilius, J. inous*
D. brevifolia—**L:** *Zizina labradus*
D. daphnoides—**L:** *Hypochrysops halyaetus*
D. divaricata—**L:** *Hypochrysops halyaetus, Jalmenus inous, Neolucia agricola*
D. mimosoides (Narrow-leafed Bitter Pea)—**L:** *Neolucia agricola*
Dendrolobium umbellatum (Horse Bush)—**L:** *Rapala varuna, Anthene lycaenoides, Catochrysops panormus*
Derris trifoliata—**H:** *Hasora hurama*
Derris sp.—**N:** *Pantoporia consimilis*, **L:** *Danis danis*
Desmodium heterocarpon—**L:** *Catochrysops amasea, Everes lacturnus, Zizina labradus*
Desmodium sp.—**L:** *Zizina labradus*
Dillwynia sp.—**L:** *Neolucia agricola*
*Dipogon lignosus (Dolichos Pea)—**L:** *Lampides boeticus*
*Dolichos sp.—**L:** *Lampides boeticus*

Erythrina sp. (Coral Trees)—**L:** *Candalides absimilis*
Eutaxia microphylla (Mallee Bush-pea)—**L:** *Neolucia agricola*
Flemingia lineata—**L:** *Catochrysops panormus, Freyeria putli*
Gastrolobium microcarpum (Poison Bush)—**L:** *Jalmenus inous*
Glycine clandestina (Twining Glycine)—**L:** *Zizina labradus*
*G. max (Soybean)—**L:** *Zizina labradus*
G. tabacina (Native Soybean)—**Pi:** *Eurema alitha*
G. tomentella (Woolly Glycine)—**L:** *Zizina labradus*
Gompholobium ecostatum (Dwarf Wedge-pea)— **L:** *Lampides boeticus*
Hardenbergia violacea (False Sarsaparilla)—**L:** *Zizina labradus*
Indigofera australis (Australian Indigo)—**L:** *Lampides boeticus, Zizina labradus*
I. colutea (Rusty Indigo)—**L:** *Freyeria putli*
I. hirsuta (Hairy Indigo)—**L:** *Freyeria putli*
I. pratensis—**L:** *Jamides phaseli, Lampides boeticus, Famegana alsulus*
Indigofera sp.—**Pi:** *Eurema hecabe*
Jacksonia scoparia (Dogwood)—**L:** *Hypochrysops ignitus, Candalides cyprotus*
J. sternbergiana (Stinkwood)—**L:** *Hypochrysops halyaetus, Neolucia agricola*
Kennedia prostrata (Running Postman)—**L:** *Lampides boeticus*
K. rubicunda (Dusky Coral Pea)—**L:** *Lampides boeticus*
*Lathyrus odoratus (Sweet Pea)—**L:** *Lampides boeticus*
Lotus australis (Australian Trefoil)—**L:** *Lampides boeticus*
*Lupinus sp.—**L:** *Zizina labradus*
*Macroptilium atropurpureum (Siratro)—**L:** *Euchrysops cnejus*
*M. lathyroides (Phasey Pea)—**L:** *Zizina labradus, Euchrysops cnejus*
*Medicago sp. (Lucernes)—**L:** *Zizina labradus*
Millettia pinnata (Pongamia)—**H:** *Hasora chromus, Badamia exclamationis*, **N:** *Phaedyma shepherdi*, **L:** *Rapala varuna, Candalides absimilis, Anthene seltuttus, A. lycaenoides, Jamides phaseli*
Mucuna gigantea (Burny Vine)—**H:** *Hasora discolor*, **N:** *Phaedyma shepherdi*
*M. novoguineensis—**H:** *Hasora discolor*
*Phaseolus vulgaris (Common Bean)—**L:** *Jamides phaseli, Lampides boeticus, Euchrysops cnejus, Zizina labradus*
Phylacium bracteosum—**N:** *Neptis praslini*
*Pisum sativum (Garden Pea)—**L:** *Lampides boeticus, Zizina labradus*
*Psoralea pinnata (African Scurf-pea)—**Pa:** *Papilio demoleus*
Pultenaea acerosa (Bristly Bush Pea)—**L:** *Neolucia agricola*
P. largiflorens (Twiggy Bush Pea)—**L:** *Neolucia agricola*
P. rigida—**L:** *Neolucia agricola*
P. tenuifolia (Slender Bush Pea)—**L:** *Lampides boeticus, Zizina labradus*

P. villosa (Hairy Bush Pea)—**L:** *Neolucia agricola*
*Robinia pseudoacacia (False Acacia)—**N:** *Polyura sempronius*, **L:** *Candalides absimilis*
Sesbania cannabina (Sesbania Pea)—**Pi:** *Eurema hecabe*, **L:** *Theclinesthes miskini*, *Lampides boeticus*, *Euchrysops cnejus*
S. javanica—**Pi:** *Eurema hecabe*, **L:** *Theclinesthes miskini*
Sesbania sp.—**L:** *Theclinesthes miskini*, *Euchrysops cnejus*
Swainsona formosa (Sturt's Desert Pea)—**L:** *Lampides boeticus*
S. galegifolia (Smooth Darling Pea)—**L:** *Lampides boeticus*
S. greyana (Hairy Darling Pea)—**L:** *Lampides boeticus*
S. stipularis (Orange Darling Pea)—**L:** *Lampides boeticus*
Swainsona sp. (Darling Peas)—**L:** *Zizina labradus*
Templetonia retusa (Cocky's Tongue)—**L:** *Lampides boeticus*
Tephrosia rufula—**L:** *Jamides phaseli*
*Trifolium pratense (Red Clover)—**L:** *Zizina labradus*
*Trifolium sp. (Clover)—**L:** *Zizina labradus*
Trigonella sp.—**L:** *Zizina labradus*
Vandasina retusa—**L:** *Hypochrysops apelles*
*Vicia faba (Faba Bean)—**L:** *Lampides boeticus*, *Zizina labradus*
*Vicia sativa (Vetch)—**L:** *Lampides boeticus*
Vigna caracalla (Snail Vine)—**L:** *Jamides phaseli*, *Lampides boeticus*, *Euchrysops cnejus*, *Zizina labradus*
V. luteola (Dalrymple Vigna)—**L:** *Euchrysops cnejus*
*V. unguiculata (Cowpea)—**L:** *Euchrysops cnejus*
V. vexillata (Wild Cowpea)—**L:** *Euchrysops cnejus*
*Virgilia oroboides (Cape Virgilia)—**L:** *Lampides boeticus*, *Zizina labradus*
*Wisteria sinensis (Chinese Wisteria)—**H:** *Hasora khoda*, **L:** *Candalides absimilis*, *Lampides boeticus*
Wisteria sp.—**N:** *Polyura sempronius*

Elaeagnaceae
Elaeagnus triflora (Milla Milla Vine)—**L:** *Rapala varuna*

Proteaceae
Members of this large Australian family host only a few species of blues and hairstreaks (Lycaenidae).
Banksia sp.—**L:** *Hypochrysops ignitus*
Buckinghamia celsissima (Ivory Curl Flower)— **L:** *Deudorix diovis*, *Rapala varuna*, *Candalides absimilis*
Conospermum taxifolium (Variable Smoke-bush)— **L:** *Candalides cyprotus*
Grevillea baileyana (White Oak)—**L:** *Hypochrysops ignitus*
G. bracteosa—**L:** *Candalides cyprotus*
G. huegelii (Comb Grevillea)—**L:** *Candalides cyprotus*
G. juniperina—**L:** *Candalides cyprotus*
Hakea leucoptera (Needlewood)—**L:** *Candalides cyprotus*
Macadamia integrifolia (Queensland Nut Tree)— **L:** *Deudorix diovis*, *Candalides absimilis*, *Nacaduba berenice*, *Erysichton lineata*, *Prosotas dubiosa*, *P. felderi*
M. tetraphylla (Rough Shelled Bush Nut)—**L:** *Nacaduba berenice*

Macadamia sp.—**L:** *Deudorix diovis*
Stenocarpus sinuatus (Wheel of Fire)—**L:** *Deudorix diovis*
Stenocarpus sp.—**L:** *Pseudodipsas eone*
Xylomelum scottianum (Native Pear)—**L:** *Theclinesthes miskini*

Lythraceae (Crepe Myrtles)
Lagerstroemia indica (Crepe Myrtle)—**N:** *Polyura sempronius*
*L. speciosa (Queen's Myrtle)—**L:** *Arhopala centaurus*, *A. micale*, *Anthene seltuttus*
Thymelaeaceae (Rice Flowers)
Pimelea ligustrina (Tall Rice Flower)—**L:** *Candalides xanthospilos*
P. linifolia (Slender rice Flower)—**L:** *Candalides xanthospilos*
P. stricta (Erect Rice Flower)—**L:** *Candalides xanthospilos*
Pimelea sp.—**L:** *Candalides heathi*

Melastomataceae (Melastoma family)
Melastoma affine (Blue Tongue)—**L:** *Hypochrysops miskini*

Combretaceae (Damson Trees and allies)
Lumnitzera racemosa (Black Mangrove)—**L:** *Hypochrysops apelles*, *H. narcissus*, *Hypolycaena phorbas*
Terminalia arenicola (Brown Damson)—**L:** *Hypochrysops ignitus*
T. catappa (Indian Almond Tree)—**H:** *Badamia exclamationis*, **L:** *Hypochrysops apelles*, *H. narcissus*, *Arhopala centaurus*, *A. madytus*, *Petrelaea tombugensis*
T. melanocarpa (Beach Almond)—**L:** *Arhopala centaurus*, *A. madytus*, *Hypolycaena phorbas*
T. microcarpa (Damson)—**H:** *Badamia exclamationis*, **L:** *Hypochrysops apelles*, *Arhopala centaurus*, *A. madytus*
T. muelleri (Mueller's Damson)—**L:** *Hypochrysops apelles*, *Arhopala centaurus*, *A. micale*
T. oblongata (Yellow-wood)—**H:** *Badamia exclamationis*
T. subacroptera (Damson)—**L:** *Hypochrysops cyane*
Terminalia sp.—**L:** *Hypochrysops narcissus*

Myrtaceae (Eucalyptus family)
Although a very large family in the Australian flora, the Myrtaceae host relatively few butterflies, including Lycaenidae (mainly hairstreaks) and skippers (all flats). Many are host plants for various moths.
Acmena sp. (Lilly Pilly)—**H:** *Chaetocneme beata*, *Netrocoryne repanda*, **L:** *Arhopala micale*, *Hypolycaena phorbas*
Agonis flexuosa (Willow Myrtle, Peppermint)—**L:** *Hypochrysops ignitus*
Angophora costata (Apple Gum)—**L:** *Hypochrysops cyane*
A. floribunda (Rough-barked Apple)—**L:** *Hypochrysops apelles*
Corymbia intermedia (Pink Bloodwood)—**L:** *Arhopala centaurus*
C. ptychocarpa (Swamp Bloodwood)—**L:** *Arhopala centaurus*

C. tessellaris (Moreton Bay Ash, Carbeen)—**L:** *Arhopala centaurus*
Corymbia sp. (Bloodwood)—**L:** *Jalmenus daemeli*
Eucalyptus acmenoides (White Mahogany)—**L:** *Hypochrysops miskini*
E. drepanophylla (Narrow-leafed Ironbark)—**L:** *Hypochrysops apelles, Theclinesthes miskini*
E. melanophloia (Silver-leafed Ironbark)—**L:** *Jalmenus daemeli*
E. moluccana (Grey Box)—**L:** *Hypochrysops cyane*
E. polycarpa (Inland Bloodwood)—**L:** *Theclinesthes miskini*
E. torelliana (Cadaghi Tree)—**L:** *Theclinesthes miskini*
Eucalyptus sp.—**H:** *Chaetocneme denitza*, **L:** *Hypochrysops ignitus, Arhopala centaurus, Jalmenus daemeli, Theclinesthes miskini*
Lophostemon confertus (Brush Box)—**H:** *Chaetocneme beata, C. denitza, Netrocoryne repanda*, **L:** *Hypochrysops miskini*
L. grandiflorus (Northern Swamp Mahogany)—**H:** *Chaetocneme denitza*, **L:** *Hypochrysops cyane*
L. suaveolens (Swamp Mahogany, Swamp Box)—**H:** *Chaetocneme denitza*, **L:** *Hypochrysops ignitus, H. miskini, H. narcissus*
Melaleuca leucodendra (Weeping Teatree)—**L:** *Hypochrysops cyane*
M. quinquenervia (Paperbark Tree)—**L:** *Arhopala centaurus*
Rhodomyrtus trineura—**L:** *Hypochrysops miskini*
Ristantia pachysperma—**L:** *Arhopala micale*
Syzygium bamagenese—**H:** *Chaetocneme critomedia*
S. cormiflorum (Bumpy Satinash)—**L:** *Arhopala micale*
S. francisii (Giant Water Gum)—**L:** *Erysichton lineata*
S. oleosum (Blue Lilly Pilly)—**L:** *Erysichton lineata*
S. puberulum (White Satinash)—**L:** *Jamides cytus*
S. tierneyanum (Bamaga Satinash)—**L:** *Arhopala micale*
S. wilsoni (Purple Powderpuff)—**L:** *Hypolycaena phorbas, Anthene seltuttus*
Syzygium sp. aff. *erythrocalyx*—**L:** *Arhopala micale*

Rhizophoraceae (Mangrove)

Bruguiera exaristata (Rib-fruited Orange Mangrove)—**L:** *Hypochrysops narcissus*
B. gymnorhiza (Large-leafed Orange Mangrove)—**L:** *Hypochrysops apelles*
Ceriops tagal (Yellow Mangrove)—**L:** *Hypochrysops apelles, H. narcissus, Hypolycaena phorbas*
Rhizophora stylosa (Red Mangrove)—**L:** *Hypochrysops apelles, H. narcissus, Hypolycaena litoralis*

Santalaceae

Choretrum glomeratum (Berry Broombush)—**L:** *Hypochrysops ignitus, Ogyris otanes*
C. spicatum (Spiked Sourbush)—**L:** *Hypochrysops ignitus, Ogyris otanes*
Exocarpos aphyllus (Leafless Ballart)—**Pi:** *Delias aganippe*, **L:** *Hypochrysops ignitus*
E. cupressiformis (Native Cherry)—**Pi:** *Delias aganippe*, **L:** *Hypochrysops ignitus*
E. latifolius (Broad-leafed Native Cherry)—**H:** *Chaetocneme beata*, **L:** *Hypochrysops ignitus*
E. strictus (Pale-fruit Ballart)—**Pi:** *Delias aganippe*
Leptomeria preissiana (Currant Bush)—**L:** *Ogyris otanes*
Santalum acuminatum (Quandong)—**Pi:** *Delias aganippe*
S. lanceolatum (Northern Sandalwood)—**Pi:** *Delias aganippe, D. argenthona*
S. spicatum (Sandalwood)—**Pi:** *Delias aganippe*

Loranthaceae (Mistletoes)

Mistletoes are one of the most important larval food plants for Australian butterflies. Almost all species are attacked by species of jezabels (*Delias* sp.) and numerous blues, especially the azures (*Ogyris* sp.). Very few other Lepidoptera or other herbivores attack these parasitic plants, which are probably chemically protected. Although common names have been recognised for some species, often based on the host tree preferences, many are generally referred to simply as 'mistletoe'.

Amyema bifurcata (Bloodwood Mistletoe)—**Pi:** *Delias argenthona, D. nigrina*, **L:** *Hypochrysops digglesii, Ogyris amaryllis, O. genoveva, O. iphis, O. oroetes, O. zosine*
A. cambagei (She-oak Mistletoe)—**Pi:** *Delias aganippe, D. argenthona, D. nigrina*, **L:** *Ogyris amaryllis, O. genoveva, O. zosine, Erysichton palmyra*
A. congener (Variable Mistletoe)—**Pi:** *Delias harpalyce, D. nigrina*, **L:** *Hypochrysops digglesii, Ogyris abrota, O. amaryllis, O. genoveva, O. zosine, Candalides margarita, Erysichton palmyra*
A. conspicua (Alphitonia Mistletoe)—**L:** *Hypochrysops digglesii, Ogyris genoveva, O. zosine, Candalides margarita*
A. fitzgeraldii (Pincushion Mistletoe)—**L:** *Ogyris amaryllis*
A. linophylla (Bulloak Mistletoe)—**Pi:** *Delias aganippe*, **L:** *Ogyris aenone, O. amaryllis, O. ianthis*
A. lucasii—**Pi:** *Delias nigrina*, **L:** *Ogyris amaryllis*
A. mackayense (Mangrove Mistletoe)—**L:** *Ogyris amaryllis*
A. maidenii (Pale-leaf Mistletoe)—**L:** *Ogyris amaryllis, O. barnardi, O. zosine*
A. melaleucae—**Pi:** *Delias aganippe*, **L:** *Ogyris amaryllis*
A. miquelii (Box Mistletoe)—**Pi:** *Delias aganippe, D. argenthona, D. harpalyce, D. nigrina*, **L:** *Hypochrysops digglesii, H. cyane, Ogyris aenone, O. amaryllis, O. genoveva, O. ianthis, O. iphis, O. olane, O. oroetes, O. zosine, Candalides margarita, Erysichton palmyra*
A. miraculosa—**L:** *Ogyris amaryllis, O. barnardi*
A. pendula (Drooping Mistletoe)—**Pi:** *Delias argenthona, D. harpalyce*, **L:** *Ogyris amaryllis, O. genoveva, O. olane, O. oroetes, O. zosine,*
A. preissii (Wire-leaf Mistletoe)—**Pi:** *Delias aganippe, D. harpalyce*, **L:** *Ogyris amaryllis*

A. quandang (Grey Mistletoe)—**Pi:** *Delias aganippe, D. argenthona, D. harpalyce, D. nigrina,* **L:** *Ogyris amaryllis, O. barnardi, O. genoveva, O. ianthis, O. iphis, O. zosine*

A. sanguinea (Blood Mistletoe)—**Pi:** *Delias argenthona,* **L:** *Hypochrysops digglesii, Ogyris amaryllis, O. zosine*

A. thalassium (Mangrove Mistletoe)—**L:** *Ogyris amaryllis*

Amylotheca dictyophleba (Scrub Mistletoe)—**Pi:** *Delias nigrina,* **L:** *Candalides margarita*

Benthamina alyxifolia (Shiny-leaf Mistletoe)—**Pi:** *Delias nigrina,* **L:** *Candalides margarita*

Decaisnina signata—**Pi:** *Delias argenthona,* **L:** *Ogyris zosine, Candalides gilberti*

Dendrophthoe curvata (Curved Mistletoe)—**Pi:** *Delias argenthona, D. mysis, D. nigrina,* **L:** *Hypochrysops digglesii, Ogyris zosine, Candalides margarita*

D. glabrescens (Smooth Mistletoe)—**Pi:** *Delias argenthona, D. aruna, D. mysis, D, nigrina,* **L:** *Hypochrysops digglesii, H. elgneri, Ogyris genoveva, O. ianthis, O. iphis, O. zosine*

D. homoplastica—**L:** *Hypochrysops digglesii*

D. vitellina (Long-flowered Mistletoe)—**Pi:** *Delias argenthona, D. mysis, D, nigrina,* **L:** *Hypochrysops digglesii, H. narcissus, Arhopala centaurus, Ogyris abrota, O. aenone, O. genoveva, O. ianthis, O. iphis, O. zosine, Hypolycaena phorbas, Candalides margarita, Erysichton palmyra*

Diplatia furcata (Bottlebrush Mistletoe)—**Pi:** *Delias argenthona,* **L:** *Ogyris aenone, O. amaryllis*

D. tomentosa—**L:** *Hypochrysops narcissus, Ogyris aenone*

Lysiana exocarpi (Harlequin Mistletoe)—**L:** *Ogyris aenone*

L. subfalcata—**Pi:** *Delias nigrina*

Muellerina celastroides (Coast Mistletoe, Banksia Mistletoe)—**Pi:** *Delias argenthona, D. nigrina,* **L:** *Hypochrysops digglesii, Ogyris abrota, O. zosine, Candalides margarita*

M. eucalyptoides (Creeping Mistletoe)—**Pi:** *Delias harpalyce, D. nigrina,* **L:** *Ogyris abrota, O. genoveva, O. ianthis*

Viscaceae (Mistletoes)

Korthalsella breviarticulata (Short Jointed Mistletoe)—**Pi:** *Delias nysa*

K. rubra (Ruddy Mistletoe)—**Pi:** *Delias nysa*

Notothixos incanus (Downy Mistletoe)—**L:** *Hypochrysops narcissus*

N. leiophyllus (Golden Mistletoe)—**Pi:** *Delias ennia*

Notothixos sp. **L:** *Hypochrysops elgneri*

Celastraceae

Celastrus subspicata (Large-leafed Staff Vine)—**L:** *Bindahara phocides*

Hippocrateaceae

Salacia chinensis (Lolly-berry Vine)—**L:** *Deudorix epijarbas, Bindahara phocides*

S. disepala—**L:** *Deudorix epijarbas, Bindahara phocides*

Euphorbiaceae (Spurges and allies)

Adriana quadripartita (Coast Bitter-bush)—**L:** *Theclinesthes albocincta, T. hesperia*

A. tomentosa (Eastern Bitter-bush)—**L:** *Theclinesthes albocincta*

Alchornea ilicifolia (Native Holly)—**Pi:** *Appias paulina*

Breynia cernua—**Pi:** *Eurema hecabe*

B. nivosa* (Snow Bush)—Pi:** *Eurema hecabe*

B. oblongifolia (Coffee Bush)—**Pi:** *Eurema hecabe*

Briedelia penangiana—**N:** *Neptis praslini*

B. tomentosa—**L:** *Anthene lycaenoides*

Croton insularis (Silver Croton)—**H:** *Chaetocneme beata*

Drypetes deplanchei (Yellow Tulipwood)—**Pi:** *Appias paulina*

Drypetes sp.—**Pi:** *Appias melania*

Glochidion apodogynum (Cheese Tree)—**L:** *Hypochrysops ignitus*

G. ferdinandi (Cheese Tree)—**L:** *Arhopala micale, Candalides helenita*

G. harveyanum (Buttonwood)—**L:** *Hypochrysops miskini*

G. philippicum (Little Cheese Tree)—**L:** *Philiris nitens*

Macaranga inamoena—**L:** *Megisba strongyle*

M. involucrata (Brown Macaranga)—**L:** *Philiris nitens, P. sappheira*

M. tanarius (Nasturtium Tree)—**L:** *Philiris nitens*

Macaranga sp.—**H:** *Chaetocneme critomedia*

Mallotus paniculatus (Turn-in-the-Wind)—**L:** *Megisba strongyle*

M. philippensis (Red Kamala)—**L:** *Megisba strongyle*

M. polyadenos (Green Kamala)—**H:** *Chaetocneme critomedia*

Petalostigma pubescens (Bitter Bark, Strychnine Tree)—**L:** *Hypochrysops apelles*

Phyllanthus tenellus (Hen and Chicken)—**Pi:** *Eurema hecabe*

Rhamnaceae

Alphitonia excelsa (Soap Tree, Red Ash)—**L:** *Hypochrysops apelles, H. delicia, H. ignitus, Rapala varuna, Psychonotis caelius*

A. incana (Hairy Sarsaparilla)—**L:** *Psychonotis caelius*

A. obtusifolia—**L:** *Hypochrysops cyane*

A. petriei (Pink ash, Sarsaparilla)—**L:** *Psychonotis caelius*

Pomaderris andromedifolia—**L:** *Hypochrysops byzos*

P. aspera (Hazel Pomaderris)—**L:** *Hypochrysops byzos*

P. cotoneaster (Cotoneaster)—**L:** *Hypochrysops byzos*

P. eriocephala—**L:** *Hypochrysops byzos*

P. ferruginea—**L:** *Hypochrysops byzos*

P. intermedia (Tree Pomaderris)—**L:** *Hypochrysops byzos*

P. lanigera (Woolly Pomaderris)—**L:** *Hypochrysops byzos*

Pomaderris sp.—**L:** *Hypochrysops byzos, H. ignitus*

Ventilago ecorollata—**Pi:** *Eurema puella*

Malpighiaceae

Rhyssopterys timorensis—**H:** *Allora doleschallii, Badamia exclamationis,* **L:** *Hypochrysops polycletus, Anthene lycaenoides*

Tremandraceae
Tetratheca hispidissima (Slender Tetratheca)—
  H: *Exometoeca nycteris*
T. hirsuta (Black-eyed Susan)—**H:** *Exometoeca nycteris*

Sapindaceae (Soapberries and allies)
Plants of this family are fed on by numerous species of blues and hairstreaks (Lycaenidae) and very few other butterflies.
Alectryon connatus (Grey Bird's Eye)—**L:** *Jalmenus pseudictinus*
A. coriaceus (Crab's Eyes)—**L:** *Deudorix diovis, Candalides absimilis, C. consimilis, Nacaduba berenice, Erysichton lineata, Prosotas felderi, Sahulana scintillata*
A. diversifolius (Scrub Boonaree)—**L:** *Hypochrysops ignitus, Jalmenus daemeli, J. ictinus, J. pseudictinus, Nacaduba berenice, Theclinesthes miskini*
A. subcinereus (Wild Quince)—**H:** *Netrocoryne repanda*
A. tomentosus (Hairy Bird's Eye)—**L:** *Deudorix diovis, Prosotas dubiosa*
Allophylus cobbe—**L:** *Ionolyce helicon, Megisba strongyle*
Arytera divaricata (Coogera, Rose Tamarind)—
  L: *Nacaduba berenice*
A. foveolata (Pitted Coogera)—**L:** *Deudorix diovis, Nacaduba berenice*
A. lauteriana (Corduroy Tamarind)—**L:** *Erysichton lineata*
A. pauciflora (Pink Tamarind)—**L:** *Candalides helenita, Anthene seltuttus, Nacaduba berenice, Jamides aleuas*
Atalaya hemiglauca (Whitewood Atalya)—
  L: *Theclinesthes miskini, T. serpentata*
A. salicifolia (Scrub Whitewood)—**L:** *Candalides absimilis, Nacaduba berenice*
A. variifolia (Wing-leaf Whitewood)—**L:** *Theclinesthes miskini*
Cupaniopsis anacardioides (Tuckeroo)—**L:** *Hypochrysops ignitus, Arhopala micale, Hypolycaena phorbas, Deudorix diovis, Rapala varuna, Candalides absimilis, Anthene lycaenoides, A. seltuttus, Nacaduba berenice, N. kurava, Erysichton lineata, Prosotas felderi, Sahulana scintillata*
C. parvifolia (Small-leafed Tuckeroo)—**L:** *Deudorix diovis, Nacaduba berenice*
Cupaniopsis sp.—**L:** *Arhopala centaurus*
Diploglottis australis (Native Tamarind)—**L:** *Deudorix diovis*
Dodonaea humilis (Dwarf Hop-bush)—**L:** *Hypochrysops ignitus*
D. lanceolata (Hop-bush)—**L:** *Hypochrysops ignitus*
D. triquetra (Common Hop-bush)—**L:** *Hypochrysops ignitus*
D. viscosa (Hop-bush)—**L:** *Hypochrysops ignitus*
Dodonaea sp. (Hop-bush)—**L:** *Hypochrysops ignitus*
Elattostachys microcarpa (Scrub Tamarind)—
  L: *Nacaduba berenice, Erysichton lineata*
Guioa acutifolia (Glossy Tamarind)—**L:** *Pseudodipsas cephenes, Hypochrysops miskini, Nacaduba berenice*
Harpullia hillii (Blunt-leaf Tulip)—**L:** *Deudorix diovis, Candalides absimilis*
H. pendula (Tulipwood)—**L:** *Deudorix diovis, Candalides absimilis, Erysichton lineata, Prosotas dubiosa, P. felderi, Catopyrops florinda*
H. ramiflora (Claudie Tulipwood)—**L:** *Deudorix diovis, D. epirus*
Jagera pseudorhus (Foambark)—**L:** *Rapala varuna, Nacaduba berenice, Erysichton lineata*
*Koelreuteria elegans (Chinese Raintree)—**L:** *Candalides absimilis*
Lepidopetalum subdichotomum—**N:** *Pantoporia venilia*
*Litchi chinensis (Lychee)—**L:** *Deudorix diovis, D. epijarbas, Rapala varuna, Anthene lycaenoides, Prosotas dubiosa, P. felderi*
Sarcopteryx martyana (Scrub Tamarind)—**L:** *Deudorix epijarbas*
S. stipata (Steelwood, Corduroy)—**L:** *Jamides aleuas*

Anacardiaceae
Blephocarya involucrigera (Rose Butternut)—
  H: *Chaetocneme critomedia*
Buchanania arborescens (Satinwood)—**L:** *Arhopala micale*
B. obovata (Green Plum)—**L:** *Arhopala centaurus*

Meliaceae
Xylocarpus moluccensis (Cedar Mangrove)—**L:** *Arhopala micale*

Rutaceae (Citrus family)
The Citrus family is the main host family for swallowtails of the genus *Papilio*. The only other butterflies feeding on plants of this family belong to the lycaenid genus *Nesolycaena* (opals), all of which feed on species of *Boronia*.
Boronia eriantha (Sandstone Boronia)—**L:** *Nesolycaena medicea*
B. glabra (Glabrous Boronia)—**L:** *Nesolycaena albosericea*
B. kalumburensis—**L:** *Nesolycaena caesia*
B. lanceolata—**L:** *Nesolycaena urumelia*
B. lanuginosa—**L:** *Nesolycaena urumelia*
B. obovata—**L:** *Nesolycaena albosericea*
B. odorata—**L:** *Nesolycaena albosericea*
B. rosmarinifolia (Forest Boronia)—**L:** *Nesolycaena albosericea*
B. wilsonii—**L:** *Nesolycaena caesia*
Bosistoa medicinalis—**Pa:** *Papilio fuscus*
*Choisya ternata (Mexican Orange Blossom)—
  Pa: *Papilio aegeus*
*Citrus aurantium (Seville Orange)—**Pa:** *Papilio aegeus, P. canopus, P. demoleus, P. fuscus*
*C. aurantifolia (Sweet Lime)—**Pa:** *Papilio aegeus, P. anactus, P. canopus, P. demoleus, P. fuscus*
C. australasica (Finger Lime)—**Pa:** *Papilio aegeus, P. anactus, P. fuscus*
C. australis (Native Lime)—**Pa:** *Papilio aegeus, P. anactus, P. demoleus*

C. garrawayae (Mt White Lime)—**Pa:** *Papilio aegeus, P. ambrax, P. anactus, P. fuscus*
C. glauca (Desert Lime)—**Pa:** *Papilio anactus,*
C. inodora (Large-leaf Lime)—**Pa:** *Papilio aegeus, P. ambrax, P. anactus, P. fuscus*
*C. limon (Lemon)—**Pa:** *Papilio aegeus, P. anactus, P. canopus, P. fuscus*
*C. paradisi (Grapefruit)—**Pa:** *Papilio aegeus*
*C. reticulata (Mandarin)—**Pa:** *Papilio aegeus, P. canopus, P. fuscus*
*C. sinensis (Orange)—**Pa:** *Papilio aegeus, P. anactus, P. canopus, P. fuscus*
*Citrus sp.—**Pa:** *Papilio ambrax, P. anactus, P. canopus, P. demoleus, P. ulysses*
Clausena brevistyla—**Pa:** *Papilio aegeus, P. ambrax, P. fuscus*
Dinosperma erythrococca (Tingle Tongue)—**Pa:** *Papilio aegeus*
D. melanophloia (Black-barked Doughwood)—**Pa:** *Papilio aegeus*
Eriostemon australasius (Pink Wax Flower)—**Pa:** *Papilio aegeus*
Flindersia australis (Crows Ash, Australian Teak)—**Pa:** *Papilio aegeus*
F. bennettii (Bennett's Ash)—**Pa:** *Papilio aegeus*
F. bourjotiana (Silver Ash)—**Pa:** *Papilio ulysses*
F. collina (Leopard Ash)—**Pa:** *Papilio aegeus*
F. ifflaiana (Hickory Ash)—**Pa:** *Papilio aegeus*
F. laevicarpa (Dirran Scented Maple)—**Pa:** *Papilio aegeus*
F. oppositifolia (Mountain Silkwood)—**Pa:** *Papilio aegeus*
F. pimenteliana (Maple Silkwood)—**Pa:** *Papilio aegeus*
F. schottiana (Bumby Ash)—**Pa:** *Papilio aegeus*
Geijera parviflora (Wilga)—**Pa:** *Papilio aegeus, P. anactus, P. fuscus*
G. salicifolia (Narrow-leafed Wilga)—**Pa:** *Graphium macleayanum, G. sarpedon, Papilio aegeus, P. ulysses*
Glycosmis trifoliata (Orangeberry)—**Pa:** *Papilio aegeus, P. fuscus* **L:** *Neopithecops lucifer*
Halfordia kendack (Saffron Heart, Kerosene Wood)—**Pa:** *Papilio fuscus, P. ulysses*
Halfordia sp.—**Pa:** *Papilio aegeus,* **L:** *Pseudodipsas cephenes*
Leionema ambiens (Forest Phebalium)—**Pa:** *Papilio aegeus*
L. dentatum (Toothed Phebalium)—**Pa:** *Papilio aegeus*
*Limonia acidissima (Wood Apple)—**Pa:** *Papilio anactus*
Melicope bonwickii (Yellow Evodia, Yellow Corkwood)—**Pa:** *Papilio ulysses*
M. elleryana (Pink Princess Corkwood)—**Pa:** *Papilio ulysses*
M. rubra (Little Evodia)—**Pa:** *Papilio ulysses*
M. vitiflora (Northern Evodia)—**Pa:** *Papilio ulysses*
Melicope sp.—**H:** *Chaetocneme beata,* **Pa:** *Papilio ulysses*
Micromelum minutum (Lime Berry)—**Pa:** *Papilio aegeus, P. canopus, P. fuscus*

*Murraya koenigii (Curry-leaf Tree)—**Pa:** *Papilio aegeus, P. ambrax, P. fuscus*
M. ovatifoliolata (Native Murraya)—**Pa:** *Papilio fuscus*
Phebalium distans (Mt Berryman Phebalium)—**Pa:** *Papilio aegeus*
Philotheca myoporoides (Long-leaf Wax Flower)—**Pa:** *Papilio aegeus*
*Poncirus trifoliata (Japanese Bitter Orange)—**Pa:** *Papilio aegeus, P. anactus*
*Zanthoxylum ailanthoides (Japanese Prickly Ash)—**Pa:** *Papilio aegeus, P. ambrax, P. fuscus*
Z. brachyacanthum (Satin Wood)—**Pa:** *Papilio aegeus, P. ambrax, P. fuscus*
Z. nitidum (Prickly Ash)—**Pa:** *Papilio aegeus, P. ambrax, P. fuscus*
Z. ovalifolium (Oval Leafed Liana)—**Pa:** *Papilio ambrax*
Zanthoxylum sp.—**Pa:** *Papilio aegeus, P. fuscus*
Zieria laevigata (Smooth Zieria, Twiggy Midge Bush)—**Pa:** *Papilio aegeus*
Z. smithii (Lanoline Bush)—**Pa:** *Papilio aegeus*

Zygophyllaceae
Tribulus cistoides (Caltrop)—**L:** *Zizeeria karsandra*
T. terrestris (Goat's Head Burr)—**L:** *Zizeeria karsandra*

Oxalidaceae
Oxalis corniculata (Yellow Sorrel)—**L:** *Lucia limbaria*
O. exilis (Shady Wood-sorrel)—**L:** *Lucia limbaria*
O. perennans (Grassland Wood-sorrel)—**L:** *Lucia limbaria*
Oxalis sp.—**L:** *Lucia limbaria*

Tropaeolaceae (Nasturtium family)
*Tropaeolum sp. (Nasturtium)—**Pi:** **Pieris rapae*

Araliaceae
*Hedera helix (English Ivy)—**L:** *Candalides consimilis*
Polyscias elegans (Celerywood)—**L:** *Candalides consimilis*
P. sambucifolius (Elderberry Panax)—**L:** *Candalides consimilis*

Loganiaceae
Strychnos lucida (Strychnine Bush)—**L:** *Deudorix democles, D. smilis*
S. minor—**L:** *Deudorix democles*

Gentianaceae
Centaurium spicatum (Spike Centaury)—**N:** *Junonia villida*

Apocynaceae
A family of mostly poisonous species eaten only by larvae of tiger and crow butterflies (Nymphalidae: Danainae) and the Hamadryad (Nymphalidae: Tellervinae).
*Adenium obesum (Desert Rose)—**N:** *Euploea core*
*A. multiflorum (Impala Lily)—**N:** *Euploea core*
*Carissa grandiflora (Natal Plum)—**N:** *Euploea core*
C. ovata (Kunkerberry, Currant Bush)—**N:** *Euploea core*

Ichnocarpus frutescens—**N:** *Euploea core*
*Mandevilla sp.—**N:** *Euploea core*
*Nerium oleander (Oleander)—**N:** *Euploea alcathoe, E. core*
Parsonsia alboflavescens—**N:** *Euploea alcathoe*
P. brisbanensis—**N:** *Euploea core*
P. eucalyptophylla (Gargaloo)—**N:** *Euploea core*
P. ferruginea (Possum Scrub)—**N:** *Tellervo zoilus*
P. latifolia (Green-leafed Silkpod)—**N:** *Tellervo zoilus*
P. straminea (Common Silkpod, Monkey Rope)—**N:** *Euploea core, Tellervo zoilus*
Parsonsia sp.—**N:** *Euploea core*
*Plumeria acutifolia (Frangipani)—**N:** *Euploea core*
*Trachelospermum jasminoides (Star Jasmine)—**N:** *Euploea core*
*Trachelospermum sp.—**N:** *Euploea core*

Asclepiadaceae
A family of mostly poisonous species eaten only by larvae of tiger and crow butterflies (Nymphalidae: Danainae).

*Araujia hortorum (Mothvine)—**N:** **Danaus plexippus*
*Asclepias curassavica (Redhead Wild Cotton)—**N:** *Danaus petilia, *D. plexippus*
Asclepias sp.—**N:** *Euploea alcathoe, E. core, *Danaus plexippus*
Brachystelma glabriflorum (Bush Potato)—**N:** *Euploea core, D. petilia*
*Calotropis gigantea (Giant Rubber Bush)—**N:** *Danaus petilia, *D. plexippus*
C. procera (Rubber Bush)—**N:** *Danaus petilia*
Ceropegia cumingiana—**N:** *Euploea core*
*Cryptostegia grandiflora (Rubber Vine)—**N:** *Euploea core*
*C. madagascariensis (Purple Rubber Vine)—**N:** *Euploea core*
Cynanchum carnosum (Mangrove Waxflower)—**N:** *Euploea core, Danaus affinis, D. petilia, Tirumala hamata*
C. christineae—**N:** *Danaus petilia*
C. floribundum (Native Pear)—**N:** *Danaus petilia*
C. leptolepis—**N:** *Tirumala hamata*
C. liebiana—**N:** *Danaus petilia*
C. ovalifolium—**N:** *Danaus affinis*
*Cynanchum sp.—**N:** *Euploea core*
*Gomphocarpus cancellatus (Broad-leafed Cotton Bush)—**N:** *Danaus petilia, *D. plexippus*
*G. fruticosa (Narrow-leafed Cotton Bush)—**N:** *Danaus petilia, *D. plexippus*
*G. physocarpus (Wild Cotton)—**N:** *Danaus petilia, *D. plexippus*
Gunnessia pepo—**N:** *Euploea core*
Gymnanthera cunninghamii—**N:** *Euploea core*
G. oblonga (Native Rubber Vine)—**N:** *Euploea alcathoe, E. core*
Heterostemma acuminata—**N:** *Tirumala hamata*
*Hoya archboldiana—**N:** *Euploea core*
H. australis (Native Hoya)—**N:** *Euploea core*
*H. carnosa (Indian Rope Hoya)—**N:** *Euploea core*
*H. cumingiana—**N:** *Euploea core*
H. macgillivrayi—**N:** *Euploea core*
Marsdenia australis (Doubah, Native Pear)—**N:** *Euploea alcathoe, E. core, Danaus petilia*
M. coronata (Slender Milk Vine)—**N:** *Euploea core*
M. glandulifera (Fraser Island Milk Vine)—**N:** *Euploea alcathoe*
M. geminata—**N:** *Euploea sylvester*
M. fraseri (Narrow-leafed Milk Vine)—**N:** *Euploea core*
M. hemiptera (Rusty Milk Vine)—**N:** *Euploea core*
M. micradenia (Little Milk Vine)—**N:** *Euploea core*
M. microlepis (Northern Milk Vine)—**N:** *Euploea core*
M. pleiadenia (Downy Milk Vine)—**N:** *Euploea sylvester*
M. rostrata (Common Milk Vine)—**N:** *Euploea core*
M. suaveolens (Scented Milk Vine)—**N:** *Euploea core*
M. velutina (Hairy Silkpod)—**N:** *Tirumala hamata*
M. viridiflora (Native Pear)—**N:** *Euploea core*
Rhyncharrhena linearis (Climbing Purple Star)—**N:** *Danaus petilia*
Sarcostemma australe (Caustic Vine)—**N:** *Euploea core*
S. esculentum—**N:** *Danaus genutia, D. petilia*
Secamone elliptica (Corky Milk Vine)—**N:** *Euploea core, Tirumala hamata*
*Stapelia grandiflora (Carrion Plant)—**N:** **Danaus plexippus*
*S. variegata (Starfish Flower)—**N:** **Danaus plexippus*
*Stephanotis sp.—**N:** *Euploea core*
Tylophora barbata—**N:** *Euploea core, Danaus petilia*
T. grandiflora (Small-leafed Tylophora)—**N:** *Euploea core, Danaus petilia*
T. paniculata (Thin-leafed Tylophora)—**N:** *Euploea core, Danaus petilia*

Convolvulaceae
Erycibe coccinea—**N:** *Neptis praslini*
Evolvulus alsinoides (Tropical Speedwell)—**N:** *Junonia villida*
Ipomoea batatas (Sweet Potato)—**N:** *Hypolimnas bolina*

Boraginaceae
Cordia dichotoma (Glueberry Tree)—**N:** *Phaedyma shepherdi*, **L:** *Arhopala micale*
Ehretia acuminata (Koda Tree)—**N:** *Phaedyma shepherdi*, **L:** *Erysichton lineata*

Verbenaceae (Verbena family)
Avicennia eucalyptifolia (Smooth-barked Grey Mangrove)—**L:** *Hypochrysops narcissus*
A. marina (Grey Mangrove)—**L:** *Hypochrysops apelles, H. epicurus*
Clerodendrum costatum—**L:** *Pseudodipsas eone*
C. floribundum (Lolly Bush)—**L:** *Hypochrysops ignitus, Hypolycaena phorbas*
C. inerme (Scrambling Clerodendrum)—**L:** *Hypolycaena phorbas*
Clerodendrum sp.—**Pa:** *Graphium sarpedon*, **L:** *Anthene lycaenoides*

Faradaya splendida (Potato Vine)—**L:** *Pseudodipsas eone, Hypochrysops miskini, Arhopala micale, Hypolycaena phorbas, Anthene lycaenoides*
*Lantana camara (Lantana)—**N:** *Junonia villida*
*Phyla canescens (Lippia)—**N:** *Junonia villida*
P. nodiflora* (Carpet Weed)—N:** *Junonia villida*
Stachytarpheta jamaicensis* (Snakeweed)—N:** *Junonia villida*
Verbena bonariensis* (Purpletop)—N:** *Junonia villida*
V. gaudichaudii (Native Vervain)—**N:** *Junonia villida*
V. officinalis* (Vervain)—N:** *Junonia villida*
V. rigida* (Veined Verbena)—N:** *Junonia villida*

Lamiaceae (Mint family)
Hyptis suaveolens (Horehound, Mintweed)—**N:** *Junonia villida*
Lavandula officinalis* (Lavender)—N:** *Vanessa kershawi*
Prostanthera nivea (Snowy Mint Bush)—**L:** *Candalides heathi*
Westringia fruticosa (Native Rosemary)—**L:** *Candalides heathi*
W. rigida (Stiff Westringia)—**L:** *Candalides heathi*

Plantaginaceae (Plantain family)
*Plantago debilis (Shade Plantain)—**L:** *Candalides heathi*
P. lanceolata* (Ribwort)—N:** *Junonia villida*, **L:** *Candalides heathi*
P. major* (Greater Plantain)—N:** *Junonia villida*
Plantago sp.—**N:** *Junonia villida*, **L:** *Candalides heathi*

Oleaceae (Olive family)
Jasminum aemulum (Native Jasmine)—**N:** *Polyura sempronius*
Notelaea longifolia (Mock-olive)—**H:** *Netrocoryne repanda*

Scrophulariaceae (Snapdragon family)
Angelonia salicariifolia—**N:** *Junonia orithya*
*Antirrhinum sp. (Snapdragon)—**N:** *Junonia orithya, J. villida*
Buchnera gracilis—**N:** *Junonia orithya*
B. linearis (Blackrod)—**N:** *Junonia orithya*
Derwentia derwentiana (Derwent Speedwell)— **L:** *Candalides heathi*
D. perfoliata (Digger's Speedwell)—**L:** *Candalides heathi*
Russelia equisetiformis* (Coral Plant)—N:** *Junonia villida*
Stemodia florulenta (Blue-rod)—**N:** *Junonia villida*, **L:** *Candalides heathi*
Striga curviflora—**N:** *Junonia orithya*
S. parviflora—**N:** *Junonia orithya*
Veronica sp.—**N:** *Junonia villida*

Myoporaceae
Eremophila longifolia (Emubush)—**L:** *Candalides heathi*
E. deserti (Turkeybush)—**L:** *Candalides heathi*
Myoporum parvifolium (Creeping Boobialla)— **L:** *Candalides noelkeri*

Acanthaceae (Acanthus family)
Asystasia gangetica (Chinese Violet)—**N:** *Doleschallia bisaltide, Hypolimnas alimena, H. bolina, H. misippus, Junonia orithya*
Asystasia sp.—**N:** *Hypolimnas bolina, Junonia orithya*
Brunoniella acaulis (Blue Trumpet)—**N:** *Junonia orithya*
B. australis—**N:** *Junonia orithya*
B. spiciflora—**N:** ?*Junonia orithya*
Dipteracanthus bracteatus—*Yoma sabina*
Dipteracanthus sp.—*Hypolimnas bolina*
Graptophyllum pictum* (Caricature Plant)— **N: *Doleschallia bisaltide, Hypolimnas alimena*
Hemigraphis alternata* (Red Ivy)—N:** *Doleschallia bisaltide, Junonia hedonia, Junonia orithya*
Hygrophila angustifolia—**N:** *Hypolimnas bolina, Junonia hedonia, J. orithya, J. villida*, **L:** *Zizula hylax*
H. costata (Glush Weed)—**N:** *Junonia hedonia*, **L:** *Zizula hylax*
Hypoestes floribunda—**N:** *Junonia orithya*
Justicia sp.—**N:** *Junonia orithya*
Pseuderanthemum variabile (Pastel Flower)— **N:** *Doleschallia bisaltide, Hypolimnas alimena, H. bolina, H. misippus, Junonia orithya*
P. bicolor* (Shooting Star)—N:** *Doleschallia bisaltide*
Pseuderanthemum sp.—**N:** *Junonia orithya*
Rostellularia adscendens—**N:** *Junonia orithya*
*Ruellia tuberosa—**N:** *Junonia hedonia*, **L:** *Zizula hylax*
Ruellia sp. (Christmas Pride)—**N:** *Doleschallia bisaltide, Hypolimnas bolina, Yoma sabina, Junonia villida*
Strobilanthes dyerianus* (Persian Shield)— **N: ?*Doleschallia bisaltide*
*Sisophyllus (Bedding Conehead)—**N:** *Doleschallia bisaltide*
*Thunbergia alata (Black-eyed Susan)—**N:** *Junonia orithya*

Goodeniaceae (Dampiera and Goodenia family)
Goodenia grandiflora—**N:** *Junonia villida*
Goodenia sp.—**N:** *Junonia villida*
Scaevola aemula (Fan Flower)—**N:** *Junonia villida*

Rubiaceae (Gardenia family)
Myrmecodia beccarii (Ant Plant)—**L:** *Hypochrysops apollo*
M. tuberosa (Ant Plant)—**L:** *Hypochrysops apollo*
Nauclea orientalis (Leichhardt Tree)—**L:** *Hypochrysops elgneri*
Richardia brasiliensis* (White Eye)—N:** *Hypolimnas bolina*

Dipsacaceae (Scabious or Teasel family)
Scabiosa atropurpurea* (Purple Pincushion)— **N: *Junonia villida*

Asteraceae (Daisies and Asters)
Ammobium alatum (Stem Daisy)—**N:** *Vanessa kershawi*
Arctotheca calendula* (Capeweed)—N:** *Vanessa kershawi*
*Artemisia sp.—**N:** *Vanessa kershawi*

Carduus sp. (Thistles)—**N:** *Vanessa kershawi*
Cassinia quinquefaria—**L:** *Hypochrysops ignitus*
Chrysocephalum apiculatum (Yellow Buttons)—
   N: *Vanessa kershawi*
C. semipapposum (Clustered Everlasting)—**N:** *Vanessa kershawi*
C. sp. aff. *apiculatum*—**N:** *Vanessa kershawi*
Epaltes australis (Spreading Nut-heads)—**N:** *Junonia villida*
Galinsoga parviflora* (Potato Weed)—N:** *Hypolimnas bolina, Vanessa kershawi*
Gamochaeta pensylvanica (Cudweed)—**N:** *Vanessa kershawi*
Helichrysum rupicola (Everlasting Daisy)—**N:** *Vanessa kershawi*
H. scorpioides (Button Everlasting)—**N:** *Vanessa kershawi*
Olearia axillaris (Coast Daisy-bush)—**L:** *Hypochrysops ignitus*
Onopordum acanthium* (Scotch Thistle)—N:** *Vanessa kershawi*
O. illyricum* (Illyrian Thistle)—N:** *Vanessa kershawi*
Rhodanthe chlorocephala (Paper Daisy)—**N:** *Vanessa kershawi*
Synedrella nodiflora (Cinderella Weed)—**N:** *Hypolimnas bolina*
Xerochrysum bracteatum (Golden Everlasting)—
   N: *Vanessa kershawi*

MONOCOTYLEDONS

The distinction between monocotyledons and dicotyledons is now eschewed by many botanists, because the monocotyledons are believed to represent just one group within the remainder of the flowering plants, all of which are dicotyledons. However, the division remains a very useful one for understanding butterfly host plant preferences. With a very few exceptions, the only species that feed on monocotyledons are skippers of the subfamilies Trapezitinae (ochres) and Hesperiinae (typical skippers) and members of the nymphalid subfamilies Satyrinae (browns) and Amathusiinae (owls). Moreover, members of these subfamilies never feed on dicotyledons.

Arecaceae (Palms)
The vast majority (85 per cent) of palms eaten by butterfly larvae are non-native. For most, the only butterflies attacking them are palm skippers (*Cephrenes* sp.). Other palm-feeders, which are mainly restricted to native palm species, include a few other tropical skippers, tropical browns and even one hairstreak. Common names are generally provided only for native species, as nurseries normally provide Latin names for cultivated species, and almost all are attacked.

Acoelorrhaphe wrightii*—H:** *Cephrenes augiades, C. trichopepla*
Aiphanes coralina*—H:** *Cephrenes augiades*
Archontophoenix alexandrae (Alexandra Palm)—
   H: *Cephrenes augiades, C. trichopepla, Sabera caesina*
A. cunninghamiana (Bangalow Palm)—**H:** *Cephrenes augiades, C. trichopepla*
Archontophoenix sp. aff. *alexandrae*—**H:** *Cephrenes augiades*
*Areca triandra—**H:** *Cephrenes augiades, C. trichopepla*
Arenga australasica (Australian Sugar Palm)—
   H: *Cephrenes augiades*
A. engleri*—H:** *Cephrenes augiades*
Astrocaryum alatum*—H:** *Cephrenes augiades*
*Attalea allenii—**H:** *Cephrenes trichopepla*
Bactris ottostapfeana*—H:** *Cephrenes augiades*
Beccariophoenix madagascariensis*—H:** *Cephrenes augiades, C. trichopepla*
Bentinickia nicobarica*—H:** *Cephrenes augiades*
Bismarkia nobilis*—H:** *Cephrenes trichopepla*
Brahea brandegeei*—H:** *Cephrenes augiades, C. trichopepla*
*Butia capitata—**H:** *Cephrenes augiades, C. trichopepla*
B. eriospatha*—H:** *Cephrenes augiades*
Calamus caryotoides (Lawyer Vine)—**H:** *Sabera caesina,* **N:** *Elymnias agondas*
C. moti (Lawyer Vine, Wait-a-while)—**H:** *Cephrenes augiades, Sabera fuliginosa*
*Calamus sp. aff. *vitiensis*—**H:** *Cephrenes augiades*
Calyptronoma dulcis*—H:** *Cephrenes augiades*
Carpentaria acuminata (Carpentaria Palm)—
   H: *Cephrenes augiades*
Carpoxylon macrospermum*—H:** *Cephrenes augiades*
Caryota albertii (Native Fish-tail Palm)—**L:** *Deudorix epijarbas*
Chamaedorea cataractarum*—H:** *Cephrenes augiades, C. trichopepla*
C. microspadix*—H:** *Cephrenes augiades*
Chamaerops humilis*—H:** *Cephrenes augiades*
Chrysophila guagara*—H:** *Cephrenes augiades*
C. warscewiczii*—H:** *Cephrenes augiades*
Clinostigma samoense*—H:** *Cephrenes augiades*
Coccothrinax alta*—H:** *Cephrenes augiades*
C. martii*—H:** *Cephrenes trichopepla*
*Cocos nucifera (Coconut Palm)—**H:** *Cephrenes augiades, C. moseleyi, C. trichopepla*
*Copernicia alba—**H:** *Cephrenes augiades*
C. prunifera*—H:** *Cephrenes augiades, C. trichopepla*
*Dekenia nobilis—**H:** *Cephrenes augiades*
Dictyosperma album*—H:** *Cephrenes augiades, C. trichopepla*
*Dypsis baronii—**H:** *Cephrenes augiades, C. trichopepla*
D. cabadae*—H:** *Cephrenes augiades*
D. darainii*—H:** *Cephrenes augiades, C. trichopepla*
D. decaryi*—H:** *Cephrenes augiades, C. trichopepla*
D. lastelliana*—H:** *Cephrenes augiades*
D. lutescens*—H:** *Cephrenes augiades, C. trichopepla*
*Dypsis sp. 'Mahajangi'—**H:** *Cephrenes augiades*
Elaeis guineensis*—H:** *Cephrenes augiades*
E. oleifera*—H:** *Cephrenes augiades, C. trichopepla*

Euterpe sp.—**H:** *Cephrenes augiades*
Gaussia attenuata—**H:** *Cephrenes augiades*
Gronophyllum microcarpum—**H:** *Cephrenes augiades*
Gulubia hombronii—**H:** *Cephrenes augiades*
G. macrospadix—**H:** *Cephrenes augiades*
Heterospathe delicatula—**H:** *Cephrenes augiades*
H. elata—**H:** *Cephrenes augiades*
H. negrosensis—**H:** *Cephrenes augiades*
H. woodfordiana—**H:** *Cephrenes augiades*
Howea belmoreana (Curly Palm)—**H:** *Cephrenes augiades*
H. forsteriana (Kentia Palm)—**H:** *Cephrenes augiades, C. trichopepla*
Hydriastele wendlandiana (Clumping Palm)—**H:** *Cephrenes augiades*
Hyophorbe lagenicaulis—**H:** *Cephrenes augiades, C. trichopepla*
H. verschaffeltii—**H:** *Cephrenes augiades, C. trichopepla*
Jessenia minuta—**H:** *Cephrenes augiades, C. trichopepla*
Laccospadix australasica (Walking-stick Palm)—**H:** *Cephrenes augiades*
Latania verschaffeltii—**H:** *Cephrenes trichopepla*
Licuala silvania—**H:** *Cephrenes trichopepla*
L. spinosa—**H:** *Cephrenes augiades*
L. ramsayi (Queensland Fan Palm)—**H:** *Cephrenes augiades*
Livistona australis (Cabbage Palm, Fan Palm)—**H:** *Cephrenes augiades, C. trichopepla*
L. benthamii (Bentham's Fountain Palm)—**H:** *Cephrenes trichopepla*
L. chinensis—**H:** *Cephrenes augiades, C. trichopepla*
L. decipiens (Ribbon Palm)—**H:** *Cephrenes augiades, C. trichopepla*
L. drudei (Halifax Fan Palm)—**H:** *Cephrenes augiades, C. trichopepla*
L. fulva—**H:** *Cephrenes augiades*
L. mariae (Central Australian Cabbage Palm)—**H:** *Cephrenes trichopepla*
L. merrillii—**H:** *Cephrenes augiades*
L. muelleri (Dwarf Fan palm)—**H:** *Cephrenes augiades, C. trichopepla*
L. nitida (Canarvon Gorge Palm)—**H:** *Cephrenes trichopepla*
L. rotundifolia—**H:** *Cephrenes trichopepla*
L. saribus—**H:** *Cephrenes augiades*
Lytocaryum weddellianum—**H:** *Cephrenes augiades*
Mauritia flexuosa—**H:** *Cephrenes trichopepla*
M. peruviana—**H:** *Cephrenes trichopepla*
Nannorrhops ritchieana—**H:** *Cephrenes trichopepla*
Neoveitchia storckii—**H:** *Cephrenes augiades*
Normanbya normanbyi (Black Palm)—**H:** *Sabera caesina*
Oenocarpus sp.—**H:** *Cephrenes augiades*
Orbignya cohune—**H:** *Cephrenes augiades, C. trichopepla*
Phoenix acaulis—**H:** *Cephrenes trichopepla*
P. canariensis—**H:** *Cephrenes augiades, C. trichopepla*
P. dactylifera—**H:** *Cephrenes trichopepla*
P. loureirii—**H:** *Cephrenes augiades, C. trichopepla*
P. reclinata—**H:** *Cephrenes augiades, C. trichopepla*
P. roebelenii—**H:** *Cephrenes augiades, C. trichopepla*
P. rupicola—**H:** *Cephrenes augiades*
P. sylestris—**H:** *Cephrenes augiades, C. trichopepla*
Pinanga bataanensis—**H:** *Cephrenes augiades*
P. coronata—**H:** *Cephrenes augiades*
P. dicksonii—**H:** *Cephrenes augiades*
P. kuhlii—**H:** *Cephrenes augiades*
P. merrillii—**H:** *Cephrenes augiades*
P. urosperma—**H:** *Cephrenes augiades*
Pritchardia affinis—**H:** *Cephrenes augiades, C. trichopepla*
P. beccariana—**H:** *Cephrenes augiades, C. trichopepla*
P. hillebrandii—**H:** *Cephrenes augiades, C. trichopepla*
P. macrocarpa—**H:** *Cephrenes trichopepla*
P. maideniana—**H:** *Cephrenes augiades*
P. minor—**H:** *Cephrenes augiades, C. trichopepla*
Ptychosperma ambiguum—**H:** *Cephrenes augiades*
P. bleeseri—**H:** *Cephrenes augiades*
P. elegans—**H:** *Cephrenes augiades, C. trichopepla*
P. furcatum—**H:** *Cephrenes augiades*
P. lauterbachii—**H:** *Cephrenes augiades*
P. lineare—**H:** *Cephrenes augiades*
P. macarthurii—**H:** *Cephrenes augiades*
P. salomonense—**H:** *Cephrenes augiades*
P. sanderianum—**H:** *Cephrenes augiades*
Raphia australis—**H:** *Cephrenes augiades*
R. farinifera—**H:** *Cephrenes augiades*
Ravenea rivularis—**H:** *Cephrenes augiades, C. trichopepla*
Rhapidophyllum hystrix—**H:** *Cephrenes trichopepla*
Rhapis excelsa—**H:** *Cephrenes augiades, C. trichopepla*
R. humilis—**H:** *Cephrenes trichopepla*
Rhopaloblaste augusta—**H:** *Cephrenes augiades*
Rhopalostylis baueri (Norfolk Island Palm)—**H:** *Cephrenes augiades*
R. cheesemanni—**H:** *Cephrenes augiades*
R. sapida—**H:** *Cephrenes augiades*
Roystonea venezuelana—**H:** *Cephrenes augiades*
Sabal domingensis—**H:** *Cephrenes augiades, C. trichopepla*
S. mauritiiformis—**H:** *Cephrenes augiades*
S. mexicana—**H:** *Cephrenes augiades, C. trichopepla*
S. minor—**H:** *Cephrenes trichopepla*
S. palmetto—**H:** *Cephrenes augiades, C. trichopepla*
S. rosei—**H:** *Cephrenes trichopepla*
S. uresana—**H:** *Cephrenes augiades*
S. yapa—**H:** *Cephrenes augiades, C. trichopepla*
Satakentia liukiuensis—**H:** *Cephrenes augiades*
Scheelea butyracea—**H:** *Cephrenes augiades, C. trichopepla*
S. cephalotes—**H:** *Cephrenes augiades*
S. zonensis—**H:** *Cephrenes augiades, C. trichopepla*
Serenoa repens—**H:** *Cephrenes trichopepla*
Syagrus amara—**H:** *Cephrenes augiades*
S. comosa—**H:** *Cephrenes augiades*
S. sancona—**H:** *Cephrenes trichopepla*
S. schizophylla—**H:** *Cephrenes augiades, C. trichopepla*
S. romanzoffiana—**H:** *Cephrenes augiades, C. trichopepla*
Thrinax excelsa—**H:** *Cephrenes augiades*
T. radiata—**H:** *Cephrenes augiades*

Trachycarpus fortunei—**H:** *Cephrenes augiades, C. trichopepla*
*T. martianus—**H:** *Cephrenes augiades*
*T. wagneranus—**H:** *Cephrenes augiades*
*Trithrinax acanthocoma—**H:** *Cephrenes augiades*
*Veitchia joannis—**H:** *Cephrenes trichopepla*
*V. merrillii—**H:** *Cephrenes augiades*
*Verschaffeltia splendida—**H:** *Cephrenes augiades*
*Vonitra fibrosa—**H:** *Cephrenes augiades*
*Washingtonia filifera—**H:** *Cephrenes augiades*
*W. robusta—**H:** *Cephrenes augiades, C. trichopepla*
Wodyetia bifurcata (Foxtail Palm)—**H:** *Cephrenes augiades, C. trichopepla*
*Zombia antillarum—**H:** *Cephrenes augiades, C. trichopepla*

Pandanaceae (Pandanus)
Pandanus sp.—**N:** *Taenaris artemis*

Flagellariaceae
Flagellaria indica (Whip Vine)—**H:** *Rachelia extrusa, Telicota anisodesma, T. augias, T. ohara,* **L:** *Hypolycaena phorbas, Candalides absimilis, Anthene lycaenoides*

Cyperaceae (Sedges and Swordgrasses)
Sedges, particularly the familiar Swordgrass or Saw-sedges, are major host plants of many ochres (Hesperiidae: Trapezitinae) and a few browns (Nymphalidae: Satyrinae), especially the swordgrass browns (*Tisiphone* sp.). Several typical skippers (Hesperiidae: Hesperiinae) may also feed on sedges.

Carex appressa (Tall Sedge)—**H:** *Oreisplanus munionga, Hesperilla ornata,* ?*Telicota eurychlora,* **N:** *Melanitis leda, Heteronympha cordace*
C. brunnea (Greater Brown Sedge)—**H:** *Hesperilla ornata*
C. gaudichaudiana (Lizard's Tail or Fen Sedge)—**H:** *Taractrocera papyria*
C. hubbardii—**H:** *Signeta tymbophora*
C. longebrachiata—**H:** *Oreisplanus munionga, Hesperilla ornata,* **N:** *Heteronympha banksii*
C. polyantha (Creek Sedge)—**H:** *Taractrocera papyria, Telicota eurychlora,* **N:** *Melanitis leda*
Cladium procerum—**H:** *Telicota eurychlora*
Cyperus decompositus—**H:** *Hesperilla sexguttata*
C. javanicus—**H:** *Hesperilla sexguttata*
C. microcephalus—**H:** *Hesperilla sexguttata*
Gahnia ancistrophylla (Curly-leaf Swordgrass)—**H:** *Hesperilla donnysa, Antipodia atralba, A. dactyliota*
Gahnia australis—**H:** *Antipodia dactyliota*
G. aspera—(Rough Saw-sedge)—**H:** *Hesperilla donnysa, H. idothea, H. malindeva, H. ornata, Telicota ancilla,* **N:** *Tisiphone abeona, T. helena*
G. clarkei—**H:** *Hesperilla donnysa, H. idothea, H. ornata, H. picta,* **N:** *Hypocysta metirius, Heteronympha mirifica, Tisiphone abeona*
G. decomposita—**H:** *Hesperilla chrysotricha, H. donnysa*
G. deusta (Mallee Saw-sedge)—**H:** *Hesperilla chrysotricha, H. donnysa, H. flavescens, Antipodia atralba*
G. erythrocarpa—**H:** *Hesperilla donnysa, H. ornata,* **N:** *Tisiphone abeona*
G. filifolia—**H:** *Hesperilla donnysa, Antipodia chaostola*
G. filum (Chaffy Saw-sedge)—**H:** *Hesperilla chrysotricha, H. donnysa, H. flavescens*
G. grandis (Brickmakers' Sedge)—**H:** *Hesperilla crypsargyra, H. donnysa, H. idothea, H. ornata, Antipodia chaostola,* **N:** *Tisiphone abeona*
G. insignis—**H:** *Hesperilla crypsargyra*
G. lanigera (Desert Saw-sedge)—**H:** *Hesperilla donnysa, Antipodia atralba, A. dactyliota*
G. melanocarpa (Black-fruit Swordgrass)—**H:** *Hesperilla idothea, H. mastersi, H. ornata,* **N:** *Tisiphone abeona, Heteronympha banksii*
G. microstachya (Slender Saw-sedge)—**H:** *Hesperilla chrysotricha, H. crypsargyra, H. donnysa, Antipodia chaostola,* **N:** *Tisiphone abeona*
G. radula (Thatch Saw-sedge)—**H:** *Hesperilla chrysotricha, H. donnysa, H. idothea, H. ornata, Antipodia chaostola,* **N:** *Tisiphone abeona*
G. sieberiana—(Red-fruit Swordgrass)—**H:** *Toxidia peron, Signeta tymbophora, Oreisplanus perornatus, Hesperilla chrysotricha, H. crypsargyra, H. donnysa, H. idothea, H. ornata, Antipodia chaostola,* **N:** *Tisiphone abeona, T. helena*
G. subaequiglumis (Bog Swordgrass)—**H:** *Hesperilla donnysa, H. idothea,* **N:** *Tisiphone abeona*
G. trifida (Coastal Saw-sedge)—**H:** *Hesperilla chrysotricha, H. donnysa, H. idothea,*
Gahnia sp. aff. *radula*—**H:** *Hesperilla mastersi*
Gahnia sp. (Sword grasses or Saw-sedges)—**H:** *Dispar compacta*
Lepidosperma angustatum (Sword Sedge)—**H:** *Motasingha trimaculata*
L. carphoides (Black Rapier Sedge)—**H:** *Motasingha trimaculata*
L. concavum (Sand-hill Sword Sedge)—**H:** *Motasingha trimaculata*
L. viscidum (Sand-hill Sword Sedge)—**H:** *Motasingha trimaculata*
Scirpus polystachyus (Large-headed Club-rush)—**H:** *Oreisplanus munionga*
Scleria ciliaris (Hairy Nutrush)—**H:** *Telicota eurotas*
S. levis—**H:** *Hesperilla sarnia*
S. mackaviensis—**H:** *Hesperilla crypsigramma, H. furva, H. sarnia*
S. polycarpa (Common Nutrush)—**H:** *Telicota eurotas*
S. sphacelata (Razorgrass)—**H:** *Hesperilla crypsigramma, H. furva, H. sarnia*
S. sumatrensis (Sumatran Nutrush)—**H:** *Telicota eurotas*
Scleria sp. (Nutrush)—**H:** *Hesperilla sarnia*
Uncinia tenella (Delicate Hook Sedge)—**N:** *Nesoxenica leprea*

Poaceae (Grasses)
Grasses are the food plants for almost all typical skippers (Hesperiidae: Hesperiinae), several ochres (Hesperiidae: Trapezitinae) and most browns (Nymphalidae:

Satyrinae). It is certain many specific records have been overlooked. As identification of grass species is a highly specialised skill, hence many records relate to 'unidentified grasses'.

Alexfloydia repens (Floyd's Grass)—**H:** *Ocybadistes knightorum*, **N:** *Hypocysta metirius*
Austrodanthonia pencillata (Slender Wallaby Grass)—**N:** *Heteronympha penelope*
A. pilosa (Velvet Wallaby Grass)—**N:** *Heteronympha penelope*
Austrodanthonia sp. (Wallaby Grass)—**H:** *Taractrocera papyria*
Austrostipa elegantissima (Feather Spear-grass)—**H:** *Croitana arenaria, C. croites*
A. eremophila (Rusty Spear-grass)—**H:** *Herimosa albovenata*
A. flavescens (Coast Spear-grass)—**H:** *Croitana croites* **N:** *Geitoneura klugii*
A. platychaeta (Spear-grass)—**H:** *Croitana arenaria, C. croites*
A. scabra (Spear-grass)—**H:** *Anisynta cynone, Herimosa albovenata, Taractrocera papyria*
A. semibarbata (Fibrous Spear-grass)—**H:** *Herimosa albovenata*
Brachypodium distachyon* (False Brome)—H:** *Anisynta cynone, Ocybadistes walkeri*, **N:** *Geitoneura klugii, Heteronympha merope*
Bromus catharticus* (Prairie Grass)—N:** *Heteronympha merope*
B. stamineus* (Brome Grass)—H:** *Ocybadistes walkeri*
Chrysopogon aciculatus (Mackie's Pest)—**H:** *Neohesperilla crocea*
C. fallax (Golden Beard-grass)—**H:** *Telicota colon*
Chrysopogon sp. (Beard-grass)—**N:** *Melanitis leda*
Cymbopogon citrata* (Lemon Grass)—H:** *Taractrocera ina*
C. refractus (Barbed-wire Grass)—**H:** *Taractrocera ina*
Cynodon dactylon (Couch Grass)—**H:** *Anisynta cynone, Taractrocera papyria, Ocybadistes walkeri*, **N:** *Hypocysta metirius, Heteronympha merope*
Dichanthium sericeum (Queensland Blue-grass)—**N:** *Mycalesis perseus*
Echinopogon caespitosus (Bushy Hedgehog-grass)—**H:** *Taractrocera papyria*
Ehrharta calycina* (Perennial Veldt Grass)—H:** *Anisynta sphenosema, Taractrocera papyria*, **N:** *Geitoneura klugii*
Ehrharta erecta* (Panic Veldt Grass)—H:** *Ocybadistes walkeri*, **N:** *Heteronympha merope*
E. longiflora* (Annual Veldt Grass)—H:** *Anisynta sphenosema, Taractrocera papyria*, **N:** *Geitoneura minyas*
Ehrharta sp.* (Veldt Grass)—N:** *Geitoneura minyas*
Enteropogon acicularis (Curly Windmill Grass)—**H:** *Croitana arenaria*
Entolasia marginata (Bordered Panic)—**H:** *Toxidia rietmanni, Signeta tymbophora*
Eriachne pallescens—**N:** *Hypocysta metirius*
Eulalia aurea (Silky Browntop)—**H:** *Taractrocera anisomorpha*
Heteropogon triticeus (Spear-grass)—**N:** *Melanitis leda, Mycalesis perseus*
Heteropogon sp. (Spear-grass)—**H:** *Neohesperilla xanthomera*
Imperata cylindrica (Bladey Grass)—**H:** *Taractrocera papyria, Ocybadistes walkeri, Suniana lascivia, Arrhenes dschilus, Telicota ancilla*, **N:** *Melanitis leda, Mycalesis terminus, Ypthima arctoa*
Ischaemum australe—**H:** *Toxidia peron, Ocybadistes hypomeloma, Telicota colon, Pelopidas agna*, **N:** *Mycalesis sirius*
I. triticeum—see *I. australe*
Joycea pallida (Silvertop Wallaby Grass)—**N:** *Geitoneura klugii*
Leersia hexandra (Swamp Rice-grass)—**H:** *Suniana sunias, Arrhenes marnas, Parnara amalia, P. bada*, **N:** *Melanitis leda*
Leersia sp. (Rice-grass)—**H:** *Suniana sunias*
Leptaspis banksii—**H:** *Telicota brachydesma*
Lolium perenne* (Perennial Ryegrass)—N:** *Argynnina hobartia*
Lolium sp.*—H:** *Ocybadistes walkeri*
Melinis minutiflora* (Molasses Grass)—N:** *Melanitis leda*
Microlaena stipoides (Weeping Grass)—**H:** *Anisynta sphenosema, Pasma tasmanica, Toxidia doubledayi, Taractrocera papyria, Ocybadistes hypomeloma*, **N:** *Geitoneura acantha, Oreixenica lathoniella, Heteronympha merope, H. paradelpha*
Miscanthus sinensis* (Chinese Silvergrass)—H:** *Telicota colon*
Ophiuros exaltatus (Canegrass)—**H:** *Telicota colon*, **N:** *Melanitis leda*
Oplismenus hirtellus (Basket Grass)—**H:** *Toxidia rietmanni*
Oplismenus sp.—**H:** *Toxidia doubledayi, T. rietmanni*, **N:** *Mycalesis terminus, Heteronympha mirifica*
Oryza sativa* (Rice)—H:** *Taractrocera ina, T. papyria, Pelopidas agna, P. lyelli, Parnara bada*
Oryza sp.—**H:** *Parnara amalia*
Oryzopsis miliacea* (Rice Millet)—H:** *Anisynta cynone*
Ottochloa gracillima (Slender Shade Grass)—**H:** *Toxidia doubledayi, T. rietmanni*, **N:** *Hypocysta metirius, Heteronympha mirifica*
Panicum maximum* (Guinea Grass)—H:** *Taractrocera ina, Ocybadistes walkeri, Suniana lascivia, S. sunias, Arrhenes dschilus, Telicota colon, T. mesoptis, Pelopidas lyelli, Borbo impar*, **N:** *Melanitis leda, Mycalesis perseus, M. sirius, M. terminus*
Paspalum conjugatum* (Sour Grass)—H:** *Taractrocera ina*
P. dilatatum* (Paspalum)—H:** *Taractrocera papyria*
P. paniculatum* (Russell River Grass)—H:** *Pelopidas agna*
P. urvillei* (Vasey Grass)—H:** *Taractrocera ina, Suniana sunias, Telicota ancilla*
P. vaginatum* (Saltwater Couch)—H:** *Ocybadistes walkeri*
Pennisetum clandestinum* (Kikuyu)—H:** *Taractrocera papyria, Ocybadistes walkeri*, **N:** *Heteronympha merope*

P. pedicellatum (Hairy Fountain Grass)—**H:** *Pelopidas lyelli, Borbo impar,* **N:** *Melanitis leda*
Phragmites australis (Common Reed)—**H:** *Taractrocera papyria, Telicota ancilla, T. colon,* **N:** *Melanitis leda*
Poa ensiformis (Purple-sheath Tussock-grass)—**N:** *Oreixenica correae, O. lathoniella*
P. fawcettiae (Smooth Blue Snowgrass)—**N:** *Oreixenica orichora*
P. gunnii (Tasmanian Snowgrass)—**N:** *Oreixenica ptunarra*
P. hiemata (Snowgrass)—**N:** *Oreixenica correae, O. latialis, O. orichora*
P. labillardieri (Large Tussock Grass)—**H:** *Anisynta tillyardi, Pasma tasmanica,* **N:** *Geitoneura klugii, Oreixenica lathoniella, O. ptunarra*
P. morrisii (Velvet Tussock-grass)—**N:** *Geitoneura klugii*
P. poiformis (Coastal Tussock Grass)—**N:** *Heteronympha merope*
P. queenslandica (Queensland Grass)—**H:** *Toxidia andersoni*
P. rodwayi (Velvet Tussock Grass)—**N:** *Oreixenica ptunarra*
P. sieberiana (Grey Tussock Grass)—**N:** *Geitoneura acantha*
P. tenera (Slender Tussock Grass)—**H:** *Anisynta monticolae, Dispar compacta, Signeta flammeata,* **N:** *Geitoneura acantha, G. klugii, Heteronympha banksii, H. merope, H. paradelpha*
Poa sp. aff. *sieberiana*—**H:** *Anisynta cynone*
Poa sp.—**H:** *Anisynta dominula, Dispar compacta, Toxidia parvula, Taractrocera papyria,* **N:** *Argynnina cyrila, Oreixenica kershawi, Geitoneura klugii, Heteronympha banksii, H. penelope, H. solandri*
Rottboellia cochinensis (Itch Grass)—**H:** *Borbo cinnara, B. impar*
Saccharum officinarum* (Sugarcane)—H:** *Arrhenes dschilus,* **N:** *Melanitis leda*
Schizachyrium perplexum—**H:** *Neohesperilla xiphiphora*
S. pachyarthron—**H:** ?*Neohesperilla crocea*
Setaria paspalidioides—**H:** *Taractrocera anisomorpha*
*Sorghum bicolor (Sorghum)—**H:** *Taractrocera anisomorpha*
S. halepense* (Johnson Grass)—H:** *Telicota ancilla, T. colon, Pelopidas lyelli,* **N:** *Melanitis leda*
S. verticilliflorum* (Wild Sorghum)—H:** *Taractrocera ina, T. dolon, Suniana sunias, Telicota mesoptis,* **N:** *Melanitis leda*
S. vulgare* (Sorghum)—N:** *Melanitis leda*
Sorghum sp. (Sorghum)—**H:** *Telicota ancilla, T. colon, Pelopidas agna, P. lyelli*
Stenotaphrum secundatum* (Buffalo Grass)—H:** *Toxidia peron,* **N:** *Melanitis leda*
Tetrarrhena juncea (Wirey Rice-grass)—**H:** *Toxidia andersoni, Signeta flammeata,* **N:** *Oreixenica kershawi*
Tetrarrhena sp. (Wire-grass)—**H:** *Signeta flammeata*
Themeda triandra (Kangaroo Grass)—**H:** *Neohesperilla senta, Ocybadistes hypomeloma,* **N:** *Melanitis leda, Mycalesis perseus, M. sirius, M. terminus, Hypocysta adiante, H. pseudirius, Ypthima arctoa, Geitoneura acantha, G. klugii, Heteronympha merope, H. penelope*
Thuarea involuta (Beach Grass)—**H:** *Ocybadistes walkeri*
Triodia mitchellii (Buck Spinifex)—**H:** *Proeidosa polysema*
T. microstachya (Hummock Grass, 'Spinifex')—**H:** *Proeidosa polysema*
T. pungens (Soft Spinifex)—**H:** *Proeidosa polysema*
Triodia sp. aff. *pungens*—**H:** *Proeidosa polysema*
Urochloa decumbens* (Signal Grass)—H:** *Taractrocera ina*
*Vulpia sp. (Silver Grass)—**N:** *Geitoneura klugii*
Unidentified grasses—**H:** *Anisynta monticolae, Pasma tasmanica, Dispar compacta, Toxidia doubledayi, T. inornata, T rietmanni, T. melania, T. parvula, T. peron, T. thyrrhus, Signeta flammeata, S. tymbophora, Croitana croites, Taractrocera dolon, Ocybadistes flavovittatus,* **N:** *Orsotriaena medus, Hypocysta angustata, H. euphemia, H. irius, H. pseudirius, Argynnina cyrila*

Zingiberaceae (Gingers)
Alpinia caerulea (Native Ginger)—**H:** *Notocrypta waigensis*
Hornstedtia scottiana—**H:** *Notocrypta waigensis*

Haemodoraceae (Kangaroo Paw family)
Phlebocarya ciliata—**H:** *Motasingha trimaculata*

Hemerocallidaceae (formerly in Phormiaceae or Liliaceae—Flax Lilies)
Dianella caerulea (Blue Flax Lily)—**H:** *Toxidia peron*
Dianella sp.—**H:** *Toxidia peron*

Iridaceae (Native Irises)
Wild irises are host plants for just one genus of ochres (Hesperiidae: Trapezitinae), *Mesodina*.
Patersonia drummondii—**H:** *Mesodina hayi*
P. fragilis (Swamp Iris)—**H:** *Mesodina halyzia*
P. lanata—**H:** *Mesodina cyanophracta*
P. glabrata (Leafy Purple Flag)—**H:** *Mesodina halyzia*
P. macrantha—**H:** *Mesodina gracillima*
P. occidentalis (Long Purple Flag)—**H:** *Mesodina cyanophracta, M. halyzia*
P. sericea (Silky Purple Flag)—**H:** *Mesodina aeluropis, M. halyzia*
P. umbrosa (Yellow Flag)—**H:** *Mesodina cyanophracta*

Agavaceae (Agave family)
Cordyline australis* (Cabbage Tree)—H:** *Sabera dobboe*
C. cannifolia (Palm Lily)—**H:** *Sabera dobboe*
C. fruticosa—**H:** *Sabera dobboe*
C. stricta (Narrow-leafed Palm Lily)—**H:** *Sabera dobboe*

Xanthorrhoeaceae (Grass Trees and allies)
These plants are attacked only by skippers (ochres) of the genus *Trapezites*. Some authorities classify *Lomandra* in a family by itself (Lomandraceae), and *Acanthocarpus* and *Xerolirion* in the family Laxmanniaceae (or Dasypogonaceae), the former of which may include also *Cordyline* (above).

Acanthocarpus canaliculatus—**H:** *Trapezites sciron*
A. preissii (Prickle Lily)—**H:** *Trapezites atkinsi, T. argenteoornatus*
A. robustus—**H:** *Trapezites argenteoornatus*
A. verticillatus—**H:** *Trapezites argenteoornatus*
Lomandra caespitosa (Mat-rush)—**H:** *Trapezites sciron*
L. collina (Sand Mat-rush)—**H:** *Trapezites sciron*
L. confertifolia (Mat-rush)—**H:** *Trapezites eliena, T. luteus, T. maheta, T. phigalioides, T. praxedes, T. symmomus, T. taori*
L. densiflora (Soft Tussock Mat-rush)—**H:** *Trapezites luteus, T. phigalia*
L. fimbriata (Mt Lofty Mat-rush)—**H:** *Trapezites phigalia*
L. filiformis (Wattle Mat-rush)—**H:** *Trapezites eliena, T. heteromacula, T. luteus, T. maheta, T. macqueeni, T. petalia, T. phigalia, T. phigalioides, T. symmomus*
L. glauca (Pale Mat-rush)—**H:** *Trapezites phigalia*
L. hystrix (Slender Mat-rush)—**H:** *Trapezites iacchus, T. maheta, T. symmomus*
L. laxa (Delicate Mat-rush)—**H:** *Trapezites praxedes*
L. longifolia (Spiney-headed Mat-rush)—**H:** *Trapezites eliena, T. heteromacula, T. iacchoides, T. iacchus, T. luteus, T. petalia, T. phigalioides, T. praxedes, T. symmomus*
L. multiflora (Many-flowered Mat-rush)—**H:** *Trapezites eliena, T. iacchus, T. luteus, T. maheta, T. petalia, T. phigalia*
L. nana (Small Mat-rush)—**H:** *Trapezites phigalia*
L. obliqua (Twisted Mat-rush)—**H:** *Trapezites phigalia, T. praxedes, T. symmomus*
L. spicata (Rainforest Mat-rush)—**H:** *Trapezites genevieveae, T. praxedes, T. symmomus*
Lomandra sororia (Sword Mat-rush)—**H:** *Trapezites phigalia*
Lomandra sp. (Mat-rush)—**H:** *Trapezites heteromacula, T. taori, Toxidia peron, Dispar compacta*
Romnalda strobilacea—**H:** *Trapezites symmomus*
Xerolirion divaricata (Basil's Asparagus)—**H:** *Trapezites waterhousei*

Smilacaceae
Smilax australis (Barbwire Vine)—**L:** *Pseudodipsas cephenes, P. eone, Hypochrysops ignitus, H. miskini, Hypolycaena phorbas*

Dioscoreaceae (Wild Yams)
Dioscorea transversa (Native Yam)—**H:** *Tagiades japetus*

Orchidaceae (Orchids)
*Cattleya sp.—**L:** *Hypolycaena danis*
Dendrobium bigibbum (Cooktown Orchid)—**L:** *Hypolycaena danis*
D. caniculatum (Teatree Orchid)—**L:** *Hypolycaena danis*
*Phalaenanthe sp.—**L:** *Hypolycaena danis*
*Phalaenopsis sp.—**L:** *Hypolycaena danis*
*Renanthera sp.—**L:** *Hypolycaena danis*
*Vanda sp.—**L:** *Hypolycaena danis*

First published in 2010

Copyright © Albert Orr and Roger Kitching 2010

All rights reserved. No part of this book may be reproduced or transmitted in any form or by any means, electronic or mechanical, including photocopying, recording or by any information storage and retrieval system, without prior permission in writing from the publisher. The Australian *Copyright Act 1968* (the Act) allows a maximum of one chapter or 10 per cent of this book, whichever is the greater, to be photocopied by any educational institution for its educational purposes provided that the educational institution (or body that administers it) has given a remuneration notice to Copyright Agency Limited (CAL) under the Act.

Jacana Books, an imprint of
Allen & Unwin
83 Alexander Street
Crows Nest NSW 2065
Australia
Phone: (61 2) 8425 0100
Fax: (61 2) 9906 2218
Email: info@allenandunwin.com
Web: www.allenandunwin.com

Cataloguing-in-Publication details are available
from the National Library of Australia
www.librariesaustralia.nla.gov.au

ISBN 978 1 74175 108 6

Design by Nada Backovic
Illustrations by Albert Orr
Maps by Roger Kitching
Typeset in 11/13.5 pt Adobe Garamond Pro by Bookhouse, Sydney
Printed in China at Everbest Printing Co.

10 9 8 7 6 5